EDINBURGH
AND THE
REFORMATION

To Maureen

EDINBURGH
AND THE
REFORMATION

MICHAEL LYNCH
Department of Scottish History
University of Edinburgh

JOHN DONALD PUBLISHERS LTD
EDINBURGH

ISBN 0 85976 069 3

The publisher acknowledges the financial assistance of the Scottish Arts Council in the publication of this volume.

Thanks are also owing to Twenty-Seven Foundation Awards, and to the Isobel Thornley Bequest Fund, for grants making publication of this volume possible.

Phototypesetting by Burns & Harris Limited, Dundee
Printed in Great Britain by Bell & Bain Ltd, Glasgow

Foreword

THIS is a book which is intended to serve both as a monograph and a reference work. The ordinary reader can happily avoid or only lightly dip into the appendices. Professional historians and the sceptical may wish to examine more closely the evidence which is contained in them. The conclusions I have drawn from this evidence will not convince or please everyone. That is inevitable, even desirable, when a period like the Reformation or a figure like John Knox are involved. But judgement of them, as of any other period or historical figure, should be based on evidence rather than myth, prejudice or folk lore. Discussion of Knox or Edinburgh's reformation or criticism of the conclusions drawn about them here will, I hope, be based on the balance of the evidence which has now come to light.

The opening chapters in the first part of the book are designed to introduce the reader to the main twists and turns in the maze which Edinburgh's history in the Reformation period resembles. It is not until the third part that a fuller guide to the maze is offered. By then it should have become apparent that the route through it is tortuous and, at times, unexpected. Only a minority of protestants, it will have been argued, supported Knox to the hilt; more than half the town held stronger loyalties to Mary, Queen of Scots than to Knox. The definitions of 'protestants' and 'catholics' which are given in part three try to absorb these facts and to point the way towards a less black and white view of Scottish burgh society as it was affected by the Reformation.

This is a study of one city and it tries to show how closely local and national history were intertwined, but often in an unexpected way, in what is supposed to be one of the best-known periods in Scotland's past. It and studies of other localities which will surely follow in the future should underline the fact that Scotland had not one but many reformations. What would be understood as the Scottish Reformation has been left in its conventional capitals but Edinburgh's own reformation has been set apart by their absence.

Preface

THIS book has been a long time in the making and owes much to others. The research for it began in 1969 and later emerged as a doctoral thesis of the University of London. It has undergone considerable changes since then. Part one, which looks at the city itself as well as its reactions to the Reformation, is largely new; parts two and three have been rewritten; the appendices have been revised and recast. The idea for the book first came from Professor A. G. Dickens, who guided and encouraged an initially reluctant postgraduate student into the study of the Reformation in the Scottish burghs. It owes more to him than he would admit or even suspect. The first breakthrough in that research — in discovering the details of a protesant coup and catholic counter-coup in the town in 1559 — owed a great deal to the painstaking, expert help of Dr. Walter Makey, Edinburgh City Archivist, in deciphering what at times approached the indecipherable. His help and advice, always generously given, have continued through many hours spent in Edinburgh's records. Any student of Edinburgh history owes much to Dr. Makey; I owe more than most. I must reserve a particular and special debt of gratitude to Professor Gordon Donaldson. He has read the whole of the text, saving me from grievous error on a number of occasions, and offered advice on many points, too many to acknowledge individually. I have benefited immeasurably from his unrivalled knowledge of this period and from exposure to his meticulous scholarship, which is a model any historian would do well to emulate. The faults which remain are indelibly my own.

I wish to thank the Company of Scottish History and the editors of the *Scottish Historical Review* and the *Bulletin of the Institute of Historical Research* for their permission to reproduce in appendices i and ii material which first appeared in their journals. Particular thanks go to Dr. James Kirk for his generous permission to include details from his doctoral thesis relating to the members of Edinburgh kirk sessions in the 1570s and to Dr. Marcus Merriman for a guiding hand through the difficult waters of the 1540s.

The material in the book has been gathered mostly in a series of expeditions to Edinburgh and London. These would have been impossible without, on the one hand, the assistance of the staffs of the Scottish Record Office, the

National Library of Scotland, the Public Record Office and the British Library, and, on the other, the benefit of a series of grants from the University College of North Wales, Bangor. A generous grant from the British Academy allowed me to make a final expedition to Edinburgh and met the costs of typing and preparation of the typescript and maps.

I owe a considerable debt to John Tuckwell of John Donald Publishers, for his advice, guidance and, above all, his patience in seeing this book into print. He remained sanguine as the project was overtaken by the demand suddenly made on me of a move to Edinburgh and new teaching commitments. My thanks go to Mrs. Barbara Morris, Map Curator of the Department of Geography of the University of Edinburgh, who expertly prepared the maps and to Mrs. Doris Williamson, Secretary to the Department of Scottish History, who produced a long and intricate typescript with remarkable speed and accuracy. The jacket illustration is reproduced by courtesy of Edinburgh City Libraries, to whom go my thanks also. My last and greatest debt is to my wife, Maureen, who has read the whole text many times over and influenced almost every page of it. Acknowledgement is not enough; I ask her to accept the dedication instead as token repayment.

Michael Lynch

Abbreviations and Conventions

ALL sums of money are given in £s Scots unless otherwise stated. With dates the year is deemed to have begun on 1 January. Names have generally been modernised. A square bracket in any list or appendix, usually referring to occupation, indicates that this was found in another source; a rounded bracket, usually a variant of a name, indicates the version found in the original. The following abbreviations have been used in the text and appendices:

Ab. Prot. Bk. King	Abstracts of the protocol books of Alexander King, Edinburgh City Archives.
Ab. Prot. Bk. Guthrie	Abstracts of the protocol books of Alexander Guthrie, Edinburgh City Archives.
Ab. Prot. Bk. John Guthrie	Abstract of the protocol book of John Guthrie, Edinburgh City Archives.
APS	*The Acts of the Parliaments of Scotland*, eds. T. Thomson and C. Innes (Edinburgh 1814-75).
B.	Burgess.
Bannatyne, *Memorials*	Richard Bannatyne, *Memorials of Transactions in Scotland, 1549-73* (Bannatyne Club, 1836).
Bannatyne, *Memorials* (Dalyell ed.)	Richard Bannatyne, *Journal of the Transactions in Scotland*, ed. J. G. Dalyell (Edinburgh, 1806).
B. & G.	Burgess-ship and guildry.
BIHR	*Bulletin of the Institute of Historical Research.*
BGKE	MS Buik of the General Kirk of Edinburgh, 1574-5.
BL	British Library, London.
BOEC	*Book of the Old Edinburgh Club.*
Broughton Court Book	*Court Book of the Regality of Broughton and Burgh of the Canongate, 1569-1573*, ed. M. Wood (Edinburgh, 1937).
Buchanan, *History*	G. Buchanan, *The History of Scotland*, trans. J. Watkins (London, 1827).

BUK	*Acts and Proceedings of the General Assembly of the Kirk of Scotland*, ed. T. Thomson (Bannatyne & Maitland Clubs, 1839-45).
Burghs Conv. Recs.	*Records of the Convention of the Royal Burghs of Scotland*, ed. J. D. Marwick (Edinburgh, 1866-90).
Calderwood, *History*	*History of the Church of Scotland by Mr. David Calderwood* (Wodrow Society, 1842-9).
Canongate Bk.	*The Buik of the Kirk of the Canagait, 1564-1567*, ed. A. B. Calderwood (Scottish Record Soc., 1961).
CSP Foreign, Eliz.	*Calendar of State Papers Foreign, Elizabeth*, eds. J. Stevenson and others (1863-1950).
CSP Roman	*Calendar of State Papers, Rome*, ed. J. M. Rigg (1916-26).
CSP Scot.	*Calendar of State Papers relating to Scotland and Mary, Queen of Scots, 1547-1603*, eds. J. Bain and others (1898-1969).
CSP Spanish	*Calendar of State Papers, Spanish*, eds. G. Bergenroth and others (1862-1954).
De La Brosse Report	'Report by De la Brosse and D'Oysel on Conditions in Scotland, 1559-1560', ed. G. Dickinson (Scottish History Society *Miscellany*, ix, 1958).
Diurnal	*A Diurnal of Remarkable Occurrents that have passed within the country of Scotland, since the death of King James the Fourth till the year 1575* (Bannatyne & Maitland Clubs, 1833).
Edin. Accts.	*Edinburgh Records: The Burgh Accounts*, ed. R. Adam (Edinburgh, 1899).
Edin. Burgs.	*Roll of Edinburgh Burgesses and Guild-Brethren 1406-1700*, ed. C. B. B. Watson (Scottish Record Society, 1929).
Edin. Recs.	*Extracts from the Records of the Burgh of Edinburgh* (Scottish Burgh Records Soc., 1869-92).
Edin. Tests.	MS Register of Edinburgh testaments, Scottish Record Office.
Edin. Tests.	*The Commissariot Record of Edinburgh: Register of Testaments* (Scottish Record Society, 1897-9).
Epistolae Regum Scotorum	*Epistolae Jacobi Quarti, Jacobi Quinti et Mariae Regum Scotorum*, ed. T. Ruddiman (Edinburgh, 1722-4).
Exch. Rolls	*The Exchequer Rolls of Scotland*, eds. J. Stuart and others (Edinburgh, 1878-1908).

Faculty of Advocates, *1532-1943*	*The Faculty of Advocates in Scotland, 1532-1943,* ed. F. J. Grant (Scottish Record Society, 1944).
Hamilton Papers	*The Hamilton Papers,* ed. J. Bain (Edinburgh, 1890-92).
Haws, *Scottish Parish* *Clergy*	C. H. Haws (Ed.), *Scottish Parish Clergy at the* *Reformation, 1540-1574* (Scottish Record Society, 1972).
Herries, *Memoirs*	*Historical Memoirs of the Reign of Mary Queen of* *Scots and a portion of the Reign of King James VI* *by Lord Herries,* ed. R. Pitcairn (Abbotsford Club, 1836).
Hist. Estate Scot.	'Historie of the Estate of Scotland' (Wodrow Society *Miscellany,* i, 1844).
Hist. King James VI	*The Historie and Life of King James the Sext,* ed. T. Thomson (Bannatyne Club, 1825).
HMC Edinburgh	*An Inventory of the Ancient and Historical Monu-* *ments of the City of Edinburgh* (Royal Commis- sion on the Ancient Monuments of Scotland, Edinburgh, 1951).
JC	MS Justiciary court records, Scottish Record Office.
Keith, *History*	R. Keith, *History of the Affairs of Church and* *State in Scotland* (Spottiswoode Society, 1844- 50).
Knox, *History*	*John Knox's History of the Reformation in* *Scotland,* ed. W. C. Dickinson (Edinburgh, 1949).
Knox, *Works*	*The Works of John Knox,* ed. D. Laing (Edin- burgh, 1846-64).
K.P.	King's party.
Lesley, *History*	J. Lesley, *The Historie of Scotland,* eds. E. G. Cody and W. Murison (Scottish Text Society, 1888-95).
Lesley, *History* (Bann. ed.)	J. Lesley, *The History of Scotland from the Death* *of King James I in the Year 1436 to the Year 1561* (Bannatyne Club, 1830).
Letters & Papers, *Henry VIII*	*Letters and Papers (Foreign and Domestic) of the* *Reign of King Henry VIII,* eds. J. Brewer and J. Gairdner (London, 1862-1910).
Lord Provosts	*The Lord Provosts of Edinburgh,* ed. M. Wood (Edinburgh, 1931).
M.	Magister.
Mary of Lorraine Corresp.	*The Scottish Correspondence of Mary of Lorraine* (Scottish History Society, 1927).

Melville, *Diary*	*The Autobiography and Diary of Mr. James Melville*, ed. R. Pitcairn (Wodrow Society, 1842).
Melville, *Memoirs*	*The Memoirs of his Own Life by Sir James Melville of Halhill* (Bannatyne & Maitland Clubs, 1827).
Mothe-Fénélon, *Correspondance diplomatique*	La Mothe-Fénélon, B. de S. de, *Correspondance diplomatique*, ed. A. Teulet (Bannatyne Club, 1840).
Moysie, *Memoirs*	D. Moysie, *Memoirs of the Affairs of Scotland from 1577 to 1603* (Bannatyne & Maitland Clubs, 1830).
MS Co. Recs.	MS Edinburgh council register.
MS Guild Reg.	MS Edinburgh guild register.
Mt.	Merchant.
NLS	National Library of Scotland, Edinburgh.
Original Letters of John Colville	*Original Letters of Mr. John Colville, 1582-1603*, ed. D. Laing (Bannatyne Club, 1858).
Papal Negs.	*Papal Negotiations with Mary Queen of Scots during her reign in Scotland, 1561-1567*, ed. J. H. Pollen (Scottish History Society, 1901).
Paul, *Scots Peerage*	*The Scots Peerage*, ed. Sir J. Balfour Paul (Edinburgh, 1904-14).
Pitcairn, *Trials*	*Criminal Trials in Scotland from 1488 to 1624*, ed. R. Pitcairn (Edinburgh, 1833).
Pitscottie, *Historie*	R. Lindesay of Pitscottie, *The Historie and Cronicles of Scotland* (Scottish Text Society, 1899-1911).
PRO	Public Record Office, London.
Q.P.	Queen's party.
RMS	*Registrum Magni Sigilli Regum Scotorum*, eds. J. M. Thomson and others (1882-1914).
RPC	*The Register of the Privy Council of Scotland*, eds. J. H. Burton and others (1877-98).
RSCHS	*Records of the Scottish Church History Society.*
RSS	*Registrum Secreti Sigilli Regum Scotorum*, eds. M. Livingstone and others (1908-).
Sadler Papers	*The State Papers and Letters of Sir Ralph Sadler*, ed. A Clifford (Edinburgh, 1809).
SHR	*The Scottish Historical Review.*
SHS	Scottish History Society.
Spottiswoode, *History*	*History of the Church of Scotland*, by John Spottiswoode, eds. M. Russell and M. Napier (Spottiswoode Society, 1847-51).
SRO	Scottish Record Office, Edinburgh.

SRS	Scottish Record Society.
TA	*Accounts of the Lord High Treasurer of Scotland,* eds. T. Dickson and Sir J. Balfour Paul (1877-1916).
Teulet, *Papiers d'état*	*Papiers d'état, pièces et documents inédits ou peu connus relatifs à l'histoire de l'Ecosse au XVIe siècle,* ed. A. Teulet (Bannatyne Club, 1852-60).
Teulet, *Relations politiques*	*Relations politiques de la France et de l'Espagne avec l'Ecosse au XVI siècle,* ed. A. Teulet (Paris, 1862).
Thirds of Benefices	*Accounts of the Collectors of Thirds of Benefices, 1561-1572,* ed. G. Donaldson (Scottish History Society, 1949).
Warrender Papers	*The Warrender Papers,* ed. A. I. Cameron (Scottish History Society, 1931-2).

Contents

Maps:

1. Edinburgh, Leith and Surrounds. Edinburgh's port lay two miles
    away at Leith. The Canongate, immediately to the east, was a quite
    separate burgh, with its own council, guilds and parish church. St.
    Cuthbert's formed a separate parish to the west, and the suburbs of
    Bristo and Portsburgh lay outside Edinburgh's jurisdiction.   4

2. Edinburgh from the West Port to the Lawnmarket. The burgh had
    for long been divided into four quarters. By the 1570s each quarter
    worshipped separately and had its own elders. The city was not,
    however, subdivided into separate parishes until 1598. Two new
    churches, Greyfriars and the Tron, were built in the early seven-
    teenth century to hold the swelling congregations of the two
    southern parishes.   12

3. Edinburgh from St. Giles' to the Netherbow. Edinburgh's popula-
    tion within its walls was about 12,500 in 1560. By 1635 it was close
    to 25,000 but accommodated largely by building upwards rather
    than outwards, making Edinburgh one of the most densely
    populated cities in Northern Europe as well as the second or third
    largest in the British Isles. There were over a hundred closes and
    wynds running off the High Street. Stewart's Close, the boundary
    between the two northern quarters, ran under the present City
    Chambers.   13

4. The Canongate. Edinburgh's jurisdiction ran some way beyond the port — or gate — at the Netherbow, allowing the king's lords to hold their famous 'creeping parliament' of 1571 within the capital but outside its walls. The Canongate, with gardens at the backs of its houses and a population of less than 2,000, stood in sharp contrast to its overcrowded neighbour. The Abbey Church remained in use as its parish church after the Reformation but catholics had occasional access to the mass in the chapel royal until 1567.   27

The maps have been compiled from Gordon of Rothiemay's map of 1647 and Kerr's composite plan of 1918, together with other evidence drawn from Hollar's view of 1670 and the Map of the Siege of Leith of 1560. The exact property boundaries and the extent of the built-up area in 1560 are often uncertain but there are good grounds for believing that they were much the same as in 1647 and that the doubling of the burgh's population between these dates was dealt with mostly by building upwards on the same sites.

Part One

Edinburgh Society

1

The Burgh Community: Pressures and Responses

EDINBURGH was by the middle of the sixteenth century a city which was threatening to burst its narrow seams. The town ran for a thousand yards from west to east along the spine of a ridge gently sloping down from the Castle to the great port, or gate, at the Netherbow, reconstructed in the course of the civil wars in 1571. On each side of the High Street, which was first paved in 1532, the ridge sloped steeply away, covered by a series of narrow closes and close-packed timber-fronted houses. A natural boundary was formed to the north by the Nor' Loch, which was increasingly becoming an open sewer, while to the south the town had already spilled over the old city wall built in the 1420s and beyond what had in past times been the wealthier, more spacious suburb of the Cowgate up to the line of a new wall. This was the so-called Flodden wall which was still not completed in 1560. Even so, the burgh was hardly four hundred yards wide from north to south and the total area within its walls comprised only one hundred and forty acres. It was largely within these limited bounds that there was contained the bulk of a population which was large enough for most of the sixteenth and seventeenth centuries for Edinburgh to lay claim to being one of the two largest cities in the British Isles outside London.

There is a paradox here. The tendency has almost always been for historians, and particularly recent Scottish historians, to stress the smallness and intimacy of all the Scottish burgh communities in this period, and Edinburgh among them. It is true that a number of contemporary observers did compare Edinburgh's size unfavourably: Froissart at the end of the fourteenth century thought the town had fewer than four hundred houses; a French visitor in the early 1550s likened Edinburgh in size to the small provincial city of Pontoise. Yet others pointed out the remarkable density of the burgh's population; the duc de Rohan in 1600 and David Buchanan half a century later claimed that there was no other town of its size so populous. Certainly by the standards of recent historians of the early modern town Edinburgh's population was large; it rivalled that of Norwich, the largest city in England outside London, and was akin to a city the size of Bremen.[1]

Precisely how large it was is difficult to quantify exactly but Edinburgh's population within the walls was certainly very close to twelve thousand in 1560. The figure, as we shall see, would rise to somewhere between fifteen and eighteen thousand if greater Edinburgh was taken account of, by including the separate jurisdiction of the burgh of the Canongate and other nearby baronies just outside the walls, like Bristo. The significant point is that Edinburgh's population more than doubled in the century after 1540. The bulk of that increase probably came after the last serious outbreak of the plague in 1584. Because the burgh was engaged until the 1630s in a long series of jurisdictional disputes with a number of its near-neighbours, which prevented significant growth into the surrounding hinterland, the only way to accommodate this dramatic rise in population was to expand not outwards but upwards. The soaring tenements in the Lawnmarket at the head of the High Street of four, five and six storeys, and eventually of fourteen and more, belong to the period after 1580. Edinburgh was fast in process of becoming a prosperous, thriving and bustling metropolis while yet retaining many of the restrictive habits and most of the dimensions of the old medieval burgh. The town's walls serve as a reminder that the reformation took place within the context of the closeted thinking of a medieval burgh.

This was a society which, nevertheless, continued to cherish the old idea of itself as a small and close-knit community. It was an idea, of course, which had a religious dimension to it as well as a social or economic one. The burgh was seen as a *corpus christianum;* its council had responsibilities towards the spiritual as well as the secular welfare of its inhabitants. Most of the organisations within burgh society had the same double aspect to them. The craft guilds were religious societies as well as privileged groups monopolising their skills. The reformation did little or nothing to alter either of these aspects; the craft altars in St. Giles' disappeared but not the religious ethos of the guild. Edinburgh society throughout the sixteenth century and beyond remained paternalistic and deeply conservative.

At the same time, however, the religious changes which took place did so within the context of developments which were increasingly putting many of the old assumptions about the organisation of burgh life under strain. The town's swelling population made some of the arrangements laid down in the *Statuta Gildae* of the twelfth century increasingly impractical. The old practice of the town, or at least of the free burgesses in it, meeting together in an annual head court had probably been abandoned for the better part of a century. The council's fears of craft insurrections after the riots of 1560 and 1561 resulted in the curtailing of the old right of an offender to appear before it accompanied by all the brethren of his craft.[2] The increasing sophistication and prosperity of certain crafts had led to large numbers of leading craftsmen being admitted to

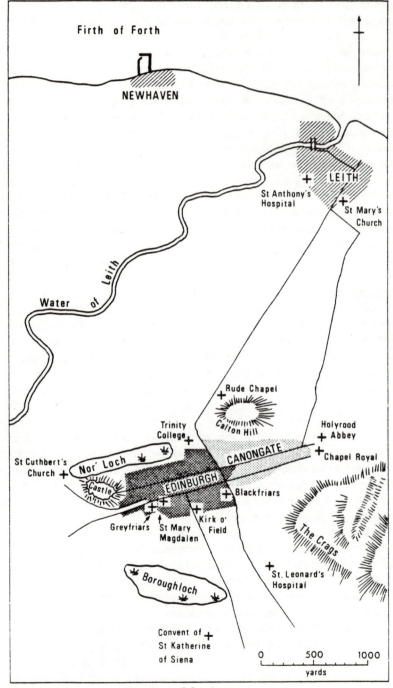

Map 1

the prestigious and formerly exclusive merchant guildry, and as a result the line between merchant and craftsman was having to be redrawn in a process completed by the revision of the town's constitution in the decreet-arbitral of 1583. Price inflation, kindled by the harvest failures of the late 1560s, set alight by the economic blockade of the town during the civil wars and kept smouldering by Morton's debasement of the coinage in the 1570s, induced the council to cling desperately to the traditional but increasingly ineffectual practice of fixing food prices. In addition, a series of externally imposed political crises, ranging from the invasion of the town on three separate occasions by the Lords of the Congregation in 1559 and 1560 to the traumatic siege of the burgh in the wars of the early 1570s, helped to intensify the natural conservatism of the burgh establishment.

Yet while the town expanded its population and became increasingly diverse in character, as it flourished in its roles as a centre for the royal court and the law with the development of a central court for civil justice in the fifteenth century, it clung to the old but necessary myth of seeing itself as a corporate society. The town's existing institutions were stretched to meet the growing pressures on them just as its buildings were stretched to accommodate a growing population. The changes which took place were cosmetic rather than fundamental and this applied as much to the celebrated decreet-arbitral, often seen as the hallmark of a hard-won democracy for the crafts, as to anything else. Power remained in much the same hands in the 1580s as it had in the 1540s. There was just one real difference — there was more of it. Edinburgh is a good illustration of the cardinal principle that the larger a town was or became in the sixteenth century, the more oligarchic its government was likely to be.[3]

If Edinburgh's physical smallness was one of its most surprising features in this period, the other was the fact that it did not control a *contado* around itself. Its port, the vital artery for its trade both with the east coast and overseas, with France, Flanders and the Baltic, lay two miles away at Leith. The burgh's jurisdiction over its own port was complicated, uncertain and acrimonious. It formed the basis of what John Knox in his *History* called the 'auld hatrent' between Leith and Edinburgh and brought the burgh into a series of disputes with a number of influential figures who held rival interests or saw an opportunity for profit. This increasingly expensive and worrying legal tangle was not firmly resolved to Edinburgh's satisfaction until 1639.[4] Predictably, the burgh also had its difficulties with the Canongate, a separate ecclesiastical burgh of regality which stretched eastwards from the port at the Netherbow down to the abbey and royal palace at Holyrood. These lasted until Edinburgh finally gained the superiority in 1636. With its more spacious lay-out and relaxed atmosphere the Canongate increasingly became a residential suburb for courtiers and members of the central administration. There were continual minor disputes over the rights of the Canongate's skilled craftsmen to sell their wares on the High Street. Edinburgh took the Canongate to court in 1573 and, to its dismay, lost.[5] The Canongate also acted as an annoying safe haven, tantalisingly just outside Edinburgh's jurisdiction, for burgesses seeking to evade their civic duties and also for catholics. There were further minor irritations caused by clusters of craftsmen and brewers who were not burgesses living outside the West Port and two of the other gates on the south side until the town acquired the superiority of Portsburgh by purchase in 1648.[6] All these nagging jurisdictional worries helped to keep the burgh an inward-looking society, clinging to the letter of the law wherever its economic privileges and monopolies were involved.

A third feature, but one much more difficult to assess in its effect, was the large number of noble houses within half a day's ride of the burgh. Two contemporary observers claimed that there were as many as a hundred.[7] A number of local lairds, like the Napiers of Merchiston, were burgesses but their influence in the political affairs of Edinburgh was surprisingly small. A number did sit on the town council from time to time but there were no ruling cliques in the sixteenth century like the Menzies family in Aberdeen, which virtually monopolised the office of provost until the 1590s.[8] The progress of the Reformation probably had a good deal to do with the influence of local lairds in many burghs but far less so in Edinburgh where the stakes were higher and the players more formidable.[9] The key factor in Edinburgh politics was often the intervention of the crown itself or of a faction within the court. The two most powerful outside influences came from the two rival noble houses of Morton at Dalkeith and the staunchly catholic Setons.[10] Crown or court managed to impose a nominee as provost of the burgh for fully twenty-five years after 1553 but interference with the lower levels of the ruling establishment was much rarer, occurring only a handful of times in the period. Each of these occasions, however, is noteworthy — Mary of Guise's imposition of bailies on the town in 1559, countered by the Congregation's wholesale replacement of the council two weeks later; the three interventions by her daughter, Mary, Queen of Scots, in burgh politics between 1561 and 1566; the forcing into exile of the council by the queen's lords in 1571; and the purge of radical supporters of the short-lived Ruthven regime forced upon the council by James Stewart, earl of Arran, in 1583. Between these low-points the council had to put up with a fairly consistent barrage of threats, bullying and noble violence on its streets. External threats and externally imposed crises were things the burgh simply had to live with in the middle quarters of the sixteenth century.

It would be easy enough to go one stage further in describing reformation Edinburgh by sketching a picture of a city divided within itself, of merchant against craftsman, catholic against protestant, magistrates against unruly mob. All of these patterns did occur but only sporadically and they seldom linked up, one with the other. Burgh life had to go on and the town was too small in its size and its thinking to admit permanent divisions within it, whether of an economic or a religious complexion. It was not the internal tensions within burgh society which set the tone of Edinburgh's reformation. There is little trace in the 1550's of the pattern which had been common in most of the German cities of protestant ideas being fostered by the craft guilds, partly as a policital lever against the town establishment.[11] Certain of the crafts remained catholic strongholds for most of the 1560s but the tension which existed between merchants and crafts did not take on the mirror image of a struggle by catholic craftsmen against a protestant-dominated merchant oligarchy. The key to understanding the burgh's complicated and shifting reactions during the reformation period lies rather in coming to grips with the recurrent but unpredictable pressures put upon it from outside. The court and the labyrinth of factions within it — and, at times of crisis, outside it — together with the open door of the resident English agent, Thomas Randolph, a classic example of an ambassador of 'ill-will',[12] brought a quite unique set of pressures to bear in the first half of the 1560s on what was by instinct an inward-looking society. Edinburgh reluctantly but inexorably became the cockpit for the shifting factionalism of Scottish politics. Hard-line protestant and catholic factions pursuing a definite party line did exist in the burgh but they remained distinctly minority parties throughout the 1560s. The reaction of the majority of the burgh's inhabitants to the succession of political crises thrust upon them was understandably confused. It may well be objected that this judgement is still, in the last resort, a subjective one, despite the new evidence which has come to light throwing doubt on many of the old black and white assumptions about the inevitable progress of protestantism in John Knox's own 'school of Christ'. Two lines of defence could be erected against this charge. It is clearly time that we knew a good deal more about Edinburgh and its reformation to balance what we already know about Knox. If the resulting conclusions do not confirm that Edinburgh's reformation can continue to be written as a biography of its first protestant minister, they are, it might well be said, less likely to surprise students of the patchy spread of Calvinism in other European societies, such as in the Netherlands. Neither Knox nor reformed protestantism should be thought of as some kind of irresistible force unless one is equally prepared to conceive of an immovable object — not catholicism but localism. The form which localism took was a formidable combination of passivity and what the presbyterian historian, David Calderwood, liked to call Edinburgh's 'religion', the love of its burgesses for 'their particular'.[13] In reality and in history dramatised irreconcilables usually have a way of working out some kind of compromise but not without doing some damage to the original postures. The more one discovers about the equivocal reactions of the burgh's inhabitants, both rich and poor, influential and insignificant, to the external pressures put on the town and the internal pressures which they produced, the more plausible this conclusion seems to become. Edinburgh's protestantism was largely the product of outside forces. It is hardly surprising that the result was that burgh protestantism was as fickle a creature as burgh politics. Edinburgh's reformation was not a story of triumphant and uncompromising progress; it was a stop-go affair for most of the 1560s, shot through with ambiguities and compromises.

NOTES

1. P. H. Brown, *Scotland in the Time of Queen Mary* (1904), 45; P. H. Brown (ed.), *Early Travellers in Scotland* (1891), 75, 93; P. H. Brown (ed.), *Scotland before 1700 from Contemporary Documents* (1893), 314; R. Mols, *Introduction à la demographie historique des villes d'Europe du XIVe au XVIIIe siècle* (Louvain, 1954-6), ii, 510.

2. *Edin. Recs.*, iii, 95

3. See W. G. Hoskins, 'The Elizabethan merchants of Exeter', in S. T. Bindoff, J. Hurstfield & C. H. Williams (eds.), *Elizabethan Government and Society: Essays presented to Sir John Neale* (London, 1961), 165.

4. Knox, *History*, 1, 239; J. C. Irons, *Leith and its Antiquities* (1898), i, 245-8, 390, 408; ii, 80, 82, 91; M. Wood, 'Survey of the development of Edinburgh', *BOEC*, xxiv (1974), 28.

5. *RPC*, ii, 220, 260ff; Wood, 'Survey of the development of Edinburgh', 29; A. H. Anderson, 'The regality and barony of Broughton, 1592-1600', *BOEC*, xxiv (1974), 2-3.

6. Wood, 'Survey of the development of Edinburgh', 29.

7. Brown, *Early Travellers*, 83, 93.

8. D. Macniven, 'Merchant and Trader in Aberdeen in the Early Seventeenth Century' (Aberdeen M. Litt., 1977), 105.

9. See I. B. Cowan, *Regional Aspects of the Scottish Reformation* (Hist. Assoc. pamp., 1978), 28-9. This short but important pamphlet has added a new dimension to the historiography of the Scottish Reformation.

10. See *Early Travellers*, 82, 136.

11. See, for example, B. Moeller, *Villes d'Empire et Réformation* (Geneva, 1966), 21, 32-7; M. U. Chrisman, *Strasbourg and the Reform* (London, 1967), 113, 292-4; A. G. Dickens, *The German Nation and Martin Luther* (London, 1974), 150, 156-7, 187-8.

12. G. Mattingly, *Renaissance Diplomacy* (London, 1955), 198-208.

13. Calderwood, *History*, v, 177-8.

2

Government and Society

ESTIMATES of Edinburgh's population in the sixteenth century vary almost as much as the processes of guesswork by which they have been arrived at. For the late 1550s they range from a low figure of 9,000 souls to an eyebrow-raising one of 30,000.[1] The majority, however, opt for the area between 9,000 and 15,000.[2] These disparities can probably be traced to the different Edinburghs which these estimates try to encompass. The permanently resident population within the walls could, given conservative assumptions about the size of households, be calculated as falling just above or below the five-figure mark. The figure, however, expands with the lens used on the microscope. Account should be taken of the town's floating population of greater and minor nobility, most of whom did not have their own town houses — according to a tax roll of 1635 their lodgings accounted for as many as 4% of Edinburgh households;[3] of the growing army of lawyers, administrators and professional men, most of whom were not taxed and are always a hidden surplus to be added on to the evidence of any tax roll; and the swelling colonies of artisans who lived just outside the town walls who also, having no burgess status, would tend not to appear on a tax roll. If a figure for greater Edinburgh is looked for, then the Canongate, which had 1,250 adult communicants in 1567, should be included along with South Leith, where the only help available is an estimate that it had a population in excess of 4,000 by the middle of the seventeeth century.[4]

It is not possible to obtain either a reasonably precise figure for Edinburgh's population or a statistically satisfactory one since all of the chains of evidence and deduction break down at some point which can only be bridged by guesswork. Most historians' estimates have been based on a muster roll of 1558, which had on it 717 craft masters and servants and 736 merchants and their servants.[5] This was not a total muster, however, of all able-bodied men in the town between the ages of sixteen and sixty which would permit the use of a multiplier to calculate the total population.[6] Its purpose was to defend the town against a prospective English invasion, and responsibility for this fell only on burgesses and their servants or apprentices. It is not even a reliable list of burgesses. Some had been granted exemptions from muster by the crown. More significantly, the point has rather been missed in previous estimates that the muster unaccountably covered only three of the four quarters of the burgh. The missing north-east quarter was the smallest in the town but it did account for about 16% of its population.[7] Three of the fourteen incorporated crafts were also not included.[8] Even if fairly accurate guesses were made to compensate for these gaps in the roll,[9] the resulting total would remain a slippery base on which to reconstruct an estimate of total population. A surer but still unsatisfactory method would be to vet the muster roll to find the total number of burgesses, both merchants and craftsmen, in the town. If the same allowances are made for gaps in the roll, it seems likely that there were about 768 burgesses in 1558, made up of about 367 merchants and 401 craft masters.[10] The break in the chain of evidence comes in trying to estimate the proportion of inhabitants who were burgesses. The best evidence available is that of an annuity tax of 1635 which indicates that some 30% of householders were burgesses.[11] This may seem a high figure, particularly if compared with the number of freemen in a contemporary English town,[12] but is to be expected in a Scottish burgh. The difficulty lies in the fact that there was no fixed quota of privilege. Entry to burgess-ship and to burgess-ship and guildry was controlled by the council through the dean of guild and, as one of the major sources of burgh revenue, was liable to fluctuate considerably. About 337 new burgesses were admitted in the course of the 1550s — and this in itself would lend evidence to a total number of burgesses a little over double that — but the new protestant regime, desperately short of funds for its reformed programme, admitted as many in the first four years after 1560. From the continuing but often incomplete evidence of the 1570s and 1580s,[13] it is obvious that more burgesses were being admitted than twenty or thirty years earlier but it is in a process of peaks and troughs, which suggests that the main consideration remained the pressures of finance rather than of a rising population. It is likely that the qualifications tend to cancel each other out and leave fairly safe the original assumption that much the same proportion of householders to burgesses existed in 1558 as in 1635. This would mean that there were a little more than 2,500 households or a population of about 12,000 in the town in the mid-sixteenth century.[14]

This convoluted calculation is, however, reasonably close to the 2,239 households which were counted by the kirk session in a census made in 1592 for a voluntary contribution to augment the stipends of the town's ministers,[15] particularly if it is remembered that 'gentlemen' and their lodgings, who were excluded from the census, accounted for 4% of Edinburgh's households in 1635. The session also tantalisingly added its estimate of the burgh's population but it is an estimate which is again an artificial one for demographic purposes. There were, it solemnly concluded, exactly eight thousand and three 'persones of discretion' in the town, divided almost exactly between the north and south sides of the High Street. There are two difficulties in this. Part of the population within the walls on the south side and a good deal outside it belonged in the separate parish of St. Cuthbert's so that it does not even give a figure for the adult population within the walls, still less for one outside. The other problem lies in deciding precisely what the phrase means and how many of the lower layers of burgh society — remembering it was drawn up for a collection — it might exclude. Yet even if the further reaches beyond the Cowgate are ignored and the estimate is taken at face value to mean the total number of adult communicants within the walls, it can be deduced that Edinburgh proper, despite the body-blow of 1,400 deaths[16] from the plague in the outbreak of 1584, must have had a population approaching 15,000 by the 1590s.[17] This would seem to be a realistic figure if compared with the recent soundly based estimate of 20,000 to 25,000 as Edinburgh's population within its own jurisdictions in 1635.[18]

The significance of a town of this size is not particularly revealed by comparing it with the other Scottish burghs of the period. Their populations are often even more difficult to assess with any accuracy; estimates of Aberdeen's population in the 1590s range from 4,000 to well over 7,000. The firmest comparison of burgh populations — though once again unsafe for calculating the actual size of populations — often comes from tax or stent rolls. The first detailed Edinburgh stent roll is that for 1583, which lists 1,245 taxpayers, residents paying over £100 Scots in rent or owning more than 2,000 merks of moveable property. The first of a series of seventeenth-century Aberdeen rolls lists 460.[19] So Aberdeen's taxable population amounted to less than 38% of Edinburgh's. It is easier to conceive of Edinburgh's importance by comparing it with other early modern towns in England and abroad than by trying to think of its wealth, population and influence in terms of multiples of other Scottish burghs. Its wealth and political significance were of a different dimension. Equally, a number of its institutions, although they bore a superficial resemblance to burghal practice elsewhere in Scotland, in fact went their own distinctive way.

Edinburgh in the sixteenth century was certainly larger than the important provincial towns of Bristol, York and Exeter. There is a striking parallel between its size and that of Norwich, the second city in England after London until it was overtaken by Bristol in the second half of the seventeenth century. Norwich's population rose from about 8,500 in 1524 to 13,000 in 1569, 17,000 in 1579 after substantial immigration of refugees from the Low Countries, and 25,000 by 1625.[20] Norwich's increase in population was also absorbed largely within the same walls, and both towns suffered severely from recurrent outbreaks of the plague. The comparison tilts considerably in Edinburgh's favour if the suburbs of greater Edinburgh are taken into account. In European terms, although the burgh could not rival an Augsburg or Cologne, still less the giants of the sixteenth century like Amsterdam, Venice or Milan, it was much the same size as Erfurt or Bremen in the Holy Roman Empire, Delft or Dordrecht

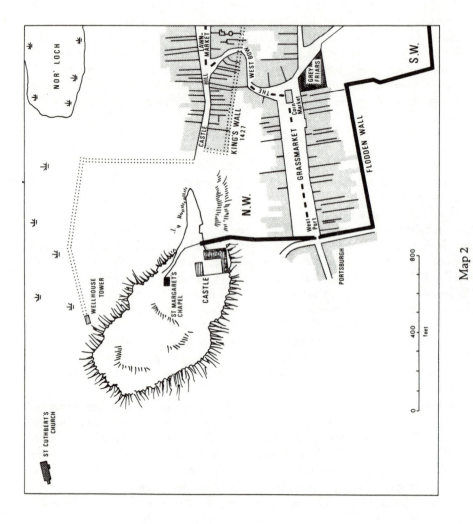

Map 2

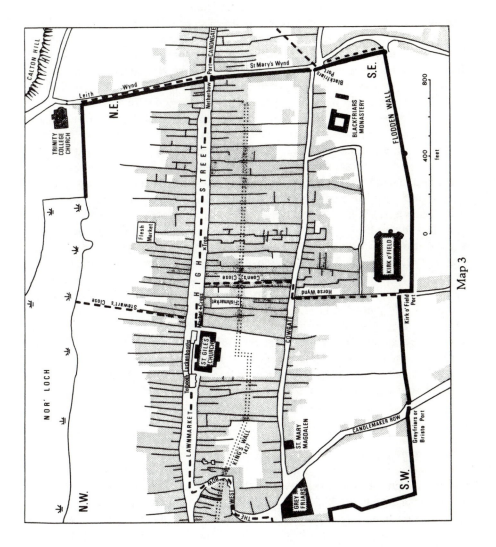

Map 3

in the Netherlands, or Geneva before its influx of refugees, and a good deal larger than Zürich.[21]

The most dramatic rise in population probably coincided with the period of most intensive building and rebuilding in the first thirty years of the seventeenth century. By 1635 the number of households within the burgh had risen to just over 3,900. Between 1592 and 1635 the number of households in the south-east and south-west quarters, the area between the High Street and the Flodden Wall, which had the greatest room for expansion, almost doubled. The soaring tenements of the north side of the Lawnmarket, originally called the 'land mercat', above St. Giles', allowed the north-west quarter to expand by almost 60%, but in the north-east quarter, between St. Giles' and the Netherbow, the increase was only half that.[22] This rapid expansion was a controlled chaos; building regulations were strict and remained in the hands of the Neighbourhood Court presided over by the dean of guild. The wealthiest parts of the burgh lay on the north-west side of the High Street down to and just beyond St. Giles' and on the south-east side, once far enough removed from the stench of the fish market, which lay just below St. Giles', for most of the way down to the Netherbow. The poorest areas lay near the walls on the south-west side lodged between the competing smells of the candlemakers near the Greyfriars Port and the maltmen around the West Port and the foot of the Castlehill.[23] Yet the strains of a growing population had not particularly altered the city's shape or character. A burgess born in 1500 would have had little difficulty in finding his bearings in 1650. Some of the markets had been moved to the lower part of the High Street; a new tolbooth had been constructed inside the west end of St. Giles' but the old one in front of the church remained; the herringbone layout of the town remained, of the High Street flanked by a series of narrow closes and alleys which were certainly no cleaner by the second half of the seventeenth century when an English visitor compared the town with a comb 'whose teeth on both sides are very foul, though the space between them is clean and sightly'.[24] Apart from the more fashionable parts of the High Street, rich and poor, merchants and craftsmen continued to live cheek by jowl with one another, hemmed in by the same walls and the same introverted thinking which went with them.

The same burgess would have had even less difficulty in fitting into the conventions of life and work in the town. The old distinctions between merchants and craftsmen, although redrawn by the revised constitution imposed on the town by the crown in 1583 in the decreet-arbitral, for the most part remained. Both groups remained dedicated to the mission of preserving the burgh as a fortress of economic privilege open only to those who inherited their freedom or paid dearly for it. The town council was expanded in size by the decreet but not in substance or attitude. It remained a paternalistic and privileged body with exclusive control over all aspects of burgh life, still concerning itself with the minutest details of trade and craft regulations and policing the burgh. The details might range from solemnly adjudicating on the virginity of the daughter of a burgess, on which turned her right to pass on her burgess rights to a prospective husband, to forcing the fleshers to remove carcasses and offal to the convenient waters of the Nor' Loch.

Although a great deal has been written about the duties and concerns of the council in the sixteenth century,[25] very little is known about its internal workings or its membership. It had met twice a week, on a Wednesday and Friday, since at least the mid-1550s. After 1560 the meetings were held in the mornings after the sermon. By 1584, because of the increasing demands on its time, it also began sitting on a Tuesday afternoon.[26] Its meetings in the council chamber of the tolbooth were confidential and its minutes seldom better than laconic. The body which controlled burgh politics was a fairly small and select oligarchy controlled by the merchants. About a quarter of the 357 merchants listed on a tax roll of 1565 sat on the council at some time in their lives. The number actively involved in burgh affairs at any one point, however, was much lower; it probably was not much more than thirty-five or forty, about double the available seats on the council. Only a little more than fifty merchants served on the council in the course of the 1550s. This was also, to a large extent, a self-perpetuating oligarchy. A complicated process of cross- and self-election had been established by various acts of parliament since 1469 and this almost invariably ensured considerable continuity between one council and the next. It is difficult to describe a normal pattern in Edinburgh since almost every annual election had its own peculiarities, encouraged by growing irregularities in procedure, especially during the 1560s, but the pattern should have taken the following course. Each Michaelmas the old and new councils met together to elect the provost, four bailies, treasurer and dean of guild. To be more precise, these seven office-holders were elected from the body of ten retiring and two new merchant councillors. The same meeting selected two craftsmen to sit on the council from a leet of six drawn up by the deacons of the incorporated crafts. The old office-holders continued as ordinary members of the new council. The provost should have been elected but seldom was, and for twenty-five years after 1553 he was not only a nominee imposed from outside, but not even a merchant burgess. Often, to the dismay of the crafts, the elections were weighted still more heavily against them by the presence of assessors, usually burgh-based lawyers, who should not have been entitled to vote but did on occasion. The most influential of these shadowy figures was Alexander Guthrie, town clerk of the burgh from 1558 until his death in 1582 and the first of a long family oligarchy of Edinburgh town clerks. To his catholic enemies the town clerk of the new protestant regime came to be known as 'King Guthrie'.[27]

The merchant oligarchy which dominated Edinburgh politics was a fairly small but not a closed one. Son tended to succeed father but it was rare for two brothers to sit side by side on the same council. Council meetings in Edinburgh were never quite the intimate family meetings enjoyed by the Strasbourg council in the eighteenth century.[28] Nor was there a formally defined patriciate of ruling families, although there were half a dozen who were consistently prominent in burgh government. Its doors were not locked and bolted against outsiders. Indeed the two most influential men in burgh politics in the quarter of a century after 1560 were both newcomers. Adam Fullarton, who emerged as the leader of the protestant party in 1559 and commanded the king's men exiled from the burgh a dozen years later, had originally secured his entry into the burgh establishment by marrying into an old influential family; Alexander Clark, a confidante of the English ambassador, Thomas Randolph, in the 1560s and provost of the burgh for six successive years after 1578, had secured burgess-ship and guildry by being a client of James Stewart, earl of Moray.[29] All offices were, in theory, open to all merchants. No distinction was made, as in English towns, between those eligible to sit on the council and those eligible for major office. In practice a distinction was drawn; the wealthier a merchant was, the more likely he was both to sit on the council and to hold office. Only six of the twenty-four richest merchants in the burgh in the 1560s did not serve on the council at some time in their lives. The scale of political influence steadily recedes the lower down the merchant community one goes; forty-nine of the first eighty merchants were elected, sixty of the first one hundred and thirteen, seventy-three of the first one hundred and seventy-six. The poorer half of the merchants, the one hundred and eighty-one assessed below £10 in the tax roll of 1565, yield only fourteen who ever reached the council chamber. It is striking, however, that a number of these small men became bailies, and they included a number of important men in the protestant regime of the 1560s — Edward Hope, Archibald Graham and David Somer. By the 1580s this general pattern of a council dominated by wealthy merchants was becoming even more pronounced. The actual numbers of wealthy men reaching the council did not increase — twenty of the first twenty-seven on a tax roll of 1583 — but it is noticeable that rather fewer middle-ranking merchants and distinctly fewer smaller merchants were coming on to the council by the 1580s.[30] The reason for this was that the wealthier merchants were tending to cling to power longer. In the 1560s it was unusual to serve for much longer than ten years; those whose service stretched for more than fifteen were few and far between. Yet by the late 1570s this practice was becoming much more common. A number of men who came on to the council in the second half of the 1560s were still there in 1585 — and an older and more short-tempered set of burgh rulers may explain a good deal in the tempestuous 1580s. What is certain is that the lines of power and privilege were drawn a good deal more starkly by then than they had been in the 1550s or 1560s.

It is clear from the point at which the regular series of council minute books begins in 1551 that two craftsmen sat on the council. The craft deacons could also be called in for any matters which impinged on the common good of the burgh. It was the deacons who drew up a leet of craft candidates for the council but their selections were not always accepted. The council resisted all their efforts to widen the range of craftsmen eligible for election. Half of the fourteen incorporated crafts were excluded in practice. Craft councillors were drawn largely from the six wealthiest and most respectable guilds, the hammermen, skinners, furriers, goldsmiths, tailors and barbers.[31] The decreet of 1583 did not drastically alter or widen this circle of privileged crafts. The six new deacon councillors were drawn invariably from these same six crafts plus the cordiners, who were the only craft to rise in status as a result of the revised burgh constitution.

The craftsmen who were admitted to the council were not very typical men. They were carefully vetted for their respectability and, in the early stages after 1560, for their protestant convictions, which had a scarcity value. Only thirty craftsmen had put their names to a subscription list of 'faithful brethren' in 1562 but more than two-thirds of the men who became craft councillors in the 1560s came from that list. But protestantism and respectability had to go hand in hand; one was not enough without the other. The prominent protestant baker, David Kinloch, was rejected in 1569, and one of the loudest of the voices raised against him was the wealthy and highly influential protestant merchant, James Baron. Crafts which dealt with 'mennis sustentation' would not have fitted well into a council which had a clear interest in keeping food prices artificially low.[32] The craft councillors were part of a small but influential and wealthy craft aristocracy which was clearly emerging in the thirty years before the decreet of 1583. Most of them were not craftsmen but craft employers and members of the merchant guildry. Increasingly the distinction drawn between them and their merchant colleagues on the council became an artificial one. A number, like the ever-present protestant activist, James Young, who was deacon of the hammermen ten times over as well, made a useful sideline in their taverns. In 1575 the regent Morton imprisoned a number of the richest merchants in the town for exporting bullion. Among their number was a skinner, Thomas Aikenhead. He had gained his guildry in 1567 but remained deacon of his craft until 1571 and was twice a craft councillor between then and the decreet. For a man like this, the transition from craft aristocracy to merchant, as redefined in 1583, was a smooth and natural one. He, like a number of other ex-craftsmen, became a bailie after the decreet.[33] All of the councils for the rest of the 1580s had an ex-craftsman as one of the bailies.[34] The merchant oligarchy which dominated Edinburgh's government was widened in 1583 but not changed either in its interests or character. The decreet did not give power to the craftsmen but to a craft aristocracy. There was no sudden democratisation of burgh government as a result.

It is not surprising to find that the political establishment took on an almost exclusively protestant complexion after the Reformation of 1559-60 but the dominance of radical protestantism was neither as sweeping nor as wholesale as many historians — of different religious persuasions[35] — have assumed. The town came to be governed not only by a protestant oligarchy in the sense of a radical, self-elected minority party, able, because of its inherited powers

C

as councillors, to impose its will on a largely conservative or acquiescent majority, but by a fairly broad-based protestant establishment which remained for the better part of the 1560s a loose coalition of interests. The religious changes did not involve a change in the kind of men who habitually sat on the council except for a brief period in the crisis of the autumn of 1559 and spring and summer of 1560 when a makeshift caretaker council took charge. The reformation did not mark any political revolution in burgh politics.

A number of protestants had infiltrated the council chamber by the 1550s but there is no evidence to suggest that they acted or were looked upon as a separate faction governed by religious interests. There was no bifurcation of burgh politics, whether inside or outside the council chamber, into catholic against protestant until the Congregation invaded the town for a second time in October of 1559, deposed the elected council and substituted a radical protestant one, made up of a highly unusual mixture of large and minor merchants, in its place. In a sense the events of 1559 and 1560 continued to colour burgh life for a long time after. The struggle between protestant and catholic activists continued, often in a bad-tempered but rarely a violent way. It was not fought out, however, in the council chamber; that was dominated by continual shifts in the balance of power between protestant radicals and protestant pragmatists which for the most part resulted in co-operation in the ordinary business of governing and the uncontroversial parts of a programme of protestantisation but which could at times flare up into bitter disagreements. In 1563, after one of these shifts, matters became so tense that the rules for conducting business had to be tightened up; interruptions were forbidden and only the bailies might call a speaker.[36] It is hardly the picture of a single-mindedly radical caucus dedicated to implementing its programme. Much the same pattern of a tension between moderates and radicals emerged again in the early 1580s, but this time the struggle was unrelenting and much more bitter in tone. This was largely because the issues involved in council politics were, almost for the first time, bound up with ecclesiastical politics. The activities of Edinburgh's radical ministers and their dismissal in 1584 sucked the council into the full force of the Melvillian controversies. It is a strange twist of irony that while the issues which threatened to bring the council into head-on conflict with James VI in 1584 were religious ones, the issues which caused greatest difficulty in the council's relations with his mother were not. The picture which will emerge from the complicated story of Mary's personal reign is of a body trying, like other bodies in the early 1560s including the General Assembly,[37] to settle into regular relations with the crown, but having, again like the General Assembly, a series of internal disagreements over the precise nature of that relationship. The key to understanding Edinburgh politics in the Marian period lies in calculating reactions within the town to increasing interference in burgh government by the crown. This interference was all the more difficult to deal with because it took the form of infiltrating the council not, for the most part, with catholics but with moderate, trustworthy protestants. The policy of the catholic queen was not to back the burgh's hard-line catholics against a protestant council but to ignite the underlying conflict between different shades of protestants within the council itself. It was a tactic which, it will be seen, came very close to success.

The councils of the second half of the sixteenth century had to deal with increasing crown interference to a degree which seems far beyond that experienced by other burghs.[38] In addition, it is clear that they became increasingly overworked. The poor were always with Edinburgh, but the strains of political crisis had increased their numbers to alarming proportions by 1562,[39] and the combination of plague and famine in 1569, followed by the enormous economic dislocation caused by the civil wars of the early 1570s, brought about a social crisis of major proportions which the stretched resources of the burgh found impossible to cope with. Bread riots never in fact materialised but craft riots, the other spectre which always haunted the council, did. The first major challenge to the new protestant regime came in the form of a series of riots by craftsmen and apprentices in the last months of 1560 and the summer of 1561. The fevered imagination of the new and still insecure protestant council suspected that a catholic conspiracy was afoot but the detailed evidence makes this look most unlikely. The first — and only — explicitly catholic riot to worry the city fathers did not come until 1565 when an ex-chaplain of St. Giles' was found saying mass in a private house and dragged to the market cross. The sight of a well-known and respected local priest being subjected to the horseplay of a protestant mob proved too much for a number of catholics who had lain low until then. A violent and large-scale struggle broke out on the High Street and was only stopped by the intervention of the provost and a force of heavily armed soldiers. Edinburgh was never closer to religious civil war. This, the Tarbot affair, had all the hallmarks of a spontaneous riot rather than a conspiracy to use violence on the streets to undermine the council's position. The first examples of riots which did have such an explicitly political aim in mind did not come until the 1580s, when they took a rather different form. By then the conspiracy was not catholic but a radical protestant one. There is evidence to show an unusual alliance between the dwindling band of radicals on the council, on the run ever since Morton's fall, and the growing forces of popular radicalism outside the traditional preserves of power in the burgh. It is ironical that the most serious internal challenge to the council's authority did not come with the Reformation but with the second Reformation, as it is sometimes called, twenty years later.

The council's worries, however, were usually reserved for more mundane things. It had a nominal control over the prices of all food and drink consumed in the town. Particular attention was lavished on the three key items in the Edinburgh shopping basket, bread, oats and ale. This led to a running battle with the town's bakers and maltmen but the council steadily was forced to concede ground. It managed until 1580 to cling to the symbolic fourpenny loaf but only by reducing its weight.[40] It was the combined effects of the debasements of the coinage during the Morton period and the catastrophic effects of the siege of the town in 1571-2 which put an end to any hopes of sustaining a cheap food policy. Even so, Edinburgh did not produce a regular and compulsory poor rate until the late 1580s, when a monthly contribution on all householders was instituted in co-operation with the kirk session.[41] An earlier attempt, encouraged by the act of parliament of 1574, had foundered badly. The council had finally agreed, under pressure from the session, to implement a compulsory weekly collection in May 1575 but the kirk session minutes of the period are littered with exhortations to the city fathers to put the system into effect. The kirk's own voluntary collections on Saturdays at the door of St. Giles' seem to have borne more fruit; in the twelve months after the records began in April 1574 the kirk's collectors handed in over £861. The collectors even jockeyed with each other for positions near the more lucrative east door. After the council put its own system into operation, the kirk's contributions fell dramatically, and the complaints mounted. The session complained that some of the congregation who lived outside the jurisdiction of provost and bailies and had promised to contribute weekly, had still not paid a penny; it reported that many inhabitants who had formerly agreed to a voluntary assessment now disputed the amount of their weekly alms; it hauled before it one worthy burgess who had been heard making complaints — which ring down the ages — that the poor supported by the kirk had more to spend on wine than honest hard-working folk. Poor relief, which might have been expected to have been the area of most fruitful co-operation between council and kirk, became an embarrassment to both. The failure of the council's system and the bad feelings it stirred up had the unfortunate effect of calling into question the efficacy of the kirk's efforts. Its weekly collection dropped by more than half to a miserly £7 8s in the summer and autumn of 1575. It was forced to admit that many of those receiving its alms did not need them while many of the deserving poor literally went begging. The council abandoned its own attempts in 1576, grumbling that the community was not willing to be taxed to support its poor. The poor and responsibilities for them were an area where the council and the burgh church simply got in each other's way, and although the kirk session records peter out late in 1575 there are hints that the miserable experience of the past year had induced a crisis of confidence in its own abilities.[42]

This confusion over the poor was not a product of the 1570s. Successive protestant councils of the 1560s had exhorted the town, crafts and the ranks of the faithful, in turn, for funds. They had had only limited success and had been forced back on a combination of continuing many of the old *ad hoc* methods which had existed before 1560, like diverting sales taxes on wine, and reallocating some of the investments of burgesses in the mass. By 1565 the crafts had agreed to deal with their own poor but the council still encountered serious resistance, even to a voluntary rate on the rest of the burgesses, some of it coming from catholics because support of the poor was linked with support of the town's ministers. The council's difficulties over a poor rate were one of the most important of the factors shaping its relations with Mary, Queen of Scots. It had first set its sights on the scheme for a new poor hospital in 1562, to be built, it hoped, on the site of the old yard of the Black Friars. When it petitioned the queen to hand over the lands and income of the friary, Mary had promised that this would be done whenever 'sufficient provisioun' had been made by the town for building costs. The campaign for funds met with sufficient, if limited, response from the protestant establishment to gain the formal grant for the hospital by March 1563. The queen was willing to co-operate with the kind of protestantism that the hospital scheme exemplified, deeply concerned with its civic responsibilities and by instinct socially conservative. The fact that it figured more and more in her calculations can be illustrated by two incidents. In December 1564 there was the strange sight of Adam Fullarton, the leader of the protestant party in the burgh since 1559, appealing directly to the queen to force the council to implement a compulsory poor rate because the voluntary system had been widely resisted and was sustained by only a 'few nowmer'. His appeal had its desired effect since the council agreed a fortnight later to implement a quarterly tax on all inhabitants to support the poor and the ministry. But when it, in turn, ran into difficulties when a number of prominent catholics refused to contribute, it also turned to the queen for help. There could hardly be a clearer reminder of the fact that the primary concern of the town council was the business of governing, and help given to it in this task would be welcome whatever its source.[43]

The problem of funds was eased a little towards the end of the 1560s by the gift to the town of Trinity College, which ironically had been secured by a catholic, or only recently ex-catholic, provost, the laird of Craigmillar. It was helped as well by increasingly frequent bonuses provided by gathering in more of the old revenues of the kirk in the burgh, not least by the deaths of old chaplains of St. Giles' who had received pensions throughout their compulsory retirement.[44] The collection for the hospital, however, had reverted to a voluntary basis by 1568 and the system of collecting poor relief in the 1570s did not differ much after the abortive efforts of 1575 from that first instituted in 1561.[45]

A good deal of the resistance to the imposition of a compulsory poor rate on the town can be explained by the fact that general direct taxation of the inhabitants by the council was not a recognised practice at this point in the town's history. The bulk of burgh revenue, the so-called common good, continued to come from a wide range of indirect sources — a figure as high as twenty-nine is given in the volume, *Edinburgh, 1329-1929*[46] — ranging from the annual lease or tack of the common mills, petty customs and risk ventures involving foreign cargoes, known as the wild adventures, to the rents paid by goldsmiths and other traders for their booths in the High Street and the fees paid for pasturing sheep and cattle on the Boroughmuir. The council was constricted by its inability to tax except in times of emergency and by the meagreness of its land holdings around the town. The inevitable result was that the relationship between ordinary expenditure and ordinary revenue was always precarious. It is hardly surprising that every outside political crisis in the period brought in its wake a further financial crisis for the burgh. The town's poverty throughout the 1570s is easier to understand when it is realised that the troops levied by the council exiled in Leith during the civil wars in 1571 and 1572 were paid for only by a substantial loan of 10,000 merks from one of the burgh's merchants. It took the town seven years to repay the loan and it managed to do so only by setting the common mills, one of the steadier sources of revenue, in tack.[47]

It was not only political crisis that strained the town's meagre resources. When Edinburgh was offered the superiority of Leith in 1565, the council had great difficulty in raising the required 10,000 merks. It managed to raise the bulk of it in the form of a forced loan on the burgh, but took a further eighteen months to pay the full amount to the crown.[48] In 1568 the harbour at Leith and the road to the port were in a shocking state of disrepair but the coffers of the common good were empty. The repairs were paid for only by suspending repayment of the loan on the superiority of Leith. Money was a highly sensitive subject even when it was needed for essential repairs or obligatory ceremonial occasions. The craft deacons objected to the sum raised for the celebrations organised for the return of the queen in 1561, and the council was closeted together for three days before it delivered its collective judgement on the sum to be spent in connection with the baptism of her son in 1566.[49] The one major source of revenue which could be expanded was the sale of burgessship and guildry. The accounts of the dean of guild, who was responsible for the upkeep of St. Giles', show that the income from this source realised more in the one year 1560-61 than for the whole of the 1550s in order to meet the spiralling costs of reorganising and refurbishing the interior of the old church.[50] Such an enormous inflation of honours could not be allowed to go on for long without damaging the social and economic fabric of the burgh. Both the resources and the room for manoeuvre of the town council were strictly limited in financial matters. It is here that the picture of an omnicompetent governing body able to rule without let or hindrance — painted with gusto by the eighteenth-century historian, Hugo Arnot, who likened the council to a despotic monarchy[51] — is at its most suspect. The notion that Edinburgh's town council or that of any of the Scottish burghs was a closed oligarchy answerable only to itself crumbles on closer inspection. In practice its range of activity rested on broad consent, whether it involved the further protestantisation of burgh society or the more mundane and frequent question of the burgh's finances. In both the council remained circumscribed by the old idea of the common good.

NOTES

1. The high figure is given in Brown, *Scotland in the Time of Queen Mary*, 52, and is backed, surprisingly, in S. G. E. Lythe, *The Economy of Scotland in its European Setting, 1550-1625* (1960), 117. The more recent work, S. G. E. Lythe & J. Butt, *An Economic History of Scotland, 1100-1939* (1975), 6, has, however, suggested that the total is more likely to be in the lower end of the range.

2. For the lower end of this more limited range, see I. F. Grant, *The Social and Economic Development of Scotland before 1603* (1930), 351. For the higher end, see J. Ridley, *John Knox* (1968), 3; W. S. Reid, 'The coming of the Reformation to Edinburgh', *Church History*, xlii (1973), 27.

3. I am very grateful to Dr. Walter Makey for the considerable, detailed information he has given me regarding the annuity tax of 1635.

4. See *Canongate Book*, 71; *APS*, VI, i, 441, 446; M. Flinn (ed.), *Scottish Population History from 17th Century to 1930s* (1977), 138.

5. MS Co. Recs., ii, fos. 126v-131r, 132r-137v; the totals are given in *Edin. Recs.*, iii, 23-5.

6. The usual multiplier lies somewhere between the 4.75 suggested in T. P. R. Laslett, 'Size and structure of the household in England over three centuries', *Population Studies*, xxiii, no. 2 (1969), 207, 211, and the 4.2 put forward by D. V. Glass & D. E. C. Eversley (eds.), *Population in History: Essays in Historical Demography* (London, 1965), 177. What indications there are for household size in Edinburgh in the seventeenth century would not differ appreciably from these guidelines; the poll tax returns for one of the Edinburgh parishes in 1694 show average household size ranging from 4.1 to 4.7; see M. Wood, 'Edinburgh poll tax returns', *BOEC*, xxz (1945), 95-6.

7. It had 220 of the 1,245 inhabitants taxed in 1583 and 58 of the 357 merchants taxed in 1565; see apps. xi & xii.

8. These were the fleshers, wrights and masons, who had 40, 19 and 13 masters respectively in 1583.

9. This is attempted in my thesis, 'Edinburgh and the Reformation' (London Ph.D., 1977), 16-7.

10. See my thesis, 17-18, for details.

11. This is based on a sample of surnames from A-D in the annuity tax toll of 1635. Again, I am grateful to Dr. Makey for this information.

12. Cf. Hoskins, 'Elizabethan merchants of Exeter', 164.

13. These figures are taken from an analysis of the guild register and yield considerably higher returns than the printed dean of guild accounts, which are extant only for the 1550s and part of the 1560s; see *Edin. Accts.*, ii, 4ff.

14. This is using a multiplier of 4.7.

15. 'The division of the town of Edinburgh within their own paroshine thereof in eight seuerall congregations', Edinburgh City Archives, MS Moses Bundles, no. 195, doc. no. 7029.

16. Moysie, *Memoirs*, 53-4; T. C. Smout, *A History of the Scottish People, 1560-1830* (1969), 163.

17. This is using a multiplier of 1.7 to include children and adding a further 4% to take account of 'gentlemen'.

18. See W. H. Makey, *The Church of the Covenant: Revolution and Social Change in Scotland, 1637-1651* (1979), 153.

19. L. B. Taylor (ed.), *Aberdeen Council Letters*, i (1942), 392-406. The nearest Edinburgh tax roll to this date is one of 1605, which has 1,168 inhabitants on it; I am grateful to Mr. James Brown for providing me with this information. For estimates of Aberdeen's population, cf. W. Kennedy, *Annals of Aberdeen from the Reign of King William the Lion to the End of the Year 1818* (Aberdeen, 1818), i, 186-7; G. D. Henderson, *The Founding of Marischal College, Aberdeen* (Aberdeen, 1946), 80. Macniven declines, perhaps wisely, to make a guess; see 'Merchant and Trader', 95-103.

20. J. F. Pound, 'Government and Society in Tudor and Stuart Norwich, 1525-1676' (Univ. of

Leicester Ph.D., 1975), 1-4; W. G. Hoskins, *Provincial England: Essays in Social and Economic History* (London, 1963), 72.

21. See Mols, *Demographie historique*, ii, 510, 511, 521, 527; N. Birnbaum, 'The Zwinglian Reformation in Zürich', *Past and Present*, xv (1959), 29; E. W. Monter, *Calvin's Geneva* (New York, 1967), 2. Geneva had a population of 10,300 or thereabouts in 1537.

22. This is based on a comparison of the parishes set out in the kirk session census of 1592 and the much fuller annuity tax roll of 1635. In the first and second of the proposed eight parishes, which roughly corresponded to the south-east quarter of the burgh, there were 535 households in 1592 and 1,051 in 1635; in the third and fourth parishes, which roughly comprised the south-west quarter, there were 597 and 1,157; in the fifth and sixth, the old north-west quarter, there were 520 and 899; the seventh and eighth, the old north-east quarter, had 594 and 794. The boundaries of the proposed parishes of 1592 are given in MS Moses Bundles, no. 195, doc. no. 7029, and of the quarters of 1635, each of which had by then been sub-divided into three, in C. B. Watson, 'List of owners of property in Edinburgh, 1635', *BOEC*, xii (1924), 93-145.

23. These generalisations are based on a comparison of the tax rolls of 1565 and 1583 (see apps. xi & xii) and the annuity tax roll of 1635.

24. Brown, *Early Travellers*, 280.

25. They are discussed most fully in *Edinburgh, 1329-1929* (1929), 319ff.

26. *Edin. Recs.*, ii, 223; iv, 225, 345.

27. *APS*, ii, 95, c. 5; 107, c. 12; 244, c. 28; 497, c. 26; see Grant, *Social and Economic Development*, 376-82. The episode involving Guthrie has been recounted, but wrongly dated, in M. Wood, 'Domestic affairs of the burgh: unpublished extracts from the records', *BOEC*, xv (1928), 47-8; see MS Co. Recs., 14 March 1562, iv, fo. 24r.

28. The only established instances of this practice in this period are Edward & Wm. Little, Henry & Wm. Nisbet, and Alex. & Nicol Uddart, although it is certainly possible of the many Adamsons on the council; cf. F. L. Ford, *Strasbourg in Transition* (Cambridge, Mass., 1958), 182-3.

29. See app. v for details of both.

30. The tax roll of 1583 reveals that 39 of the first 84 on it, 50 of the first 181 and 58 of the first 225 served on the council at some time during the period. The remaining bulk of smaller merchants yield only 11, but more than half of those had ended their civic careers well before the 1580s.

31. Between 1551 and 1570 there were 11 hammermen, 7 goldsmiths, 6 skinners, 5 tailors, 4 barbers and furriers and 1 wright as craft councillors; between 1572 and 1583 there were 8 skinners, 4 goldsmiths and hammermen, 3 tailors and wrights, and 2 barbers.

32. *Edin. Recs.*, iii, 263-4; MS Co. Recs., iv. fo. 246r.

33. *Edin. Burgs.*, 23; *Edin. Recs.*, iv, 469, 578.

34. See *ibid.*, iv, 578-60; they were Wm. Harvie, tailor (1584-5), John Wilkie, skinner (1585-6), Michael Gilbert, goldsmith (1586-8), Wm. Smail, tailor (1588-9) and David Fairlie, tailor (1589-90).

35. It is striking that the committed Roman Catholic viewpoint, best seen in Fr. Antony Ross, 'Reformation and repression', *Innes Review*, x (1959), 355, shares the assumption of presbyterian historiography, seen, for example, in Reid, 'Coming of the Reformation', 31-5, that the history of Edinburgh's reformation is best told in terms of the steady and systematic protestantisation of burgh society, apparently without let or hindrance.

36. *Edin. Recs.*, iii, 172.

37. D. Shaw, *The General Assemblies of the Church of Scotland, 1560-1600: their Origins and Development* (1964), 13, 38-42.

38. This is a subject which has received surprisingly little study, apart from recent work on Aberdeen. There were, in this case, only a handful of occasions in the sixteenth century when the crown interfered in the burgh's affairs to a serious degree; see Macniven, 'Merchant and Trader', 109-10. This was, it seems, the more common pattern, although further research may qualify this impression.

39. See *Edin. Recs.*, iii, 145

40. *Ibid.*, iv, 184.

41. *Edin. Recs.* (1589-1603), xix, 17, 170.

42. *Edin. Recs.*, iv, 9, 39, 48-9; *APS*, iii, 86-8. The amounts of the kirk's weekly collection are entered regularly throughout the minutes of the kirk session; see BGKE, fos. 24v, 27v, 34v, 38v, 54v, 55r, 57r, 58r, 59r, 62r, 65r, 66r, 67r, 70r-71r, 76r, 77v.

43. *Edin. Recs.*, iii, 103, 110-11, 145-7, 180, 191; MS Co. Recs., 12 May 1565, iv, fo. 129v. See M. Lynch, 'The "faithful brethren of Edinburgh": the acceptable face of protestantism', *Bulletin of Institute of Historical Research*, li (1978), 198, for the text of the kirk session's appeal for funds in 1562 to build a poor hospital; see also *RSS*, v, 1275.

44. See, for example, *Edin. Recs.*, iii, 243-4, 245, 256; MS Co. Recs., iv, fos. 208v-209v.

45. Cf. *Edin. Recs.*, iii, 102, 247-8; iv, 154, 164, 203, 327.

46. *Edinburgh, 1329-1929*, 336.

47. MS Co. Recs., v, fos. 7v-10r, 54v-55r.

48. *Edin. Recs.*, iii, 207-8, 213, 224, 227-9; MS Co. Recs., iv, fos. 171v, 222r; see Wood, 'Survey of the development of Edinburgh', 28.

49. *Edin. Recs.*, iii, 120, 223, 226, 245-6.

50. Cf. the income realised from this source by the dean of guild with his expenditure on St. Giles' (*Edin. Accts.*, ii, 4-82, 118ff; see also *Registrum Cartarum Ecclesie Sancti Egidii de Edinburgh* (Bann. Club, 1859), xlv-xlix).

51. H. Arnot, *History of Edinburgh* (Edinburgh, 1779), 495.

3

The Burgh Church

EDINBURGH and its surrounding area could boast an impressive list of churches, chapels and religious houses. Within or just outside the burgh there were three collegiate churches, a Franciscan and a Dominican friary, poor hospital and a number of private chapels.[1] A little further away, to the west of the Castle, lay the parish church of St. Cuthbert's; it included within its bounds parts of the burgh to the south of the Cowgate. To the east lay the abbey at Holyrood, which was pressed into service as the catholic parish church for Edinburgh in the months between July and October 1559 when, in accordance with the amnesty drawn up between Mary of Guise and the Lords of Congregation, the city was allowed to practise both the mass and the new protestant service, presided over by the ex-Dominican friar, John Willock, in St. Giles'. The queen's private chapel at Holyrood became a refuge for catholic worship, which was occasionally open to outsiders, for much of the 1560s but the abbey church remained the parish church for the Canongate. Also within the bounds of the burgh of the Canongate and so within the jurisdiction of the abbot of Holyrood were the Rude Chapel in the Greenside and the two chapels, each with poor hospital attached, of St. Leonard and St. Thomas.[2] Immediately to the south of the town lay the Dominican convent of St. Katherine of Siena, which enjoyed the patronage of the Seton family.[3] The two friaries which lay just inside the town walls in the Cowgate, the Black Friars and Grey Friars, had suffered some damage when an English army under the command of the earl of Hertford had raided the town in 1544, but the damage which was done to them and the rest of the town has often been exaggerated. It seems likely that both friaries remained largely intact until they were ransacked by a mob in June 1559 shortly before the Congregation entered the town.[4] The loyalist council headed by Lord Seton stepped in, however, to prevent the same thing happening to the Abbey at the hands of a mob anticipating the entry of the Congregation in April 1560. It does not seem likely that this kind of image breaking or violent iconoclasm was encouraged by most protestants of influence in the burgh either before 1559 or during the reforma-

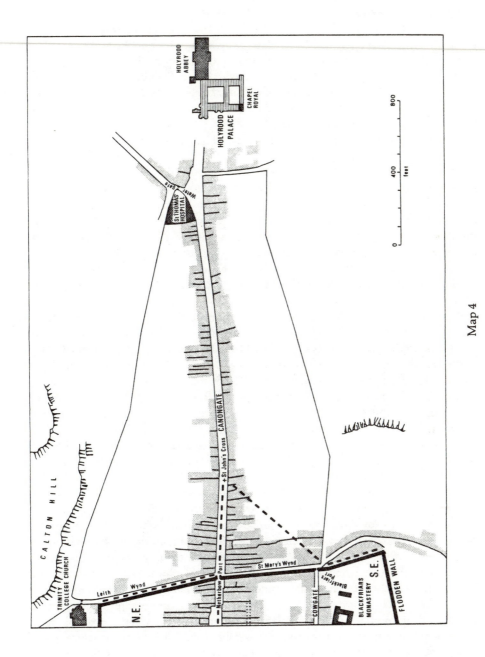

Map 4

tion crisis itself. Knox himself complained of 'temporisers' in the protestant riot on St. Giles' day in 1558. Edinburgh's mixed council, which remained in being until the elections of October 1559, was as concerned as any undilutedly catholic town council, like that in Aberdeen, to preserve the town's religious places.[5]

The legacy the protestant council expected to inherit in 1560 was, on the face of it, considerable. St. Giles' had been erected to collegiate status in 1466 on the substantial teinds of the parishes of Dumbarney and Kirknewton in Fife; further endowments by burgesses and burgh incorporations had followed. This legacy might be supplemented by the income from a variety of religious foundations within the town's jurisdiction. The largest prize was the Black Friars, where the income was 500 merks a year.[6] But the prospect of the new church laying its hands on the whole income of the old soon dissolved, and the protestant city fathers focused their hopes on securing the lands and income of the old church within the burgh itself. Various difficulties, however, proved to lie in the way of even this emasculated inheritance, which did not come into the council's hands until 1567 and even then not in full. Yet along with these new and fragmented revenues came major responsibilities, both old and new, particularly since the burgh undertook to support its own ministers. In financial terms, the reformation proved to be a double-edged blessing for the burgh.

As well as the great church of St. Giles', Edinburgh had two other collegiate churches, both only a few minutes' walk from it. Trinity College, which had been founded by Mary of Gueldres in 1460, lay immediately adjacent to the Leith Wynd Port on the north-eastern edge of the town and the Church of St. Mary in the Field, usually known as the Kirk o' Field, which was a much older foundation, lay just inside the walls on the south-east side. St. Giles', however, was the parish church of the burgh and had since 1400 been the subject of considerable investment by burgesses and neighbouring lairds. The church, as a result, had greatly increased in size and shape, particularly in the first half of the fifteenth century, and this process of reconstruction had become part of a concerted attempt by the town to have St. Giles' erected into a collegiate church. The intimate links between the town and its parish church were reinforced by the erection of altars within the church. It has been estimated that there were more than forty by 1560 and a great proportion of these had been erected or re-endowed in the period after 1466. Many had been donated by private patrons but since 1475, when the masons and wrights obtained a grant from the town council of the Chapel of St. John the Baptist, it had become the practice for each craft once it was formally incorporated to endow an altar and chaplainry in St. Giles'. By 1522 every one of the fourteen craft guilds had its own altar and chaplain. The terms of the charters establishing these bequests had, with time and especially since 1466, become more exact and prescriptive. The degree of control exercised by guilds over their chaplains was considerable; each of the craft deacons acted as kirkmaster for his craft with full rights of presentation and dismissal, able to regulate the hours of devotions, and in charge of the weekly penny donated by every master of the craft and halfpenny by every servant to furnish the altar and support the chaplain. The large merchant guildry had not one kirkmaster but four and it is clear from the terms of one of its charters that the office expected as much a pious patron as a vigilant treasurer.[7]

Patronage of many of the individual benefactions and most of the collective ones ultimately resided in the town council which, through the office of the dean of guild, also exercised considerable influence over the duties of the provost and prebendaries and was responsible for the upkeep of the fabric. The office of dean of guild was one for pious and wealthy men; James Carmichael, who held the office for half of the 1550s, was one of the principal benefactors in the enlarging of the Altar of the Blessed Virgin in 1556.[8] It is difficult, though, to unravel the thoughts of his successor, James Baron, when he took up the office in 1555; he had been a convinced protestant since the early 1540s. He next returned to the office with the protestant council imposed upon the town by the Lords of Congregation in 1559 and 1560. His main task then, ironically, was to supervise the dismantling of the institutionalised catholic ritual embodied in the complicated network of aisles and side altars so devotedly cultivated by his predecessors. Baron was a bizarre exception to the rule: a protestant patron and supervisor of the catholic cult of the town. It is striking that none of the other deans of guild of the decade before the Reformation came back on to the council in the years after it; they, like Carmichael, were convinced catholics.

This also provides a clue to the difficulties the new protestant regime of the 1560s had with the craft deacons. The craft was a miniature of the Christian community of the burgh. The masters, journeymen and apprentices existed as a religious fellowship as well as a trade incorporation. They were collectively bound to meet certain obligations to their altar and chaplain, to attend the funerals of their fellows and to take part in religious processions. The focus of their identity and independence as a craft was their altar in St. Giles'. The religious responsibilities of the deacon as kirkmaster made him a miniature of the dean of guild. The numbers of protestant craftsmen were few in the early years both before and after 1560; the number who had been deacons of their crafts was fewer still. It is clear that the majority of leading craftsmen remained unapologetic catholics. When the vestments and holy vessels of the skinners' altar were put up for sale by the council in August 1560 they were bought by a master of the craft, John Loch, who became its deacon a year later. He did not buy them as souvenirs; he was caught having mass said in his house in 1565.[9] It was not simply the money of burgesses which was invested in the mass;[10] it was also the collective identity of each of the craft guilds. One of the major problems for the new protestant regime was to find new outlets for the religious devotion of the craftsmen.

The force of catholic piety in the years immediately preceding the Reformation should not be underestimated. It has been pointed out that the surviving accounts of the dean of guild after 1552 reveal that only trifling sums were by then being devoted to the shrine of St. Giles'.[11] It is an obvious point but largely an unfair one; the days of massive investment of capital in St. Giles' as well as the need for it had been over since the 1520s, perhaps even since the 1450s.[12] The bulk of the revenue for the upkeep of the church and the numerous shrines within it came not from conspicuous acts of pious generosity which would be recorded in the accounts but from long-established and mostly small rents and annuals collected on property, mostly within the burgh, and from a bewildering *ad hoc* system of fines, entry fees and weekly contributions. This was one of the reasons why the new protestant regime found it so difficult to realise the income of the old church in the burgh. Permanent endowments were small and St. Giles' was not alone in this respect; the total annual revenue for the eight major altars of the Church of St. Nicholas in the catholic stronghold of Aberdeen amounted to less than £43.[13]

Historians of the Scottish Reformation have until recently been remarkably reluctant to consider any pattern other than that of a long, drawn-out and steady decay of catholic institutions paralleled by a long and steady growth of protestantism.[14] Yet it would certainly be a mistake to think of the 1550s in the stark terms of a spiritual crisis within the old burgh church which was increasingly unable to fulfil the needs of its parishioners. There are a number of signs which point towards a healthy civic catholicism. The worst corruptions of the old church were largely absent in the burghs where supervision of the clergy was close and rigorous. There is evidence of continuing endowment of the Black Friars in the mid-1550s. The hammermen were spending large sums in enlarging their altar in St. Giles' in 1552. The Magdalen Chapel in the Cowgate, founded by a wealthy merchant in the early 1530s, was re-endowed to the tune of £2,000 by his widow in 1553 and the hammermen added a further 500 merks; her daughter in turn invested a further £1,000 in 1555 to provide a regular income for a hospital.[15] There are a number of individual cases which show that influential men who later emerged as prominent members of the protestant establishment were still cast in the role of pious catholics in the second half of the 1550s. The other significant donor to the altar of the Blessed Virgin in 1556 along with James Carmichael was the laird of Blackbarony, Andrew Murray, who came on to the council in 1562 and celebrated his arrival by appearing among the ranks of the 'faithful brethren' who contributed to the poor hospital. From pious catholic to pious protestant in six years — it is not an unusual pattern in other city reformations of the sixteenth century. A historian of the reformation in the German cities in the early 1520s might ask why he took so long. The council itself was undoubtedly still an active catholic patron: it rebuilt the song school in 1554; in 1555 it provided a new building on the edge of the town for a grammar school; it made a series of attempts to deal with the poor in the second half of the 1550s.[16] Its first concern when the Congregation threatened to invade the town in June 1559

was to preserve its prized collection of religious relics and its expensive investments in the church's furniture.[17] This was the context out of which the new
church had to grow. The deeply conservative and paternalistic ethic of the
post-reformation burgh church stemmed very largely from the shape of traditional civic catholicism, which was still alive and well in the 1550s. This was
the base on which the protestant ethic was built and it was also its straitjacket.
The reformation in Edinburgh clearly followed one of the guiding principles of
other reformations of the sixteenth century: it succeeded most readily where it
changed least.

The first two protestant councils, which held power uninterruptedly from
the return of the Lords of Congregation in April 1560 until Queen Mary's first
intervention in burgh politics immediately after the election of October 1561,
were packed with a far larger *corpus* of radical men than most of their
successors in the 1560s. They did not, however, approach the complex
business of the protestantisation of burgh life with a simple and single-minded
zeal. Much of the initial eighteen-month period in power was spent in finding
out by process of trial and error what the new protestant council might and
might not do. Its first action, a week after English soldiers first entered the town,
was to order the repair of St. Giles', where altars had again been thrown down
by some of the protestant lords. Its second — and its first mistake — was to
impose a tax of £1,600 on the burgh to meet the expenses of the Congregation.[18] The new regime had great difficulty in raising this relatively small
amount. One wealthy merchant was imprisoned and then hauled before the
freshly re-established congregation in St. Giles' for refusing to pay. Eventually
the bailies were forced to resort to a money broker. There are clear indications
that the new regime had miscalculated; the extentors, the burgesses appointed
to assess the burden of individual taxation, were all protestants and most were
not established figures in burgh society; there are hints that some prominent
catholic loyalists were singled out for penal assessments. The mistake was not
repeated; the auditors appointed to review the tax a month later were a more
balanced body and this was to set the pattern for most of the rest of the
1560s.[19]

On 8 May 1560, the day that the new council made arrangments to house
the town's minister, John Knox, it also instructed its treasurer to cease all
payments out of the common good to chaplains and prebendaries. On 26 May
the council went one stage further by instructing all heritors of property in the
burgh on which annuals were due to chaplainries to stop paying them. In effect
it had banned all private and public patronage of the old burgh church. On 12
July it assumed full control of the Franciscan and Dominican properties in the
burgh and all income due from them. Collectors were appointed to uplift the
revenues to support the town's new ministry. Knox, who had been appointed
the burgh's minister when the Congregation first occupied the town in 1559,
was promised a stipend of £400 but seems to have had to settle for half of that.
John Cairns had been a reader in the privy kirk, the congregation of early

protestants which began to meet in the burgh for worship and readings from Scripture in the mid-1550s. His appointment was now formally recognised, with a stipend of £40; this was increased to 100 merks in 1561.[20] The payments were made by the dean of guild, who was given oversight of the revenues from the old ecclesiastical foundations in a logical extension of his interests in the burgh church. It is clear that in the heady days of the summer and autumn of 1560 the new protestant regime in Edinburgh was moving steadily towards a new burgh church founded on the revenues of the old. Its vision of a 'truly reformit' church clearly mirrored the financial arrangements for a reformed national church envisaged in the First Book of Discipline, which was under discussion by the Reformation Parliament and still in process of revision.[21] The dream of protestant visionaries already appeared to be becoming a reality in the burgh of Edinburgh.

Appearances were deceptive. The transfer of funds from the old burgh church to the new proved consistently difficult to operate in practice, even in the free market economy allowed to operate until a little after the return of Mary, Queen of Scots, in August 1561. The council had made an elementary tactical error in appearing to release heritors from the obligations to the burgh church and then demanding them anew. The response was poor and the council was forced to repeat its ordinance for the collection of annuals in April 1561. The problem was intractable because it was largely a practical one; the old revenues were, for the most part, made up of small property rents which were cumbersome to collect, particularly in a town with an active market in property. As late as 1569 the council found itself driven to desperate lengths to pay for the ministry; a number of burgesses were shut up in the tolbooth until they agreed to pay. It was forced to turn to other expedients. It was common for Knox or Cairns to be paid from the 'readiest money' available; a half of Knox's salary for 1560-61 came from the rental of the burgh mills.[22] These *ad hoc*, often desperate, measures continued to operate intermittently throughout the 1560s despite a series of schemes which came and went to place the payment of the ministry on a sounder footing. The new regime was in a quandary over the form this financial settlement should take. Should it be genuinely voluntary and limited only to the faithful, a new brand of pious giving to supplant the old? Or should it take the innovatory form of a specific tax, which might also embrace other godly interests such as relief of the poor? Should it be only on burgesses or on all inhabitants able to pay it? The story of the financing of the new burgh church in the period after the reformation and indeed well into the seventeenth century is one of a continuous oscillation between these possibilities and usually of settling uneasily somewhere in between. The new church, which had seemed to promise a direct and simple faith, and a cheap faith at that, proved to be expensive and demanding.

The first crisis in the finances of the new church came in 1562 when the council decided to acquire another minister to help to deal with its growing congregation. The man approached was the ex-Dominican friar, John Craig, who was minister of the Canongate. Within the next eighteen months the council tried no less than three separate schemes to finance its new responsibilities, each meeting with only limited success. The normal system used to pay national taxation was that the merchants were assessed individually in the quarter of the burgh in which they lived and the craftsmen paid a fixed proportion of the total, usually set at a fifth. In June 1562 the council tried to adapt this system used for national taxation to local voluntary taxation for the new church. Each of the bailies was to convene the merchants of his quarter and ask each one individually what he would give in the form of a voluntary but regular contribution, and each of the deacons was to do the same with members of his craft. The system was an unhappy marriage of voluntary piety and traditional taxation. As the crafts swiftly pointed out, it was designed to raise specific rather than regular sums; the craftsmen were unwilling to give their collective piety free rein in case their total contribution exceeded their traditional proportion of a fifth of all taxation and created an unwelcome precedent. It was clear within a year that the system was not working; Craig and Cairns had not been paid for six months. In June 1563 the council resorted to a direct appeal to the faithful to support their ministers until some 'better order' could be established. This did have a precedent — the appeal made by the kirk session in November 1562 to the 'faithful brethren' of the town for a new poor hospital.[23] Yet the obvious difficulty was the narrow basis for such an appeal. The contributors to the hospital numbered only one hundred and sixty; more than a fifth of them were lawyers or local lairds who would not necessarily be as generous towards the ministers as they had been to the poor. The ranks of the brethren had in any case their fair share of outspoken critics of the ministers, like Euphemia Dundas who accused Knox of having been caught with a common prostitute in the same month as the appeal was launched.[24] Reading between the lines of the council's next pronouncement on the subject, in November 1563, it is obvious that piety, left to itself, was not enough; Craig and Cairns, it pointed out, had not been paid for the better part of a year. It was at this point that the council turned to the most drastic of its expedients to date. After 'long reasoning' it decided to impose what amounted to a household tax of four shillings a year to be collected in two instalments. New taxes were bad enough; flat-rate taxes were an unheard-of imposition in burgh society. The scheme crumbled almost as soon as it was implemented. By April 1564, two months after the first instalment fell due, members of the council were being sent out among the faithful with a collecting can.[25]

Between May 1564 and January 1565 the council tried each of the three systems again. All communicants were ordered to appear, one quarter after another, before the full council to declare the amount of their 'voluntary' contributions. Six months later, councillors were again sent out with the begging bowl 'to travell among the faythful'. Finally, in January 1565, a compulsory quarterly tax was levied on all inhabitants of the burgh. There were two significant differences distinguishing it from the scheme of 1563. The first was that the tax aimed to solve two problems rather than one; the council's failures to establish both a voluntary poor rate and a voluntary system of donations to the ministry were swept together. The second was that an additional element had entered the ring—it was at the express instruction of the queen. The crafts agreed to take care of their own poor and to bear a reasonable share of paying for the ministry, and reluctant catholics were cajoled.[26] It is striking that the most significant advance to date towards permanently endowing the new burgh church stemmed from the intervention of the queen. Successive protestant councils up to 1565 had proved unable to implement a reformed programme based either on voluntary piety or compulsory taxation or even on a mixture of the two.

Since early 1562 the new protestant regime had had to lower its sights. A significant slice of the revenues it had seized in 1560 passed out of its control when the income from all monastic lands within the burghs reverted to the crown in February 1562.[27] Knox, who was the town's first minister, was paid by the Collector of Thirds of Benefices after November 1561, although Craig and Cairns continued to be paid directly by the burgh.[28] Step by step, however, the diverted lands and revenues were allowed to trickle back into burgh hands. In August 1562 the council successfully secured the return of the yard of the Franciscan friary for use as a new burial ground. The yard and income of the Dominican friary were recovered by March 1563 after the kirk session had shown it could raise the funds to build a new hospital.[29] It is fairly obvious that the council expected an early recovery of the rest of its lost income from November 1565 onwards, when it ordered a full inventory of the revenues of the old church and rashly promised to increase Knox's salary in anticipation. It had to wait until the last months of Mary's personal reign but in March 1567 Edinburgh, along with a number of other burghs, finally received the remaining lands and revenues of the old church within the town. Trinity College, which was not included because it lay outside the town, passed into the burgh's hands eight months later.[30]

It was with the burgh's recovery of most of the local income of the old burgh church that the second significant step was taken towards obtaining a regular income for the ministry — and again it was with the help of the queen. It was realised that the kirk rents, even if efficiently collected, could not sustain the combined burdens of ministry, poor relief and education. In 1567 the privy council ordered the burgh to resurrect its tax of 1565. The way was pointed towards the future although the future took some time to come. Little was done during Moray's regency; by 1570 the council had progressed only as far as persuading the crafts to put a firm figure on their still voluntary 'benevolence'. By the mid-1570s, however, it is clear that all of the stipends of the burgh's growing collection of ministers were met by the burgh itself.[31]

This was a burden which increased steadily with time. The combined salaries of Craig and Cairns, together with their household expenses and those of Knox, were less than £400 a year. By 1578 the annual bill for salaries alone exceeded £1,000. The ambitions of the council to secure the best ministers it could and to keep them proved expensive. James Lawson, who was appointed in 1573 to replace Knox, was paid 400 merks, which increased to £400 in 1575; John Durie was paid 200 merks when first appointed but was receiving £200 by 1577; Walter Balcanquhal was paid £100 in 1574 but his stipend doubled within three years; John Cairns, who probably remained a reader, received 200 merks in the 1570s, more than three times his original stipend in 1560.[32] The town's income from the old church did not stretch to anywhere near these sums; the accounts of the Collector of Kirk Rents for 1574 and 1575 reveal that kirk rents scarcely met a third of the burgh's outlay on its ministers. Most of the balance had to be made up by taxation. Between 1574 and 1577 a regular tax known as the common collection was levied on all inhabitants of substance. The merchants were stented in their quarters; the crafts paid a fixed proportion of the merchants' quota in accordance with the formula laid down in 1570. The tax was supplemented by a voluntary contribution from the judges of the Court of Session, the lawyers and their clerks, but this was not always forthcoming.[33] The system was abandoned in the early 1580s in the face of growing opposition to it, especially among the crafts, and once again the familiar pattern of late payments of stipends and recourse to the burgh treasurer for temporary funds reasserted itself. The shortfall came to be met not by a regular and specific tax but by adding on the required amount to the next national tax imposed on the burgh.[34] Edinburgh's ministers were wealthy men by any standards but the result was that the burgh church of the 1580s, just like that of the 1560s, was in a state of near-permanent overdraft.

The sums involved in these early abortive schemes may not seem large. The compulsory household tax of 1563 could not have raised more than £400. The voluntary offer of the crafts in 1570 was probably part of an effort to raise £500 a year. The annual target required in the 1570s to supplement the kirk rents was in the region of £600. These are amounts which, it has been pointed out, were only a thirtieth — or a sixth in real terms — of the vast sums raised in the 1640s to pay the stipends of the burgh's ministers.[35] It was not the amount of money involved, however, which was the most important issue at stake, but the principle of taxation for burgh purposes itself. It took a very long time for burgh society to accept the principle of direct taxation for religious or quasi-religious purposes. The reluctance of the town to pay for its ministers was one of the most serious of the obstacles in the way of the protestantisation of burgh society. It demonstrates once again the truth of the axiom, now put into a mirror image, that the reformation was slowest to succeed where it attempted any fundamental change. And change which touched the pockets of burgesses was fundamental indeed.

It is true that on the face of it the actions of the protestant regime brought to power in April 1560 were as ruthless as they were radical. Within three months not only were contractual payments to chaplains stopped and kirk rents frozen but a number of apparently irrevocable steps were taken. The sacred vessels, relics and vestments of the old church, which had been put into safekeeping when the Congregation first entered the town in 1559, were auctioned off to the highest bidder. Not even those which belonged to craft altars escaped. The next council, elected in October 1560, increased the pace of protestant reforms: the Sunday flesh market was abolished; it ordered booths and taverns to close during the Sunday sermon; Sabbatarianism was imposed not only on all inhabitants of the town but also on all visitors to it; the deacon of the fleshers, the fourth or fifth largest craft in the burgh, was dismissed from office for adultery. Six months later, in the wake of a series of craft riots, this council went a stage further: it tried to revive the payment of kirk rents for godly purposes; attendance at the sermon was enforced; a compulsory poor rate was threatened; all ex-priests and ex-religious who had not conformed to the new faith were ordered to leave the town immediately. Within a year of its being swept to power, John Knox, the preacher of the new regime, could use his privileged position in the pulpit of St. Giles' to ram home the point:

> What adulterer, what fornicator, what known mass-monger or pestilent papist durst have been seen in public?[36]

Yet how far had the new protestant regime progressed towards a reformed city before Mary's return? The idea of a religious revolution ruthlessly imposed on burgh society by a regime of radical protestants passes over most of the ambiguities involved in Edinburgh's reformation and the actual nature of authority available to the burgh's rulers. The regime's financial ambitions for both the ministry and the poor were already in process of being compromised — both by their own radicalism and because they ran up against burgh precedent. Most of the other aims of the reformed programme were limited in scope and effect for the same reasons. It had become clear before Mary returned that the council could not supplement the authority of the kirk session in breaches of morality to the point of dismissing office-holders; the unfortunate deacon of the fleshers was the first and last sexual offender to lose his office in the 1560s. Ministers, like the unfortunate Paul Methven of Jedburgh, might continue to fall for such misbehaviour but burgh office-holders escaped with a fine. The council's attempts to enforce attendance at the sermon came at a point where considerably less than a quarter of the adult population of the burgh, some 1,300, took communion; the reluctant might be brought to St. Giles' but they could not be forced — or allowed — to communicate. When the council issued its proclamation against priests and friars in March 1561, it admitted the failure of its previous tactics of persuasion and deplored the continuing influence of catholic clergy in holding 'the sempill pepill in blindness and errour'.[37]

The reissue of this proclamation six months later, after Mary's return, brought the council into head-on confrontation with the queen, in an episode of which Knox makes great play in his *History*. The affair led to the forced resignation of the provost and magistrates but it did not lead to a catholic counter-revolution. There was little difference in the protestant complexion of the council which finally emerged. Mary's interventions in burgh affairs were, in fact, limited in number and in scope. She made judicious interventions in council elections from 1564 but only rarely in order to infiltrate catholics on to the council. She moved, on occasion, to protect catholic priests, like the Dominican friar, John Black, accused of committing adultery with the wife of a prominent protestant burgess in 1562, and James Tarbot, an ex-chaplain of St. Giles', caught saying mass in the town in 1565.[38] While it is true that the hand of the queen was significant in limiting the horizons of the burgh church and its allies on the council, particularly in its treatment of catholic clergy, it is important to understand that her hand was used only sparingly and was not always necessary. The most effective checks on a policy of protestant expansionism came not from the queen but from within burgh society itself.

The major catholic challenge to the new regime proved to come not from Marian intruders or the old chaplains and prebendaries of St. Giles', most of whom conformed or left, but from the stubbornly catholic master of the grammar school, William Roberton, who persistently refused to take communion under the new rite or even attend the sermon. Ironically, the protestant council which returned to the town in 1560 had paid Roberton's quarterly stipend even before it had made arrangements for Knox himself. When the council tried to dismiss Roberton two years later, it ran into a series of legal technicalities and found that he had a good deal of influential support within the burgh. The affair became a test-case which dragged on for a number of years until the council finally admitted defeat.[39] Time proved that the council was not able to implement a blanket religious test on all office-holders, just as it was not able to rid itself of its contractual obligations to its old chaplains. Catholic relics were easy enough to dispose of but not the contracts of catholic chaplains or schoolmasters. Equally, it found that harassing catholic priests was one thing but harassing catholic burgesses quite another. A wholesale exclusion of catholics either from burgh office or burgh privileges did not lie within the competence of the new regime. The repercussions of these limitations for the shape of the new church were serious. Its transition from a 'privy kirk' in the 1550s to a burgh church in the 1560s became less a matter of expanding a radical core than casting a much wider net, which allowed some of the catch to slip in and out of it almost at will. The ranks of the brethren as a result included supporters of Roberton, bitter personal enemies of Knox, even crypto-catholics.[40] As the privy kirk took on a 'public face', as Knox put it, it took on the form of a comprehensive burgh church, distinguished for the most part by a protestantism which was diluted rather than dynamic, pious rather than radical. The transition from one to the other had come too early to be effective; the radical core of convinced protestants was too small and vulnerable to impose its will even on a passive majority. Victory had not come as the climax of a carefully engineered campaign within the town, as it had in most of the German and Swiss cities in the 1520s, but almost by accident, brought about by outside forces. It took the resulting burgh church the better part of a generation to shake off the price of its victory in 1560.

The core of the new burgh church almost certainly remained the early enthusiasts of the 1550s or before, just as its court, the kirk session, owed much of its organisation to the practices adopted in the privy kirk of the mid-1550s. Knox has described in great detail how the burgh's early protestants met in secret and closed conventions in houses or in the fields for readings from scripture and elected from within their own ranks some, as Calderwood adds, like William Harlaw, a tailor from the Canongate, and the ex-Dominican friar, John Willock, 'to occupy the supreme place of exhortation and reading', and others 'to be elders and helpers unto them for the oversight of the flock and some to be deacons for the collection of alms to be distributed to the poor of their own body'. As the privy kirk grew into a burgh church it elected elders and deacons to support the minister but they were drawn, Knox makes clear, from 'men of good conversation and honest fame *in the privy kirk*'.[41] A pure protestant pedigree presumably remained a precondition of spiritual office for some time to come. The electoral procedure, which is far more precisely laid down than that in the Book of Discipline,[42] also seems to have been designed to ensure that the early converts did not let slip their grip on the developing church. The old members of the session played a large part in nominating the new; they drew up the leets of elders and deacons, although each consisted of double the number of vacant places. The congregation continued to have a direct voice in the election process; it was allowed to add names to the leets or veto existing ones as well as casting its votes. The principle of congregational democracy extended, so Knox claimed, one stage further: the candidate receiving 'the moniest votes' would have 'the first place in the eldership and so proceeding till the number of twelve be complete', so that 'if a poor man exceed the rich man in votes, he precedes him in place'.

There is striking corroboration in the fragments of evidence which remain of the membership of the privy kirk of Knox's claim that wealth and status were not pre-requisites of office. All of the elders and deacons whose names are known came from well beneath the social status expected of a member of the town council. Two of them were merchants but only on a small scale; John Cairns, who later became a reader in St. Giles', was probably the son of a Leith skipper; the remaining three were craftsmen but only one of them was a craft master. It was a most unlikely collection in a society so conscious of rank and privilege — minor merchants, a craftsman, craft apprentices; only one of the six a member of the guildry; none with any experience of burgh office; none a burgess, if they had even reached that lowly rung on the ladder of burgh society, for more than three years.[43] A godly — and classless — society must have seemed near at hand.

There is evidence as well to substantiate Knox's claim that the Edinburgh kirk session did actually follow the remarkable system of election he described, which extended far beyond the closeted dealings of council elections or the notional democracy of the annual head court of the burgh, when all burgesses assembled to adjudicate on matters concerning the common good. When the session records first become available to us, they describe a procedure operating in 1574 which closely follows Knox's description. There are differences, but only of a minor kind: the congregation was first assembled not on a Sunday but a Thursday; the leet did contain exactly double the number of vacancies, but not in the prescribed quantities. The ambitions of the candidates had been given free rein; all but six of the fifty-six set their sights on the eldership. It is also clear that by 1574 the pressure on limited space within St. Giles' had forced the swelling congregation to assemble in their quarters in different parts of the church to cast their votes. By that time three elders and four deacons had been assigned to each of the quarters of the burgh but it is not clear from the minutes whether each quarter only voted for its own elders and deacons — a system which certainly operated when the burgh was later split into four parishes, each with its own session.[44]

There are good grounds for seeing the privy kirk as a revolutionary cell operating outside the established machinery and expectations of burgh society.[45] Yet like the radical town council which emerged in the reformation crisis of 1559, its like was not seen again — at least not for a generation. The privy kirk met not only in the fields like the persecuted Covenanters of the later seventeenth century, but in the commodious houses of its wealthy merchant brethren. Its meetings were closer to private conventicles than to the hedge sermons which preceded the outbreak of the first major crisis in the Netherlands in 1566,[46] and it was their hosts, the established merchants, who became virtually the proprietors of the kirk session. The merchants' partners were Edinburgh's legal establishment. Although the first leet of 1574 was drawn from a fairly wide cross-section of society — seventeen of the prospective elders were craftsmen and more than half of the merchants were smaller men, with even cramers or booth owners among them — the elders who were elected came from a much more select group. Six lawyers had stood for election, including the clerk register. Along with them stood three of the four retiring bailies of the council of 1573-4 and three of the old ordinary councillors. This formidable array of talent swamped the opposition. The result was that five of the six lawyers became elders as did four of the merchants on the old council and one on the new. All of the six merchants made elders had previously been bailies and all were drawn from the loftier reaches of the merchant hierarchy. The one craftsman who became an elder was a baker but one who virtually monopolised the deaconship of his craft in the 1570s and had been one of the leading activists in the king's party during the civil wars. There was certainly no hint in this or any of the other kirk session lists of the 1570s or 1580s, whether of elders or deacons, of apprentices or craft servants like those in the early days of the privy kirk. The eye of the needle was wide enough, on the other hand, for both merchant prince and lawyer to pass through with accustomed ease.

There can be little doubt from the lists which are extant for the 1570s that the eldership was dominated by a coalition of wealthy lawyers and merchants, most of whom had an impressive record of council service behind them. Much the same co-operation existed between these two groups on the session as between merchants and assessors on the council. Although no session minutes as such remain for the 1560s, there are strong hints in the contribution list drawn up by the kirk session in 1562 that this formidable alliance had formed as early as then. The list does not say who were actually on the session at the time but the list taken as a whole — with almost exactly half of both the merchant and legal establishments represented on it — gives the firm impression that that was where power lay from the very early days of the new burgh church.[47]

Occasionally a merchant appeared as an elder before beginning his career on the council, or a craftsman who never rose to the top of his craft, but usually it was not done without impeccable references — John Johnston was the brother of the laird of Elphinstone, Henry Charteris was the son of a former dean of guild, and the craftsman, John Freir, was the brother of a writer to the signet. If the elder's social connections were not impressive, then almost invariably his protestant ones were: the otherwise obscure figure of Matthew Forester was the brother of a merchant who had been in the inner circle of the protestant party since 1559; Patrick Rig was one of the two elders on the session of 1574 who were brothers-in-law of Edward Hope, who had a protestant pedigree stretching back to the 1540s. The same pattern operated amongst the deacons: the Charteris family and its in-laws were represented on all the sessions of the 1570s for which evidence exists. The combination of extended family connections and like-thinking men undoubtedly gave to the session much of its sense of continuity and internal dynamic. This was important because the Edinburgh session did not resort to the council's practice of re-selecting itself year after year or to the tactic increasingly used by other sessions, particularly as the seventeenth century progressed, of swamping itself with members of the sitting town council. The elections of 1574 and 1575 saw a complete turn-over in membership; not a single elder or deacon served for two consecutive years. None of the four lists extant shows more than three of the sitting council on the session: in 1574-5 there were two bailies and a councillor, in 1575-6 one bailie and a councillor, in 1573-4 a single bailie and in 1584-5 no members of the council at all. Yet if the same men did not crop up year after year, the same kind of men undoubtedly did.

The session was not quite the comfortable club which this might imply. A natural tension tended to exist within it and this derived in large measure from the differences in social origins between elders and deacons. As with the elders, there tended to be more merchant deacons than craftsmen. The majority of them, however, were middle-ranking or smaller merchants. What was quite clear was that none of them had previously sat on the council and most never would. For a select few the office was a stepping stone towards a future civic career, but for most it provided hard and pious work rather than new-found influence. The crafts never provided more than six of the sixteen deacons and they came always from the same seven or eight crafts — the skinners, tailors, baxters, barbers, hammermen, goldsmiths, cordiners and wrights. Even the large number of craft candidates in 1574 were drawn from the same guilds, which were, with the obvious exception of the baxters, almost exactly the same crafts as gained direct representation on the council in 1583. There can be little doubt that the session offered a political outlet to some quite lowly men — ordinary master craftsmen, inland merchants, even booth owners — who did not ever rise very high in their craft or the merchant community. But this outlet had its limits; there seemed to be little room on the session for the candlemaker or the bonnetmaker, the humblest of the master craftsmen. The session was also a very obvious breeding ground for radicalism, particularly among the smaller men it drew on. It was this development which threatened the accustomed balance — or imbalance — of interests on the session and the relationship which had developed over the years between it and the town council. The challenge, as we shall see, could not be allowed to go unheeded.

Although the original system of congregational democracy had seemed to prove no barrier to the advancement of the burgh establishment within the session, the electoral system described by Knox seems to have come to an end in 1575. The leets drawn up by the old session, even after they had been offered to the congregation 'to agment or diminishe', contained exactly the number of vacancies, twelve elders and sixteen deacons. The congregation did not elect but approve. In 1584 the pattern was taken another — and probably much more significant — stage further. The kirk session was actually chosen by the town council and craft deacons sitting together in the council chamber. This took place in a very particular context, shortly after the purging from the council of the last traces of a radical faction which had been closely associated with the Ruthven lords, who had briefly come to power in 1582-3. The session bore all the signs of being a safe and trustworthy body; four of its six merchant elders had been on the town councils of 1580-82, which had co-operated readily with Esmé Stewart. There was every reason to suppose they would co-operate with his colleague, Arran. The old council of 1583-4 had been seriously split over the agonising question of whether it should endorse Archbishop Adamson's letter condemning the town's radical ministers, who had fled into exile in England after the storm of protest which followed the passing by parliament of the so-called 'Black Acts', which aimed to restore greater power over the church to the crown. None from this council was allowed on to the new kirk session. Although this system of direct election lapsed, probably immediately after the fall of Arran in 1585, it did point the way of things to come. It returned in the 1620s when, in each of the four elections within

Edinburgh to correspond to its four parishes, the bulk of the council could comfortably outvote each kirk session.[48] There are good grounds for supposing that the kirk session was not immune to the general drift of burgh institutions towards a concentration of power in a largely self-selecting oligarchy.

It was only natural that the session should adopt a number of the practices and habits of the town council. Elections were held, not in August as recommended by the Book of Discipline,[49] but in October, usually a week after the council's own elections. This was a sensible working arrangement, although it tended to encourage retiring members of the council, including bailies, to stand for the eldership; there was often, as a result, a closer link between the session and the old town council rather than the sitting one. It was also sensible for the session to sit on a Thursday rather than a Sunday, as stipulated by Knox,[50] since the council sat on the days before and after. It was a rare meeting that went by without some of its members being delegated to petition the council the following day on some pressing matter. Other habits were obvious imitations of council practice: like the council, the old session in effect chose the new; proceedings were confidential; the number of craftsmen who became elders was in practice limited to two, the same number as allowed on the council until 1583.

Like the council, the session seemed to be at its happiest and most unanimous when it was regulating the minutest details of the workings of society and its lowliest members. In nineteen months it solemnly adjudicated on more than one hundred and thirty cases of fornication or adultery, including some where the offence had been committed more than six years beforehand. Occasionally the offender was someone as illustrious as Mr. Thomas Craig, a senator of the College of Justice and cousin of the burgh's second minister up until 1573, John Craig.[51] Usually they were humbler and, more often than not, female. The other and more creditable side of the coin is that the session increasingly acted as the conscience of the burgh establishment. It did not shrink from continually cajoling the council into implementing an effective system of poor relief, even if ultimately to little effect. Its acts of charity ranged from paying the bills for a badly burned child and a slater who had broken his leg falling from a roof, to granting twenty shillings to both an ex-friar for 'tua sarkis' and a webster who needed a nurse for his infant child, and paying for the education of a foundling.[52] It was in these kinds of dealings, once removed from the embarrassing question of a poor rate, that the kirk session worked most closely with the town council and came closest to the reformed ideal of the two jurisdictions, church and state, working in partnership.[53]

There were limits to the scope of this co-operation and to the investigative powers of the session. Only the civil magistrate possessed the power of excommunication and banishment from the town and this was used sparingly. There is no trace in the council minutes of any catholic burgesses, as distinct from regular or secular clergy, being banished before 1569.[54] In arguing that council and session acted in concert in a policy of dedicated repression, Fr. Antony Ross has pointed to the significance of the career of Robert Drummond, the guild officer, as a kind of municipal catholic catcher. Yet Drummond and the session did not always see eye to eye; he was actually dismissed in 1569 for misbehaviour before the session.[55] The session had to work with a council which was, for the most part, compromised by its own conservatism to the point where it proved reluctant to resort to the unusual step, which excommunication involved, of withdrawing burgess status. This was a body happy enough to pursue a policy of limited co-operation with a catholic queen and with men, at times, on it who had catholic relations and even catholic wives. It was not likely that such a body would always be willing to act as a rubber-stamp for an over-zealous kirk session.

There are other grounds for wondering whether the much-vaunted efficiency of the kirk session was not more mythical than real. The enthusiasm of its own members was not inexhaustible; twice within four months in 1575 it was forced to deplore the failure to attend meetings regularly. Within the same period it hauled before it a catholic candlemaker who admitted not having attended communion in St. Giles' once in the previous fourteen years. It is difficult when confronted with the curious case of Henry Easton to argue that the system of communion tickets, which evolved in the 1560s and was supposed to act as a check on recusancy, was infallible.[56] It is equally difficult to follow the logic of the argument that the size of the Scottish burghs made a thorough-going campaign of religious repression possible, that a man might hide in a city the size of Paris or London but hardly in Edinburgh.[57] It was larger than both Zürich and Geneva, the setting for other conspicuous attempts to set up a well disciplined 'school of Christ'. The difficulties of sheer organisation in regulating an adult population of between six and eight thousand inhabitants plus a floating population of professional men, traders, visitors and vagrants, were immense. One of the most intractable problems for the town council was the unfortunate habit of its neighbours of banishing vagrants and miscreants into an adjoining jurisdiction; the kirk session also suffered from this practice of its neighbours of exporting human flotsam. Its jurisdictional problems also worked in the opposite direction. The session's powers ended at the Netherbow, and a number of catholic burgesses seem to have taken refuge in the slightly more relaxed environs of the Canongate. Those harassed by the Canongate kirk session might, if they had the right connections, take refuge in the houses of members of the court or central administration or, further afield, in the Seton household.[58] The area around Edinburgh offered ample opportunity for undermining municipal uniformity. It is difficult to see how Edinburgh could in these circumstances hope to emulate the efficiency of the closed Calvinist monastery of the Genevan city state. Even within the town, the physical geography of multi-storeyed tenements separated by narrow closes was not ideal for sifting a largely unenthusiastic population. The point has been made often enough that burgh society provided a favourable environment for the growth of early protestant cells.[59] It does not seem to have been realised that it was just as useful to the catholic cells which undoubtedly persisted after 1560, even if seldom breaking surface as outright recusancy. The kirk session only gradually penetrated the two most important incubators of burgh catholicism, the household and the craft.

The sessions of the mid-1570s had to deal less with catholics than with Marians. Almost a quarter of its time was taken up, even two and a half years after the fall of the Castle in 1573, with the problem of inhabitants of the town who had become involved in one way or another with the losing side in the civil wars. This was a highly emotive business since the houses and property of a number of leading burgesses who had been forced out of the town by the Marian party had been systematically burned and looted. For the most part the session dealt brusquely and efficiently with self-confessed offenders. It is very noticeable that a large proportion of the unfortunates called before it were drawn from the lowest reaches of burgh society, men who do not appear in other contemporary records, were not burgesses and were beneath the threshold of tax payers. The wealthier and usually more committed queen's men did not escape the session's attention but were often dealt with in a manner which was markedly more discreet and patient. It was when it was dealing with men of substance, in this and other matters, that internal divisions within the session were liable to come to the surface. The two most acrimonious meetings of the session, when matters were actually pressed to a vote, both stemmed from the bad feeling left over from the period of forced exile and siege. In one, the session had to decide whether that august person-age, Thomas MacCalzean of Cliftonhall, a senator of the College of Justice, should be forced to appear barefoot and in sackcloth to confess his fault at the pillar of St. Giles'. In the other, the session was highly embarrassed when one of its elders, the highly respected leader of the king's party in exile, Adam Fullarton, was accused by a member of the influential Fairlie family, which had been deeply involved with the Marian cause, of having exploited his position during the troubles for the purposes of peculation.[60]

MacCalzean had been an elder of the kirk and one of the burgh's early protestants; so had Fullarton. They ended up on opposite sides in the civil wars. Henry Nisbet and Fullarton, both stalwarts of the king's party in the wars, were elected elders in 1574. They ended up as bitter opponents in the Melvillian crisis of 1584.[61] The session, like the council, was never a wholly united body single-mindedly bent on a protestant crusade although it did come closer to that ideal than the council. The thread of consistent radicalism and consistent hostility to any taint of Erastianism, whether offered in the form of Mary or Arran, was rare indeed. John Preston was one of the most outspoken of the elders who defied James VI when summoned to Falkland in 1584. But his history was a curious one; he had co-operated with Mary of Guise to the point of becoming a bailie on the loyalist council headed by Lord Seton in 1559, and enjoyed the confidence of her daughter enough for her to nominate him to the council in 1565, although he was a commissioner to the General Assembly at the time.[62] Even for Fullarton, the most distinguished protestant in the burgh for fully twenty-five years, the thread was not unbroken — he had turned to Mary, almost certainly on behalf of the session, to help to cajole a reluctant council in the perennial problem of the poor. Yet these were the kind of protestant allies, the men of influence, on whom the new burgh church and Knox chiefly relied. The protestant establishment — as represented in both council and kirk session — was not as unremittingly hostile to Mary as was Knox himself. These differences of emphasis could, at a time of severe crisis, lead to real divisions. The fragments of evidence which exist suggest that the kirk session split in 1571, when a handful of its members, like a handful of the council and a large wedge of the burgh establishment, chose to remain behind in the town to co-operate with — or at least to acquiesce in — the coup of the queen's lords.[63] The burgh's ministers were split as well; Knox left but John Craig remained. The session certainly split again in the summer of 1584, when three of its members agreed to subscribe to Adamson's letter; the affair also produced divisions within the council but, both there and in the merchant community as a whole, the bulk of the establishment closed ranks under pressure from the court against its own radical ministers. Craig was invited back to the pulpit of St. Giles'. These internal divisions mirrored the growing tension which was coming to the surface in the 1580s — between a kirk session overawed by the strident cries of its smaller men and a town council more oligarchic and authoritarian than ever. Erastianism, compromise and conservatism were the hallmarks of Edinburgh's rulers. Knox and the reformation may have made them protestants but found it much more difficult to change their most basic instincts.

NOTES

1. See *HMC Edinburgh*, 25-71, 125-6, 129-44, 216-8, 249; Arnot, *History of Edinburgh*, 243-58, 267-71, 277. For a full list of the various foundations, see D. E. Easson, *Medieval Religious Houses, Scotland* (London, 1957), 116, 118, 131, 136, 152, 164-5, 175-8, 214, 220-21.

2. For the history of the Hospital of St. Leonard, see H. M. Paton & J. Smith, 'St. Leonard's lands and hospital', *BOEC*, xxiii (1940), 111-46.

3. See *Liber Conventus S. Katherines Senensis prope Edinburgum* (Abbotsford Club, 1841).

4. See W. Moir Bryce, 'The Black Friars of Edinburgh', *BOEC*, iii (1910), 54-5, 59-60; H. Maxwell, *Edinburgh: a Historical Study* (Edinburgh, 1916), 126; but cf. *HMC Edinburgh*, 125. The evidence is itself partly conflicting; cf. Lesley, *History*, ii, 405-6; *Hist. Estate Scot.*, 61; *Diurnal*, 269.

5. G. Dickinson (ed.), *Two Missions of Jacques de la Brosse* (SHS, 1942), 91; Knox, *History*, i, 128; *Edin. Recs.*, iii, 66; see B. MacLennan, 'The Reformation in the burgh of Aberdeen', *Northern Scotland*, ii (1974-7), 127.

6. I. B. Cowan, *The Parishes of Medieval Scotland* (SRS, 1967), 51, 123, 217; Easson, *Medieval*

Religious Houses, 220; Makey, *Church of the Covenant*, 114; Moir Bryce, 'Black Friars', 69. See also MS Accounts of Collectors of Kirk Rents, 1573-1612 (unfoliated); the income from this source is prominent, for example, in the accounts of 1575.

7. J. C. Lees, *St. Giles', Edinburgh* (1889), 49, 57, 78-80, 86-8; *Edinburgh, 1329-1929*, 76-7; *Registrum Cartarum Ecclesie Sancti Egidii de Edinburgh* (Bann. Club, 1859), xciv-v, lists 44 altars but estimates vary because of difficulty over names; see Easson, *Medieval Religious Houses*, 220; J. D. Marwick, *Edinburgh Guilds and Crafts* (Scot. Burgh Recs. Soc., 1909), 48.

8. Lees, *St. Giles',* 82-3; *Edin. Accts.*, ii, 65.

9. *Edin. Recs.*, iii, 70; *Edin. Accts.*, ii, 91-2, 117-8; W. Angus, 'The incorporated trade of skinners of Edinburgh', *BOEC*, vi (1913), 32; see app. vi for details of Loch.

10. This point is strongly emphasised in R. Nicholson, *Scotland: The Later Middle Ages* (Edinburgh, 1974), 471.

11. *Ecclesie Sancti Egidii*, xliv.

12. See Lees, *St. Giles',* 48ff.

13. Kennedy, *Annals of Aberdeen*, 24ff.

14. Honourable and important exceptions are G. Donaldson, *The Scottish Reformation* (1960) and Cowan, *Regional Aspects of the Scottish Reformation.*

15. More than £66 was spent by the hammermen on their altar in 1552-3; see J. Smith, *The Hammermen of Edinburgh and their Altar in St. Giles' Church* (1907), xxxvi, 151-4; T. Ross & G. B. Brown, 'The Magdalen Chapel, Edinburgh', *BOEC*, viii (1916), 40, 51, 76; T. Ross, 'The Magdalene Chapel and the Greyfriars Churches, Edinburgh', *Trans. Scot. Ecclesiological Soc.*, iv (1912-13), 97-8; *HMC Edinburgh*, 41-4.

16. *Edin. Recs.*, ii, 192, 197, 210, 285; *RSS*, iv, 3144, 3268; D. B. Horn, 'The origins of the University of Edinburgh', *Edin. Univ. Journal*, xxii (1966), 218, 223. Cf. Reid, 'Coming of the Reformation', 42, where an attempt is made, on distinctly flimsy evidence, to detect Knox's influence at work on developments in the burgh's care of its poor from 1555 onwards. The privy kirk started, according to Knox himself, by looking after its own poor rather than acting as a pressure group or agency for the care of the burgh's poor as a whole (Knox, *History*, ii, 277).

17. *Edin. Recs.*, iii, 42-5.

18. *Ibid.*, iii, 62-3; *Hist. Estate Scot.*, 83.

19. *Edin. Recs.*, iii, 63-4; MS Co. Recs., iii, fos. 33v, 75v; for fuller details of the extentors, see Lynch, 'Thesis', 69.

20. *Edin. Recs.*, iii, 64, 65, 68. The dean of guild's accounts for May-Oct. 1560 show that Knox was paid £200 for half of his year's stipend but the quarterly payments after Dec. 1560 were only for £50 (*Edin. Accts.*, ii, 115; *Edin. Recs.*, iii, 87, 97, 98, 109, 123). Dr. Makey has rightly pointed out that Edinburgh offered Knox a princely stipend before the ministry as a whole was properly provided for. The answer to his rhetorical question, 'And did they not actually pay it?', may well be 'yes and no', however, rather than 'yes'; see *Church of the Covenant*, 149. The figures are conveniently condensed in R. Miller, *John Knox and the Town Council of Edinburgh* (1898), 31-3.

21. See J. C. Cameron (ed.), *The First Book of Discipline* (1972), 3-14.

22. *Edin. Recs.*, iii, 105-6, 262; *Edin. Accts.*, i, 358; Miller, *John Knox*, 33.

23. *Edin. Recs.*, iii, 131, 136, 161; T. A. Kerr, 'The early ministry of John Craig at St. Giles', 1562-1566', *RSCHS*, xiv (1962), 3-4; Reid, 'Coming of the Reformation', 41; Lynch, 'Faithful brethren', 198.

24. *Edin. Recs.*, iii, 162, 164; see app. ii for the list of contributors.

25. *Edin. Recs.*, iii, 174, 177-8.

26. *Ibid.*, iii, 178, 191, 193, 195, 197.

27. Knox, *History*, ii, 328-32; *RPC*, i, 202.

28. See Donaldson, *Thirds of Benefices*, 54, 128, 131, 141, 191, 297.

29. *Edin. Recs.*, iii, 146; Easson, *Medieval Religious Houses*, 131; *RSS*, v, 1275; J. D. Marwick, *History of the Collegiate Church and Hospital of Holy Trinity, 1460-1661* (Edinburgh, 1911), 50; Reid, 'Coming of the Reformation', 40; Lynch, 'Faithful brethren', 195.

30. *Edin. Recs.*, iii, 208; *RMS*, iv, 1802; *RSS*, v, 2296, 3146, 3334; *Edinburgh, 1329-1929*, 39-40; Easson, *Medieval Religious Houses*, 221.

31. *Edin. Recs.*, iii, 229, 278; iv, 56-7. The 'Buik of assignationis of the ministeris and reidaris stipendis', printed in *Register of Ministers, Exhorters and Readers and of their Stipends after the Period of the Reformation* (Maitland Club, 1830), xvii, shows that Edinburgh's three ministers and one reader in 1576 were 'sustenit be the toun'; see also Makey, *Church of the Covenant*, 118.

32. *Edin. Recs.*, iv, 7-8, 28, 56, 74. See MS Accounts of the Collector of Kirk Rents for 1574 and 1575 for details of Lawson's and Durie's early stipends.

33. *Edin. Recs.*, iv, 46, 56, 99, 109, 193; see MS Accounts of the Collector of Kirk Rents for 1574-5 and 1577-8.

34. *Edin. Recs.*, iv, 56, 146, 196.

35. The amount raised in 1574 was £631 (MS Accounts of Collector of Kirk Rents); see also Makey, *Church of the Covenant*, 118.

36. *Edin. Recs.*, iii, 42-4, 64, 65, 70, 101-3, 105-7; Knox, *History*, ii, 4; Angus, 'Edinburgh skinners', 32.

37. *Edin. Recs.*, iii, 65, 80, 90, 101; MS Co. Recs., 19 Sept. 1567, iv, fo. 203r; *CSP Scot.*, i, no. 967. For Methven, see Knox, *History*, ii, 66-8; *Fasti Ecclesiae Scoticanae* (ed. H. Scott), ii, 124.

38. *Edin. Recs.*, iii, 125, 131, 133, 195-6. Cf. Reid, 'Coming of the Reformation', 38. See ch. 6 for further details.

39. *Edin. Recs.*, iii, 131-2, 139, 141-5. The Roberton affair is discussed more fully in ch. 6.

40. See app. ii for a list of the 'faithful brethren'. The overall complexion of the protestant establishment of the town, as it had emerged by 1562, is discussed in ch. 10; the motives of the less than faithful amongst the ranks of the brethren are discussed in ch. 11.

41. The italics are mine; see Knox, *History*, ii, 277-8; also Calderwood, *History*, i, 304.

42. Cf. *First Book of Discipline*, 175.

43. Calderwood, *History*, i, 303-4; they are listed in app. iv.

44. BGKE, fos. 21r, 22v-23v; members of the kirk session are listed in app. iii.

45. Makey, *Church of the Covenant*, 152, 165.

46. G. Parker, *The Dutch Revolt* (London, 1977), 73-6; J. H. Elliot, *Europe Divided, 1559-1598* (London, 1968), 39-40.

47. See app. ii.

48. Makey, *Church of the Covenant*, 157. I am considerably in Dr. Makey's debt for his patient explanations of the seemingly ever-changing number of parishes in early seventeenth-century Edinburgh and the complex changes in electoral practice of their kirk sessions.

49. *First Book of Discipline*, 175; see W. R. F. Foster, *The Church before the Covenants* (1975), 68.

50. Knox, *History*, ii, 278.

51. BGKE, fo. 8r; the senator, who allegedly had stubbornly catholic inclinations, is discussed in T. A. Kerr, 'John Craig, 1512-1600' (Edinburgh Ph.D., 1954), 4-5.

52. BGKE, fos. 11r, 24v, 27v, 34v, 37r, 38v, 54v, 55r, 57r, 58r, 61v, 62r, 68v, 71r, 76r.

53. See Makey, *Church of the Covenant*, 149; Foster, *Church before the Covenants*, 83-4.

54. MS Co. Recs., 8 July 1569 & 6 Oct. 1570, iv, fos. 243r, 264v.

55. Ibid., 2 Nov. 1569, iv, fo. 248r; see Ross, 'Reformation and repression', 359n.

56. BGKE, fos. 55r, 67r, 70v; see app. vi for details of Easton.

57. See Ross, 'Reformation and repression', 360n.

58. *Canongate Book*, 41; W. Forbes-Leith, *Narratives of Scottish Catholics under Mary Stuart and James VI* (1885), 178; see app. vi for the Canongate's catholics. Certain prominent catholic burgesses of Edinburgh, who bitterly opposed the new regime but seem to have avoided outright recusancy, moved to the Canongate; see, for example, Herbert Maxwell in app. viii.

59. The point was stressed in Ross, 'Reformation and repression', 355, and, more recently, in D. E. Meek & J. Kirk, 'John Carswell, superintendent of Argyll: a reassessment', *RSCHS*, xix (1975), 2-3.

60. BGKE, fos. 32r, 53; see app. vii for details of Fullarton and app. viii for MacCalzean, the Fairlies and the large number of minor figures the session dealt with in the aftermath of the war, like the apprentice baxter, John Heriot.

61. MacCalzean had been an elder in 1571 when the queen's lords took over the town and remained in office. Nisbet had been a member of the king's party town council elected in Oct. 1572 while the siege of the Marian stronghold of the Castle was still going on; he engaged in a bitter dispute with another of the town's protestant veterans, Edward Hope, over the town's exiled radical ministers in 1584 (Calderwood, *History*, iv, 141ff). The significance of the dispute is discussed in ch. 8.

62. See ch. 6 for the significance of Mary's leet of 1565 and app. x for details of Preston.

63. As well as MacCalzean, who remained as an elder, the well-known printer, Thomas Bassenden, continued in office as a deacon; see app. viii.

4

Merchants and Craftsmen

DAVID Calderwood was careful to bracket Edinburgh's merchants and craftsmen together in their common devotion to the 'religion of Edinburgh . . . their
particular'. He castigated with equal fervour the vested interests of merchants
trading with catholic Spain and of craftsmen trying to preserve their Monday
market in 1592. Both merchants and craftsmen were monopolists who
cherished the privileged positions given to them in burgh society. It is a point
that seems to have been missed subsequently. Historians of the Scottish town
seem to have become obsessed with the notion that burgh society from the
later fifteenth century was seriously divided by an endemic conflict between
merchants and craftsmen. A thriving industry grew up in the nineteenth
century devoted to the pursuit of the 'blue blanket', originally the Banner of the
Holy Ghost dedicated to the altar of St. Eloi in St. Giles' and by the sixteenth
century the rallying point for craft demonstrations. The most authoritative
work on the merchant guildry is still a highly partisan account commissioned
by the town council to prove a legal point.[1] It is hardly surprising that the
effect of the study of the details, and too often the minutiae, of merchant and
craft guilds has been to over-emphasise the disputes and social differences
which existed between them.

This is an important point to settle. If the Reformation took place against a
background of a deeply divided urban community, as in certain of the North
German cities in the late 1520s and early 1530s, it might be expected to have
become enmeshed in the craftsmen's political struggles against the ruling
oligarchy. There is certainly no trace in the Scottish towns of the pattern so
familiar in many of the German imperial cities of a political alliance between
protestant preachers and craftsmen to promote protestantism and, occasionally, also craft interests. There are, however, so it has been argued, indications
of an alliance between Mary of Guise and catholic craftsmen in the second half
of the 1550s.[2] The thesis, however, turns on two specific instances in 1556 and
1559 and both are suspect. Mary was not trying to effect a shift in the balance
of power in the burgh in favour of the crafts but using them to try to extract

49

more revenue from a merchant-dominated council. The craftsmen were not the allies of the Queen Regent but her pawns in a more elaborate game. There is a fundamental consistency throughout the troubled times which came before and followed the revolt of 1559 and 1560; no party or faction sought to ally itself with the craftsmen. No one played the craft card — not Mary, Queen of Scots, despite the fact that she returned to Edinburgh in 1561 only a month after the second of two serious riots of what Knox called 'ungodly' craftsmen; certainly not Knox himself after his brief holy alliance with the 'rascal multitude' in the summer of 1559; not even the queen's lords when they took over the town in 1571, despite the large numbers of craftsmen who supported them. The first firm hint of a political alliance between the court and Edinburgh's craftsmen did not come until the early 1580s, when James Stewart, earl of Arran, seems to have moved in their direction in order to check the spread of popular radicalism. As a result, the two major developments of 1583, the revised burgh constitution, which gave the crafts greater representation on the council, and the purging of the radical pro-Ruthven faction from the council, were linked. Arran's most loyal supporters in the dishing of the radicals in the council elections which followed the decreet-arbitral were the newly promoted deacon councillors. This alliance with Arran, however, was short-lived and unusual. It does not seem to indicate a ready-made politics of resentment within burgh life in the reformation period which was ripe for exploitation by outside interests.

There are other grounds for scepticism. Historians of Scottish burghs have rather neglected to realise how wary other urban historians of the early modern period have become in deducing too much about how society and government worked in a town from its supposed general characteristics. The centenary volume *Edinburgh 1329-1929* did, it is true, suggest that Edinburgh's social conflicts in the sixteenth century had been exaggerated, but the thought was not pursued. Recent work on Aberdeen has pointed in the same direction.[3] The myth persists, however, despite the fact that few urban historians would now be happy with the assumption that a social or political dichotomy in urban life need follow on from an economic one. There are two further reasons why it seems unlikely that Scottish burgh society revolved around a lasting and bitter conflict between its merchants and craftsmen. The terms themselves are vague and amorphous. A merchant might mean an overseas trader, combining wealth and influence, or a seed seller in a booth in the market place, combining poverty with obscurity. A craftsman might be a wealthy goldsmith, perhaps a money broker to the crown, or a candlemaker, excluded from political influence even in craft circles and shunted to the furthest southern suburb of the town. The divisions within these two groups were starker and more significant than the differences between them. The term 'merchants' and 'craftsmen' are a convenient shorthand but they do not of themselves comprehend more than a third of burgh society, nor do they always explain the way it worked. The other reason is that there was no fixed ratio between the two. It has often been pointed out that there was a high degree of uniformity in burgh life in Scotland.[4] Burgh privileges were long-established and exhaustively set out in the Laws of the Four Burghs and *Statuta Gildae* of the twelfth and thirteenth centuries; subsequently one burgh tended to ape the practices of another and, more often than not, the model was Edinburgh. Yet what has often been forgotten is that the proportions of craftsmen to merchants varied conspicuously from burgh to burgh. So too did their relative standing. Like was not copying like.

Some fifteen years after the Reformation the émigré bishop of Ross, John Lesley, in an uncharacteristically shrewd observation, remarked of the citizens of Dundee that it was difficult to discern 'quither they be richer in outlandis geir and merchandise, or in their awne labour and industrie'. Perth, according to its royal charter of 1556, was 'chiefly upheld by the fortunes, order and policy of the tradesmen', who made up the bulk of the burgess population and rivalled its merchants in their tax assessments. In Glasgow the town's crafts-men outnumbered the merchants by 361 to 213 in 1604.[5] In Edinburgh the numbers were more even, though not as even as has often been concluded from the muster roll of 1558, which included apprentices and servants as well as masters; there were 527 'neighbours', or merchants and traders who were subject to individual assessment before the decreet, in the tax roll of 1581, and 489 from the incorporated crafts in 1583. Just as relative numbers varied, so did the degree of organisation. Brechin had no organised crafts before the seventeenth century, whereas Dumfries had no merchant guild throughout the period, even though its crafts had joined together in one aggregate corporation before the end of the sixteenth century. Most of the larger burghs had seven incorporated crafts but Edinburgh issued charters of incorporation, or seals of cause, to fourteen crafts between 1475 and 1536. Its merchant guildry, although founded by the thirteenth century, was not incorporated until 1518.[6] It is difficult to see how conflict between the two groups could have taken the same form in such different circumstances.

The blanket formula of 'merchants and craftsmen' has tended to obscure the point that the question of what groups there were within the boundaries of the Scottish town is not a simple one. They were chameleon-like; they vary, as do individual members of each of them, depending on the kind of lens on the microscope that is used to examine them. Politically, burgh society rested on the relationship between its magistrates and citizens. The most obvious social characteristic of burgh life was the yawning gap between the free burgesses, who included both merchants and craftsmen, and the cluster of other groupings which collectively comprised the 'unfree', apprentices, journeymen, merchant and craft servants and the unskilled labourers. The latter were the hidden majority, who appear in kirk session records but seldom elsewhere. It is they who were the under-privileged in the sixteenth-century burgh and not the craftsmen. It is only when the economic focus of the lens is put on that the picture narrows to the free burgesses and is marked by the familiar division between merchants and craft masters. The rivalry between them was largely confined to disputes over their respective commercial privileges and their respective share in burgh government. The argument that this tension was significant largely turns on the peculiarly broad definitions on which it is founded. It is not surprising that historians have unearthed deep and lasting conflict with tools as crude as these.

Who were the merchants? It is not — at least on these terms — the classic picture of a small, closely knit body, bound together by wealth, power and inter-marriage. It has been estimated that Elizabethan Exeter, a town with a population of about 10,000, had about a hundred merchants. Edinburgh, which was about a quarter as large again, had more than three times as many merchants in 1565.[7] The discrepancy is explained by the fact that Edinburgh's merchants included not only those engaged in foreign trade but also the retailers of goods within the town itself. The merchants ranged from wealthy overseas traders, operating mostly in France, Flanders and the Baltic down to very humble booth owners. The range of wealth within the merchants is well illustrated by the tax roll of 1565 to raise money for the purchase of the superiority of Leith; 70% of the total raised by the merchants in 1565 came from the wealthiest quarter of the merchant community and over 60% from the top third. In terms of absolute personal wealth, the disparity could range from the monumental £29,064 left by William Birnie in 1569 to a few pounds or even less. The inventory of Birnie's goods in the hands of his agent in Dieppe provides a study in miniature of Scottish exports in the sixteenth century; there was £10,000 worth of salmon, herring, cod, hides, wool and grain. Birnie's fortune compares very favourably with the total of just over £37,000 left by John MacMorran, who was described by Calderwood as the richest merchant of his day, when he died in 1596, almost thirty inflation-ravaged years later.[8] By that time the value of the Scots pound against the pound sterling had dropped from a fifth to almost a twelfth. It is also noticeable that most of MacMorran's fortune came from shares in shipping; Birnie's came from merchandise. Birnie, however, stood head and shoulders above his contemporaries. The point was made, not unfairly, by an English memorandum of 1580 that a Scots merchant was regarded as wealthy if he was worth £1,000 sterling. Certainly the average Edinburgh overseas merchant was worth nothing like the average Bristol or Exeter merchant's estate, both of which were a little above £1,900 sterling, or even the estate of the average provincial English merchant of £1,428.[9] The average estate of the top third of Edinburgh's merchants was not much over £2,000 Scots in this period, although more than a score have been found who left more than £5,000.[10] This was enough, however, to ensure that wealth and power lay within a relatively small section of the merchants, who did fit the classic pattern. Their numbers would not have been significantly more than a hundred and twenty in the 1560s. As well as monopolising 70% of merchant wealth, they accounted for more than two-thirds of those who sat on the council. It is no coincidence that this was also the group which formed the bulk of the protestant establishment by 1562. By contrast, the lower half of the merchants was a distinctly under-privileged body. Their assessment in 1565 only just crept over the total for the dozen largest merchants in the burgh; less than half of them were members of the merchant guildry; only one in thirteen ever reached the council chamber.

It is almost as misleading, in the search for the general social characteristics of Scottish burghs, to talk of the craftsmen as if they were a self-contained group or even class. The leading goldsmith in Edinburgh, Michael Gilbert, who became a burgess in 1549, left £22,667 when he died in 1590. Gilbert was the prototype for the latter and better-known goldsmiths and money brokers, Thomas Foulis and George Heriot. Although he, like Birnie, stood on his own, craftsmen in Edinburgh did range from the very comfortably off, like the saddler, George Richardson, or the tailor, John Simpson, who left £3,574 and £2,631 respectively, to the humble or the poverty-stricken. Yet Richardson was not the wealthiest member of his craft in the 1580s, only the third or fourth. The wealthiest flesher in the burgh, Harry Burrell, who was an elder of the Canongate kirk session in the 1560s, left £2,022;[11] he paid a quarter of the tax levied on the forty members of his craft in 1583. Almost exactly the same pattern of wealth and influence reproduced itself with the crafts as with the merchants. The poorer half of the 496 craftsmen on the tax roll of 1583 accounted for only 15% of the assessment on the crafts, and their share was less than that of the half dozen wealthiest of their fellows. The top 15% of craftsmen accounted for 56% of the wealth of all craftsmen and filled as many places on the council as all their fellows put together. There could hardly be a clearer illustration of a craft aristocracy. Some crafts were also distinctly wealthier than others and the increasingly sophisticated demands of the market in the second half of the sixteenth century underlined the growing divide. Just over fifty craftsmen paid more than the average overall assessment in 1583. Two-fifths of this craft aristocracy were tailors. Edinburgh had as many as 142 tailors and drapers in 1583, coincidentally almost exactly the same number as Norwich, and this would suggest a considerable demand for fine clothing from beyond the burgh as well as from the court. They also included seven goldsmiths, five skinners, four baxters and surgeons or barbers, and three saddlers and shoemakers. Add to this the three drapers, two dyers or litsters, and a hatmaker, who were not, strictly speaking, craftsmen, and the picture is clearly that of an expanding and increasingly sophisticated market, whose demands were the source of the accumulation and concentration of wealth among a select band of craftsmen.

It is clear enough that both the merchant and craft communities rested on a social pyramid with a very broad base and a sharply tapering apex, which was probably more exaggerated in Edinburgh than in other Scottish burghs. It is this distinctive structure which should be borne in mind in any discussion of the consequences of the incorporation of craft guilds or their political development. Incorporation brought increasing responsibility to the craft for the discipline of its own members, the quality of its products and even for the care of its own poor, but this did not usually mean that the craftsmen as a whole were gaining increased independence or power. The same is true of the apparent growth of craft representation on town councils, usually in the second half of the sixteenth century. These newly won responsibilities and privileges on the council and within the craft itself did not accrue to the bulk of craftsmen or even craft masters.

This was hardly surprising. The granting of seals of cause ensured that the craft drew the same legal distinctions as the burgh itself: the same discrimination between free and unfree, with their respective privileges and lack of them. A typical charter, granted to the Edinburgh websters, stipulated that only 'freemen of the craft that are burgesses' could elect their deacon. Any one craft was the burgh in microcosm — a privileged group of freemen burgesses, some of whom formed a still further privileged inner circle of guild brethren; below them were a variety of under- and unprivileged, the apprentices, journeymen, craft servants and labourers. Movement up the scale was intentionally made a long and expensive process. Mastership of the craft, like burgess-ship, only went to well-defined, model citizens:

> able qualified men, and that they be married, dwelling within the burgh, having sufficient substance, with stob and stake.[12]

A number of devices combined to bar the likelihood of rapid advance within the social community of the craft. Entry fees to the craft were rising steeply in the sixteenth century, particularly towards the end of it. This was made starker by the savage differential rates imposed on outsiders; the Edinburgh skinners charged ten shillings to sons of burgesses and £5 to all others in 1533 but by 1596 were demanding £5 and £40. The period of apprenticeship was also weighted in favour of freemen's sons. Crafts usually stipulated that a master could only have one apprentice at a time, although no limit was put on the number of journeymen he could employ. There were, as a result, often more tied servants in a craft than masters. The precise proportions varied from craft to craft because of the different technical demands each made; the most labour-intensive were the hammermen, baxters and bonnetmakers.[13] Craft masters, as a breed, were as unashamed monopolists as established merchants. They were wedded to the same static view of society with its twin notions of inherited privilege bound up with service, which pervaded the whole of burgh life. There was no sign of this slackening in the sixteenth century, despite an expanding population.

The revised Edinburgh constitution of 1583 did not open the doors to all-comers or break down the medieval walls of privilege. Quite the opposite; entry fees continued to rise and one of the basic assumptions of the decreet was that 'the son, daughter, or apprentice can be in no better estate nor their father or master was by their right'. The trend in the sixteenth century was not towards democratisation of the crafts but a shoring up of their position as privileged enclaves. The danger to such a community, in the eyes of both the magistrates and the guilds, was precisely those who were not contained within these concentric circles of social and economic monopoly and privilege: the swelling hordes — or so they seemed in a period of expanding population — of outland men, untied journeymen and labouring poor. In one of its recurrent outbursts, the Edinburgh council branded the

> great multitude of journeymen or taskmen of the crafts . . . as . . . nothing else but idle vagabond persons, bound to no master, troublers of the quiet estate of this common weal . . . and bear no burden with the town.

The advantage of the craft guild to the town council was that its masters became collectively as well as individually responsible for their members. Craft entry was restricted, by order of the council, to those who were 'bound to ane master as a feed servant for meat and fee for year or half year, who shall answer for him to the magistrates as law will'.[14] In return for standing as surety for these potential troublemakers, the craft master was delegated considerable powers. A servant usually had to pay a booking fee to the craft, which was also rising. He had to pay weekly contributions.[15] His wages were regulated by the craft itself and they seem, from the example of the Edinburgh skinners, to have remained static in a period of rapidly rising prices. Inflation forced home the stark differentials of life within the craft; top-grade masters seem to have enjoyed a three-fold increase in wages in the sixteenth century; a labourer's wage increased by about 60%; but the craft servant in the skinners still earned a shilling a day along with his keep.[16] The effect of these elaborate regulations was to tie the craft servants and apprentices firmly to their masters. The master's household was just as useful as his craft in providing a unit of stability, capable of imposing civic discipline at the behest of the magistrate or moral example at the bidding of the kirk session.

The craft guild provided the last link in the interlocking chain of authority which permeated burgh life. Both the magistracy and the deaconship of the craft had acquired a semi-religious character well before 1560, and both retained it after the Reformation. The craft worshipped together both before and after 1560; the old practice of the deacon compelling moral offenders to appear before the congregation was continued. The customary attendance of the whole craft at funerals and at church was tightened up. The enforcement of dues to a craft altar had long been vested in council and craft jointly; the deacon was used to 'poind with an officer of the town'. The same technique of joint supervision with officers of the craft was used by the kirk session. It was as applicable to enforcing religious and moral uniformity as it was to safeguarding the burgh's system of economic privilege. Just as much as the council, the session made use of the inducement of the shared fine, one half to go to itself and the other to the craft. The enforcement of discipline by craft and session was not a one-way traffic of meting out a double dose to moral deviants; the statutes of the Glasgow weavers threatened members who canvassed for election not only with permanent loss of their freedom but a guest appearance at the pillar of the kirk as 'a person seditious and mover of trouble'.[17] The structure and constitution of the craft guild and the merchant guildry came to be reinforced by the kirk session as well as by the council. Much the same reciprocal guarantees existed between craft and session as between craft and magistrates. The nature of authority in the Scottish burgh lay deeply embedded in an interlocking relationship of council, kirk session and merchant and craft guilds. It was this peculiarly close triangular relationship which characterised the burgh reformation in Scotland, giving it an extra dimension which can only loosely be called Calvinist. It was certainly not a feature which was copied from Geneva, which was until late in the sixteenth century a city without guilds.[18] The trinity was all the more secure because of the natural identity of interests of the men who controlled each part of it. Paternalism went hand in hand with monopoly and privilege.

It is fairly safe to conclude that the closed doors behind which the craft met and the internal discipline it had to hand helped to give an important focus and direction to the reformed church in the burgh.[19] But this took time. There is no evidence to suggest that protestantism had taken any Edinburgh craft in its grip before 1559 and much to indicate that catholicism continued to exercise a strong hold over many after 1560. The deacon of the skinners bought the sacred vessels and vestments belonging to his craft when they were put up for auction in 1560 in order that they might be used again. The craft guild acted as a privy kirk in miniature for catholicism in the 1560s rather than for protestantism in the 1550s.

The most striking evidence for the persistence of catholicism comes in the records of the hammermen craft. It provides a graphic illustration of a craft in serious internal conflict throughout the 1560s, with the council seemingly unable to intervene decisively in a long-running power struggle within the craft. The hammermen were the second largest craft in the burgh, with seventy-two masters in 1560. It was an unwieldy conglomerate, ranging from wealthy and prestigious saddlers and cutlers to humbler and dirtier blacksmiths, lorimers and pewterers. By 1568 each of the six constituent trades which made up the craft had its own two representatives on a twelve-man inner council of masters. It was also difficult to control because of its unusually high proportion of servants; its records bristle with repeated threats of the penalties for disobedience to the deacon and masters. The first signs of real trouble came on the very day that the Congregation first appeared outside the city gates in 1559. One of the masters, George Small, a saddler, seized the opportunity to demand that the council remove the sitting deacon.[20] His petition was not well received but it did point the way towards a stormy future. Small was one of a limited but very active inner circle of protestant activists in the craft, mostly made up of saddlers and cutlers. They ran into bitter opposition after 1560 from an equally militant but larger body of catholics, drawn from a wider range of the craft, but whose spokesmen were mainly smiths or pewterers. The council was twice forced, in desperation, to intervene to dismiss catholic deacons in the 1560s. The craft was not effectively purged until after the civil wars of the early 1570s.

The initial reaction of the conservatives in the craft to the reformation crisis and its aftermath seems to have been a willingness to compromise. The deacon who was attacked by Small in June 1559, James Cranston, was prepared to deal with the Lords of Congregation and the protestant council they imposed on the town four months later. William Brocas, the first of the two deacons removed by the council after 1560, was one of the delegation of craftsmen who offered to co-operate with the new regime in setting up a church which would be 'a mirrour and exempill to all the rest of the realme' in November 1560. There was no immediate adoption of hard-line positions across a religious divide when the reformation came. The deacon Brocas was standing in for at this meeting was William Harlaw, who had shot to prominence, gaining burgess-ship, guildry and office near-simultaneously in 1560, because of his protestant leanings. It was not until 1562 that their religious differences had driven a wedge between them.

There were a number of reasons why this should have been so. Important issues were still to be clarified. What would happen to the craft's funds devoted to its altar, which had been expensively refurbished only half a dozen years before? Would it have to continue paying its old chaplain? These were questions very similar to those facing the town as a whole, and each guild was confronted with them. The dilemmas of the Edinburgh hammermen were especially acute, however, because they had not one chaplain but two, and not just an altar but a quite separate chapel with a poor hospital attached to it as well. To make matters more complicated still, one of the chaplains, Sir Thomas Williamson, had been imprisoned in Roslin Castle and the craft was forced to appoint a replacement, William Barber, in November 1559. By October 1560 the craft was calling Barber 'thair minister of the Magdalen Chapel and collector to the beidmen' of the hospital. The point is not that Barber suddenly appeared as a reformed minister but that a replacement chaplain was conveniently renamed to meet changed circumstances. Continuity was the keynote of the way the hammermen approached the reformation crisis. One postscript remained; like the burgh, the craft was forced to continue paying its old chaplain until he died, although Williamson had to bring a legal action against the hammermen to prove his point. A more difficult legal problem surrounded the question of the Magdalen Chapel in the Cowgate itself. It was a recent foundation and its charter had set down the duties of its chaplain and frequency of services in great detail. The hammermen were not the founders but only the patrons of the chapel. The family of the merchant founder was an influential one and had invested further considerable sums in it as late as 1555. Part of this investment was in the form of a lease on property in Edinburgh and on lands outside the burgh in Cousland near Dalkeith and Carnwath in Lanarkshire. This was why Barber's reappointment in 1560 gave him 'full power to uplift annuals and mails of the hospital'. The craft seems, however, to have had difficulty in extracting rents from its tenants in the 1560s. The hammermen, anxious to hold on to their recently acquired property, found themselves the target of a barrage of rival interests — a new protestant council, an old and influential catholic family, a former chaplain and inmates of the hospital anxious to assert their rights and tenants eager to shed their obligations.[21] With so much at stake, it is not surprising that they tried to proceed with caution.

By the time of the craft election in May 1562 this united front had broken down. It was customary for the old deacon to recommend the new to the masters as a whole for adoption; he would at least be instrumental in drawing up a short-list of suitable candidates. In 1562 the retiring deacon complained to the council that the 'old order' had been ignored. A group of forty masters, just over half the craft, had ignored his advice and drawn up their own leets. Their choice was Brocas. The council promptly shut him up in the tolbooth and replaced him with James Young, who had proved his reliability by his membership of the protestant council which was imposed on the town with Archibald Douglas of Kilspindie as its provost when the Lords of Congregation took over the town in 1559. The records of the craft simply ignored the incident and noted that Young was elected, miraculously, by the unanimous votes of the whole craft. They do reveal, however, that the town council did more than simply dismiss Brocas. The craft was purged; Young was surrounded by a craft council of like-minded men. There was room on it for only one of the six candidates in the original election. Numbers in the craft suddenly jumped; an extra eleven masters were accepted during Young's tenure of office in what looks like a deliberate attempt to alter the balance of power within the craft. Nonetheless, the Brocas affair refused to go away. It became so serious that it was referred to the privy council three months later and Brocas took the opportunity to pledge his loyalty to the queen and to declare that no protestant council would ever seduce him 'fra his faith'. Young and his faction did, however, manage to maintain their grip on the craft for the next half-dozen years. But in 1568 the council was again forced to intervene when the masters elected a pewterer, John Wilson, 'a man of na religion', as their deacon to replace Young. Within three weeks a second election was held and Alexander Thomson, a cutler like Young, invested in office. This time the purge was not so effective. Wilson could not be displaced from the council of the craft and he was swept back into power in the following three years. Steadily the influence of the protestant faction was whittled away. More than half of the craft councils for the years 1569 and 1570 came out on the side of the queen's party in 1571. Thirty-two members of the craft as a whole can be positively tied to the queen's men. Wilson himself stayed in the town and craft elections were held in the occupied town in 1572. The loyalist hammermen were not just passive Marians. It is striking how many of them were singled out for particularly harsh treatment in the legal proceedings which followed the wars: Patrick Anderson, who had been on the council of the craft in 1570, headed a list of forty-seven inhabitants indicted for active conspiracy; the blacksmith, William Henderson, was actually forfeited by parliament for treason in 1573; he and the catholic saddler, George Smith, were both in the Castle when it finally fell. The counter-revolution in the craft's affairs came only after the return of the king's party to the town which swept Young and his confederates back to power.[22]

The internal divisions within Edinburgh's hammermen provide a vivid picture of a community within burgh society in conflict in the aftermath of the Reformation. There are indications that the skinners had a number of stubborn catholics in their ranks and both the goldsmiths and baxters had a substantial wedge of queen's men among them, but it seems likely that the hammermen's disputes were unusual both for their bitterness and their explicitness. The struggle within the craft was not, like that in the more privileged atmosphere of the council chamber, between radical and moderate protestants; it was between radical protestants and catholics. To some extent, these religious differences latched on to existing tensions within the craft between wealthy saddlers and cutlers and the humbler trades. What is striking is how little these arguments within the craft corresponded to events outside it. The reformation crisis brought uncertainty and compromise rather than an exclusive protestant regime; the decisive return to power of the conservatives came during the explicitly protestant regency of the earl of Moray. Much of this struggle took place behind closed doors, self-absorbed and out of reach of a bemused council. It broke surface in 1562 and 1568 but only came explicitly into the open during the civil wars when it found wider political issues on which it could refocus. Although there were a number of early committed protestant hammermen, it is difficult to see how the closed doors of the craft helped the growth of protestantism. Its inbred atmosphere first helped the craftsmen to submerge their differences and then to kindle them. It also made it very difficult for the council to intervene decisively. The council's failures with the hammermen in the 1560s once again demonstrate its natural limitations; craft councillors could be controlled fairly easily but disaffected deacons and master craftsmen posed a formidable problem. Protestantism, it found, could not be expected to sweep over burgh life like a tidal wave; it had to infiltrate each separate compartment of society. Some closets proved harder to penetrate than others.

If it was religion which brought the council into conflict with the hammermen, it was usually prices which strained its relations with other crafts. In theory the craft underlined one of the most cherished ideas in burgh life — the concept of the common good or 'common weill'. The incorporated craft was responsible for the quality of its wares as well as the conduct of its members. It seems, though, at first sight, that the dominant feature of relations between the two bodies was an unrelenting, close supervision by the council. From 1496 town councils were required by act of parliament to set prices on staple foods and to appoint examiners to enforce them. Even such a comparatively small burgh as Arbroath could produce an impressive list of 'flesh prissers' and 'tunners of ale'. By the middle of the sixteenth century parliament's indictments of craftsmen had become wholesale and obsessive, speaking of 'the exhorbitant prices that everie craftsman within burgh raisis'. Commissions were set up by the privy council in 1535 and 1550 to investigate the dearth. Within the burghs themselves, however, the degree of interference varied significantly from craft to craft. The pattern was what one might expect in any early modern town: attention tended to be concentrated on the baxters, fleshers, shoemakers and tailors, the producers of food and clothing. Supervision of these crafts came very early, often long before incorporation; the Aberdeen council established a system of marks for their baxters in 1398 but did not grant a seal of cause until 1534. It was also more intensive.[23]

The council's supervision concentrated on precisely those trades, with the possible exception of the cordiners, where the degree of technical skill required was at its lowest. Its concern was far more with price-fixing than quality control. The result was that it did not come into conflict with all the crafts but only a select few, particularly the baxters and fleshers. Edinburgh and the Scottish burghs as a whole were not a society plagued by frequent craft riots. The legendary blue blanket when it did go up usually involved one craft rather than the craftsmen as a whole. The dispute was usually about price-fixing: the baxters rioted in 1551 and the fleshers in 1553 in protest at the council's policy of holding down food prices to artificially low levels in a period of acute shortage.[24] Of all the well-known riots in this period only one has the convincing credentials of a full-scale craft riot. In August 1543 a number of craftsmen were imprisoned in the Castle for an armed demonstration in the council chamber. It is possible that there was a background of friction between the council and the crafts but the real cause can better be understood if it is remembered that it took place when opposition was mounting against the policies of the earl of Arran, who, since being made governor in January 1543, had concluded an unpopular alliance with England and indulged in a series of alarming flirtations with protestant preachers. The leader of the demonstration was not a craftsman but a well-known conservative merchant, Francis Tennant; the point of parading the blue blanket around the council chamber was that it was the Banner of the Holy Ghost. This was why the privy council intervened so quickly; it was a political demonstration, not a craft riot.[25] The first of the two riots of 1560 and 1561 was triggered off by the dismissal of a deacon of the fleshers for adultery but its origins cannot be separated from a series of skirmishes this craft had had with the council over the shifting of the day and site of the traditional Sunday flesh market. The second riot did involve a wide range of craftsmen, but stemmed from the heavy-handed actions of the new protestant regime rather than a clash over traditional privileges. Neither was a conspiracy of craftsmen against a merchant-dominated council.[26] It is only the riot of 1582, which indirectly led to the revised burgh constitution, that can give comfort to a conspiracy theory. By 1578 the craft deacons were convening on a regular basis, electing their own convener and sometimes sending their own commissioners to lobby parliament.

By 1581 they were meeting quite openly in St. Giles' and had hired an expensive lawyer to look after their interests. It was probably no coincidence that the man they chose to look after their interests, David McGill, had close connections with Esmé Stewart, who was now duke of Lennox, and James Stewart, soon to be made earl of Arran. The records of the Convenery show that the deacons had carefully planned a campaign to make Edinburgh 'ane haill toun without any divisioun' focusing on the annual election in 1582 for two months before it. By coincidence these same months had seen the demise of Lennox. It seems, however, that the Ruthven lords, newly come to power, were anxious not to give Arran a chance to build up an interest among the craftsmen of the capital and acted quickly in setting up a commission. The concessions gained by Edinburgh's craftsmen in 1583 had a good deal to do with the tangled history of the rise and fall of the Ruthven lords and the vulnerability of the burgh to pressure from the crafts in that period.[27]

The riot of 1582, although it embodied long-felt grievances over craft representation, was a very special case. It did not typify the general relations between council and crafts in the sixteenth century. Craftsmen were not singled out for paternalistic treatment and there was not a widespread reluctance to accept regulation and inspection of crafts or their products. The prices of merchandise, particularly wine, were as strictly regulated as crafts-men's goods; the council appointed wine masters annually and there were periodic drives against wine sellers, who included both merchants and crafts-men.[28] On market days the rights of both groups were protected. It was the council's job to defend privilege; any permanent breach of the walls of merchant or craft privilege would have cracked the whole edifice of burgh monopoly and authority. The burgh and the guild constitution were too closely tied to leave room for serious or lasting tension between the magistrates and the crafts.

This relationship had to operate within certain defined limits. The Dundee baxters successfully applied to the crown in 1561 for a summons of reduction against their magistrates, who had enacted that master bakers take an annual oath binding them to make bread at a price fixed by the council without reference to the market price of wheat. The summons stated that

> . . . the provest and bailies of quhatsuevir burgh can not lefulie nor rychtueuslie prescribe any reule to ony mannis conscience, nor caus compell him to sweir to kepe and observe any act or ordinance sett furth be thame, bot the maist that thai may do of the law is, to sett furth thair lefull statutis, actis and ordinances as thai may conforme to thair privilege and fredomes of our said burgh.[29]

Even in the context of a closely knit urban community, neither the authority of the magistrates nor burgh law was absolute. The town council could not increase its control over the crafts simply by issuing a stream of municipal regulations. Dundee and other Scottish towns were not alone in this; sixteenth-century Ulm had exactly the same trouble with its bakers.[30] It is not easy, then, to talk loosely of an increase in magisterial authority over the crafts in the sixteenth century. Nor, however, is it easy to draw hasty conclusions about an increase in the powers of the crafts, either in the form of an increasing independence in the conduct of their own affairs or their undoubted increasing representation on town councils. The council's authority was conditioned by the intricate network of 'privilege and freedomes' held by the burgh; the movement towards greater guild autonomy and representation was conditioned by the structure of the craft guild and its constitution.

It seems hard to square what in many burghs seem to have been mutually contradictory developments: the merchants were increasing their grip on the guildry, at times to the exclusion of the craftsmen; yet, at the same time, an increasing number of craftsmen were coming on to town councils, as in Perth, where by 1556 they made up half the council. This will remain a conundrum unless it is realised that the movement within the craft guild was towards the concentration of power and privilege in the hands of a select few. The result of incorporation was to vest a certain amount of self-regulation of crafts in the hands of their deacons. The statutory amount of power possessed varied not only from burgh to burgh but from craft to craft. The Aberdeen crafts were generally granted fairly comprehensive powers. In Dundee, the authority of the deacons was limited by their members' right to appeal above their heads to the provost and bailies. In Edinburgh, the arrangements appear to have been less generous: the council usually reserved the right, as they did with the skinners, to appoint and dismiss the deacon.[31] There is no evidence, however, in the craft's minute book that the council ever exercised this right in practice, and the cases in which it dismissed deacons were rare. There was not regular interference by the council either with the deacons or in their duties. It was the purpose of granting letters of incorporation to shift the burden of ordinary administration away from an increasingly over-worked town council. The growing delegation of authority by town councils to craft deacons in the century before the Reformation was part of a more general revision of the traditional arrangements by which burghs were governed as they underwent a significant increase in their populations. By the 1560s the characteristically medieval practice of any inhabitant being able to come before the full council was being curtailed; the case had first to be vetted by the bailies. Craftsmen were no longer allowed to accompany a colleague pressing his suit before the council. In practice, this vetting of ordinary business involved increasingly heavy responsibilities being vested in both burgh magistrates and craft deacons; their authority increased in proportion. It was not the policy of town councils to control the craftsmen by direct means. They could do so more effectively by indirect control through the deacons; the considered response of the Edinburgh council to the riots of 1560 and 1561 was to rely on the deacons to prevent full-scale meetings of craftsmen, which had led to 'tumults and uproris'.[32]

There were two sides to this arrangement: the deacons had to remain answerable to the burgh magistrates and, just as important, they had to be answerable for all of their members. To meet their responsibilities, it was common for them to erect a small disciplinary body within the craft; the Dundee websters provided in their charter for a 'quorum of five', which was to include the chaplain to their altar and would be called by him 'if any one year after year misconduct himself'. In Edinburgh the usual practice was for four quartermasters and the treasurer to assist the deacon, but in the second half of the sixteenth century the numbers tended to increase, although this varied from one craft to another; the small goldsmith craft continued with its council of four, the skinners increased their body to eight in 1579 and the hammermen to twelve in 1568.[33] There was a marked tendency after the Reformation for what had previously been a fairly *ad hoc* system to become more formal and regular, to evolve into what amounted to a burghal authority in miniature. The consolidation of the authority of this inner circle gave extra impetus to the development of an aristocracy within the craft.

The significance of the Edinburgh decreet-arbitral of 1583 has usually been seen in the increased representation it gave to the crafts on the council. A number of its other provisions have been largely ignored. Up until 1583 the system of appointing the deacon was, in practice, that the outgoing holder of the office had sole power to nominate a leet which was then presented to the masters. The new arrangements provided that the retiring deacon actually drew up the leet in consultation with the council. Usually they looked no further than the inner circle around the deacon. The decreet gave its blessing to the long-term movement towards a concentration of power in the deacon and his council. This was again a common pattern in other European towns; in Strasbourg the retiring master and his council chose their own successors from 1551 onwards. Nor surprisingly, the Edinburgh decreet was used as a model for other burghs to copy. Aberdeen's constitution was revised on similar lines in 1587. The decreet also made a substantial dent in craft independence. It was more crucial to the craftsman if they wanted to preserve their autonomy that they retained the right to meet *as* a craft than that they gained further, but still token, representation on the council. However, in the revised constitution, at the same time as being granted the one they were permanently deprived of the other:

> nather the merchants amang themselffis, nather the craftis and thair dekynis or visitouris, sall haif or mak any particulare or generall conventiouns, as dekyins with dekyins, dekyins with thair craftis, or craftis amang themselves, for les to mak privat lawes or statutes . . .

The thinking behind the decreet, and it is difficult to imagine anything else given the fact that it was occasioned by a serious craft riot, concentrated on an attempt to curb craft politics at its roots.[34]

Politically, the winners were the craft aristocracy, the losers the ordinary craftsmen. In the same way, the gap between richer and poorer merchants also widened, though over a longer period. The incorporated guild, far from undermining the council's grip on the burgh, complemented and enhanced it. Increasingly in the second half of the sixteenth century, the distinctive feature of Edinburgh society was not the contrast between merchants and crafts but between those in authority and those subject to them. Society was organised not only as a series of groups but also as a series of group disciplines[35] — not only of council and burgesses, kirk session and congregation, but also the merchant guildry and the craft incorporation. It was by careful use of the enclosed structure of the guildry and the craft guilds that the myth of a corporate society could be maintained. This also explains how, as the town expanded, its government became not less but more authoritarian in nature.[36] The rising craft aristocracy was absorbed into the merchant oligarchy. It was the privileged, as ever, who inherited power in Edinburgh.

NOTES

1. Calderwood, *History*, v, 178. See J. Colston, *The Guildry of Edinburgh: Is It an Incorporation?* (1887).

2. Reid, 'Coming of the Reformation', 28-9.

3. The pitfalls are ably set out in Birnbaum, 'The Zwinglian Reformation in Zürich', 28; see *Edinburgh, 1329-1929*, 272, and Macniven, 'Merchant and Trader', 125. Few historians would still be happy with the extravagant generalisations of Hume Brown (see *Scotland in the Time of Queen Mary*, 144ff), but the myth of a bitterly divided burgh community persists; see S. G. E. Lythe, 'Life and labour in Dundee from the Reformation to the Civil War', *Abertay Historical Soc. Publications*, v (1958), 17.

4. See Grant, *Social and Economic Development*, 128, 133-4; D. Murray, *Early Burgh Organization in Scotland* (1924), i, 8. A note of caution is, however, sounded in W. M. Mackenzie, *The Scottish Burghs* (1949), 96, that local history is liable to be influenced, above all else, by localism.

5. Lesley, *History*, i, 53; Perth's charter is printed in A. J. Warden, *The Burgh Laws of Dundee* (1872), 236; for Glasgow, see Murray, *Early Burgh Organization*, i, 484n, and Smout, *History of the Scottish People*, 173-4.

6. Grant, *Social and Economic Development*, 412; W. McDowall, *History of the Burgh of Dumfries, with Notices of Nithsdale, Annandale and the Western Border* (Edinburgh, 1867), 145, 368; Marwick, *Edinburgh Guilds and Crafts*, 63-4.

7. See Hoskins, 'Elizabethan merchants of Exeter', 164. There were 357 merchants on the Edinburgh tax roll of 1565 (see app. xi), but a sizeable number of others gained exemptions (see *Edin. Accts.*, i, 54-60), so that the full total was close to 400. By 1581 there were 527.

8. *Edin. Tests.*, 10 March 1569 and 23 July 1596; Calderwood, *History*, v, 382; G. Donaldson, *Scotland: James V to James VII* (1965), 251.

9. *CSP Scot.*, v, no. 368; Hoskins, 'Elizabethan merchants of Exeter', 172; W. K. Jordan, *Philanthropy in England, 1480-1660* (London, 1959), 336, 376.

10. This average figure is an impressionistic one since a systematic search was not undertaken. The search, however, did cover most of the prominent burgesses in the town who died before 1600. Fuller details are given in Lynch, 'Thesis', 24n, or in the appendices noted below; all are to be

found in *Edin. Tests.* Five estates of more than £20,000 were uncovered — Birnie, John Dougal (vii), the goldsmith, Michael Gilbert (viii), MacMorran (x), and the wife of John Provand (iii); four of between £10,000 and £12,500 — Gilbert Dick (x), Adam Fullarton (v), Alex. Park and Janet Fleming, the widow of Wm. Craik (viii); eight of between £6,750 and £10,000 — Henry Charteris (iii), Alan Dickson (v), Wm. Fowler (viii), John Howieson (vii), James Johnston of Kellebank, James Ross (vii), Wm. Speir and Thomas Uddart; and seven of between £5,000 and £6,000 — James Baron (v), John Dougal (vii), James Forman (vii), the wife of James Inglis (vii), Wm. Inglis (iii), James Lowrie and John Main (iii). This list, however, significantly understates the collective wealth of the Edinburgh establishment: a large number of leading merchants do not have testaments recorded, especially in the period up to c.1580; where a testament is extant, it will only indicate money and moveable goods. The average estate increased appreciably in the early 17th century.

11. See Edin. Tests., 31 Jan 1592, 27 May 1590, 28 Jan. 1580 & 26 Jan. 1591 for Gilbert, Richardson, Simpson and Burrell respectively.

12. *Edin. Recs.*, i, 33; ii, 216.

13. Angus, 'Edinburgh skinners', 47-8; Marwick, *Edinburgh Guilds and Crafts*, 45ff; H. Lumsden, *History of the Skinners, Furriers and Glovers of Glasgow* (Glasgow, 1837), 22. The Edinburgh muster roll of 1558 provides the number of servants in some, but not all, of the crafts (see *Edin. Recs.*, iii, 25).

14. *Edin. Recs.*, iv, 278-9, 413.

15. See *ibid.*, i, 203-4, for the Edinburgh websters' seal of cause of 1521, which is a good illustration of the powers delegated to craft masters, and Lumsden, *History of Glasgow Skinners*, 26, for an ordinance of 1571 about fees.

16. Lythe, *Economy of Scotland*, 30; Angus, 'Edinburgh skinners', 46.

17. R. Lamond, 'The Scottish craft gild as a religious fraternity', *SHR*, xvi (1916), 210; C. A. Hunt, *The Book of the Perth Hammermen, 1518-1568* (Perth 1889), lxiv; W. F. Gray, 'The incorporation of candlemakers of Edinburgh, 1517-1584', *BOEC*, xvii (1930), 95; W. Campbell, *History of the Incorporation of Cordiners in Glasgow* (Glasgow, 1883), 67; R. D. McEwan, *Old Glasgow Weavers: being records of the Incorporation of Weavers* (Glasgow, 1908), 15.

18. Monter, *Calvin's Geneva*, 159.

19. See J. Kirk, 'The development of the Melvillian movement in late sixteenth century Scotland' (Edinburgh Ph.D., 1972), 11-12.

20. Smith, *Hammermen of Edinburgh*, 173-4; MS Hammermen Recs., ii, fos. 4v, 6r, 7r; *Edin. Recs.*, iii, 45.

21. *Ibid.*, iii, 90-92; Ross, 'The Magdalene Chapel', 98-9; Ross & Brown, 'The Magdalen Chapel', 40, 76; Smith, *Hammermen of Edinburgh*, 172; see app. v for Small and app. vi for Brocas.

22. *Edin. Recs.*, iii, 134-5; MS Co. Recs., iv, fo. 30r; cf. MS Hammermen Recs., 3 May 1562, i, fo. 215v; see also *RPC*, i, 216. The lists of members of the council of the craft elected 1568-70 are given in MS Hammermen Recs., i, fos. 231v, 232r, 233r. See app. vi for the catholic hammermen, Brocas and Smith, app. v for its protestant activists, Harlaw and Young, and app. viii for its queen's men, Anderson, Henderson and Wilson.

23. *APS*, ii, 238, 351, 487; *RPC*, i, 94-5; L. A. Barbé, *Sidelights on the History, Industries and Social Life of Scotland* (London, 1919), 245-6; G. Hay, *History of Arbroath* (Arbroath, 1876), 113; E. Bain, *Merchants and Craft Guilds, a History of the Aberdeen Incorporated Trades* (Aberdeen, 1887), 212-3, 216-7.

24. *RSS*, v, 1362, 1400; Pitcairn, *Trials*, i, 360; JC 1/6, 17 Sept. 1551. For the fleshers' case, see *TA*, xi, 186; *Edin. Recs.*, ii, 177.

25. See JC 19/1, 17 Aug. & 10 Oct. 1543, where fifteen entered pledges. Only eleven are listed in the document cited by A. Pennecuik, *An Historical Account of the Blue Blanket or Craftsmen's Banner* (Edinburgh, 1826), 75. Pennecuik's account was accepted by both J. Colston, *The Incorporated Trades of Edinburgh* (Edinburgh, 1891), xxxii-iii, and Grant, *Social and Economic*

Development, 429. For the political background in the late summer of 1543, see M. H. Merriman, 'The struggle for the marriage of Mary, Queen of Scots: English and French intervention in Scotland' (London Ph.D., 1975), 68-79.

26. The riots of 1560 and 1561 are discussed more fully in ch. 5.

27. MS Act Book of Deacons of Crafts, i, fos. 6v, 7, 14r; *Edin. Recs.*, iv, 240, 255-6; Calderwood, *History*, iii, 635.

28. See MS Co. Recs., 31 May 1564, iv, fo. 104r, for an example of the annual appointment of wine masters, and JC 1/12, 13 June 1565, for an example of the frequent judicial action taken against burgesses, including here six tailors, for selling wine at above the fixed price.

29. Warden, *Burgh Laws of Dundee*, 338.

30. E. Naujocks, *Obrigskeitsgedanke, Zunftverfassung und Reformation* (Stuttgart, 1958), 46.

31. See Hunt, *Perth Hammermen Book*, vii-xii; Bain, *Merchant and Craft Guilds of Aberdeen*, 98; Warden, *Burgh Laws of Dundee*, 100; Angus, 'Edinburgh skinners', 51.

32. Warden, *Burgh Laws of Dundee*, 34-5; *Edin. Recs.*, iii, 156-7.

33. Warden, *Burgh Laws of Dundee*, 510-11; MS Goldsmiths' Recs., fo. 8v; Angus, 'Edinburgh skinners', 54; MS Hammermen Recs., i, fo. 231v.

34. *Edin. Recs.*, iv, 268, 270-71; cf. Chrisman, *Strasbourg and the Reform*, 7; Bain, *Merchant and Craft Guilds of Aberdeen*, 332.

35. Smout, *History of the Scottish People*, 95.

36. See Hoskins, 'Elizabethan merchants of Exeter', 165.

Part Two

Burgh Politics and National Crisis

5

Politics and Protestantism in the 1550s

EDINBURGH had in the 1540s a foretaste of a number of the pressures inflicted upon it in the dozen years or so which followed the reformation crisis. In 1544 the town was overrun by an English army under the command of the earl of Hertford. The instructions from the English privy council to burn and lay waste the town were not, however, carried out to the letter and accounts of the damage to the burgh have often been exaggerated; it seems to have been only its southern fringes along the Cowgate and Holyrood to the east which suffered badly. Damage to life and goods was probably at least as serious as that to buildings. One English account claimed that between 120 and 140 inhabitants, almost a tenth of the number of men the town could put under arms in 1558, were killed in the initial assault and that a further four or five hundred fell for the loss of a mere seven Englishmen in a second attack. Although the claims of military commanders should always be treated with scepticism, even a fraction of Hertford's estimated kill would have been a grievous blow to a town the size of Edinburgh. £10,000 sterling worth of merchandise, mostly grain, was seized from the warehouses of Leith along with two ships in its harbour. Yet military force only followed where economic sanctions against the town had failed. The seizure of a number of ships in 1543 had created such bad feeling that the townspeople threatened to hold an English emissary, Sir Ralph Sadler, as a hostage for their safe return. Sadler in return had threatened an economic blockade of the Forth which would 'utterly beggar the town', coming, as it did, at the vital time in the year for the French wine trade.[1]

The various attempts to force the burgh's merchants into a pro-English party, combined with the uncertainties generated by the earl of Arran's flirtation with protestant preachers and an English alliance, inevitably had some effects. There are a number of indications that the burgh was in something like a state of internal turmoil in 1543. In August, a number of armed men, among them two members of the formidable and, as time would prove, consistently conservative, merchant family, the Tennants, burst into the council chamber parading the Banner of the Holy Ghost. The privy council was sufficiently alarmed by this outburst to intervene immediately to bring the rioters before the justiciary court, and by the prospect of a wavering council to impose on it a client of Cardinal David Beaton, Sir Adam Otterburn, as provost at the elections two months later. Nonetheless, Sadler reported, the merchants still 'murmur amongst thaim selfes'.[2] The only ingredient which was missing in 1543 for a full rehearsal of the crises of 1559 or 1571 was a significant protestant party within the burgh. A firm peg on which to hang either protestant-tinged noble factionalism or intervention by a foreign power did not yet exist.

Although the regular series of council minutes begins in 1551, it offers little help in unravelling the tangled complex of pressures on the burgh during the last years of Arran's tenure as governor or the first years of the regency of Mary of Guise. The town council itself had been subjected to the influence of the shifting factions centring around Mary, Beaton and Arran since the beginning of the minority of Mary, Queen of Scots. It had to suffer a series of nominees as provost since the crisis of 1543, none of them a burgess, despite the act of parliament of 1537, which had detailed the 'almaist ruynous' consequences of intruding outsiders into burgh office. Even nominees did not have security of tenure; Sir Adam Otterburn was dismissed from office in the mutual recriminations which followed the English sack of the town in 1544.[3] Life remained uncertain and, at times, frightening in the second phase of the 'rough wooing'. The devastating English victory at Pinkie in 1547 had ended with the scattered remnants of the Scots being chased to the gates of Edinburgh. The string of English garrisons which were set up in the Lothians and Borders after Pinkie threatened to strangle the burgh's trade. Edinburgh and its port seemed for a few months to be likely additions to those garrisons. From early in 1548 the English forces settled down to a war of attrition in the Lothians. The result was that, although Edinburgh was never actually besieged, it was put under economic siege; the countryside within a two-mile radius of the town, which included the burgh's mills, was burned and laid waste. The concomitant of Protector Somerset's concerted attempts to create an English pale in central and southern Scotland was an increasing number of French troops, concentrated around Edinburgh and Leith. To the town the antidote was almost as unwelcome as the disease. Although Arran tried to prevent the burgh being turned into a base camp for the French army, there were a series of clashes on the streets which ended with the French being driven out of the burgh.[4] The seeds were sown for the burgh's double-edged fears eleven years later.

The end of the rough wooing seems to have brought a more settled period to the burgh. The most obvious sign of this was that merchants returned to the office of provost. Yet this only came after the sitting provost and two of his bailies had been summarily dismissed from office in June 1550 for their part in a trifling affair involving the brother of Mary of Guise. If it was a more settled period, it came to an end in October 1553, when Sir William Hamilton of Sanquhar, another client of Arran, who had by now been elevated to the French duchy of Châtelherault, was made provost in what was probably a last desperate attempt to hold Edinburgh opinion. This was not the only irregularity in this election; the established and elaborate election process was circumvented by the co-option of two of the bailies, Duncan Livingstone and William Muirhead, and the dean of guild. It seems likely that the other two bailies, although they might have been arrived at by due process, were also vetted; at least one of them, John Preston, had been a Châtelherault nominee before.[5] Edinburgh's politics was a sensitive barometer of the state of court politics; it was not surprising that the Châtelherault period ended, like that of Mary of Guise half a dozen years later, with an attempt to pack the town council.

It would be a mistake, however, to believe that burgh politics would have been more settled if only left alone. There was in the early 1550s a distinct sharpening of tension between the council and some of the crafts, largely as a result of its deliberate policy of holding food prices down to artificially low levels in a period of acute and sustained shortages. There was, as a result, a riot involving the baxters in 1551, and a number of fleshers were put to an assize in 1553. The only one to profit from these incidents was Châtelherault; it was wholly in character that the fine of five hundred merks imposed on the baxters went into his pocket. If craft or court politics did not provide ammunition for the tortuous internal wranglings of the burgh establishment, then personalities would. Francis Tennant had taken the chance to demonstrate against the council's co-operation with Arran's policies in 1543 but his dis-affection in the 1550s was based on personal pique and he became a lonely and sullen figure relegated to the background of burgh politics. Although this mal-content found new targets to grumble at after 1560, his criticisms of the new regime were only marginally more bitter than those of the old. At times, however, disputes centred around personalities could blow up into something more serious. The classic example of this in the 1550s was the struggle which developed between two merchant families, the Littles and the Barons, for the office of water bailie of Leith, which sucked in Mary of Guise because one of the contenders was a client of hers. The dispute went as far as the regent almost being forced into her first active intervention in council affairs; she threatened a bailie, the dean of guild and four councillors with dismissal.[6] This affair is a good illustration of the point that in a tight-knit, closed society the politics of personality was always potentially combustible. The most difficult situation to deal with was one where personal or family interests combined with other loyalties or interests.

This was the reason why the Little affair was the major flashpoint during the regency of Mary of Guise before 1559. It was a period which saw a con-tinuation of what had by now become the customary interference with burgh government as well as an escalation of the internal tensions within the burgh. The regency coincided with what seems to have been a rising tide of claims from the crafts ranging from the fundamental, the role in the annual election process, to the trivial but symbolic, such as a key to the charter chest. The campaign intensified after the passing of an act of parliament in 1555, which abolished the office of craft deacon as well as other craft privileges. Yet the argument that has been made out that Mary was playing for the support of the crafts turns on two specific instances.

In 1556 she granted a charter to the craftsmen which effectively nullified the act of 1555. This was done in the context of increasing pressure on the merchant-controlled council to hold down the prices of food and wine, an outright ban on the export of fish and the forced import of bullion. The council had two cards to play — the offer of four thousand merks plus some lavish entertainment for the regent in exchange for a settlement of these disputes or an outright refusal to agree to pay any taxes. The charter can be seen as another means used by Mary to put pressure on the council. This is not to deny that the crafts were not grateful for this concession. They predictably claimed a right to vote in the first dispute to arise between Mary and the burgh, which happened to be over the right to nominate the water bailie of Leith. This was another reason why the council allowed the affair to go to the brink before it pulled back. The 1556 episode seems more likely to have been part of a manoeuvre by the regent to extract more revenue out of the burgh rather than, as some have argued, a last stand for catholicism and the French alliance. It would also be a mistake to imagine that the craftsmen made only gains; part of the arrangement was that they had to pay their own arrears of tax.[7]

In September 1559, the next time that the craft deacons claimed voting rights and when control of the burgh *was* at issue, the argument has more substance. It can be argued that the crafts were used as part of an elaborate scheme of the regent to gain a tighter grip on the burgh in a period of intensifying crisis. Yet not all of the craftsmen who held office in 1559 were inclined to resist the second and decisive occupation of the town by the Lords of Congregation in October 1559. The regent, it is true, had raised the crafts' hopes but it is easier to talk in terms of a resultant inflation of expectations on the part of the crafts, which would express itself in a series of election disputes throughout the 1560s, than of an explicit alliance between Mary of Guise and Edinburgh's craftsmen. It was the new protestant regime of the 1560s rather than the one which held power in the second half of the 1550s which suffered more severely, but not because it was protestant.

The relations between the regent and Edinburgh's merchant community were also characteristically ambivalent. A number of them profited from her assumption of authority in 1554, even though her administration had a distinctly French tinge to it.[8] The merchants were not unwilling to act as money lenders to the crown; thirty-three of the wealthiest of them agreed to lend £1,000 to Mary's principal French adviser, Henri Cleutin, sieur d'Oysel, in December 1554, which was recovered from the burgh's share of the first of Mary's major subsidies. Yet by October 1555 the burgh's merchants were reluctant to extend the same facility again despite the threat of imprisonment if they refused. The demand produced internal tensions since it was the bailies who were put in the awkward and invidious position of being Mary's agents and the potential gaolers. It does seem, however, that the pressure paid and the loan was made.[9] Even before this latest forced exaction there had been hints of the 'grudge or murmour of the pepill' from James Henderson, the former propagandist for Somerset who had returned to Scotland to hold office under the regent and a man well qualified to testify to Edinburgh opinion.[10] The prospect of a continual drain of revenue to the crown in the un-precedented form of a perpetual tax, as mooted in 1556, and the reality of five separate tax demands made between September 1556 and December 1557 must have strained loyalty to the limit. The burgh had to resort to extraordinary methods of raising revenue, of taxing burgesses' sons who had not yet gained their freedom, and a tax on rents and land within the burgh. Even so, it had difficulty in extracting this level of taxation; the £1,200 which the burgh negotiated to absent itself from the army which marched to the Border in September 1557 remained unpaid in July 1558.[11] The burden fell heavily on Edinburgh, which was asked to raise a disproportionately large number of men for the abortive invasion of 1557 as well as to repair the still uncompleted Flodden Wall, and most heavily on its merchants, who bore what was in-creasingly becoming an unfairly heavy share of burgh taxation.

The danger in a catalogue of grievances lies in overstatement. It would be possible to present a picture of a town bowed under the weight of taxation, its merchants forced into making loans to the crown, its magistrates threatened with peremptory dismissal, the merchant-dominated council threatened with being swamped with craftsmen, its trading monopoly threatened by Mary's actions over the superiority of its port of Leith from January 1556 onwards.[12] Yet it would be an overstatement to see these accumulated grievances in terms of the longer-term factors which led to the burgh's disaffection from the regent in 1559. It is as well to remember that conditions seemed to point in her favour when she came to power in 1554. She must have seemed a welcome relief from the grasping clutches of Châtelherault, who had spent much of his last months in office wringing dry the profits from justice; his victims included a score of Edinburgh burgesses, whose offences ranged from outright collaboration with the English in the 1540s, like James Henderson, to merely technical mis-demeanours, like that of William Birnie.[13] The link, of course, was that they were two of the wealthiest merchants in the town and could well afford to pay. It was symptomatic of Mary of Guise's different approach that she did not reproach Henderson for his past but appointed him to office.[14] Conciliation and good government were the keynotes of her administration. What dis-affection there was stemmed from her actions in raising revenue. Yet it is difficult to believe that Mary would have pushed either the question of craft representation on the council or the matter of the superiority of Leith to the point of seriously antagonising Edinburgh's merchants while she remained dependent on them as money brokers. The catalogue of grievances presented by the Congregation in October 1559, when they deposed the regent and the town council, had an air of hindsight and self-justification about it.[15] At the same time, there can be little doubt that Edinburgh was not one of the burghs enjoying a relationship with the regent which could be described as one of mutual trust.[16] The pressures on Edinburgh during the first three and a half years of Mary's regency provide a background for understanding the burgh's reactions to the crisis of 1559 and 1560 but the search for definite causes must be taken up with the shorter term.

It might be thought that a more direct link might be made with the repercussions of the theft of the image of the town's patron saint, St. Giles, probably sometime in July 1558. The council was ordered by the archbishop of St. Andrews, John Hamilton, under pain of excommunication, to replace it before the annual procession on the feast day of St. Giles on 1 September. The council refused to accept the responsibility for doing this and appealed directly to Rome; a tribunal was set up, which was still sitting shortly before the Congregation first entered the burgh in June 1559. If Knox is to be believed, Edinburgh approached the Reformation with a quasi-protestant town council under threat of excommunication for maintaining 'that God in some places had commanded idols and images to be destroyed'. This is most doubtful. It is the first illustration of the fact that Knox's claims about the motives involved in Edinburgh politics in the Reformation period must be treated with the utmost caution. The rather different conclusions which have recently been drawn from the affair are more convincing; the dispute was a technical one and it provides little evidence for supposing that religious considerations operated in it. Excommunication, if it could conceivably have been enforced, would have had very serious consequences for a trading community; the inability to collect debts, for instance, would have brought commerce to a grinding halt. It is also difficult to believe that one council would have attacked the doctrinal efficacy of images while the next, a mere ten months later, would have anxiously stored away the town's collection of religious vestments and relics. If one town council doubted the devotional value of the statue of St. Giles in its collegiate church, why was its successor so keen to preserve his arm bone?[17] It would, in any case, be difficult to construct a protestant caucus out of the town council of 1557-8. It is true that fifteen of the eighteen burgesses on it later appeared on the protestant subscription list of 1562, but only three of them had emerged to declare for the Congregation in October 1559. Seven of them, on the other hand, specifically refused to co-operate with the protestant lords and were summarily dismissed.

The excommunication affair is a significant illustration of the dangers involved in too readily linking the pressures on the burgh in the period up to 1559 with the assumption that the 1550s saw a growing groundswell of protestant opinion. An earlier theft of images from St. Giles' in 1556 *had* been firmly dealt with. The assize which convicted the culprits included two of the burgesses appointed to the council by the Congregation in 1559; coincident-ally, one of them, John Spens, was also one of the bailies on the council put under sentence of excommunication in 1558.[18] There are no grounds for supposing that the council was becoming lax in its vigilance against iconoclasm or that its attitude had been softened by fellow travellers on it. There is also precious little evidence to show that the protestant element on the councils of the second half of the 1550s was victimised by Mary of Guise.[19] The six members of the council threatened with dismissal by her in 1556 over the appointment of a water bailie of Leith did, it is true, have among them the three most important protestants in the burgh in the second half of the 1550s, James Baron, Edward Hope and Adam Fullarton. They also included two men who later emerged as hard-line members of the catholic party in the 1560s, John Spottiswood and James Lindsay. The wine merchants who fell victim to Mary's policy of holding down prices in 1555 included Richard Strang, a member of the pro-Congregation council of 1559-60, but also Herbert Maxwell, one of its most bitter opponents. It is difficult to believe that the illustrious Thomas MacCalzean was dismissed for any other reason in 1556 than insubordination. He was probably, as he later claimed, an early protestant but still had to be forced to pay his share of the tax imposed by the Congregation on the burgh in 1559, did not leave with them in November, and even rented his house out to the returning hard-line catholic provost, Lord Seton, shortly afterwards. MacCalzean's guiding principle, even in the reformation crisis was, as with so many others, business as usual.[20] It is a largely fruitless exercise either to try to interpret Mary's dealings with the burgh before the crisis of 1559 as a catholic regent reacting to a protestant-tinged council or to try to accommodate all the burgh's internal disputes in the 1550s within a religious framework.

This remains the case even into 1559. The council which was elected in October 1558 did not have an easy year in office. There was continual friction between it and the provost, Seton, who had now returned from France. This culminated in the ordering into ward of one of the bailies, Alexander Baron, and Alexander Guthrie, the common clerk, the throwing into irons of two sons and a servant of one of the councillors, Thomas Thomson, and the imprison-ment of a second bailie, David Forester, in the Castle and then at Dunbar. Once again, the clash seems to have been one of personalities rather than of religious differences; Forester certainly supported the Congregation later in 1559, and it would be possible to make out a plausible case for Thomson and Guthrie as protestant sympathisers, but not for Baron, who was imprisoned in turn by the bailies of the new regime in 1562 for 'evill speiking of the gude toun' to the queen. The Forester incident was regarded by the council with such seriousness that they forecast it might set off an 'upror and insurrection of the common pepill of this burgh to the greit hurt of the commoun weill of the samyn'. They could not have been reassured by Seton's counter-threat to resist any trouble 'with his kyn frendis'.[21]

The imminent entry of the Congregation into Edinburgh in June 1559 refocused and partly recast this growing antipathy between Seton and his council. The threatened riot did take place, but in the form of an iconoclastic attack on the Blackfriars and Greyfriars, which changed the accusation against Seton from one of provoking a riot to one of abandoning his charge to the 'rascall people'.[22] The council took fright; it decided to take the matter of the town's ecclesiastical vestments and valuables into its own hands. There was no hint in Edinburgh of Dundee's reaction to the pressure put upon it by protestant ideas and image-breakers; there the council auctioned off its relics and vestments in August 1559 on condition that the buyers altered them enough to make them unusable 'in papistrie herefter'. Edinburgh's city fathers, like those of Aberdeen, hid their treasures away for a better day.[23]

The safeguarding of the town's religious places seems to have been the council's first consideration in June 1559, but it entailed a dualistic, not to say ambivalent, policy. On the one hand, the council was concerned to reassure Mary that it retained a firm grip on the town; it seems likely that this was why Seton was blamed for the riot of 14 June. The precedent that was in both Mary's and the council's minds was Perth which grew more alarming as time went on.[24] The iconoclastic riot of 11 May, during which Perth's churches and friaries had been looted, had been followed by a short-lived armistice; the town had been re-occupied by Scots soldiers in French pay, its bailies dismissed, and a number of burgesses exiled.[25] The approaching army of the Congregation, however, brought with it the prospect of anarchy in the town if the council did not comply, as St. Andrews and Dundee had done, in removing 'all monuments of idolatry'.[26]

The council of 1558-9 seems to have had a larger protestant element within it than its predecessor. At least a third of its members can safely be classed as protestant sympathisers. It also seems likely that this was not a secret, for the commissioners who were sent to treat with the Congregation at Linlithgow on 29 June were noticeably taken from the protestant contingent on the council.[27] It would be difficult to argue, however, that this council was split into religious factions, each following different courses. Although the burgh's protestants openly adopted Knox as their minister on 7 July, the council resisted the appeal from a protestant hot-head to dismiss one of the deacons as a man who 'refusit to serve his God'. The council was neither persuaded nor suddenly taken over by its protestants. The members who dealt with the Congregation's negotiators, Ruthven and Sandilands of Calder, on 12 July were more representative of the council as a whole and included men who went different ways in the next crisis.[28]

There was neither a purge nor a period of one-party government during the

Congregation's first occupation of the town in July 1559. This deliberately ambivalent policy, which partly reflected the council's own composition, must have seemed to have paid when the Congregation agreed to leave the burgh on 24 or 25 July. Their departure, however, indirectly produced another problem. It was at this point that Mary devised the plan of holding a kind of mass religious referendum in the town rather than acquiesce in the arrangement originally arrived at with the Congregation that the mass should continue to be said, but only in Leith and Holyrood, and a protestant service be held in the great church of St. Giles'. The scheme was ingenious but dangerous. It pleased neither the council nor the burgh's protestants, who protested that 'Goddis treuthe . . . sal be subiect to voiting of men'. It also created further difficulties for Seton, who was forced to walk a tightrope between the prospect of further antagonising the council if its authority was diminished by such an innovation and baulking Mary's scheme to gain a tighter religious grip over the burgh. Seton's problem, however, was taken out of his hands, since the town 'utterly refused to choose againe'.[29] In the intervening period until September 1559 the council, with Forester now restored, met fairly regularly and as a near-complete unit, with the notable exception of Seton himself, who attended only once during this period.[30] It was also in this period that the peculiar situation persisted of one friar, the Dominican, John Black, celebrating the mass at Holyrood and an ex-friar, probably also a Dominican, John Willock, preaching in St. Giles'. This was an arrangement which was not unique in the sixteenth century; it had been imposed on a number of Upper German cities by the Emperor, Charles V, in 1548, but not without difficulty. It was not likely, however, to last in an unstable political situation. The most worrying feature for the council, since it lay outside their control, must have been the provocative behaviour of French troops who were able to come and go as they pleased.[31]

Mary's next opportunity to regain control of the burgh came with the council elections of September and October 1559. Her first tactic was to turn once again to the craft deacons. Its effect was to recast the issues at stake and to unite the majority of the council in opposition. It was not religion but the burgh constitution which was at stake in the election of 1559. On 20 September the deacons, backed by a proclamation from the queen, claimed the right to vote in the forthcoming election. Two days later, they tried again, presenting a further writing from Mary, which clearly anticipated her alternative tactic — a leet. The council, in the meantime and against the wishes of Seton, took the unusual step of formally replacing any of its members who were away on business, including one who had been away only a week.[32] It looks as if the council, which had already been in serious conflict with its provost, was desperately trying to pack its depleted ranks in an attempt to resist pressure from three sides — from Seton, the crafts and Mary of Guise. Up to a point its blocking tactics succeeded, but this success made inevitable Mary's other tactic — a leet.

It was the leet and the repercussions which flowed from it which brought to an end the dualistic administration of 1558-9 and polarised opinion within the burgh. A number of sources report the forcing of a leet of provost and bailies on the town 'against all ordour of election' at the Michaelmas election and their removal by the Congregation on 22 October after their entry into the burgh.[33] Although the council register does not record either coup, it does, from its recitation of the council members present at most meetings, confirm that there were two councils and establish the membership of both of them.[34] The first council, which again had the regent's loyal ally, Seton, as its provost, did not hold office long. The first accusation by the Congregation of election-rigging came in a long list of articles of grievance of 3 October. This was the council which, according to the minutes, first met on the 6th. It met again on the 14th, making a timely decision to move the town's artillery into the Castle. The Congregation entered the town four days later and on the 21st called a convention of the nobility which deposed the regent. Interference in burgh elections not only in Edinburgh but also in Perth and Jedburgh was one of the pretexts that were used.[35]

According to the testimony of John Preston, one of Mary's original nominees, to a full-scale inquiry commissioned by her daughter and Francis II, which took evidence in the town four months later, it was at this point that he and his colleagues were asked to continue in office but refused; they were forcibly replaced by four new bailies and 'aultres douze pour le conseil'. This, however, was not quite accurate; two members of the Seton council, Alexander Park and John Spens, did take up the Congregation's offer. A third, Luke Wilson, co-operated to the point of helping to assess the tax liability of one of the burgh's quarters. This new protestant council, with Archibald Douglas of Kilspindie, the brother of the sixth earl of Angus and grandson of the famous 'Bell-the-Cat', installed as its provost, met on 27 October along with the craft deacons in order to levy a tax of two thousand merks on the burgh to help to meet the Congregation's crippling financial burden of having five thousand men under arms. The purge did not end there. Three deacons — of the wrights, baxters and skinners — were removed. Yet the purge here was far from total; at least five other deacons complied. It is a striking fact which says little for the notion that in the 1550s the craftsmen were broadly for Mary of Guise and the merchants against her, that the burgh office-holders who were craftsmen acquiesced more readily in the Congregation's wishes than those who were merchants.[36]

The combination of a succession of heavy defeats suffered by the Congregation between 31 October and 6 November, their failure to woo the Captain of the Castle, Lord Erskine, and a steady defection from their own ranks made their military position untenable and dismayed their supporters within the burgh. Food was running short and the morale amongst the inhabitants as a whole was low enough to be turning into outright hostility to the occupying army. The protestant lords evacuated the town at midnight on the 6th and most of their town council must have gone with them. They were not alone in fleeing the town. Two separate English accounts point to a mass exodus of 'the most part of the substancial men' as one occupying army seemed set to begin where the other had left off. The fears of the inhabitants seemed to have been realised when French troops were quartered on the town after Mary's return on 7 November but damage seems to have been limited and confined to property. It seems likely that the Seton council did not re-establish control until after the 'French rage' had spent itself; it did not meet until 13 November. The catholic counter-coup was completed by the re-consecration of St. Giles'.[37]

The disruption which was caused by the occupation and re-occupation of the burgh in October and November 1559, however, can be exaggerated. It seems likely that the exodus, like that before the siege of October 1571, was only temporary. The regent was anxious to conciliate rather than punish and her offer of an amnesty was designed to speed a return to the situation most likely to favour her administration — business as usual. Trade was not paralysed; more than forty Edinburgh merchants promptly set sail for France and had the misfortune to be attacked by pirates off the coast of Northumberland. To complete the irony, they included Luke Wilson, who had been a member of the original Seton council, had acted as an extentor for the Congregation after they occupied the town and had cheerfully resumed his seat on the Seton council on 21 November until called to account by it after the de la Brosse inquiry had completed its investigations. Reprisals were limited to those who were actual collaborators. The eight hauled before the council included one of the deacons who had agreed to impose a levy on the town to help to finance the Congregation, two of those who had helped collect it and two maltmen, who probably had provisioned the army.[38] Yet, even if the actual disruption was small, the experience had been traumatic. The scars and fears of the 1540s had been reopened. Thomas Randolph, the most astute of William Cecil's agents in Scotland, recognised as much when he drew up a memorandum for his master's attention a month later: what should be done, he asked, if a burgh offered to surrender to an English expeditionary force? Cecil's answer was unequivocal: all Scottish towns must remain in 'Scottis handes'.[39] The English, at least, had learned from the mistakes of the 1540s.

The Seton council resumed control over a town which had now shed all traces of the bipartite administration and religious arrangements of the late summer and autumn of 1559. The mass was restored, St. Giles' reconsecrated and the town's ecclesiastical vestments and valuables returned. The purge of burgh protestants from offices in the royal gift, like those in the Mint, was swift but the repercussions for other burgesses were slower to materialise and probably were not far-reaching.[40] There was no hint of anything like the systematic dragnet instituted by returning king's men in 1572. The damage to the town had been caused, not by fellow burgesses, but by outsiders. The crisis of 1559 and 1560 lacked the animus and the moral certainties produced by the civil wars.

The end of the Seton council was in sight by 1 April 1560, when Mary of

Guise retreated into Edinburgh Castle and the French behind their fortifications at Leith. Its last entry in the minutes was on 30 March, but it managed to deal firmly with a mob of looters after the French withdrawal and was still in control when an English messenger arrived in the town on 3 April. The Kilspindie council had regained control by 9 April, when a large number of English soldiers entered the town, although its first entry in the minutes was not until the 16th. It then proceeded to pick up the pieces of administration, first ordering the repair of St. Giles', where altars had recently been thrown down by some of the protestant lords and next granting a further tax on the town for the Congregation, this time for £1,600.[41] Edinburgh's counter-reformation was over.

The Kilspindie council's resumption of power was vigorous, but not un-equivocal. Payments were quickly made to the town's ministers, Knox and Willock, while the siege of Leith continued; at the same time the town stopped paying its chaplains to say mass. Yet the day before this apparent watershed in Edinburgh history, the treasurer had duly paid the quarterly fee of the master of the grammar school, William Roberton, who subsequently emerged as one of the most stubborn of the catholic opponents of the new regime.[42] Even at the moment of protestant victory, dramatic change and continuity stood un-easily side by side. It was the story of much of Edinburgh's reformation. The town could put only three hundred men under arms — a fifth of its potential manpower — to help in the siege of Leith. It had difficulty in extracting the tax earmarked for the Congregation from a reluctant community. Eventually it was forced to borrow money to meet its commitments. The reasons for this reluctance were significant. Some prominent catholic loyalists, like the bailie of the deposed Seton council, Herbert Maxwell, had punitive levels of taxation imposed on them; Maxwell was eventually paid back a half of the original assessment after strenuous appeals. The men chosen by the returning protestant regime to implement the tax came mostly from outside the existing circle of privilege and respectability. A good example was Michael Christison, a small merchant who had emerged in the privy kirk in the 1550s. He was elevated to the guildry for his services but this could not disguise the fact that he and most of his colleagues must have been seen as protestant *arrivistes* bent on imposing arbitrary and penal taxation on their betters. This was a policy which was liable to produce bitter conflict within the burgh community. The new regime pulled back from it. When it appointed auditors to review the tax a month later, it looked beyond its protestant loyalists. Two of the established merchants it chose illustrate the indirect consequences of this shift of policy. One was Andrew Stevenson, one of the half-dozen wealthiest men in the town, who proved willing enough to adopt a nominal protestantism but who also had a wife with strong catholic loyalties. The second was John Spottiswood, who later emerged as part of a catholic faction in burgh affairs; his first, and by no means his last, clash with protestant authority came only three days after his appointment.[43] Conciliation meant that the new regime was forced to turn to men like these.

The history of the Scottish Reformation, it should be remembered, was not marked by full-scale purges of catholics from office. Protestants and catholics sat side by side in the privy council, the administration and the law courts; they mixed freely, as events turned out, at the royal court when it returned to Scotland. The burghs were not exempt from this pattern. This is not to say that the new protestant regime in Edinburgh did not try to change matters — it clearly did in the summer of 1560. Even then, in the first flush of victory, it found that it could not swim against the tide. Throughout the 1560s it had particular difficulty in two areas with a comprehensive programme of protestantisation. It would find it very difficult to dislodge catholic or crypto-catholic office-holders, particularly schoolmasters; and it seems to have realised almost from the beginning that certain functions, particularly those of tax assessment and audit, would have to remain open to respected and established burgesses, in whom the community as a whole could have confidence. Protestantisation in Edinburgh as elsewhere had to stop short of a wholesale promotion of protestants regardless of their status.

Edinburgh politics had been polarised along religious lines by Mary of Guise's leet and the Congregation's coup of October 1559. Both sides in the struggle had interfered with elections and ridden rough-shod over burgh privileges. Knox had also criticised the regent for the poor quality of her appointees: he characterised Seton as 'most unworthy of any regiment in any well ruled commonwealth' and dismissed his bailies as 'some as meet for their office as a sowtar to sail a ship in a stormy day'. There was some truth in this. Seton was unpopular in the town, had neglected his duties in the past and was, according to a different source, 'wearie of his office'. Some of the office-holders were more conspicuous for their links with the court than their service to the town. Two of the bailies were very short of experience and the dean of guild was so decrepit that he never took up office.[44] Yet the Congregation's alternative regime made a poorer showing still. Inexperience riddled its membership. Ten of its fourteen ordinary councillors were new men and more than half of them never appeared on the council again; there was not another set of bailies with so little experience of office until the Marian coup of 1571. The Seton appointees, whatever their other faults, were at least still drawn from the upper strata of the burgh's merchants. Together they could muster twenty-three servants; the Kilspindie office-holders could manage fourteen and James Baron provided half of these by himself. Kilspindie's bailies paid only a third of the tax their rivals did. The Congregation had been forced to dig deeper still for some of the councillors; three of them were not even members of the guildry and one of these, John Bell, was a seed seller and, from the evidence of tax rolls, the smallest merchant to appear on the council in the second half of the sixteenth century.[45] Mary of Guise had been guilty of tactlessness and favouritism; the protestant lords, who had in the second half of 1559 generally taken care to stress the need for government by the well born, seemed to be threatening the Edinburgh establishment itself.

The Congregation's difficulties in establishing protestant government in the town were, in a sense, surprising given the number of incidental factors which seemed to be flowing in their favour in 1559. Certain of their claims must have met with a sympathetic response: the prospect of dearth and the town's inability 'to susteane thowsands of strangers'; the impending threat of the 'planting of men of warre in our free towns', which materialised with the French re-occupation of the town in November 1559. The crisis year had seen the exaggeration of two worrying prospects for the town; the question of the superiority of Leith had cropped up again and the prospect of further rioting in the town had sharpened the fears of the more substantial burgesses about Mary's tactic of supporting the rights of the crafts in burgh elections, which now took on the appearance of an appeal for popular support. The threat to the independence and integrity of burgh authority, first raised by her proposal for a popular vote on religion, culminated in her forced leet of October. In 1559 it must have seemed to many of the inward-looking merchant establishment that this was the most disturbing element of all: the potential break-up of the burgh's elaborately woven system of monopoly, privilege and control.[46]

Yet disaffection was one thing and outright rebellion another. Very few of the larger merchants reacted to the extent of openly going over to the Congregation. Trade, after all, did continue. The 'French rage' proved worse in expectation than in reality. The prevailing reaction of both the merchants and the burgh as a whole to the events of 1559 was a natural and apprehensive uncertainty.[47] The majority of the deacons were not so attached to Mary as to refuse to co-operate with the Congregation. The majority of the merchants were not so convinced by the propaganda of the Congregation as to flock into its ranks. Events were confused and allegiances less than clearcut.

It is difficult to try to superimpose on this ambivalent picture the notion either of a mounting sense of grievance against Mary of Guise or a rising tide of protestant feeling. The reformation crisis had not brought to the surface large numbers of hidden protestants. The burgh's protestants had been embarrassed by the regent's suggestion that heads be counted to determine the town's religion. Their efforts to bridge the gap between being a tolerated minority and becoming, in effect, a political party had met with mixed fortunes. Many of them could not have relished suddenly being thrown into the spotlight. Others patently opted for the course of safety or profit: Thomas MacCalzean had agreed to become the custodian of the town's most treasured religious relics and the landlord of its catholic provost; merchants who had co-operated with the protestant party when it took over the town turned unhesitatingly to the catholic council and the regent to look after their interests whenever it faltered.[48] The burgh establishment forced compromises on the new protestant regime when it returned to power. The events of 1559 point not to a swelling and increasingly confident protestant element but to a beleagured and often nervous minority, brought to power by circumstances outside its control rather than by its own strength.

Yet protestantism, it must be remembered, had been infiltrating Edinburgh society for fully a quarter of a century. Half a dozen heretics had been detected in the burgh and its port as early as 1534, and a further campaign in 1538 and 1539 netted three more along with some English protestant literature. Calderwood, as distinct from Knox, maintains that there were a number of other secret 'professors' before 1540, and with his help it is possible to trace fifteen of them. The effects of the brief period of Arran's sponsorship of protestant preachers, if not protestantism outright, are debateable. Sadler confidently reported to Henry VIII in the middle of 1543 that the town of Leith 'be noted all to be good Christians'. The end of Arran's exclusive period in power, however, brought this expansion to an abrupt end: by the end of 1543 the papal legate was able to report 'great changes' in the men of Leith. There are few signs in Edinburgh itself, however, of any dramatic effects. Knox complained that it continued 'to be drowned in superstition'. Although there were fears of iconoclastic rioting against the religious houses, as had happened in Perth and Dundee, those involved in an attack on the Blackfriars were outsiders, who were firmly repulsed by the assembled town after the alarm was raised. The same impression is reinforced by the hostile reception given to a protestant preacher six months earlier.[49] Edinburgh's protestants were still in the early 1540s to be counted in handfuls.

Edinburgh is a good example of the general argument that protestantism in the Scottish towns went to ground between the early 1540s and the mid-1550s.[50] There is little or no trace of activity in the years in between. It would be wrong to conclude from this, however, that protestantism took root in Edinburgh seriously only after Knox's well-known ten-day preaching campaign in May 1556.[51] This would ignore the early protestants themselves, who they were and what positions they held in burgh society. It is possible to compile a list of about thirty-three protestant sympathisers, who had direct links with Edinburgh, Leith or the Canongate in the period up to 1556.[52] A number of them were not significant figures and disappeared without trace. At least four fled to England and seem not to have returned. Of those from the burgh itself, five had died before 1559 and two more by the very early 1560s. It is true, on the face of it, that only a handful of these early heretics had gained positions of influence within the burgh: Patrick Lindsay had been on the council once in the 1540s; Robert Watson's father had held office three times between 1536 and 1541; Edward Hope had come on to the council in 1552 and James Baron in 1555. Yet most of the very early protestants, those who can be traced to the period before the 1550s, were far from being nonentities. They included the master of the grammar school, the wife of the common clerk of the burgh, a Leith skipper, two advocates, the administrator of the Mint, and Arran's personal physician. Most of the remainder were merchants. Patrick Lindsay is the only craftsman who can be identified before the setting up of the privy kirk in the mid-1550s but he was far from a typical one. He was the business partner of James Henderson, the English apologist of the 1540s, who had extensive trading interests in the Netherlands.[53] Francis Aikman and James Sim were both apothecaries, and Sim and Baron had both figured amongst the half-dozen largest contributors to the d'Oysel loan in 1554; Aikman had lent money to the town in the aftermath of the English sack of the town in 1544.[54] Most but not all of these merchants were wealthy men; John Main was only a cramer and, like Edward Hope, was assessed at just under half the merchant average in 1565. One very obvious reason why so many of them were not in positions of influence in the 1540s was that they were quite young. Knox specifically referred to 'young William Adamson', who became a burgess in 1542; Hope only reached burgess status in 1540 and survived well into the 1580s; Main did so in 1535, Cant in 1536, William Johnston, the advocate, in 1538, and Baron not until 1547.

It is clear that protestantism first took root in a small but influential coterie of wealthy merchants and professional men. Some of them had links with Arran. Significantly for the future, it had captured a number of younger men, most of them sons of the merchant establishment. By the mid-1550s, however, a different pattern was emerging. The movement was still obviously gaining recruits from the sons of wealthy merchant families and continuing to suck in to it the wives of influential men; it had recruited the wife of the common clerk of the burgh in the 1520s and 1530s, and one of Knox's 'dear sisters of Edinburgh' was the wife of the man who held the same office from 1558 until his death in 1582. A different breed of protestants was, however, coming to the surface. All of the elders or deacons of Edinburgh's privy kirk given by Calderwood were significantly smaller men. Two of them were small merchants and one the son of a Leith skipper; the other three were all craftsmen but only one of them had reached the status of master of his craft. Only one of the six was a member of the merchant guildry and only one ever held burgh office, but not until the 1570s. It is clear that they were a new wave of converts from their age. They were of a younger generation again; none had become a burgess before 1552 and two were still serving their apprenticeships. It was from this point that Edinburgh protestantism first took on what was to be its characteristic dual pattern until the 1580s of a small caucus of influential merchants and an outer circle of smaller, less influential men. It may well be that it was the effect of Knox's visit in 1555 and 1556 which extended the breadth of appeal of the movement and that it was he who first attracted into it the ordinary craftsman or apprentice.

It is difficult to see, however, how Knox's first contact with the burgh was much of a turning-point in the history of Edinburgh protestantism beyond this one limited point. It still clearly lacked widespread popular support. It was still dominated by the same kind of men, and often the same men, as almost twenty years before. This is indeed the most important point to grasp about the early heretics of the 1530s and early 1540s. On the face of it, only three of them — Baron, Hope and David Borthwick — could be said to be significant figures in the progress of protestantism in the burgh, either in the crisis of 1559-60 or after it. Yet, paradoxically, the first tentative steps taken before 1545 were immensely significant. A whole network of links can be traced between these early heretics and the most prominent protestant figures in Edinburgh twenty or thirty years later. Almost half of the inner circle of the protestant party of the 1560s had family links, either direct or indirect, with them; Martin Balcaskie married a daughter off to one of the most prominent of these later protestant party men and Francis Aikman married off two. The Baron, Hope and Guthrie family connections left few untouched. Edinburgh protestantism had survived into the 1550s because it was, above all else, a tightly-knit family circle. This was why Knox so assiduously cultivated his 'sisters of Edinburgh' and was even prepared to refer one's marital difficulties to a higher authority, Calvin himself. At least three of them were the wives of very significant men indeed — Alexander Guthrie, the common clerk, James Baron, a dean of guild in the mid-1550s, and James McGill, appointed clerk register by Mary of Guise and made president of the burgh in 1556.[55] Knox did not create or even alter the basic strengths of burgh protestantism; he courted it as it was.

The early English connection does not seem particularly significant. Only a handful of Edinburgh burgesses were genuine collaborators with the English occupying armies in the 1540s. A number had their alleged misdemeanours in the 1540s cast up in the last months in office of Arran in 1554; but Arran was more concerned with the profits of justice he might still make while he had the chance than with punishing genuine collaborators. It was no coincidence that it was almost exclusively wealthy merchants who were brought to justice. It is true that among his victims were three members of the Kilspindie council — David Forester, John Ashlowaine and Alexander Guthrie — but it is difficult to believe that there was substance to his charges that they had actively become involved with the earl of Glencairn or Patrick, Lord Gray, during the 'rough wooing'.[56] Only Durham and James Henderson were both undoubted collaborators and men of influence in the burgh. The most significant connection which can be established is that between the protestant goldsmith, Patrick Lindsay, and James Henderson. Yet Lindsay's brother, James, who allegedly was also involved in the Glencairn rebellion of 1544, became a leading figure in the catholic party of the 1560s as well as a member of the Seton council of 1559-60.[57] The case of Edinburgh amply bears out the dangers which have been pointed to in pressing too hard on the link between collaboration with the English in the 1540s and early receptivity to reformed ideas.[58] Even so, the English connection should not be rejected outright. Bishop Lesley specifically linked the spread of English protestant literature with the growth of preaching in private houses in Edinburgh later in 1558. The one surviving testament of an early protestant to itemise books reveals an impressive English collection; Marjorie Roger, who was the wife of the leader of the burgh's protestants in 1559, Adam Fullarton, and was herself almost certainly one of Knox's 'sisters', had copies of Tyndale, Cranmer, Jewel, Becon, Foxe and two editions of Hooper in her library. Her husband was one of the six merchants on the Kilspindie council of 1559 who, although the English trade was a minor feature in Edinburgh's interests, had traded with England since the early 1550s.[59]

Most of what were to become the characteristic features of Edinburgh protestantism were already present by the mid or later 1550s — its links with England, as yet probably only tentative; its connections with the administration; the fact that, although it was not confined to a single social group, its locus and strength were. It was the distinctive nature of its development, behind a few closed doors, which gave it a small but firm foothold in burgh society. The faithful met in the houses of the wealthy merchants amongst them. The very structure of the house cell and the tight family circle made for the inbred nurturing of protestant ideas rather than their widespread dissemination. This was the most significant of the patterns which flowed from Edinburgh's early protestants — by 1555 the initiative had been established within a small circle of established burgesses, and they did not relinquish it or vastly extend the circle until the later 1560s. For some time after 1560 the criterion of protestant respectability continued to be how long one had held a party card.

When protestantism is seen as a close, conservative group moving by degrees rather than a swelling movement moving rapidly towards mass conversion, its reactions to the reformation crisis become more understandable. It was, when the Congregation first entered the town in July 1559, still in a distinct minority in all parts of Edinburgh society. It was on the defensive. The protestant coup which came three months later was not the triumphant climax to a long campaign. Burgh protestantism did not rise to claim power; it was given it. The only hint of it flexing its muscles before the crisis was the riot on St. Giles' day in 1558. The statue of the town's patron saint was the natural centrepiece of the annual religious procession on the first day of September. Considerable but apparently unsuccessful pressure, including the threat of excommunication, had been brought to bear on the council to replace it after it was stolen less than two months before the date of the procession. Knox in his account tries to tie together the excommunication affair and the riot itself, which broke out as the procession wound its way through the streets. He implies that the 'tragedy of St. Giles' was a natural climax of the anti-catholic feeling in the burgh, which engulfed even the council. This is almost certainly a figment of Knox's imagination. His rollicking account of the riot missed out what undoubtedly would have been the highlight of the procession — the heretics who were taking part in it and were due to recant their errors when it arrived at the market cross. The riot certainly embarrassed both the catholic authorities and the regent who was present. It was probably more significant that it threatened to split the burgh's protestants themselves. Knox singled out David Forrest, who had been a much-respected figure in burgh protestantism for over fifteen years and held office in the privy kirk, as one of the 'temporisers that day' who tried to stop the rioters. It seems obvious that their conservative-minded leaders were alarmed that control was slipping away from them. Protestantism did not have an elaborate programme; it had for most of the 1550s been dominated in Edinburgh and elsewhere by sober, committed converts meeting to pray and preach in private conventicles. After the execution of Walter Miln in 1558 there was a resurgence of iconoclastic protestantism, which brought a new urgency and shrillness but which, at least in Edinburgh, threatened the natural leaders of the movement. The riot and the new strains it epitomised were another reason to move forward only slowly and cautiously.[60] What was in prospect was not the imminent collapse of catholicism but the opening up of the natural divisions within protestantism itself.

Yet by October and November 1559 events had moved on and issues had moved on with them. The rival Seton and Kilspindie regimes politicised Edinburgh catholicism and protestantism. What was offered now was the politics of commitment. It seems that the majority of the burgh's population, irrespective of whether they were merchants or craftsmen, did not wish to take up either offer. It took some time for Edinburgh society to catch up with the politicisation of religion which took place in the second half of 1559. In the meantime, the dominant impression to be gained from the new and detailed evidence which has come to light is of a widespread lack of commitment to either party. For the merchants, this was balanced by a willingness to be swayed by the concerns that were closest to the real interests of the burgh's merchant oligarchy. Both parties had, however, threatened the burgh's constitution and its well-being. This produced, on both sides, apart from the zealots at either extreme, allegiance which was qualified, ambivalent and transitory. Edinburgh, for the most part, saw the events of 1559 and 1560 more as a crisis of burgh society than a crisis of faith.

NOTES

1. *Sadler Papers*, 20, 24, 95, 121, 325, 363-4, 368-9, 494; *Hamilton Papers*, ii, nos. 14, 27, 57, 73, 217, 232-3, 350.

2. JC 19/1, 17 Aug. 1543; Pitcairn, *Trials*, i, 330. Further and increased pledges for the fifteen involved were entered 10 Oct. (see JC 19/1). See also *Hamilton Papers*, ii, no. 73.

3. *Edin. Recs.*, iii, 296-9; *Lord Provosts*, 16-7; *APS*, ii, 349; *Hamilton Papers*, ii, no. 298; see also M. H. Sanderson, '"Kin, freindis and servandis": the men who worked with Archbishop David Beaton', *Innes Review*, xxv (1974), 43, for details of Otterburn.

4. *CSP Scot.*, i, nos. 129, 290; Teulet, *Papiers d'État*, i, 196; M. L. Bush, *The Government Policy of Protector Somerset* (London, 1975), 26.

5. *Letters & Papers, Henry VIII*, xix(i), no. 483; *RPC*, i, 100-1; *Mary of Lorraine Corresp.*, 339; *Lord Provosts*, 17-18; *Edin. Recs.*, ii, 190; MS Co. Recs., ii, fo. 24.

6. *RSS*, v, 1362, 1400; JC 1/6, 17 Sept. 1551; Pitcairn, *Trials*, i, 360; *TA*, xi, 186; *Edin. Recs.*, ii, 198, 221-2; iii, 162; MS Co. Recs., ii, fo. 76v.

7. *Edin. Recs.*, ii, 188-9, 230-32, 234-6, 263; see esp. the council minute of 25 Jan. 1556 and the testimony of Thomas Boyce, the crafts' spokesman; see also *APS*, ii, 497-8; *Edinburgh, 1329-1929*, 277. The argument that there was a specific alliance between the regent and Edinburgh's craftsmen can be found in both Reid, 'Coming of the Reformation', 28-9, and Grant, *Social and Economic Development*, 430, 433.

8. See *RSS*, iv, 2746, 2750, 2757, 2889, 2910, 3068, and R. Marshall, *Mary of Guise* (London, 1977), 203-4.

9. *Edin. Recs.*, ii, 206-7, 214-5, 221-3; an entry of 22 Nov. 1555 stipulated that the names of those who lent money to the regent be registered (MS Co. Recs., ii, fo. 62v).

10. *Mary of Lorraine Corresp.*, 403.

11. The total was well in excess of £4,000. This was made up of 1,000 merks for remaining away from a border raid together with the burgh's share of the cost of the embassy of Kilwinning to France in Sept. 1556; £208 as its share of the general tax of Nov. 1556; £2,250 for the marriage of Mary, Queen of Scots and Francis; a further £1,200 for a licence for absenting itself from Fala Muir plus an undisclosed amount for equipping 300 men; and a further undisclosed sum for repairing the town walls in Dec. 1557; see *APS*, ii, 604; Buchanan, *History*, 390; *Edin. Recs.*, ii, 249-51, 256-7; iii, 2-4, 9-10, 14-15; *TA*, xi, 374.

12. Cf. Reid, 'Coming of the Reformation', 28-9, who follows much this line of argument; see also Knox, *History*, i, 239; Calderwood, *History*, i, 527; *CSP Foreign, Eliz.*, ii, no. 9; J. C. Irons, *Leith and its Antiquities* (1898), i, 231-41.

13. *RSS*, iv, 2074, 2234, 2388, 2445, 2507, 2544, 2557, 2611, 2627, 2672, 2702.

14. *Ibid.*, iv, 2743, 3068.

15. See *CSP Foreign, Eliz.*, ii, no. 9, for the Congregation's case.

16. See Donaldson, *James V to James VII*, 86.

17. Knox, *History*, i, 127; *Edin. Recs.*, iii, 42-4. Fuller accounts of the excommunication affair are given in P. J. Murray, 'The excommunication of Edinburgh town council in 1558', *Innes Review*, xxvii (1976), 24-34, and W. J. Anderson, 'The excommunication of Edinburgh town council, 1558', *ibid.*, x (1959), 289-94.

18. The other member of the assize who became a member of the council set up by the Congregation in 1559 was John Ashlowaine; see JC 1/9, 7 Dec. 1556; Pitcairn, *Trials*, i, 393-4; *Edin. Recs.*, ii, 251-2. The council was more successful than other accounts have made out; cf. Reid, 'Coming of the Reformation', 30-31; Murray, 'Excommunication of Edinburgh town council', 26.

19. Cf. Reid, 'Coming of the Reformation', 29.

20. *Edin. Recs.*, ii, 244-5, 255; iii, 62; MS Co. Recs., 29 Oct. 1559, iii, fo. 27r; JC 1/7, 4 May 1555, fos. 41v, 42r; Pitcairn, *Trials*, i, 377; *TA*, xi, 276; cf. Reid, 'Coming of the Reformation', 29.

21. *Edin. Recs.*, iii, 31-4, 37-8. For Baron's brush with the council in 1562, see MS Co. Recs., iv, fo. 35v. Thomson was called before the council in Feb. 1560 after the de la Brosse inquiry into the events of Oct. 1559 (ibid., iii, fo. 31v); he, Forester and Guthrie were all prominent protestant activists throughout the 1560s (see app. v).

22. *Hist. Estate Scot.*, 61; Knox, *History*, i, 192; *Diurnal*, 269.

23. *Edin. Recs.*, iii, 42-4; D. H. Fleming, *The Reformation in Scotland: Causes, Characteristics, Consequences* (1910), 319, 321; MacLennan, 'Reformation in the burgh of Aberdeen', 127.

24. Mary had written to the council on 14 May (*Edin. Recs.*, iii, 36-7).

25. *Hist. Estate Scot.*, 58-9; Knox, *History*, i, 172-80; Knox, *Works*, vi, 23; Keith, *History*, i, 200; Spottiswoode, *History*, i, 274; Donaldson, *James V to James VII*, 93.

26. Knox, *History*, i, 182-3.

27. It is likely that seven of this council had protestant sympathies: James Baron, David Forester, John Spens and James Young, all members of the council imposed upon the town by the Congregation four months later; Thomas Redpath, Andrew Slater and Thomas Thomson were protestant activists in the 1560s (see app. v for details of all seven). The delegation sent to negotiate with the Congregation comprised the four whom the protestant lords nominated later in the year, the common clerk, Alex. Guthrie, whose wife was close to Knox (see app. iv), Michael

Gilbert, who helped to raise the burgh's second tax to finance the forces of the Congregation in May 1560, and a prominent tailor, Archibald Dewar, who was on the subscription list of 1562 (*Edin. Recs.*, iii, 44, 64).

28. Three who certainly remained loyal to Mary of Guise were James Curle and James Lindsay, both members of the council deposed by the Congregation in Oct. 1559, and James Carmichael, who gave evidence at the subsequent inquiry (*Edin. Recs.*, iii, 45-6; *De La Brosse Report*, 110).

29. *Hist. Estate Scot.*, 64-5, 67; *Diurnal*, 269-70; Knox, *History*, i, 202-6; *CSP Scot.*, i, nos. 500, 504; *Edin. Recs.*, iii, 46-9; Donaldson, *James V to James VII*, 94.

30. On 24 August (MS Co. Recs., iii, fo. 23r).

31. Knox, *History*, i, 211, 213-4; *Hist. Estate Scot.*, 65, 67; Ridley, *John Knox*, 342-3. See also Moeller, *Villes d'Empire et Réformation*, 91, and F. Lau & E. Bizer, *A History of the Reformation in Germany to 1555* (London, 1969), 236-7.

32. *Edin. Recs.*, iii, 52-7; MS Co. Recs., iii, fos. 17r, 23v.

33. See *Hist. Estate Scot.*, 70; Knox, *History*, i, 242; *De La Brosse Report*, 92ff; Herries, *Memoirs*, 45; Calderwood, *History*, i, 542.

34. Full details of both councils are given in Lynch, 'The two Edinburgh town councils of 1559-60', *SHR*, liv (1975), 117-39.

35. *CSP Foreign, Eliz.*, ii, nos. 20, 111; Knox, *History*, i, 249, 251-2; Calderwood, *History*, i, 541-5; cf. *CSP Scot.*, i, no, 566, which gives the date of the deposition as 23 Oct.

36. *De La Brosse Report*, 121-2; MS Co. Recs., iii, fos. 26v, 27r; see the Kilspindie council list of 1559-60 in app. i.

37. Knox, *History*, i, 259-60, 262, 275; *Diurnal*, 54-5, 271-2; Herries, *Memoirs*, 46; *Sadler Papers*, 554; *CSP Foreign, Eliz.*, ii, nos. 211, 234; MS Co. Recs., iii, 27v; *Edin. Recs.*, iii, 59-60; Keith, *History*, i, 251; *Hist. Estate Scot.*, 73.

38. *RPC*, i, 430-31; MS Co. Recs., 16 Feb. 1560, iii, fo. 31v.

39. PRO, SP 52/1, 12 Dec. 1559, fo. 298r; see *CSP Scot.*, i, no. 595.

40. *Edin. Recs.*, iii, 59-60; *RSS*, v, 715, 720.

41. *Diurnal*, 56-7; Knox, *History*, i, 311; G. Dickinson (ed.), 'Journal of the Siege of Leith, 1560', in *Two Missions of Jacques de la Brosse* (SHS, 1942), 89, 91, 95; *Hist. Estate Scot.*, 83; *Edin. Recs.*, iii, 62; MS Co. Recs., iii, fo. 33r. The tax was agreed on 29 April 1560 and not 30th, as given in the printed record (ibid., fo. 33v).

42. Roberton was paid on 7 May (MS Co. Recs., iii, fo. 34r; see also *Edin. Recs.*, iii, 63-4, 65).

43. *CSP Scot.*, i, no. 756; *Edin. Recs.*, iii, 63-4; MS Co. Recs., iii, fos. 33v, 35r-36r, 75v. See app. iv for Christison, app. vi for Spottiswood and app. viii for Stevenson.

44. Knox, *History*, i, 242; *Hist. Estate Scot.*, 61; see also *CSP Scot.*, i, nos. 566, 596(4), 616; see Lynch, 'Two Edinburgh town councils', 126-7, for further details.

45. The evidence as to servants comes from the muster roll of 1558 and as to tax assessments from the stent roll of 1565 (see MS Co. Recs., ii, fos. 126v-130v; the 1565 roll is reproduced in app. xi).

46. Calderwood, *History*, i, 511; Knox, *History*, i, 223, 240-41; *CSP Scot.*, i, nos. 469, 471, 734; *Hist. Estate Scot.*, 58; *Edin. Recs.*, iii, 30-31, 34-5; *Mary of Lorraine Corresp.*, 426-8.

47. See *CSP Scot.*, i, no. 662; *Hist. Estate Scot.*, 63.

48. See *Sadler Papers*, 663-4, 673, 677, 685-6.

49. *Ibid.*, 242; R. K. Hannay, 'Letters of the papal legate in Scotland, 1543', *SHR*, ix (1914), 18, 21; *Hamilton Papers*, i, nos. 298, 301(1), 337; ii, nos. 11, 15; *Two Missions of Jacques de la Brosse*, 20; Knox, *History*, i, 43; Calderwood, *History*, i, 108.

50. See Cowan, *Regional Aspects of the Scottish Reformation*, 11, 14-7.

51. Cf. Ridley, *John Knox*, 232.

52. See app. iv.

53. *TA*, viii, 118; *Mary of Lorraine Corresp.*, 93.

54. *Edin. Recs.*, ii, 206-7; Aikman was not repaid until 1553 (MS Co. Recs., ii, fo. 16v).

55. See Knox, *Works*, iv, 233-4, 245, 247, 251; also Ridley, *John Knox*, 169, 236, 263.

56. I am grateful to Dr. M. H. Merriman for his advice on this point; see *RSS*, iv, 2234, 2293, 2611.

57. Merriman, 'The struggle for the marriage of Mary, Queen of Scots', 30, 216, 247ff; *RSS*, iii, 1461; iv, 746, 2445, 2507, 2557, 2627, 2672, 2702; Prot. Bk. King, ii, fo. 157. A number of other burgesses were granted remissions in the same period in 1554 for absenting themselves from hosts (*RSS*, iv, 2388, 2544, 2074).

58. See M. H. Merriman, 'The assured Scots: Scottish collaborators with England during the Rough Wooing', *SHR*, xlvii (1968), 33-4.

59. Lesley, *History* (Bann. ed.), 269; see Edin. Tests., 30 Jan. 1584 for Marjorie Roger's testament. The other protestant merchants with English connections were John Ashlowaine, David Forester, Alex. Guthrie, Richard Strang and John Johnston, all members of the Congregation's council of 1559; James Sim (see app. iv) and Luke Wilson, who acted as an extentor for the Congregation's first tax of 1559, were two more with trading contacts with England (*CSP Scot.*, i, nos. 363, 366, 373, 373(1), 382, 405; *Edin. Recs.*, ii, 175).

60. Cf. the accounts of the riot given in Knox, *History*, i, 127-9; Buchanan, *History*, 395-6; Lesley, *History*, ii, 383.

6

The Politics of Conciliation:
Mary, Queen of Scots and the Burgh

EDINBURGH'S first protestant town council to be elected by normal and due process took office, apparently without incident, in October 1560, a month after the close of the Reformation parliament.[1] At least in terms of the wealth and social standing of its members, the new council was a much more respectable body than the one it replaced. Of the sixteen merchants on it who can be traced in the tax roll of 1565, only three fell much below the average merchant contribution of £11; half of them paid twice the average or more, and six of them more than three times the average. A third of this new council was drawn from the twenty-five or so wealthiest merchants in the burgh. It was also almost certainly protestant to a man; every member of it, with the exception of Somer and Graham who both later proved themselves as activists, is to be found in the subscription list of 'faithful brethren' of November 1562. Yet, as a whole, it lacked experience; five of its six merchant office-holders had only one or two years' council service behind them. The ordinary council emphasised the point more clearly; half of them had either a single year's experience or none at all. The new regime had progressed beyond the social *parvenus* turned to by the Congregation in the crisis of 1559; it had still to shed the image of *arrivistes*.

This, then, was the council that had to deal with the various difficulties that the setting up of 'the face of the reformed kirk' involved in practice as well as with the chaos left by the events of the previous fifteen months. Both sets of problems were complicated and exaggerated by the fact that Edinburgh was a capital city, a metropolis and a market town. While it is true that within a year the burgh's religious problems would be complicated by the appearance of what became an occasional catholic chapel less than half a mile outside its jurisdiction, the arrival of Mary, Queen of Scots, did not mark the beginning of the new regime's difficulties. It was in the aftermath of the parliament of August 1560 that the town had to decide on what attitude to take to the number of practical problems which resulted from its position as the largest and by far the most important of the Scottish burghs. Some of these questions were dealt with in a series of civic ordinances proclaimed, as precedent dictated, by the new council after taking office: the burgh's strict Sabbatarianism should apply not only to its own inhabitants but to all visitors and strangers. In effect, the ordinances of 30 October were directed mainly against the continuation of the flesh market, which had traditionally been held on a Sunday. A series of further difficulties resulted from this; the site of the flesh market had to be changed as well, since on its new day it clashed with the main food market. This was done without consulting the craft deacons, which produced the inevitable formal protest and, more seriously, a refusal by the fleshers to pay their mails and dues to the common good.[2]

The second half of 1560 was a worrying time for the burgh authorities. The town was under considerable financial strain; it was still filled with 'brokin men of weyr' and masterless men who might well turn a minor brawl into another full-scale riot. The threats of the laird of Restalrig to be 'evin with yow' after his mistress had been carted through the town for adultery were taken seriously, as well they might be, since another prisoner, the parson of Penicuik, had been broken out of ward in the tolbooth a few days before.[3] The council was clearly worried by these incidents; they illustrated the weakness of burgh authority if it was not grounded on the consent of the burgh's inhabitants. A strongly worded proclamation was issued on 5 September, which condemned the activists driven by a 'particular hatrent' of some of the new establishment; it was also directed, though, at what was a more serious and intractable problem, the deliberate non-co-operation of others, leaving the bailies and burgh officers in an isolated and vulnerable position. These two themes recurred with regularity in the early 1560s and with frequency in the early days of the establishment of the new protestant regime.

It was against this worrying background that the new council became involved in the first of a series of serious riots, which plagued its year in office. On 22 November William Harlaw, the deacon of the hammermen, appeared before the council to plead the case of John Sanderson, the fleshers' deacon, who had been condemned to be carted and banished for adultery. Sanderson's offence was, at worst, a technical one; he had obtained a divorce from his wife, but from the old church courts. Despite the fact that the case was adjourned, there was a minor demonstration in the flesh house on the 22nd. There was a more serious riot, involving about sixty craftsmen, apprentices and unfree the next day, after the council refused to release Sanderson and ordered the carting to be carried out. A justiciary court was convened with remarkable speed and six craftsmen were called before it on 27 November, accused of organising both disturbances. Four more, including Sanderson himself, were summoned the next day and two of them came to trial on 19 December.[4] The identity of the alleged ringleaders has never been established, but historians have tended to accept Knox's denunciation of the riot as another example of 'the rascal multitude, inflamed by some ungodly craftsmen'.[5]

The evidence does not really bear this out. The six accused on 27 November comprised the deacons of the hammermen and tailors, Harlaw and James Norval; two fleshers, John Ur and James Henryson; a pewterer, John Wilson, and a drummer, Walter Osborne. Three of the four summoned on the 28th were again from the hammermen craft: John Rhind, another pewterer, who had been deacon of the craft three years before, and two craft masters, James Fraser and Walter Wight, who were tried three weeks later. What is noticeable is that two of the accused had been among the spokesmen for the crafts on 22 and 23 November. Despite the fact that a third of the first assize was made up of members of the old council of 1559-60, not all six were convicted; Harlaw, Henryson and Osborne were convicted on both charges, Wilson on one of them, and the others were acquitted. Again, in the second trial, there were no blanket convictions; Fraser was acquitted on all charges and Wight found guilty only of being involved in the riot of the 23rd. While it is true that a number of prominent conservatives, like Alexander Skene and Edmund Hay, pleaded on behalf of the accused at the first trial, so did David Kinloch and Michael Gilbert, two of the three most prominent protestant craftsmen in the burgh in the 1560s. If the conspirators were all religious conservatives, it would be difficult to understand why Knox was asked to intercede on their behalf. In fact Knox had some reason to intervene; Harlaw was a militant convert, who remained a prominent activist throughout the 1560s. Both he and Fraser were appointed as collectors for the poor in the first attempt at a voluntary collection on a large scale in April 1561. At the same time, there can be little doubt that some of the others involved were convinced catholics. The Rhind family remained stubbornly antagonistic to the new regime throughout the 1560s, Wilson became a test case in his own right when he was dismissed from office in 1568 for his religious views, and Osborne was convicted of treason in 1572 for fighting for the queen's party.[6]

It seems clear that, despite Knox's allegation, the Sanderson disturbances of November 1560 are not easily seen as religious riots. Both protestant and catholic craftsmen were involved in them. Nor were they riots of the 'rascal multitude'; three sitting deacons were implicated as well as two other prominent members of the hammermen craft. It is also wrong to suggest that there is no record of any punishment inflicted: Sanderson was deprived of office and his goods escheated; it seems likely that Harlaw, although he held on to his office, was deprived of his burgess-ship for a short time; Wight was still in the Castle early in January 1561, when his wife petitioned the council for his release.[7] The riots are better understood as the culmination of a series of disturbances which had thoroughly alarmed two successive councils and as part of a series of skirmishes with the fleshers. Despite the fact that the council could point to the ordinance of 10 June against adulterers, whoremongers and brothel-keepers, an ordinance which some, but not all, of the deacons had agreed to, there can be little doubt that its interpretation of it in the Sanderson case *was* extreme, as the craft protest of 23 November alleged. The deacons, of course, had had little objection to the pleasing spectacle of Restalrig's mistress being carted under the same ordinance, but a colleague was, in their view, a different matter. Although the council did not have the grace to admit it, its policy towards sexual offenders who were also office-holders did change as a result of the Sanderson affair. James Nicol, a sitting councillor, escaped with a fine for fornication with his servant in 1567, and the then deacon of the tailors, Alexander Sauchie, was only fined for adultery; neither was dismissed from office.[8]

The Sanderson riots did almost mark a turning point in the affairs of the burgh. The submission of the crafts on 28 November and 6 December showed that the deacons were willing to approve and stand by laws against the saying or hearing of the mass, but were not prepared to accept an over-strict inter-pretation of the morality laws. Yet the deacons were as concerned in their own way with the problem of authority and the dangers of lawlessness from the 'rascal multitude'; they spoke in impressive terms of what was in effect a *corpus christianum* threatened by false rumours and 'wikit memberis'. It is difficult to decide how much of this should be taken at face value; the council does seem to have accepted that there was not a full-scale conspiracy against it by the deacons, but how many of them could realistically be expected to fulfil their side of the bargain in establishing a reformed society? It is certainly difficult to see how William Brocas, one of the petitioners on 28 November, could believe in a kirk that would be 'a mirrour and exempill to all the rest of this realme'; Brocas was the catholic hammerman who boasted to the privy council two years later that the council had not seduced him 'fra his faith'. Brocas, though, was not typical of the leading craftsmen who made this offer; the deacons of the goldsmiths, skinners and masons all appeared on the sub-scription list, as well as Kinloch and Young. Harlaw was not the only protestant activist among the deacons; Robert Henderson, deacon of the barbers, was involved, like Harlaw, in the Riccio murder. The same deacons very willingly agreed to the proclamation against priests and friars passed in March 1561, the proclamation that led to such trouble after Mary's arrival.[9] The craft petition of November 1560 was a unique offer of 'broderlie amity', extended by the protestant-dominated leaders of the crafts to a merchant-dominated protestant council. The council, however, had convinced itself of the dangers of craft riots and was unwilling to allow its reformation to extend to a revolution in burgh politics. It did make sure that in the future the laws against fornication and adultery were operated with more discretion but it drew back from more radical solutions. The reformation did little to change the most cherished ideas of how burgh society should be run.

Yet it is possible to see that the Sanderson riot did impress upon the new regime the need to co-operate more fully and frankly with the craft deacons. It seems clear that the side-effects of the council's efforts to produce a reformed society by legislation had not been fully worked out. The traditional practice of an offending craftsman being accompanied by his whole craft when he appeared before the council could not be allowed to continue without the prospect of almost weekly craft demonstrations; in practice this meant a greater reliance than before on the deacons. The council was concerned about the difficulty of persuading 'men of honeste and judgement' to take office, yet its treatment of Sanderson and its suspicions of the role of the deacons in the affair were self-defeating. A number of the difficulties which arose out of the Sanderson affair were of the council's own making and produced by its own insecurity. It did try to tread more warily in the future. When a series of ordinances were proposed five months later, envisaging the confiscation of religious holdings within the town, compulsory attendance at the sermon and a variety of schemes for relief of the poor, unilateral action was not taken; each deacon was given a copy of the ordinances to present to his craft and ordered to report back with their answers.[10]

The council, to give it credit, did also anticipate the possibility of trouble arising from the Robin Hood procession which had been banned by parliament in 1555; it sensibly took the precaution of consulting the deacons before taking action against the craft apprentices who had ignored the warning and run riot through the streets. The deacons were willing to co-operate in 'extreme punischment' of the apprentices, provided it was kept as a burgh matter and not referred to a higher court. But the council seems to have lost its nerve; five weeks later it applied to the justice clerk to set up an assize to try the rioters of 11 March, and it did this without consulting the deacons. The apprentices were duly convicted on 20 July. The next day another of the rioters, James Gillone, was put to an assize, convicted and condemned to death, although the original ordinance of 23 April had specified only banishment. It is difficult to comment directly on the charge made in the *Diurnal* that this assize was packed by the council, as there is no trace of it in the justiciary record. The assize of 20 July, however, was not obviously packed. The opinions of seven of its fifteen members can be traced with some certainty; four were protestants, of varying hues, and three were political or religious conservatives.[11]

It is difficult to explain this collective change of mind precisely; the council was very concerned about an outbreak of violence during the convention of nobility which met in May 1561; it probably had its suspicions about who the 'papists' were who 'hunt for occasions of brogle'. James Dalyell, a leading conservative, had been hauled before the council only two months before for threatening it in graphic terms. Yet the riot was less dangerous than the council's reactions to it. Their hard line misfired badly. The day set for Gillone's execution saw a much more serious riot which lasted for fully six hours; for most of that time the bailies were imprisoned in their tolbooth and were rescued only by the intervention of the Constable.[12] The rioters of 21 July were not like those of the earlier Robin Hood disturbances, although apprentices were again involved. Of the six who were convicted and put to the horn on 8 August, three were tailors and three belonged to the hammermen craft;

all of them were masters of their craft and two of them had held office in the burgh. Retribution did not rest there; seven other craftsmen were convicted of failing to render assistance to the magistrates during the riot. They included the deacons of the goldsmiths, baxters and wrights — all three of them were at least nominal protestants. Three more craftsmen were drawn into the net the next day when sureties of £100 each were entered for them as well as the seven convicted.[13] Again it is hardly surprising that the deacons should have turned to Knox for help; it is also not surprising that they should have been disappointed by his refusal. After 1560 Knox had little to offer protestant craftsmen. He proved to be as much a conservative in burgh politics as the men on whom he relied to push through his reformation.

After the two major disturbances of 1560 and 1561, the Sanderson and Gillone riots, the council had flailed about itself without discrimination or discretion; it had cited before a series of assizes three of the four craft collectors for the poor of April 1561, two of the relatively few craftsmen who were willing to subscribe to the contribution list of November 1562, and an ex-colleague on the council. A number of other prominent craftsmen had become involved in the affairs. Although the council had apparently, after the Sanderson affair, recognised the need for a rapprochement with the deacons, it seems to have panicked under pressure. The alternative explanation offered by Knox that they were a series of catholic-inspired conspiracies is misleading and does not hang together. Once again the flashpoint which turned a minor stir into a full-scale riot was a shift in policy by the council. It is true that there was probably some connection between the two sets of disturbances, as Knox maintains: two craftsmen — Fraser, and the flesher, James Henryson — were directly involved in both. But it also looks as if some old scores were being paid off; Knox's reference to 'some known unhonest craftsmen' is revealing in itself. Kinloch, who had spoken up for Harlaw and the others at their trial in November 1560, was himself singled out for suspicion six months later; Morrison was deprived of his burgess-ship on 18 July, two days before his trial; Nicol Rhind was an old enemy of the provost, Kilspindie. The episode also left some new scores to be settled; one of the accused of 8 August was Nicol Young, whose murder early in 1564 indirectly produced a major crisis for the protestant regime. In the short term the affair petered out rather miserably; the council suffered a serious loss of face when it was forced to agree not to pursue any of the actual rioters of 21 July, but the session inevitably had the last word.[14]

In a sense a good deal too much has been made of the riots of 1560 and 1561; they were not religious riots, although some 'ungodly' craftsmen were involved in them. If they had been, they would have been a good deal more serious. In another sense, not enough has been made of them; the involvement of a number of protestant craftsmen in them points to the inconsistent relationship between the council and the two sets of deacons of 1560-61 and 1561-62. This in turn stemmed very largely from the inconsistent stop-go policy of the new council, very conscious of its authority and vulnerability, feeling its way, but not always with sensitivity. The riots only developed after and as a result of a series of shifts of policy and tactics by the council; this was exaggerated by its failure to co-operate consistently with the deacons and by an element of victimisation which had crept into its dealings. The council became concerned not only with maintaining its own authority but with saving face. The conspiracy was probably largely in the minds of the new regime.

The nine months before the return to Scotland of Mary, Queen of Scots had seen two serious craft riots. The new protestant regime in Edinburgh had been put in severe difficulties. It is significant that there was no attempt by Mary to exploit this situation. Calderwood does refer to 'seditious craftsmen' who appealed to her for a pardon for their involvement in the riot immediately she returned, but nothing seems to have come of it. This was probably the first case of the queen taking Lord James's advice not to press 'matters of religion' since tumults would inevitably result. Whatever the real nature of the riots of 1560 and 1561, there does seem to have been fear in a number of quarters that further disturbances would break out after her arrival. William Maitland, writing to Cecil on 10 August, agreed that the suppression of catholicism must remain the first priority, but emphasised that it must be done by 'indirect meanis'.[15] Mary did not succumb to the temptation of intervening on the crafts' behalf in the council elections of October 1561 either, despite the provocative position taken by the merchant-dominated council. The council had rejected the leet of candidates for the two craft representatives on the council presented by the deacons and substituted a nominee of its own, John Weir; this was a breach of established practice and eventually the council conceded the point. The response of the deacons was to challenge the presence of assessors during the election process.[16]

Whether Mary had accepted the advice of Maitland and Lord James to play matters coolly—and the composition of her privy council would strongly suggest she did — there can be little doubt that both Knox and the new protestant regime in Edinburgh had some reason to fear for their positions. A number of conservatives had been appointed to important burgh offices in the royal gift in 1560 and early 1561; this must have given some reason to suppose that there would be further intervention in burgh affairs. It has been pointed out that Knox himself seems to have shunned the possibility of co-operation with the queen from the outset; his reasoning must have included the possibility of his own banishment.[17] The other element that entered into their calculations must have been the symbolic impact of the mass, even if it were only within the precincts of the chapel royal. This must have seemed uncomfortably close to the dual arrangements of 1559. In the past six months the council had managed to secure the agreement of the crafts to the expulsion of stubborn ex-priests, monks and friars from the town, to compulsory attendance at prayers and the sermon, to a theoretically voluntary collection system for the poor and to the annexation of church lands within the burgh.[18] The growth points for a godly society, even if it were not a perfect one, and for its wider acceptance had been forged. It is difficult to be precise about the extent of this hold on the population as a whole. The Easter communion of 1561 had, according to Randolph, been attended by 1,300 people after rigorous vetting. This would account for less than a quarter of the adult population of the burgh. The much smaller parish of the Canongate was able to muster about 1,000 communicants by early 1564 and 1,200 by 1566.[19] Unlike Maitland or Lord James, Knox and the protestant regime could not afford the luxury of accommodation; the framework for their godly society was promising but precarious.

On 31 August Knox preached a violent sermon against the saying of the mass at Holyrood.[20] The events of the following six weeks indicate forcibly that this was the opening shot in an organised campaign. The initial target was the queen's official entry into the burgh two days later. The celebrations were a mixture of expensive pageantry and pointedly protestant propaganda; a six-year-old boy emerged from a globe to present her with a bible, the 'Psalm Book' and four stanzas of welcoming reverential doggerel, but only after she had been subjected to a pageant comparing a priest offering the mass to the story of Korah, Dathan and Abiram, who were swallowed up for making an unnatural sacrifice at the altar of the Lord.[21] The real focus of the campaign, however, was the municipal election. Randolph seems to have been well briefed in advance; he wrote to Cecil on 24 September about the 'great expectation' surrounding these elections and the great set-piece sermon Knox would give on the following Sunday, 28 September, on the duty of magistrates in a Christian commonwealth. Four days later, the newly elected council duly demonstrated its devotion to its Christian duty by reissuing the ordinances of June 1560 and March 1561, which branded together priests and 'huremongaris, adulteraris and fornicatouris' as unfit to stay in a godly society. The bait was taken. On 5 October Mary ordered the council to dismiss the provost and bailies, which was done, after some demurral. Knox makes a great deal of capital out of the affair, maintaining that it was the established practice for a new council to proclaim the municipal statutes and ordinances. While Bishop Keith, the episcopalian historian writing in the eighteenth century, was wrong to deny that such a custom existed, it would be misleading to think that that precedent was quite so simple as Knox outlined it. It was not usual practice only to proclaim one particular statute. The statutes which were normally proclaimed were invariably concerned with food prices and minor details of civic life, as in 1560 and 1562. These ordinances were not reissued in 1561 until 5 November.[22] The controversy over the proclamation has thrown a smoke-screen over the whole affair, obscuring the real issue, which has been overlooked: who were the four bailies who reissued the ordinance and were dismissed along with Kilspindie? None of them had sat on the old council of 1560-61. Two of them, Forester and Kerr, had served on the radical Kilspindie council of 1559-60, but the other two had not been on the council since 1557. None of them could have been chosen by due process. This sudden and mysterious appearance of four new bailies was unusual and highly irregular; there is not another example of it in the 1560s.

These maneouvrings cast Knox's charge that the deposition of Kilspindie and the four bailies by Mary was 'against all law' in a very different light. There are two possible interpretations of the adoption of these four hard-line protestants as bailies in October 1561: it may simply be that the resolve of the protestant establishment was being stiffened by this injection into it from the top; or it may be that their election and immediate reproclaiming of the ordinance against priests and friars was a deliberate tactic in the campaign against Mary. In terms of propaganda, Knox and his colleagues could scarcely lose; either the royal proclamation of 25 August 1561 forbidding any alteration or innovation in the state of religion, which came to be the cornerstone of Mary's religious policy, would be interpreted to include the two ordinances of June 1560 and March 1561 and the precedent for a local godly society reaffirmed, or Mary would be tempted into a repeat of her mother's indiscretion of 1559 of forcing a set of new bailies on the town, which had provided one of the pretexts for her deposition in the second phase of the revolution of 1559. There is some evidence that may underline the second theory, although it has to be treated with caution; Herries, not always an unimpeachable source, refers to the proclamation as a ruse to 'project a beginning of a tumult to bring the Queen in contempt'. If this was the case, the plot partly misfired; Mary did order the dismissal of five office-holders but did nothing more. She blacklisted the radicals, but did not produce a 'white list' to replace them. Perhaps surprisingly, she did not turn to her catholic appointees of 1560 and early 1561. The omission was partly accidental; a leet of three for the provostship was made up but not presented in time. This list does show both her inexperience and the fact that she had not as yet learned from all her mother's mistakes; it included the hated Seton. This delay produced a situation which posed a difficult problem for the crafts as the council's new choice as provost was Thomas MacCalzean, an advocate and assessor.[23] Mary did not make the same mistakes again: her next major intervention in a burgh election, in 1565, was well-timed, judicious and comprehensive.

The net result of the purge of early October 1561 was not great; it was far from a municipal 'coup d'état'.[24] The new office-holders were solidly protestant. There was a difference of opinion amongst the councillors over the attitude that they should take to this intervention by Mary, but the split for the moment was neither serious nor lasting. It is noticeable that Randolph did not bother to report the outcome of the affair until 24 October.[25] On balance, neither Mary nor Knox and the protestant regime made an appreciable gain or loss from the episode; it is best summed up as a draw.

It is difficult to accept Knox's implied charge that the result of this incident was a state of anarchy in the burgh: it is true that there were a number of brawls in the town in the following three months, some of them with more of a religious tinge than others, but is is difficult to see them as reflecting much more than the usual difficulties faced by the burgh's magistrates when faced with *force majeure*. The royal proclamation of August 1561 was awkwardly double-edged and did create friction. Randolph expected it to be reissued in stronger terms after a high mass in the chapel royal on All Saints' Day, which caused further friction between Knox and Lord James and Maitland, whom he had blamed for the dismissal of Kilspindie and his bailies.[26] Shortly afterwards, a resident of Leith, William Balfour, who interrupted John Cairns' examination of intending communicants in St Giles' and was unwise enough to repeat his criticisms in the tolbooth, was convicted by a very protestant-looking assize for contravening the proclamation.[27] Knox was still willing to condone a protestant-tinged disturbance but equally ready to condemn a catholic one; and the town council seems to have been quite able to secure convictions under the proclamation. The only interference with its jurisdiction came when it again attempted to enforce its own proclamation against priests and friars by imprisoning the Dominican friar, John Black, who was promptly removed to the protection of the Castle on Mary's instructions. This was not the simple case of fornication the following lines might suggest:

> He took a black whoor to wash his black sarks
> Committing with her black fornication.

Black had been a thorn in the side of the new regime ever since 1559. What made matters embarrassing was that the woman involved was the divorced wife of a prominent protestant merchant who came on to the council six months later.[28] These incidents took place against the background of a sustained campaign from the pulpit of St. Giles' and a counter-campaign, which the council was slow in checking, emanating from the pen of the catholic ex-schoolmaster of Linlithgow, Ninian Winzet, whose tracts were circulating freely in the burgh in the spring and summer of 1562.[29]

The most serious breakdown of order came in December 1561 when a major fracas developed when the earl of Bothwell 'played the riot' in the town by forcing his way into the house of Cuthbert Ramsay, whose daughter-in-law was suspected of being Arran's mistress. The whole town was alerted and a guard put on Randolph's house. As well as being a reply in kind for an earlier attack on Bothwell by Châtelherault's men, the incident was part of an old family quarrel; Ramsay was married to that formidable lady, Agnes Stewart, a mistress of James IV, and, as sometime countess of Bothwell, Bothwell's own grandmother.[30] The attack did not act as a flashpoint for internal tensions within the town itself and was not among the more serious of a long series of noble feuds in the sixteenth century which used the High Street as their battleground. Despite these disturbances, a case can hardly be made out either for a breakdown of municipal authority or for undue interference with it. It would certainly not be appropriate to talk in terms of a developing tension between the council and Mary in late 1561 or 1562.

There was, however, a good deal of shadow boxing between them. The council was finally forced to take expensive action over the ruinous state of the old tolbooth by a combination of threats from the queen and the Court of Session to quit the town. The council's immediate response to a royal instruction to deal with 'certane seditious personis' in the burgh was to remove the figure of St. Giles from the town's standard; its more considered response, tongue in cheek, was to impose what was in effect a religious test on office-holders as the best method to deal with this problem. This, though, was not primarily part of an attempt to protestantise the town council;[31] the councils of 1560-61 and 1561-62 were satisfactory enough bodies. Nor did it draw an immediate response from Mary. The act was not repealed until January 1564 in the very different circumstances of an aftermath of the protestant disturbances of late 1563 and Knox's inflammatory letter inviting all his brethren to congregate in support of two burgh activists cited to appear before the Court of Justiciary.[32] The ordinance must be read in the context of the craft elections of May 1562 and the opening of the campaign against William Roberton, the catholic master of the grammar school, which began a few days earlier. The council's major difficulties were again with the hammermen; the retiring deacon reported to the council that forty — fully half of the masters of the craft — had ignored his advice and proceeded to choose their own leets and deacons for the coming year. Four of the six nominees — Brocas, Wight, Gotterson and Fraser — had been involved in one or other of the riots of 1560 and 1561. The new deacon, Brocas, was a particularly objectionable choice since he made little attempt to disguise his catholic sympathies. He was dismissed by the council and replaced by James Young, perhaps the most prominent of the small circle of militantly protestant craftsmen in the 1560s. The dispute simmered on; Brocas broke out of the tolbooth in October but was caught and censured for this, the latest in a long line of brushes with the bailies, which had been exacerbated by his testimony before the privy council some two months before.[33]

The council's other major problem — the case of the master of the grammar school — was again largely of its own making. The council's efforts to dismiss William Roberton, who had held his post since 1547, began in April 1562. Roberton was certainly seen as a test case; he had refused to conform to the extent of attending sermon or communion. Again, Mary did not intervene immediately in Edinburgh affairs; she had little need to. The council found the affair more complicated than it had bargained for; it ran into a series of legal technicalities and found that Roberton had a good deal of influential support within the burgh. The list of twenty-two witnesses who were prepared to testify on his behalf includes many names one might expect, but also some one might not. There were a number of political or religious conservatives on it: James Carmichael had given evidence to the de la Brosse inquiry in February 1560 and been purged from office after 1560; Alexander Skene had been called before the council in 1561 for taking communion according to the Roman rite.

Yet some of them — John Marjoribanks, a sitting bailie, Edward Henderson, the master of the song school, Alexander Sim, later one of the commissaries of Edinburgh, and Alexander Bruce, deacon of the barbers — were equally willing to put their names to the contribution list of 'faithful brethren' drawn up by the kirk session four months later. This seems to indicate the presence and strength of a moderate protestant opinion, unwilling to accept the blanket implementation of a religious test on all office-holders without regard to their merit, even if they were obdurate papists. It was not until January 1564 that Mary intervened, to counter the council's most effective ploy to date — simply to stop paying Roberton. This did not bring an immediate response and the instruction had to be repeated, this time successfully, five months later. The affair dragged on miserably for the rest of the 1560s. Pressure was re-applied by the ultra-protestants on the council after Mary fell from power in 1567 and Roberton was forced to retire, although he was given a pension. It was then, however, that the uncompromising protestants among Edinburgh's rulers ran up against a third obstacle in their campaign against their catholic schoolmaster — the law. Roberton raised an action in the Court of Session and was awarded judgement against the town in 1569. He returned to teach Edinburgh's youth well into his old age.[34]

Both the Roberton and the Brocas affairs, in their different ways, demonstrate that Mary did not interfere unnecessarily in the burgh's affairs and indicate at the same time the reasons she did not do so. Natural conservative forces, reinforced by the constraints of the civil law, made it very difficult for a reforming council to implement a godly programme once it began to impinge on the interests of office-holders. In a sense the moral of the Sanderson affair was being restated. Despite the fact that the council had largely been taken over by fairly vigorous protestant enthusiasts, its power base was a narrow one. Both among the craft masters and in the lower levels of the burgh administration,[35] there were strong conservative tinges. Mary applied pressure on a different point and one which proved to be more sensitive, the issue of crown intervention in the annual election process.

The potential divisions within the protestant establishment which had briefly appeared in October 1561 opened up more clearly a year later in a pro-tracted and bad-tempered election process, complicated by royal interference. Little of it appears in the printed council records. The old and the new councils met together on 25 September in the first episode of the customary controlled procedure to hear a letter from the queen naming Kilspindie as provost in place of the present incumbent, Thomas MacCalzean. The membership of the old council was supplemented by three assessors, two replacements for absentee merchant councillors, three newly elected merchant councillors and two new craft councillors. It was decided to delay a reply for a week and in the mean-time the old council continued to sit, hearing the latest instalment in the con-tinuing saga of the Roberton case on 3 October. Three days later an increasingly impatient Kilspindie asked a further joint meeting of the old and new councils if he was to be admitted as provost; the deacons, despite their protests, were excluded. This meeting was seriously split: four of the seven retiring office-holders together with two of the three assessors and a merchant councillor were willing to accede to Mary's letter; but a majority, nineteen of the twenty-six, composed of the remaining ten retiring councillors, three of the four retiring bailies, all the newly elected councillors and an assessor, objected and tried to delay for a further two weeks 'to reason' with the queen. The situation was further complicated by a formal protest against these delaying tactics from Kilspindie, who resorted to the support of the craft deacons, who might have tipped the balance in his favour. This in turn produced a counter-protest from James Baron and Richard Strang, on behalf of the reluctant majority, against the participation of the deacons in the election process. It is as well to remember the ironies in this situation, which had brought about such a serious internal split in the protestant regime; the protestant laird whom the Lords of Congregation had imposed on the town in 1559 was now backed by a catholic queen; he was opposed by the bulk of the merchants who formed the protestant party. There is no further trace of the dispute in the council record. By 23 October a new set of bailies had been installed, although the trappings of office were not handed over to them until two weeks after that.[36]

The eventual composition of the new council confirms the seriousness of the internal dispute within the council over its response to the queen's letter. The three retiring office-holders and five new nominees who advocated a hard-line policy had to be admitted to the new council if due process was to be followed, and this was done. The process had started on the assumption that the new office-holders would be found, as was usual, from the body of the old ordinary council; this did not happen. All eight of the ordinary councillors who followed the hard-line policy on 6 October were excluded; the only councillor to gain promotion was the only one who was prepared to follow a softer line, John Spens. The other three bailies were co-opted from outside; ironically two of them, Forester and Dickson, had been dismissed along with Kilspindie twelve months before. The fourth, Andrew Slater, was a consistent protestant activist throughout the second half of the 1560s. The council had purged itself in order to produce a body able to work with the queen.

It would be a mistake to see the composition of this council as a defeat for the queen simply because of the return of Kilspindie. She had, after all, backed his return for the simple reason that he knew how to rule the town.[37] What it did illustrate was a serious split within the protestant establishment over the attitude it should take towards the queen's influence over burgh elections. The danger here lies in over-statement; the new council of 1562-3 was no less protestant than its predecessor. It was willing to accommodate a degree of royal intervention in certain areas of its business, but not in religious matters. The new council demonstrated its protestant orthodoxy by renewing the campaign against adulterers and fornicators on 6 November and, if anything, proved more vigorous in its pursuit of catholic burgesses. On 12 November the first of a series of catholics was hauled before it for having his child baptised at Holyrood; a number of critics of Knox, including Francis Tennant, a former provost of the burgh, were dealt with firmly; it started proceedings against twenty-two inhabitants found attending mass at Holyrood on 8 August 1563, despite the embarrassing detail that they included the wives of some prominent members of the protestant establishment.[38]

The difficulty that the new regime faced in October 1562 was that the issue at stake was not religion. Their dilemma was not made easier by the fact that Mary's choice was Kilspindie, the provost who had piloted the burgh to protestantism; a nominee like Seton or a choice issue like the threat of papistry would have united them in opposition. But the question here was the rather amorphous one of burgh privilege, and it was complicated by the factor of personal loyalty to Kilspindie and his threat to use the craft deacons to secure a majority for himself. This election demonstrated two important general points; it was when religion was not an issue that the new establishment was at its most vulnerable. To some extent the establishment's unity was more apparent than real; once other factors, like personal ambition, personal loyalties or burgh privilege, were brought into play its unity became very brittle indeed.

By the second half of 1562 it does seem that opinion had moved within a section of the protestant establishment from a position of implacable hostility to Mary to a realisation that burgh life and burgh authority had to go on and the crown would have to be accorded some say in these matters. As a result, things do seem to have quietened down; the years of Kilspindie's tenure, from October 1562 until his dismissal in August 1565, have been described as 'comparatively uneventful'.[39] This is generally true. A more or less normal pattern of relations was being established between the council and the queen in this period. It would be wrong to think of this relationship as a compromise; that is what it certainly was not. It was, though, something like a *modus vivendi*; the council was allowed, within certain limits, to explore new avenues for the enforcement of protestant orthodoxy. At times, it overstepped the mark. Even the purged council of 1562-3 yielded to this temptation; Mary's angry refusal to receive commissioners from the burgh to discuss the vexed question of jurisdiction over Leith, despite the council record's professed ignorance of the cause, was almost certainly due to the imprisoning in the tolbooth of yet another friar accused of violating the proclamation of August 1561.[40] At the same time, the council was anxious to pursue the less controversial aspects of a godly society; it set its sights in 1562 in particular on the scheme for a proposed new poor hospital. This kind of concern, the more respectable face of protestantism, was encouraged by Mary. A council petition of August 1562 asking for the return of the lands and incomes of the Black Friars had met with the response from Mary that this would be done whenever ' sufficient prouision' had been made by the town for the building of a hospital. The resulting campaign to produce promises of financial support from the 'faithful brethren' of the burgh was successful enough to gain the formal grant of the hospital from the queen by March 1563.[41]

The kind of protestantism that the hospital scheme exemplified, a protestantism of civic responsibility and social conservatism, was not naturally hostile to the queen and figured more and more in her calculations and policy towards the burgh. The degree of her success in this area can be illustrated by two incidents: in December 1564 there was the strange sight of Adam Fullarton, Knox's most important ally in the burgh in the 1560s, appealing directly to the queen to force the council to implement a compulsory poor rate since the voluntary system had been widely resisted and only sustained by a 'few nowmer'. In turn, when the council ran into difficulties with the collection of the new quarterly tax on all inhabitants for the poor and the ministry, it appealed to the queen five months later to force a number of leading catholics, including James Lindsay, Herbert Maxwell and Alexander Skene, to contribute.[42] There could hardly be a clearer illustration of how the expectations that both religious parties in the burgh had of Mary had changed in the three years since her arrival.

This *modus vivendi* could be interrupted, though, by other factors and this was what happened in two serious, drawn out, but separate affairs beginning in August 1563 and February 1564. Protestant tempers had been raised by the flagrant celebration of the mass by a number of prominent catholic leaders at Easter 1563.[43] Knox had been temporarily mollified by the judicial action taken against them but the sight of a large-scale celebration of the mass at Holyrood by Edinburgh's catholics on 8 August provoked a riot the following Sunday. Patrick Cranston and Andrew Armstrong appeared before the Court of Justiciary on the same day as the twenty-two catholic worshippers. Neither was a very significant figure, although both had long and chequered careers as protestant activists. Knox's account of the incident is disarming but unconvincing; they were merely picketing the chapel, noting down the names of the recusants, had followed the worshippers as they went into the chapel and had remonstrated with the priest that he was defying the law by saying mass when the queen was not present. Yet both the accused were carrying pistols, and Armstrong's subsequent career makes him look like a most unlikely peaceful picketer. Both had sureties entered for them and duly appeared again on 23 and 24 October, when the trial was adjourned until 13 November.[44] In the meantime Knox had tried to drum up support for the two among the Congregation throughout the country. It is clear that he did not have a great deal of success. This again casts considerable doubt on the amount of popular support he was able to draw on in Edinburgh itself. Knox is equivocal about this; on the one hand he talks of 'the few brethren . . . within the town' in early October, but on the other hand boasts of a thronging mass of supporters who turned out to support him two months later, when he was called before the privy council.[45] If Knox's account of the December incident can be accepted, it is the first example of a mass protestant gathering in Edinburgh; there had been large gatherings with some protestant overtones before, such as during Mary's first entry into the town in 1561, and there had been minor demonstrations of an explicitly protestant character before, like Robert Norval's horseplay before the trial of Archbishop Hamilton in May 1563 for breaking the proclamation of 1561. This was something on a different scale and it was also obviously not an exclusively Edinburgh occasion. It was only now, in the face of a major demonstration against her authority, that the queen demanded a revocation of the ordinance of July 1562 enforcing a religious test on burgh office-holders.[46]

There is no mention in the council register of an election in October 1563 but the new council had seen a certain shift of balance again, bringing on to it six of the group that had pursued a hard-line policy against royal intervention the year before. What is more, they did not simply return to the ordinary council. This was balanced, though, by the removal of four of the same group who had remained on the council, either as retiring office-holders or as new nominees.[47] There seems to have been a conscious balancing of forces at this election; two others from the hard-line faction were allowed to remain as well, Nicol Uddart, who was promoted as a third bailie, and John Marjoribanks, who continued on the ordinary council. The result was that exactly half — eight of the sixteen merchants on the council — were drawn from the hard-liners. The return of these men is best explained in terms of a desire to avoid a hardening or institutionalising of the split of October 1562 which might have resulted from their exclusion from the council for any longer time. The overall complexion of the new council was again firmly protestant. Its role in the demonstration of December 1563 is not known, although conclusions might be drawn from Mary's demand for the repeal of the ordinance of July 1562; but this was not the most serious challenge to its authority during its term of office. The council was severely shaken by the repercussions of what on the face of it appeared to be a much more innocuous incident, the Nicol Young affair.

In February 1564 Young, a tailor, who had been involved in the craft riot of 1561, was set upon by a group of six inhabitants, most of them protestants; they included Arthur Grainger, who had been on the council of 1561-2, and William Paterson, a prominent protestant merchant.[48] On 15 February the council was presented with a petition from Paterson for his release from the tolbooth. A majority of the nine members of the council present agreed to release him despite a protest from two bailies, Glen and Spens, of the legal dangers that were involved if Young were to die. This was precisely what happened; Young did die shortly afterwards and by the middle of May the whole of the council found itself indicted.[49]

The pursuers in the action seem to have had different aims in mind.[50] The laird of Merchiston was intent only on prosecuting David Somer, the only bailie present on 15 February who had agreed to Paterson's release, probably to exonerate his brother, who was on the council; the father and brother of the victim, using the argument of collective responsibility, set their sights on all the nine members of the council who had been present; James Young, who was in the embarrassing position of being a member of the protestant inner circle in the burgh as well as an aggrieved relative, was appalled at the way the affair got out of hand. Eventually, after legal arguments, the accused were whittled down to four; the two bailies who had taken the precaution of entering a formal protest escaped, as did Cuthbert Ramsay, who boasted that neither the pursuers nor the queen's advocates would accuse him. The reason was simple: Ramsay was a prominent Marian. Six other members of the council were bound over for a further fifteen days.[51] So those tried on 6 June were reduced to four: David Somer, Edward Hope, James Baron and James Adamson. All four were prominent members of the protestant party.

The assize chosen to try the case was an interesting one. Naturally, because of the nature of the case, it was composed of prominent burgesses, but it contained a larger proportion of known religious or political conservatives than any other up to this date. Membership of assizes had never since 1560 been confined to protestants, but no other assize list before 1564 had a majority of known conservatives.[52] The motives may well have been partly personal; Bellenden, the justice clerk, was related to one of the pursuers, Napier of Merchiston. But Bellenden was also described by Knox as 'not the least of the flatterers of the Court'. It may well be that a section within the court as well as the burgh's catholic party seized what was a welcome opportunity to put the burgh's protestant regime firmly in its place. The voting followed near-absolute religious lines: only two of the thirteen members of the assize returned different verdicts on the three charges brought against the defendants.[53] The balance of forces on the assize was otherwise clearly drawn; eight voted to convict, five to acquit. Seven of the eight who convicted were demonstrably conservatives of one kind or another. James Forret, Edward Kincaid, John Spottiswood and the pewterer, John Wilson, all supported the queen's party in the civil wars. So did Herbert Maxwell who, along with James Lindsay, had been on the Seton council of 1559-60. James Carmichael's distinguished civic career had come to an abrupt end after he gave evidence to the de la Brosse inquiry in 1560. Both Lindsay and Spottiswood had determined catholic wives.[54] On the other side, of the five, Adam Fullarton and Archibald Graham were part of the protestant inner circle; Patrick Hardy was a cordiner, who had appeared on the subscription list of 1562, as had Thomas Todmer; it is not clear who James Johnston was — he might be James Johnston of Kellebank, of the Cottis, or of Westray; all three were connected with the protestant establishment.[55] Not surprisingly, Somer protested that the verdict had been 'partiale gevin'.

Burgh administration did not, however, grind to a halt during or after the trial; Kilspindie had personally entered pledges for the reappearance of all nine accused on 10 June. According to the justiciary record, the four convicted on the 10th were pledged on 2 July, each on a punitive surety of £1,000. They had been held in the Castle until then but both Somer and Adamson were present at a council meeting on 28 June. Council business seems to have gone on regardless both during and after the trial. Knox and Craig were confident enough about the state of things in the town to leave for a preaching campaign in the north in mid-August.[56] This calm, however, was deceptive; the new regime had been severely rattled by the Nicol Young affair. Although the council, with consummate cheek, duly elected the man at the centre of the affair, William Paterson, as a bailie in October 1564, the experience proved too much for a number of others; eight of the ten ordinary councillors retired from office. The experience of this council's year in office had shown that it could ride out a crisis stemming from the cry of 'defence of religion' fairly comfortably if it did not take matters beyond the point of confrontation with the queen. It was far more vulnerable to the less predictable clash of family, personal and religious loyalties involved in the Young affair, particularly after the catholic party in the burgh latched on to the possibilities of exploiting it.

There is a good deal to show that after the dust of the Young affair had settled there was a continuing, working rapprochement between Mary and the town. The privy council quickly settled a dispute between the craftsmen and the council over procedure at the next election. The new council concentrated on civic improvements, on details of administration. Where the queen did intervene, it was to preserve order in the town; a likely skirmish between Seton and Maitland on the High Street in October 1564 was forestalled; an appeal two months later from the leading spokesman for the protestant party for a compulsory poor rate to check the increasing numbers of destitute as a result of the severe shortage of food, which affected the burgh throughout most of 1564 and 1565, was answered favourably. This was done despite objections and resistance from the catholic party in the burgh.[57]

Once again this emerging pattern of a *modus vivendi* was interrupted by an outbreak of religious chauvinism; and, once again, the trouble stemmed from the ordinances of June 1560 and March 1561. In April 1565 one of the old chaplains of St. Giles', James Tarbot, was found conducting mass in a private house. It sounds, from the account in Knox's *History* by his continuator, as if there had been an organised witch-hunt, in which at least one of the bailies was involved, to stop a repetition of the celebration of the mass at Easter, as had happened two years before. Tarbot was dragged to the market cross, forcibly dressed in his vestments, his hands tied to his chalice and he was bombarded with eggs — since supplies were still not plentiful it is doubtful if the estimate of 10,000 eggs of Randolph's source, Alexander Clark, can bear much credence.

The treatment of Tarbot before he was actually tried was undoubtedly an intensification of the tactics of popular protestantism. Up till now the burgh's protestant activists had contented themselves with attacking the physical symbols of catholic practice; the drowning of the idol of St. Giles' in the Nor' Loch in 1558; the mocking of Archbishop Hamilton's procession before his trial by Robert Norval, 'a merry man', in 1563. Where there had been violence, as in the assault on Cuthbert Ramsay's house in 1561, personal motives had been involved as well as religious, and burgesses had only been marginally involved. The Tarbot affair was a serious one and it is evident that there was a feeling among many in the burgh that this went too far. Randolph testified that the assize that convicted Tarbot the next day was split between catholics and protestants. According to Knox's *History*, a further bout of egg throwing was stopped by 'some papists'. Their intervention almost produced what would have been the first explicitly religious confrontation between catholics and protestants on the streets of the burgh. Knox's continuator laconically refers to 'some tumult' but Clark estimated that the protestant mob numbered three or four hundred and admitted that what precipitated the riot was not further horseplay at the priest's expense but a physical threat to his life. Edinburgh's first and only catholic riot was triggered off by the sight of a respected local priest at the mercy of a protestant mob carrying staves. The situation was only quietened by the appearance of the provost with a number of halberdiers.[58]

Mary's reactions to the Tarbot affair can be properly judged only if it is realised how near it had brought Edinburgh to the brink of open violence in the streets. It is difficult to accept a good many of Randolph's conclusions about the affair because of his vested interest in reporting a great upswell of protestant feeling as a result of it. It's not easy to reconcile his informant's assertions that there was a 'greater rage' among 'the faithful' than at any time since late 1559 with Moray's disastrous failure to find support in the burgh only four months later, at the end of August. His informant, Alexander Clark, was, after all, a client of Moray.[59] It is easier to believe that Moray and Châtelherault would have used any armed invasion of the burgh ordered by the queen to remove its magistrates, particularly one led by that old enemy of the Hamiltons, the earl of Lennox, as a pretext to ally themselves with a section of the burgesses who were prepared to defend themselves by force. It is not certain how many would have taken up arms, but again the source may not be reliable. Clark, as well as being on the council, was one of the four captains of the burgh's protestants who mustered on the Crags, which lay just outside the town, early in July. If there was an attempt by the Moray faction in the months leading up to the Darnley marriage on 29 July to win armed support within the burgh, it was not conspicuously successful. On the contrary, it does look as if Edinburgh's protestants were divided; Knox's *History* complained that information about the musters on the Crags had been passed on to the queen, not by catholic supporters but by 'false brethren'.[60] The Tarbot affair had not had the effect of galvanising the brethren into action.

It is not clear from the sources available how long Mary toyed with the idea of a strong show of force in Edinburgh. It could not have been long. Tarbot was apprehended on 15 April; Clark's letter was probably written on the following Sunday, the 22nd; it was passed on by Randolph a week later. On the 22nd, Clark was anticipating the arrival of a force of Marian nobles led by

Lennox and Athol on the following Thursday or Friday, 26 or 27 April. Knox's *History* published a 'threatening' letter from Mary at Stirling to the town council dated the 24th, which demanded that the council's letter expressing their regrets about the Tarbot riot be backed by the arrest of the ringleaders. The council sent a large delegation to the queen, who was still at Stirling on the 30th, trying to avoid her taking action against 'certane principale nychtbouris'. By 12 May the council was turning to her for assistance in compelling a number of reluctant members of the catholic faction to pay their contribution to the poor relief tax. About the same time the rumours had spread through the town that Mary was on the verge of abandoning catholicism.[61] The threatened armed entry into the burgh did not take place, nor were the provost and bailies dismissed; no action seems to have been taken against the prominent burgesses who were apparently behind the Tarbot riot, although Mary's actions over the next few months should be read in terms of her suspicions about those behind the disturbances of April 1565. The only action that does seem to have been taken was that the process against Tarbot and the two burgesses, John Loch and John Kennedy, who were taken with him, was set aside. Clark tries to make a good deal of capital out of this, suggesting that the 'most part' of the burgh was enraged by it. Yet Loch and Kennedy were comparatively small fry[62] and both the council and the protestant establishment must have considered themselves fortunate to have escaped so lightly. The measures that Mary eventually took were mild when considered against the seriousness of the Tarbot affair, which was not just another isolated instance of the victimisation of priests or friars. Both the measures and the council's attitude to Mary as shown shortly afterwards do not support the notion that a breach was opening up between her and the burgh or its council.

In saying this, it has to be realised that the protestant establishment in Edinburgh was always a coalition; it held within it an often uneasy balance between radical activists and moderates. Perhaps the only way to understand the growing discrepancies in evidence which can be seen in the Tarbot affair and which increase in the period up to and after the murder of Riccio in March 1566 is to realise this and to understand that Knox's *History* and, to a lesser extent, Randolph's dispatches up to his forced departure in March 1566, are largely accounts of its activist wing. When the council records fall silent during the crisis month of July 1565,[63] it is largely the account in Knox's *History* that has to be relied upon. Early in July 'a great part' of the burgh's protestants met on the Crags to elect captains. The *History* does not explain why. It was hardly surprising that, in view of the Tarbot affair and Moray's growing disaffection, Mary took the prospect of armed insurrection within the capital seriously. After the bailies, just as they had done ten weeks before, neglected to take action against the ringleaders, the four captains were apprehended by direct means; they were pledged before the justiciary court on 13 July and appeared again on 26 July and 15 August.[64] The four captains — 'King' Guthrie the town clerk, Andrew Slater, Gilbert Lauder and Clark himself — contained few surprises. Clark and Guthrie had both been consistent supporters of the English connection since 1560; they were both on intimate terms with Randolph. They and Slater were key figures in the protestant establishment; Lauder, though, was not. He was the son of one of the queen's advocates; he was no longer a merchant and did not figure prominently in burgh politics before or after 1565. While it is easy enough to identify the leaders of the protestant activists in the town, it is difficult even to guess at their numbers. Certainly very few burgesses became involved in the Moray conspiracy proper; of those who did, one was significant — William Paterson, the man at the centre of the Nicol Young affair and now a sitting bailie, who was convicted in December 1565 for supplying the rebels with money. Ironically, the assize contained one of Young's relations.[65] Two of the others who fled had close connections with the burgh. Paterson was probably involved in the same chain of supply as the two notaries who had passed money on from Randolph to Moray, John Johnston and James Nicolson. Johnston was a useful ally as clerk to the privy council and had been linked with the burgh's protestants since 1559. Nicolson was connected to the burgh's protestant party by marriage.[66] There is no evidence, though, of general support for Moray in any section of burgh society when he rode into the town at the head of the rebel lords on 31 August.[67]

On the face of it this does not seem surprising. Only eight days before, Mary's patience had finally worn out; she dismissed Kilspindie and replaced him with a catholic, the laird of Craigmillar, labelled by Knox as 'a right epicurean'. Randolph promptly predicted, with some relish, that this would lead to 'cumber'. An attempt to silence Knox had been stoutly and bluntly resisted by the whole council and thirteen of the fourteen craft deacons. The tax of £1,000 raised on the town proved difficult to extract from the burgesses; extentors were appointed promptly on 24 August, and although a licence to remain absent from the host to pursue the rebels was granted two days later, the money was not forthcoming. The council was forced to resort to donations from its own members, a loan from Guthrie and a swift collection of the revenues from the common mills; this in turn was resisted by the current farmers of the mills. Melville pointed to the discontentment of the 'maist part' of the burgh with the Marian administration.[68] An argument has sometimes been constructed that would explain the burgh's reluctance to help Moray in late August and early September 1565 as largely due to the long split between him and Knox and that Mary's brusque treatment of the burgh continued after her return on 19 September.[69] Another extent of £1,000 was demanded; a number of leading merchants — estimates vary from seventeen to thirty — were summoned before the privy council and imprisoned after being denounced for financing the rebels. Sir James Balfour, who was an increasingly influential voice in Mary's privy council, personally threatened them with execution and six were singled out to be taken to the Castle. Matters culminated in a leet from the queen to infiltrate the council with a number of catholics. This heavy-handed treatment was part of Mary's catholic policy that she had been increasingly moving towards since early in 1565, and in Edinburgh it proved counter-productive; the seeds were sown of widespread discontent that would erupt within the following six months in the Friar Black affair and the Riccio murder.[70]

Things were not quite so simple. The election of September and October 1565 was indeed a significant one in the history of the burgh's relations with the Marian administration; but as well as a stick a number of carrots were on offer. The town emerged well from the series of financial demands made on it. The account in Knox's *History* is confused but it seems that it was at Craigmillar's suggestion that the tax of £1,000 was supplemented by a much larger sum, negotiated on the basis of the grant of the superiority of Leith to the burgh. This was a subtle manoeuvre, which took account of both the crown's desperate need for cash and the burgh's problems with its jurisdiction over its port. It was a distinct twist on the attempts of Mary's mother to exploit the superiority to the burgh's disadvantage in 1559. Although the grant was only, in theory, to act as security for repayment of the loan, the town must have been confident that its jurisdictional difficulties with Leith were at an end. The opportunity was grasped eagerly; the superiority was claimed in the tolbooth on 10 October, only six days after the formal grant was made, despite the fact that it was not due to take effect for a further six months. The role of Craigmillar in the deal must have eased his reappointment as provost. Although there is no direct evidence to prove it, it may well be that another attractive proposition was dangled before the burgh; the council suddenly on 12 October ordered that an inventory be made of the remaining church lands and revenues within the burgh, although they were not granted by the crown until March 1567.[71]

The key to Mary's policy, however, was her leet of 26 September. The crown had two distinct problems in trying to intervene in burgh elections: one was how to gain influence without antagonising significant sections of opinion; the other was to whom to turn to do this. This leet was an interesting one and was not quite as it was described in Knox's *History*, 'a number of papists, the rest not worthy'. It did have its share of conservatives: James Carmichael had denounced the protestant coup of 1559 at the de la Brosse inquiry; six of Mary's other ten nominees had been on the notorious Seton council of 1559-60, but not all of them were still catholics. Seven of the eleven had appeared on the protestant subscription list of 1562.[72] Of course, this should not always be taken at its face value; Curle and Little who figured on it were almost certainly hostile to the radical elements within the new regime, as were Carmichael and Leach. The former three were all involved, in one way or another, with the Marian party during the civil wars. Curle was a frequent visitor to France, at least once in the company of Seton; he became an exile there in the 1570s.[73] Yet others were less easy to brand as 'papists'; Wilson, despite the fact that he had been on the Seton council early in October 1559, had been one of the extentors appointed to raise £1,600 for the Congregation. Both Preston and Spens were by 1565 highly respectable members of the protestant establishment; it can hardly be a coincidence that both were chosen in 1565 as commissioners to the General Assembly. There is no reason to doubt that John Sim was not an orthodox protestant; he certainly suffered in 1571 for his loyalties to the king's party. The one remaining Marian nominee, James Nicol, is difficult to judge; he had only received his guildry in 1563 and come on to the council a year later.[74] Yet taken as a whole, there is little room for doubting that Mary's nominees were overwhelmingly of a protestant complexion. If the leet was not dominated by catholics, the alternative claim in the *History* that it was made up of nonentities is just as suspect. Preston, on the contrary, had the longest and most distinguished record of anyone who sat on the town council in the 1560s; he had served near-continuously since 1549. Spens had been on the council, without a break, since 1557; Sim had been on the council from 1554 to 1557 and had come back on to it as a bailie in 1564; Wilson had been twice burgh treasurer in recent years; Gilbert was the wealthiest craftsman in Edinburgh; Livingstone, in effect, was Knox's paymaster. Even if Nicol lacked experience, he was a perfectly proper choice as a bailie since he had been on the previous 1564-5 council. The case that the protestants on the leet were 'not worthy' was preposterous.

In one sense, Mary's tactics were less provocative than those used by her mother six years before. The four bailies and the treasurer whom she nominated were all perfectly respectable choices and did not seriously interfere with due process. Two of the five had not been on the old council but had been on that of 1563-4. In another sense, though, Mary's leet went a good deal further than her mother's; it did not seek to nominate only the provost and bailies but all the office-holders, both the new craft councillors and all the new merchant councillors. The remaining five places on the council would have been filled by retiring office-holders. The significant point about this was that the leet would have secured a *continuing* Marian interest on the council. Apart from the provost, Mary was careful not to infiltrate catholics or conservatives directly into high office straight away; Carmichael and the others were planted in the influential position of dean of guild, who had some say over merchant nominees to the council, and on the ordinary council. It is clear that Mary carefully avoided pushing too hard too quickly; the plan was for future growth rather than immediate results. Her other problem was one that she shared with the protestant establishment: how to persuade men to take office. A number of her choices had some connection with the court: Curle had been appointed custumar in 1560; Livingstone had recently secured his appointment as sub-collector of thirds of benefices for Lothian; Leach had been rewarded before this for his services to both Mary and her mother; Gilbert was all but unofficial goldsmith to the queen; Spens had been granted an exemption from hosts and taxation only two weeks before. The crucial factor in persuading Carmichael, Curle and Wilson to accept office was probably the renegotiation of the lucrative lead mines contract, which fortuitously came up for renewal in August 1565.[75]

The leet, had it been fully implemented, would not have resulted in a municipal *coup d'état* but it would have redrawn the lines of the coalition which controlled burgh politics in the 1560s. A coalition of radical and moderate protestants would have turned into a coalition of moderate protestants, some with an attachment to the court, and moderate catholics. In fact, the leet was not accepted as it stood; Carmichael, Curle and Wilson were rejected. Preston was moved to the key post of dean of guild; a new treasurer and two new bailies were found. Yet Mary does not seem to have been dissatisfied with the result; the changes escaped censure despite the implied threat in her original letter of 26 September if her nominees were not accepted. The two new bailies — Fowler and Stevenson — were both at least nominal protestants, having appeared on the subscription list of 1562; but Stevenson's wife was a catholic and both he and Fowler had a role, albeit largely passive, in the queen's party during the civil wars.[76] The leet of September 1565, despite the alterations made to it, was not as unsuccessful as some have thought; all four bailies performed their duties in a manner that was satisfactory to the crown. Spens was compensated in August 1566 for damage he had suffered during the siege of Leith in 1559; Nicol and Fowler were considered reliable enough to sit on the assize which convicted Thomas Scott and two Edinburgh burgesses of the murder of Riccio.[77] Although the council as a whole was still protestant, if the subscription list of 1562 is used as a guide, it was purged of most of the activists; David Forester was the only one on it to be implicated in the Riccio affair. The success of the leet was not due to the fact that it followed an overtly catholic policy, but rather to the fact that Mary's policy was still equivocal, had an eye for self-interest and attempted for the moment merely to reshuffle the political and religious coalition which controlled the burgh.[78] The end result was not so short of Mary's objective; it did produce a council mostly made up of moderate-minded men.

This reinterpretation of Mary's treatment of the burgh in September and October 1565 does suggest an alternative explanation of the movement of opinion in the town after the Tarbot affair. The lesson of both the Tarbot and the Crags affairs had not been to demonstrate a broadly based protestantism that was becoming more confident and belligerent. On the contrary, it had shown that the prospect of religious riots on the streets and of armed rebellion against the queen split protestant opinion. A large section, probably a majority, of the burgh's protestants disapproved of activism and were unwilling to be pushed into it. It would be wrong to think of this as a permanent split; protestant unity could always be restored, though perhaps only temporarily, by a convincing cry of 'defence of religion'. This was what happened when Knox was threatened with a temporary restraint on his preaching in August 1565; the protestant coalition on the council closed ranks to defend Knox and the burgh's right to appoint its own ministers. This was the first and only attempt to muzzle Knox and seems to have come from Darnley rather than Mary herself. It was a serious miscalculation, made more embarrassing by John Craig's refusal to preach while Knox was suspended.[79] The royal intervention in the burgh election process only a month later had all the signs, on the other hand, of a carefully calculated scheme, which only partly misfired. On this interpretation, the failure of the town to support Moray when he entered the town on 31 August is more readily explained in terms of a widespread reluctance to become involved in protestant activism. It is a mistake to think of Edinburgh as a hotbed of radicalism; the town shared the general reluctance of Scottish society as a whole to take political risks for the sake of protestantism.

It is likely that in the capital there were two other factors that encouraged this feeling; many of the protestant establishment were close enough to Randolph to know that by August there was no prospect of English intervention and it seems likely that the Crags affair should be considered as the pro-Moray coup that failed. The timing of the musters, the links of the leaders with both Moray and Randolph, do strongly suggest that the burgh's protestant activists were preparing to join the growing Moray conspiracy which had some prospect of success in July.[80] After one conspiracy of a militant minority against the queen had been discovered, it was unlikely that the burgh would indulge in another.

The effect of the Friar Black and Riccio affairs was rather different. Early in February 1566, Friar John Black, who was by now a marked man, was attacked, probably from behind, and badly wounded. It is very likely that the four men accused of this assault — Andrew Armstrong, James Young, Thomas Brown and William Johnston, all of them protestant activists and all of them involved in the Riccio murder just over a month later — were guilty. The record of the proceedings brought against them is complex and confused and does not fully appear in Pitcairn's summary;[81] they first appeared before the Court of Justiciary on 12 February, were pledged and reappeared six days later, when the process was delayed a further day for legal arguments to be heard. Young seems not to have been brought to trial; an assize list for Armstrong had all those returning guilty verdicts, seven of the thirteen members, deleted and the whole list is marked 'absentes'. Only Brown and Johnston seem actually to have come to trial and only Johnston was convicted, but only by his own confession. It seems clear that the courts had difficulty with an assize made up of Edinburgh burgesses in securing a conviction even for the most outrageous assault on a catholic friar or priest. Reluctance to appear and reluctance to convict was not confined to protestants; James Carmichael tried to avoid sitting on Armstrong's assize. There were a number of catholics on the Brown and Johnston assize — James Dalyell, David Logan, a baxter, James Forret, Cuthbert Ramsay, John Graham and Archibald Leach.[82] Although the record of the voting is confused, only Ramsay and Graham of these five found both guilty. The fact that a convinced Marian like James Forret would vote to convict all four defendants in the Nicol Young case, would help to convict the ex-priest and Ruthven retainer, Henry Yair, of the murder of Riccio but would not convict a fellow-burgess for a religiously motivated assault unless presented with an actual confession is remarkable;[83] it must either speak volumes for the fear of Armstrong's 'protestant murder gang'[84] or testify to a general desire of most conservatives in the 1560s to lie low. Equally, the full flavour of the first assault on Friar Black is not caught unless it is realised that the 'murder gang' included a man who had been a burgh commissioner to the General Assembly and was the most influential protestant craftsman in Edinburgh in the 1560s.

The atmosphere in the town was heightened by rumours of a restoration of the mass in St. Giles', the declaration of a general fast for the two Sundays preceding the coming meeting of parliament early in March and the final expulsion of Randolph. Although there are no entries in the council register between 11 January and 19 March, it seems most unlikely that burgh administration had ground to a halt during the whole of this period.[85] The suggestion that the whole council and all the craft deacons turned out with Craigmillar to rush down to Holyrood when news of Riccio's murder broke in the town seems well-founded.[86] But who among Edinburgh's protestant party were involved in the events of the night of 9 March? This is a factor that has not been considered either in the controversy as to whether or not Knox and Craig had prior knowledge of the Riccio murder or whether the town shared in the general effects it had in reuniting the protestant party in Scotland.[87]

The burgesses who were involved in one or other of the two murders on 9 March included, of course, all four of the Armstrong murder gang as well as a number of names that were by now familiar, like Patrick Cranston, Knox's 'zealous brother' of 1563. Ridley argues that they were part of a band of five hundred men who kept watch in the courtyard at Holyrood and turned back the provost and his followers; this seems to be based on a misreading of a passage in Knox's *History*, 'having about four or five hundred men in warlike manner'. It seems clear both from the text and from other sources that this refers to the townspeople who were led by Craigmillar down to Holyrood and not to any of those involved in the conspiracy.[88] Although there is in fact no indication as to how many from the burgh were involved apart from a laconic remark from Randolph about 'divers of Edinburgh', the conspiracy was not confined to a few activists whose significance lay only in the fact that they were readily available as an armed gang. The departure of Knox on 17 March in the wake of the protestant lords was followed the next day by the entry of Mary into the town with a force estimated at up to eight thousand men and by, according to Knox's *History*, a series of 'outrages' on the inhabitants.[89] Four days later a proclamation was made at the market cross summoning eleven burgesses and William White, the Canongate cordiner, to appear on a charge of high treason for keeping guard outside Holyrood on the night of the murder. These twelve were only those who had had the prudence to flee the town. The list included all four involved in the earlier assault on Friar Black; Young and Brown were held for most of Monday 11 March but then released, but all four absconded when news arrived of Mary's march on the town from Dunbar on the 18th. Guthrie had left with the clerk register, James McGill, and Bellenden shortly before her arrival, although the last entry in his protocol book was for 7 March, the day parliament opened and two days before the murder. According to the *Diurnal*, between twenty and thirty were put into the tolbooth between 19 and 21 March. These were not all burgesses; Knox's *History* refers to 'certain gentlemen' among the group who were held for a total of fourteen to sixteen days, first in the tolbooth and then in Holyrood.[90] Three of this group — Thomas Scott, the under-sheriff of Perth, and two burgesses, William Harlaw, a saddler, and John Mowbray, a merchant — were brought to trial on 1 April. Despite being convicted, they were saved from execution by the intercession of Bothwell and banished.[91] Between 30 March and 20 April a series of pledges were entered on behalf of nine prominent burgesses, who were to re-enter ward on six or twenty-four hours' warning on pain of a fine of £1,000; three of them, Robert Watson, Robert Cunningham and Edward Hope, had been among those warned on 22 March and must have decided to return to the burgh. It is likely, from the coincidence of dates, that the others were from the group that had been held since about 19 March.

There were twenty-one burgesses in all who were suspected of being involved in the Riccio conspiracy.[92] A number of the others nearer to the centre of the conspiracy had close links with the burgh—James McGill and his servant William Cheyne; and the lawyers, John Sharp and James Millar.[93] It is remarkable that only one of the twenty-one implicated was a member of the sitting town council, David Forester. Yet only seven of the twenty-one did not hold office within the town at some time during the 1560s. Four of them — Young, Harlaw, Redpath and Henderson — were influential craftsmen. The other ten comprised, to a large extent, the core of the protestant party in the 1560s. It is easier to list the members of the protestant inner circle who were not implicated than it is to try to describe the widespread influence and responsibility that these men had in the first years of post-reformation Edinburgh. Three further points about them are important: the fact that so few of them were on the council of 1565-6 tends to confirm the amount of progress that Mary had made before the Riccio affair in influencing the composition of Edinburgh's government. This would lead one to suspect that the protestant party approached the Riccio affair not only as a device to re-secure wider protestant unity but also to regain their influence in burgh affairs. Once again, as in 1565, the conspiratorial group had within it the men most closely associated with Randolph and the English connection: this time not only Clark and Guthrie, but also Fullarton and Graham. Two more general conclusions also follow: Randolph, from the safety of Berwick, tantalisingly drew a connection between the burgesses involved in the Riccio affair and the abortive Moray coup of the year before: 'I judge as many like to take hurt as were in the former action'.[94] His allusion is more useful for 1565 since more evidence is available for 1566; the connection can be established through Clark and Guthrie but it is likely that it was more widely spread than that. The motive in both 1565 and 1566 was broadly the same, although it became more pressing as time went on: the need to counteract Mary's largely successful redrawing of the lines of loyalty and self-interest within the burgh establishment. In national politics there was a considerable difference in the nature of the support for the Moray conspiracy and the Riccio affair in the following year. Noble factionalism, ambition and, for a few, protestantism combined to weave a very tangled web of loyalties in 1565 and 1566. In Edinburgh the pattern was simpler and the link between the two conspiracies more direct. The burgh's protestant activists were involved in both but they remained a small minority, driven on by fear as much as by religious conviction.

This new evidence about the involvement of Edinburgh's protestant inner circle in the Riccio affair would also add considerably to the weight of circumstantial evidence which points to the likelihood that Knox and Craig were party to the conspiracy.[95] There can be little doubt that Guthrie had prior knowledge of the conspiracy; Clark and Graham were attached to Moray and Maitland respectively; if they were involved, men like Hope, Cunningham and Young would not be far behind. It is still not clear how close they were to the centre of the plot; the most serious offence that any of them was charged with was detaining the queen in Holyrood. But it is fairly obvious what lines of communication were used in involving them, if only on the fringes of the affair. This evidence not only indicates that more were involved but that they were much more influential than has been realised. It would have been strange indeed if Knox had not been aware of the activities of the men who were his closest colleagues in the burgh in the 1560s.

Any conclusion that the Riccio affair helped to heal the breaches in the protestant party in the burgh can only be impressionistic, but it did not immediately restore the hardliners to the council. The dismissal of Guthrie after his flight to England and his replacement as common clerk by a Marian nominee, David Chalmer, did bring a predictable protest from the council; Chalmer first presented himself on 3 April but was stalled for a further two days. The appointment was eventually accepted only, as one of the Marian nominees for the last election, John Preston, put it, 'for feir of horning' and it was strongly opposed by Craigmillar.[96] This was the second time that Mary had failed to realise that even a moderate council would resist any direct interference with burgh privilege; the dismissal of Guthrie and the attempt to silence Knox in August 1565 touched on a very sensitive area, which, for the town, changed the issues at stake. If this was a technical miscalculation, the election of October 1566 revealed the longer-term strategy behind the leet of September 1565. Two of the former nominees to the council, Livingstone and Little, were now put forward as bailies; Craigmillar was to be continued as provost, as were the dean of guild and treasurer. Mary had obviously been reasonably satisfied with the restraint shown by the council of 1565-6; only one outsider was proposed by her and, ironically, this was Clark, who probably shared in the restoration to favour of his master, although he was not granted a remission for his part in the Riccio affair for another three months.[97] The council's reaction was prickly; even continuity, if it was imposed from outside, was unpalatable. It demurred when it first received the queen's instructions on 1 October and it took a personal interview with her and a further letter to persuade it to comply. The cumbersome election process was already under way when the first instruction arrived; an entry of 27 September lists three members 'of the new counsale'. The objection was not to the bailies who, as Mary's second letter caustically pointed out, 'were na strangearis bot of thame ye yourself haid schoisin in lytis', but to the continuation of the provost, treasurer and dean of guild. This can be gleaned from the fact that the council on 4 October had to fill the three vacancies on the ordinary council which they, as retiring officers, would have filled. Despite the fact that the council was reasonably content with Craigmillar, as well it might have been, it did not want him to continue in office.[98]

It is not easy to generalise about the council that eventually emerged; two died in office and another was replaced for lack of diligence in his duties.[99] The impression that loyalties on it were fairly evenly divided is perhaps best illustrated by the fact that six of its members would eventually join the king's party in Leith and six others would remain in the town during the civil wars.[100] It is equally difficult to generalise about relations between it and Mary; the *modus vivendi* continued, probably eased by Knox's long absence in England between December 1566 and July 1567.[101] Mary's policy of considered concessions continued: a number of burgesses were pardoned for the Riccio murder along with the main conspirators on 24 December; the reformed church gained a series of concessions between October 1566 and March 1567.[102] These culminated, for Edinburgh, in the settlement of two outstanding questions; on 13 March the town, along with a number of other burghs, was finally granted the remaining lands and revenues in the burgh that had belonged to the old church. This brought to an end a campaign which had been going on since 1562 and which had had a firm expectation of success since at least November 1565, when Knox's stipend had been increased in anticipation. Equally important, the income from the source was to be supplemented by the resurrection of a tax on the burgh for sustaining the ministry. Although the town did make moves to capitalise on its new assets about five months later, nothing was done about the proposed regular tax until the 1570s.[103]

Yet, if the schemes for a reformed society could now be placed on a firmer financial footing, the other major concession that Mary had made to the burgh, the grant of the superiority of Leith, had gradually soured. The town had been delayed on three separate occasions from taking possession of the superiority, in April and October 1566 and again early in 1567 until the following April. The town had also had great difficulty in raising the full amount of the loan; the council paid off 300 of the 2,000 merks that had been obtained from the crafts in November 1566; the amount was only paid in full to the crown in March 1567, significantly just before the grant of the church lands and revenues. The council then apparently managed to scrape the money together only by borrowing £1,200 of it from a consortium of merchants headed by James Baron; the loan was still unpaid in April 1569.[104] Until April 1567 the queen's growing attachment to Bothwell had only affected the burgh indirectly, with the possibility of the revival of the consistorial court of the archbishop of St. Andrews in Edinburgh to hear the divorce. The effects of the Bothwell coup, however, were real and alarming. The Castle, which had been handed over to Mary on 21 March, now came into Bothwell's hands. Equally alarming, though in a different way, was his assumption of the superiority of Leith.[105] This was a reversal of Mary's policy over the previous eighteen months and, given the time and money which the town invested in the prospect of settling its jurisdictional problems with Leith, it must have figured as prominently in the burgh's thinking as the removal from the Castle of the earl of Mar, whose tenure had been reassuring in troubled times.

During the confusing and dangerous situation between the seizure of the queen by Bothwell on 24 April and Mary's defeat and capture at Carberry Hill on 15 June 1567 the town as a whole was concerned with its own safety rather than its investment in Leith. There was no repetition of the public outcry against Bothwell that had followed the murder of Darnley. Evidence as to the precise degree of support that was given to the confederate lords allied against the queen varies in detail but not in substance; in this instance, there seems little reason to doubt Knox's *History*, which lamented that the burgesses did not join the lords 'as was expected'. Huntly's complaints about being forced to retreat into the Castle because of the level of support for Moray in the burgh had an air of self-justification and exaggeration about them. In fact, the town scrupulously complied with the letter of the law; the town gates were shut but no resistance was made at the arrival of the confederate lords on 11 June. The council's prompt dispatch of excuses to the queen at Dunbar showed that it had learned from experience how to conduct itself in times of uncertainty. At the same time, there can be little doubt that opinion, even if it was only passive opinion, had swung against Mary.[106] The successive scandals of the past year had shocked even catholic Europe. Edinburgh's burgesses — catholics or moderates as well as ultra-protestants — had added cause to take offence since these scandals had been taking place on their doorstep. Yet this movement of opinion was not irrevocable. A very substantial number of burgesses from a broad spectrum of Edinburgh society were prepared to support the queen's party only three years later and this tends to suggest that the most telling reasons for the burgh's disaffection from the queen in the spring of 1567 were short-term or local and had much to do with the effects of the Bothwell coup. By the time of Langside in May 1568 the burgh's conservatives had partly rallied.[107] Moderate opinion would follow in time. But the two opposing factions in Edinburgh and the town as a whole played no significant part in the events leading up to the revolution of 1567.

After the débâcle at Carberry Mary was led into Edinburgh and taunted with abuse from some of the crowds which lined the streets. This highly unpleasant reception, so different from that given to her on her arrival from France just six years before, should not be allowed to obscure the loyalties much of Edinburgh still felt towards its queen or the very real achievements of Mary's policies during her personal reign. There were mistakes, but it was on the whole a success story. She had certainly offended against the burgh's morals, which were as much ingrained as Calvinist,[108] and she had also misunderstood the real strengths behind Knox's standing in Edinburgh. He was not only a protestant activist in a town which was little inclined towards activism; he was also the burgh's pastor and could draw upon more than one set of loyalties. Mary never quite appreciated this. Yet the burgesses' attitude to Knox was equivocal and this left room for manoeuvre. There was no attempt by her to play either the craft or the ultra-catholic card. Her support in the burgh did not rest only with its meaner men or its catholics but penetrated deep into the merchant establishment. There was a change in her policy from 1565 onwards but not, at least in Edinburgh, towards a polarisation of religious opinions. It was more a shift of emphasis from a fairly permissive *modus vivendi* with minimal interference in burgh affairs to an interventionist policy, which was carefully balanced by concessions, both collective and individual. Edinburgh does not seem to have been the only burgh where this was attempted. Her aim was a moderate and non-partisan administration and she came very close to achieving it in 1565 and 1566. Marian policy recognised and built on the fact that Edinburgh protestantism, and particularly the protestantism of the burgh establishment, suffered for most of the 1560s, if not beyond, from a split personality.

NOTES

1. There is no trace of an election in the council minutes, which show a gap between 26 Sept. and 14 Oct; the first list of members of the new council is not given until 15 Nov. (MS Co. Recs., iii, fos. 50r, 58r; *Edin. Recs.*, iii, 83-4).

2. *Edin. Recs.*, iii, 85-6, 103-5.

3. *Ibid.*, iii, 37-8, 63, 76, 79-82.

4. *Ibid.*, iii, 89, 93; Calderwood, *History*, iii, 121; Knox, *History*, i, 355; JC 1/11, 27 Nov. & 19 Dec. 1560.

5. Knox, *History*, i, 355-6; see Ridley, *John Knox*, 382; Brown, *John Knox*, ii, 108; W. S. Reid, *Trumpeter of God: a Biography of John Knox* (New York, 1974), 210-11.

6. Knox, *History*, i, 358; MS Co. Recs., iii, fo. 77r; see app. v for Harlaw and app. viii for Osborne and the Rhinds.

7. MS Co. Recs., iii, fo. 67v; iv, fos. 2r, 42r. Harlaw was made B.&G. 26 Dec. 1560; he is given as a deacon again on 9 April 1561. Cf. Ridley, *John Knox*, 382.

8. *Edin. Recs.*, iii, 65, 80, 90; MS Co. Recs., 19 Sept. 1567, iv, fo. 203r.

9. *Edin. Recs.*, iii, 90-95, 101-2; *RPC*, i, 216; see app. v for Henderson and app. vi for Brocas.

10. *Edin. Recs.*, iii, 77, 95, 105-7.

11. *Ibid.*, iii, 107-8, 116, 117-8; JC 1/11, 20 July 1561; Pitcairn, *Trials*, i, 409-10.

12. *Edin. Recs.*, iii, 107; MS Co. Recs., iv, fo. 24r; Wood, 'The domestic affairs of the burgh, 1554-1589', 47-8; Calderwood, *History*, ii, 123, 125; *Diurnal*, 65, 283; Knox, *History*, i, 357-8.

13. Pitcairn, *Trials*, i, 410; JC 1/11, 9 Aug. 1561.

14. MS Co. Recs., iv, fo. 12r; Pitcairn, *Trials*, i, 399; Knox, *History*, i, 358-9.

15. Calderwood, *History*, ii, 143; D. M. Rose, 'Mary Queen of Scots and her brother', *SHR*, ii (1905), 157-62; M. Lee, *James Stewart, Earl of Moray* (1953), 81; *CSP Scot.*, i, no. 1001; BL, MS Cott. Calig. B. x, fo. 152r (see *CSP Scot.*, i, no. 1004).

16. *Edin. Recs.*, iii, 122-5, 131.

17. Lee, *James Stewart*, 88; Donaldson, *James V to James VII*, 109; Ridley, *John Knox*, 388-9; see ch. 9.

18. See *Edin. Recs.*, 24 March, 2 & 23 April 1561, iii, 101-2, 103, 105-7.

19. *CSP Scot.*, i, no. 967; *Canongate Book*, 18, 25, 43, 51, 63, 71.

20. Knox, *History*, ii, 12; *Diurnal*, 66; Lee, *James Stewart*, 88-9; Ridley, *John Knox*, 390-91.

21. *CSP Scot.*, i, nos. 1013, 1017; *Edin. Recs.*, iii, 121-2; D. H. Fleming, *Mary Queen of Scots* (1897), 255-6; Lee, *James Stewart*, 89; Reid, 'Coming of the Reformation', 36.

22. *CSP Scot.*, i, no. 1023; *Edin. Recs.*, iii, 65-6, 84-5, 101-2, 125-8, 154; Knox, *History*, ii, 21-2; Keith, *History*, ii, 93; cf. Brown, *John Knox*, ii, 167n.

23. Knox, *History*, ii, 22; Calderwood, *History*, ii, 156; Herries, *Memoirs*, 59; *Edin. Recs.*, iii, 125-7.

24. Lee, *James Stewart*, 90. The episode is badly confused in Reid, 'Coming of the Reformation', 38, which refers to the replacement of the five office-holders by a set of catholic ones, who were in turn replaced by a third set of bailies with the protestant veteran, James Baron, as provost. There is no evidence for this suggestion. The errors seem to arise from the misreading of a letter from Randolph to Cecil of 11 Nov. 1561, which predicted the restoring of Kilspindie and the original bailies as the result of a fracas at a high mass on All Saints' Day; the two are not connected in the brief extract given in *CSP Scot.*, i, no. 1041, but see BL, MS Cott. Calig. B. x, fo. 194r.

25. *CSP. Scot.*, i, no. 1035.

26. Knox, *History*, ii, 23; *CSP Scot.*, i, no. 1041; BL, MS Cott. Calig. B. x, fo. 194; Lee, *James Stewart*, 90; Ridley, *John Knox*, 395.

27. JC 1/11, 31 Dec. 1561; Pitcairn, *Trials*, i, 416-8. Pitcairn traces only three 'of any note' on this assize; he misses Richard Strang and John Johnston, both members of the Kilspindie council of 1559-60, and the protestant activists, Andrew Armstrong and David Kinloch (see apps. v & vii).

28. This was John Weston, who had been given his guildry by right of his wife, Katherine Ewart, in 1549 (*Edin. Burgs.*, 521; she is given as Ewing in *Edin. Recs.*, iii, 133); see also Knox, *Works*, ii, 594.

29. *CSP Scot.*, i, no. 1077; *CSP Foreign, Eliz.*, iv, nos. 855, 883; Winzet, *Tractates*, pp. xxxviii, xli; *Edin. Recs.*, iii, 170; A. Lang, *John Knox and the Reformation* (1905), 218-9.

30. *CSP Scot.*, i, nos. 1049, 1056; *Diurnal*, 70; R. Gore-Browne, *Lord Bothwell, a Study of the Life, Character and Times of James Hepburn, 4th Earl of Bothwell* (London, 1937), 28, 46, 140-42; Prot. Bk. King, iv, fo. 152. Ramsay was a leading merchant and Marian (see app. viii); he was one of the catholic exiles who gave evidence in Paris in 1576 for the nullification of Bothwell's marriage to Mary (*CSP Roman*, ii, nos. 429, 430; A. Fraser, *Mary Queen of Scots* (London, 1969), 448).

31. *Edin. Recs.*, iii, 130, 133, 136-7, 140-41, 163; Wood, 'Domestic affairs of the burgh', 3; cf. Reid, 'Coming of the Reformation', 38.

32. It was repealed 27 January 1563/4 but the literal transcription from the original given in *Edin. Recs.*, iii, 141, has misled Reid, 'Coming of the Reformation', 38, into thinking it was

repealed in Jan. 1563. The other study touching on this episode, M. H. Sanderson, 'Catholic recusancy in Scotland in the 16th century', *Innes Review*, xxi (1970), 92, does not mention this delay.

33. MS Co. Recs., iv, fos. 30r, 46r; *Edin. Recs.*, iii, 133-5; *RPC*, i, 216; see Pitcairn, *Trials*, i, 435 (JC 1/12, 1 Oct. 1563). There were 66 masters in the craft in 1558 (*Edin. Recs.*, iii, 25).

34. *Edin. Recs.*, iii, 131-2, 133, 135, 139, 141-5, 149, 190, 193-4, 196, 215, 227; iv, 342. The judgement of 1569 was recorded in *Balfour's Practicks*, ed. P. G. B. McNeill (Stair Society, 22, 1963), ii, 411. See also W. C. A. Ross, *The Royal High School* (Edinburgh, 1934), 3-4. I am grateful to Professor Gordon Donaldson for pointing out these references.

35. See ch. 9.

36. MS Co. Recs., iv, fos. 43v, 44, 46r, 47r; *Edin. Recs.*, iii, 149-51. The advocates of a policy of accommodation were MacCalzean (ex-provost), Acheson (ex-bailie), Guthrie (ex-dean of guild), Wilson (ex-treasurer), Spens (an ex-councillor), Moscrop and James Watson, assessors; the reluctant majority was made up of the three other ex-bailies, the rest of the retiring ordinary council of 1561-2, including the craft councillors, together with the five new nominees and the other assessor, Richard Strang.

37. Reid, 'Coming of the Reformation', 38; cf. *Edin. Recs.*, iii, 148; *Lord Provosts*, 22.

38. *Edin. Recs.*, iii, 152-3, 162, 164; Pitcairn, *Trials*, i, 435. See ch. 9 and app. vi for further details; for Tennant, see app. viii.

39. *Lord Provosts*, 22.

40. *Edin. Recs.*, iii, 11 & 18 Sept. 1563, 169-70; JC 19/2, 10 Sept. 1563.

41. *Edin. Recs.*, iii, 145-7; *RSS*, v, 1275; see M. Lynch, 'The "faithful brethren of Edinburgh": the acceptable face of protestantism', *BIHR*, li (1978), 198, for the kirk session's resolution of Nov. 1562.

42. *Edin. Recs.*, iii, 191; MS Co. Recs., iv, fo. 129v.

43. Knox, *History*, ii, 70; *Diurnal*, 75; Ridley, *John Knox*, 422; Lee, *James Stewart*, 115-6.

44. Knox, *History*, ii, 87-8; Calderwood, *History*, ii, 230; *CSP Scot.*, ii, no. 36; Ridley, *John Knox*, 428-9; Pitcairn, *Trials*, i, 434-5; JC 1/13 & JC 19/2, 1 Oct. 1563. For details of Armstrong's and Cranston's later activities, see app. v. See also JC 19/2, 23 & 24 Oct. There is no trace of a further appearance by them on the next appointed day, 13 Nov., although the court did sit on that day. It is possible that proceedings were held over until after Knox's appearance before the privy council in mid-Dec.

45. Knox, *History*, ii, 88-9, 93; *CSP Scot.*, ii, no. 36; Ridley, *John Knox*, 429; see also Calderwood, *History*, ii, 243-4.

46. Knox, *History*, ii, 76; *Diurnal*, 67-8; MS Co. Recs., 27 Jan. 1564, iv, fo. 37r; *Edin. Recs.*, iii, 140-41; cf. Reid, 'Coming of the Reformation', 36.

47. Glen and Somer were co-opted as bailies, and Park as treasurer; Baron, Hope and James Adamson returned to the ordinary council, and John Adamson, Harwood, Thomson and Weston retired from it.

48. JC 19/2, 19 Feb. 1564. They reappeared before the court 11 Aug. 1564 except for one, who had fled to Jedburgh (JC 1/12; Pitcairn, *Trials*, i, 452).

49. MS Co. Recs., iv, fos. 95v, 96r. Although only nine of the council were present — the others were James Adamson, Baron, Hope, Park, Preston, Ramsay and Somer — pledges were entered for twelve of its members on 18 & 19 May (JC 19/2).

50. The details here, unless otherwise annotated, are all taken from the account of the trial given in Pitcairn, *Trials*, i, 442-50.

51. These were Bruce, Dickson, Gilbert, Graham, Marjoribanks and Alex. Napier; probably through a printing error only Marjoribanks is noted by Pitcairn (*Trials*, i, 442n; see JC 1/12, 6 June 1564).

52. See ch. 9.

53. Knox, *History*, ii, 101. The two odd men out on the assize were Thomas Henry and John Wilson, who both acquitted on one charge and convicted on two.

54. *De La Brosse Report*, 110-11. Most of these men are discussed in ch. 11 and detailed in app. viii; see app. vi for Spottiswood, his wife, Bessie Marjoribanks, and Lindsay's wife, Margaret Ramsay.

55. Kellebank appeared on the subscription list; he and Cottis were both on the council in the 1560s; Westray was involved in the Riccio conspiracy (*RPC*, i, 436, 463).

56. JC 1/12, 6 June 1564; JC 19/2, 2 July 1564; MS Co. Recs., iv, fo. 105v; *Edin. Recs.*, iii, 183-4; T. A. Kerr, 'The early ministry of John Craig at St. Giles', 1562-1566', *RSCHS*, xiv (1962), 6.

57. *Edin. Recs.*, iii, 185ff; MS Co. Recs., iv, fos. 111r-112r, 129v; *CSP Scot.*, ii, no. 110; Reid, 'Coming of the Reformation', 42.

58. Cf. the account in Knox, *History*, ii, 141-2, and that of Clark in *CSP Scot.*, ii, nos. 169, 171(1); see also Calderwood, *History*, ii, 571. The authorship of Book V of Knox's *History*, which covers the period July 1564-August 1567, is uncertain. It may have been written by Knox's secretary, Richard Bannatyne, or even by David Calderwood, who published the work in 1644. It was, however, probably based on notes gathered by Knox himself. See the introduction to Croft Dickinson's edition of the *History*, i, lxxxviii-cix.

59. *CSP Scot.*, ii, nos. 171(1), 245; Knox, *History*, ii, 163; Lee, *James Stewart*, 146. Clark had been made B.&G. at Moray's request a few months earlier (*Edin. Burgs.*, 109).

60. *CSP Scot.*, ii, no. 171(1); Teulet, *Relations Politiques*, ii, 196; JC 1/12, 26 July 1565; JC 19/2, 15 Aug. 1565; Knox, *History*, ii, 153.

61. *CSP Scot.*, ii, nos. 171, 171(1), 176; *Edin. Recs.*, iii, 195-7; Knox, *History*, ii, 142-3. Clark's letter is only marked 'this Sunday'; from internal evidence it is more likely that it was written on 22 April rather than 29th (see PRO, SP 52/10, fos. 89r-90v).

62. See app. vi for details.

63. There are no entries between 30 June and 3 Aug. 1565; see MS Co. Recs., iv, fo. 130; *Edin. Recs.*, iii, 198.

64. Donaldson, *James V to James VII*, 118; Lee, *James Stewart*, 137ff; *TA*, xi, 376, 380; JC 19/2, 13 July & 15 Aug. 1565; JC 1/12, 26 July 1565; see app. v for details.

65. JC 1/12, 4 Dec. 1565; John Young, a tailor, was on the assize. Paterson continued to serve as a bailie throughout Aug. & Sept. 1565 (MS Co. Recs., iv, fo. 130v).

66. Knox, *Works*, vi, 27; *Diurnal*, 81, 87; *CSP Scot.*, ii, nos. 240, 243; *RSS*, v, 2508; *RPC*, i, 158. See app. v for further details of Johnston and Nicolson.

67. *CSP Scot.*, ii, no. 245; Knox, *History*, ii, 163; *Diurnal*, 82.

68. The only absentee when the council met to defend Knox on 23 Aug. was the deacon of the barbers; *Edin. Recs.*, iii, 199-203; MS Co. Recs., iv, fos. 130v, 131r, 132r, 133v, 134r; Knox, *History*, i, 113; *Lord Provosts*, 22-3; *CSP Scot.*, ii, no. 246; Melville, *Memoirs*, 150.

69. As in Lee, *James Stewart*, 146ff; Reid, 'Coming of the Reformation', 38.

70. Knox, *History*, ii, 169-71; *Diurnal*, 83-4; Teulet, *Papiers d'État*, ii, 108; *Edin. Recs.*, iii, 206-8. This is the outline of the argument followed in Lee, *James Stewart*, 149-51, 165, 170.

71. *Edin. Recs.*, iii, 207-8, 210; *Diurnal*, 84; *RSS*, v, 2358, 3334; Wood, 'Survey of the development of Edinburgh', 28.

72. Knox, *History*, ii, 170-71. The seven were Curle, Gilbert, Little, Preston, Sim, Spens and Wilson.

73. *CSP Scot.*, iv, no. 782; *CSP Roman*, ii, nos. 429, 430; Fraser, *Mary Queen of Scots*, 448; see app. viii for Carmichael, Curle and Little.

74. *Edin. Recs.*, iii, 198, 211; *Thirds of Benefices*, xl; *Edin. Burgs.*, 379; see app. vii for Sim.

75. *RSS*, v, 807, 1659, 1956, 2316; *RPC*, i, 232, 373-7, 400-401.

76. *Edin. Recs.*, iii, 207; see app. viii for Fowler and Stevenson and app. vi for Stevenson's wife, Helen Johnston.

77. Cf. Reid, 'Coming of the Reformation', 38; see *RSS*, v, 3043; Pitcairn, *Trials*, i, 480; JC 1/13, 1 April 1566.

78. Cf. the arguments in Donaldson, *James V to James VII*, 110, 113, and Lee, *James Stewart*, 149-50.

79. See Ridley's interpretation of this incident (*John Knox*, 439-41); also Kerr, 'Thesis', 62; Lang, *John Knox and the Reformation*, 247.

80. *CSP Scot.*, ii, nos. 241, 249, 257; *CSP Foreign, Eliz.*, vii, no. 1451. Cf. Donaldson, *James V to James VII*, 118, with Lee, *James Stewart*, 137, 147.

81. See Pitcairn, *Trials*, i, 475-6; JC 1/12, 12 & 18 Feb. 1566.

82. See ch. 11 for a fuller discussion of this point and apps. vi and viii for details of individual catholics mentioned.

83. See Pitcairn, *Trials*, i, 448, 481; individual verdicts are given in the Young case but not with Yair; see JC 1/13 for the Yair entry, which is undated but follows an entry of 31 July 1566.

84. Ridley, *John Knox*, 452.

85. *CSP Scot.*, ii, nos. 335, 352; *Diurnal*, 88; Ridley, *John Knox*, 444; *Edin. Recs.*, iii, 211n; MS Co. Recs., iv, fo. 143v. A series of men, however, were admitted as burgesses between 1 Feb. & 1 March (*Edin. Accts.*, ii, 213-4).

86. See Knox, *History*, ii, 180n; 35 torches were paid for eight days later (*Edin. Recs.*, iii, 214); there were, including the common clerk, 20 on the council and 14 craft deacons.

87. See Ridley, *John Knox*, 448-9; Lee, *James Stewart*, 165; Brown, *John Knox*, ii, 304-10; Tytler, *History of Scotland*, iii, 215-8, 403-9; see *CSP Scot.*, ii, no, 363, for the document on which the collusion of Edinburgh's two ministers turns.

88. Knox, *History*, ii, 180; Ridley, *John Knox*, 446, 450. See Pitcairn, *Trials*, i, 484-5, for the testimony of James Young and Andrew Armstrong (see app. v), both of whom claimed to have been in Craigmillar's party with 'mony ma'; see also *Diurnal*, 91, which testifies that when the alarm sounded every man 'past to armour'.

89. *CSP Scot.*, ii, no. 363; *Diurnal*, 94; Knox, *History*, ii, 183-4; Ridley, *John Knox*, 450.

90. *Diurnal*, 96-7; Pitcairn, *Trials*, i, 483-5; Knox, *History*, ii, 183-4; see Prot. Bk. Guthrie, iv, fos. 10, 12r.

91. Knox, *History*, i, 357-8; ii, 184; Pitcairn, *Trials*, i, 480; *RPC*, i, 447; *Diurnal*, 97-8; Spottiswoode, *History*, ii, 39. Both Harlaw and Mowbray later returned to Edinburgh.

92. *RPC*, 30 March & 1 April 1566, i, 442, 444; JC 1/13, 8 & 20 April. See app. v for details.

93. See app. v for details of McGill, Millar and Sharp; Cheyne was a burgess (*Edin. Burgs.*, 105; *RPC*, i, 463).

94. *CSP Scot.*, ii, no. 363.

95. See Ridley, *John Knox*, 448-50.

96. MS Co. Recs., iv, fo. 145; *Edin. Recs.*, iii, 212.

97. Lee, *James Stewart*, 173; Donaldson, *James V to James VII*, 122; *RSS*, v, 3149.

98. MS Co. Recs., iv, fos. 156v, 157v; *Edin. Recs.*, iii, 216-7, 219-20.

99. *Ibid.*, iii, 228, 237; MS Co. Recs., iv, fo. 198r.

100. The king's men were Robert Abercrombie, John Harwood, John Preston, John Sim, Alex. & Nicol Uddart; the queen's men were Alan Dickson, Wm. Fowler, Arthur Grainger, Edward Little, Andrew Stevenson and James Mossman, who joined the council after Carberry.

101. Ridley, *John Knox*, 461-2; *CSP Scot.*, ii, no. 563; *BUK*, i, 84-8.

102. *RSS*, v, 3149; *RPC*, i, 487, 494; Donaldson, *James V to James VII*, 125.

103. *RSS*, v, 3334; see also *ibid.*, v, 3342, 3368, 3374, 3386, 3417, 3419, 3452; *Edin. Recs.*, iii, 229, 240-41, 262, 277-9; iv, 56-7.

104. *Ibid.*, iii, 213, 224, 227, 228-9; see MS Co. Recs., iv, fos. 171v, 222r, 230r, 234r, 235v, 238v, 239r.

105. *CSP Scot.*, ii, nos. 461, 498; *Diurnal*, 107; Donaldson, *James V to James VII*, 123, 128-9; Donaldson, *Scottish Reformation*, 73.

106. Lee, *James Stewart*, 191; Knox, *History*, ii, 209; *CSP Scot.*, ii, no. 523; Spottiswoode, *History*, ii, 57; Herries, *Memoirs*, 93; *Hist. King James VI*, 11-12.

107. See Alex. Acheson, James Curle, Sebastian Danelour, Herbert Maxwell, the two Moscrops and Francis Tennant in app. viii.

108. Lee, *James Stewart*, 199.

7

The Wars between Leith and Edinburgh

AFTER the murder and burial of the Regent Moray in January and February of 1570 the focus of the intermittent, shifting, but increasingly bitter struggle between the king's and queen's lords moved to Edinburgh, where it would remain for the next three years and three months until the rendering of the Castle in May 1573. Despite its obvious importance, this watershed in the political and religious history of post-Reformation Scotland has been subjected to surprisingly little detailed study. This is no doubt due in part to the tangled and distasteful nature of the wars, of skirmishes, murder and judicial murder, reprisals and counter-reprisals.[1] Even so, there has been no serious attempt to examine the composition of the rival king's and queen's parties after Langside,[2] nor any attempt to evaluate the effect this traumatic three-year period had on the capital. The two are linked in that it is difficult to imagine a comprehensive study of the civil war period without a more thorough knowledge of what happened in Edinburgh during this time and of the reactions of its inhabitants.

It was later argued, with the benefit of hindsight, by an English memorandum of 1579 that the whole period from James's coronation until the Pacification of Perth in 1573 was a 'continuance of civil wars'. Yet it is difficult to detect many signs of the coming political crisis within Edinburgh itself, apart from prudent preparations in strengthening the walls and an attempt by the council three months after Langside to discover the likely allegiance of the crafts in 'this present troublis'. The burgh's catholic party did not drum up very significant support for Mary in the period up to Langside and the only hint of civil insurrection within the town itself was a demonstration at the Netherbow in October 1568, which was led, not by a Marian, but by the ubiquitous protestant craftsman, James Young.[3] For much of 1568 and at least the first half of 1569 Edinburgh was absorbed in its own double crisis; since April 1568 there had been severe food shortages in the burgh, which were followed by a serious outbreak of the plague in October 1568. Both lingered on until July or August 1569.[4] It is as well to remember that the burgh was only slowly

125

recovering from this serious social and economic crisis when it was enmeshed in its most serious political crisis of the century.

It was not until the political vacuum between the death of Moray in January 1570 and the appointment of Lennox as regent six months later that there were serious attempts by each faction to ensure the commitment of the burgh itself; the first came from the queen's lords in April. The burgh, before the burial of Moray, had appealed to Morton to establish a sitting of the Court of Session and was reassured by the calling of a convention of nobility for 4 March in the town. But the apprehensions of the burgesses were revived, and fully shared by Thomas Randolph, the English ambassador, when the lords who assembled for the funeral dispersed on 18 February and the rival faction assembled at Linlithgow on 3 March. A strict watch was set during the convention and it was thought wise to continue it on 22 March after the king's lords had once again left the town.[5] When news came that Fleming and Maitland had arrived at Seton's house at Niddry, only ten miles away, news that persuaded William Kirkcaldy of Grange, who had accepted Mary's surrender at Carberry and had been appointed Governor of the Castle after Langside, that the time had come to release his prisoner, the staunch Marian, Lord Herries, Randolph decided it was time to leave. His long-standing connections with the protestant faction in the burgh were more likely to prove embarrassing than guarantee his safety in a situation where the town was desperately trying to arrive at a *modus vivendi* with the queen's lords. On 12 April the council, after a good deal of discussion, agreed to a request from them to enter the burgh with the guarded reply that the 'hale nobelities of this realme' was welcome, though on certain limited conditions. Once again, despite his removal to Berwick, Randolph seems to have been privy to the inner workings of the town council; his memorandum to Cecil is more revealing than the subsequent laconic council minute.[6]

There was a good deal of uncertainty within the town as to the intentions of the queen's lords. Rumours flew about that Châtelherault, who had not long returned from France, was putting pressure on Kirkcaldy of Grange to make Seton provost of the town and Captain of the Castle in his place. Despite denials from Grange, these were bound to revive memories of the circumstances of Seton's last term of office in 1559-60, which were sharpened once again by Seton's short temper and loose tongue. His threat to enter the town, by violence if necessary, exactly repeated the bluster of May 1559. The comparison is a very real one, for even Châtelherault admitted, some four months later, that already more damage had been done to towns and to individuals than in the wars of the 1540s or the reformation crisis.[7] The fears of the burgesses were strengthened by Herries' demand for the keys to the ports and his assertion of the right of the lords to recruit within the town. Both demands were resisted, probably because they did not have Grange's backing. It was not until eleven months later, at a crucial point in the heightening tension, that a recruiting drum was beat in Edinburgh's streets. The last of the Marian lords left the town on 28 April for Linlithgow before the imminent arrival of Morton together with Sussex's forces. The episode was not forgotten: fifteen months later, four burgesses were accused of plotting the English invasion.[8]

The significance of the episode of April 1570 was not only that it was the first attempt to win over the town, both physically and in its adherence. It also produced the first real internal differences of opinion within the burgh. It seems likely, though, that the divisions which Sussex reported were more about the tactics that should be adopted in the face of threats and provocation rather than outright and declared allegiance to one party or the other. The response of the activist wing of the protestant faction — two of the four later arraigned by the queen's lords in July 1571, Cunningham and Brown, had distinguished themselves on the night of the Riccio murder — was abrasive and uncompromising; it tried to encourage Morton to eject Huntly and Châtel-herault by himself. But only John Harwood of the four was on the council, whose composition is revealing; it contained almost the whole range of opinions as they later crystallised. It had on it Fullarton, Slater, Chisholm, Dick and William Harlaw, all later staunch supporters of the king's party and singled out for forfeiture or denunciation as rebels in August 1571.[9] Four others on it — John Acheson, Alexander Uddart, William Little and John Preston — had similar sympathies, although they were not always un-qualified. It also contained two who later proved to be outright Marians, Andrew Stevenson and the second craft councillor, James Norval. Acheson's attitude cannot have been a simple one. Like at least three others on the council — William Fowler, and the two bailies, Simon Marjoribanks and Henry Nisbet — he had been preoccupied over the previous three months with an embargo on his goods and ships in France and Flanders.[10] It is significant that, whatever their eventual declared sympathies, only six members of the sitting town council were prosecuted by the Marian lords when they returned to the burgh in 1571. The collective and considered response of the council was muted and ambiguous; after the lords left the town the council found itself saddled with an embarrassing promise to readmit them when they desired and to act in a neutral fashion. It seems likely that Bannatyne's explanation is sub-stantially true; the council had not been able or willing to take a hard line with the Marian lords, it had been manoeuvred into inviting them in the first place and into making the promise that they would be allowed to return, so that divisions within both the council and the town developed over whether the promise was binding and what it meant.[11] The effect, of course, was to make more difficult the council's relationship with Grange, a man to whom they were in a sense committed as they had refused Moray's request to displace him as its provost at the last election in October 1569.

Maitland had predicted that Moray's death would bring about a redistribu-tion of allegiance of the two factions and a certain re-casting of issues, based on the 'regiment' of the realm. The demands of the queen's lords on the burgh were bad enough; the high-handed tone in which they were made, with the hapless council being pilloried for daring to 'prescribe ane order to the nobilitie of the realm' reflecting the conviction of the queen's lords of the right to hold sway over the 'meaner sort', was almost guaranteed to antagonise the Edinburgh establishment or that of any of the burghs.[12] The short occupation of the town by the Marian lords in April 1570 reproduced the fears of 1559; the key issue again was not religion or ideological preference, but self-preservation. Issues had indeed been recast; the one which dominated all others was the 'regiment' of the burgh.

The return of Morton to the burgh on 29 April, reinforced by Lennox two weeks later, meant that it was the turn of the king's lords to try to secure the burgh's loyalty. Morton reported that a muster of 1,500 men of the town had been held immediately, each being made to swear allegiance to the king. However, it is likely, given these numbers, that this promise was as badly kept as a second one to refrain from approaching any of the Marians or the queen herself to arrange the release of the merchandise held in France.[13] Throughout July and August 1570 tension persisted, unaffected by Lennox's appointment as regent. Grange's intentions were still in doubt as his programme of fortification continued; Randolph's opinion of him wavered almost from day to day. The town was a hotbed of rumour; there was word of the goods held in France, the imminent return of Mary, an invasion by the Duke of Alva from the Netherlands, a plot by Grange to hang the leading king's men among the burgesses, and — a more likely prospect — the return of the queen's lords. Grange was equally susceptible to rumour; his preparations became near-frantic when he heard that Sussex was planning to lay siege to the Castle.[14]

The phoney civil war period continued until the end of 1570, with actions largely governed by fears rather than realities. James McGill, the clerk register, and Archibald Douglas of Glenbervie had been left in the burgh by Lennox on 9 August. McGill's election as provost on 3 October was, Herries maintains, designed to forestall a suspected attack by Huntly and Kerr of Fernihurst, which was also the reason for Lennox's hasty return. This seems a likely explanation, as such an attack would have threatened the convention due to meet on the 13th to confirm Lennox's appointment. The new council that was elected along with McGill looks like a more resolute body; there is no evidence that any one of them had Marian sympathies.[15] It seems that precautions were taken to ensure the election of two craft councillors who favoured the king's lords, with the first ticket from the craft deacons being refused. The precautions were justified; two on the original ticket, Alan Purves and George Smith, did remain in the burgh during its occupation, whereas the two eventually chosen, Mungo Brady and James Inglis, both moved to Leith.[16]

By this time the question of the arrested goods in France was, in the eyes of the king's lords, becoming serious, as the continuing plight of the merchants pointed to one of two courses: either they abandoned the king's lords to seek redress or the lords themselves took action to seek redress on their behalf at the expense of those who were suspected of having engineered the manoeuvre.[17] The whole episode points to two patterns that would become common during the civil wars. It was difficult to reach agreement in a situation where both parties, as a king's party memorandum frankly admitted, did not hesitate to 'take advantage of others'; these matters of personal interest would have to be settled either before or in any agreement ending the wars. At the same time, material and personal considerations tended to produce allegiance which was marginal, hedged or temporary. The dilemma of Archibald Stewart was particularly acute; he was a close personal friend of Knox and notionally a supporter of Lennox, but after his marriage to Helen Acheson, the widow of the richest merchant in Edinburgh of his day, he had seen a large proportion of her merchandise in France arrested by her husband's agent, William Aikman, at the instigation of Sebastian Danelour, a Marian dependant. But even after Stewart agreed to deliver money to Grange after his goods had been released, doubts persisted as to where his real loyalties lay. By January 1571 it seems that Mary had herself begun to realise that the exercise might prove to be counter-productive. The Marian agent, John Chisholm, agreed with this analysis, advising Grange in February to beware of the merchants for 'the most part of them are nothing worth'. It says much for the confused motives of the burgh's merchants that when Morton and McGill arrived in Berwick on 18 April 1571, at a time when events in the burgh were fast approaching crisis point, they found there three of the sitting town council, anxiously trying to negotiate passports to reach their arrested merchandise. At least two of the three, John Acheson and Nicol Uddart, later proved themselves devoted supporters of the king's party.[18] The reactions of the merchants in the impending crisis should not be over-simplified; a number of the most prominent among them faced an acute conflict of interests.

The reaction of the craftsmen to the situation in the burgh was not straightforward or uniform either. Both Bannatyne and Calderwood accuse the deacons of crafts of conniving with Grange in the next event to shake the burgh, the 'outrage' of 21 December, when Grange broke into the tolbooth to release one of his men held for assault. It may well be that both the English government and the king's lords subsequently made great play with the incident for propaganda purposes, but initially both Lennox and the town council made little of it for fear of provoking fresh disturbances within the town. The council minutes did not even mention it and the regent duly renewed the abstinence when it lapsed nine days later. The one who refused to remain quiet was Knox, whose sermon of 24 December roundly condemned Grange, implying that he was a murderer and cut-throat. On the face of it, the involvement of the deacons seems plausible; Knox's second sermon of 31 December recalled the craftsmen's riots of 1560 and 1561.[19] But both Bannatyne's and Calderwood's accusations are very vague, as is the account in the *Diurnal*; no names are given anywhere. The same deacons had refused to give a pledge of support to Grange only four months before. Only four of the deacons were queen's men and only two of those can be shown to have remained in the town beyond January 1572.[20] Although the deacons were not

K

to prove to be as staunchly for the king's party as the sitting council, they were far from being Grange supporters to a man and their collective involvement in the fracas of 21 December seems unlikely. Of course there were individual and possibly influential craftsmen who were closely linked with Grange; one of them was Walter Wawane, an ex-deacon of the tailors, who led a procession from the Castle through the streets of the burgh to St. Cuthbert's Church on 27 February shortly before the meeting of the General Assembly. It should not be concluded from this that the tailors were predominantly queen's men.[21]

By March 1571 relations between Grange and the burgh were deteriorating almost by the day. On the 19th Grange, in response to a proclamation from the regent forbidding the townspeople to enter into his service, had the recruiting drum beaten through the streets. This was a serious development, for it had been avoided throughout the occupation of the town by the queen's lords the previous April. The next day, some of his men occupied Holyrood. Food supplies belonging to Edinburgh merchants were seized in Leith. More seriously still, on 28 March his men took and fortified the steeple of St. Giles'. As before, there seems to have been divisions within the council as to how to react to the worsening situation. One of the bailies, John Sim, was censured by his colleagues on 30 March for releasing a man held for assault under threat from 'the lordis'. Obviously Sim did not want a repetition of the incident of 21 December. On 8 April Grange went one step further; he prevented a proclamation from the regent forbidding any dealing with him being read at the market cross. In its place he had a proclamation of his own read out five days later, which fell just short of declaring unequivocally for the queen's lords. There could, however, have been little doubt as to what his intentions were with a steady stream of Marian lords arriving in the burgh from 5 April onwards for their convention.[22]

By 16 April this process had gone far enough for the English agent, William Herlle, to report to Burghley that the town was now in Grange's hands, although the council had tried to reassure Lennox of their loyalty on the 14th and repeated their assurances to Morton and McGill on the 20th. But Morton and McGill could not have been encouraged at finding three of the council in Berwick on their own business on the 18th. Matters did not improve with the departure of some of the Marian lords; a series of minor incidents followed. The Hamiltons arrived on the night of 19/20 April. That was enough in itself to persuade some of Knox's friends to keep a watch on his house. Their fears were realised when James Inglis, one of the craft councillors and a staunch king's man, was taken into the Castle by Arthur Hamilton of Myreton only two days later. His arrest provoked both the council and the deacons to appeal to Grange for his release. On the 25th there was a bloody brawl between some young men of the town and Grange's men guarding the steeple. Two days later, Grange had the town's artillery taken into the Castle. On 28 April the final provocation to the council came with the arrest of the provost, James McGill.[23]

The months of March and April 1571 had revealed an essential conflict of interests between Grange and the council. Grange, unconvinced of
the success of the French manoeuvre to bind the leading overseas merchants to
the Marian cause, was ever suspicious of the town and ready to see danger particularly in the jealously guarded privileges of the burgesses to watch and
ward. His arrest of eight burgesses, all armed, on the night of 28/29 April confirmed his suspicions.[24] It was these seditious activities of Lennox's supporters,
so his proclamation of 30 April maintained, that jeopardised the formerly
good relations between the town and the Castle. The concern of the council
was obviously to prevent a state of anarchy developing in the town and
maintain their own authority, but also to keep access to the town open. With
the arrival of Morton at Dalkeith on 27 April and the first exchange of fire
between the rival forces at the Netherbow port on the 29th, this precarious
modus vivendi began to break down.[25]

The beginning of 'the wars between Leith and Edinburgh' has been dated by
Calderwood as the skirmish on 29 April. Yet there was *not* an immediate coup
within the burgh. The last entry in the council register, a rather optimistic
interpretation of the meaning of Grange's proclamation, was made on 1
May.[26] On the same day the keys of the gates were taken from the bailies and
construction of a buttress above the butter tron started; work on a second
buttress at the West Bow began the following day. On the 3rd, after the arrival
of Châtelherault, accompanied by 400 men, the tolbooth and the house of its
keeper, Andrew Lindsay, were occupied and the resident scribes forced to
move; the next day, further defensive work on St. Giles' was begun, this time
on the structure itself. Knox was finally persuaded to leave the town on 5 May,
but the motives involved were as much concerned with avoiding a violent
clash between soldiers and townspeople as with his safety. The pulling down
of houses near the Netherbow to improve the town's defences began shortly
after. On 10 May a curfew was declared and a number of suspected supporters
of the regent were taken into protective custody on the 13th for the duration of
the siege. Forced labour on the fortifications began the next day. The frantic
preparations ensured that the holding of the famous 'creeping parliament' in
the Canongate in competition with the Marian parliament in the tolbooth on
14 and 16 May was no more than a symbolic gesture, even if there was an
accompaniment of cannonfire.[27]

However, it is significant that during this time the town council was not
dismissed. Grange, according to the *Diurnal*, had second thoughts about his
proclamation of 29 April ordering all supporters of the regent to leave the
town within six hours. Even though the order was repeated in a second
proclamation on 10 May, the policy of the occupying lords was equivocal.
John Sim and 'certane of the counsall' were actually refused permission to
leave the burgh to join the regent at Leith. Rather than be exiled, some suspected king's men were temporarily taken into the Castle and duly released on
20 May after the siege of the burgh was raised. It does seem that there was a

hiatus in the normal day-to-day activities of the council during the actual period of hostilities; even preaching and prayer were suspended between 14 and 19 May. But after 20 May the peculiar situation of before resumed; Craig continued to preach in St. Giles' and did so until 12 June.[28] The threads of day-to-day burgh administration were picked up again; the burgh register of deeds, which had broken off after 23 April, resumed on 26 May, with John Adamson, later a very committed king's man, still acting as a bailie.[29] On 30 May Hew Lauder, one of the staunchest Marian supporters in the town, was created a burgess and guild, the last entry in the guild register until August 1572.[30] John Robeson's protocol book shows that the provost, James McGill, and all four bailies were still acting in an offical capacity on 4 June, two days after the first really serious skirmish of the wars at Edmonston Edge, where McGill's servant, Adam Wauchope, was killed. It is not clear exactly when the town council was expelled. The indictments against queen's party burgesses are not very specific and bracket the dismissal of the council and the general expulsion of their fellow burgesses together, in the months of April, May and June 1571. The one drawn up against John Newlands is a little more precise, mentioning 'at the leist June'.[31] The systematic demolition of houses at the head of the Canongate had started on or about 9 June. From the complaints of the king's lords, now at Stirling, on 14 June, it is obvious that large numbers had already left the town and that the council house had been completely taken over. The *Diurnal* dates the exodus in the period up to 6 June. Yet the protocol book of Alexander Guthrie, the town clerk, has entries for 1, 5, 7 and 9 June, with Mungo Fairlie officiating on each occasion. It is true that Guthrie and Fairlie were later called to account for remaining in the town, but Fairlie did not become a pawn of the queen's party until after he had capitulated to their threats more than a month later. It seems likely that the town council was only dismissed sometime between 9 June and the proclamation of the 13th requiring all the inhabitants to acknowledge only the sovereignty of the queen. This would also indicate that there was only a vacuum of about ten days until a new provost, bailies and council were appointed on 20 June.[32]

It seems that, given these new-found circumstances, there needs to be some reinterpretation of motives. The council and probably a large proportion of the eventual exiles were not anxious to rush off to join Morton, although the council was concerned to re-pledge its loyalty to the regent, particularly after a formal request for entry into the town had been refused on 12 May.[33] McGill was still in the town when his servant was killed at Edmonston Edge on 2 June. It seems plausible that the council was anxious to cling on, if not to power, at least to office until the temporary crisis, as it hoped it would be, subsided. This was not the first time that the town had been occupied by the Marian lords and precedent pointed to the likelihood of their survival. If the indictments of 1573 are to be accepted, there was from April 1571 onwards the new and added difficulty of large-scale and fairly continuous riots, mostly of craftsmen; the estimate of one thousand rioters, however, looks like judicial exaggeration.[34]

The prospect of a breakdown of order would have been more likely to have encouraged the ruling establishment to stay on rather than to leave.

From Grange's and the Marian lords' point of view, there was much to be said for keeping on at least the framework and trappings of burghal administration and authority; a powerless town council, however disaffected, was better than none. The absence of any mention of atrocities in any of the contemporary sources and the fairly gentle treatment given to suspected supporters of Lennox underline the argument that the queen's lords were aware of the dangers of anarchy and concerned to avoid conjuring up chilling memories of the reoccupation of the town by French troops in November 1559. It was the king's party that was put in difficulty by such tactics; its proclamation of 20 May was at pains to stress that it wished the proper administration of the burgh to continue along with the law courts, parliament and the court itself. The bishop of Galloway, taking Craig's place in the pulpit, pushed the point home, emphasising the town's absent ministers.[35] It looks as if the queen's lords changed their minds about a policy of immediate exclusion, preferring to allow the sitting council to continue as long as was necessary to effect a fairly smooth takeover. Although the town remained an armed camp, it was at least in name not under martial law. Burgh administration did continue.[36]

The queen's lords also attempted to take over the normal processes of central administration, though perhaps with less success. The three clerks of the Court of Session were forbidden to leave the burgh on 14 May.[37] Maitland boasted to Beaton that the king's lords would find it difficult to re-establish the court as the clerks, papers and processes were all held in Edinburgh; the result, he considered, would be 'a great hinder in thair authoritie'.[38] The last entry in the court book was for 6 April but somehow it turned up in Leith, where proceedings began again on 12 November 1571.[39] The last dated testament in the register of testaments of the commissary court of Edinburgh was for 30 April;[40] the register of acts and decreets of the same court broke off on 2 May.[41] But the commissary court's register of deeds and protests continued until 18 June after a break between 3 May and 6 June, with Clement Little, one of the three commissaries still performing his duties. No reprisals were taken against Little for this; he was a member of an extremely respectable Edinburgh family which was strongly pro-regent, and he formally resumed his duties at Leith five months later along with the other commissaries.[42]

The Marian manoeuvre met with only limited success; the registers of the Court of Session remained in the town, but the justiciary court book and most of the books and papers of the commissary court appeared in Leith shortly after the king's proclamation of 23 October that all the administrative processes of the crown and the courts of justice be transferred to Leith. The desertion of the commissaries was only remedied by the queen's party late in April 1572, when they were formally dismissed and substitutes appointed. By that time, the action was more of a gesture than a practical step towards answering the administrative details of ruling the town; a number of wills made in Edinburgh during the occupation were registered at Leith, both before and after the raising of the siege. The support of lawyers was one of the most important weapons available to the king's party.[43]

Nonetheless, there does seem to have been a serious attempt made by the queen's lords to set up an alternative administration in Edinburgh in the summer of 1571, both in central and municipal government. The custumar, Robert Watson, a consistent protestant activist throughout the 1560s, was replaced on 20 July by Cuthbert Ramsay, one of the new bailies. As well as a new loyalist council and officials, a new kirk session was also appointed, although only two of its members can be traced.[44] Other officers of the kirk were also replaced; Robert Cunningham, the collector of kirk rents, was not allowed to leave the burgh until he had handed over and settled his accounts.[45] These efforts at establishing their credibility as a new regime and the stress on maintaining as much as possible of a continuity in burgh life and administration pointed to the increasing likelihood that the Marian lords were set for a long stay in the town.

The capture of Edinburgh, together with the changes that had been made within it in June 1571, shortly after the raising of the first siege, dictated both the military and diplomatic tactics of the king's lords for the rest of the wars. Lennox had explained to Elizabeth on 28 May that his first priority was still to recapture the Castle and town. A plan had been devised by mid-June to spread his limited manpower over the country as a whole yet still retain some pressure on Edinburgh. The beginnings of the protracted campaign to cut the town off from its supplies of food and fuel can be traced to the latter half of the same month. As the appointed dates of the second set of rival parliaments in August approached, the tempo of the near-daily minor but bloody skirmishes increased. Sir William Drury, the marshal of Berwick, reported on 4 August that the king's lords intended to attack the town about a week later to forestall the parliament, but the assault was postponed. Despite Lennox's gloomy estimates, mostly for Elizabeth's benefit, of the forces and firepower necessary to take the town, it was certainly not impregnable. Calderwood thought that the Netherbow could have been taken during a running skirmish on 16 June, and a carefully devised surprise attack on the same port on 22 August was foiled only by a passer-by raising the alarm. The warning did not go unheeded twice; the port was considerably strengthened almost immediately.[46] The skirmishing around the town increased during the meetings of the rival parliaments at Stirling and Edinburgh. Fifty king's men, including some of the exiles, and twenty queen's men from the burgh were captured in the same affray on 30 August.[47] The increasing frequency and scale of these actions was interrupted by the night raid of the queen's lords on Stirling on 3 September, which resulted in the death of Lennox. The botched Stirling coup was the turning point in the wars. The sustained and full-scale siege of Edinburgh began in earnest only after the Stirling parliament and the election of Mar as regent on 5 September.[48] After that the focus of the king's lords remained firmly fixed on the town.

The situation in Edinburgh also ended any remaining hopes of a temporary truce; the queen's lords would agree to one only on the basis of the maintenance of the existing *status quo*, together with satisfactory military precautions, whereas the king's lords were unlikely to agree to anything less than the *status quo ante* of January 1571, when Lennox had last left the town. Their differences centred on the point that 'no innovation . . . be made in the town either in the name of one authority or the other'. To the queen's party this meant the continuation of the intruded council and the exclusion of the armed Edinburgh band as well as the king's lords, except as private individuals. The exiles could not agree to there being 'nothing publicly executed in Edinburgh' on this basis and the regent had too few forces available to risk antagonising the three hundred strong Edinburgh band. Lennox was willing to allow Grange's soldiers to remain in the Castle, but could not contemplate allowing them even into the upper parts of the town, although pressed by Drury to do so; nor could he agree to try to prevent the return of the exiles.[49] Much of the force of Lennox's case as presented to Elizabeth rested on his claim that the 'most part' of the burgh's inhabitants supported the king and had been expelled as a result. The only proper course, he maintained, was *first* to regain the town and then to renegotiate a truce. This remained the negotiating position of the king's party; Mar was still holding to it in January 1572.[50]

While it is very doubtful, at least in July 1571, that Lennox's claim was factually true, it was certainly pressure on him from the exiles and the value of their support, both in terms of men and money, that obliged him to hold to a hard line over the truce and the terms on which the town might be reopened. The 'Edinburgh band', the exiles in arms at Leith, had been formed on 23 June 1571, only three days after the intrusion of a new council on the town. Its elected leader was an obvious choice; Adam Fullarton, the expelled dean of guild, was the undisputed secular leader of Edinburgh's protestant party. The relative numbers of the rival armed groups of burgesses are difficult to ascertain precisely. According to the *Diurnal*, the queen's men in the town paraded the new bailies through the town and mustered five hundred men in the Greyfriars' yard on 7 July, and the exiles responded with a muster of two or three hundred men at Leith. This would, however, only account for half of the able-bodied men in the burgh who mustered in May 1570. The loyalty of the burgesses was crucial to both sides. Maitland admitted just before the first siege that he had only a hundred men who were not either mercenaries or from the town. Although Bannatyne claimed that the king's men numbered over four thousand at the start of the siege of October 1571, John Case's estimates were more precise and realistic: the king's party, he reported, was then a thousand strong, including one hundred of the exiles; the queen's party had about seven hundred men in the town, which would confirm the figure given in the *Diurnal*.[51]

The desperate need of the queen's lords to supplement their men under arms helps to explain the contradictory stream of proclamations which flowed out of Edinburgh. On 25 June, their treatment of the townspeople took a new turn with a proclamation threatening the confiscation of the goods of those who had left and a summons of forfeiture against the provost, McGill. Yet a second proclamation, of 13 July, invited all the inhabitants of the burgh to return, even those who had fought for the king's party. On the 20th, the stick was re-applied, threatening all who moved to Leith with death. The author of the *Diurnal* is inconsistent at this point; although he claims that those who remained were ready to join in every skirmish with relish, he also admits that eighty burgesses fled after and in spite of the threats contained in the proclamation of 20 July.[52] It seems likely that the queen's lords had by now three objects in mind: to keep as many burgesses within the burgh as possible; to isolate them from their fellows, first halting the daily passage of burgesses between the burgh and Leith and secondly sifting those who had remained to ensure their loyalty; and denouncing those who had already left. It was the last of these policies which embittered the exiles.

The process of reprisal and counter-reprisal began in earnest with the arraigning of four prominent burgesses for maintaining the king's authority on 18 July, the day after Captain Culane, a distinguished and respected soldier, had been executed in Leith.[53] With the meetings of the rival parliaments in August 1571 the process accelerated. On 18 August thirty burgesses were denounced as rebels by the Marian parliament; perhaps surprisingly, only four of the thirty were members of the excluded council. Among the long list of forfeitures produced on 29 August were seventeen Edinburgh burgesses.[54] The rival Stirling parliament contented itself with forfeiting only five burgesses, including two of the new bailies.[55] The processes of escheat and forfeiture of burgesses of the queen's party did not begin in earnest until after the privy council resumed sitting in Leith on 13 September. By contrast, the processes of the queen's lords against the exiles were already well in hand by then.[56]

The preparations for the siege of the burgh went on for a full month after the Stirling parliament. The artillery of Dumbarton and Stirling castles was only moved on 3 October. However meagre the resources of the attackers, the combination of preparations for the siege and propaganda from the king's side triggered a further exodus from the burgh. A proclamation of the Stirling parliament, presented to Maitland on 27 September, represented an improvement in their propaganda tactics; it cleverly combined the prospects of the inevitable success of the king, the 'rysing sone', and the stability which would only come when that happened.[57] The *Diurnal* goes so far as to say that scarcely ten per cent of the inhabitants remained in the town during the siege of October 1571, so widespread was the expectation of Mar's victory. Alexander Guthrie, the town clerk, was one of those who chose this moment to take flight.[58] In response, Grange resorted to a policy of laying waste the countryside around the town. The closes on the east side of the burgh, still the most vulnerable part of his defences, were blocked up, to the dismay of their owners, and a new gate constructed at the Netherbow; houses on the outskirts of the town, in the Potterrow, were burned to the ground. His preparations, particularly in stockpiling food, had been thorough; Case estimated that he had ample supplies to last the winter, and shortages became severe only after May 1572.[59]

On the eve of the siege and in the midst of frantic preparations for it inside a largely deserted town, the Marian lords took the time and trouble to set in motion the annual election process on 3 October. Why should they have bothered? The answer lies in the fact that the exiles had already elected a new council; an entry for 2 October in the protocol book of John Robeson shows that McGill had been re-elected provost and that Adamson and Acheson, two of the bailies of the council of 1570-71, had been re-elected. Six of the seven office-holders of this new body had served on the council dismissed in June. The imputed challenge to the authority of the queen's lords was clear. The character of the queen's bailies, however, reflected the limited talent available in the crisis of October 1571; not one of them had been on the council before.[60]

The expected swift capture of the town did not materialise. According to both Bannatyne and Calderwood the siege began on 9 October, but matters did not begin in earnest until the regent's artillery started its bombardment on the 16th. This lasted only four days and was not followed up with an assault on the walls. The king's forces withdrew down the Canongate on the 20th and fell back on Leith the next day. Bannatyne is unable to explain the precise reasons for this sudden retreat, but the town had proved a tougher nut to crack than either the king's lords or Drury had expected. The lords now maintained that 3,000 extra foot and 200 horse were necessary in addition to their existing men to take town and Castle; some of the estimates of their English advisers were more extravagant still. The tactics of the lords changed to a policy of slow attrition, although here as well there was a good deal of over-optimism; Morton maintained on 25 November that the town was without food, fuel or cash.[61]

Although Morton in particular had hopes of a successful assault on the unwalled side of the town, the tempo of the wars had distinctly slackened. The first serious skirmish for almost eight weeks took place on 10 December. The occasional bloody skirmish could not disguise the fact that this was for the most part a period of phoney war; prisoners openly walked the streets of Leith, licences were granted by the regent to Edinburgh burgesses to return to the town to fetch their goods. By 13 December the king's lords had realised that these licences were being used as an excuse to continue trafficking with the beleagured town and withdrew them temporarily. The problem of cutting the town off was not a simple or clear-cut one; the size of the town and ease of access to it from all sides put a complete economic blockade beyond their limited resources.[62] It was unrealistic to expect that the burgh's patterns of commerce and trade, which were so based on trafficking between Leith and

Edinburgh, would be easy to block off. If goods could be collected from the burgh, could rents? The difficulty for the king's lords was to control the loyalties of a large population, most of whose support was convenient or enforced, marginal or temporary.

The first attempt of the king's party at trying to assess the individual loyalties of the inhabitants came in October 1571, when the provost and council in exile were instructed to make a roll of those who were still in the town so that they might be excluded from trading with other burghs. This, of course, could affect only the merchants in the town. The difficulties in drawing up an accurate list were not eased by the fact that access to and from the town was not difficult and that, according to the same proclamation, a number of the wealthiest of the merchants had quietly moved to various parts of the country. The privy council sitting at Leith did make some attempts to ensure at least the neutrality of such men; John Spens, a prominent member of the council in the earlier 1560s who had been shown favour by Mary, had pledges entered to guarantee that he remained safely out of the way at Penicuik. The serious business of large-scale denunciations, escheats and forfeitures did not begin until early in 1572; only seven inhabitants were escheated between September and December 1571.[63] Matters quickened a little in the first half of January 1572 when a further eight were escheated, including one of the sitting bailies, Peter Martin, whose office made him an obvious target.[64] The list of 195 inhabitants who were summoned to appear at Leith on 31 January brought a larger dimension to the efforts of the king's party. It certainly produced some response from the edgy remaining loyalists; what is difficult is to be sure how great the response was. Although Bannatyne claims that 'a grit part found souertie', the numbers to be found in the justiciary court book are sparse.[65] On the other hand, the only evidence to indicate any attachment to the queen's party for a large number of burgesses is their inclusion on this list. The order given in the list should not be taken too literally; the first name on it was Thomas MacCalzean, who was readmitted to the Court of Session a month later after turning up in Leith. MacCalzean's distinction lay not in his being a leader of the queen's party in the burgh but in his impeccable sense of timing in being the first to be granted a formal remission by the king's party.[66] It seems reasonable to conclude that the warning produced a sizeable reaction among the ranks of the inhabitants, which had swollen again since the abortive siege of October 1571, despite a counter-proclamation from the Castle on 21 January warning all the exiles to present themselves in the burgh.[67]

It was from this point onwards that the dual campaign of attrition and victimisation of the burgesses gained momentum. As the formal threats of denunciation and forfeiture by the Castilians could carry little conviction in the circumstances, a new tactic was devised to put pressure on the exiles. On 3 February the house of the provost, James McGill, was thrown down; he was the first victim in a notorious campaign which continued over the next five months. The next to suffer, about a fortnight later, was Nicol Uddart, the major financier of the king's party. In all, perhaps as many as fifty houses were demolished. Their owners do not all seem to have been fervently committed king's men; they certainly did include some activists, like Fullarton and David Kinloch, some of the bailies of the council in exile, like John Acheson and Andrew Slater, but also many of the waverers, trimmers or marginally committed. They included Uddart, who lent money to both sides, and Helen Acheson and Michael Gilbert, who had been pressured into supporting the queen's lords early in 1570 by the arresting of their goods in France.[68] The authors of the *Diurnal* and the *History of King James the Sext,* who seem to have remained in the town throughout, maintain that it was done to supplement the town's dwindling fuel supplies. It is true that the weather continued very cold and that coal was very scarce, particularly after the king's forces sabotaged the machinery of the coal pits around the town. While it is possible that this may have been the reason for the first of the demolitions, it can hardly explain the continuing activities of the 'Captain of the Chimneys' and his band into the spring and early summer of 1572. In February the council in exile had petitioned the privy council, pointing out that the demolition campaign was designed to force the exiled burgesses to lend money to the Castilians and asked that a proclamation be issued banning such loans. It looks as if this was yet another tactic of the queen's party to gain the financial support of the wealthier merchants which misfired. An anonymous report, endorsed by Drury, claimed that fifty of the largest houses in the town were being ransomed for 50,000 merks. Much of the animus and a good deal of the propaganda of the exiles stemmed from this campaign.[69]

The other object of the exiles' anger was the inhabitants of the Canongate; the same petition of 25 February claimed that the majority of its inhabitants were trading with the enemy. About six weeks later they were all evicted as part of an attempt to draw a two-mile strip of no-man's land around the town. The shock for them did not end there; not only were they forcibly moved to Leith, but when there they had to pay taxes towards the upkeep of the regent's forces. It is not clear how heavy this burden was on the exiles of both Edinburgh and the Canongate; the only indication comes in the testament of a fairly wealthy merchant, John Morrison, whose debts included £8 as two months' wages for a man of war. It is noticeable that Morrison owed this to the town, which must have continued to bear the responsibility for taxing its own burgesses and for financing the Edinburgh band. This, though, was taxation on an unprecedented scale.[70]

The attempt at putting a stranglehold on the burgh's food supplies continued with the destruction of the town mills early in April, which provoked the queen's lords into an unsuccessful attempt to burn down the mills around Leith. The blockade was not watertight; despite the severity of the penalties against it, smuggling of food certainly continued. Despite the occupation of houses in the surrounding area by the king's forces, the Castilians did have some success in running the blockade, although their attempts were the product of increasing desperation; on 18 June the house of Alexander Pirie, a maltman near Merchiston, was raided, probably with his own connivance.[71] Even so, the struggle, which by now was for the stomachs rather than the hearts and minds of the remaining inhabitants, had its effects.

Prices in the beleaguered burgh had risen substantially by May 1572, as the anonymous author of the *Diurnal* complained. Ale, at 10d a pint, was more than twice the statutory price of 1569, but other commodities were still surprisingly cheap. The prices of wheat, barley and meal were still below the peak reached during the dearth and plague of 1569. The Marian administration in the town, clearly worried by the rocketing price of malt, issued a proclamation in June holding the price of ale down to a quarter of its market rate and malt to the unrealistically low level of 20s a boll — which was a pious attempt to set the clock back more than fifteen years. The effect of the proclamation, as the *Diurnal's* author drily remarked, was only to make drink scarcer. Prices continued to rise into July 1572, but not at a uniform rate. It can be inferred from the 10d pint of May that the market price of a boll of malt was then about £7; less than two months later, it had risen to £10. Over the same period wheat increased five-fold in price and salt four-fold, but meal by only a half and meat by a third.[72] The phenomenal increases in bread prices can be explained by the deliberate campaign waged by both sides from April 1572 onwards to break down the mills around the town.

Price inflation at Leith also varied from one commodity to another; meal and salt were less than half the price fetched in the burgh, mutton and bread almost a third of the Edinburgh prices, which would point to the fact that the queen's party had not been particularly successful in sabotaging the mills around the Water of Leith. But malt, which stood at £6 a boll in July 1572, must have been almost as scarce in Leith as it was in Edinburgh. It seems clear that the dramatically steepening curve in the price of wheat and salt between May and July 1572 can explain both the exodus of the burgh's poorer inhabitants and the continuing problems which the king's party had with traders running the blockade; the edict against inhabitants of the Canongate having dealings with the rebels was reissued on 12 July. Profit margins which ranged from sixty-six per cent on malt to a hundred and fifty per cent on mutton and bread could not be ignored lightly.[73] Although the shortages in the town in the crisis months of June and July 1572 must have had catastrophic results, it would be as well to remember that general price levels, both in Edinburgh and Leith, had risen seriously during the wars. The return of the exiles to the town did not bring about a fall in prices, although the end of the wars did produce a settling effect. The market price of wheat fell from its peak of £10 a boll in July 1572 to £3 a boll by December 1573. Even so, this figure was almost as much as its price during the dearth of 1569. The result was that, whereas the burgh had managed to hold on to the symbolically significant 4d loaf up until 1571, by late 1573 it conceded the 6d loaf, which by 1587 had become the 8d loaf, when the price of wheat returned to £6 a boll. The price of mutton, even in Leith, was three times what it had been fifteen years earlier.[74] Increasing economic hardship was an inevitable and general consequence of the wars.

There was a fairly steady stream of refugees out of the town from February 1572 onwards. Yet the attitude of both parties to them had changed. It was now the king's party rather than Grange that had fears of a fifth column developing; a proclamation of 3 May, aimed at the most recent arrivals, threatened them with death if they stayed in Leith. Life from now on became extremely hazardous for what the *History of King James the Sext* called the 'neutrall people of Edinburgh'.[75] On the other hand, it was by now clear that Grange was happy enough to have the demands on his dwindling food supplies diminished. While Bannatyne may be exaggerating in saying that the poor were 'put out of the town' in May, it is difficult to see how they could physically survive in a situation of rampaging price inflation. By mid-June the Castilians were even rooting out the young able-bodied apprentices and servants who had been left behind by their masters to protect their goods and property. The Castilians' response to a further king's party proclamation of 21 June was two-fold; those who wished to leave were allowed to do so, but a counter-proclamation tried to enforce a distinction between those who would fight and those who merely wanted to remain in the burgh. Drury admitted that the response to this proclamation had been disappointing; the refugees were now limited to women and children. It is clear that the rump of those who still remained in the burgh from late June onwards were committed Marians.[76]

Throughout the winter and spring of 1571-2 there had been near-continual pressure on the king's party to agree to a truce. In the meantime, the attitude of the exiles had hardened. After the last major affray before the truce six of the queen's men who had been captured were executed after a summary trial, including an ageing schoolmaster and ex-priest, William McKie. The house of David Kinloch, who had been one of those who clamoured most loudly for harsh treatment, was demolished the following day.[77] The spiralling effect of reprisals and counter-reprisals made it difficult for Mar to negotiate on the basis of a return to the *status quo ante* of January 1571. The exiles were reluctant to return to a situation so dependent on Grange's good will. So the precedents of 1570 and 1571 were produced again for Elizabeth's benefit: the breach of the tolbooth in December 1570; the use of the Castle as a refuge for Marian sympathisers during the winter of 1570-71; Grange's threats against the craftsmen. There was some force in these arguments, for Maitland himself pointed out in August 1572 that the Castle was always 'able to cast the ballance', but an equally telling point was the fear of the future role of the loyalist rump left in the town. One of the major calculations which affected the policy of both Mar and Morton for the rest of 1572 was their belief that a 'great faction of the townsmen' remained faithful to Grange.[78] Their fears of a fifth column were well-grounded, as the queen's men in the burgh had not been a hapless rabble pressed into military service. A half of the burgh establishment as well as half of the able-bodied men in the town had supported the queen's cause. The upper reaches of Edinburgh society were as thoroughly permeated by Marianism as the lower. The wars between Leith and Edinburgh were, in a very real sense, a civil war which split Edinburgh society in two.

Matters were still cast in the balance. The truce drawn up on 30 July had been virtually forced on both parties by the English and French ambassadors. It was a fragile settlement, even for a two months' truce. The proposed solution to the vexed question of the retention of the profits from forfeited lands was no more than a pious hope; it was vague on the precise municipal arrangements that followed from the town being 'sett at sic libertie as it wes' in January 1571. A rejoinder from Mar the very next day seemed to dispute the right of burgh office-holders appointed during the troubles to collect customs, one of the primary duties of the bailies.[79] It was around the issue of proper authority within the burgh that the first disputes regarding the truce crystallised.

This was hardly surprising. A bond had been drawn up by the exiles on 2 July, which amounted to a mutual covenant to redress the damage done to themselves, their town and their God. Their objective was as plain as their resolution: to restore 'the whole policie within that town'.[80] It is a remarkable document and a clear expression of the fact that the Edinburgh band, the core of the exiles, had now developed into a win-the-war party and would not be content with anything which fell short of that. On the evening of 31 July, a few hours after the truce had been formally declared, the exiles returned, parading up the Canongate, led by their ministers, John Brand and John Durie, and armed to the teeth. They amounted in all to five hundred hagbutters and sixty pikemen. It was their arrival which transformed the military situation within the town. When they assumed their traditional duties, as burgesses, to watch and ward, the Castilians protested that the truce had not been intended to be a justification for the burgh being guarded 'as ane town of war' by their enemies. It is not clear whether Mar was aware of or encouraged the entry of the exiles, but he was happy to defend their actions subsequently. The only party which could benefit from this inevitable conflict between the constitution of the town and the privileges of its burgesses on the one hand and the terms of the truce strictly interpreted on the other were the king's lords. The taxing of the burgh a week later, even if it was to raise more soldiers, was technically within the power of the bailies, but imposing free quarter on the inhabitants who had remained in the town was more difficult to justify.[81]

It is a matter of inference to say exactly when the council-in-exile resumed its duties and responsibilities in the town displacing the queen's party council, but it had certainly done so by 22 August. It was helped in proving its legal continuity by its possession of the official books of council and guildry. Although there is no trace of a council register for this period, both the guild register and the burgh register of deeds turned up in the possession of the exiled council and were restarted on 22 August and 14 September. The man in charge of the recovery of the burgh was Adam Fullarton, who, as well as being dean of guild and captain of the Edinburgh band, was now also president in the absence of McGill.[82] Given these developments, it was most unlikely that the regent would agree either to remove the king's party's armed supporters from the town or to allow, as the Castilians put it, 'the merchands and craftis to reule and aggrie among thameselffis, as thai wont of auld'. So far as the king's party was concerned, the armed Edinburgh band was legally entitled to be in the burgh and the normal processes of burgh administration had been resumed. It was even less likely that Mar would agree to the Marian demand made two days later, on 27 August, for a discharge of all goods of the inhabitants seized during the troubles.[83]

The kirk session-in-exile did not lose time either in re-establishing itself in the town; on 4 August a letter was sent from the 'kirk and brethren of Edinburgh' to Knox, who was still in St. Andrews, inviting him to return to replace the less committed John Craig.[84] Again the resumption of control by the exiles led to complaints from the Castle. Grange complained to Killigrew particularly that those who had remained during the crisis were being coerced into submitting to the session. It is clear that the long list of ninety-two penitents preserved in English state papers, dated November 1572, are the same men referred to by Calderwood for two months earlier; the three he mentions by name are also on the later list. The formal bill of submission of '29 or 30' penitents, noted by Bannatyne, which was handed to Killigrew early in October, itemises the same three men. This was done after they had declared to the superintendent of Lothian that their action was voluntary.[85] It is quite likely that this was indeed the case; no judicial action had yet been taken against most of the penitents, whose purpose was to urge the session to intercede on their behalf. It was only in a few cases a matter of double jeopardy. The Edinburgh session did not engage on large-scale submissions until September 1573, after the judicial processes were largely over. It did not anticipate the decision of the General Assembly, which sat in the burgh from 20 October, to bring to 'amendment of lyff' or excommunicate all notorious offenders. At the same time, it is obvious that Edinburgh and its experiences exercised a decisive influence on the strident atmosphere at the Assembly, an influence which was exaggerated still further by the absence of most of the nobility and lairds.[86]

A solidly king's party council was elected in October 1572, headed by the veteran protestant activist, Lord Lindsay; three of the sitting bailies were re-elected. Although no council minute book is extant, it is obvious from the frequency and regularity of entries in the register of deeds and in the protocol books that council business was now back on a normal footing.[87] Despite the fact that the new council was composed of exiles, it seems that Lindsay's appointment was designed to keep their zeal in check. One source claims that he was 'purposelie' created provost and it was he who was behind a proclamation of 22 November forbidding the molesting of those who had remained in the burgh. Although the partisan author of the *Diurnal* claims that he did this so that 'he may obtene all thair favouris', it is more likely that this was done to discourage a flight into the Castle by the rump of the Marian faction in the burgh. All judicial proceedings against queen's party burgesses were held off until the following February and the majority were not begun until after the fall of the Castle.[88] Less gentle treatment was given in town business; the council deliberately enforced an ordinance that those who had remained behind should lose their freedom by refusing to grant burgess-ship to a son whose father had done so.[89]

Despite the fact that the king's party, thanks to the exiles, was now in control of the town, Killigrew privately considered that, on balance, it had lost from the truce, which had been extended three times before hostilities broke out again on 1 January 1573. The Castle was now revictualled; there were still strong rumours of the imminent arrival of Alva; the upper part of the town was vulnerable to excursions from the Castle. Although Killgrew's dispatches suggested a state of normality, the new situation brought not less physical disruption to the town but more. The combination of preparations for a siege of the Castle and the damage from cannonfire or deliberate fire-raising by the Castilians certainly caused more damage to property; in one raid alone, Pitscottie estimated that eighty lodgings in the Cowgate were destroyed. Despite the construction of elaborate defences in the upper part of the High Street, they were breached in a series of raids into the heart of the town, in which both property and food supplies were destroyed. St. Cuthbert's was set on fire on 17 January and St. Giles' attacked on 7 February. The maltmen's area around the Castlehill and outside the West Port was particularly badly hit.[90]

The decisive factors, however, were no longer to be found in the relative strength of the king's and queen's men in and around Edinburgh. The increasing likelihood of English intervention and the collapse of the queen's party elsewhere in the country after the Pacification of Perth on 23 February isolated the Castilians. The expected date of English intervention, although first predicted by Killigrew as the end of February, did not materialise until early in April, when a band of English pioneers landed at Leith. The rest of the proceedings, assuming there would be no intervention from France or Spain, were a formality. The Castle fell on 28 May. The last months of the siege had taken place against a highly charged atmosphere in the town; memories of St. Bartholomew were not allowed to fade. Both Morton and Killigrew had tried to dampen the righteous desire for vengeance of the restored exiles, but it was allowed freer expression after the Castle had fallen. It is difficult to resist the feeling that the two goldsmiths, Mossman and Cockie, who were executed along with Grange, were the chosen sops to appease this feeling. Their offences were no more heinous than those of other burgesses who had remained in the

Castle, like Cuthbert Ramsay. The king's administration had little reason to be merciful; it had been severely embarrassed by the quality of the coin minted in the Castle, which compared very favourably with its own produced at Dalkeith.[91]

The large-scale trials of burgesses, which began on 31 July, probably drew on the evidence drawn up by the exiles in the form of another roll.[92] The severity of the fines imposed on the convicted, however, has been exaggerated by the *Diurnal*; the minimum imposed at this time was not twenty merks but ten. In fact, the size of the fines exacted in August and September 1573 was rather less than those imposed before the fall of the Castle. The scale of fines dropped dramatically as time went on; £10 was the maximum penalty exacted after 1574.[93]

The process of satisfying the kirk session also dragged on, at least until October 1575. It began on a large scale, according to the *Diurnal*, in September 1573.[94] It seems that no one was exempt from this process, not even the most respectable members of the protestant establishment. Even those who had merely remained in the town after June 1571 had to comply. It is noticeable, however, that the more prominent citizens, like Moscrop, Lauder or Dickson, were treated, if not less stringently, at least with more tact and considerable patience. The sticking-point for many of them, like MacCalzean, was not repentance but public repentance. He was prepared to buy his sackcloth or donate its price to the poor but not to wear it.

Although the session reserved its most righteous denunciations for those who had looted their neighbours' goods or helped to demolish houses in the burgh, there is room to doubt whether this was the most significant damage inflicted on the fabric of Edinburgh society during the civil wars. At most, fifty houses were demolished between February and July 1572. Nor should the king's party propaganda that the town had been turned into 'another Liddesdale' be too easily accepted. There were fears of anarchy not only in Edinburgh but also in Leith; Drury in July 1572 reported that neither set of magistrates dared to enforce justice. Burgh life did not cease to function in Edinburgh. On the contrary, every attempt was made to carry on an illusion of normality: the council was continued; bailies continued with their usual duties, including the giving of sasines; the kirk session continued. The commissaries who went to Leith were replaced. Even the traditional feature of burgh life that had been banned again after the riots of 1560, the Robin Hood pageant, was re-introduced. Of course, part of the motivation behind this was to undermine or block the alternative town council and king's administration which were being set up in Leith; the clerks of the Court of Session and some of the members of the sitting town council were detained in the town despite the officially declared policy of expelling king's party supporters. Much of the negative half of the policy failed. Certain of the books of the council must have been smuggled out of the town — the burgh register of deeds, the commissary registers, the guild register — along with the justiciary court books. Even craft elections seem to have been held at Leith in May 1572.[95] But it would be hard to be so certain that the positive half of the policy also failed.

To lay too much stress on the disruption caused by the coup of June 1571 would be to misunderstand the nature of an essential part of the queen's party support within the town. The sympathy of the older generation within the merchant establishment was as important to the Marian cause as the physical presence of the craftsmen, apprentices or day labourers in their limited forces. There is no suggestion in any source to justify the suggestion that the queen's lords pandered to the crafts to woo them over.[96] The Marian coup of 1571 was in no sense a social revolution. It was a return to the old order. It brought back into positions of prominence a large number of leading figures in the old establishment, who had spent the 1560s in a number of guises ranging from outright hostility to the new regime to a conservative acquiescence in the more acceptable parts of its programme. It is difficult to imagine that their support would have been so forthcoming if the burgh had been under a state of martial law.

It is also doubtful if trade was severely interrupted. Overseas trading could still be carried on through Leith, unlike the situation in 1559, as well as through the numerous small ports along the Forth. Merchants who at least nominally supported either side continued to travel to France to import wine.[97] Many overland merchants seem to have moved to Leith, where the novel possibilities of provisioning a sizeable army and latterly an English army compensated for their partial loss of a market in Edinburgh. Some of the loans to the king's party were in the form of merchandise, particularly cloth.[98] What was more serious was the strain which was put on the normal processes of commerce. Edinburgh was a society which functioned on credit; the average overseas trader, by the evidence of the testaments, was owed two to three times the amount of merchandise which he had in stock at any one time. Part of the reason for this was that certain commodities, particularly wine, were seasonal. The only sizeable merchant to die in the civil war period and whose testament is extant was William Fowler, who faced the added complication of owning a large amount of property within the burgh. Fowler, as a result, was owed substantial sums by burgesses and notables of both parties. James McGill owed him six months' rent and it is possible that it was for one of the two houses of McGill's torn down in 1572.[99] These difficulties were not just personal ones. Drury in September 1571 shrewdly remarked that 'money is the man in Scotland'. Credit was beginning to dry up for both parties as early as this because of the interruption to the normal ebb and flow of commercial transactions. Maitland only a little earlier had complained that loans from merchants were more difficult to obtain. The financial aid given to the queen's party was not confined to committed Marians like Archibald Seinyeor. Michael Gilbert, and his son-in-law, Nicol Uddart, two of the most respected and wealthy men in the town, played the role of honest broker, lending to both sides. They offered to arrange the transfer of funds from London to Edinburgh for the bishop of Ross at a lucrative rate of exchange. At that point, the most profitable course seemed also to be the safest. As time went on, though, more pressure had to be applied by the queen's party to squeeze further funds out of the burgh. Although the demolition campaign was simply vindictive in certain cases, like that of McGill, it should also be seen as a last desperate attempt to force the wealthier burgesses to extend their credit to the queen's party.[100] Although these tactics in the first half of 1572 were a failure, others that were used in the second half of the year during the truce were not. The subsequent inquests into the Castilians' backers revealed that the main domestic source of finance was those to whom the royal jewels had been laid in pledge. The findings proved highly embarrassing. The major backers were Alexander Clark and Archibald Stewart. Clark had been a client of Moray and one of the protestants in the town supposedly most committed to the English connection. Stewart was an old and valued friend of Knox. Their relationship was very close indeed. Knox, when Stewart visited him as he lay on his death-bed in November 1572, was so pleased to see his old friend that he ordered a fresh cask of wine to be opened in honour of the occasion. It is a scene which reveals a good deal about the interplay of interests and religious or political ideas in the Reformation period. Protestant merchant and protestant reformer might agree on the ideas themselves but not always on the priority they should be given. Even in Knox's last hours, Stewart presumably took the view that sentiment or politics should not interfere with business.[101]

The response of the king's party to the same problem of finance differed in its details. Loans were also forthcoming. Taxes were raised on the exiles of Edinburgh and the Canongate; Maitland complained in August 1572 that the extension of these taxes to the inhabitants of Edinburgh after the return of the exiles to the burgh would raise another company of soldiers. Another lucrative source was the mint set up at Dalkeith in March 1572.[102] The lowering of the silver content in the coinage and the vigorous campaign that was waged against the handling of the coin minted in the Castle must have exaggerated the spiralling pattern of price inflation. This continued and even worsened after the exiles' return. Prices, however, did not rise evenly on all commodities. There was a general price rise which was much steeper for bread, ale and oats; these were the commodities which had particularly suffered from the campaign of mutual attrition during the wars, with the demolition of the common mills and the firing of the malt barns around the Castlehill and outside the West Port. It has been argued that severe price inflation in Scotland did not come until the Morton period.[103] Yet an explanation that rests wholly on the successive debasements of the coinage, which began in 1572, ignores the peculiar cumulative effects of the circulation of two sets of coin of different intrinsic values combined with severe and artificially induced food shortages. Prices after the rendering of the Castle remained as high as during the dearth and plague year of 1569. By the later 1580s the prices of the civil war period, apart from the last desperate days of July 1572, were accepted as normal. There can be little doubt that the long crisis of the wars had accelerated the rate of price inflation. It was not only during the wars that Edinburgh's inhabitants were worst hit by its effects; the subsequent campaign against coin minted in the Castle was directed most obviously at the townspeople.[104] It seems incontrovertible that it was the poorest sections of burgh society who were most badly hit. The most lasting legacy of the civil wars was that they increased the already yawning gulf between rich and poor in the burgh.

NOTES

1. The fullest account of the civil war is still the one given in P. F. Tytler, *History of Scotland* (Edinburgh, 1828-43); see iii, 343-4; also Ridley, *John Knox*, 492. A highly colourful and sometimes instructive account is given in J. Grant, *Memoirs and Adventures of Sir William Kirkcaldy of Grange* (Edinburgh, 1849).

2. A remarkable insight into the composition of the queen's men at Langside is provided in G. Donaldson, *Mary, Queen of Scots* (1974), 121-39; see also his introduction to *RSS*, vi, p. vii.

3. *CSP Scot.*, v, no. 437; *Edin. Recs.*, iii, 246, 250-51, 258; MS Co. Recs., iv, fos. 225v, 226r.

4. The outbreak of plague is first mentioned in the council minutes on 5 Oct. 1568. Although it seems to have slackened by late Dec., and Calderwood testifies that it had died out by Feb. 1569, there was a further outbreak late in May 1569. A council proclamation of 1 July still referred to 'this dangerous tyme of pest' and it was not until late Dec. 1569 that the council allowed those who had been exposed to the disease out of quarantine (*Edin. Recs.*, iii, 247, 253-5, 256, 258-9, 261, 267; MS Co. Recs., iv, 242v; Calderwood, *History*, ii, 477; *Diurnal*, 147).

5. *Diurnal*, 156-7, 159, 161, 163; *CSP Scot.*, iii, nos. 122, 142; *Edin. Recs.*, iii, 268-70; Ridley, *John Knox*, 489.

6. *Diurnal*, 167-8; *Edin. Recs.*, iii, 271; *CSP Scot.*, iii, nos. 161, 183; see Donaldson, *Mary Queen of Scots*, 122, for the motives of Grange and Maitland.

7. *CSP Scot.*, iii, nos. 190, 193, 408; Bannatyne, *Memorials*, 38; Calderwood, *History*, ii, 558, 560; *Edin. Recs.*, iii, 38.

8. Bannatyne, *Memorials*, 33, 176; *Edin. Recs.*, iii, 271; Calderwood, *History*, ii, 554; *Diurnal*, 172, 202, 233; see Hew Brown, Robert Cunningham and John Harwood in app. vii and Mungo Fairlie in app. viii.

9. *CSP Scot.*, iii, no. 209; *Diurnal*, 171, 238-9, 244.

10. The seizure was first reported in Jan. 1570, but there was no specific mention of the merchants involved until Feb. 1571; see *CSP Scot.*, iii, nos. 80, 627; also nos. 264, 382.

11. Bannatyne, *Memorials*, 39-40; *Hist. King James VI*, 56.

12. *CSP Scot.*, iii, no. 156; Bannatyne, *Memorials*, 32-3.

13. *CSP Scot.*, iii, no. 264; *Diurnal*, 173, 175; Bannatyne, *Memorials*, 40-41.

14. *Diurnal*, 174, 184; *CSP Scot.*, iii, nos. 307(1), 312, 330, 339(1), 342(1), 345, 390, 417; Calderwood, *History*, iii, 10.

15. Herries, *Memoirs*, 130; *CSP Scot.*, iii, nos. 486, 503, 522. McGill was only persuaded to accept office on 20 Oct. (*Edin. Recs.*, iii, 277-8); Mungo Fairlie, one of the bailies, developed Marian sympathies under pressure (see app. viii).

16. MS Co. Recs., iv, fo. 263v; *Edin. Recs.*, iii, 277.

17. *CSP Scot.*, iii, no. 538; see Wm. Aikman and Sebastian Danelour in app. viii.

18. *CSP Scot.*, iii, nos. 609, 627, 639, 703; see Helen Acheson and Archibald Stewart in app. viii and John Acheson and Nicol Uddart in app. vii.

19. Calderwood, *History*, iii, 20-21; *CSP Scot.*, iii, nos. 585, 591; Bannatyne, *Memorials*, 71-2, 76-7; *Diurnal*, 197; cf. Ridley, *John Knox*, 495-6.

20. The four queen's men were John Cunningham, Cuthbert Matheson, George Smith and John

Wilson of the tailors, websters, wrights and hammermen. The deacons of the masons and cordiners, Murdo Walker and John Nicolson, were king's men; it is likely that Thomas Aikenhead and Nicol Sim of the skinners and goldsmiths were, like their brothers, John and Alex., also king's men. See apps. vii & viii; also *CSP Scot.*, iii, no. 422.

21. This is discussed more fully in ch. 12.

22. *Diurnal*, 203, 205-8; Calderwood, *History*, iii, 33; *Edin. Recs.*, iii, 284; Bannatyne, *Memorials*, 109-10; *CSP Scot.*, iii, no. 698.

23. *Ibid.*, iii, nos. 699, 703; *Edin. Recs.*, iii, 284-5; Bannatyne, *Memorials*, 111-13; Ridley, *John Knox*, 499.

24. *Diurnal*, 209-10; Bannatyne, *Memorials*, 113; see David and Captain Adamson and Andrew Henryson in app. vii.

25. *Edin. Recs.*, iii, 285; Bannatyne, *Memorials*, 113-5; *Diurnal*, 209-10.

26. Calderwood, *History*, iii, 70-71; *Edin. Recs.*, iii, 285; cf. Bannatyne, *Memorials*, 113-5.

27. *Ibid.*, 117-8, 120, 122-3; Calderwood, *History*, iii, 72-3; *Diurnal*, 211, 213-5; *RPC*, xiv, 98; Ridley, *John Knox*, 500.

28. *Diurnal*, 211, 213, 216, 224; Bannatyne, *Memorials*, 113-5, 133; Knox, *Works*, vi, 599; T. A. Kerr, 'The later ministry of John Craig at St. Giles', 1567-1572', *RSCHS*, xiv (1962), 96.

29. See MS Burgh Register of Deeds, ii, fo. 18v, although Adamson's name has been filled in in a different hand. An entry of the same date in Prot. Bk. Guthrie, vi, fo. 72, shows Adamson officiating as a bailie in a transfer of property.

30. MS Guild Register, i, fo. 101v; see *Edin. Burgs.*, 298.

31. Prot. Bk. Robeson, fo. 119; see *Diurnal*, 218-9; *CSP Scot.*, iii, no. 779. The indictments were drawn up against Patrick Anderson and 46 others and John Newlands (JC 26/1, 31 July & 3 Nov. 1573); they are summarised in their entries in app. viii.

32. *CSP Scot.*, iii, nos. 790, 798, 799; *Diurnal*, 220, 226; Bannatyne, *Memorials*, 164-5, 170; cf. Prot. Bk. Guthrie, vi, fos. 73r-74v.

33. See Bannatyne's account of their motives (*Memorials*, 121).

34. This was given in the indictment drawn up against Newlands; see app. viii.

35. *CSP Scot.*, Châtelherault to Alva, 10 Aug. 1570, iii, no. 408; also no. 805; *RPC*, xiv, 100; Bannatyne, *Memorials*, 138-41.

36. Cf. Ridley, *John Knox*, 501.

37. Bannatyne, *Memorials*, 123; see George Gibson, Robert Scott and John Wallace in app. vii.

38. Maitland to Beaton, 28 Aug. 1571, *Misc. Papers illustrative of events in the reigns of Queen Mary and King James VI*, 66.

39. See JC 1/13, 12 Nov. 1571; the volume is unfoliated. The court returned to Edinburgh on 21 Oct. 1572.

40. See MS Register of Testaments, ii, fo. 170r, for the testament of David and John Honeyman, dated 30 April 1571; there is an undated entry after that, followed by one for John Wallace of Craigie on 30 July. The first entry made at Leith, for John Espye, was not until 22 Nov. 1571 (fo. 174v).

41. MS Register of Acts and Decreets, 2 May 1571; it resumed at Leith 6 Dec. 1571. The volume is unfoliated.

42. See MS Register of Deeds and Protests; there are entries for 6, 11 & 18 June; it resumed at Leith 2 Nov. 1571. The volume is unfoliated. See Clement Little and his brother, William, in app. vii.

43. *RPC*, ii, 85, 91; *Diurnal*, 295; Donaldson, *Mary Queen of Scots*, 137. An exception was made for Robert Scott, who was specifically instructed by McGill, the clerk register, to remain in the burgh to safeguard the register books of the Court of Session until the end of the troubles (*RPC*, ii, 138).

44. *Diurnal*, 234; see Thomas MacCalzean and Thomas Bassenden in app. viii.

45. Bannatyne, *Memorials*, 190-91.

46. *CSP Scot.*, iii, nos. 767, 821, 852, 862, 892; *Diurnal*, 226, 239-40; *Hist. King James VI*, 86-7;

Calderwood, *History*, iii, 100; Bannatyne, *Memorials*, 178; see Thomas Barrie in app. viii.

47. *CSP Scot.*, iii, nos. 899, 904, 914; *Diurnal*, 246; *Hist. King James VI*, 88-9; see Francis Tennant in app. viii.

48. *CSP Scot.*, iii, nos. 912-4, 921(3), 940.

49. *Ibid.*, iii, nos. 807, 808, 810, 836(1).

50. *Ibid.*, Lennox to Elizabeth, 27 July 1571, iii, no. 843; Mar to Hunsdon, 15 Jan. 1572, iv, no. 111.

51. *Diurnal*, 227, 231; Herries, *Memoirs*, 138; *CSP Scot.*, iii, nos. 264, 917; iv, nos. 13(1), 14, 15, 19; cf. Bannatyne, *Memorials*, 192.

52. *Diurnal*, 227, 232-3, 235.

53. *Ibid.*, 233; Bannatyne, *Memorials*, 176; *CSP Scot.*, iii, no. 840; Calderwood, *History*, iii, 113. See the entries for Thomas Brown, Robert Cunningham and John Harwood in app. vii and Mungo Fairlie in app. viii.

54. *Diurnal*, 238-9, 244. The four from the council, who were also among those forfeited on 29 Aug., were John Adamson, Michael Chisholm, Adam Fullarton and Mungo Russell (see app. vii).

55. *CSP Scot.*, iii, nos. 898, 899; *Diurnal*, 245-6; Bannatyne, *Memorials*, 185-6; Calderwood, *History*, iii, 137. See Gilbert Balfour of Westray, Thomas Hamilton of Priestfield, Herbert Maxwell, and John and Patrick Moscrop in app. viii.

56. *RPC*, ii, 81; see *RSS*, vi, 1286ff.

57. *CSP Scot.*, iii, nos. 914, 941(3), 949; *Diurnal*, 251-2; *Hist. King James VI*, 95; see Bannatyne, *Memorials*, 188-90; *RPC*, ii, 93.

58. Although *Diurnal*, 252, is not unambiguous on this point, it seems fair to conclude from the independent figures of the total numbers of queen's men left in the town, including nobles, retainers and mercenaries, given by both Case and Maitland (see *CSP Scot.*, iii, no. 917; iv, no. 15) that the hard core of support for the queen's party among the townsmen could not have been significantly more than this. The accumulated evidence from subsequent justiciary processes for conspiracy or treason would not reveal a total of more than a hundred, which was the size of the force commanded by Gilbert Balfour of Westray in Oct. 1571.

59. *Diurnal*, 250-51; *CSP Scot.*, iii, no. 956; nos. 7, 13(1).

60. *Diurnal*, 250; Prot. Bk. Robeson, 2 Oct. 1571, fo. 124. Apart from two odd references to a town council of Edinburgh at Leith in *RPC*, ii, 87, 120, Robeson's protocol book is the only source for the council in exile from when it was elected in Oct. 1571 until it re-established itself in Edinburgh in Aug. 1572. Of its office-holders, all except Andrew Slater had been on the council dismissed in June 1571; cf. *Lord Provosts*, 26. John Aitkin's protocol book is the only source, apart from a single entry in *RSS*, vi, 1431, for the queen's party council elected in Oct. 1571.

61. Bannatyne, *Memorials*, 192-5; Calderwood, *History*, iii, 153; *CSP Scot.*, iv, nos. 22, 55, 66, 68; *Diurnal*, 251-2.

62. *CSP Scot.*, iv, nos. 63, 82; *Diurnal*, 256; *RPC*, ii, 102, 104; Buchanan, *History*, 509.

63. *RPC*, ii, 87-8, 90, 93; *RSS*, vi, 1260, 1271, 1274, 1286, 1288, 1295, 1346; see Thomas Andrew, Gilbert Balfour, Wm. Curle, Helen Leslie, Cuthbert Murray, and John and Patrick Moscrop in app. viii.

64. *RSS*, vi, 1416, 1420, 1423, 1431, 1437; see Matthew Aikman, Thomas Bassenden, John Clavie, Matthew Easton, Alex. Ellis, Alex. Job, Peter Martin and John Wilson in app. viii.

65. Bannatyne, *Memorials*, 218-21 (Univ. MS, fo. 81); see also the Dalyell ed., 313-20 (Advocates MS, fo. 238). Fourteen appeared promptly before the justiciary court (see JC 1/13, 1 Feb. 1572).

66. Bannatyne, *Memorials*, 229; cf. Reid, *Trumpeter of God*, 277.

67. *Diurnal*, 286-7.

68. *Ibid.*, 257-8, 288, 295, 299, 301, 307; *CSP Scot.*, iv, nos. 148-9; see app. ix for details.

69. *Diurnal*, 262, 288; *CSP Scot.*, iv, no. 149; *Hist. King James VI*, 103; *RPC*, ii, 120ff.

70. *Ibid.*, ii, 120ff; *CSP Scot.*, iv, no. 239; *Diurnal*, 293; see Morrison's entry in app. vii.

71. Bannatyne, *Memorials*, 230; *CSP Scot.*, iv, nos. 239, 250(1); *Hist. King James VI*, 100;

Pitscottie, *Historie*, ii, 277; *Diurnal*, 301-2.

72. Cf. *Diurnal*, 147, 299, 302, 306; see also *Edin. Recs.*, iii, 11, 265; Calderwood, *History*, iii, 213; Pitscottie, *Historie*, ii, 260. This was below the market price as it had stood in 1557, when it was two merks a boll.

73. *Diurnal*, 306; *RPC*, ii, 157.

74. For bread and wheat prices see *Diurnal*, 147, and *Edin. Recs.*, iii, 265; iv, 2, 8, 499. Mutton, which had sold for between 6s and 8s in 1557, had risen to 16s by 1564 and reached 20s in Leith in 1572; the price in Edinburgh was over 50s (*ibid.*, iii, 11, 180; *Diurnal*, 306).

75. *Hist. King James VI*, 103; *Diurnal*, 295; see also Herries, *Memoirs*, 139.

76. Bannatyne, *Memorials*, 234; cf. *Diurnal*, 295, 302; also *RPC*, ii, 149; *CSP Scot.*, iv, nos. 369-71.

77. *Ibid.*, iv, nos. 358, 363; *Diurnal*, 264, 300-1; *Hist. King James VI*, 107-8; Pitcairn, *Trials*, 1, ii, 32; JC 1/13, 13 June 1572. Nine burgesses involved in the same affray, but fortunate enough not to have been captured, received far lighter treatment after their convictions ten months later, even though they included one of the ringleaders of the loyalist burgesses, Peter Thomson (*ibid.*, 9 Feb. 1573; Pitcairn, *Trials*, 1, ii, 40).

78. *CSP Scot.*, iv, nos. 275, 417.

79. *Ibid.*, iv, nos. 399, 407; Bannatyne, *Memorials*, 240-46; *Diurnal*, 308-11; *CSP Foreign, Eliz.*, x, nos. 473, 505; Ridley, *John Knox*, 510.

80. See Bannatyne, *Memorials*, 247-9.

81. *Ibid.*, 246-7; *Diurnal*, 311-2; *Hist. King James VI*, 119; *CSP Scot.*, iv, nos. 407, 415, 418(1), 423(1).

82. MS Guild Register, i, fo. 101v (see *Edin. Burgs.*, 47, under George Barclay); MS Burgh Register of Deeds, ii, fo. 22r.

83. *Diurnal*, 313-4; *Hist. King James VI*, 120.

84. Knox, *Works*, vi, 623; Bannatyne, *Memorials*, 253-5; Ridley, *John Knox*, 510; Kerr, 'The later ministry of John Craig', 98-9.

85. See PRO, SP 52/53, fo. 254; the first 31 are given in *CSP Scot.*, iv, no. 487. This is not the original document but a copy, in an English hand, which may explain some of the peculiar renderings of names in it. See also Bannatyne, *Memorials*, 274, and cf. Dalyell, ed., 404. The bill was presented before the renewal of the truce on 8 Oct. (*Diurnal*, 316).

86. *Ibid.*, 317-20, 336-7; Bannatyne, *Memorials*, 276-9; *BUK*, i, 50-54; *CSP Scot.*, iv, no. 463.

87. See Burgh Register of Deeds, ii, fos. 22v-43r; Prot. Bk. Wm. Stewart, younger, fos. 2r-116v; Prot. Bk. Aitkin, iii, fos. 1r, 6r, 24v; Prot. Bk. Robeson, fos. 177, 184, 185; Prot. Bk. Wm. Stewart, elder, 18 & 23 Oct. 1572.

88. *Hist. King James VI*, 124-5; *Diurnal*, 331-2; *RPC*, ii, 172; see also *ibid.*, xiv, 324. The first major judicial process against burgesses began on 4 Feb. 1573 (see JC 1/13; Pitcairn, *Trials*, 1, ii, 39-40).

89. See *Edin. Burgs.*, 5. Ironically, the son, John Neill, had served in Leith; see app. vii.

90. *CSP Scot.*, iv, nos. 439, 520, 576; *Diurnal*, 325-7; Bannatyne, *Memorials*, 298-9; Pitscottie, *Historie*, ii, 298; *Hist. King James VI*, 125-8.

91. *CSP Scot.*, iv, nos. 567, 586, 588, 596, 603, 666, 679, 712; *Diurnal*, 261, 312, 328-9, 333; *Hist. King James VI*, 140-41; *RPC*, ii, 172; Donaldson, *James V to James VII*, 166.

92. JC 26/1, 31 July 1573 (see the entry for Patrick Anderson in app. viii); *Hist. King James VI*, 147-8.

93. *Diurnal*, 336; cf. *TA*, xiii, 329-48. See Wm. Melville or John Thomson in app. viii. The significance of the size and timing of fines on queen's party burgesses is discussed more fully in ch. 12.

94. *Diurnal*, 337. Penitents appeared before the Edinburgh kirk session throughout the period (April 1574-Oct. 1575) for which its records are extant.

95. Calderwood, *History*, iii, 257; *CSP Scot.*, iv, no. 388; *Diurnal*, 263; see MS Goldsmiths' Recs., fo. 9r.

96. E. S. C. Percy, *John Knox* (1937), 415.

97. See Andrew Craig in app. vii and Edward Little in app. viii.

98. *TA*, xii, 363.

99. Fowler was owed rent by John Muir and Alex. Sim, who had left for Leith, and various sums of money by a number of queen's party burgesses, including Gilbert Balfour, Edward Little and Alex. Sauchie; see app. viii.

100. *CSP Scot.*, iii, nos. 917, 941; iv, no. 149; *Diary of John Leslie, Bishop of Ross* (Bann. Misc., iii), 131; see Gilbert in app. viii and Uddart in app. vii.

101. *CSP Scot.*, iv, no. 728; *RPC*, iii, 388-90; Knox, *Works*, vi, 636-7. To add to the irony, Stewart was on the militant council re-elected in Oct. 1572 at the time.

102. *CSP Scot.*, iv, nos. 218, 418(1); *Diurnal*, 261.

103. R. Mitchison, *A History of Scotland* (London, 1970), 134-5, 145.

104. *APS*, iii, 92-3; *Diurnal*, 344-5; *CSP Scot.*, iv, no. 96; Moysie, *Memoirs*, 18.

8

The Reigns of Morton, Lennox and Arran,
1572-85

THE period of Morton's regency saw a distinct turning-point in Edinburgh politics. When it began, in November 1572, the struggle between the king's and queen's parties in the burgh was nearly at an end and this in turn had settled the running feud between the protestant and catholic parties which had been going on since 1559. By the time of Morton's execution, in June 1581, the town was again enmeshed in factional politics. Yet this factionalism was not another round in the same struggle; almost without exception, the new factions developed from within the body of younger and respectable merchants who had provided the core of the king's party. New issues formed in the course of the 1570s and the early 1580s and new factions formed in response to them. The Melvillian problem was one of these issues, but not the only or even the most important one.

The most telling of the factors that led to the polarisation of the merchant establishment was Morton himself. The civil wars had not ended when the first clash arose between the burgh and the Morton administration; the loyalist town council was surprised, even dismayed, by a decision awarded against it in the Court of Session in a jurisdictional dispute with the Canongate, which had helped to frustrate the blockade of the town during the wars. A more personal source of grievance, particularly for those whose houses had been demolished during the siege, was Morton's failure to make good his promise to hand over half of the proceeds gained from the remissions granted to queen's men from the town. The first serious clash between Morton and the kirk session came over the licence which he granted to Robert Gourlay to export corn in a period of dearth; the affair was all the more embarrassing as Gourlay was also an elder. Although the English ambassador, Sir Henry Killigrew, reported that the incident had produced 'some little grudging' between the regent and the ministers, it is difficult to believe that it weighed very heavily in the longer term; the kirk had more pressing reasons for its growing disenchantment with Morton.[1]

A much more serious affair, and one which was cast up in the recriminations which followed Morton's fall from power, began in December 1574, when a number of merchants were summoned to appear before the privy council for exporting gold and silver. The *Diurnal* names eight merchants who were imprisoned on their own expenses as a result early in February 1575. They were certainly, as another source remarks, 'merchands of wealth'; they were the very cream of Edinburgh society. What was equally to the point was that four of them — the two Uddart brothers, Henry Nisbet and John Morrison — were on the council.[2] This became an issue in itself when they were kept in prison for over five months; it is likely that they were not released until the middle of August 1575.[3] The council had not been treated in such a cavalier fashion since it had suffered at the hands of Seton in 1559. It is not clear whether they were actually brought to trial; there is no trace of them in the justiciary records, but there is mention in the *Treasurer's Accounts* of an assize for those 'indytit for awaytaking of gold'. The impact of the affair, however, was much wider; the eight were only a sample picked out as examples to the merchant community. The original letters of summons were issued on a 'great multitude' of Edinburgh merchants, and an unextracted council minute of October 1575 reveals another thirty-six of them. They included, by the combined evidence of two tax rolls of 1581 and 1583, eighteen of the wealthiest thirty merchants in the burgh.[4] It was small wonder that the affair became so bitter or that these merchants might boast that just as they had set Morton up, so they could pull him down; they were the former core of the king's party at Leith. It did not go unnoticed by the dedicated Scotland watchers; the French ambassador in London, de la Mothe Fénélon, briefly accepted a rumour of Morton's death as a result of the affair and reported that Killigrew had been sent on an emergency mission to Scotland. The affair ended, predictably, in a financial exaction; after their first offer was rejected as 'na offer', the merchants agreed to a composition of ten thousand merks.[5] The eight burgesses had, in effect, been hostages for holding the bulk of the Edinburgh establishment to ransom.

The bullion affair was not the only dispute that blew up between Morton and the merchants. A number of money changers were hauled before the privy council in January and February 1575; the offence of 'trafficking' was probably much the same as the one that had involved Nisbet and the others but less important, since they were all smaller men. In February 1575, Robert Watson, another of the most prominent men in the king's party, was summoned along with other merchants from other burghs for 'barrelling of beif, butter, talloun', presumably for export in a period of acute food shortage. Another group of merchants were imprisoned for disputing proclamations issued against the import of salt and expensive wines. This was not the last clash between Morton and the burgh's influential wine lobby. In 1579 a group of merchants from Edinburgh and Dundee were called before the privy council for refusing to supply the court with cut-price wine; at least two of them, John Morrison and James Ross, had previously been involved in the bullion affair. The action again had wider repercussions, since the bailies were accused, probably justifiably, of failing to operate the acts regulating wine prices.[6] The thorny question of the superiority of Leith, which had been purchased on reversion at great expense and inconvenience in 1565, was again brought up in 1577, probably as the pretext for a further financial demand.[7] Edinburgh's grievances during the Morton regency were not confined to the merchants. Morton's tinkering with the coinage affected Edinburgh's inhabitants more seriously than most, since it was they who were most likely still to be in possession of the coin minted in the Castle during the siege.[8]

Yet it would be an exaggeration to think of Edinburgh as being totally hostile to the Morton regency. The town did not lose all of its battles with the Canongate over its jurisdiction. Morton was not inflexible; the town consented to a tax on it less grudgingly once Morton had bowed to pressure to postpone a justice ayre involving large numbers of its inhabitants for supplying the Castilians during the siege.[9] He agreed to postpone the action on a number of the merchants summoned in the bullion affair to avoid damaging their trading activities.[10] More significantly, there were a number of influential burgesses who had good reason to adhere to Morton. The captain of the Edinburgh band at Leith, Adam Fullarton, was granted the lucrative contract for the lead mines along with Morton's kinsman, Douglas of Parkhead, for the unusually long period of twelve years in 1576. It is likely that John Robertson, another wealthy merchant, was a partner in the same deal. John Provand, who was given burgess-ship and guildry free at the regent's request in 1576, was suspected of having been Morton's accomplice in poisoning the earl of Atholl in 1579. He was one of the first to be questioned by the privy council after Morton was put into the Castle in January 1581 and fled about ten weeks later along with other merchants and Morton supporters, who were suspected of planning to stage a counter-coup.[11] Alexander Clark, the provost of the burgh during the period of Morton's final fall, reacted differently; the reason was the skeleton in his cupboard, the loan he had made to Grange in the final stages of the siege of the Castle in the second half of 1572 and the royal jewels that he had kept as security. Morton had cleared up this embarrassing matter for Clark and gained his loyalty in return. Clark's concern, particularly when rumours started to circulate that Morton would be tried for crimes that had been committed during his regency, was to make sure that his name remained cleared, and this must explain a good deal of his flexibility as provost during much of the Lennox and Arran periods in the first half of the 1580s.[12]

Not all of Morton's supporters in the burgh bent so far with the wind as Clark. A substantial body of burgesses — estimates of their numbers vary from fifty-two to over a hundred and fifty — were forced to leave the town during Morton's trial in May 1581.[13] It is not possible to discover who these men were but it would seem unlikely from evidence for later in the 1580s that they were all outside the inner circles of power in the burgh. Just before the annual election in October 1580, John Durie, the most outspoken of the burgh's ministers, had appealed that no member of either the Morton or the Esmé Stewart factions be allowed on to the council.[14] The indications are that his advice went unheeded. By 1580 burgh politics had been swallowed up in the factionalism that enmeshed Scottish politics as a whole.

Evidence to support this conclusion comes from the intricate jigsaw of council membership, which underwent more frequent and drastic changes in this period than it did in the difficult years of the 1560s. The Morton interest on the council was clearly revealed in the dismissal of five of its members along with Douglas of Parkhead by the conservative earls of Argyll and Atholl after their coup in April 1578 and by Morton's leet five months later after he had returned to power. It included, predictably, Provand, Clark and Robertson. John Acheson, John Arnot, Michael Chisholm, Andrew Slater and John Johnston, the brother of the laird of Elphinstone, were also members. Arnot, Slater, Chisholm and Johnston were the men, along with Adam Fullarton, who were nominated by the radical Ruthven lords shortly after their successful coup in 1582.[15] The history of Edinburgh in the period from the first fall of Morton in 1578 to the fall of the Ruthven lords in 1583 centred on the successive promotion and exclusion of two distinct political factions within the burgh establishment. Edinburgh politics were in a highly volatile state long before they were exposed to the crisis which followed the passing of the 'Black Acts' in 1584.

It was only natural that after the deposition of Morton in March 1578 it should have been the disaffected among the merchants who were turned to. Three of the men promoted — William Little, William Napier and Henry Nisbet — had been excluded from the council since their imprisonment by Morton in 1575. It was this faction that was returned to power in the election of October 1580 despite Durie's plea. Although there is no trace of the election process in the council record, the details are suspicious; all of the new bailies were co-opted on to the council and only one of the retiring ordinary council survived. The pattern is clear enough; factionalism had been developing ever since 1575, centring around the figure of Morton himself. The anti-Morton faction, which had a brief taste of power in the short-lived coup of April 1578, was reduced, with the return of Morton to influence at court, to a subsidiary role from then until October 1580. It was, however, not totally excluded; Alexander Uddart, David Williamson, Henry Nisbet and Little all remained on the council. The trend so evident in the election of 1580 was confirmed by that of 1581. It seems clear that Lennox and Arran did not themselves bring about the polarisation of burgh politics but only built on a split that was already there.

It is difficult to know quite how to characterise the ideas or interests of the men to whom both Lennox and Arran turned. Although the preponderance of influential opinion in the burgh had been in favour of excluding Morton, their support for the conservative earls of Atholl and Argyll was not conspicuously enthusiastic and it would be misleading to think of them as a catholic faction.[16] They did, however, find themselves increasingly out of sympathy as time went on with the men who might have been thought to be their most natural allies against Morton — the ministers. Edinburgh's radical ministers, Lawson, Durie, Balcanquhal, and Pont, the minister of St. Cuthbert's, were unrelenting in their bitter opposition to the successive regimes of Morton, Lennox and Arran. They had been well represented in the series of committees which drafted the Second Book of Discipline as a blueprint for the reorganisation of the church along presbyterian lines. They vied with each other in the outspokenness of their criticisms of Lennox from the pulpit of St. Giles'. Balcanquhal was ordered before the privy council in 1580 for deploring the fact that French courtiers could 'impugne the truthe . . . upon the streets of Edinburgh' and was cited before the General Assembly by the king less than a year later for insinuating that Lennox had brought popery not only into the court but his own household. Durie was threatened with imprisonment more than once before he was banished from the town in 1582 for calling Lennox and Arran 'abusers of the king'. Pont helped to draw up the act of the General Assembly which approved the Ruthven Raid. Lawson, despite pleas from the provost for circumspection, openly hailed the Ruthven regime as a deliverance from bondage and, after its fall, equally openly deplored the hounding of Andrew Melville into exile in England. This concerted chorus of protest from the pulpit came to a head with the passing of the 'Black Acts' in May 1584. Despite an explicit warning from the privy council, Lawson and Balcanquhal openly criticised the parliament, and Balcanquhal and Pont even entered a formal legal protest when the acts were proclaimed at the market cross on the following day. To prevent arrest Lawson and Balcanquhal followed Melville on the road south. Pont followed later, no doubt because it took him time to disentangle his complicated business affairs; he managed to combine the ministry of St. Cuthbert's with the provostry of Trinity College and being a senator of the College of Justice. Durie was the only one of Edinburgh's ministers not to go into exile as a result of the crisis of 1584, but he had little choice; he had already been banished to Montrose. Religious radicalism had brought the burgh's ministers almost to the point of self-destruction.[17]

The majority of the merchants who had been driven into opposition to Morton in the second half of the 1570s did not take the same high road to 1584 as the ministers. It was substantially this same body of men who proved willing to support Lennox as well as Arran. Most of them were not convinced that protestantism was under as great a threat from Lennox as their minsters maintained. They saw Arran's government as a return to a *via media* after the extremes of the Ruthven Raid.[18] They were increasingly embarrassed by the interventions of the privy council in burgh affairs as a result of the outbursts of their ministers. Their appeals to Lawson not to associate the burgh too closely with the Ruthven Raid had gone unheeded. When the crisis point had been reached with the calculated storm of protest from the pulpit of St. Giles' over the Black Acts, they had played for time rather than openly silence their own ministers. Their behaviour up to this point had been characterised by pragmatism and moderation. It was dictated by expediency rather than by principle. They found, however, that they could not escape from the shockwaves of the crisis of 1584. Two of the exiled ministers sent a letter justifying their actions to both the council and the kirk session. The council, still trying to extricate itself as best it could from the affair, passed the letter on to the king without comment. It was then asked by James to endorse a reply to the ministers which had been drafted by Archbishop Adamson of St. Andrews.[19] The moderates had a cause forced upon them.

The wider issues at stake were neatly illustrated in a dialogue between two Edinburgh merchants, Edward Hope and Henry Nisbet, over the implications of the letter. The extracts in the printed version of Calderwood's *History* give Hope, a veteran protestant heretic of the 1540s, a great deal more to say as well as the better of the argument: it was 'conscience that makes men refuse'; should men not obey 'the Great King' before 'an earthlie king'? Nisbet, who, as a bailie, had been confronted with the dilemma face to face, had four points of substance to make and they could well comprise the manifesto of the moderate faction in Edinburgh politics by the mid-1580s. He did not share the fears of the ministers about the legislation of the parliament of 1584 since it had also explicitly confirmed 'both the doctrine and ministration of sacraments presently preached'; he criticised them for having more regard for their own consciences than the good of their flock, pointed out that the primary duty of magistrates was 'obedience to established laws' and set down the cardinal principle of Edinburgh government — 'it is the king we have to do with'. The ministers and their allies were clear enough as to what they thought of these 'slyders from the truthe' and, as time went on, rewrote the history of the previous few years in terms of a deliberate conspiracy by them against the true church. The first letter from the exiled ministers alluded to the silent opposition of some of their congregation over the previous three years; the second letter, which was to the council, complained of 'wolves' invading the corridors of power. These were the men whom Hope accused of 'casting the burthen' of the affair on the king when, in fact, it was 'devised in your own bowels'.[20] By 1584 the divisions in burgh politics had taken on an explicitly religious complexion.

Even so, it has been the other faction in burgh politics, which stood firm behind Morton and turned, in relief, to Ruthven, the men who held to radical protestantism and the English connection, that historians have tended to emphasise. Lee argued that the merchants were alarmed by Morton's arrest in 1581 because of a fear that trade with England might suffer as a result. Conyers Read, citing the hounding out of the town of Robert Montgomery, bishop of Glasgow, after his excommunication by the Edinburgh presbytery in June 1582, maintained that 'it was clear enough that the preachers had the burghers behind them'. Donaldson, more cautiously, has paraphrased the council's agreement 'to gif their concurrence' to the Ruthven coup in September 1582 because of the 'popular support' within the burgh for Durie, who had been banished for an attack on the Lennox administration.[21] Durie was allowed to return a few days later and was greeted by a throng of inhabitants — Calderwood estimated their numbers at 2,000 — singing psalms pointedly in front of Lennox's residence.[22] There can be no doubt that it was this faction which enjoyed popular support in the town, and support on a scale that was unknown before the 1580s. But popular support in itself had never been enough to guarantee power in Edinburgh. The key question was still, as it had been in the 1560s, the attitude of the establishment. Both factions drew on a core of fairly respectable merchants, but the pro-Arran group, as it solidified in the aftermath of the Ruthven regime, was noticeably more entrenched in the uppermost layers of the establishment. Little, Napier, Williamson, James Ross, the two Uddarts and the two Nisbets all came from the top twenty-five or so of the merchant establishment. The only men in the rival faction in this class were John Dougal, Mungo Russell and John Robertson. The radicals may have had popularity; the moderates had wealth and privilege.

Which one had power? Viewed in this light, the evidence for the whole of the period from Morton's fall at the end of 1580 to Arran's capture of the key positions of captain of the Castle and provost of the burgh in October 1584 is distinctly equivocal. Although the puritan English agent, Sir Robert Bowes, reported in January 1581 that the town had 'offered liberally for [Morton's] delivery', the council itself contained four of his most bitter personal enemies, Alexander Clark the provost, Alexander Uddart and William Napier, who were both bailies, and Henry Nisbet. Although the provost and bailies had, shortly after their election, assured Bowes of their continuing loyalty to the 'amity', less than three months later Bowes had to admit that only a remnant of an English party remained. Randolph, who was sent to make a more hard-headed appraisal of the state of affairs, bluntly reported that Edinburgh 'bears no goodwill to Morton'.[23] Although a substantial but unidentifiable body of burgesses was forced to leave the town during Morton's trial, it is clear that the majority of the members of the council were not distressed by his fall.

The election of October 1581 saw a further shift away from the ex-Morton interest. The majority of this council agreed in May 1582, albeit under pressure, that Durie should leave the town at least temporarily. Clark and Henry Charteris, one of the bailies, had to suffer an outburst of personal abuse from Andrew Melville as a result. Yet the council of 1581-2 was not prepared to acquiesce in all of Lennox's actions. Another of its bailies was Gilbert Dick, a more robust presbyterian than most of his colleagues, who had tried to put into practice Balcanquhal's campaign from the pulpit against the sexual licence of Lennox's followers in the brothels of the Cowgate. About a month before the Durie affair reached its crisis point Dick had been removed from office, apparently on a technicality. The council objected, probably not because Dick had the 'great love of the godly' but because his removal prejudiced the liberties of the burgh.[24] Equally, the council was prepared to protest against the banishment of a number of burgesses in the wake of the Durie affair. It appears, though, from the evidence that is available, that is was left to the kirk session rather than the council to push the case of Durie himself.[25]

It has to be remembered that it was this same council that was in office during the Ruthven coup. Its agreement to accept the aims of the Ruthven lords can be taken out of context; it should be balanced against its carefully expressed hope that their entry should 'nocht putt in perill' the town. The lords themselves were certainly not convinced by this expression of loyalty. The leet which they proposed on 28 September contained only two members of the sitting council, Andrew Slater and John Johnston, the brother of the laird of Elphinstone. They clearly preferred to return to the safer option of the core of the ex-Morton faction.[26]

Although the council, rather characteristically, did not accept the leet in full, it accepted enough of it to swing the balance of power away from the Lennox faction; three of the four bailies had been on the leet. The most contentious issue that arose during its period in office was the banquet that was held in honour of the French ambassador, de la Mothe Fénélon, in February 1583. The evidence is rather contradictory, both as to who invited Fénélon and who actually attended the banquet in spite of a fast proclaimed by the kirk session in retaliation. The English agents, Bowes and Davison, reported that Clark and 'some few merchants' had issued the invitation. Fénélon himself claimed that he had been entertained by 'all the chiefs' of the town, including the provost. According to Spottiswoode, the magistrates were nearly excommunicated as a result. From what is known of the composition of the council, it seems that Calderwood's is the most likely explanation: three of the bailies and most of the council boycotted the banquet. It is likely that the odd-man-out among the bailies was William Fairlie, whose two brothers, Mungo and David, had both compromised themselves during the civil wars; he himself had long been a personal enemy of Adam Fullarton and had been banned from the communion table as a result in 1574. Equally, it seems more plausible that pressure for the banquet came not from the council but from a number of wealthy merchants whose 'god is their gaine'. Remembering that the next election saw the return in strength of what had now become a pro-Arran faction, who were drawn from the wealthiest section of the merchant establishment, it seems likely that these were the prominent members of Edinburgh society to whom Fénélon alluded. The banquet was an attempt by the excluded and more moderate members of the merchant establishment to embarrass the substantially pro-Ruthven council. There can be no doubt, though, that at the same time there was considerable popular feeling against both Fénélon and Maineville; David Kinloch, one of the most militant of the Edinburgh band during the civil wars and a highly influential craftsman, led a mob which tried to assault Maineville and his private chaplain.[27]

It was obvious after the eclipse of the Ruthven lords in the summer and autumn of 1583 that the council's days in office in its existing form were numbered. Personal scores were settled first, however; Dick was forfeited for murder. Despite rumours of an early purge of office-holders in the burghs, little else happened until a leet was presented to the council on 25 September. Unlike the Ruthven leet of the year before, this time there were no half-measures. Clark was continued as provost but all the other offices went to men who were co-opted on to the council; all the new councillors, both merchants and craftsmen, were also nominees; only one from the old ordinary council survived. This was as comprehensive a purge as any since 1559. It is not surprising that James Lawson, in the second of his letters to the council from exile in 1584, talked of the 'wolves' who had infiltrated it.[28] The coup did not go uncontested; pro-Ruthven candidates were put up for all the major offices. The balance was swung, however, by the newly nominated councillors, by replacements for absentees, and by the six new deacon councillors, who were admitted to the election process for the first time.[29] It is important to note that the implementation of the decreet-arbitral coincided with and was an important constituent of the coup of September and October 1583.

It would be an over-simplification to think of the craftsmen as committed to Arran, despite a laconic remark by Calderwood that Lennox and Arran 'fostered the feud between the merchants and craftsmen'. At least three of the deacons who had protested bitterly in October 1583 against the participation of assessors in the election were committed radicals.[30] It is true that certain of the craftsmen on the council of 1583-4, particularly Alexander Oustean and William Harvie, were energetic supporters of the new regime, but Oustean was also one of those who refused to sign the king's letter to the exiled ministers in June or July of 1584.[31] It is more likely that what the crafts saw as the issue at stake in 1583 was not a commitment to either of the Ruthven or the Arran factions but to the decreet itself, and a personal debt to Arran, who had backed the crafts' case since 1582.[32]

It was this purged and nominated council that had to contend with the most serious of the running disputes between the burgh's ministers and the administration. The council started off on a policy of restoring order to the town by re-enacting an old statute to banish any inhabitant convicted of 'common tulyie'. Yet even this council, which Bowes described as pro-court and pro-French in sympathies, was reluctant to commit itself to removing Durie permanently. It became more difficult to maintain this position with every fresh outburst from the pulpit. The appeal made in January 1584 to the king to allow Durie to return until the next meeting of the General Assembly was made by two of the ministers and two members of the session. It is noticeable that the two representatives from the council who accompanied them were only ordinary councillors; one of them, Michael Chisholm, belonged to the Ruthven rump that had remained on the council. It seems likely that the session was a good deal less reticent than the council in the crisis that deepened after the parliament of May 1584, which had precipitated the flight of Lawson and Balcanquhal.[33]

A number of radicals were forced to leave the town early in June. It seems likely that some members of the kirk session were among them; John Adamson, one of the eighteen listed by Calderwood, certainly was. They included a number of very prominent burgesses, like Fullarton, Primrose, John Dougal and Andrew Napier, as well as smaller men. A further hundred and twenty or hundred and forty were threatened with the same fate on the pretext of an incident that went back to the Lennox period, probably towards the end of 1582, and some of them were actually banished shortly afterwards.[34] The combined effect of all of these pressures was considerable, but not wholly successful. Both the council and the kirk session were split, but not in the same proportions. Calderwood states that all of the council agreed to subscribe the king's reply to the exiled ministers drafted by Archbishop Adamson except six, whom he names, and 'other three of the kirk'. Only three of those named, however, were actually on the council.[35] According to Spottiswoode, sixteen of the principals' eventually signed the letter. As the total membership of the council, apart from the newly created deacon councillors, was nineteen, this evidence would again point to three who held out — William Little, Andrew Slater and the provost, Alexander Clark, as well as the tailors' deacon, Alexander Oustean. For Clark, the letter seems to have been the last straw and put an end both to his 'courting', which had been assiduously cultivated ever since the fall of Morton, and to his tenure of the office of provost.[36]

It would appear that a larger proportion of the kirk sesson refused to submit to pressure; eleven of its twenty-eight members were summoned to Falkland on 28 June for a personal interview with James, during the course of which they were accused of treason. Only two, who seem to have been the most outspoken among them, are named by Calderwood but their names are significant. One was John Blackburn, a small and probably fairly young merchant, who had first come to prominence during the civil wars. The other was a more surprising figure; he was John Preston, a man who was now seventy-one years of age and whose long and distinguished civic career stretched back to 1549. Although he had never become involved in the more questionable activities of the protestant party, Preston had been one of the most respected members of the protestant establishment and had represented the burgh over a long period at the General Assembly and the Convention of Royal Burghs.[37] The contrast between Blackburn and Preston was not an isolated one. It was repeated over and over again among the burgesses who were banished or pledged on their good behaviour during the course of 1584. The radical presbyterian supporters of the exiled ministers were mostly smaller merchants or craftsmen but they also numbered among them some of the grand old men of Edinburgh protestantism — Preston, Adam Fullarton, Edward Hope. The widows of two of the most influential men in shaping the course of Edinburgh's reformation, James McGill and Alexander Guthrie, were banished in September 1584 along with the wives of the exiled ministers.[38] The most serious opposition in the burgh to the treatment of the ministers, the 'Black Acts' of 1584 and the increasing interference in burgh affairs came not from the council, which had been systematically purged in 1583 and 1584, but from the kirk session and a small but dwindling band of veterans of the reformation crisis and the early 1560s, who had steadily lost influence in the burgh since the civil wars. The remnants of the protestant regime of the early 1560s had now to turn to quite different allies from the well-heeled merchants they had relied on during the crisis of 1571-3. The strength of radical protestantism now lay, not in the corridors of power, but in its grassroots appeal amongst the crafts and smaller merchants.

The problem of the 'spyte' of the Melvillian-dominated session was dealt with after the council election of 1584, which was again pre-empted by a leet naming all six office-holders as well as Arran himself as provost.[39] One of the victims was John Preston. The last traces of the pro-Ruthven council of 1582-3 were removed and a solidly pro-Arran faction elected. It had become established practice for the election to the kirk session to follow in the two or three weeks after the council election process was completed. From the limited evidence that is available it seems that it was often the pattern that retiring members of the council stepped on to the session, as in October 1575. Since the retiring councillors were almost Ruthven supporters to a man, this may have forced the Arran faction into preventive measures. It was also an opportunity not to be missed to gain control of the session, since at least three of its most prominent members — Blackburn, John Johnston of Elphinstone and John Adamson — had been banished from the burgh. An ordinance of 14 October imposed a system of direct election of the session by the council. The device that was used, of the council and deacons descending on each of the four quarters of the burgh, now declared to be separate parishes, was one that would be used again and refined from the 1620s onwards. It was a system that was unique to Edinburgh in this period[40] and this probably reflects the unique problem that Edinburgh posed for the court in the early 1580s. It probably did not survive the fall of Arran.

The result of the purging of the session was a rather strange body. The elders were respectable enough; they included what seems to have been the statutory two craftsmen, four advocates and six fairly well-to-do merchants. It was usual for the deacons to be drawn from less prosperous sections of burgh society than the elders and they often had limited experience of office. The deacons nominated in 1584 exaggerated both of these tendencies; they contained some very small men indeed, both merchants and craftsmen, and not one of them had ever held burgh office. A number had only very recently been given burgess status. Melvillianism may temporarily have been sifted out of the kirk session, but only at the expense of a good deal of the drive and enthusiasm which seem to have come from its meaner men.[41]

Part of the same pattern of exerting stricter and more direct control over an expanding and often temperamental population were two other reorganisational schemes put through by the same council. The events of the previous four years had shown up the deficiencies of the town's arrangements for a night watch, particularly when the king was in residence at Holyrood. From November 1584 a system of thirties rather than quarters was used. The direct nomination of the dean of guild's council by the town council and the reformulation of the burgess oath, as well as changing the medieval legacy of the head courts of the burgh, introduced a political dimension which had not been there before.[42]

By the end of 1584 and the beginning of 1585 the two ministers of St. Cuthbert's had been dismissed. On 9 December Nicol Dalgleish was tried and convicted of concealing a letter from Balcanquhal; Robert Pont was banished less than three weeks later, although his position was complicated by the fact that he also held the provostry of Trinity College, which took a further six months to settle.[43] Yet the purge did not end the king's problems with Edinburgh's ministers or the town's reluctance to accept the dictates of the court on religious matters. Ultra-protestantism continued, but with a difference. The crisis of 1584 was the last in which the political generation of the early 1560s played a serious role. Of course, the obvious reason for this was that a good many of them were dead by then. David Forester had died in 1572, James McGill in 1579, Alexander Guthrie in 1582.[44]

There is a more significant explanation, which goes a long way towards explaining the gradual eclipse of militant protestantism among Edinburgh's merchants, a process that must have seemed very unlikely in 1573. Killigrew's well-known remark—'Methinks I see the noblemen's great credit decay . . . and the barons, burghs and such-like take more upon them' — whatever its truth in the longer-term, was certainly an understandable one to make in the context of the victory of a militant party, bound to political protestantism and the English alliance. It was a remark that had a profound effect on the assumptions that lay behind English foreign policy towards Scotland for the next ten years. A myth was cultivated of a pro-English party which would hold 'the repose of the two realms before their particular interests' and an important element of this party was thought to be the reliability of the 'best affected burgesses of Edinburgh'. It was the persistence of this myth which allowed Bowes in particular to compose outrageously over-optimistic assessments of the situation in Scotland in the second half of 1580 for the benefit of his masters. It took Randolph to make a more realistic analysis and to realise how much Edinburgh's attitude to the politics of the English connection had changed since his period of residence in the early 1560s.[45]

The four key agents of the English connection in the 1560s had been Alexander Guthrie, Adam Fullarton, Alexander Clark and Archibald Graham. Guthrie had acted as a source of information for Randolph as early as October 1560. Three months later Clark recited a record of his service in a letter to

Cecil. The links that Clark and Graham had with the English interest were probably dictated at first by their masters; they were clients of Moray and Maitland, the apostles of the pro-English policy of the Congregation after 1559. Relations between Clark and Randolph, however, went a good deal further than those between ambassador and trusted informant; Randolph described Clark as his 'treasurer' and enjoyed exchanging ribald gossip about the court.[46] Fullarton was close to both Randolph and Killigrew but his contacts extended to the highest reaches of the English privy council; the list of his 'verre good freindis' — Burghley, Walsingham, Leicester, Bedford, Hunsdon, Hatton — was nothing short of spectacular.[47] All four had become involved at one time or another during Mary's personal reign in conspiracies which had English foreknowledge or tacit support. Clark and Guthrie had been two of the elected leaders of the Congregation who mustered on the Crags in 1565 in the prelude to the Moray conspiracy. All four had been involved in the Riccio affair, and Guthrie deeply enough for him to flee to England along with James McGill in its aftermath. Yet after Randolph left Scotland, under duress, in 1566, relations between the 'English interest' in Edinburgh and England seem never to have been so close again, apart from a brief period from 1572-3. There was certainly never again quite the same influential protestant caucus in the burgh to which English foreign policy could turn, in desperation, to run the 'violent course'. Both early in 1581, in the period of the failing fortunes of Morton, and in the autumn of 1583 after the eclipse of the Ruthven lords, an emergency English mission failed to arouse a significant pro-English party in the town.[48]

A variety of factors, not the least of them complacency, combined to open up a 'Scottish gap' in general and a split within Edinburgh's merchant community in particular. The four elements that comprised the English connection — nobles, lairds, ministers and the 'better sort' of burgesses — were an unstable coalition at best. The ministers were not slow to criticise English pensioners, and their increasingly outspoken sermons did not endear them to the more prosperous among the merchants, who remained heavily dependent on trade with France.[49] The lesson of the civil wars, that the merchants would commit themselves to political action only if there was a guarantee that English policy would be carried through to a conclusion and tangible results would follow, had never wholly been taken to heart. The striking unanimity of the 'Edinburgh band' in 1572 had been produced by a set of distinctly peculiar circumstances, which were not easily reproduced in the growing factionalism of Scottish and Edinburgh politics after the wars.

The individual leaders of the English connection either faded from active politics, like Graham, or were compromised. Guthrie seemed, as time went on, to be absorbed in the task of passing on his office of common clerk of the burgh to his son rather than in risking the family inheritance by coming out strongly for one faction or the other in the unstable situation which persisted after 1578. Relations between Clark and Morton deteriorated seriously in a relatively short period between January and February 1581 when Clark's position as provost was under threat and his past dealings with Morton were under investigation. After that point Clark, despite repeated assurances of his continuing loyalty to the English connection, pursued a bewilderingly flexible course. Clark's deviation was a matter of choice and had happened before, in 1569, but the eclipse of Adam Fullarton's standing in the burgh paradoxically can be traced to the English connection itself. The peak of Fullarton's career had come after his return to the burgh as the leader of the Edinburgh band, when he was made one of the lords of the articles in the parliament of April 1573.[50]

It was natural that it should have been Fullarton who was turned to, both as a client of Morton and as one who, as he said himself in 1584, had laboured 'nycht and day' for the amity,[51] to seek redress for the serious losses which Edinburgh merchants sustained from English pirates in the 1570s. Archibald Graham had been chosen for much the same reasons, as a client of Maitland and key figure in the English connection, to seek settlement of a piracy case in the 1560s. The Graham affair had also shown the dangers of failure; the case dragged on for more than seven years and Randolph warned of growing disenchantment with England.[52] There had been a second warning in the failure of John Ferguson in the mid-1570s.[53] Fullarton was the third and most serious casualty. His appointment in May 1577 kept him in England for more than two and a half years, during which time Morton's position slipped steadily away. The final settlement of the piracy disputes took ten years' litigation in the Admiralty Court, and even then the Scots secured less than a quarter of their original claim.[54] The long delays were a natural breeding-ground for disaffection. There was a growing suspicion that Fullarton had been pressing his own case rather than that of the merchants as a whole and this led to a bitter personal split between him and John Provand, another of Morton's most loyal supporters in the burgh. Provand even began to spread rumours that Fullarton had slipped away to Flanders with the proceeds. He and a number of other merchants brought an action against Fullarton which dragged on until 1582; it is significant that the others involved included William Fairlie, William Nisbet and David Williamson, all members of the anti-Morton and anti-Ruthven faction on the council in the early 1580s. The effects of piracy were probably not as serious as some of the more plaintive petitions to the English privy council made out but at least a quarter of the uppermost layer of the merchant establishment did suffer from them.[55] The dispute was the more bitter because it was, at least ostensibly, a family affair; a Dundee petition complained of the damage inflicted on members of the 'one household of faith'.[56]

The miscalculations of English policy in the piracy disputes exaggerated what was a more serious miscalculation, the failure to realise that radical protestantism had, at best, only a slippery grip on the burgh establishment. English policy, always through its puritan agents on the lookout for 'the better sort', became committed to fostering not an Edinburgh connection but one faction in burgh government, which increasingly had as its allies a radical element outside the natural circles of power. It failed to adapt itself to the growing rift between the bulk of the wealthy merchant establishment and the more outspoken of the ministers, which can be traced back to the 1570s. As one faction displaced another on the council, so the attachment to the 'amity' moved from the real to the notional.

Fullarton never returned to the town council, and during the various crises of the early 1580s he played only a marginal role in Edinburgh politics. His fall from grace was all the more startling for a man who, after the death of James Baron in 1569, had emerged as the undisputed secular leader of Edinburgh protestantism. It would be an exaggeration to see the eclipse of the pro-Morton and pro-Ruthven faction as being as sudden or dramatic as Fullarton's, but there can be little doubt that by the Arran period the threat to the moderate merchant establishment lay more outside the council chamber than inside. The centre of gravity of Edinburgh's caucus of activists had shifted perceptibly downwards as the unifying issues of the civil wars had given way to the more confusing ones of the later 1570s and the early 1580s. This shift did not significantly alter, even after Arran's fall. Some of the old Ruthven faction did return to the council in 1586; Balcanquhal returned in 1585, and new Melvillian ministers took the places of the old. Nonetheless, there was a difference. The old backbone of radical protestantism had been irreversibly weakened and no new graft could restore it completely. James VI's problem in the future did not lie with a disaffected and militant caucus on the council but with an amorphous radical mass outside it. The vital — and dangerous — link between militant protestantism and the merchant establishment had gone.

NOTES

1. *RPC*, ii, 220, 260ff; *Hist. King James VI*, 148; *Diurnal*, 336; *CSP Scot.*, iv, no. 788(1); Donaldson, *James V to James VII*, 148, 167-9. Gourlay was an elder rather than a deacon, as Killigrew reported; see BGKE, fos. 5r-6v and app. iii.

2. *TA*, xiii, 46-7; *Edin. Recs.*, iv, 32; *CSP Scot.*, vi, no. 26; *Diurnal*, 343; *Hist. King James VI*, 151; SRO, MS Privy Council Register of *Acta* (PC 1/7), fo. 348; see *RPC*, ii, 709, 718, 727, 730, 731, 737. One of the eight, Thomas Aikenhead, was a skinner; the other seven all appeared among the first fifteen merchants in the tax roll of 1583.

3. See MS Co. Recs., v, fo. 50v; *Edin. Recs.*, iv, 40; *CSP Scot.*, v, nos. 186-7.

4. *TA*, xiii, 46, 68; MS Co. Recs., 20 Oct. 1575, v, fos. 54v, 55r; see *Hist. King James VI*, 151. A letter from Morton to Borthwick of 27 Jan. 1575 instructed, however, that action only be taken against twenty or twenty-four of the principals in the meantime (NLS, MS Balcarres Papers, 29.2.9a., no. 17). The eighteen wealthy merchants were Gilbert Dick, John Dougal, Mungo Fairlie, John Harwood, Wm. Little, Simon Marjoribanks, David Morris, John Morrison, Wm. Napier, Henry Nisbet, John Robertson, James Ross, Mungo Russell, Bartilmo Somerville, Alex. & Nicol Uddart, Thomas Vaus and Luke Wilson.

5. *Correspondence Diplomatique de la Mothé Fénélon*, vi, 464, 472; but cf. *CSP Scot.*, v, nos.

169, 176; also *ibid.*, v, no. 187(1); MS Balcarres Papers, no. 13; MS Co. Recs., v, fo. 55r.

6. *TA*, xiii, 49, 52; MS Register of *Acta* (PC 1/7), fos. 293-5, 324; *RPC*, ii, 712, 721, 736; iii, 116-8; Pitscottie, *Historie*, ii, 319; MS Balcarres Papers, no. 11; see *Diurnal*, 343.

7. Commissioners were sent from the burgh to Stirling on 18 Dec. 1577, not on 23 Dec., as given in *Edin. Recs.*, iv, 61; cf. MS Co. Recs., v, fo. 84.

8. *APS*, iii, 92-3; *Diurnal*, 344-5; *CSP Scot.*, v, no. 96; Moysie, *Memoirs*, 18; Mitchison, *History of Scotland*, 135.

9. *RPC*, ii, 577; *CSP Scot.*, v, nos. 223, 226; *Edin. Recs.*, iv, 45-7; see *TA*, xiii, 329-48, which lists, among others, 94 from the area immediately adjoining the burgh, who were fined for supplying the rebels as a result of the justice ayre held in Feb. and early March 1576.

10. MS Balcarres Papers, nos. 15, 17.

11. *RPC*, ii, 506, 626; iii, 769; *Edin. Burgs.*, 407; *CSP Scot.*, v, nos. 760, 761, 776.

12. *RPC*, iii, 388-90. Ironically, the nominee of the confederate lords for provost, Archibald Stewart, had been involved in the same transaction; see app. viii.

13. Cf. Calderwood, *History*, iii, 556; *CSP Spanish*, iii, no. 97.

14. *CSP Scot.*, v, nos. 606, 608.

15. *Edin. Recs.*, iv, 71, 84-5, 248.

16. *Ibid.*, iv, 81; *RPC*, iii, 10; Calderwood, *History*, iii, 418-9; *CSP Scot.*, v, no. 351; see Donaldson, *James V to James VII*, 174.

17. The elaborate process of drafting the Second Book of Discipline, together with useful biographies of the radical ministers involved in it, is valuably summarised in Kirk, 'Thesis', esp. 231-4, 363, 564-7, 609-10, 633-4, 648-9. At times the committees resembled a meeting of the Edinburgh presbytery as it evolved a few years later in 1581. See also *BUK*, i, 592, 594-6; Calderwood, *History*, iii, 583-5, 620, 642-3, 677-9, 722-6, 762, 764; iv, 2, 13, 64-5; *RPC*, iii, 335; *CSP Scot.*, vi, nos. 113, 120, 122, 130, 142; vii, 146.

18. See Donaldson, *James V to James VII*, 173, 181.

19. Calderwood, *History*, iv, 73-91; *CSP Scot.*, vii, nos. 157, 171, 180, 193, 196, 416.

20. Cf. the Small MS of Calderwood's History (NLS, Advocates MS 33.6.1), 209-34, with the short extract printed in *History*, iv, 141-3; see esp. pp. 217, 225-6, 229, 234. See also *History*, iv, 74, 78.

21. Cf. M. Lee, 'The fall of Regent Morton: a problem in satellite diplomacy', *J. Of Modern History*, xxviii (1956), 126-7; C. Read, *Mr. Secretary Walsingham and the Policy of Queen Elizabeth* (Oxford, 1925), ii, 179; Donaldson, *James V to James VII*, 179. See also *CSP Scot.*, v, no. 655; vi, no. 130; Calderwood, *History*, iii, 629, 631; viii, 222-4; *Edin. Recs.*, iv, 240-41, 244-5.

22. Calderwood, *History*, viii, 226; *CSP Scot.*, vi, no. 160.

23. *Ibid.*, v, nos. 614, 655, 708; Calderwood, *History*, iii, 483.

24. *Ibid.*, iii, 620, 775; viii, 222-3; Spottiswoode, *History*, ii, 288; *Edin. Recs.*, iv, 234-5; *CSP Scot.*, vi, nos. 104, 125, 218. Dick had already survived being tried for illegally imprisoning a royal messenger two years before (JC 6/1 & JC 2/1, 1 Jan. 1580).

25. *Edin. Recs.*, iv, 237-8; *CSP Scot.*, vi, no. 130; *RPC*, iii, 488; Calderwood, *History*, viii, 225.

26. *Edin. Recs.*, iv, 245, 248.

27. *CSP Scot.*, vi, nos. 306, 330, 336, 386; Spottiswoode, *History*, ii, 298; Calderwood, *History*, iv, 317; BGKE, 7 Dec. 1574, fo. 32r; see Mungo and David Fairlie in app. viii and Kinloch in app. vii.

28. *CSP Scot.*, vi, nos. 605, 644; vii, no. 196; *Edin. Recs.*, iv, 289-91; Calderwood, *History*, iv, 78.

29. MS Co. Recs., vii, fos. 15, 18v, 19r, 20v; *Edin. Recs.*, iv, 289-91.

30. Calderwood, *History*, iv, 411; *Edin. Recs.*, iv, 250-55; MS Co. Recs., 2 Oct. 1582, vi, fo. 208r; see John Bairnsfather, Edward Galbraith and Gilbert Primrose in app. x.

31. See *Edin. Recs.*, iv, 301, 319-21, 339-40; MS Co. Recs., 1, 3 & 11 June 1584, vii, fos. 90v, 92r; Calderwood, *History*, viii, 269.

32. See Calderwood, *History*, iii, 635.

33. *Edin. Recs.*, iv, 295-6, 314; *CSP Scot.*, vi, nos. 654, 675, 718; vii, no. 146; Calderwood, *History*, iv, 2, 72; *RPC*, iii, 617.

34. *CSP Scot.*, vii, nos. 167-8, 180; Calderwood, *History*, viii, 260; see also iv, 2; *RPC*, iii, 488; see app. x for details.

35. Calderwood, *History*, viii, 269. The three members of the council were Wm. Little, a bailie, Andrew Slater, a councillor, and Alex. Oustean, one of the new deacon councillors; see app. x.

36. Spottiswoode, *History*, ii, 318; *CSP Scot.*, vii, no. 171.

37. Calderwood, *History*, iv, 122-4; viii, 262-7; *Edin. Recs.*, iv, 380; see Preston's entries in apps. vii & x.

38. Calderwood, *History*, iv, 126-41, 200; *CSP Scot.*, vii, no. 308.

39. *CSP Scot.*, vii, no. 158.

40. *Edin. Recs.*, iv, 355-6, 359. I am grateful to Dr. W. H. Makey for this information; the complicated relationship between town council and kirk session has been expertly analysed by him in *The Church of the Covenant*, 154-64.

41. See app. iii for the membership of the kirk session of 1584-5; the point is discussed more fully in ch. 3.

42. *Edin. Recs.*, iv, 358, 362-3, 384, 387-8.

43. *RPC*, iii, 701-02; Calderwood, *History*, iv, 211, 245; *Original Letters of John Colville*, 74; *CSP Scot.*, vii, no. 479; Pitcairn, *Trials*, 1, ii, 136-8; JC 2/2, 8 & 9 Dec. 1584.

44. See app. v for details of all three; for McGill, see also *CSP Scot.*, v, no. 434.

45. *Ibid.*, iv, no. 476; v, nos. 160, 595, 606, 614, 698, 708.

46. Their gossip was too ribald for the Victorian editor of English state papers; see esp. PRO, SP 52/10, Clark to Randolph, [22?] April 1565, fos. 89r-90v; cf. *CSP Scot.*, ii, 171(1); see app. v for details of the four.

47. *CSP Scot.*, vii, no. 285.

48. *Ibid.*, ii, no. 352; v, nos. 651, 653; vi, no. 660.

49. *Ibid.*, v, nos. 116, 470, 512, 698; vii, no. 109.

50. *Edin. Recs.*, iv, 111, 130; *CSP Scot.*, ii, no. 1142; see esp. *ibid.*, 11 Jan. & 8 Feb. 1581, v, nos. 660, 708; *Diurnal*, 331.

51. *CSP Scot.*, vii, no. 285.

52. See *ibid.*, i, nos. 938, 1034; ii, nos. 81, 112, 196, 234, 419, 422, 425-6, 431, 444-5, 454; *RPC*, i, 430-32.

53. See *CSP Scot.*, iv, 783, 787, 788(1); *Edin. Recs.*, iv, 14; for Ferguson, see app. vii.

54. *CSP Scot.*, ix, nos. 413, 417.

55. *Edin. Recs.*, iv, 22, 168-9; *RPC*, iii, 269, 322, 497-8; *CSP Scot.*, v, nos. 356, 394; vi, 268, 367, 430, 552. Eight of the first twenty-nine merchants on the 1583 tax roll were affected — Robert Abercrombie, Gilbert Dick, Wm. Napier, Wm. Nisbet, John Provand, Bartilmo Somerville, Nicol Uddart and David Williamson. See also *Warrender Papers*, i, 142, 166-7.

56. *CSP Scot.*, vi, no. 429.

Part Three

Parties and Party Men

9

The Old Establishment and the New

THE oligarchy which controlled Edinburgh politics was a small and select body. About a quarter of the merchants on the tax roll of 1565 sat on the council at some time in their lives; a little more than fifty merchants served on it in the 1550s.[1] It is likely, though, that the number actively involved in burgh affairs at any one point was no more than thirty-five to forty, about double the available seats on the council. The very structure of elections ensured, as it was meant to, a large element of self-perpetuation; it also, through the device of promotion on to the council of two new merchant members each year, contained a built-in means of transferring power from one generation to the next. At times, the divine right of heredity operated more obviously; Archibald Graham simply took his father's seat on the council when his political career came to an end in 1555.[2]

The effect of the municipal coups of October 1559 and April 1560 was to interrupt this pattern severely; if those who came on to the council as a result of one or other of the Marian leets of 1565 and 1566 are discounted, only twenty-two of the merchants who had served on the council in the 1550s survived the coup. The natural processes of death and old age accounted for a further fifth of the old regime of the 1550s; at least half a dozen had died by 1560 and a further three had retired from active politics.[3] Only a rough net estimate is possible, but it seems that the reformation crisis resulted in the purge of about half of the burgh establishment. It is certainly the case that more than half of the Seton council of 1559-60 were excluded from the council in the 1560s. They included two of the much criticised bailies, Maxwell and Little, the dean of guild, Thomas Uddart, although he had little taste for office in any case, five of the merchant councillors and both the craftsmen. Three more from the council of 1558-9 were victims of the purge. In many city reformations of the sixteenth century the reformation was carried through by an oligarchy which was able to paper over its own differences in order to cling on to power. Direct intervention by successive protestant and catholic invading armies, each imposing a purged administration on the town,

172

removed the possibility of a united front persisting amongst Edinburgh's ruling class. Purges and splits were imposed on the burgh by external forces. The new, protestant establishment was, however, to find that it could not govern without at least the tacit consent of the old.

The immediate result of the Congregation's purge was a partial vacuum. Nine of the twelve merchants on the Kilspindie ordinary council and one of the bailies had their first taste of office as a result of the coup of October 1559; only three of the remainder had been on the council more than twice before. What must have been striking about the new protestant regime was its unprecedented inexperience of burgh affairs. It does seem unlikely, however, that protestants had deliberately been frozen out in the 1550s, since both of the key figures in the nurturing of protestantism in the 1550s, James Baron and Edward Hope, were regular members of the council during that period. A second feature of the Kilspindie council was even more striking; it was drawn from a much wider range of the merchants than was usual and even included some cramers. Edinburgh's reformation, however, did not result in a permanent downward shift of power within the merchant class. The pattern of the Kilspindie council was not repeated. Half of the *arrivistes,* mostly the lower half, never held council office again, although they were admitted to lesser duties.

The council of 1560-61 went a long way towards establishing the social respectability of the new regime. The average assessment of its members in the 1565 tax roll was exactly two and a half times the merchant average; it had only three newcomers, James Aikman, John Uddart and John Adamson, all of them younger members of leading merchant families. The consolidation of the new regime continued over the first half of the 1560s; it tended to take the form of the continuous presence of a rump of committed protestants together with the re-admittance of a select number of the old establishment and the first appearance of younger men. The latter process is the more striking; in the years between 1561 and 1564 seven of the old guard returned to the council and thirteen appeared on it for the first time. The process was one of trial and error; about a third of the newcomers were given a fleeting taste of office and quietly dropped. It would be an exaggeration to think of a solid and totally committed protestant regime emerging in the early 1560s. The effect of the queen's intervention in burgh elections was great enough for the whole process to have to be gone through again after 1567: there were five newcomers added to the protestant core in 1567, five in 1568 and four in 1569. There was almost as great a difference between the councils of the early and late 1560s as there was between those of before and after 1559. This was a process that was accelerated by civil wars and the purge of queen's men that followed them; none of the Marians survived but there was also only a handful of the protestant veterans of the early 1560s remaining in power ten years later.

There was undoubtedly a systematic purge of conservatives from the council after 1560. Yet an analysis that rests only on council membership may produce an impression of too sharp a break. Involvement in burgh affairs was not confined to those who sat in the council chamber. There were a number of occasional but nonetheless important civic duties to be fulfilled; the most regular of these were the duties of auditor and extentor, who usually numbered sixteen and twelve respectively. Other tasks which were delegated to a committee of burgesses ranged from settling boundary disputes to preparing the town's defences. The demands of the reformed programme also increased these opportunities from 1561 onwards with the more permanent offices of collectors for the poor and the ministry, as well as occasional inventories of the annuals, rents and lands of the old church within the burgh. All of these secondary duties in theory allowed a wider participation in civic affairs, although in practice some of them, like the auditors of the bailies' and dean of guild's accounts, were handled almost exclusively by members of the council. In addition, a fairly wide range of burgesses, much wider than the select group who were drawn upon for council office, sat on assizes in the Court of Justiciary as well as on burgh courts.

The purge did not extend beyond council service. A number of members of the old establishment continued to perform these secondary duties: Richard Gray, who had testified before the de la Brosse inquiry in February 1560, was nevertheless an adjudicator in a neighbourhood dispute in 1561 and an extentor in 1564; Thomas Uddart acted as an auditor in 1562 and 1563 and William Lawson in 1563; John Dougal was an extentor in 1564.[4] Of course, it might be argued that this was not a high price for the new establishment to pay to provide itself with a front of respectability. Yet if that was the case, the new regime went a good deal further than it needed to. Most of the excluded merchants of the hard-line Seton council of 1559-60 continued to serve in these minor positions: James Curle was an auditor in 1562 and 1563 and an extentor in 1566; James Lindsay was an auditor in 1562, 1563, 1565 and 1567 and an extentor in 1562, 1566 and 1567. This applied even to the much-criticised bailies: Herbert Maxwell and Edward Little were both auditors in 1565 and Little an extentor in 1564. They were allowed to do this in spite of the fact that they formed the core of the rival catholic party in the burgh. Other members of the same faction were given the same opportunities: James Carmichael, another de la Brosse witness, was an auditor in 1562 and 1563; John Spottiswood was actually an auditor shortly after the Congregation returned to the burgh in April 1560 as well as in 1562 and 1563.[5] John Charteris, the veteran of the Seton council, was not re-employed, but his catholic son was used as an extentor in 1561; William Brocas, the catholic hammerman, was an adjudicator along with Richard Gray in 1561; Adam Allan was an auditor in April 1567.[6] The admission of conservatives and outright catholics to this range of responsibilities began on a consistent basis in the spring of 1561 and continued at least until the autumn of 1567. The revolution of 1567 seems to have brought a new broom to the minor offices in burgh administration.[7] There were other offices, however, like those of craft deacons, which lay at best at the outer fringes of the council's control. Here the council found it very difficult to keep catholics out of office — and away from power. John Loch became deacon of the skinners in 1561 and William Brocas of the hammermen in 1562. In certain cases things did not improve with time; it was in the late 1560s that the conservatives regained control of the hammermen craft.[8]

Obviously it was felt that it would have been politically unwise to carry through a total purge of burgh administration. Attention was concentrated on the council itself. Although council meetings were held in closed session, it was part of the burgh tradition that some open government was necessary, particularly where the town's finances were concerned. This was all the more necessary in a period like that between 1560 and 1567 when an unusually large number of financial demands were being made on the burgesses in the form of extents. The new regime did not try to protestantise the whole range of burgh government. Where it was trying to implement its reformed programme, it *was* forced to rely on a fairly select band of committed protestants. This was particularly true of the collectors for the ministry, where the weight of authority had often to be added to the arts of persuasion to exact 'voluntary' contributions; here men like James Baron, David Forester and John Preston were resorted to. In a real sense, though, the old processes of taxation and audit continued to be administered neutrally; this should be borne in mind when considering the complaints of contemporary catholic apologists of the deliberate victimisation of catholics through over-taxation.[9] The one excursion into partisan tax assessment, when the Congregation entered the town in 1560, was a disastrous failure.

The other serious complaint that was made was of the inability of catholics to gain justice from civil magistrates.[10] It is very difficult to pass judgement on this in one way or another. It should be realised, though, that Edinburgh's new regime had a particular situation to bear in mind: the presence within the burgh and even at times within its own tolbooth of the Court of Justiciary. An analysis of the assize lists of the justiciary court also reveals the same use of catholics and conservatives after 1560. William Aikman and John Young, both members of the council in the second half of the 1550s, were on two of the assizes which dealt with the craft riots of 1560 and 1561.[11] Most of the catholic veterans of the Seton council were used with some consistency: Maxwell, Little, Lindsay and Archibald Leach were called to serve on a total of eight assizes between 1562 and 1567, dealing with cases which ranged from sheep-stealing to the Nicol Young affair and the trial of protestant activists for the first assault on Friar Black. Other prominent figures in the catholic party appeared along with them, including Carmichael, Spottiswood, Cuthbert Murray, Cuthbert Ramsay and James Dalyell. Like Murray, some of those used were known practising catholics: John Graham was one of a formidably catholic-looking assize which tried Thomas Brown and William Johnston for the attack on Friar Black; John Aldinstoun, although called, failed to turn up for the trial of their partner-in-crime, Andrew Armstrong. Certain trials, like those dealing with the Black and Young affairs, were obviously packed with catholic sympathisers.[12] Equally, others, like the trial of the catholic rioter, William Balfour, in 1561 were packed with protestant burgesses.[13] In general, though, assize lists probably give a nearer representation of the natural balance of forces in Edinburgh in the years after 1560 than any other source.

Unlike the minor range of duties in burgh government, catholics continued to serve on assizes after the revolution of 1567. Maxwell, Murray and Lindsay all served on the various assizes dealing with the murderers of Darnley in the last three months of 1567. Ramsay served on the trial of a fellow burgess, Hercules Methven, convicted of importing counterfeit coin early in 1568. It is likely that a number committed themselves at Langside, yet right up until the middle of 1570 others who had been more careful continued to be called on to assizes; Ramsay absented himself in December 1569 but Dalyell did appear for the trial of a baxter for adultery in June 1570. It was often the case that burgesses failed to turn up when called for service, but this was not confined to catholics; the duty was a time-consuming, unpopular and even dangerous one. In May 1568 a number of burgesses were fined for failing to attend the trial of the Hamiltons; they included David Somer and Herbert Maxwell, leading lights of both the burgh's factions.[14]

There was one further obstacle to the wholesale protestantisation of the burgh establishment; certain important burgh offices lay in the royal gift. The office of custumar was awarded to James Curle in October 1560; Henry Charteris, the son of the Seton councillor, John Charteris, gained the post of tronarship. Royal patronage was extended to other members of the catholic party: Herbert Maxwell was made general of the Mint in January 1560. Francis Tennant gained two offices in the queen's household as a reward for turning over to Mary a set of dispatches intended for Throckmorton; Sebastian Danelour was given the vacant position of clerk to the commissariat of Edinburgh and Gilbert Balfour of Westray made master of the queen's household in 1565.[15] William Aikman was given the influential office of overseer in Dieppe in 1565; it was this appointment that allowed him to apply pressure on certain of the burgh's merchants to force them into the queen's party in the civil wars.[16] Other members of the party, like Dalyell, Leach and the other Seton craft councillor, Robert Fyndar, were done a variety of minor favours, as well as two of the old establishment, William Lawson and James Wallace.[17]

Burgh life was not controlled by one administration, but by two: by court and town. This imposed a further set of limitations on the new regime. It was only the upper echelons of burgh office-holders that were purged of catholics in the first half of the 1560s. Even the offices that lay within the town council's limited patronage were not fully protestantised. The case of the catholic master of the grammar school, William Roberton, was not an isolated one; the master of the song school, Edward Henderson, was described in an English memorandum of 1570 as 'papist'; Alexander King, who was still, according to Calderwood, 'a malicious papist' when he returned to Scotland in the 1580s, was clerk of the burgh court throughout the 1560s until his promotion to procurator fiscal early in 1567; Edmund Hay; still a faithful catholic in 1579 according to his brother, was twice an assessor in the 1570s.[18] The old establishment survived in a variety of forms alongside the new after 1560. It was this that made Mary's attempts to infiltrate its members back on to the council in 1565 all the more dangerous. The old establishment was not fully laid to rest until after the civil wars. It was ironical that by that time most of the new establishment had passed on as well.

NOTES

1. There is not full information on four of the councils of the 1550s but the total number of councillors is not likely to have been substantially more than this since a number of the gaps would have been filled by retiring office-holders.

2. MS Co. Recs., ii, fo. 45v.

3. For further details see Lynch, 'Thesis', 255.

4. *De La Brosse Report*, 113; MS Co. Recs., iv, fos. 5r, 20v, 55r, 97r, 108r; *Edin. Accts.*, i, 376.

5. MS Co. Recs., iii, fo. 35r; iv, fos. 20v, 39v, 55r, 108r, 143r, 164, 186r, 198r; *Edin. Accts.*, i, 377, 437-8; *De La Brosse Report*, 110.

6. MS Co. Recs., iv, fos. 5r, 14v, 186r; see app. vi for Allan, Brocas and Charteris.

7. There are, however, very few lists for the period 1568-70, although no obvious catholics appear on them; see MS Co. Recs., iv, 229r, 270r.

8. See app. vi for Loch and Brocas and ch. 4 for a fuller discussion of the hammermen.

9. MS Co. Recs., iv, fos. 69r, 91r, 99v, 120r, 266v; *Papal Negotiations*, 465.

10. Forbes-Leith, *Narratives of Scottish Catholics*, 74.

11. JC 1/11, 19 Dec. 1560 & 8 Aug. 1561.

12. See JC 1/11, 6 May 1562 (Pitcairn, *Trials*, i, 425); JC 1/12, 6 June 1564, 30 July 1564, 21 Oct. 1564, 26 Oct. 1565 and 18 Feb. 1566 (439-40, 442-50, 456, 466, 475-6); JC 1/13, 1 April 1566 (481); see app. vi for Aldinstoun and Graham.

13. JC 1/11, 24 Dec. 1561 (Pitcairn, *Trials*, i, 416-8).

14. JC 1/13, 22 Oct., 10 & 12 Dec. 1567, 17 Jan. & 20 May 1568, 6 Dec. 1569, 14 June 1570 (Pitcairn, *Trials*, 1, ii, 10-11, 13).

15. *RSS*, v, 733, 807, 808, 815, 1015, 2323, 2712, 3354; see also *ibid.*, vi, 13, 401, 522; *CSP Scot.*, i, nos. 958, 964. Balfour and Danelour were exempted from the heavy burgh tax of 1565 (*Edin. Accts.*, i, 54).

16. *RSS*, v, 1897; see app. viii for Aikman, Helen Acheson and Archibald Stewart.

17. *RSS*, v, 821, 839, 943, 1714, 1956.

18. *Edin. Accts.*, i, 306; BL, MS Cott. Calig. C. ii, fo. 174v (see *CSP Scot.*, iii, no. 601); Calderwood, *History*, iv, 414; MS Co. Recs., iv, fo. 180r; *Edin. Recs.*, iv, 57, 71; Forbes-Leith, *Narratives of Scottish Catholics*, 146.

10

Protestantism and the Protestant Party

IN August 1561, shortly before Mary's arrival at Leith, William Maitland of Lethington wrote to Cecil analysing the likely effect her return would have on the state of protestantism. His analysis was a subtle and discriminating one; protestants, he maintained, 'be not all alike' and were not all equally 'bent to maneteyne' the reformed religion. He distinguished four groups of likely waverers: those who were still dependent on the French faction; the 'covetous'; the 'inconstand', who were liable to be overawed by the court and the 'countenance of theyr princesse'; and the complacent.[1] Maitland's letter is a useful reminder, first that the nature of protestantism cannot be easily generalised about, and secondly that the return of the queen led to a regrouping of the factions within Scottish politics. Both are relevant to the way that protestantism developed in Edinburgh in the 1560s.

The development of the Reformation in Scotland after the crisis of 1559 and 1560 depended on the use of the more important towns as growth points for the spread of reformed ideas.[2] While the significance of the burghs to the new faith has been pointed to often enough, there has been little done in the way of a closer examination of the speed and nature of the spread of protestantism in them. The reason for this has usually been a lack of detailed evidence, but the same is true of Edinburgh, despite its voluminous collection of municipal records and the frequency of very specific references to it in most of the contemporary accounts of the reformation period. The most recent account of Edinburgh's reformation takes little account of either of Maitland's main points; it talks rather vaguely of a 'protestant element' in burgh government, which 'despite Mary, seems successfully to have held a dominant position from 1560 on'. This element was apparently largely derived from the 'leading merchants', although the same historian earlier detected its origins in the burgh's 'lower middle class'.[3]

Protestantism had been slow to establish itself in any numerical strength in Edinburgh before 1559, and as late as 1565 there is room for doubting if it was accepted by the majority of the population. While it is difficult to resist the argument that the city's protestants exercised an influence out of all proportion to their numbers,[4] neither their numbers nor the reasons for their influence have ever been made clear. There are a number of sources which can be used to build up a picture of the spread of protestantism in Edinburgh in the 1560s including Knox's *History*, the anonymous *Diurnal of Occurents* and official justiciary records, but the most important single document is the list of one hundred and sixty 'faithful brethren of Edinburgh' in 1562, the contributors to the proposed new poor hospital. The list is appended to a resolution of the kirk session to raise funds for the building of a hospital on the site of the Black Friars' yard.[5]

The importance of the document goes beyond showing the very real concern of the newly established religion for the social problems of the burgh; it is the only surviving record of the Edinburgh kirk session before 1574 and its contribution list gives the first semi-official indication of the nature of the spread of protestantism within Edinburgh society. Although the list itself gives no indication of the status of the contributors, except in a few cases where there may be a need to distinguish between burgesses of the same name, almost all of those on it are readily identifiable from other sources, a fact which is significant in itself. This reveals that rather more than half of the 'brethren' were merchants; about a fifth belonged to the professional classes, most of them lawyers; a further fifth were craftsmen; in addition there were seven local lairds or heritors who held burgess status and five women.

Yet an analysis along these lines conceals as much as it reveals. The 'merchants' of the Scottish burghs encompassed a much wider section of the population than in most urban societies; they ranged from the large overseas merchants, trading mostly in France and Flanders, down to the humble booth-owners or cramers, merchants only in the sense of selling goods within the town. Equally, it has not been sufficiently understood by historians of the Scottish burgh how wide a group the craftsmen comprised; they ranged from the humble craft master to the prosperous craft employer, who was, more often that not, a member of the merchant guildry long before the decreet, or to the odd individual, like the goldsmith, Michael Gilbert, whose fortune rivalled that of Edinburgh's two greatest merchant princes of the sixteenth century, William Birnie and John McMorran. The tax roll of 1565[6] confirms how stark the disparity of wealth among the burgh's merchants could be and how finely tapered the economic pyramid was at its apex. Contributions ranged from £2 to £60; almost exactly half of the merchants on the roll were assessed at £5 or less; the total amount they paid was only slightly more than that paid by the two dozen wealthiest merchants in the town. The merchant princes were rivalled only by the lawyers. The prominence of this group in Edinburgh society in the sixteenth century is partly masked by the fact that they did not pay tax. They appear in 1565 because it was a loan rather than a tax, and between them the thirty-one lawyers paid as much as the two dozen richest merchants in the burgh.

Where, from within this wide spectrum, did the 'faithful brethren' of 1562 come? The answer is quite clear. The vast majority of the merchants on the list came from the ranks of the wealthier overseas merchants. There is a striking correlation between wealth and professed protestantism; fourteen of the top twenty-four merchants in the town appeared among the 'brethren'; twenty-five of the top forty-three; forty-seven of the top eighty, who were assessed at £20 or more in 1565; fifty-seven of the one hundred and thirteen who paid more than the average assessment. A half of the upper crust of the burgh's merchants appeared on the list. The women were also the widows of fairly wealthy merchants. There was left amongst the merchants a largely silent majority of smaller men and cramers; there were only thirty 'brethren' amongst the remaining two-thirds of the merchant community and only fifteen from the lower half of the merchants, the one hundred and eighty-one whose assessment fell beneath £10. It is hardly surprising that the appeal from the kirk session contained the pious hope that godliness would 'aboundantlie incresse' the donor's 'substance'. The prominence of the lawyers among the burgh's protestants was perhaps also to be expected since Edinburgh was a capital city and this was to be a typical pattern of seventeenth century kirk sessions. Yet it is striking that it should have been so complete — twenty-one of the thirty-one lawyers on the 1565 roll figures on the contribution list — and that it should have emerged as early as 1562. The pillars of the new kirk were the prosperous merchant and the lawyer.

The craftsmen among the 'brethren' tended, with the exception of the baxters, to come from the wealthier, more respectable guilds. All of them were of burgess status and masters of their crafts; most also belonged to the prestigious merchant guildry. They included the sitting craft councillors and the current deacons of seven of the fourteen incorporated crafts; nineteen of the thirty craftsmen on the list held burgh office in the 1560s. Yet the list also illustrates the difficulties that protestantism had in penetrating certain of the crafts. The only hammerman on it was the ubiquitous James Young. Although there were other committed protestants in the craft, like William Harlaw and George Small, they were badly outnumbered, as the support for the catholic, William Brocas, in 1562 indicated. The fleshers were another craft which caused the council much concern; their deacons for most of the 1560s were men who supported the queen's party in the civil wars. There were no cordiners, websters or walkers on the list and no representatives of the unincorporated crafts. Nor did it include James Lawson or John Cunningham, the men who effectively controlled the bonnetmakers and wrights in the 1560s and later emerged as queen's men. There is no trace, curiously, of the protestant activists immortalised by Knox in his *History* — Robert Norval, Patrick Cranston or William Harlaw. Most conspicuously of all, there is in 1562 no sign of the apprentices and craft servants who had held office in the privy kirk in the second half of the 1550s.

The 'faithful brethren' were not drawn from a representative cross-section of

Edinburgh society or made up only of activists. Their composition distinctly resembled that of the ruling groups in the burgh in the 1560s — a council dominated by the larger merchants, together with the legal interest and a small, select group of local lairds, plus a fairly small craft aristocracy. The privy kirk had taken on a 'public face' and respectability at the same time. The pattern was already set for the future; there was little difference between the 'brethren' of 1562 and the composition of the eldership of the session in the 1570s. Protestantism, it is now clear, was firmly rooted within the burgh establishment by 1562 and the elaborate mechanisms of cross and self-election meant that it was difficult to displace, despite direct intervention by the queen in 1561, 1565 and 1566. The list also shows that the burgh's protestants had powerful friends within the privy council; James McGill, Robert Richardson and John Spens of Condy had all been on the committee set up early in 1562 to inquire into the incomes of all 'prelates and beneficed men' within the town.[7]

The fact that the most distinctive feature of Edinburgh's protestants in 1562 was their respectability was not altogether to be expected. The crisis of 1559 had produced a radical council drawn from a far wider range of merchants than was usual, even including some cramers. Yet the pattern established by the Kilspindie council of 1559-60 was not repeated. After the crisis of 1559 and 1560 was over, the social composition of the ruling oligarchy reverted to much the same as it had been before 1559, although some individuals were purged from it. Most of the newcomers disappeared into relative obscurity. The contribution list of 1562 distinctly reinforces this impression and demonstrates how quickly, once the initial crisis was past, protestantism was received into the burgh establishment. The council was dominated by the 'brethren' throughout the 1560s; only two members of the councils of 1560-62 and 1563-4 were not drawn from them, only one of the council of 1562-3. At least two-thirds of all the councils between 1564 and 1569 were subscribers to the list of 1562; most of the remainder were men who had reached burgess status since then.

The comparative ease with which this was done is more easily explained when it is realised how loosely the term 'protestant' has to be used to encompass all of the 'brethren'; far from all of them were enthusiasts. A few, like Alexander Skene and Edmund Hay, were out-and-out catholics seeking to demonstrate their new-found godliness; some, like Andrew Stevenson and James Watson, had catholic wives; a number, like James Lindsay, James Carmichael, James Curle and Cuthbert Ramsay, were prominent political opponents of the new regime throughout the 1560s. The list included half a dozen of the burgesses who had led the resistance to the council's attempts to remove the catholic master of the grammar school four months before. It even had on it one of Knox's most outspoken personal critics, Euphemia Dundas; she was called before the council a few months later for openly accusing him of consorting with a common whore.[8] Some of these are extreme examples but they do illustrate how widely drawn the coalition was that made up

Edinburgh's 'protestant' establishment. It was a coalition that might agree over the schemes of the new kirk which, like the proposed poor hospital, were not far removed from the traditional concerns and policy of the burgh; this particular scheme had been floated since 1552. The coalition might also largely close ranks when either burgh privilege or the independence of the burgh's kirk was involved, such as when the positions of the town clerk and burgh minister were threatened in 1565 and 1566; both Guthrie and Knox could rely on the burgh's cultivated jealousy of its own privileges rather than support which was merely sectarian. It was also only to be expected that considerable support would be found among the upper strata of burgh society for a protestantism of civic responsibility and social conservatism. Yet the coalition was liable to split when confronted with more difficult political issues, such as the intervention of the queen in burgh affairs or the harassment of catholics. Only a minority of the protestant establishment was willing to resort to protestant activism. The seriousness of the split that developed in the later 1560s is well illustrated by the fact that twenty-three of the 'brethren' supported the queen's party in the civil wars and thirty-five were king's men.

One of Knox's latest biographers has argued that it was characteristic of him to emerge as the member of a party.[9] It is surprising that it has never been pointed out that Knox's base was in Edinburgh and that it also lay in an organised party. It was not the protestant establishment as a whole, as represented on the contribution list or on the councils of the 1560s, which comprised this party. Unequivocal support for Knox was confined to a small minority of activists. For most of the 1560s the party was controlled by an inner circle of about twenty, most of them merchants. Who were these men? Knox's own account is quite misleading. Most of the familiar names from the pages of his *History* — Robert Norval, his 'merry man', Andrew Armstrong and Patrick Cranston, his 'dear brethren', who were involved in the riot in the chapel royal in 1563, William Harlaw and John Mowbray, convicted for their part in the events on the night of the Riccio murder — were in fact minor figures with little or no influence. Only one of them — Harlaw — ever held burgh office and the merchants among them belonged to the lowest rungs of the social ladder. Only one of them — Mowbray — was respectable enough to figure amongst the 'faithful brethren'. The hard core of the party lay elsewhere.

What role did the minor party men play in protestant politics? They were certainly among the 'secret miscreants', as the Jesuit observer, Nicholas de Gouda, called them, who were only too willing to resort to the tactics of organised riot or assault. It is difficult to judge how successful they were in the first half of the 1560s in intimidating a largely unsympathetic population, but intimidation was certainly one element in protestant activism.[10] The party, however, did not always operate on the basis of an inner ring of influential conspirators, who directed, or at least condoned the activities of its wilder men. Murder or assault was not confined to a lunatic fringe of insignificant zealots. James Young, the most prominent craftsman in the party and a one-time commissioner to the General Assembly, was not afraid of getting catholic blood on his hands. William Paterson, an otherwise highly respectable merchant, was arraigned for the murder of a catholic craftsman in 1564; his record certainly did not cast a blight on his political career — he was promptly elected a bailie. When it mattered, the grandees of the party were willing to risk dirtying their own hands; thirteen of the inner circle were suspected of being involved in the events that centred around the murder of Riccio. Only a small handful of the party's grandees were not at some time or another in the 1560s involved or implicated in direct and illegal action to further the protestant cause.

The pattern of protestant direct action changed as the 1560s went on and the party found its position increasingly thrown into question by the intervention of the queen in burgh affairs. The focus of the party's activities shifted from harassment of catholic priests and worshippers, which had at least a veneer of legality about it, to involvement in factional politics inside and outside Mary's court. This was a new and dangerous direction for the burgh's protestant enthusiasts to take. They had had very little of an active role in the revolt of the Lords of Congregation in 1559. There had been far less of a direct connection between local protestant lairds or nobles and the burgh's protestants in the reformation crisis than in many other towns and this remained the case for most of the first half of the 1560s. The key moment, which vividly demonstrated the change, came in July 1565; a number of the burgh's activists were caught drilling in secret at the precise moment the Moray conspiracy was coming to the boil. When their leaders were brought before the Court of Justiciary an impressive queue of protestant lesser nobility formed to offer pledges, including Robert Campbell of Kinzeancleuch, Lord Lindsay of the Byres, George Douglas of Borg, Patrick Bellenden of Stenness, the brother of the justice clerk, one of the sons of Walter Kerr of Cessford and a son-in-law of Patrick, Lord Gray.[11] A number of these men had long-standing connections with Knox; more still became involved in one or other of the conspiracies of 1565 and 1566, the abortive coup which ended in the knockabout farce of the Chaseabout Raid and the grimmer affair which resulted in the death of Riccio and almost of the queen herself, together with her unborn child. By 1565 the burgh's protestant party had become a kind of fifth column inside the capital for protestant factionalism.

This was high politics to become involved in. Why did the protestant party risk it? One answer is that it still had much of its morality of 1559, an inward-looking and anxious minority; the other is that it had since then remained a tightly knit group, held together by office, but from 1565 onwards held together more tightly still by the prospect of displacement from office. Every council up to 1565 had on it a significant caucus of its members: the Kilspindie council of 1559-60 had ten; the council of 1560-61 eight; 1561-2 seven; 1562-3 seven; 1563-4 eleven; 1564-5 eight. The seriousness of the threat contained in Mary's first leet of 1565 can be shown by the fact that the party's representation on the council shrank to four; the council of 1566-7, after her second leet, also had only four. By the time of the Riccio conspiracy the party was under siege.

From the evidence of the 1565 taxation roll, it seems that this inner circle of committed activists were fairly respectable men, but not as respectable as the 'faithful brethren'. Fifteen of the merchants were assessed on the roll, and eight of them did belong to the top third of merchants assessed at more than £10. Yet only one, James Baron, belonged amongst the cream of Edinburgh society; four of the group were only average-sized merchants and three more were rather less than average. The evidence of their overall economic standing contrasts quite strikingly with the dramatic demonstration of support for the king's party given by so many of the burgh's wealthiest merchants during the civil wars. It is true that just about half of the town's leading merchants were prepared to subscribe to at least a nominal protestantism by 1562. What is questionable is that they were prepared to give Knox their 'full support'; a number of the leading families in Edinburgh society, the Uddarts, the Aikman's and the Achesons, appeared in their numbers on the subscription lists but not among the inner circle of activists.[12] Yet by 1572 the process of the politicisation of protestantism had gone far enough for them to be conspicuously represented in the ranks of supporters of the king's party. This conversion of the leaders of Edinburgh society to wholehearted support for ultra-protestantism and, by implication, for Knox, should not, however, be exaggerated. It was, as we shall see, far from total and it did not last.

Any account of the progress of protestantism in Edinburgh during the 1560s cannot simply be a story of its growth. There are, in any case, no reliable gross figures on which to base such an account. Speculation along these lines must necessarily be an imprecise as well as a largely unprofitable exercise, for it eschews the key point that there were a number of faces of protestantism in Edinburgh in the 1560s. This seems to have been the case in all of the Scottish burghs. The 'faithful brethren' of the subscription list represented its most respectable face, in a protestantism of civic responsibility and social conservatism, which was far removed from the 'rascal multitude' of 1559. The political activism of the protestant party was another face, but one which was not generally accepted among the leading merchants before the civil wars. To be more precise, activism was a two-faced phenomenon; the party was controlled by middle-ranking merchants and prominent craftsmen, but since the mid-1550s smaller merchants and craftsmen seem to have swollen the ranks of the enthusiasts. The events of late 1558 and 1559 had shown that the burgh had by then its own share of 'rascall people',[13] and it was the force within this popular element which the respectable half of the party tried to channel and direct.

Although much the same basic dichotomy between protestantism and a protestant party probably existed in many of the other burghs, it took its starkest form in Edinburgh because certain conditions obtained there that were not so conspicuously present elsewhere. The proximity of the court on the one hand, and the close and continuous links between the party and committed protestants on the privy council and in the administration like James McGill, John Johnston and James Nicolson, combined to heighten the dilemma in which the party found itself after the return of Mary. The fact that four of the key members of the party — Guthrie, Clark, Graham and Fullarton — were closely associated with Randolph and the English connection had the same effect. Johnston and Nicolson were the go-betweens of Randolph and Moray in 1565 and fled to England to avoid capture. Guthrie was close enough to the centre of the Riccio conspiracy to have to flee to England with McGill in 1566. If Edinburgh's protestant party depended on any one group for its progress and contacts, it was not on neighbouring lairds but on this small circle of well-placed lawyers.[14]

By 1565 the party was forced to adapt itself to the challenge posed by Marian politics since what threatened to develop was a polarisation of opinion between itself and the more general body of irenic and accommodating protestant feeling that prevailed within the burgh establishment. The growing pains of Edinburgh protestantism largely derived from the effect of Mary's policies. It was characteristic of the party that it chose the path of confrontation in reply, and it was this attitude which by the early 1570s broadened and intensified into the overriding ethos of the king's party. For most of the 1560s, however, despite the existence of a rival catholic party in the burgh, it was only occasionally that the bitter relations between the two factions broke out into anything more serious. For the most part the rival parties indulged only in shadow-boxing with each other. The protestant party was usually less concerned with its catholic opponents than the more persistently worrying problem of how best to chase its own paler shadows. The major difficulty the party faced was that burgh protestantism was always a broad church. It was often too broad for the taste of the protestant party or its mentor, John Knox.

NOTES

1. BL, MS Cott. Calig. B. x, fo. 152; see *CSP Scot.*, i, no. 1004.
2. *First Book of Discipline*, 51.
3. Cf. W. S. Reid, 'The middle class factor in the Scottish Reformation', *Church History*, xvi (1947), 146, and his 'Coming of the Reformation', 33-4, 38.
4. Lee, *James Stewart*, 43n.
5. The list is given in full in app. ii.
6. See app. xi.
7. See Knox, *History*, ii, 329.
8. *Edin. Recs.*, iii, 162, 164. This is discussed more fully in ch. 11; details of catholic recusants are to be found in app. vi.
9. Ridley, *John Knox*, 523.
10. *Papal Negotiations*, 129-39.
11. See JC 1/12, 26 July 1565; JC 19/2, 13 July & 15 Aug. 1565.
12. Cf. Reid, 'Coming of the Reformation', 34.

13. The phrase is used in the anonymous account, *Hist. Estate Scot.*, 61, to describe the riot in which the burgh's friaries were looted before the Congregation's first entry into the town late in June 1559; it might equally have been applied to the St. Giles' Day riot of Sept, 1558; cf. Knox, *History*, i, 162, for his well-known account of the 'rascal multitude' at Perth in May 1559.

14. Cf. Cowan, *Regional Aspects of the Scottish Reformation*, 28.

11

Catholicism and the Catholic Party

EDINBURGH'S catholics found themselves in an ambivalent position in the early 1560s. The support that the burgh had given to the Congregation in 1559 had stemmed for only a committed minority from religious conviction. There had been little evidence of widespread religious disaffection amongst the inhabitants in the 1550s, yet the town as a whole had had more reason than most to be glad to see the departure of the French after the Treaty of Edinburgh.[1] The municipal coups of October 1559 and April 1560 had not been wholly unwelcome, but they had resulted in a narrowing of the already narrow power base on which the town council rested. All of the councils of the second half of the 1550s had had their share of protestants; no council in the 1560s had on it anyone who can be shown to have been a committed and devout catholic. Yet, even if they were purged from the council, catholics were not excluded from office in the burgh, which in a number of cases lay within the royal gift; they were not excluded from sitting on the assizes of the Court of Justiciary; they continued to serve in minor but necessary functions as auditors, extentors and collectors. The mass had been proscribed by the Reformation parliament but the legislation remained unratified until it was enacted as of new in 1567. Mary's proclamation of 1561 had in certain areas only served to enshrine a state of uncertainty or ambiguity; the legality of marriage or baptism by catholic rite was debatable. This point became less academic when it became clear that what amounted to a rival local church had been set up in the chapel royal. In a sense, the situation that had obtained between the Congregation's first and second occupations of the town in 1559 was reproduced after 1561; the reformed service was held in St. Giles' and the mass at Holyrood.[2]

Most historians would agree that Edinburgh remained a predominantly catholic town at least in the first half of the 1560s. Some have been more particular, claiming that not only the mass of the inhabitants but also the majority of the burgh's wealthier and more respectable citizens remained catholic in sympathies.[3] To some extent, this last point can be disproved by an analysis of the 'faithful brethren' of November 1562; the list of names that the kirk session drew up included a fraction over half the merchant establishment. In a number of cases, however, the choice of a nominal protestantism over outright recusancy was obviously only a tactical one. The wealthier and more respectable a burgess was, the more likely he was, it seems, to do this. The perils of excommunication — banishment, an inhibition on collecting debts — were enough to ruin even the most prosperous merchant. Recusancy was a luxury which few active traders or heads of households could afford.

Edinburgh's protestant establishment proves, on closer examination, to have been a curious collection of conservatives, trimmers and activists. Yet this was really not so surprising. St. Giles', even with John Knox in the pulpit, was not an assembly line churning out identikit protestant enthusiasts. Protestants came in a number of different shades. Exactly the same qualification must be borne in mind when seeking out the burgh's catholics in the 1560s. There are no reliable figures as to their numbers; the estimates made by the Jesuit, Father William Crichton, and the Spanish ambassador in London, Guzman de Silva, that 9,000 attended communion at Holyrood at Easter 1566 and more than 12,600 a year later, even if accurate, would have included inhabitants from the surrounding area as well as Edinburgh itself. It remains a mystery, however, how catholics in such numbers could have fitted into the confines of a small, private chapel. Very little is known about the actual size of the chapel royal but it did manage to accommodate the queen's household, which probably numbered about fifty, and twenty-six outsiders at the mass which led to arrests in 1563. It is difficult to believe that the chapel would have held many more than this. Both estimates, in any case, amounted to considerably more than the total adult population of both Edinburgh and the Canongate combined. The offical returns for the parish of the Canongate, which worshipped next door in the Abbey Church at Holyrood, showed that between nine hundred and a thousand took communion by the protestant rite in 1565.[4] This seems to represent a more realistic sense of statistics. There was undoubtedly widespread sympathy for the old faith but the extent of it is not to be measured by the counting of heads in the chapel royal or elsewhere. The evidence which does exist leaves the impression that comparatively few risked indulging in catholic practices; sixty-two have been traced, about a quarter of them living in the Canongate rather than in Edinburgh itself.[5]

Very little is known, though, even about this comparatively small number of recusants. Pitcairn, in printing a list of twenty-six of them accused of attending mass at Holyrood in August 1563, commented that their names 'may perhaps be considered interesting, though persons moving in the lower ranks of society'. On the face of it, this does seem a fair impression; they included five or perhaps six merchants; the others were made up of craftsmen, even though some were not listed as such, and women. But Pitcairn did not print the names of those who entered pledges on behalf of these catholic worshippers and they contain much more revealing information. Three of the women, Katherine Bryce, Isobel Curror and Helen Johnston, were pledged by their husbands. These men must have been particularly embarrassed by their wives' indiscretion; they were all at least nominal protestants and had figured on the subscription list of 1562. Two of them, James Aikman and James Watson, had sat on the council since 1560. Watson had actually been on the council when his wife attended mass at Holyrood in August 1563, and Aikman returned to it within a fortnight of his wife's appearance before the Court of Justiciary on 1 October. The third was Andrew Stevenson, who came on to the council two years later and remained on it for most of the second half of the 1560s. Two conclusions are possible about this affair and both are likely. It was often the case that families were split along religious lines — the two prominent Edinburgh families, the Barons and the Littles, each had a catholic and a protestant wing; even Knox's own colleague, John Craig, had a cousin who remained a convinced catholic all his life. Even more frequently it was the habit of other members of the establishment to subscribe to a nominal, even dutiful, protestantism as heads of their households but they would themselves avoid the taint of recusancy and the financial risks associated with it.

The merchants who became involved, either directly or indirectly, in this affair were certainly not all minor figures; Aikman and Watson were average sized merchants according to the evidence of the taxation roll of 1565, but Stevenson was one of the wealthiest men in the burgh. Cuthbert Murray and Adam Allan, who were both indicted in 1563, were assessed at two and two and a half times the merchant average in 1565. Only John Brown and Henry Kerr were small men, paying about one quarter and one sixth the average rate. Bessie Hill was the wife of the Islay herald, Peter Thomson, who had been captured by the Congregation in November 1559 and remained a loyal Marian throughout the 1560s and the civil war.[6] Not all of the craftsmen were nonentities either; John Aldinstoun and Thomas Clarkson had both headed their crafts in the second half of the 1550s. William Brocas, to the dismay of the council, had been elected deacon of the hammermen in May 1562 and had fought a running battle with it for six months after his dismissal; both he and George Smith, another member of the same craft, had been summoned before the privy council in August 1562, so that the council's treatment of them could be scrutinised. Brocas had taken the opportunity to proclaim that the council would never seduce him from his faith; he might have said the same for the bulk of his craft.[7]

If one incubator of catholicism was the craft guild, the other was the household. A number of the worshippers, as might be expected, were related. Adam Allan had married into the Stevenson family and Bessie Tod, like Katherine Bryce, had married into the Watsons. Four members of the Clarkson family were cited; along with John and Thomas were John's son-in-law, John Paterson, and Margaret Galloway. The evidence does not indicate that those who remained devout catholics were all from the older generation. It is true that a number of the worshippers must have been in late middle age: Isobel

Curror's husband had been made a burgess in 1530; Thomas Clarkson had been a freeman of his craft in 1531; the husbands of Bessie Young and Christian Pinkerton had gained their burgess-ships in 1531 and 1538; Harry Young had also been made a burgess in 1538. But John Charteris and Cuthbert Murray had only gained their burgess-ship in the mid-1550s and Walter Scott in 1560; Henry Kerr must have been in his twenties since his father had been forty-two in 1560 when he testified to the de la Brosse inquiry.[8] Other catholic devotees confirm the same impression: John Graham, John Spottiswood and John Kennedy were all made burgesses in 1555; Henry Easton did not reach this status until 1567; George Smith's son was not made a burgess until 1586. Both Graham and Charteris had children of baptismal age in 1561 and 1562. It is obvious that the catholic problem was not one that would simply fade away with time and the passing of the older generation. The sample of the burgh's catholics that is available indicates that they were drawn fairly evenly from all ages, largely because catholicism was entrenched in certain families. The craft concentrated catholicism in pockets which were difficult to winkle out quickly; the household was where stray catholicism might linger on.

The evidence also shows that they were drawn from all ranks of Edinburgh society. There were in all ten merchants and thirteen women, ten of them merchant's wives. The merchants who became involved ranged from the wealthiest in Edinburgh in the 1560s, like Andrew Stevenson, to the humblest, like John Graham. There were six advocates or notaries and two school-masters; at least four of them were ex-priests or chaplains. The fifteen Edinburgh craftsmen included four baxters and four hammermen but were drawn from nine different crafts in all. Their experience of burgh office was not impressive; only one of the merchants, John Spottiswood, had been on the council before 1560 and only three of the craftsmen had been deacons of their crafts. Only two, Brocas and Loch, gained office after 1560.

It seems likely that outright recusancy was a limited problem by the mid-1560s. The only figure for attendance at a protestant communion in Edinburgh is Randolph's for Easter 1561 of thirteen hundred; communicants in the adjoining parish of the Canongate increased from nine hundred in 1565 to twelve hundred by 1566, which must have accounted for a very substantial proportion of its population.[9] Yet not all the catholics who can be traced were actually recusants in the strict sense of the word. Alexander Skene was released from ward by the town council in July 1561 provided he attended the sermon and repented before the session. Obviously he took the threat of banishment seriously and his attempt at a front of protestant respectability was successful enough for him to be included among the list of 'faithful brethren' of the burgh sixteen months later. Yet Skene remained a convinced catholic who evidently continued to attend mass and was eventually excom-municated for this in 1569. Edmund Hay was another devout catholic who trimmed to the point of being included on the subscription list. Others drew the line differently, at times even idiosyncratically; one schoolmaster, who had been a priest, agreed to make his children attend protestant services, even said that he accepted the doctrines of the new church, but refused to take communion.

Catholicism was difficult to root out because it did not confine itself to recusancy. Crypto-catholicism could take a number of forms, ranging from positive co-operation with the protestant regime on the less controversial parts of its programme, through a ritual attendance at the sermon and even communion to avoid the economic and social perils of public censure, excommunication and banishment, to an outright hostility which might express itself in political or personal terms. It seems fairly safe to assume that a number, if not most, of the catholics who have been traced also paid minimum observance to the services of the new kirk; five of the six merchants called before the Court of Justiciary in October 1563 for attending mass at Holyrood were included in a tax roll two years later and so must still have been trading. The fact that John Graham was a persistent offender did not hinder him from gaining his guildry in 1568; no objection was made to the granting of a free burgess-ship to David Hoppringle in 1568 despite the confrontation between him and the council over his marriage less than two years before. There does not seem to have been any attempt to attach a religious test to burgess rights and privileges; the first test came only after the civil wars of 1571-3, when a father's right to pass on his burgess right to his son was declared invalid because he had remained in the town during the siege. Even that was a political test rather than a religious one. It was not until 1587 that an addition was made to the burgess oath making religious orthodoxy a prerequisite of burgess status.[10] By then it was protestant radicalism and not catholicism which was the target.

There are grounds for wondering whether the much-vaunted efficiency of the kirk session was more mythical than real. It has been argued that the size of the Scottish burghs made a thorough-going campaign of religious repression possible, that a man might hide in a city the size of Paris or London but hardly in Edinburgh.[11] The argument, however, anticipates; the town's physical geography of multi-storeyed tenements separated by narrow closes was not ideal for sifting a largely unenthusiastic population. It is more likely that it made the problem, once it had become a more limited one, easier to deal with. The case of Henry Easton, who successfully avoided attending communion for fourteen years yet was granted a burgess-ship in 1567, demonstrates that the system of communion tickets which evolved in the 1560s did not catch all the burgh's recusants in its net. It is possible that Easton found it easier to do this because he was a member of a craft that was not formally incorporated. Yet the difficulties of sheer organisation in regulating an adult population of between six and eight thousand inhabitants, plus a floating population of professional men, traders, visitors and vagrants, were immense. There were loopholes even after the formal process of excommunication had been gone through; the kirk session complained in 1574 that a number who had been banished from the burgh were openly walking the streets.[12]

It should also be remembered that Edinburgh was a city the size of Norwich; it was larger than both Zürich and Geneva. It could be argued that much of Zürich's problem in enforcing religious orthodoxy lay not so much in the city itself but its *contado*, where both catholicism and Anabaptism flourished; but at least the surrounding territory lay within Zürich's jurisdiction.[13] This was not the case with Edinburgh; Alexander Skene argued in 1561 that he had taken communion by the catholic rite but had done so outside the town and the bailies' jurisdiction. The area around Edinburgh afforded ample opportunity for undermining municipal uniformity, not only in the queen's private chapel, but in the Seton household and in the private houses of members of the court or central administration; as late as 1582 Father John Hay could still recommend Leith as the safest port of entry for catholic priests because of its proximity to the Seton residence.[14] A third aspect of the problem was more intractable; perhaps as many as one quarter of Edinburgh's overseas merchants might at any one time be abroad on business. In the 1550s it is likely that a number of the burgh's merchants had come into contact with heretical opinions in Dieppe, Rouen or La Rochelle. In the 1560s Edinburgh's protestant regime was faced with a mirror image of the same problem; this was particularly so because the Scots staple at Veere was controlled by a strictly orthodox catholic, George Hackett.[15] After 1570 a whole variety of economic pressures were put on the burgh's overseas merchants via their agents in France and the Netherlands to give help to the queen's party. It was almost impossible to control the habits of the merchants without placing an unacceptable degree of restriction on their trading activities.

Although the Canongate had certainly resorted to formal excommunication by 1566, there is no trace in Edinburgh, in the absence of its kirk session records, of anything like a systematic campaign of excommunication or banishment of persistent offenders until 1569. In January a temporary pulpit was set up in the tolbooth 'for preiching to the papists'. Six months later, the council issued a proclamation forbidding contact with ten named and other unnamed catholics, who had been excommunicated for 'abiding at and mainteyning of the mess'. Not all of them left the town immediately; the council had to issue a further proclamation in October ordering them to leave within forty-eight hours. The fact that three of them were allowed to return to the town for a short time twelve months later indicates that the process had been gone through with.[16] Yet there is no indication in the council register of any burgesses, as distinct from clerics, being banished for their religious opinions before 1569. It is certainly true, however, as the catholic controversialist, Nicol Burne, alleged, that priests and friars were murdered or assaulted on Edinburgh's streets or subjected to 'banisin, impresoning, and harling thame on sleddis'. A number of burgesses were also imprisoned for taking part in catholic baptismal or marriage services and it is fair to argue that the bailies were exceeding their authority in detaining them. Yet Winzet in his *Buke of*

Four Scoir Thre Questions of 1563 is not unambiguous; he referred to the banishing of 'Christiani and trew Scottismen fra thair roumes and possessiones' by burgh magistrates, who, he claimed, had 'only power to puniss thair awin comburgessis in an viii s. unlaw or siclyke'.[17] He does not specifically accuse magistrates of banishing burgesses. It is clear enough that outsiders, and particularly priests, were regarded as fair game. The burgh's own catholics, however, could shelter behind burgh privileges, which could not be tampered with lightly. It is, of course, always possible, as has been claimed by Fr. Ross, that records may be missing or may not even have been kept regarding the harassment of catholics in the town; the activities of Robert Drummond, the guild officer, must, in the absence of kirk session records before 1574, remain a subject for speculation. Yet if Drummond was a kind of municipal catholic-catcher, his career did not always run smooth; he was dismissed in 1569 for 'misbehaving' before the session.[18] It is also true that there is a suspicious absence of references in burgh records to a few, but only a few, of these catholics. The balance of probabilities is simply that they came from the lowest ranks of burgh society which records usually ignore.

There is a danger, however, in arguing from isolated incidents and negative evidence. A recent general survey of catholic recusancy in Scotland in trying to explain the comparative absence of serious persecution has suggested two main possible lines of argument: either the amount of recusancy 'was not sufficient to warrant a full-scale attack' on it or there was 'real difficulty in operating the machinery of repression'.[19] Both of these possibilities certainly operated in Edinburgh in the 1560s. Recusancy was muted and sporadic; it tended to rise and fall with changes in the political situation or with the opportunities to express itself. Priests were plentiful enough but masses were not. It also seems clear, from the Sanderson case, that both the session and the council ran into difficulties in operating a strict interpretation of a pure and godly society in cases of morals. The council's attempts to protestantise its schoolmasters also aroused opposition, again not all of it coming from committed outright catholics. The people who were prepared to involve themselves in what turned out to be a successful campaign to maintain the catholic master of the grammar school included a number of the 'faithful brethren', a large slice of the professional men in the town and even a sitting bailie.[20] The limitations and restraints placed on the burgh's protestant regime were not all external ones. A wholesale policy of repression and protestantisation did not depend only on the willingness of the magistrates to co-operate; it could be implemented only with the consent of the burgh establishment as a whole. This was the third, and probably the most important, of the barriers in the way of a full-scale war of attrition against catholics.[21]

Crypto-catholicism might, of course, take other forms. A series of burgesses were hauled before the council, particularly between 1560 and 1563, accused of slandering either the ministers or magistrates. It has been argued that these were isolated instances and that those involved had 'little backing'. Some were

P

obviously nonentities, but not all of them.[22] Peter Douglas, who renounced his burgess rights after being imprisoned for disobedience to one of the bailies of the re-established Kilspindie council in May 1560, was the brother-in-law of Archibald Graham, one of the inner circle of the protestant party. It seems likely that Douglas retained catholic sympathies for some time; he acted as a surety for Archibald Trench when he was caught attending mass at Holyrood in 1563.[23] Alexander Baron, put in 'faust ward' in June 1562 for 'evil speaking' of the town to the queen, had been on the council from 1556 to 1560, when his career came to an abrupt halt; he was a member of the other branch of the Baron family from his cousin, James, another member of the protestant inner circle.[24] Francis Tennant, who was imprisoned for slandering the ministry in June 1563, had been provost of the burgh in 1550. Tennant, though, seems to have been only as disgruntled with the new regime as he had been with the old; he had had a series of brushes with the bailies in the 1550s. His basic political sympathies, however, were clear enough; he was one of the first to support the queen at Langside.[25]

There were others with whom personal grievances probably played a more telling part rather than religious or political principles. John Cardwood was accused of slandering the ministry and magistracy in March 1561; his dis-affection no doubt was the result of the revoking of his wife's right to purchase his guildry because of her fornication before marriage.[26] The well-known case of Euphemia Dundas, who accused Knox of being caught with a whore in 1563, was not simply that of the malice of a 'gossiping woman'. She was the widow of Alexander Adamson, who had been one of the largest merchants in the burgh; she successfully carried on her husband's business after his death, was assessed at nearly double the merchant average in 1565 and figured on the subscription list of 1562.[27] Resentment and criticism of the new regime came from a variety of sources, not all of them explicitly catholic. The most intriguing of these outbursts came in March 1562, when a merchant, James Dalyell, was called before the council following a complaint by the dean of guild and the common clerk, Alexander Guthrie. His words were obviously directed at the new protestant regime in general:

> Lat thame tak thair tyme, it will be verray schort, thai are nother godlie men nor honest, thai
> profes ane thing and do ane uther, thai wald cut my throt and thai mycht, and I defy thame

and at Guthrie, 'King Guthrie' as he called him, in particular. Dalyell, it might seem, was not a very significant figure; he was a small merchant, assessed at less than half the merchant average in 1565; he had never been on the council, although he had gained burgess-ship and guildry in 1550. His opposition to the new regime did not slacken with time; he was one of the activists of the queen's party during the civil wars and was eventually captured and executed.[28]

Dalyell was one of a small group of men, mostly merchants, who formed the core of a catholic party in Edinburgh in the 1560s.[29] It was a group that was fuelled less by religious conviction than by an intense resentment against the new regime. It included a number of the members of the displaced Seton council of 1559-60; two of its leading figures had been the much-criticised bailies of that council, Herbert Maxwell and Edward Little. Five of the ordinary councillors also belonged to it — Alexander Baron, James Curle, James Lindsay, Archibald Leach, a furrier, and John Charteris, whose son had his child baptized by the catholic rite in 1561. Both Baron and Charteris, however, were dead by 1565. Other members of it were Cuthbert Ramsay, Francis Tennant and James Carmichael. Carmichael, like Maxwell and Little, testified to the de la Brosse inquiry in February 1560; all three were in their middle or late forties and seem to have taken exclusion from power very hard.[30] It is interesting that none of these men listed so far seems to have risked indulging in catholic worship; the only prominent members of the catholic faction who did so were Cuthbert Murray and John Spottiswood. It could be argued that others might be added to this group of a dozen or so. Other names do spring to mind, such as Edward Kincaid or the two craftsmen, James Forret and John Wilson; all three were members of the Nicol Young assize in 1564. Other candidates for inclusion might be the merchants, David Corsbie and Peter Martin, or the notary, Alexander King. The two most significant of its other figures, however, were the two French merchants, Archibald Seinyeor and Sebastian Danelour, who had both married into prominent burgh families. Both were undoubted Marian agents but their double-dealing became increasingly complicated as the civil wars neared. Seinyeor even had the effrontery to put himself forward as a candidate for the eldership in the kirk session elections of 1574.[31]

This was an extreme but not necessarily untypical example of the fact that the lines drawn between political catholics, crypto-catholics and nominal protestants were often very fine ones. Like Alexander Skene and Edmund Hay, four of the inner circle of the catholic party — Curle, Little, Lindsay and Ramsay — appeared on the protestant subscription list of 1562. So too did a number of the other figures on the fringes of the party, like King and Martin. One or two even served in the minor offices which were created to implement parts of the new godly programme, as collectors for the poor. Although Ramsay was the only one amongst them to reach the council before the royal leets of 1565 and 1566, there was not a total purge of catholics, in this less strict sense of the word, from civic administration. It was to be expected that most of these political catholics would continue to perform the minor but significant duties of auditors and extentors since these were functions where the traditional principle of the common good had to be seen to be operating impartially.

It was predictable because all the prominent members of the party except Dalyell and Murray had held burgh office before 1560; some, like Little and Lindsay, had a long and impressive record of service. Eleven of the thirteen central figures were still alive at the time of the tax of 1565; Tennant does not appear on the roll and Leach, as a craftsman, was not individually assessed, but of the nine remaining merchants, it is significant that only one, Dalyell, was assessed at much below the merchant average. Spottiswood was assessed at £12, Murray at £20, Maxwell at £25 and Ramsay at £60. It is when these statistics are added to those of the actual recusants and their relations that a more realistic impression of the strength of the catholic interest in Edinburgh society begins to emerge. There was certainly, in religious terms, a 'still strong catholic opinion' in the burgh which usually remained fairly subdued; its most dangerous outburst came in 1565 in reaction to the outrages perpetrated on the priest, Sir James Tarbot.[32] But the Maxwell circle was more than than; it was a tight-knit political faction which was at its most dangerous not on religious issues but on personal or political ones, like the Nicol Young affair. It would not be wholly accurate to call it a Marian party since Mary's policy did not always seek to promote it or its interests. It is arguable that its policy of non-co-operation and obstructionism was most serious in the kirk's and council's schemes for financing their godly programme; yet this was the area which Mary was most willing to encourage. Thus it was to Mary that the council turned to deal with Maxwell, Lindsay, Spottiswood and Skene when they refused to pay their contribution to the poor.[33] There can be little doubt that Mary acted as a restraining influence not only on the protestant party in the burgh but also on this catholic party. It was not only in national politics but also in burgh politics that the opposing parties had reason to be dissatisfied with Marian policy.[34] The queen waited fully eighteen months before revoking the council ordinance of July 1562 imposing a religious test on office-holders.[35] It was not until 1565 that she decided to try to infiltrate members of the catholic party on to the council. But even then her strategy was not to produce a catholic body but a mixed one, purged of the extremists of the rival party. It is characteristic that she conspicuously avoided pushing its leader into office. Maxwell had to wait until the coup of 1571 before he returned to power.

It is easier now to deal with the claims that catholics were subjected to a campaign of systematic victimisation; there were complaints made in the first half of the 1560s of discriminatory taxation and the inability of catholics to gain civil justice from magistrates. It is very difficult to substantiate or refute the charge of over-taxation in specific instances, but there is precious little evidence to back it; Maxwell had his assessment of £25 reduced to £15 on appeal in 1565 and he reached an apparently amicable agreement with the auditors over his debts to the town in January 1563.[36] It is, however, true that a number of the members of the catholic party were pursued by the council over a long period on a variety of matters. Maxwell and the council had a sustained running battle over blocking a common passage; despite the triviality of the offence, tempers ran high.[37] Many of the matters, however, stemmed from a desire to tidy up the financial affairs left outstanding after the demise of the Seton council of 1559-60. The Kilspindie council of 1559-60 and its successor made a determined effort to set the town's financial affairs in order; this involved pursuing the deans of guild of the two previous years, James

Carmichael and John Charteris, for settlement of their accounts. The council was still trying to regain the balance from James Lindsay's treasurer's account of 1558-9 in 1561 and eventually had to threaten him with imprisonment before they were settled. Both he and Maxwell were pursued for contributions, but this could again hardly be called harassment; the auditors were ordered by the council to 'aggrie ressonablie with him as thay had done with utheris'.[38] The evidence hardly points to a campaign of conspicuous victimisation and it is difficult to see how such a policy could have been carried through when catholics appeared on every list of auditors and extentors up to 1568. There is no way of discovering the composition of burgh courts, but the make-up of assize lists for the Court of Justiciary for most of the 1560s was far from exclusively protestant. Systematic victimisation of catholics could only have operated in the wake of a radical purge; for the most part, it was petty harassment which made do in lieu of a purge.

There are two factors which have tended to be ignored in assessments of the nature of catholicism in Edinburgh and other towns in the 1560s. The first is the number of established burgesses who were willing to subscribe to at least a nominal, civic protestantism from relatively early on in the 1560s without prejudice; the second is the effect of the Marian policy of accommodation. The queen's policy was not a catholic one in the sense that she invariably favoured or promoted the interests of the burgh's catholic party; nor was it anti-protestant in the sense that she invariably blocked the more acceptable schemes for producing a reformed city. Both of these factors had much the same effect; they tended to blur the starkness of the division between the two opposing parties in the burgh. Political catholicism, if it was to prove effective, had to operate within these limitations. In this sense, its dilemma was much the same as the one which confronted political protestantism. That seems to have been the main reason why there was no head-on clash between the two until after Mary's departure from Scotland.

Much the same comparison could be made between the more explicitly religious faces of protestantism and catholicism. Both worked within and were conditioned by peculiarly local circumstances: the proximity of the court and of a mixed administration; the burgh's position as a capital and a market town, balanced by its lack of jurisdiction outside its own narrow environs; the absence of a university. Catholicism in general found itself in a paradoxical position in the 1560s, with the structure of the old church continuing alongside the new. In Edinburgh, there was added to this general paradox a peculiarly local set of paradoxes, which left room for a variety of possibilities of crypto-catholicism. Despite Knox's fears about the symbolic effect of one mass,[39] the most serious of the threats to the new regime took the form of political faction rather than catholic ritual. It was catholics playing politics rather than catholics clinging to the old rites who were dangerous.

NOTES

1. Cf. Herries, *Memoirs*, 50.

2. *CSP Scot.*, i, no. 510; Knox, *History*, i, 213-4; *Edin. Recs.*, iii, 46-7; see M. Sanderson, 'Catholic recusancy in Scotland in the 16th century', *Innes Review*, xxi (1970), 88, 101.

3. See A. Lang, *John Knox and the Reformation* (1905), 142ff; Brown, *John Knox*, ii, 22-3, 108; Miller, *John Knox and the Town Council of Edinburgh*, 13; Ridley, *John Knox*, 358.

4. *Papal Negotiations*, 495-6, 520-21; *Canongate Book*, 18, 25. It is a little surprising that these estimates have been taken at face value by a number of historians; see Reid, 'Coming of the Reformation', 33-4; Cowan, *Regional Aspects of the Scottish Reformation*, 33.

5. Full details of catholic recusants are given in app. vi.

6. Pitcairn, *Trials*, i, 435; cf. the full details given in the original justiciary record (JC 1/12, 1 Oct. 1563); see also *De La Brosse Report*, 94.

7. *Edin. Recs.*, iii, 134-5; MS Co. Recs., iv, fo. 46r; *RPC*, i, 216. The catholic leanings of the hammermen craft are discussed in ch. 4.

8. *De La Brosse Report*, 114.

9. *CSP Scot.*, i, no. 967; *Canongate Book*, 18, 25, 43, 51, 63, 71.

10. *Edin. Recs.*, iv, 97; cf. Sanderson, 'Catholic recusancy', 92; see the entries for John and Richard Neill in apps. vii & viii.

11. See Ross, 'Reformation and repression', 360n.

12. BGKE, fos. 12v, 49v.

13. R. C. Walton, *Zwingli's Theocracy* (Toronto, 1967), 4.

14. *Edin. Recs.*, iii, 115; *Canongate Book*, 41, 74; Forbes-Leith, *Narratives of Scottish Catholics*, 178.

15. Reid, 'Coming of the Reformation', 28; J. Davidson & A. Gray, *The Scottish Staple at Veere* (Edinburgh, 1909), 172-3.

16. *Edin. Recs.*, iii, 259, 264; MS Co. Recs., iv, fos. 243r, 264v.

17. T. G. Law (ed.), *Catholic Tractates of the Sixteenth Century, 1573-1600* (Scot. Text Soc., 1901), 167; Ninian Winzet, *Certain Tractates* (Scot. Text Soc., 1888), i, 94-5; cf. Ross, 'Reformation and repression', 355.

18. MS Co. Recs., iv, fo. 248r; see Ross, 'Reformation and repression', 359n.

19. Sanderson, 'Catholic recusancy', 87.

20. *Edin. Recs.*, iii, 141-3.

21. Cf. Sanderson, 'Catholic recusancy', 91.

22. Reid, 'Coming of the Reformation', 33; see *Edin. Recs.*, iii, 85, 132.

23. *Edin. Burgs.*, 156; Prot. Bk. John Guthrie, fo. 18; JC 1/12, 1 Oct. 1563.

24. MS Co. Recs., iv, fo. 35v; Prot. Bk. King, v, fos. 157, 176. Alexander died in 1564 or 1565 (see *Edin. Tests.*); his brother, John, was an active queen's man in the civil war (see app. viii).

25. *Edin. Recs.*, ii, 198, 221-2, 239; iii, 162, 299; see app. viii.

26. MS Co. Recs., iii, fo. 75r; *Edin. Burgs.*, 100.

27. *Edin. Recs.*, iii, 162, 164; *RSS*, v, 787; Ridley, *John Knox*, 23, 417. She was assessed at £20 in 1565; see apps. ii and xi.

28. MS Co. Recs., 14 March 1562, iv, fo. 24r; see Wood, 'Domestic affairs of the burgh', 47-8; see app. viii for Dalyell.

29. Details of all the main members of the catholic party mentioned here are given in app. viii.

30. *De La Brosse Report*, 110, 120, 122.

31. Danelour had married into one of the branches of the Adamson family (*RSS*, vi, 2764) and Seinyeor into the Craiks; see app. viii for details of both; also Donaldson, *James V to James VII*, 120.

32. Ross, 'Reformation and repression', 358; see ch. 4 for details of the Tarbot affair.

33. MS Co. Recs., 12 May 1565, iv, fo. 129v.

34. This point is made by Ross, 'Reformation and repression', 358, 378.

35. Cf. *ibid.*, 356, and Sanderson, 'Catholic recusancy', 92, which both give the impression that the ordinance was quickly revoked under pressure from the queen. The revocation is misdated in Reid, 'Coming of the Reformation', 38; see MS Co. Recs., iv, fo. 37r.

36. *Papal Negotiations*, 465; Forbes-Leith, *Narratives of Scottish Catholics*, 74; see Ross, 'Reformation and repression', 352, 355. Edward Kincaid, James Lindsay and Edward Little, all political opponents of the new regime, were among the extentors who assessed the tax of 1565 (MS Co. Recs., iv, fos. 55v, 59r, 137v; *Edin. Accts.*, i, 376; see app. viii for details of all three).

37. MS Co. Recs., iv, fos. 28r, 115v, 184v, 210r, 257v; see Wood, 'Domestic affairs of the burgh', 49.

38. MS Co. Recs., iv, fos. 3r, 6r, 39v, 45r, 59r; *Edin. Recs.*, iii, 197.

39. Knox, *History*, ii, 12.

12

King's Men and Queen's Men

VERY little is known of the reactions of Edinburgh's inhabitants to the traumatic experience of the civil wars. Historians who have looked at the period have drawn their conclusions about the burgh from a single, laconic comment of a contemporary, Sir James Melville of Halhill, who testified that except for a few 'that taried within the town . . . the maist part of the richest men and merchandis left the town and past till Leith'. It should be remembered, however, that Melville's were the recollections of an old man, not noted for the accuracy of his memory, and lack the authenticity of a diary. They were later echoed, and their emphasis slightly altered, by Spottiswoode, writing in the early seventeenth century, who maintained that 'they were of quiet disposition and greatest substance . . . were forced to forsake their houses'. Two things have been inferred from this evidence: that the majority of wealthy merchants supported the king's party while most of the craftsmen or lower classes sympathised with the Marian party.[1] At least one of these conclusions is seriously misleading. Even so, neither the numbers nor the motives of any of these groups have ever been made clear. This is despite the fact that more evidence exists to determine the political allegiances of the burgh's inhabitants than at any other point in the sixteenth century. It is possible to build up from a whole variety of sources an unusually comprehensive picture of the reactions of all of burgh society, even of the unfree, who are, in the nature of burgh records, usually the silent and forgotten majority.

There are enough detailed sources to provide a very full picture of the queen's party. Knox's secretary, Richard Bannatyne, incorporated in his memoirs a list of one hundred and ninety-five inhabitants who were warned to appear before the Court of Justiciary at the end of January 1572;[2] he added that 'a grit part' of them 'fand souertie'. Although the justiciary records reveal only a dozen who complied the next day, a further eighty-two on the Bannatyne list may well have done so as they seem to have escaped any further judicial censure or that of the kirk. It is likely that this list originally derived from the roll of merchants which the privy council instructed the council-in-exile to draw up so that they might be blacked from trading in other burghs.[3] The list of ninety-two inhabitants who petitioned the kirk session for redress, apparently in November 1572, was probably an extended version of the list of thirty or so penitents handed to Sir Henry Killigrew in October.[4] This can be supplemented by the manuscript record of the Edinburgh kirk session, which was dealing with offenders who had remained in the burgh during the wars throughout the period for which its records are extant, from April 1574 until November 1575.[5] Two further lists are to be found in English state papers, both of the two hundred or so who were still in the Castle when it was surrendered in May 1573;[6] about twenty-five of them came from the town itself. The picture is largely completed by official records. Apart from the isolated trial after the bloody skirmish on the Crags in June 1572, judicial proceedings did not begin in earnest until February 1573, and the bulk of the offenders were not called before the Court of Justiciary until late July or August of that year; only a fraction of those cited are printed by Pitcairn, although he does note the fact.[7] The *Register of the Privy Seal* records the granting of four remissions to burgesses between May and October 1572 and a further seventeen in the first five months of 1573 but the bulk of them did not come until after the end of the siege of the Castle and the beginning of judicial proceedings. From the evidence of this source and the *Treasurer's Accounts* the proceedings were not completed until at least four years later.[8] The last important source is the protocol books; John Aitkin and William Stewart, elder, remained in the town throughout the prolonged crisis and their protocol books are an important and untapped source for the wars. It is from them and the protocol book of John Robeson, who promptly moved to Leith in August 1571, that the significant fact that both parties set up a functioning town council can be gleaned. It is also obvious from the protocol books that a number of burgesses who did remain in Edinburgh for at least part of the time escaped the judicial net.[9]

As might be expected, the sources for reconstructing the victors, the supporters of the king's party, are more fragmentary. Three of the four most important are printed; a list of thirty-nine prominent burgesses, including four of the excluded council, who were either denounced or forfeited by the queen's lords in August 1571, is given in the *Diurnal*, although Bannatyne maintained that the number was nearer a hundred. The *Register of the Privy Seal* shows that a number of king's men gained from the escheat of the goods of forfeited Marians from September 1571 onwards; the *Treasurer's Accounts* reveals that thirteen burgesses and one from the Canongate lent a total of £9,434 2s to the king's party during the wars: individual loans ranged from two hundred merks to £1,100.[10] The other source is again the justiciary records; there are a series of assize lists from November 1571, when the court was re-established at Leith, until 21 October 1572 when it was re-established in Edinburgh. It also seems a safe assumption that the major trials of Marians, which took place from February 1573 onwards, were packed with king's men. It would be dangerous to carry this assumption too far, though; ex-queen's men were represented at non-political trials as early as May 1573, before the end of the siege.[11]

From these sources it has been possible to trace a total number of four hundred and seventy burgesses or inhabitants who were in some way connected with the queen's party and one hundred and fifty with the king's party. This must represent a high proportion of the support for the Castilians; the *Diurnal* reported that five hundred queen's men mustered in Edinburgh in July 1571; Calderwood set their numbers lower, at three hundred and forty. The figure of two thousand supporters given in two sets of subsequent legal proceedings must be put down to judicial exaggeration. It is clear, though, that the respective numbers of both parties fluctuated considerably during the ebb and flow of the wars. The English agent, John Case, reported that there were only a hundred armed exiles in Leith prior to the first siege of the burgh in October 1571. He estimated at the same time that there were about seven hundred men in the town in all. It is not easy to guess how many of these were townsmen; the *Diurnal* estimated that the exodus before the siege had left only ten per cent of the population in the burgh; Maitland, on the other hand, admitted that a bare hundred of his forces were not either mercenaries or from the town. It is possible that the number of able-bodied inhabitants who still remained in the town by then had shrunk by as much as a half but it is likely that the failure of the siege brought the townspeople back in large numbers. The queen's party, at its peak, had probably about six hundred townspeople in its ranks. The author of the *Diurnal*, who seems to have stayed in Edinburgh throughout, guessed the initial strength of the exiles at between two and three hundred; Case, however, reported that less than a half of them were actually armed. By the time of its triumphant entry into Edinburgh on 31 July 1572, the 'Edinburgh band' of exiles had swollen to five hundred and sixty.[12]

It seems fair to conclude that more than three-quarters of the queen's party's sympathisers have been traced but only about one quarter of the eventual support for the king's party. It has also been possible, using a variety of burgh sources, to establish the trade or craft of all but fifty of the queen's men and all but a handful or so of the king's men; a combination of tax rolls, testaments and lists of office-holders has also given some indication of the relative wealth and status of the two groups. Perhaps surprisingly, it is from the king's party that the clearer picture emerges. Seventy-one of them were merchants or merchants' widows. The number of craftsmen was half this; there were a dozen tailors or drapers, six skinners or furriers, four hammermen and cordiners, three goldsmiths, two each from the baxters and masons, and a flesher and a bower. Of the remainder, a number, including the captains of the regent's forces, were only burgesses in a technical sense. Ten other burgesses, who figured among the owners of the houses demolished by the Castilians between February and July 1572, might have been added to the list. The balance of probabilities is that they were devoted king's men. However, the evidence for some of the victims indicates that that devotion at times post-dated the destruction of their properties. Some were victimised precisely because they were playing a double game. Unless further corroboration exists, they have not been included in these figures.[13] Once again, though, a crude analysis along these lines conceals as much as it reveals. It is the evidence of the tax rolls that is more significant.

If the roll of 1583 alone is taken as an indicator, eight of the ten wealthiest men in the burgh in the 1580s supported the king's party in the civil wars; a ninth, Michael Gilbert, wavered until his house was demolished by the Castilians early in 1572. The correlation between wealth and support for the king's party was very marked indeed: in the top five per cent of Edinburgh society, those taxed at £7 or above in 1583, there were twenty-one king's men but only five queen's men, including Gilbert; in the top ten per cent, those taxed at £4 or above, the relative numbers were thirty-one and twelve. These are quite striking figures, given the fact that the information available about the king's party is so imperfect. It is clear, though, that this enthusiasm did not permeate the whole merchant body. The 1581 roll, which comprises only merchants, gives the same indications of the commitment of the wealthiest merchants to the regents; the allegiance of twenty-five of the top forty on the roll can be established and of them eighteen supported the king and seven the Castilians. But the further one goes down the roll, the more the pattern of support veers towards the queen's party; of the middling merchants, paying between three times and a third of the average assessment, the relative figures are twenty-two and thirty-two; of the very small men, they are nine and twenty-eight.

It would seem that Melville's point that the majority of the wealthy merchants supported the king is firmly established. However, the evidence does come from tax rolls of up to ten years later and deals with an establishment closer to the time Melville was writing his *Memoirs* than to the wars themselves. A very different impression is gained from the tax roll of 1565. In it, of those who can be traced in the same upper crust of burgh society — the forty wealthiest merchants in the town — they split almost evenly, ten for the king and nine for the queen. So did the top eighty — sixteen for the king, seventeen for the queen. After that the same pattern seen in the later tax rolls gradually asserts itself: the poorer half of the merchant body, those paying two-thirds or less of the average assessment, split decisively two to one for the Castilians. Melville's conclusion needs radical revision. One half of the burgh establishment as it stood in the mid-1560s supported the queen's party. The loyalties of the merchant body taken as a whole, from merchant prince down to humble booth owner, were clearly tilted towards the queen. The merchant princes were, in fact, particularly conspicuous in their support for the queen's party; the fortunes of the two wealthiest men in the burgh, William Birnie and Michael Gilbert, helped to finance it; three of the remaining seven leading merchants — Partick Edgar, Cuthbert Ramsay and Andrew Stevenson — were closely involved with it. There were other leading personalities in the town who became involved. The town clerk, 'King' Guthrie, remained in the town along with his scribe, William Stewart. So did the clerk of the kirk session and the master of the grammar school, who ironically had originally been appointed to replace an untrustworthy catholic incumbent. So did the wealthiest maltman in the town and the only two surviving burgess provosts of the town, Thomas MacCalzean and Francis Tennant.

It has been suggested in an important revisionary essay, which remains the only serious attempt to analyse the state of Scottish society during the civil wars, that the traditional view of the aristocratic strength of the Marian party being counter-balanced by middle-class support for the king and his regents may have been exaggerated.[14] The evidence pointing in this direction is even more startling than this essay suggested. Despite a decade of John Knox in the pulpit of St. Giles' and a protestant council in power, supposedly committed to support him, the Edinburgh establishment was split down the middle by the rival calls on its loyalties in the wars. Wealth and respectability of long standing tended to gravitate towards what must have seemed the more respectable cause, the one which stressed continuity rather than the uncertainties of deposing a monarch. The most significant support for the king's party and the revolutionary regime established in 1567 came from committed protestants and the younger generation of merchants, very often men who had only reached burgess status within the preceding five years. The council-in-exile at Leith, which was elected in October 1571, neatly illustrates the two recruiting grounds for the king's party: it was headed by three veterans of the protestant party of the 1560s and four younger men, who had all come on to the council since the revolution of 1567. Wealth was not the main dividing line between the two parties; it was rather a combination of ideas and age. Edinburgh society had, on the whole, chosen to lie low during the reformation crisis. It was forced, largely by circumstances, to declare its loyalties in the long, bruising crisis of the civil wars. Its considered response, however, was as equivocal as ever.

How important were the parts played by the people of Edinburgh in the civil wars? By the middle of 1571 the most pressing problem for the king's party was finance. It is likely that the amount of financial support given by Edinburgh merchants has been seriously underestimated. The *Treasurer's Accounts* itemise a loan from Adam Fullarton, the captain of the Edinburgh band, of £324 16s 4d, but his wife's testament, made ten years later, reveals that he had lent more than six times that amount. Nicol Uddart lent the council-in-exile at least £3,000, more than double the largest amount recorded in the *Treasurer's Accounts*, to finance the Edinburgh band. The inhabitants of the Canongate were dismayed at the amount of taxation levied on them after they were forcibly moved to Leith in March or April 1573. The testament of John Morrison, an Edinburgh exile, shows that he was taxed at the rate of £4 per month. This was the burden for a fairly wealthy merchant, since he had been assessed at four times the average in 1565, but it was severe in contrast with the fiscal demands made on burgesses in normal times, even in the 1560s. By March 1572 the recurrent monthly expenditure on the seven hundred regent's soldiers based at Leith was over £4,500 and most of them were owed back pay which amounted to over £20,000 in total. Since the arrears remained at the same level three months later, it is unlikely that the burgesses in exile made a much larger contribution in loans from that point on than the total in the *Treasurer's Accounts* indicates, which amounted to about two months' expenses for the regent's forces.[15] The Edinburgh band, though, was self-financing and it gradually formed a larger and larger proportion of the forces of the king's party, reaching a peak of perhaps as much as forty per cent of it by July 1572, just before it made the breakthrough in the military stalemate by re-entering the town. Just as important as numbers was motivation; by then the band was the most committed and militant group within the king's party.

The king's men from the burgh provided their party with men, money and motivation. It is difficult to be as precise about the queen's men. They had almost exactly a hundred of the burgh's merchants in their ranks;[16] they ranged considerably in wealth and status. The wealthy provided respectability as well as a limited amount of finance. Within six months of the coup, however, money was beginning to dry up because overseas merchants had difficulty in running the blockade. Loans still filtered through, even so, at times from unlikely places. A number of apparently committed king's men were playing an elaborate double game, lending to both sides. The support of the small merchants, who were mostly purveyors of food and essential clothing, was vital because the war effort was so closely tied to the smooth running of the town's economy. Equally important for the same reason were the maltmen, who figured prominently among the queen's men; there are twenty-seven of them, along with four brewers and two mealmen. Like the merchants, they ranged from the wealthiest in the burgh, John Wilson, to the smallest; a sizeable proportion of them were not even freemen and lived outside the West Port. The merchants did not flee as a body to Leith. By remaining in large numbers, they gave a sense of normality to both the administration and economy of the town. The degree of support for the Marian coup turned on two factors: the considerable residual loyalty to the queen amongst all sectors of society and the impression which was fostered of business and town government as usual.

There is a considerable body of evidence to substantiate the conclusions of a number of historians, inferred from Melville's original comment, that the crafts played a significant role in the town's support for the queen. At one time or another during the wars the following numbers of craftsmen were implicated: forty baxters; thirty-two hammermen; twenty-eight tailors or drapers; twenty fleshers; nineteen cordiners; sixteen wrights; thirteen skinners; nine litsters; eight goldsmiths; six websters; five barbers or surgeons; three candlemakers, masons, lorimers and bowers; two bonnetmakers, walkers, coopers and furriers; and one slater and painter. It is possible, from an analysis of the muster roll of 1558 and the tax roll of 1583, to establish what proportion of each craft became involved and their relative wealth and standing. This would in some cases qualify the initial impression that might be gained from these raw figures: probably as few as one-fifth of the tailors were queen's men. The fraction might have been even smaller if it is remembered that the 1583 roll did not include apprentices. Less than a quarter of the skinners were implicated, whereas two-thirds of the cordiners, half of the fleshers, and probably just under half of the baxters and hammermen. The hammermen provide another essential clue. This was a confederate craft; it included a number of different skills within it and a wide range of wealth as a result. What is clear is that the support for the queen's party was largely drawn from the smiths, the poorest section of the craft; the queen's men included only five of the twenty hammermen who paid 10s, a third of the average assessment, or more in 1583. The same holds good for a number of the other crafts whose members were prominent in the ranks of the queen's party; only one of the twenty fleshers who were assessed at 10s or above in the same roll was a queen's man; only two of the twenty-eight skinners, four of the eleven cordiners and eight of the thirty baxters, who were assessed at 13s 4d or more; only seven of the twenty-seven tailors assessed at more than 20s. There are conspicuous exceptions, like the goldsmiths, many of whom were merely continuing their long service in the royal Mint, but, in general, it can safely be said that the queen's party drew its support either from the meaner crafts or from the poorer sections of the crafts.

There were, of course, a number of contributory factors as to why this should have been so. The wealthiest flesher in Edinburgh was Harry Burrell, who had removed himself to Leith but had prudently left his daughter and son-in-law behind to carry on the business; his precautions did not, however, prevent his house being demolished by the Castilians. Burrell was not an isolated example; David Logan's catholicism was not enough reason to persuade him to stay and he left his son behind to assume his burghal responsibilities; Mungo Russell, one of the most prominent figures in the king's party, also left his servant in the town. It was only to be expected that masters would leave and servants or apprentices would stay behind; this seems a more likely explanation than one that proposed a natural alliance between the queen's party and the craft apprentices. It was also more difficult for craftsmen than it was for the overseas merchants to establish themselves in Leith; exiled craftsmen were forced to turn to the privy council to seek permission to set up their booths in Leith in the face of opposition from its inhabitants.[17] There were also individual reasons why one group rather than another would have been reluctant to leave the town. Most of the maltmen lived just inside or outside the West Port, the area closest to the Castle; brewers, baxters, smiths, and possibly cordiners and websters as well, all worked with a fixed piece of apparatus, which would have been difficult or impossible to move.

It would be an exaggeration to conclude from the evidence pointing towards the relative poverty of the queen's men from the crafts that they were mostly nonentities; thirty-six of them had been deacons. Their support of the queen's party does illustrate the problems that the council had in the 1560s with certain crafts; the hammermen, despite the dismissal of William Brocas in 1562 and the influence in it of the two protestant activists, James Young and William Harlaw, had a queen's man as deacon four times in the 1560s; the goldsmiths were controlled by a Marian nine times in the same period, the tailors and fleshers seven times. The tailors, like the hammermen, had been taken over by queen's men after 1567 and were the craft which was most obviously purged after the wars. Nonetheless, it is fairly clear that the exiled craftsmen were mostly substantial men; eleven of the thirty-five who have been traced had held office in the town. Among the twelve tailors who were king's men, five came from the upper crust of the craft. All four of the hammermen came from the prosperous cutlers and saddlers, who formed the aristocracy of the guild. The evidence, even if it is comparatively slight for the king's men from the crafts, points towards that same dependence that the new protestant regime in the 1560s placed on a craft aristocracy, who were more reliably protestant than their fellows. The predictable name of James Young crops up in the ranks of the king's party. Yet Young was not the only influential craftsman; the baxter, David Kinloch, was one of the most militant leaders of the Edinburgh band.[18]

It might be possible, from the overall statistics, to construct an argument that it was the groups that were deprived of a voice in burgh government — the maltmen, baxters and fleshers — that were prominent among the Marians. Yet that would be a generalisation that foundered on particulars. Representation on the council was the prerogative of the aristocracy of a craft, not of its whole membership. Amongst the baxters it was Kinloch who suffered most from this policy of exclusion, yet this made no difference to his support for the merchant-dominated king's party. Another of the most vocal of the council's critics in the 1560s on craft privileges in elections was another king's man, Peter Turnet. For craftsmen like these, their burgh politics were not allowed to get in the way of their protestant politics. Some of them had gained an outlet via the kirk session; Kinloch, Burrell and the skinner, John Freir, though never on the council, were elders of the kirk at one point or another.[19] There is no evidence to show that they were offered anything more tangible by the queen's lords. Mary herself had never played craft politics and neither did the Marian party. The presence of the old merchant establishment amongst the Marians made any prospect of such a ploy even more unlikely. There may have been a coup d'état in June 1571 but there was not a social revolution. Again, as with the merchants, it is not easy to dogmatise about the role of the craftsmen in the wars since there were such wide variations among the crafts and within individual crafts. Neither the crafts nor the craft deacons were as easily persuaded into the ranks of the queen's party as Bannatyne made them out to be; only four of the deacons of 1570-71 were queen's men.[20] Even so, it is clear that it was the craftsmen who provided most of the manpower to defend the town; it was the doyens of the burgh establishment who controlled them.

Other dichotomies existed within the queen's party's support in the burgh. They were not all 'outs' seeking office. They did include a number of the old establishment, like Francis Tennant and James Carmichael, who had been excluded from the council after 1560, but ten queen's men had served on the council in the 1560s. Some of them had done so for a considerable length of time: Alan Dickson had been on it for five years running in the 1560s and John Marjoribanks and James Oliphant each for three; William Fowler and Andrew Stevenson had each served four times since 1564. Two of the bailies intruded by the queen's lords in June 1571, Cuthbert Ramsay and Thomas Hamilton, had been on the council in the 1560s. Yet those who were elected in October 1571 were an unimpressive lot; none had been on the council before. Corsbie was a very small merchant; Nisbet, although he later rose to a distinguished career, had only gained his guildry a year before. It probably says a good deal about the nature of the Marian support that none of the older, established merchants who remained risked taking office on the eve of the siege.

The Marians included the head of the catholic faction in the burgh, Herbert Maxwell, who was one of the bailies forced on the town in June 1571, but also Thomas MacCalzean, who had some basis to his claim to be one of the first protestants in the town. The case that MacCalzean put to the General Assembly in 1574 had distinct echoes of the proclamation of the queen's lords of April 1570, that the majority of them had been the 'first and . . . greatest instruments' of the establishment of protestantism. One anonymous account, in trying to condemn the punitive treatment handed out to those who had remained in the burgh, pursued the same point, arguing that the queen's party contained as many loyal protestants as its rival.[21] There was a good deal of truth in this; MacCalzean was not an isolated figure. Alexander Guthrie, who had a better protestant pedigree than MacCalzean, lingered on in the town until September or October 1571; John Moscrop, the town's procurator fiscal, who had been entrusted with the handling of the case against the catholic master of the grammar school in 1562, was a committed Marian; as many as twenty-eight of the 'faithful brethren' of 1562 supported the queen's party. Marian sympathies even extended to a few former protestant activists; alongside Guthrie in the ranks of the queen's men was Alan Dickson, who had been one of the hardline protestant bailies dismissed by the queen in 1561. Why should Patrick Thomson, the son of another key protestant party man of the early 1560s, suddenly have appeared as a militant supporter of the queen in 1571? The likely answer is a useful reminder that in burgh society, as in Scottish society as a whole, the pull of family and kin was usually more potent than that of ideas. Thomson had married into an old conservative family. He had become part of the Craik connection. The queen's party amongst the burgesses, like the nobility, was organised around a series of family connections.[22]

George Buchanan, the chief apologist of the king's party, made the point that the queen's party as a whole had very diverse origins; some came from the Hamilton faction, some were 'papists, some fenzeit protestants that have no God but geir'.[23] The same was true of the municipal queen's party; it was a coalition of different classes, groups and interests. Its aim was to preserve an essential continuity in both secular and spiritual affairs; the kirk session was continued along with the town council. Pressure was exerted on certain members of both bodies to continue in office. The new regime was not an explicitly catholic one. Yet clearly not all of the queen's men were respectable protestants. They included among them ten of those who had been caught openly practising catholic ritual in the 1560s, and five of these had been formally excommunicated and banished in 1569. There were also a number of persistent fornicators, stubborn excommunicates — though their offence is not known — and members of the old conservative establishment among them, enough to give an edge to the righteous anger of the kirk session in the recriminations which followed the end of the wars. More significantly, they included the whole of the inner circle of the catholic party in the burgh. The wars saw the reintegration of the burgh's catholics into the political life of the town. This says much for the thesis that comparatively few in this period actually saw protestantism and catholicism as locked together in a life-and-death struggle. In a close-knit society this would have meant neighbour against neighbour, merchant against partner or client. Catholics, because of the natural kindliness of burgh society, had never quite been cast in the role of untouchables. They could now return also to the highest positions in burgh government. This was part of a process which had been begun by Mary during her personal reign, the redrawing of the lines of politics and loyalty away from religious partisanship; it was taken to its conclusion by the Marian coup of 1571. That was one of the chief reasons for the breadth of the appeal of the queen's party in burgh society. It was a coalition — that was the most alarming feature to Knox and his allies who relied on the divisiveness of religious politics.

The major disadvantage of coalition politics is usually that there is a wide variation in the interests involved and degrees of enthusiasm for the cause. The situation brought about by the siege of the burgh was complicated. The majority of the merchants who went to Leith were overseas traders, whose economic interests were not necessarily adversely affected by their exile. Larger merchants usually had two warehouses, one underneath their house in Edinburgh and one in Leith; they were cut off from one market but provided with another, potentially more lucrative one. Some, like the wine importer, Andrew Craig, simply made a token appearance in Leith and then continued with their overseas trading activities. It was generally, though not always, the case that smaller merchants had more restricted horizons; many of the very small men were only booth owners. It is not surprising that they remained in some numbers in the town. The dilemma for large property owners was particularly acute; William Fowler had acted as an agent for both parties, probably in an attempt to placate each of them, but remained in the town to protect his property interests. Economic self-interest, or love of 'geir', could take a variety of forms because the interests of the various kinds of merchants ranged over a wide area; it did not simply push the merchants as a whole into one party or another.

The largest single group of merchants to suffer in the aftermath of the siege were the maltmen; twenty-seven of them were implicated and the two largest fines were exacted on maltmen. Yet all that this probably indicates is that malt was one of the commodities in greatest shortage in Edinburgh by 1572 rather than that this group had any particular attachment to the Marian cause; by June 1572 a profit of sixty-six per cent could be made from running the blockade. This example also demonstrates that it is not always the case that activism can be measured simply by tabulating the size of fines imposed. Thirteen burgesses were fined more than £50. It is true that some of them were prominent Marians; they included two of the bailies of 1571-2. Yet the third bailie, Corsbie, was fined only £20. The significant factor in explaining the harsh treatment meted out to these men was not their degree of involvement with the queen's party but the fact that ten of the thirteen had been prudent enough to seek remissions before the fall of the Castle in May 1573.[24] Penance was more expensive in the highly charged atmosphere that persisted up until the final defeat of the Castilians.

A more realistic inference can be made from the series of judicial proceedings which began early in 1573. It seems that some attempt was made in these mass trials to distinguish the different degrees of involvement with the rebels. The first list of 4 February 1573 were, with one exception, all maltmen or purveyors of food and were charged only with assisting Grange in withholding the burgh. The forty-five pledged on 17 August were again almost all maltmen, baxters or fleshers.[25] It is the trials for treason or conspiracy that reveal those who were more deeply involved; Maxwell, the two Moscrops, Hamilton and Balfour of Westray had all been important enough to have been forfeited along with the titular leaders of the queen's party, like Châtelherault, Sir James Balfour of Pittendreich and the bishop of Galloway, at the Stirling parliament of August 1571. Ramsay, Patrick Thomson and the blacksmith, William Henderson, were forfeited along with Lord Home by the Edinburgh parliament of April 1573.[26] The forty-seven indicted three months later before the Court of Justiciary had only one merchant among them; they included twelve hammermen, six skinners, five wrights, four cordiners and tailors and three websters.[27] It is noticeable that five of those who had already been convicted for being involved in the skirmish at the Crags came from the same crafts.[28] By contrast, those charged with conspiracy on 13 August were mostly merchants and included Corsbie, Dickson, John Spottiswood and Andrew Stevenson among them.[29] The final significant proceedings were those taken against the small wool merchant, John Newlands, the alleged ring-leader behind the riots in the town that had culminated in the forced exile. The kirk session record also usually distinguished between those who had merely remained in the town, those who had taken up arms and those who had sequestered or destroyed their neighbours' goods or property.

The hard core and the leadership of the queen's party were largely derived from the catholic party of the 1560; to this was added a number of individual but influential merchants and advocates like Dickson and Moscrop. The rank and file of its activists came from the smaller merchants and about half a dozen of the crafts — principally the hammermen, tailors, cordiners, skinners, wrights and goldsmiths. For the remainder, their allegiance was for the most part marginal, temporary or circumstantial. The king's party was less obviously a coalition of interests. To begin with, the interests of the merchants dictated a cautious and conservative attitude; both burgh and personal interests, the threat of a breakdown of order in the town and the sequestering of merchandise in France, might initially have pointed to a compromise with Grange. Yet once the merchants found themselves in exile, those same interests increasingly pointed in an opposite direction. The accumulated grievances of the exiles, separated from their homes, Edinburgh warehouses, rents and markets, made possible a unique conjunction of self-interest and political protestantism. There is a striking parallel here with the course of the French wars of religion in the second half of the 1560s; it has been argued that the Huguenot ministers were reluctant to enter the wars but that once they became involved they pressured for the continuation of the struggle until tangible and lasting gains would be secured.[30] The Edinburgh merchants in exile gradually developed into a win-the-war party; the demolition campaign of the Castilian 'Chimney band' and the spiralling pattern of reprisals and counter-reprisals combined to give them an animus as well as an identity of interests which the queen's party in the burgh lacked. In the reformation crisis of 1559-60 and the 1560s only a committed minority had become actively involved in the politics of protestantism. John Knox had not managed to convert more than a fraction of the burgh establishment to political protestantism in the course of the 1560s; the civil wars succeeded where Knox had failed. It was the crisis brought about by the wars which politicised the younger generation of the merchant establishment. The protestant party was finally given an issue with which it could sweep the board. It was symbolic that the titular leadership of the Edinburgh band should have gone to Adam Fullarton, the leader of the Congregation in the burgh in 1559. In a very real sense, the wars between Leith and Edinburgh were the last round in the struggle between the burgh's protestant and catholic parties which had been going on ever since October 1559.

NOTES

1. Melville, *Memoirs*, 255; Spottiswoode, *History*, ii, 158. Ridley has followed the notion that a stark dichotomy emerged in the civil war: town councils and merchants for the king, craftsmen and the poor for the queen (*John Knox*, 491); Percy argued that the craftsmen took the troubles as an opportunity to further their disputes with the merchants by backing Grange against Knox (*John Knox*, 415); Hume Brown based his argument that the majority of the well-to-do citizens were staunch supporters on the flimsy foundations of this evidence and his own prejudices (*John Knox*, ii, 254, 261). It is no coincidence that all three works have the same title. The civil war is as good an example as any of how Edinburgh's history has been distorted by the cult of personality.

2. Bannatyne, *Memorials*, 218-21 (Univ. MS, fo. 81); see also Dalyell ed., 313-20 (Advocates MS, fo. 238). There is one more on the Univ. MS list as two are given with the name of Alex. Hastie.

3. See JC 1/13, 1 Feb. 1572; *RPC*, ii, 87-8.

4. PRO, SP 52/23, fo. 254; the first 31 are given in *CSP Scot.*, iv, no. 487; Bannatyne, *Memorials*, 274; cf. Dalyell ed., 404.

5. Buik of the General Kirk of Edinburgh, fos. 1-77.

6. SP 52/25, fos. 72r-73r, 117r-118v; see *CSP Scot.*, iv, nos. 639(1), 666.

7. See JC 1/13, 13 June 1572*; 4* & 9* Feb. 1573; 1* & 2* April 1573; 3*, 13*, 17 & 26 Aug. 1573; also JC 26/1, 30 April, 31 July, 10/11 Aug. & 3 Nov. 1573. Those asterisked are printed in Pitcairn; see *Trials*, 1, ii, 32, 39-40, 42, 45, 47 & 47n.

8. *RSS*, vi, 1586, 1758, 1763, 1766, 1817ff; *TA*, xii, 265-8; xiii, 9, 115, 329-48.

9. Prot. Bk. Aitkin, i, fos. 63ff. (26 Sept. 1571-28 Jan. 1572); vol. ii for the period from then until Oct. 1572 had gone missing in this century; Prot. Bk. Stewart, elder (unfoliated; 2 June 1571 onwards); Prot. Bk. Robeson, xvii, fos. 121-85 (4 Aug. 1571-4 Feb. 1573).

10. Cf. *Diurnal*, 238-9, 244; Bannatyne, *Memorials*, 178; see also *RSS*, vi, 1256ff; *TA*, xii, 253-4, 363.

11. JC 1/13, 30 Nov. 1571; 23 Feb., 28 April, 13 June, 17 & 22 July 1572; 9 Feb. 1573, 3 Aug. 1573; see Pitcairn, *Trials*, 1, ii, 40, 45-6. Two former Marians, however, served on an assize, which tried two servants of Cockburn of Ormiston, on 8 May 1573; see Thomas Andrew and William Watson in app. viii; Andrew had still to be granted a remission.

12. *Diurnal*, 226, 231; Calderwood, *History*, iii, 111; *CSP Scot.*, iii, no. 917; iv, nos. 13, 14; cf. JC 26/1, 31 July & 3 Nov. 1573 for the proceedings against Patrick Anderson and others and John Newlands (see app. viii).

13. They are given separately in app. ix.

14. See 'The queen's party, 1568-73', ch. 5 of Donaldson, *Mary Queen of Scots*, esp. 136.

15. *TA*, xii, pp. viii, 331, 363; *Diurnal*, 293; *CSP Scot.*, iv, nos. 222, 368.

16. This figure excludes maltmen, carters, stablemen etc., who were taxed along with the merchants before 1583.

17. MS Privy Council, Register of *Acta* (PC 1/6), fo. 45; see *RPC*, ii, 100 and the entries for James Inglis, Wm. Leach, Peter Turnet, Murdo Walker and James Young in app. vii.

18. See *Diurnal*, 301.

19. *Edin. Recs.*, iii, 268-9; Freir was elected an elder in 1573 and Kinloch in 1574 (see app. iii); Burrell was an elder of the Canongate parish 1566-7 (see app. ix).

20. Bannatyne, *Memorials*, 71; see John Cunningham, Cuthbert Matheson, George Smith and John Wilson, the deacons of the wrights, websters, tailors and hammermen, in app. viii.

21. *CSP Scot.*, iii, no. 181; *Hist. King James VI*, 147.

22. Cf. Donaldson, *Mary Queen of Scots*, 125-35.

23. *CSP Scot.*, iii, no. 123.

24. *RSS*, vi, 1818, 1844B, 1846-8, 1857, 1876, 1884, 1899, 1954; cf. *ibid.*, p. ix.

25. See JC 1/13 under these two dates.

26. *CSP Scot.*, iii, nos. 897-8; iv, no. 636; *Diurnal*, 245-6, 331; Bannatyne, *Memorials*, 186; JC 26/1, [30] April 1573.

27. Ibid., 31 July 1573; see Patrick Anderson's entry in app. viii for details of the indictment.

28. JC 1/13, 9 Feb. 1573; Pitcairn, *Trials*, 1, ii, 40.

29. JC 1/13, 13 Aug. 1573; see John Adamson, younger in app. vii.

30. R. N. Kingdon, *Geneva and the Consolidation of the French Protestant Movement* (Geneva, 1967), 153.

13
Conclusion

EDINBURGH'S reformation was one of the last of the great city reformations of the sixteenth century. Even though the city did not have the independence or quasi-independence of the imperial cities or Swiss city republics, its reformation took on a highly distinctive shape, which in many respects distinguished it from that in the other Scottish burghs. To some extent this was predictable since it developed in an unusual set of conditions. Despite its size and undoubted predominance over the other burghs, Edinburgh was, until 1583, a city without a university. This meant that its reformation lacked the hothouse intellectual atmosphere of St. Andrews as well as the ultra-cautious restraint which characterised Old Aberdeen. From the beginning Edinburgh's reformation was about practicalities. The university, when it emerged, resembled neither the traditional Scottish institutions nor Geneva's Academy; it was a civic creation, controlled by the town council. It had its antecedents in the 1550s, when two lectureships had been created by the regent, Mary of Guise.[1] It was significant that both were filled by burgh lawyers. Edinburgh, before it had a university, had its own intellectual community and this was largely dominated by its legal profession. The library of the new university was based on the impressive collection of books of one of the burgh's commissaries. From very early on the lawyers had a considerable voice in the new kirk just as they had in the town council. They appeared in large numbers on the protestant subscription list of 1562 and monopolised a third of the eldership on the kirk sessions elected in 1574 and 1575. Yet even theirs — the the purpose of the 1562 appeal is significant here — was a pragmatic faith rather than an intellectualised one.

All of the Scottish burghs were subject to outside influences, but none to quite the same amount of political interference as Edinburgh, interference which became more detailed and discriminating as the sixteenth century went on. The combination of the court and the labyrinth of factions within — and, at times of crisis, outside — it, together with what was always the welcoming door for protestant extremists of the resident English ambassador, brought a unique set of pressures to bear on what was by instinct an inward-looking society. Edinburgh reluctantly, but increasingly, became the cockpit not only for English policy in Scotland but also for the shifting factionalism of Scottish politics. This came at a time when the burgh also had its own serious social and economic problems to contend with. The notion of a 'permanent crisis' is more often than not in a historian's imagination rather than real, but Edinburgh did come close to it in this period. There were a recurrent series of food shortages, outbreaks of the plague, threats to the political and economic independence of the town as well as siege and invasion to contend with between the 1540s and 1580s. It was this complex and confusing backcloth which set the tone of Edinburgh's reformation.

It is hardly surprising that there was not a unified response either from the burgh or from burgh protestantism to this combination of pressures. The first authentic voice of Edinburgh protestantism emerged in the declaration of the radical minority in the town in July 1559. It was the product of an externally imposed crisis — the occupation of the town by the Congregation and Mary of Guise's subsequent scheme for a poll of religious opinion. The crisis of 1559 brought about both the crystallisation and the politicisation of the protestants in the burgh; it turned them from a tolerated prophesying group into a political party. The strident tone of this beleaguered and vulnerable minority, which refused to allow its subscription to a larger truth to be 'subject to the voiting of men',[2] did not end in 1560. In Edinburgh, as in most the Scottish burghs, protestants had not gained power through their own strength; they had power thrust upon them. The minority party of 1559 remained a minority party for the better part of the 1560s. The result was that it continued in the 1560s, even after the prohibition of the mass, in much the same form as it had in the later 1550s, as a small, ingrown circle of activists. The new regime was unsure of its position and liable to overreact to any threat to it, whether it took the form of a craft riot, as in 1560 and 1561, or Mary's fairly conservative attempts to broaden and dilute the burgh oligarchy in 1565 and 1566.

The price of this unexpected victory was that the radical protestants, lacking widespread appeal, had to turn to the existing establishment for support. The broader and blander character of the 'faithful brethren' of 1562 is a good example of what came to be the more typical face of Edinburgh protestantism. The subscription list shows that protestantism had captured half of both the merchant and legal establishments by 1562 but also amply confirms that it fell far short of a dynamic protestantism. The scheme for a poor hospital owed something to the vision of the remarkable 'assured Scot', James Henderson, but it followed a series of attempts by a catholic council to deal with the problem of the poor in the second half of the 1550s. The proposed poor hospital was not an explicitly protestant creation but a burgh one. The other planks of the agreed programme were discipline and education, and both again built on foundations laid in the 1550s.[3] It was predictable, but nonetheless important, that the upper strata of burgh society would be attracted to the schemes of the new church which were closest to the traditional policies of the burgh. The same applied to the upper reaches of the crafts. The craft aristocracy was just as anxious to preserve the tightly structured framework of existing society and was even willing to help to propagate the myth of Edinburgh as a 'mirrour and exampill to all the rest of this realme'. It was only gradually, however, that the myth developed and overtook that of St. Andrews as the best reformed city in the realm.[4] There was less agreement over the policy of trying to attract to the burgh the most talented — and expensive — ministers in the reformed church. There was continual difficulty in meeting their stipends and growing irritation, particularly in the 1580s, at their stridency.

This protestant coalition was at its most enthusiastic and its most unanimous when it was concerned with the details of discipline, education and poor relief. The peculiarly close triangular relationship of ministry, council and guilds, which came to characterise the burgh reformation in Scotland, was largely founded on this paternalistic piety. It was certainly not a feature which was copied from Geneva, which was until late in the sixteenth century a city without guilds and without a natural or intimate bond between its pastors and the Small Council.[5] Although there was not in Scotland so explicit a theory of the city as a *corpus christianum* as there was in some of the imperial or Swiss cities,[6] it was certainly explicit enough in practice. The council worshipped together and attended a service before its meetings. The craft, before and after 1560, worshipped as a body, provided for its own poor and imposed discipline upon its own members both through the guild and the household. Yet all of this took time. A town council could only move at the speed it was allowed to by custom and convention. It could not, even if it wished to, impose a blanket religious test on office-holders or burgess rights. The closed doors and inbred religiosity of the craft guild did not provide a natural breeding-ground for early protestantism. The craft was important, not for the development of a protestant privy kirk in the 1550s, but, in certain cases, for the persistence of catholic privy kirks well into the 1560s.

It has been pointed out that the keynote of the social emphasis of the new church was its involvement in the life of the community,[7] but it was always involvement which took place within the existing institutions or conventions of burgh society. The kirk session adopted many of the practices of existing burgh courts or guild incorporations. Burgh protestantism was able gradually to build on the fact that the craft guild had long given a further dimension to the shape of the town as a Christian community. Enthusiasm could be encouraged and filtered at the same time. It was a civic protestantism and always institutionalised in its ethos. It is when more account is taken of this that the organisation of the new church at local level appears far less radical and far less dependent, in practice, on the example of the 'best reformed churches' than has often been suggested.[8] The new church was able to use the burghs as the growth points for the spread of protestantism but the policy had its price. The burghs were the most settled part of Scottish society, held together by long-established privileges and traditions. The new religion was obliged in the burghs to work within the natural constraints of burgh life. It was always first and last a burgh church.

It is surprising how little is known of Edinburgh's reformation; it does not figure prominently in the pages of Knox's *History*, and has attracted only a single article and not one monograph. What has served in its place is the cult of the personality of John Knox. It is a view of history at times so staggering in its crudity as to be scarcely credible were it not so firmly established in the popular imagination. It has come to be recognised how much John Calvin's reformation benefited from the 'myth of Geneva'.[9] Edinburgh's reformation has still not escaped from the myth of John Knox. Many historians — catholic as well as presbyterian — have felt comfortable in the assumption that Knox wielded absolute moral authority over Edinburgh society. Yet they have done this without even knowing who governed Edinburgh in the post-Reformation period. It is as if the history of Calvin's second period in Geneva from 1541 onwards was written without any reference to the overriding political struggle between Calvinists and Perrinists. The struggle in Edinburgh was as bitter and had many of the same general characteristics: it took place between un-compromising reformers and moderates; the fortunes of the two fluctuated from election to election; disputes were particularly sharp over the operation of the morality laws and how they should be applied to office-holders. The key issue, however, belonged to the peculiarly Scottish climate induced by the return of Mary and her marriage to Darnley; it stemmed directly from the crisis in which political protestantism found itself by the middle of the 1560s. Only a small, militant minority was willing to take on the role of an ultra-protestant fifth column in Mary's capital.

Only a small section of the burgh establishment was willing to accept the implications or risks of political protestantism, despite prolonged exposure to Knox's sermons, at any time before the civil war of the early 1570s. It was only then that a situation arose where the interests of burgh politics and protestant politics coincided. Even then the result fell far short of a mass conversion. The bond of the military coterie of the exiled king's party solemnly drawn up shortly before it returned to the town was a striking statement of militant protestant unity but a highly unusual one.[10] It must have seemed in 1571 and 1572 that Edinburgh's merchants had at last adopted the militant stance of the urban elements in the Huguenot movement. The conversion of a large section of the burgh establishment to radical protestantism was a temporary phenomenon, however, dependent on highly unusual circumstances. It lasted only as long as the exiles held on to their persecution complex, which briefly echoed that of the Huguenots.[11] Without a continuing threat to their survival, most of the younger established merchants who formed the core of the king's party quickly dropped their militancy as issues recast themselves in the Morton period.

Apart from this brief period during the civil war there was always at least an underlying tension between protestant activism and civic protestantism. In the 1580s this widened into an open breach, which focused on a struggle for power in the council chamber. Burgh politics were a good deal more faction-ridden in the early 1580s than they had been in the 1560s. There was more poignancy attached to the issues involved because they now, virtually for the first time, were to do with ecclesiastical polity, the role of the king and his advisers in the religious affairs of the burgh, as well as the wider Melvillian issues prompted by the passing of the Black Acts. Part of the tactical difficulty of the protestant party in the 1560s had been that, with the mass already abolished, there was no natural focus for its campaign. The progress of Edinburgh's reformation and that in the other Scottish burghs had a sense of anti-climax about it as a result. There was nothing of the typical pattern of the urban reformation of the 1520s — a popular campaign, usually directed against abuses, a disputation, followed, sooner or later, by abolition of the mass. The wider appeal to the populace, paradoxically, belonged in Edinburgh to the 1580s rather than to the late 1550s or early 1560s. Popular protestantism on a large scale did not prepare the way for the Reformation or even result quickly from it. Mass protestant demonstrations came a generation after the Reformation.

The first example of what was in any sense a theological disputation involving the burgh inhabitants again belonged to the 1580s rather than the 1560s. The dialogue of 1584 between 'two neighbours of Edinburgh', Edward Hope and Henry Nisbet, turned on the familiar Melvillian distinction made by Hope between God's law and the laws of men. Nisbet's attitude to the Black Acts was straightforward and practical: parliament, he claimed, had confirmed the existing doctrine and worship of the kirk; the burgh had no alternative but to conform to the wishes of the crown.[12] There can be little doubt that Nisbet also spoke for a large section of the burgh establishment when he expressed his irritation with the intemperate demands of the radical ministers.

The confrontation between these two men was also a symbolic one. Hope was a veteran not only of the reformation crisis but of the burgh's first faltering steps towards protestantism in the early 1540s. Nisbet was a much wealthier merchant, who had come to a position of influence in the burgh towards the end of the 1560s after the deposition of Mary; his family had been split in its allegiances during the civil war and he had become increasingly disaffected from Morton as the 1570s went on and was ready to co-operate with both the Lennox and Arran regimes in the 1580s. The younger generation of merchants who came on to the council in the later 1560s and the 1570s were an important constituent of the many-sided reaction against what was seen as the extremes of Melvillianism.[13] In its essence, this was the same struggle between moderate and militant protestantism as had been going on since the early 1560s and this was reflected in some of the personalities involved — the veterans of the old protestant party, Hope, Fullarton and Slater — against the moderates and Marian nominees of the 1560s, Andrew Stevenson, Luke

Wilson and Alexander Uddart. Men like these, usually prosperous members of old merchant families, had noticeably come back into favour after 1578; they even brought with them old leaders of the queen's party in the civil war, like Hew Lauder and William Nisbet, Henry's brother. The point has often been made that the radicalism of the 1580s was not a new phenomenon; the same essential issues, it is argued, were at stake then as in the first years of the new church. This is true at least to the extent that there was considerable continuity between the committed protestants of the 1560s and the radicals of the 1580s. The men of 1560 who survived turned out, for the most part, to defend the kirk in 1584. They brought along with them many of the sons of their old colleagues; there was a strong family tradition in radicalism. Yet it is often forgotten that the radicals were not the only ones with predecessors; their moderate opponents also had twenty-five years' tradition to fall back upon of consistent criticism of extremism. Moderation also ran in families and especially in the leading families of the Edinburgh establishment. What was new about the struggles of the 1580s was the size and popular appeal of the radical movement and the fact that power within it had decisively tipped towards its meaner men. The Reformation and its repercussions had largely been debated within the privileged confines of the burgh establishment. The repercussions of the Melvillian crisis were debated in a much wider forum and the struggle over them threatened to engulf burgh society as a whole.

The history of Edinburgh's reformation is a tortuous one and one in which the crisis of 1559-60 did not bring a clear-cut victory to Knox and the committed reformers. There was always formidable resistance to a protestantism of extremes. The protestantism which prevailed amongst the burgh establishment was pious and paternalistic but it did not, for the most part, see itself as engaged in an eternal struggle with the Anti-Christ, whether in the guise of stubborn catholics or pallid protestants. It is at times difficult to remember this when reading Knox's *History* or a number of biographies of him, where the emphasis is usually on confrontation and dramatised irreconcilables. Yet Knox is always vague about Edinburgh opinion between the extremes of the spectrum and often highly misleading. Twice, by implication, his *History* attacks one of the most respected men in the burgh for accepting office on a nominated council; among the Marian nominees of 1565 whom it labelled unworthy of office were two commissioners to the General Assembly, the sub-collector of thirds for Lothian and the wealthiest craftsman in the burgh. Political accommodation, which was a cardinal principle of successful government in Scotland,[14] had no place in Knox's scheme of things. It was, nevertheless, a recurrent pattern in Edinburgh's reformation.

There is no reason why we should continue to look at Edinburgh and its reformation only through Knox's eyes when so few in the town actually shared his forthright opinions. The Reformation brought with it important constitutional questions; Knox makes no mention of them. The moderates were always present in the corridors of power; Knox ignores them or dismisses them as unimportant. These were two of the three significant barriers in the way of the wholesale protestantisation of burgh society. The third is that Knox was not so central a figure in Edinburgh as his *History* or his hagiographers have made him out to be. He was, for one thing, not an omnipresent figure in the town in the 1560s. Often, quite simply, he was not there. There were a number of reasons for this. His uncompromising opinions were dangerous in periods of crisis. Twice, in 1559 and 1571, he had to remove himself to avoid provoking a hostile reaction in the town and left a safer substitute in the pulpit of St. Giles'. Although he declared that he found 'his estate honourable enough' as minister of Edinburgh and declined to become a superintendent, he interpreted his responsibilities to the new Church of Scotland more broadly. He accepted half-a-dozen invitations to act as a visitor or commissioner to other churches throughout the country in as many years from 1562 onwards. In 1562 he was away for four months; he was away when most of his closest allies on the council found themselves indicted before the Court of Justiciary in 1564 for turning a blind eye to a colleague who was guilty of assault and murder; late in 1565, when the repercussions of the botched Moray conspiracy remained uncertain, he took on a commission 'for so long as occasion might suffer'. Indeed, for much of the period from then until after the deposition of Mary in 1567 Knox was away: first lying low in the west after the Riccio murder, returning in December 1566, but only briefly, in order to apply to the General Assembly for a six months' leave of absence in England.[15] It is one thing to argue that Knox's domineering presence could silence all opposition; it is quite another to insist that his spectre could as well.

Knox did not have quite the same long, almost masochistic devotion to his adopted city as did Calvin. At the same time, it is true and it is important to establish that his position as the first minister of Edinburgh was perfectly secure; he might often meet criticism for his uncompromising views but his critics would for the most part close ranks if his position was threatened. It is probably true that at times he enjoyed a relationship with the council which rivalled Zwingli's in Zürich for its intimacy. It was a relationship, however, which had its limits; it did not extend to wholesale harassment of catholics or to political activism. As for his contribution to Edinburgh's reformation, that was probably a good deal more limited than historians have allowed for. One man, even Knox, does not make a reformation. Much of the overriding ethos of Edinburgh protestantism was built on foundations laid down long before Knox became the burgh's minister. It is now clear that he did not, like Calvin, succeed in bringing permanently into power a new and — at least in his terms — godly magistracy. He did not solve, and at times only exacerbated, what tensions existed between the craftsmen and the merchant-dominated council. He failed to turn fully half of the burgh establishment and rather more than half of the population taken as a whole away from their loyalty to Mary, Queen of Scots.

A balanced view of Knox will not emerge until a more balanced view of his own congregation in St. Giles' emerges as well. Revolutions breed not only revolutionaries and ideologues but also trimmers and fellow-travellers. The religious revolution of 1559-60 was no exception. The more we learn of the complex reactions of Edinburgh society to the Reformation, the more ambiguous the role of Knox becomes. Because he lacked popular support, Knox had to turn to where power lay already — to the burgh establishment. Who were his allies there? A little is already known of James Baron because of his contacts with Knox in the mid-1550s but little of the two other formative figures in Edinburgh's reformation, Adam Fullarton, the spokesman for the Congregation in 1559, and 'King' Guthrie. Both, like Baron, had wives among Knox's 'dear sisters of Edinburgh'. Fullarton is the prime example of the increasing influence the English connection had on Edinburgh protestantism; his wife's library is a good example, probably the only one we have, of the key influence of English printed books on early protestantism; he mysteriously disappeared to England for two months shortly after the Congregation retook the town in 1560; he was the living example of the 'better sort' of protestant on whom the hopes — and schemes — of English foreign policy were based. Guthrie, the town clerk for fully quarter of a century, took over the key office of dean of guild from Baron and held on to it for the rest of the first half of the 1560s. He deserves a more prominent place in the long list of town clerks in sixteenth century Europe who played an important part in the spread of the Reformation.

Yet this protestant triumvirate of Knox's closest allies in Edinburgh was not without its flaws. Baron spent a good deal of his time in the 1560s pursuing an errant wife through the church courts; Fullarton slipped off the council for fully half of the 1560s, probably because of his growing business interests; Guthrie, although he had been prepared to get blood on his hands on the night of the Riccio murder, declined to leave the town when it was taken over by the queen's lords in 1571. These men had considerable influence but neither they nor the protestant caucus which they headed were the undisputed rulers of Edinburgh in the Reformation period. Burgh government continued to draw on the majority of the burgh establishment to keep itself going and the city's reformation had to accommodate itself to this simple fact of life. Baron belonged amongst the city's top twenty merchants; so did John Preston, Andrew Stevenson and Cuthbert Ramsay. All three figured on the protestant subscription list of 1562 and were on the council in the 1560s. Preston was probably the most respected figure in burgh government; he had enjoyed the favour of Mary of Guise and found little difficulty after his conversion to protestantism in enjoying the favour of Queen Mary. He was able to reconcile being at the same time a Marian nominee and a commissioner to the General Assembly. Stevenson reached the council chamber because he was one of Edinburgh's merchant princes; he became a protestant bailie who managed to have a catholic wife at the same time. Ramsay could be a protestant councillor in the mid-1560s and a bailie of the Marian regime which took over the town half a dozen years later. Ramsay and Stevenson were as much a part of the corporate personality of Edinburgh protestantism as Guthrie and Fullarton. Knox might insist:

> In religion thair is na middis: either it is the religion of God . . . or els it is the religion of the Divill[16]

but men like these, together with the majority of the burgh establishment, spent much of their time forging a middle way.

In studies of the Scottish Reformation too little attention has been paid to the nature of Scottish society itself. Considerable emphasis has frequently been laid on the advantages the burghs brought to the growth of protestantism but remarkably little on the disadvantages. The burghs were vital to the growth of protestantism but they imposed severe restrictions on its shape. In a society so conscious of rank, tradition and precedent the Reformation was only likely to make progress where it did not disturb the existing order of things. If there were two things most dear to an Edinburgh burgess they were his privileges and the money which those privileges allowed him to make. Both seemed to be threatened by the new religion. The early programme of the protestant reformers promised a new society; it provoked a backlash. A full-scale programme of protestantisation, involving coercion, penal taxation and the withdrawal of burgess rights, impinged too far on burgh privilege and had to be abandoned for a more cautious, conciliatory approach. If there was repression, as some historians have argued, it was on a petty scale and was kept in check by the customs and conventions which governed burgh life. Other historians have maintained that there was in Scotland a uniquely successful co-operation between church and state at local level; the kirk session was, it has been argued, the most effective body in the new church. There is truth in this but also much exaggeration. Genuine co-operation did exist on a regular basis but it ground to a halt when it ran up against the simple but key factor which undermined so many of the schemes of the kirk — a lack of money. Burgh society proved time and again that it was not willing to be taxed to pay for the new church. Burgh privilege and the widespread reluctance to accept burgh taxation together fashioned a formidable straitjacket for the new burgh church. The Reformation brought protestantism to Edinburgh but it had to fall into step beside the 'religion of Edinburgh'.

NOTES

1. D. B. Horn, 'The origins of the University of Edinburgh', *Edinburgh Univ. Journal*, xxii (1966), 299-300.

2. *Edin. Recs.*, iii, 47.

3. See *ibid.*, ii, 170-71, 232, 261; iii, 50-51; *RSS*, iv, 3144, 3268.

4. *Edin. Recs.*, iii, 92; see Knox, *Works*, vi, 546; Melville, *Diary*, 60.

5. Monter, *Calvin's Geneva*, 144, 159.

6. See Moeller, *Villes d'Empire et Réformation*, 15-6.

7. I. B. Cowan, 'Church and society in post-Reformation Scotland', *RSCHS*, xvii (1971), 185, 196.

8. Most recently by J. M. Kirk, 'The influence of Calvinism on the Scottish Reformation', *RSCHS*, xix (1976), 163.

9. See A. Dufour, 'Le mythe de Genève au temps de Calvin', *Schweizerische Zeitschrift für Geschichte*, ix (1959), 497ff.

10. Bannatyne, *Memorials*, 247-9.

11. See D. R. Kelley, 'Martyrs, myths and the Massacre: the background of St. Bartholomew', *American Historical Review*, lxvii (1972), 1330.

12. See Calderwood, *History*, iv, 141-3, for a brief summary of the dialogue, although Hope is given all the best lines.

13. Donaldson, *Scottish Reformation*, 211.

14. Donaldson, *James V to James VII*, 215.

15. Knox, *Works*, vi, 122, 142-3; *BUK*, i, 51, 54, 57, 73, 84-5, 113, 130; Calderwood, *History*, ii, 282, 284, 306, 394; *CSP Scot.*, i, nos. 1132, 1136, 1157; Ridley, *John Knox*, 459; Brown, *John Knox*, ii, 176.

16. Knox, *Works*, iv, 232.

Appendices

R

Appendix i

Lists of Edinburgh town councils and deacons of crafts, 1551-1584, with index to members of the council

THE council elections were held annually in October but craft elections were held in May. The year in office of a councillor of 1562-3, for example, ran from October 1562-September 1563; that of a craft deacon of 1562-3 ran from May 1562-April 1563. The lists given in *Edin. Recs.*, iii, 289ff & iv, 575ff, are not always accurate, even when full, and should be treated with caution.

Abbreviations

C	councillor
CC	craft councillor
DC	deacon councillor (from 1583)
DG	dean of guild
(K)	Kilspindie
(KP)	king's party
nom.	nominated by leet
P	provost
PR	president
(QP)	queen's party
r	replacement
(S)	Seton
T	treasurer

The council of 1551-2

Provost:	WILLIAM CRAIK
Bailies:	PATRICK IRELAND
	WILLIAM LAWSON
	JOHN PRESTON
	ROBERT FLEMING
Dean of Guild:	JAMES CARMICHAEL
Treasurer:	ROBERT GRAHAM

The craft deacons

Goldsmiths:	MICHAEL RHIND
Hammermen:	MUNGO HUNTER

References: MS Co. Recs., ii, fos. 4v, 6r, 7v; MS Goldsmiths' Recs., fo. 8r; Smith, *Hammermen of Edinburgh*, xciii.

The council of 1552-3

Provost:	WILLIAM CRAIK
Bailies:	EDWARD LITTLE
	RICHARD GRAY
	JOHN YOUNG
	JAMES WALLACE
Dean of Guild:	JAMES CARMICHAEL
Treasurer:	ALEXANDER PARK
Ordinary council:	PATRICK IRELAND
	WILLIAM LAWSON
	JOHN PRESTON
	ROBERT FLEMING
	ROBERT GRAHAM
	JOHN DOUGAL
	JAMES ADAMSON
	RICHARD STRANG
	EDWARD HOPE
	ALEXANDER KAY
	ALEXANDER BRUCE, barber
	MUNGO HUNTER, smith

The craft deacons

Tailors:	ROBERT LINDSAY
Skinners:	WILLIAM COLDEN
Furrier:	JOHN CRAIG
Goldsmiths:	THOMAS EWING
Hammermen:	JAMES YOUNG, cutler
Cordiners:	ROBERT FLEMING
Baxters:	DAVID KINLOCH
Walkers:	JAMES STIRK

References: MS Co. Recs., iii, fos. 11v, 13r, 14v, 16v.

The council of 1553-4

Provost:	SIR WILLIAM HAMILTON OF SANQUHAR[1]
Bailies:	DUNCAN LIVINGSTONE
	WILLIAM MUIRHEAD
	WILLIAM LAWSON
	JOHN PRESTON

Dean of Guild:	JOHN SIMPSON[2]
Treasurer:	ROBERT GRAHAM

The craft deacons

Furriers:	ARCHIBALD LEACH
Goldsmiths:	THOMAS EWING
Hammermen:	JAMES YOUNG, cutler

References: MS Co. Recs., ii, fos. 19v, 21v, 23v, 24r; *APS*, ii, 603; Sir John Lauder of Fountainhall, *Historical Notices of Scottish Affairs* (Bann. Club, 1848), 73-4; MS Neighbourhood Book, 9 July 1554; MS Goldsmiths' Recs., fo. 8r.

1. See the annotated copy of *Lord Provosts*, 18, kept in Edinburgh City Archives.
2. Cf. *Edin. Recs.*, iii, 300.

The council of 1554-5

Provost:	ARCHIBALD DOUGLAS OF KILSPINDIE
Bailies:	EDWARD HOPE
	JOHN SIM
	JAMES ADAMSON
	JAMES LINDSAY
Dean of Guild:	JAMES CARMICHAEL
Treasurer:	JOHN PRESTON
Ordinary council:	JOHN SIMPSON
	ROBERT GRAHAM[1]
	JAMES BANNATYNE[2]
	ALEXANDER PARK
	ALEXANDER BRUCE, barber
	ROBERT LINDSAY, tailor

The craft deacons

Tailors:	PATRICK DURHAM
Skinners:	JAMES FORRET
Furriers:	ANDREW ELPHINSTONE
Goldsmiths:	THOMAS EWING
Hammermen:	JAMES YOUNG, cutler
Wrights:	JOHN CUNNINGHAM
Websters:	MARTIN LYELL

References: MS Co. Recs., ii, fos. 28v, 35, 37v, 39v, 41v; MS Goldsmiths' Recs., fo. 8r; Prot. Bk. King, iv, fo. 175.

1. Replaced by his son, Archibald Graham, in March 1555.
2. Replaced by Richard Carmichael, 22 March 1555.

Appendix i

The council of 1555-6

Provost:	ARCHIBALD DOUGLAS OF KILSPINDIE
Bailies:	JOHN SIM
	RICHARD CARMICHAEL
	ALEXANDER HOME
	ROBERT FLEMING
Dean of Guild:	JAMES BARON
Treasurer:	ARCHIBALD GRAHAM
Ordinary council:	EDWARD HOPE
	JAMES ADAMSON
	JAMES LINDSAY
	JAMES CARMICHAEL
	JOHN PRESTON
	JOHN SIMPSON
	ANDREW MURRAY OF BLACKBARONY
	ADAM FULLARTON
	ALEXANDER ACHESON
	JOHN SPOTTISWOOD
	JOHN LOCH, furrier
	MICHAEL GILBERT, goldsmith

	The craft deacons	*The craft visitors*
Tailors:	PATRICK DURHAM	NICOL RHIND[1]
Skinners:	JAMES ABERNETHY	THOMAS CLARKSON
Goldsmiths:	THOMAS EWING	JOHN GILBERT[2]
Hammermen:	ANDREW HAMILTON, smith	JOHN BANKS
Barbers:		ALEXANDER BRUCE
Masons:		GILBERT GREIG
Wrights:		VIRGIL CALDER
Cordiners:		WILLIAM SMITH
Baxters:		THOMAS BOYCE
Walkers:	JAMES STIRK	CUTHBERT DICK
Websters:		WILLIAM MOCHRIE

References: MS Co. Recs., ii, fos. 49v, 57r, 58r, 64r, 67r, 72r; Prot. Bk. King, v, fo. 175; Smith, *Hammermen of Edinburgh*, xciii. The deacons were abolished by an act of parliament of 1555 (*APS*, ii, 497-8); the first mention of the visitors comes on 21 Dec. 1555 and the last on 24 March 1556.

1. Given as Archibald Dewar on 24 March 1556.
2. Given as John Mossman on 24 March 1556.

The council of 1556-7

Provost:	ARCHIBALD DOUGLAS OF KILSPINDIE
Presidents:	JAMES McGILL
	THOMAS MARJORIBANKS OF RATHO

Bailies:	WILLIAM KERR, elder
	ALAN DICKSON
	JOHN PRESTON
	ALEXANDER BARON
Dean of Guild:	JAMES CARMICHAEL
Treasurer:	ALEXANDER PARK
Ordinary council:	JOHN SIM
	RICHARD CARMICHAEL
	ALEXANDER HOME
	ROBERT FLEMING
	JAMES BARON
	ARCHIBALD GRAHAM
	ANDREW MURRAY OF BLACKBARONY
	WILLIAM CRAIK
	JAMES WATSON
	JOHN YOUNG
	JAMES YOUNG, cutler
	ARCHIBALD LEACH, furrier

The craft deacons

Tailors:	JAMES NORVAL
Skinners:	JAMES FORRET
Furriers:	ARCHIBALD LEACH
Goldsmiths:	THOMAS EWING
Hammermen:	JAMES YOUNG, cutler
Barbers:	ALEXANDER BRUCE
Masons:	THOMAS JACKSON
Wrights:	ROBERT FYNDAR
Cordiners:	THOMAS HOGG
Baxters:	DAVID KINLOCH
Fleshers:	RICHARD HENRYSON
Walkers:	JAMES STIRK
Websters:	MARTIN LYELL
Bonnetmakers:	JAMES LAWSON

References: MS Co. Recs., ii, fos. 82r, 85v, 86r, 87r, 89v, 93v, 95r, 102r, 104v; Prot. Bk. King, v, fo. 210.

The council of 1557-8

Provost:	GEORGE, LORD SETON
Presidents:	JAMES McGILL
	THOMAS MARJORIBANKS[1]
	ROBERT MAITLAND OF LETHINGTON
	m. THOMAS MacCALZEAN[2]
Bailies:	ALEXANDER ACHESON
	WILLIAM LAWSON
	JAMES LINDSAY
	EDWARD LITTLE

Dean of Guild:	JAMES CARMICHAEL
Treasurer:	JAMES ADAMSON
Ordinary council:	WILLIAM KERR, elder
	ALEXANDER BARON
	ALAN DICKSON
	JOHN PRESTON
	ALEXANDER PARK
	ARCHIBALD DOUGLAS OF KILSPINDIE
	JAMES CURLE
	DAVID FORESTER
	GILBERT BALFOUR
	JOHN SPENS
	DAVID SOMER[3]
	MUNGO HUNTER, smith
	ROBERT HENRYSON, surgeon

The craft deacons

Tailors:	ROBERT LINDSAY
Skinners:	THOMAS REDPATH
Furriers:	ANDREW ELPHINSTONE
Goldsmiths:	JOHN MOSSMAN
Hammermen:	JOHN RHIND
Barbers:	NOWIE BRUCE
Masons:	HENRY LAWTIE
Wrights:	ROBERT FYNDAR
Cordiners:	JOHN BINNEY
Fleshers:	WILLIAM ROBESON
Walkers:	JAMES STIRK
Websters:	MARTIN LYELL
Bonnetmakers:	JOHN WALSH

References: MS Co. Recs., ii, fos. 102r, 104r, 107r, 108v, 113r, 114v, 116r, 117r, 120r.

1. McGill and Marjoribanks served until Seton appeared on 28 Oct. 1557.
2. Maitland became president on Seton's absence on 19 Jan. 1558; there were two presidents from 9 Feb. although MacCalzean was not named until 9 May.
3. Somer only appeared on the list of newly elected councillors of 18 Sept. 1557.

The council of 1558-9

Provost:	GEORGE, LORD SETON
Bailies:	DAVID FORESTER
	JOHN SPENS
	ALEXANDER BARON
	JAMES CURLE
Dean of Guild:	JOHN CHARTERIS, elder
Treasurer:	JAMES LINDSAY

Ordinary council:	JAMES CARMICHAEL
	JAMES BARON
	WILLIAM LAWSON
	THOMAS THOMSON
	JAMES ADAMSON
	WILLIAM PATERSON
	EDWARD LITTLE
	ALEXANDER ACHESON
	ANDREW SLATER[1]
	WILLIAM AIKMAN[1]
	JAMES YOUNG, cutler
	THOMAS REDPATH, skinner

The craft deacons

Tailors:	ALEXANDER SAUCHIE
Skinners:	JAMES INGLIS
Furriers:	ANDREW ELPHINSTONE
Goldsmiths:	MICHAEL GILBERT
Hammermen:	JAMES MUIR
Barbers:	ALEXANDER BRUCE
Masons:	DAVID GRAHAM
Wrights:	DAVID SHANG
Cordiners:	JOHN BINNEY
Baxters:	ANDREW GIBSON
Fleshers:	ROBERT GARDENER
Walkers:	JAMES HUNTER
Websters:	GEORGE HUNTER[2]
Bonnetmakers:	JAMES LAWSON (sometimes given as William)

References: MS Co. Recs., ii, fo. 131v; iii, fos. 4, 5r, 7v, 9v, 10v, 11v; MS Goldsmiths' Recs., fo. 8v. Cf. the lists given in P. J. Murray, 'The excommunication of Edinburgh town council in 1558', *Innes Review*, xxvii (1976), 32, and W. J. Anderson, 'The excommunication of Edinburgh town council in 1558', *ibid.*, x (1959), 291; both give the deacon of the barbers as Alex. Durie and of the walkers as James Stirk.

1. Slater and Aikman were replaced by m. James Watson and Edward Hope on 20 Sept. 1559; one of the assessors, Robert Crichton, who was also absent, was replaced by Alexander Guthrie.
2. Given as Wm. Mochrie from 24 March 1559.

The Seton council of 1559-60

Provost:	GEORGE, LORD SETON
Bailies:	JOHN PRESTON
	EDWARD LITTLE
	WILLIAM KERR, younger
	HERBERT MAXWELL[1]
Dean of Guild:	THOMAS UDDART[2]
Treasurer:	ALEXANDER PARK

Ordinary council:	JOHN SPENS
	ALEXANDER BARON
	JAMES CURLE
	JOHN CHARTERIS, elder
	JAMES LINDSAY
	JAMES ADAMSON
	ROBERT GLEN
	LUKE WILSON
	JAMES HOPPRINGLE
	ARCHIBALD LEACH, furrier
	ROBERT FYNDAR, wright

References: MS Co. Recs., 6 Oct., 21 Nov. 1559, 19 Jan., 1560, iii, fos. 26r, 27v, 29v; see also fos. 26v, 28r, 30v for other entries concerning Uddart, Park and Little.

1. Maxwell does not appear in the council minute book, but is given in both the treasurer's accounts and the guild register (*Edin. Accts.*, i, 304; MS Guild Register, i, fo. 50v).

2. For Uddart, who never took up office, see *ibid.*, 14 Oct. 1559, i, fo. 50v; *Edin. Accts.*, ii, 116.

The Kilspindie council of 1559-60

Provost:	ARCHIBALD DOUGLAS OF KILSPINDIE
Bailies:	DAVID SOMER
	EDWARD HOPE
	JAMES WATSON
	ADAM FULLARTON
Dean of Guild:	JAMES BARON
Treasurer:	ALEXANDER PARK
Common Clerk:	ALEXANDER GUTHRIE
Ordinary council:	JOHN SPENS[1]
	DAVID FORESTER
	JAMES THOMSON
	ROBERT KERR, elder
	JOHN ASHLOWAINE
	JOHN JOHNSTON
	JOHN BELL
	JOHN OUSTEAN
	ROBERT WATSON
	JAMES LOWRIE
	RICHARD STRANG
	ALEXANDER MORVESS
	JAMES YOUNG, cutler
	WILLIAM MORRISON, tailor

References: MS Co. Recs., 27 Oct. 1559, 16 April 1560 etc., iii, fos. 26v, 33r. See also *De La Brosse Report*, 121-2.

1. He acted as a bailie during Fullarton's absence in England, 16 April-12 June 1560 (fos. 33r-37r).

The craft deacons, May 1559-April 1560[1]

	May-Sept. 1559	27 Oct.
Tailors:	ALEXANDER SAUCHIE	SAUCHIE
Skinners:	PETER TURNET	JAMES INGLIS
Furriers:	HEW CANNY	
Goldsmiths,	MICHAEL GILBERT	
Hammermen:	JAMES CRANSTON	CRANSTON
Barbers:	PATRICK LINDSAY	
Masons:	THOMAS JACKSON	
Wrights:	ROBERT FYNDAR[2]	JOHN CUNNINGHAM
Cordiners:	ROBERT HUNTRODDS	HUNTRODDS[3]
Baxters:	JOHN ALDINSTOUN	HERCULES METHVEN
Fleshers:	RICHARD HENRYSON	
Walkers:	JAMES STIRK	
Websters:	ROBERT MEID	MEID
Bonnetmakers:	JOHN WALSH	WALSH

References: MS Co. Recs., iii, fos. 24v, 26v.
There are no further relevant entries until 26 May 1560, by which time new craft elections had taken place.

1. The first entry of the restored Kilspindie council, on 16 April 1560, refers to the 'maist part' of the deacons being present.
2. A replacement for Fyndar was to be expected after his election to the Seton council at Michaelmas 1559.
3. He returned the vestments, which he had in safekeeping, 12 Dec. 1559 (*Edin. Recs.*, iii, 60).

The council of 1560-61

Provost:	ARCHIBALD DOUGLAS OF KILSPINDIE
Bailies:	ROBERT GLEN
	ADAM FULLARTON
	DAVID SOMER
	JOHN SPENS
Dean of Guild:	JAMES WATSON
Treasurer:	JAMES LOWRIE[1]
Ordinary council:	EDWARD HOPE
	JAMES BARON
	ALEXANDER PARK
	JAMES THOMSON
	JAMES ADAMSON
	ALEXANDER GUTHRIE
	JAMES AIKMAN
	THOMAS THOMSON
	JOHN UDDART
	ARCHIBALD GRAHAM
	JOHN ADAMSON
	ALEXANDER SAUCHIE, tailor
	ALEXANDER BRUCE, barber

The craft deacons

Tailors:	JAMES NORVAL
Skinners:	GEORGE REDPATH
Furriers:	HEW CANNY
Goldsmiths:	MICHAEL GILBERT
Hammermen:	WILLIAM HARLAW, saddler
Barbers:	ROBERT HENRYSON
Masons:	JOHN INGLIS
Wrights:	JOHN CUNNINGHAM
Cordiners:	THOMAS HOGG (given twice as ROBERT)
Baxters:	HERCULES METHVEN
Fleshers:	JOHN SANDERSON[2]
Walkers:	GEORGE HUNTER
Websters:	LEONARD THOMSON
Bonnetmakers:	JAMES LAWSON

References: MS Co. Recs., iii, 35v, 39v, 40r, 42r, 44v, 45v, 58r, 59r, 64v, 69, 71v, 74r.

1. He died in office and was replaced by Luke Wilson 17 Jan. 1561.
2. He was dismissed for adultery 22 Nov. 1560; Thomas Dobie is given as deacon from 19 Feb. 1561.

The council of 2-8 Oct. 1561

Provost:	ARCHIBALD DOUGLAS OF KILSPINDIE
Bailies:	DAVID FORESTER
	ROBERT KERR, elder
	ALEXANDER HOME
	ALAN DICKSON

Dismissed by Mary 8 Oct. 1561 (*Edin. Recs.*, iii, 126).

The council of 8 Oct. 1561-62

Provost:	m. THOMAS MacCALZEAN
Bailies:	JOHN ADAMSON
	JAMES THOMSON
	JOHN MARJORIBANKS
	ALEXANDER ACHESON
Dean of Guild:	ALEXANDER GUTHRIE
Treasurer:	JOHN PRESTON[1]
Ordinary council:	LUKE WILSON[1]
	ROBERT GLEN
	ADAM FULLARTON
	DAVID SOMER
	JOHN SPENS
	JAMES WATSON

JAMES ADAMSON
JAMES BARON
JAMES JOHNSTON OF KELLEBANK
ROBERT CUNNINGHAM
ARTHUR GRAINGER
ALEXANDER PARK
EDWARD HOPE
MICHAEL GILBERT, goldsmith
JOHN WEIR, pewterer[2]

The craft deacons, 1561-62

Tailors:	ALEXANDER SAUCHIE
Skinners:	JOHN LOCH
Furriers:	ANDREW ELPHINSTONE
Goldsmiths:	THOMAS EWING
Hammermen:	JOHN ROBESON
Barbers:	ROBERT HENRYSON
Masons:	MURDO WALKER
Wrights:	PATRICK SHANG
Cordiners:	ROBERT HOGG
Baxters:	DAVID KINLOCH
Websters:	JOHN SCOTT
Bonnetmakers:	JOHN WALSH

References: MS Co. Recs., iv, fos. 13r, 18, 22, 23v.

1. Preston retired due to ill-health 25 Nov. 1561 and was replaced by Luke Wilson, who was already on the council.
2. Replaced by Peter Turnet 11 Feb. 1562 because he had been elected 'by the auld ordour' and not by craft ticket (see *Edin. Recs.*, iii, 124).

The council of 1562-3

Provost:	ARCHIBALD DOUGLAS OF KILSPINDIE
Bailies:	JOHN SPENS
	ALAN DICKSON
	ANDREW SLATER
	DAVID FORESTER
Dean of Guild:	ALEXANDER GUTHRIE
Treasurer:	JOHN PRESTON
Ordinary council:	JOHN ADAMSON
	JAMES THOMSON
	JOHN MARJORIBANKS
	ALEXANDER ACHESON
	LUKE WILSON
	m. THOMAS MacCALZEAN
	NICOL UDDART
	ANDREW MURRAY OF BLACKBARONY
	JOHN WESTON

JOHN HARWOOD
JAMES WATSON[1]
JAMES YOUNG, cutler
THOMAS REDPATH, skinner[2]

The craft deacons

Tailors:	JOHN PURVES
Skinners:	ALEXANDER WOOD
Furriers:	ANDREW ELPHINSTONE
Goldsmiths:	GEORGE RHIND[3]
Hammermen:	JAMES YOUNG, cutler[4]
Barbers:	ALEXANDER BRUCE
Masons:	JOHN PATERSON
Wrights:	PATRICK SHANG
Cordiners:	WILLIAM GASTON
Baxters:	WILLIAM NEWTON
Fleshers:	RICHARD HENDERSON
Walkers:	GEORGE HUNTER
Websters:	WILLIAM MEID
Bonnetmakers:	JAMES LAWSON

References: MS Co. Recs., iv, fos. 33, 37, 40v, 48v, 49v, 50r, 59v, 63r, 65r, 66v, 67v; MS Goldsmiths' Recs., fo. 8v.

1. Only appears 17 March 1563.
2. Temporarily replaced by Jas. Inglis, skinner.
3. He was elected deacon 3 May 1562, but the council record variously gives Michael Gilbert, Thomas Ewing and Michael Rhind.
4. Replaced by John Robeson, cutler, after his elevation to the council. Young had been appointed after the dismissal by the council of the catholic, William Brocas (see app. vi; *Edin. Recs.*, iii, 134-5).

The council of 1563-4

Provost:	ARCHIBALD DOUGLAS OF KILSPINDIE
Bailies:	ROBERT GLEN
	JOHN SPENS
	DAVID SOMER
	NICOL UDDART[1]
Dean of Guild:	ALEXANDER GUTHRIE
Treasurer:	ALEXANDER PARK
Ordinary council:	DAVID FORESTER
	ALAN DICKSON
	JOHN PRESTON
	JOHN ADAMSON
	JAMES BARON
	JOHN MARJORIBANKS
	EDWARD HOPE
	ANDREW SLATER[2]

ALEXANDER NAPIER
CUTHBERT RAMSAY
ALEXANDER BRUCE, barber
MICHAEL GILBERT, goldsmith[3]

The craft deacons

Tailors:	ALEXANDER SAUCHIE
Skinners:	JOHN FREIR
Goldsmiths:	JAMES COCKIE
Hammermen:	JOHN WEIR, pewterer[4]
Barbers:	ALEXANDER BRUCE
Masons:	JOHN PATERSON
Wrights:	JOHN CUNNINGHAM
Cordiners:	THOMAS HOGG
Baxters:	WILLIAM NEWTON
Fleshers:	WILLIAM ROBESON
Walkers:	[blank] HUNTER
Websters:	ROBERT MEID (also given as WILLIAM)
Bonnetmakers:	JAMES LAWSON

References: MS Co. Recs., iv, fos. 72r, 73v, 74v, 79r, 83, 84r, 85r, 87r, 93r, 97v, 99r.

1. Discharged for absence abroad 15 Oct. 1563 and replaced by Robert Kerr, elder.
2. Replaced, temporarily, by Archibald Graham 13 Dec. 1563; Slater returned 18 Feb. 1564.
3. Replaced, temporarily, by James Young, cutler; Gilbert returned 28 March 1564.
4. Replaced (?) by James Young from 15 Oct. 1563; the craft minute book, however, gives Young as deacon for the full year (MS Hammermen Recs., i, fo. 218r).

The council of 1564-5

Provost:	ARCHIBALD DOUGLAS OF KILSPINDIE[1]
Bailies:	ALAN DICKSON
	DAVID FORESTER
	WILLIAM PATERSON
	JOHN SIM
Dean of Guild:	ALEXANDER PARK
Treasurer:	ROBERT GLEN
Ordinary council:	JOHN SPENS
	DAVID SOMER
	ROBERT KERR
	ALEXANDER GUTHRIE
	ARHCIBALD GRAHAM
	ALEXANDER CLARK
	WILLIAM FOWLER
	JAMES LOWRIE
	JAMES NICOL
	ALEXANDER UDDART
	ALEXANDER SAUCHIE, tailor
	MUNGO HUNTER, smith

The craft deacons

Tailors:	JOHN PURVES
Skinners:	ALAN PURVES
Goldsmiths:	JAMES COCKIE
Hammermen:	MUNGO HUNTER[2]
Barbers:	JAMES LINDSAY
Masons:	JOHN PATERSON
Wrights:	JOHN CUNNINGHAM
Cordiners:	WILLIAM HUTCHESON
Baxters:	WILLIAM NEWTON
Fleshers:	JOHN BLYTHMAN
Walkers:	JAMES HUNTER
Websters:	ROBERT MEID[3]
Bonnetmakers:	JAMES LAWSON

References: MS Co. Recs., iv, fos. 107v, 109r, 112r, 113r, 115v, 116v, 118v, 119v, 123r.

1. Resigns in favour of Sir Simon Preston of Craigmillar 23 Aug. 1565 after receiving the king's and queen's writing.
2. Given as Nicol Purves from 6 Jan. 1565, but the craft minute book gives Purves as deacon for the full year (MS Hammermen Recs., i, fo. 221r).
3. Given as Wm. Meid from 6 Jan, 1565.

The king's and queen's leet of 26 Sept. 1565

Bailies:	JOHN PRESTON*
	JOHN SIM*
	JOHN SPENS
	JAMES NICOL*
Dean of Guild:	JAMES CARMICHAEL
Treasurer:	LUKE WILSON
Ordinary council:	EDWARD LITTLE*
	DUNCAN LIVINGSTONE*
	JAMES CURLE
	MICHAEL GILBERT, goldsmith*
	ARCHIBALD LEACH, furrier*

Those asterisked did sit on the council in 1565-6. Preston, however, did so as dean of guild rather than as a bailie.

The council of 1565-6

Provost:	SIR SIMON PRESTON OF CRAIGMILLAR
Bailies:	JOHN SIM
	JAMES NICOL
	WILLIAM FOWLER
	ANDREW STEVENSON

Dean of Guild:	JOHN PRESTON
Treasurer:	JOHN WESTON
Ordinary council:	DAVID FORESTER
	WILLIAM PATERSON
	ALAN DICKSON
	ALEXANDER PARK
	ROBERT GLEN
	ALEXANDER UDDART
	EDWARD LITTLE
	DUNCAN LIVINGSTONE
	JAMES BARON
	THOMAS FLEMING
	MICHAEL GILBERT, goldsmith
	ARCHIBALD LEACH, furrier

The craft deacons

Tailors:	JOHN PURVES
Skinners:	ALAN PURVES
Furriers:	JOHN WAUCHOPE
Goldsmiths:	GEORGE HERIOT
Hammermen:	NICOL PURVES
Barbers:	JOHN CHALMER
Masons:	ARCHIBALD GRAY
Wrights:	JOHN CUNNINGHAM
Cordiners:	WILLIAM GASTON
Baxters:	JOHN CRICHTON
Fleshers:	THOMAS DOBIE
Walkers:	GEORGE HUNTER
Websters:	JOHN SCOTT
Bonnetmakers:	JAMES LAWSON

References: MS Co. Recs., iv, fos. 130v, 131r, 140v, 141v, 142r, 143r, 145.

The king's and queen's leet of 1 October 1566

Provost:	SIR SIMON PRESTON OF CRAIGMILLAR*
Bailies:	DUNCAN LIVINGSTONE
	EDWARD LITTLE*
	THOMAS FLEMING
	ROBERT GLEN*
	ALEXANDER CLARK*
	ALEXANDER UDDART*
Dean of Guild:	JOHN PRESTON*
Treasurer:	JOHN WESTON*

Those asterisked sat on the council of 1566-7.

The council of 1566-7

Provost: SIR SIMON PRESTON OF CRAIGMILLAR

Bailies: EDWARD LITTLE
ALEXANDER CLARK
ALEXANDER UDDART
ROBERT GLEN[1]

Dean of Guild: JOHN PRESTON

Treasurer: JOHN WESTON[2]

Ordinary council: DAVID FORESTER
JOHN SIM
JAMES NICOL
ANDREW STEVENSON
WILLIAM FOWLER
ALAN DICKSON
WILLIAM PATERSON
JAMES OLIPHANT
NICOL UDDART
ARTHUR GRAINGER
JAMES ADAMSON
ALEXANDER PARK
THOMAS REDPATH, skinner[3]
ROBERT ABERCROMBIE, saddler

The craft deacons

Furriers: ARCHIBALD WAUCHOPE
Goldsmiths: GEORGE HERIOT
Hammermen: JOHN WEIR

References: MS Co. Recs., iv, fos. 157v, 158v, 164v, 166, 170r, 171v, 180r, 182r, 195v, 198r; MS Goldsmiths' Recs., fo. 9r; MS Hammermen Recs., i, fo, 227r.

1. Replaced by David Forester, who was already on the council, 23 July 1567.
2. He died in Feb. 1567 and was replaced by John Harwood.
3. He died in July 1567 and was replaced by James Mossman, goldsmith.

The council of 1567-8

Provost: SIR SIMON PRESTON OF CRAIGMILLAR

Bailies: ANDREW SLATER
ALEXANDER CLARK
ADAM FULLARTON
JAMES OLIPHANT

Dean of Guild: ALEXANDER PARK

Treasurer: JOHN HARWOOD

Ordinary council: EDWARD LITTLE
ALEXANDER UDDART
ROBERT GLEN

S

DAVID FORESTER
JOHN PRESTON
WILLIAM LITTLE
MICHAEL CHISHOLM
MUNGO FAIRLIE
HENRY NISBET
ROBERT FORRET
JAMES INGLIS, skinner
JAMES YOUNG, cutler

The craft deacons

Tailors:	ALEXANDER SAUCHIE
Skinners:	THOMAS AIKENHEAD
Furriers:	THOMAS DICKSON
Goldsmiths:	GEORGE HERIOT
Hammermen:	JAMES YOUNG, cutler
Barbers:	ALEXANDER BRUCE
Masons:	THOMAS JACKSON
Wrights:	PATRICK SHANG
Cordiners:	ALEXANDER DAVIDSON
Baxters:	JAMES WOOD
Fleshers:	[blank] WAUCHOPE[1]
Walkers:	THOMAS ANDREW
Websters:	LEONARD THOMSON
Bonnetmakers:	JAMES JOHNSTON

References: MS Co. Recs., iv, fos. 186v, 191r, 193r, 203v.

1. Leonard Dobie is given as deacon of the fleshers on 4 June 1567.

The council of 1568-9

Provost:	SIR SIMON PRESTON OF CRAIGMILLAR
Bailies:	ADAM FULLARTON
	ALEXANDER CLARK
	WILLIAM LITTLE
	ROBERT FORRET[1]
Dean of Guild:	JOHN HARWOOD
Treasurer:	ANDREW STEVENSON
Ordinary council:	ANDREW SLATER
	JAMES OLIPHANT
	ALEXANDER UDDART
	JAMES BARON
	EDWARD HOPE
	THOMAS DAVIDSON
	JAMES FORMAN
	JOHN UDDART[2]
	ROBERT GOURLAY
	JAMES JOHNSTON OF THE COTTIS

SIMON MARJORIBANKS
THOMAS HAMILTON OF PRIESTFIELD[3]
JAMES MOSSMAN, goldsmith
THOMAS AIKENHEAD, skinner

The craft deacons

Tailors:	ALEXANDER SAUCHIE
Skinners:	JOHN WILSON
Furriers:	THOMAS DICKSON
Goldsmiths:	JAMES MOSSMAN[4]
Hammermen:	JOHN WILSON, pewterer[5]
Barbers:	NOWIE BRUCE
Masons:	ARCHIBALD GRAY
Wrights:	JOHN CUNNINGHAM
Cordiners:	ALEXANDER DAVIDSON
Baxters:	JOHN WOOD
Fleshers:	JOHN BLYTHMAN
Walkers:	JAMES HUNTER
Websters:	JOHN SCOTT
Bonnetmakers:	JAMES JOHNSTON

References: MS Co. Recs., iv, fos. 217v, 218r, 227, 228, 229v, 231v, 232v, 242v, 244v, 245r; MS Goldsmiths' Recs., fo. 9v.

1. Replaced by Andrew Slater 1 July 1569.
2. Replaces Slater on the ordinary council 1 July 1569.
3. First appears 7 Sept. 1569.
4. Replaced by George Heriot after his election to the council.
5. Replaced by Alex. Thomson, cutler, after his dismissal by the council as 'ane man of na religioun' 8 May 1568; Wilson's original election is ignored in the craft minute book (MS Hammermen Recs., i, fo. 231v).

The council of 1569-70

Provost:	SIR WILLIAM KIRKCALDY OF GRANGE
Bailies:	SIMON MARJORIBANKS
	MICHAEL CHISHOLM
	DAVID FORESTER
	HENRY NISBET
Dean of Guild:	JOHN PRESTON
Treasurer:	THOMAS HENDERSON
Ordinary council:	ADAM FULLARTON
	ALEXANDER CLARK
	WILLIAM LITTLE
	JOHN HARWOOD
	ALEXANDER UDDART
	JOHN ACHESON
	GILBERT DICK
	WILLIAM FOWLER

ANDREW SLATER[1]
ANDREW STEVENSON[2]
JAMES MacCARTNAY
WILLIAM HARLAW, saddler
JAMES NORVAL, tailor

The craft deacons

Tailors:	WALTER WAWANE
Furriers:	THOMAS DICKSON
Goldsmiths:	NICOL SIM
Hammermen:	JOHN WILSON, pewterer
Barbers:	NOWIE BRUCE
Baxters:	JAMES FIDDES
Fleshers:	WILLIAM ROBESON

References: MS Co. Recs., iv, fos. 245, 246v, 249v, 250r, 251v, 253v, 254r.

1. Temporarily replaced by James Adamson 3 March 1570.
2. Temporarily replaced by Edward Little 3 March 1570.

The council of Oct. 1570-June 1571

Provost:	JAMES McGILL
Bailies:	JOHN ADAMSON
	JOHN SIM
	MUNGO FAIRLIE
	JAMES MacCARTNAY[1]
Dean of Guild:	ADAM FULLARTON
Treasurer:	NICOL UDDART
Ordinary council:	SIMON MARJORIBANKS
	MICHAEL CHISHOLM
	DAVID FORESTER
	HENRY NISBET
	JOHN PRESTON
	THOMAS HENDERSON
	JOHN HARWOOD
	JAMES ADAMSON[2]
	MUNGO RUSSELL
	PATRICK RIG
	JAMES INGLIS, skinner
	MUNGO BRADY, goldsmith

The craft deacons:

Tailors:	GEORGE SMITH
Skinners:	THOMAS AIKENHEAD
Goldsmiths:	NICOL SIM
Hammermen:	JOHN WILSON, pewterer
Barbers:	ALEXANDER BRUCE

Masons:	MURDO WALKER
Wrights:	JOHN CUNNINGHAM
Cordiners:	JOHN NICOLSON
Baxters:	JAMES FIDDES[3]
Fleshers:	WILLIAM ROBESON
Walkers:	GEORGE HUNTER
Websters:	CUTHBERT MATHESON

References: MS Co. Recs., iv, fos. 256r, 260v, 263v, 264r, 265r, 271v.

1. Replaced by John Acheson 2 Feb. 1571.
2. John Uddart deputised for him 4 Oct. 1570.
3. Given as James Wood from 24 Aug. 1570.

The queen's party council, 20 June-Oct. 1571

Provost:	ANDREW KERR OF FERNIHURST
Bailies:	CUTHBERT RAMSAY
	THOMAS HAMILTON [OF PRIESTFIELD]
	HERBERT MAXWELL
	HEW LAUDER
Deacon of the hammermen:	JOHN WILSON[1]

References: *Diurnal of Occurents*, 226; *Lord Provosts*, 26; MS Hammermen Recs., i, fo. 235r.

1. No election was recorded in the craft minute book, but Wilson continued as deacon, remaining in the town. He presented his accounts in April 1572.

The queen's party council, Oct. 1571-Aug./Sept. 1572

Provost:	SIR JAMES BALFOUR OF PITTENDREICH
Bailies:	DAVID CORSBIE
	WILLIAM NISBET
	PETER MARTIN
Deacon of the hammermen:	WILLIAM RAE[1]

References: Prot. Bk. John Aitkin, i, fos. 63r, 66v, 69r; see also fos. 71r, 73r, 79r, 81v, 84r. The first relevant entry is for 8 Oct. 1571. Volume one ends 28 Jan. 1572; volume two, running from 1 March 1572 until 13 Oct. 1572, has gone missing in recent years. *Diurnal of Occurents*, 250, gives the date of Balfour's election as 2 October. MS Hammermen Recs., i, fo. 236v.

1. Rae was elected by 'the masteris' gathered in the Magdalen Chapel in the Cowgate 3 May 1572.

The king's party council-in-exile,[1] *Oct. 1571-1572*

Provost:	JAMES McGILL
President:	ADAM FULLARTON[2]
Bailies:	JOHN ACHESON
	JOHN ADAMSON
	ANDREW SLATER
	MICHAEL CHISHOLM
	MUNGO RUSSELL[3]
Dean of Guild:	ADAM FULLARTON
Deacon of the goldsmiths:	ADAM CRAIG

References: Prot. Bk. John Robesoun, fos. 124-169; the period covered is 2 Oct. 1571-20 Sept. 1572.

MS Burgh Register of Deeds, ii, fo. 22r; the volume resumes on 14 Sept. 1572 after the council had re-established itself in Edinburgh.

MS Guild Register, i, fos. 101v, 102r; Fullarton's election as dean of guild at Michaelmas 1573 is said to be his third consecutive year in office.

The Minute book of the Goldsmith Craft, fo. 9v, indicates that an election was held on 3 May 1572 at Leith.

1. Both Robesoun, fo. 124, and *Reg. Privy Co.*, ii, 120, indicate that a full council and set of deacons sat at Leith; although it is very likely that the deacons who held office in Dec. 1572 had, like Craig, been elected at Leith in May, this has not been assumed.

2. He is given as such on 22 Aug. 1572; McGill had returned by 30th.

3. Only the Burgh Register of Deeds gives Russell as a bailie, on 14 Sept. 1572; Robesoun gives all the other four bailies together on 20 Sept.

The council of 1572-3

Provost:	PATRICK, LORD LINDSAY OF BYRES
Bailies:	MICHAEL CHISHOLM
	JOHN ADAMSON
	WILLIAM LITTLE
	MUNGO RUSSELL
Dean of Guild:	ADAM FULLARTON
Treasurer:	NICOL UDDART
Ordinary council:	JOHN ACHESON
	JOHN PRESTON
	ALEXANDER UDDART
	EDWARD HOPE
	ARCHIBALD STEWART
	HENRY NISBET
	WILLIAM SCOTT
	EDWARD GALBRAITH, skinner
	JAMES NICOLSON, tailor

The craft deacons

Tailors:	JOHN COOPER
Skinners:	PETER TURNET
Goldsmiths:	ADAM CRAIG
Hammermen:	JAMES YOUNG, cutler
Barbers:	ROBERT HENRYSON
Masons:	MURDO WALKER
Wrights:	PATRICK SHANG
Cordiners:	JOHN NICOLSON
Baxters:	DAVID KINLOCH
Walkers:	MATTHEW BROWN
Websters:	WILLIAM WILSON
Bonnetmakers:	WILLIAM WALKER

References: NLS MSS, no. 189 (an extract from the council minute book, which is not extant, of 12 Dec. 1572); MS Burgh Register of Deeds, ii, fos. 22v-43r; MS Guild Register, 19 Dec. 1572, i, fo. 102v; Prot. Bk. Aitkin, iii, fos. 1r-30v; Prot. Bk. William Stewart, elder, iii, 18 Oct. 1572; *Hist. King James VI*, 124; *Diurnal of Occurents*, 322; MS Hammermen Recs., i, fo. 237r.

The council of 1573-4

Provost:	PATRICK, LORD LINDSAY OF BYRES
Bailies:	SIMON MARJORIBANKS
	HENRY NISBET
	ARCHIBALD STEWART
	ALEXANDER UDDART
Dean of Guild:	WILLIAM PATERSON
Treasurer:	JAMES ROSS
Ordinary council,	JOHN ADAMSON
	MICHAEL CHISHOLM
	WILLIAM LITTLE
	MUNGO RUSSELL
	ADAM FULLARTON
	JOHN PRESTON
	WILLIAM ADAMSON
	JOHN ARNOT
	JAMES OLIPHANT
	JOHN ROBERTSON
	JOHN HARWOOD[1]
	THOMAS AIKENHEAD, skinner[2]
	WILLIAM MENTEATH, bowmaker[3]

The craft deacons

Tailors:	JOHN COOPER
Skinners:	EDWARD GALBRAITH
Furriers:	JOHN WAUCHOPE
Goldsmiths:	ADAM CRAIG
Hammermen:	JOHN ANNAND, cutler

Barbers:	NOWIE BRUCE
Masons:	MURDO WALKER
Wrights:	PATRICK SHANG
Cordiners:	ANDREW WILSON
Baxters:	DAVID KINLOCH
Fleshers:	JOHN HENDERSON
Bonnetmakers:	WILLIAM WALKER

References: MS Co. Recs., v, fos. 1, 2, 3v, 7r, 14v, 19v.

1. He first appeared, probably as a replacement, 9 June 1574.
2. Replaced by James Inglis, skinner, from 12 Feb. 1574.
3. Replaced in his absence by Robert Henderson, barber, 9 June 1574.

The council of 1574-5

Provost:	PATRICK, LORD LINDSAY OF BYRES
Bailies:	NICOL UDDART [1]
	JOHN ARNOT
	WILLIAM NAPIER
	MICHAEL CHISHOLM
Dean of Guild:	JAMES ADAMSON
Treasurer:	JAMES ROSS
Ordinary council:	SIMON MARJORIBANKS
	HENRY NISBET
	ARCHIBALD STEWART
	ALEXANDER UDDART
	WILLIAM PATERSON
	JOHN PRESTON
	RICHARD ABERCROMBIE
	HENRY CHARTERIS
	ROBERT GALBRAITH
	JOHN MORRISON
	JAMES INGLIS, skinner
	ROBERT HENRYSON, surgeon

The craft deacons

Tailors:	JOHN COOPER
Skinners:	JAMES INGLIS
Furriers:	THOMAS DICKSON
Goldsmiths:	NICOL SIM
Hammermen:	JAMES YOUNG
Barbers:	ROBERT HENRYSON
Masons:	WILLIAM BICKERTON
Wrights:	THOMAS WOOD
Cordiners:	ANDREW WILSON
Baxters:	DAVID KINLOCH
Fleshers:	CUTHBERT THOMSON
Walkers:	ALEXANDER WILKIE

Websters:	ROBERT MEID
Bonnetmakers:	EDWARD WYLIE

References: MS Co. Recs., v, fos. 18v, 21r, 23r, 32r, 43v, 52.

1. Although Nicol and Alex. Uddart, Nisbet, and Morrison were imprisoned by Morton on 2 Feb. 1575, they were not replaced on the council; three of them did, however, temporarily return to attend a meeting on 4 March. All four appeared on 9 July to petition the council, but did not return to the council itself until 23 Sept. (see *Edin Recs.*, iv, 40; *Diurnal of Occurents*, 343).

The council of 1575-6

Provost:	PATRICK, LORD LINDSAY OF BYRES
Bailies:	MICHAEL CHISHOLM
	JOHN ARNOT
	JOHN ADAMSON
	ROBERT KERR, elder
Dean of Guild:	JOHN HARWOOD
Treasurer:	MUNGO RUSSELL
Ordinary council:	NICOL UDDART
	JAMES ADAMSON
	JAMES ROSS
	ANDREW SLATER[1]
	WILLIAM ADAMSON
	ALEXANDER CLARK
	ROBERT KERR, younger
	JAMES GUTHRIE
	MARK KERR
	JOHN ROBERTSON
	GILBERT PRIMROSE, surgeon[2]

The craft deacons

Tailors:	JOHN MURDO
Skinners:	[blank] BROWN
Furriers:	THOMAS DICKSON
Goldsmiths:	GEORGE HERIOT
Hammermen:	JAMES YOUNG, cutler
Barbers:	GILBERT PRIMROSE
Masons:	MURDO WALKER
Wrights:	PATRICK SHANG
Cordiners:	JOHN NICOLSON
Fleshers:	JOHN HENDERSON
Walkers:	JOHN FAIRLIE
Websters:	JOHN SIM

References: MS Co. Recs., v, fos. 46v, 56, 58r, 59, 60r, 61r.

1. He and another unnamed councillor were temporarily replaced by Edward Little and Robert Cunningham 6 March 1576.
2. He was given, unusually, as both deacon of his craft and a craft councillor on 14 Jan. 1576.

The council of 1576-7

Provost:	GEORGE DOUGLAS OF PARKHEAD
Bailies:	ANDREW SLATER
	ROBERT KERR, younger
	JOHN ACHESON
	JOHN MARJORIBANKS
Dean of Guild:	ALEXANDER GUTHRIE
Treasurer:	JAMES ROSS
Ordinary council	PATRICK, LORD LINDSAY OF BYRES
	MICHAEL CHISHOLM
	JOHN ARNOT
	JOHN ADAMSON
	ROBERT KERR, elder
	JOHN HARWOOD
	MUNGO RUSSELL
	ALEXANDER BARCLAY
	ADAM FULLARTON
	JOHN FERGUSON
	JAMES YOUNG, cutler
	JOHN WILKIE, skinner

The craft deacons

Tailors:	JOHN MURDO
Skinners:	JOHN WILKIE
Hammermen:	ROBERT ABERCROMBIE, saddler
Barbers:	GILBERT PRIMROSE
Cordiners:	ALEXANDER DAVIDSON
Baxters:	DAVID KINLOCH
Fleshers:	JOHN HENDERSON[1]

References: MS Co. Recs., v, fos, 66v, 74r.

1. He was dismissed by the other deacons in favour of John Robeson, but was restored by the council 11 Jan. 1577 (*Edin. Recs.*, iv, 56).

The council of Oct. 1577-April 1578

Provost:	GEORGE DOUGLAS OF PARKHEAD*
Bailies:	ROBERT KERR, younger
	ALEXANDER UDDART
	HENRY CHARTERIS
	JOHN ROBERTSON*
Dean of Guild:	LUKE WILSON
Treasurer:	JAMES ROSS
Ordinary council:	ANDREW SLATER*
	JOHN ACHESON*
	JOHN ARNOT*

JOHN PROVAND*
JOHN MARJORIBANKS
ALEXANDER GUTHRIE
JOHN ADAMSON
JAMES GUTHRIE
ALEXANDER CLARK
JOHN PRESTON
THOMAS MILLAR, cutler
DAVID DANIELSTONE, goldsmith

The craft deacons

Tailors:	PATRICK SANDILANDS
Skinners:	EDWARD GALBRAITH
Furriers:	THOMAS DICKSON
Goldsmiths:	WILLIAM COCKIE
Hammermen:	ROBERT ABERCROMBIE, saddler
Barbers:	GILBERT PRIMROSE
Masons:	MURDO WALKER
Wrights:	THOMAS WOOD
Cordiners:	JAMES WATSON
Baxters:	DAVID KINLOCH
Fleshers:	JOHN PATERSON
Walkers:	ALEXANDER WALKER
Websters:	LEONARD THOMSON
Bonnetmakers:	JOHN ALEXANDER

References: MS Co. Recs., v, fos. 81v, 82r, 92r, 94r.

Those asterisked were dismissed 14 April 1578 (*Edin. Recs.*, iv, 71). The deacons were not affected by these changes.

The council of 14 April-Oct. 1578

Provost:	ARCHIBALD STEWART*
Bailies:	ROBERT KERR, younger
	ALEXANDER UDDART
	HENRY CHARTERIS
	MICHAEL CHISHOLM*
Dean of Guild:	LUKE WILSON
Treasurer:	JAMES ROSS
Ordinary council:	JOHN MARJORIBANKS
	ALEXANDER GUTHRIE
	JOHN ADAMSON
	JAMES GUTHRIE
	ALEXANDER CLARK
	JOHN PRESTON
	ROBERT KERR, elder*
	WILLIAM LITTLE*
	WILLIAM NAPIER*

HENRY NISBET*
ROBERT GALBRAITH*
THOMAS MILLAR, cutler
DAVID DANIELSTONE, goldsmith

Reference: MS Co. Recs., v, fo. 93v.

Those asterisked were the replacements appointed 14 April 1578. Robert Kerr took Douglas of Parkhead's rightful place on the ordinary council as retiring provost.

Morton's leet[1] of Sept. 1578

Provost:	ALEXANDER CLARK	(C)
Bailies:	JOHN ARNOT	
	ANDREW SLATER	
	MICHAEL CHISHOLM	
	JOHN ROBERTSON	(C)
Dean of Guild:	LUKE WILSON	(DG)
Treasurer:	JAMES ROSS	(C)
Ordinary council:	JOHN PRESTON	(C)
	JOHN JOHNSTON OF ELPHINSTONE	(C)
	THOMAS VAUS	
	ROBERT CUNNINGHAM	
	ADAM CRAIG, goldsmith	(CC)
	JAMES INGLIS, skinner	

References: MS Co. Recs., v, fo. 107; *Edin Recs.*, iv, 84-5; *Reg. Privy Co.*, iii, 36-7.

1. There were, in fact, two leets; the first, of 20 Sept., specified only the seven office-holders; the second, of 28 Sept., added four councillors and two craft councillors. It also tried, unsuccessfully, to proscribe David Williamson and Thomas Aikenhead.

The bracketed abbreviations indicate the positions of those who were elected to the council of 1578-9.

The council of 1578-9

Provost:	ARCHIBALD STEWART
Bailies:	ROBERT KERR, elder
	WILLIAM ADAMSON
	GILBERT DICK
	RICHARD ABERCROMBIE
Dean of Guild:	LUKE WILSON
Treasurer:	ANDREW STEVENSON
Ordinary council:	ROBERT KERR, younger
	ALEXANDER UDDART

JOHN ROBERTSON[1]
HENRY CHARTERIS
JAMES ROSS
ALEXANDER CLARK
JOHN PRESTON
WILLIAM LITTLE
JOHN JOHNSTON OF ELPHINSTONE
DAVID WILLIAMSON
THOMAS AIKENHEAD, skinner
ADAM CRAIG, goldsmith

The craft deacons

Tailors:	PATRICK SANDILANDS
Skinners:	JAMES INGLIS
Goldsmiths:	WILLIAM COCKIE
Hammermen:	ROBERT ABERCROMBIE, saddler, deacon convener
Barbers:	ALEXANDER BRUCE
Masons:	MUNGO TELFER
Wrights:	THOMAS WOOD
Cordiners:	WILLIAM HUTCHESON
Baxters:	JAMES WOOD
Fleshers:	THOMAS ROBESON
Websters:	JOHN STEVENSON
Furriers:	ARCHIBALD LEACH
Walkers:	ALEXANDER WALKER
Bonnetmakers:	WILLIAM SOMER

References: MS Co. Recs., v, fos. 96r, 107v, 108v, 146r; MS Act Book of Deacons of Crafts, i, fo. 6v.

1. Replaced by James Forman 27 June 1579.

The council of 1579-80

Provost:	ALEXANDER CLARK
Bailies:	WILLIAM LITTLE
	ROBERT KERR, younger
	HENRY NISBET
	JOHN ADAMSON
Dean of Guild:	LUKE WILSON
Treasurer:	ANDREW STEVENSON
Ordinary council:	ARCHIBALD STEWART
	ROBERT KERR, elder
	WILLIAM ADAMSON
	GILBERT DICK
	RICHARD ABERCROMBIE
	JOHN JOHNSTON OF ELPHINSTONE
	JAMES FORMAN
	JOHN MAIN

WILLIAM FAIRLIE
JOHN FISHER
EDWARD HERIOT, goldsmith
JOHN WILKIE, skinner[1]

The craft deacons[2]

Tailors:	NICOL RHIND	
Skinners:	PATRICK BROWN	
Furriers:	THOMAS DICKSON	(ARCHIBALD LEACH)
Goldsmiths,	GEORGE HERIOT	(EDWARD HERIOT)
Hammermen:	JOHN RICHARDSON,	(ROBERT ABERCROMBIE,
	saddler, deacon convener	saddler)
Barbers:	ROBERT HENRYSON,	
	deacon convener	
Masons:	JAMES WRIGHT	
Wrights:	THOMAS WOOD	(ANDREW WILLIAMSON)
Cordiners:	JAMES WATSON	(WILLIAM WEIR)
Baxters:	WILLIAM FIDDES	(THOMAS ANDERSON)
Walkers:	THOMAS ANDREW	(WILLIAM COUTTS)
Websters:	THOMAS BLYTH	(RICHARD DALGLEISH)
Bonnetmakers:	WILLIAM SOMER	
Fleshers:	JOHN HENDERSON	

References: MS Co. Recs., v, fos. 146, 165; vi, fos. 1r, 27r; MS Act Book of Deacons of Crafts, i, fos. 7v, 10v.

1. Replaced during his absence by Thomas Aikenhead 18 March 1580.
2. Eight of the craft deacons were dismissed (by the council of 1578-9) for remaining in the burgh during the civil wars, 26 June 1579 (see their entries in app. viii); their replacements are given in brackets.

The council of 1580-81

Provost:	ALEXANDER CLARK
Bailies:	ALEXANDER UDDART
	JAMES NICOL
	WILLIAM NAPIER
	JOHN SIM
Dean of Guild:	JOHN HARWOOD
Treasurer:	JOHN ROBERTSON
Ordinary council:	WILLIAM LITTLE
	ROBERT KERR, younger
	HENRY NISBET
	JOHN ADAMSON
	LUKE WILSON
	ANDREW STEVENSON
	JOHN JOHNSTON OF ELPHINSTONE
	ROBERT BOG
	FRANCIS KINLOCH

JOHN LOWRIE[1]
EDWARD GALBRAITH, skinner
ALEXANDER OUSTEAN, tailor

The craft deacons

Tailors:	ALEXANDER OUSTEAN, deacon convener
Skinners:	PATRICK BROWN
Furriers:	THOMAS DICKSON
Goldsmiths:	EDWARD HERIOT
Hammermen:	JOHN RICHARDSON, saddler
Barbers:	GILBERT PRIMROSE
Masons:	MURDO WALKER[2]
Wrights:	WILLIAM STEVENSON
Cordiners:	JOHN NICOLSON
Baxters:	JOHN HERIOT
Fleshers:	JOHN BLYTHMAN
Walkers:	WILLIAM WALKER[3]
Websters:	LEONARD THOMSON

References: MS Co. Recs., vi, fos. 48v, 76v, 110v, 114v, 116v, 120v, 123r, 128v, 131v; MS Act Book of Deacons of Crafts, i, fo. 11r.

1. Replaced by Henry Charteris 22 April 1581.
2. Replaced by Hew Brown after his death, 10 Feb. 1581.
3. Replaced by Thomas Andrew 18 Jan. 1581.

The council of 1581-2

Provost:	ALEXANDER CLARK
Bailies:	ROBERT KERR, younger
	HENRY CHARTERIS
	JOHN MORRISON
	GILBERT DICK[1]
Dean of Guild:	JOHN HARWOOD
Treasurer:	JOHN ROBERTSON
Ordinary council:	ALEXANDER UDDART
	JAMES NICOL
	WILLIAM NAPIER
	JOHN SIM
	JOHN JOHNSTON OF ELPHINSTONE
	PATRICK COCHRANE
	JOHN FAIRLIE
	ALEXANDER SCOTT
	ANDREW SLATER
	JOHN PRESTON
	THOMAS MILLAR, cutler
	JOHN BANNATYNE, skinner

The craft deacons

Tailors:	ALEXANDER OUSTEAN[2]
Skinners:	PATRICK BROWN[3]
Furriers:	THOMAS DICKSON
Goldsmiths:	DAVID DANIELSTONE
Hammermen:	JOHN WATT
Barbers:	GILBERT PRIMROSE, deacon convener
Masons:	MUNGO TELFER
Wrights:	JOHN STEWART
Cordiners:	JOHN NICOLSON
Baxters:	WILLIAM FIDDES
Fleshers:	JOHN HENRYSON
Walkers:	WILLIAM COUTTS
Websters:	THOMAS WRIGHT
Bonnetmakers:	PATRICK RANNALD

References: MS Co. Recs., vi, fos. 158v, 161v, 162r, 177v; MS Act Book of Deacons of Crafts, i, 12v, 13r, 16r, 17r.

1. Dick, although dismissed by a royal letter of 30 April 1582, was not replaced (*Edin Recs.*, iv, 234-5). The council made do with three bailies for the rest of its term.
2. The tailors' deacon given in the Act Book was John Young.
3. The skinners' deacon given in the Act Book was James Colden.

The council of 1582-3

Provost:	ALEXANDER CLARK
Bailies:	ANDREW SLATER
	JOHN ADAMSON
	MICHAEL CHISHOLM
	WILLIAM FAIRLIE
Dean of Guild:	JOHN PRESTON
Treasurer:	MUNGO RUSSELL
Ordinary council:	HENRY CHARTERIS
	JOHN MORRISON
	JOHN HARWOOD[1]
	JAMES FORMAN
	ALEXANDER NAPIER
	JOHN JOHNSTON OF ELPHINSTONE
	WILLIAM NISBET
	WILLIAM MAULE[2]
	ROBERT KERR, younger[1]
	EDWARD MAUCHAN
	JAMES FERGUSON, bowmaker
	JOHN BAIRNSFATHER, tailor

The craft deacons

Tailors:	WILLIAM HOPPRINGLE*
Skinners:	EDWARD GALBRAITH*

Furriers:	THOMAS DICKSON*
Goldsmiths:	EDWARD HERIOT*
Hammermen:	JOHN WATT*
Barbers:	GILBERT PRIMROSE,* deacon convener
Masons:	WILLIAM BICKERTON
Wrights:	ANDREW WILLIAMSON
Cordiners:	WILLIAM WEIR
Baxters:	ADAM NEWTON
Fleshers:	JAMES UR
Walkers:	THOMAS ANDREW[3]
Websters:	THOMAS WRIGHT
Bonnetmakers:	WILLIAM SOMER

References: MS Co. Recs., vi, fos. 199r, 203r, 208r, 210v, 212, 213, 230v; vii, 18r; *Edin. Recs.,* iv, 265-75, 289-91. Two additional councillors, John Robertson and William Inglis, appeared from 22 April 1583. The six deacons asterisked continued to sit, as deacon councillors, from 14 May 1583 until the next election to conform to the requirements of the decreet-arbitral.

1. Clark, Kerr and Harwood were replaced, in their absence, by James Ross, William Cockburn and Andrew Stevenson at the beginning of the election process on 25 Sept. 1583.
2. Maule took the place belonging to Gilbert Dick, the bailie dismissed in April and May 1582.
3. Given as William Coutts in MS Act Book of Deacons of Crafts, i, fo. 18r.

	The council of 1583-4	
Provost:	ALEXANDER CLARK*	
Bailies:	WILLIAM LITTLE*	
	HENRY NISBET*	
	JAMES NICOL*	
	THOMAS AIKENHEAD, skinner*	
Dean of Guild,	JAMES ADAMSON*	
Treasurer:	JAMES ROSS*	
Ordinary council:	ANDREW SLATER	
	JOHN ADAMSON	
	MICHAEL CHISHOLM	
	WILLIAM FAIRLIE	
	JOHN PRESTON	
	MUNGO RUSSELL	
	WILLIAM NISBET*	
	HEW LAUDER*	
	DAVID WILLIAMSON*	
	JOHN JOHNSTON OF ELPHINSTONE	
	THOMAS MILLAR, cutler*	
	WILLIAM HARVIE, tailor*	
	The craft deacons[1]	
Tailors:	ALEXANDER OUSTEAN**	(JOHN MURDO)
Skinners:	JOHN BANNATYNE**	(JAMES COLDEN)
Furriers:	THOMAS DICKSON	

Goldsmiths:	THOMAS ANNAND**	(GEORGE HERIOT)
Hammermen:	JOHN WATT, deacon convener**	
Barbers:	ROBERT HENRYSON**	
Masons:	MUNGO TELFER	(GAVIN PIRIE)
Wrights:	RICHARD BROWN	
Cordiners:	THOMAS BRUCE**	(HENRY WHITE)
Baxters:	JAMES WOOD	(ADAM NEWTON)
Fleshers:	JAMES UR	
Walkers:	WILLIAM COUTTS	(ALEXANDER WALKER)
Websters:	THOMAS WRIGHT	(JOHN STEVENSON)
Bonnetmakers:	WILLIAM SOMER	(PATRICK RANNALD)

References: MS Co. Recs., vii. fos. 20v, 21r, 85r; MS Act Book of Deacons of Crafts, i, 20v.

The members of the council asterisked (*) had been nominated by the king's leets of 22 & 24 Sept. 1583 (*Edin. Recs.*, iv, 290-92).

The deacons asterisked (**) also sat on the council under the new arrangements of the decreet-arbitral.

1. The deacons listed in the Act Book do not always agree with those in the council minutes; where they do not, they are given in brackets.

INDEX

BARON, JAMES
DG 55-6, (K) 59-60; C 56-7, 58-9, 60-62, 63-4, 65-6, 68-9.

BELL, JOHN
(K)C 59-60.

BOG, ROBERT
C 80-81.

CARMICHAEL, JAMES
DG 51-3, 54-5, 56-8, nom. Sept. 1565; C 55-6, 58-9.

CARMICHAEL, RICHARD
rC 54-5; B 55-6; C 56-7.

CHARTERIS, HENRY
C 74-5, 78-9, 82-3; B 77-8, 81-2; rC 80-81.

CHARTERIS, JOHN elder
DG 58-9; (S)C 59-60.

CHISHOLM, MICHAEL
C 67-8, 70-71, 73-4, 76-7, 83-4; B 69-70, (KP) 71-2, 72-3, 74-6, nom. Sept. 78, 82-3; rB April 78.

CLARK, ALEXANDER
C 64-5, 69-70, 75-6, 77-9; B 66-7 (nom. Oct. 66), 67-9; nom. P Sept. 1578; P 79-84 (nom. again Sept. 83).

COCHRANE, PATRICK
C 81-2.

COCKBURN, WILLIAM
rC 82-3.

CORSBIE, DAVID
(QP)B 71-2.

CRAIK, WILLIAM
P 51-3; C 56-7.

CUNNINGHAM, ROBERT
C 61-2; rC 75-6; nom. C Sept. 78.

CURLE, JAMES
C 57-8, (S) 59-60, nom. Sept. 1565; B 58-9.

DAVIDSON, THOMAS
C 68-9.

DICK, GILBERT
C 69-70, 79-80; B 78-9, 81-2.

DICKSON, ALAN
B 56-7, 61-2 (dismissed Oct. 61), 62-3, 64-5; C 57-8, 63-4, 65-7.

DOUGAL, JOHN
C 52-3.

DOUGLAS, ARCHIBALD of Kilspindie
P 54-7, (K) 59-60, 60-62 (dismissed Oct. 61), 62-5; C 57-8.

DOUGLAS, GEORGE of Parkhead
P 76-8 (dismissed April 78).

FAIRLIE, JOHN
C 81-2.

FAIRLIE, MUNGO
C 67-8; B 70-71.

FAIRLIE, WILLIAM
C 79-80, 83-4; B 82-3.

FERGUSON, JOHN
C 76-7.

FISHER, JOHN
C 79-80.

FLEMING, ROBERT
B 51-2, 55-6; C 52-3, 56-7.

FLEMING, THOMAS
C 65-6; nom. B Oct. 66.

FORESTER, DAVID
C 57-8, (K) 59-60, 63-4, 65-8, 70-71; B 58-9, 61-2 (dismissed Oct. 1561), 62-3, 64-5, 69-70; rB 66-7.

FORMAN, JAMES
C 68-9, 79-80, 82-3; rC 78-9.

FORRET, ROBERT
C 67-8; B 68-9.

FOWLER, WILLIAM
C 64-5, 66-7, 69-70; B 65-6.

FULLARTON, ADAM
C 55-6, 61-2, 69-70, 73-4, 76-7; (K)B 59-60, 60-61, 67-9; DG 70-71, (KP) 71-2, 72-3; (KP)PR 71-2.

GALBRAITH, ROBERT
C 74-5; rC April 78.

GLEN, ROBERT
(S)C 59-60, 61-2, 65-6, 67-8; B 60-61, 63-4, 66-7 (nom. Oct. 66 but dismissed July 67); T 64-5.

GOURLAY, ROBERT
C 68-9.

GRAHAM, ARCHIBALD
rC 54-5, 63-4; T 55-6; C 56-7, 60-61, 64-5.

GRAHAM, ROBERT
T 51-2, 53-4; C 52-3, 54-5.

GRAINGER, ARTHUR
C 61-2, 66-7.

GRAY, RICHARD
B 52-3.

GUTHRIE, ALEXANDER common clerk
C 60-61, 64-5, 77-8; DG 61-4, 76-7.

GUTHRIE, JAMES
C 75-6, 77-8.

HAMILTON, THOMAS of Priestfield
C 68-9; (QP)B June-Oct. 71.

HAMILTON, SIR WILLIAM of Sanquhar
P 53-4.

HARWOOD, JOHN
C 62-3, 69-71, 73-4, 76-7, 82-3; rT 66-7; T 67-9; DG 75-6, 80-82.

HENDERSON, THOMAS
T 69-70; C 70-71.

HOME, ALEXANDER
B 55-6, 61-2 (dismissed Oct. 61); C 56-7.

HOPE, EDWARD
C 52-3, 55-6, 60-62, 63-4, 68-9, 72-3; rC 58-9; B 54-5, (K) 59-60.

HOPPRINGLE, JAMES
(S)C 59-60.

IRELAND, PATRICK
B 51-2; C 52-3.

JOHNSTON, JAMES of the Cottis
C 68-9.

JOHNSTON, JAMES of Kellebank
C 61-2.

JOHNSTON, JOHN
(K)C 59-60.

JOHNSTON, JOHN of Elphinstone
nom. C Sept. 78; C 78-84.

KAY, ALEXANDER
C 52-3

KERR, ANDREW of Fernihurst
(QP)P June-Oct. 71.

KERR, MARK
C 75-6.

KERR, ROBERT elder
(K)C 59-60, 64-5, 76-7, 79-80; B 61-2 (dismissed Oct. 61), 75-6, 78-9; rB 63-4; rC April 78.

KERR, ROBERT younger
C 75-6, 78-9, 80-81, 82-3; B 76-8, 79-80, 81-2.

KERR, WILLIAM elder
B 56-7; C 57-8.

KERR, WILLIAM younger
(S)B 59-60.

KINLOCH, FRANCIS
C 80-81.

KIRKCALDY, SIR WILLIAM of Grange
P 69-70.

LAUDER, HEW
(QP)B June-Oct. 71; C 83-4 (nom. Sept. 83).

LAWSON, WILLIAM
B 51-2, 53-4, 57-8; C 52-3, 58-9.

LINDSAY, JAMES
B 54-5, 57-8; C 55-6, (S) 59-60; T 58-9.

LINDSAY, PATRICK, LORD, of Byres
P 72-6; C 76-7.

LITTLE, EDWARD
B 52-3, 57-8, (S) 59-60, 66-7 (nom. Oct. 66);
C 58-9, 65-6 (nom. Sept. 65), 67-8.
See app. viii.

LITTLE, EDWARD
rC 69-70, 75-6.
B. & G. Sept. 1567; brother of William.

LITTLE, WILLIAM
C 67-8, 69-70, 73-4, 78-9, 80-81; B 68-9, 72-3,
79-80, 83-4 (nom. Sept 83); rC April 78.

LIVINGSTONE, DUNCAN
B 53-4, nom. Oct. 66; C 65-6 (nom. Sept. 65).

LOWRIE, JAMES
(K)C 59-60; T 60-61.
Died in office.

LOWRIE, JAMES
C 64-5.
B. & G. Jan. 1565 by rt. of his father, James.

LOWRIE, JOHN
C 80-81.

MacCALZEAN, m. THOMAS
PR 57-8; P 61-2; C 62-3.

MacCARTNAY, JAMES
C 69-70; B 70-71.

McGILL, m. JAMES
PR 56-8; P 70-71, (KP) 71-2.

MAIN, JOHN
C 79-80.

MAITLAND, ROBERT of Lethington
PR 57-8.

MARJORIBANKS, JOHN
B 61-2, 76-7; C 62-4, 77-8.

MARJORIBANKS, SIMON
C 68-9, 70-71, 74-5; B 69-70, 73-4.

MARJORIBANKS, THOMAS of Ratho
PR 56-8.

MARTIN, PETER
(QP)B 71-2.

MAUCHAN, EDWARD
C 82-3.

MAULE, WILLIAM
C 82-3.

MAXWELL, HERBERT
(S)B 59-60, (QP) June-Oct. 71.

MORRISON, JOHN
C 74-5, 82-3; B 81-2.

MORVESS, ALEXANDER
(K)C 59-60.

MUIRHEAD, WILLIAM
B 53-4.

MURRAY, ANDREW of Blackbarony
C 55-7, 62-3.

NAPIER, ALEXANDER
C 63-4.
B. & G. June 1553.

NAPIER, ALEXANDER
C 82-3.
B. March 1574.

NAPIER, WILLIAM
B 74-5, 80-81; rC April 78; C 81-2.

NICOL, JAMES
C 64-5, 66-7; B 65-6 (nom. Sept. 65).
G. Oct. 1563.

NICOL, JAMES
B 80-81, 83-4 (nom. Sept. 1583); C 81-2.
B. & G. June 1567 as the son of James.

NISBET, HENRY
C 67-8, 70-71, 72-3, 74-5, 80-81; B 69-70, 73-
4, 78-80, 83-4 (nom. Sept. 1583); rC April 78.

NISBET, WILLIAM
(QP)B 71-2; 82-3, 83-4 (nom. Sept. 83).

OLIPHANT, JAMES
C 66-7, 68-9, 73-4.

OUSTEAN, JOHN
(K)C 59-60.

PARK, ALEXANDER
T 52-3, 56-7, (S & K) 59-60, 63-4; C 54-5, 57-8, 60-62, 65-7; DG 64-6, 67-8.

PATERSON, WILLIAM
C 58-9, 65-7; B 64-5, 74-5; DG 73-4.

PRESTON, JOHN
B 51-2, 53-4, 56-7, (S) 59-60, nom. 65; T 54-5, 61-3; DG 65-6, 66-7 (nom. Oct. 66), 69-70, 82-3; C 52-3, 55-6, 57-8, 63-4, 67-8, 70-71, 72-5, 77-8, 78-9 (nom. Sept. 78), 81-2, 83-4.

PRESTON, SIR SIMON of Craigmillar
P Aug. 65-Sept. 69 (nom. Aug. 65 and Oct. 66).

PROVAND, JOHN
C 77-8 (dismissed April 78).

RAMSAY, CUTHBERT
C 63-4; (QP)B June-Oct. 71.

RIG, PATRICK
C 70-71.

ROBERTSON, JOHN
C 73-4, 75-6, 78-9; B 77-8 (dismissed April 78), nom. Sept. 78; T 80-81.

ROSS, JAMES
T 73-5, 76-8, nom. Sept. 78, 83-4 (nom. Sept. 83); C 75-6, 78-9; rC 82-3.

RUSSELL, MUNGO
C 70-71, 73-4, 76-7, 83-4; (KP)B 71-2, 72-3; T 75-6, 82-3.

SCOTT, ALEXANDER
C 81-2.

SCOTT, WILLIAM
C 72-3.

SETON, GEORGE, LORD
P 57-9, (S) 59-60.

SIM, JOHN
B 54-6; C 56-7.
G. Sept. 1549.

SIM, JOHN
B 64-5, 65-6 (nom. Sept. 65), 70-71, 80-81; C 66-7, 81-2.
B. & G. Nov. 1561; see app. vii.

SIMPSON, JOHN
DG 53-4; C 54-6.

SLATER, ANDREW
C 58-9, 63-4, 68-70, 75-6, 77-8 (dismissed April 78), 81-2, 83-4; B 62-3, 67-8, (KP) 71-2, 76-7, nom. Sept. 78, 82-3; rB 68-9.

SOMER, DAVID
C. 57-8, 61-2, 64-5; (K)B 59-60, 60-61, 63-4.

SPENS, JOHN
C 57-8, (S & K) 59-60, 61-2, 64-5; B 58-9, 60-61, 62-4, nom. Sept. 65; (K)rB 59-60.

SPOTTISWOOD, JOHN
C 55-6.

STEVENSON, ANDREW
B 65-6; C 66-7, 69-70, 80-81; T 68-9, 78-80; rC 82-3.

STEWART, ARCHIBALD
C 72-3, 74-5, 79-80; B 73-4; P April 78-Sept. 79 (nom. April 78).

STRANG, RICHARD
C 52-3, (K) 59-60.

THOMSON, JAMES
(K)C 59-60, 60-61, 62-3; B 61-2.

THOMSON, THOMAS
C 58-9, 60-61.

UDDART, ALEXANDER
C 64-6, 67-70, 72-3, 74-5, 78-9, 81-2; B 66-7 (nom. Oct. 66), 73-4, 77-8, 80-81.

UDDART, JOHN
C 60-61; rC 68-9, 70-71.

UDDART, NICOL
C 62-3, 66-7, 75-6; B 63-4, 74-5; T 70-71, 72-3.

UDDART, THOMAS
(S)DG 59-60.

VAUS, THOMAS
nom. Sept. 78.

WALLACE, JAMES
B 52-3.

WATSON, m. JAMES
C 56-7, 61-3; rC 58-9; (K)B 59-60; DG 60-61.

WATSON, ROBERT
(K)C 59-60.

WESTON, JOHN
C 62-3; T 65-6, 66-7 (nom. Oct. 66).

WILLIAMSON, DAVID
C 78-9, 83-4.

WILSON, LUKE
(S)C 59-60, 61-3, 80-81; rT 60-61, 61-2; nom.
T Sept. 65; DG 77-8, 78-9 (nom. Sept. 78),
79-80.

YOUNG, JOHN
B 52-3; C 56-7.

Craftsmen

ABERCROMBIE, ROBERT saddler
CC 66-7.

AIKENHEAD, THOMAS skinner
CC 68-9, 73-4, 78-9; rCC 79-80; B 83-4.

ANNAND, THOMAS goldsmith
DC 83-4.

BAIRNSFATHER, JOHN tailor
CC 82-3.

BANNATYNE, JOHN skinner
CC 81-2; DC 83-4.

BRADY, MUNGO goldsmith
CC 70-71.

BRUCE, ALEXANDER barber
CC 52-3, 54-5, 60-61, 63-4.

BRUCE, THOMAS cordiner
DC 83-4.

CRAIG, ADAM goldsmith
CC 78-9 (nom. Sept. 78).

DANIELSTONE, DAVID goldsmith
CC 77-8.

DICKSON, THOMAS furrier
DC May-Oct. 83.

FERGUSON, JAMES bowmaker
CC 82-3.

FYNDAR, ROBERT wright
(S)CC 59-60.

GALBRAITH, EDWARD skinner
CC 72-3, 80-81; DC May-Oct. 83.

GILBERT, MICHAEL goldsmith
CC 55-6, 61-2, 63-4, 65-6 (nom. Sept. 65).

HARLAW, WILLIAM saddler
CC 69-70.

HARVIE, WILLIAM tailor
CC 83-4.

HENRYSON, ROBERT barber
CC 57-8, 74-5; rCC 73-4; DC 83-4.

HERIOT, EDWARD goldsmith
CC 79-80; DC May-Oct. 83.

HOPPRINGLE, WILLIAM tailor
DC May-Oct. 83.

HUNTER, MUNGO smith
CC 52-3, 57-8, 64-5.

INGLIS, JAMES skinner
CC 67-8, 70-71, 74-5; rCC 62-3, 73-4; nom.
CC Sept. 78.

LEACH, ARCHIBALD furrier
CC 56-7, (S) 59-60, 65-6 (nom. Sept. 65).

LINDSAY, ROBERT tailor
CC 54-5.

LOCH, JOHN furrier
CC 55-6.

MENTEATH, WILLIAM bowmaker
CC 73-4.

MILLAR, THOMAS cutler
CC 77-8, 81-2, 83-4.

MORRISON, WILLIAM tailor
(K)CC 59-60.

MOSSMAN, JAMES goldsmith
rCC 66-7, 68-9.

NICOLSON, JAMES tailor
CC 72-3.

NORVAL, JAMES tailor
CC 69-70.

OUSTEAN, ALEXANDER tailor
CC 80-81; DC 83-4.

PRIMROSE, GILBERT surgeon
CC 75-6; DC May-Oct. 83.

REDPATH, THOMAS skinner
CC 58-9, 62-3, 66-7.

SAUCHIE, ALEXANDER tailor
CC 60-61, 64-5.

WATT, JOHN smith
DC May-Oct. 83, 83-4.

WEIR, JOHN pewterer
CC 61-2.

WILKIE, JOHN skinner
CC 76-7, 79-80.

YOUNG, JAMES cutler
CC 56-7, 58-9, (K) 59-60, 62-3, 67-8, 76-7;
rCC 63-4.

Appendix ii
The subscription list of the 'faithful brethren' of Edinburgh of November 1562

(SRO, RH 9/14/8)

THERE are 160 names on the list, which is appended to a resolution of the Edinburgh kirk session of 26 November 1562 to raise funds for the building of a new poor hospital in the burgh. The resolution and list have been printed in my 'The "faithful brethren of Edinburgh": the acceptable face of protestantism', *Bulletin of Institute of Historical Research*, li (1978), 198-9. The contributors have been classified by social group and status and the sums in brackets refer to their assessments, where appropriate, in the tax roll of 1565 (see app. xi). The original list gives no indication of the status of the contributors, except in a few cases where there may be a need to distinguish between burgesses of the same name. All such details have been added, although it has not been thought necessary to give sources for the craftsmen, most of whom can be found in the printed burgess roll or held office in the burgh (see app. i). Since only a third of the contributors have a promised sum entered against their names, the subscriptions have not been given.

Classification of contributors

Merchants:
Patrick Edgar, Alex. Park, Cuthbert Ramsay, Andrew Stevenson, Thomas Uddart, Luke Wilson (£60); Alex. Acheson, James Baron (£50); James Adamson, John Adamson, Rot. Gray, Thomas Henderson, m. John Preston (£40); Alex. Clark, Thomas Davidson and his mother, m. Rot. Glen, Francis Linton, m. John Marjoribanks, Wm. Paterson, Nicol Uddart (£30); John Ashlowaine, Thomas Henry, James Laurie (£25); John Arnot, Gilbert Balfour, Andrew Barton, Hew Brown, Rot. Craig, John Dougal, Wm. Fowler, James Guthrie, John Haliday, Edward Little, Simon Marjoribanks, Peter Martin, Edward Mauchan, George Nisbet, John Norval, Alex. Uddart, John Uddart, elder, Rot. Watson (£20); John Adamson, elder, Adam Fullarton, Arthur Grainger, Alex. Home, George Hopper, Rot. Kerr, David Lyell, Andrew Slater, Thomas Thomson (£15); James Aikman, James Carmichael, Rot. Cunningham, James Curle, Alan Dickson, David Forester, Edward Home, Rot. Johnston, m. James Lindsay, Rot. Linton, Rot. Quintin, m. John Spens, David Towers, m. James Watson (£10); Gilbert MacQuhirrie, Thomas Todmer (£6); James Forman, John Herries, Edward Hope, Wm. Kerr, John Mowbray, Alex. Napier, John Sim, John Watson (£5); Rot. Dalgleish, Wm. Kincaid, John Uddart, younger (£3); John Hamilton, George Purvock (£2); David Acheson and his son, James Henderson, m. Thomas Fleming, John Heriot, Wm. Lawson, David Little, Wm. Little (brother of Clement), James Thomson.

Lawyers and professional men:
m. David Borthwick, m. Thomas MacCalzean, m. John Moscrop, burgh procurator-fiscal (*Edin. Recs.*, iii, 29) (£100); Rot. Scott (100 merks); m. Clement Little, m. Alex. Mauchan (£60); Neil Laing, later keeper of the signet (*TA*, xi, 373; see also *RSS*, v, 378), m. David McGill (£50); James Bannatyne, depute-clerk of justiciary (*RSS*, v, 1158), Alex. Guthrie, town clerk, m. Richard Strang, m. Alex. Sim, later commissary of Edinburgh (*RSS*, v, 2396), John Young, writer to the signet (*RSS*, v, 913) (£40); m. Edward Hay, Edward Henderson, master of the song school (*Edin. Accts.*, i, 306), m. Alex. Skene, John Wallace, scribe to the exchequer (*TA*, xi, 255) (£30); m. George Freir, Alex. King, m. Henry Kinross, James Millar, later justice-clerk depute (*RSS*, v, 2604; see also *TA*, xi, 207) (£10); m. Rot. Forman, Lyon king of arms (*RSS*, v, 712, 817), George Gibson, scribe of the Court of Session (Calderwood, *History*, iii, 77), m. George Hay, John Johnston, clerk of the privy council (*RPC*, i, 188n), m. James McGill, clerk register (*RSS*, v, 512), James Nicolson, clerk to the signet (*RSS*, v, 1325), m. Rot. Richardson, treasurer (*RSS*, v, 1127), m. John Spens of Condy, advocate to the privy council (*RPC*, i, 188), m. George Strang, later advocate to the privy council (*RSS*, v, 1690).

Lairds and heritors:
James Johnston of Kellebank (£40); Thomas Hamilton of Priestfield (£20); John Johnston of Cottis (£10); John Carkettle; Archibald Douglas, laird of Kilspindie, provost; John Johnston of Cottis; Andrew Murray, laird of Blackbarony.

Women:
Euphemia Dundas (£20), Widow Simpson (£15), Christine Baron [del.], Margaret Bonkle, Marian Scott.

Craftsmen:
Michael Gilbert, Alex. Mason, James Mossman, goldsmiths; John Cooper, Arch. Dewar, Rot. MacCure, John Purves, Alex. Sauchie, Lawrence Simpson, tailors; John Freir, George Redpath, Thomas Redpath, Peter Turnet, Alex. Wood, skinners; James Inglis, Thomas Thomson, furriers; James Young, hammerman; Alex. Bruce, Rot. Henderson, barbers; Gilbert Cleuch, John Inglis, masons; Patrick Shang, wright; Patrick Hardie, cordiner; George Gibson, John Hamilton, David Kinloch, Wm. Newton, Thomas Wood, baxters; Henry Burrell, flesher; John Hudson, bonnetmaker.

Status unknown:
m. Adam Lauder.

Appendix iii
The Edinburgh kirk sessions of 1573-6 and 1584-5

THE kirk session was elected annually in October shortly after the council elections. The surviving session record begins in April 1574, halfway through the year in office of the kirk session of 1573-4; the list of its members is incomplete. It ends in October 1575, shortly after the election of the session of 1575-6. The order of precedence of the members of the sessions elected in 1574 and 1575, which may be of significance in indicating the number of votes cast for each of its members, has been preserved as in the original. The session of 1584-5 was nominated by the council and deacons of crafts. Those asterisked served at one time or another on the council and are listed in the council index (see app. i).

The kirk session of 1573-4

Elders

*HENRY CHARTERIS, for the N.E. quarter [merchant; book importer and printer]
B.&G. 22 April 1573, but assessed at £15 in 1565, and at £4 in 1581 and £2 in 1583; he died in 1599, leaving £7,270 (Edin. Tests., 16 Sept. 1606); see also *RSS*, v, 3197.

*MICHAEL CHISHOLM, for the S.E. quarter [merchant]
See app. vii for further details; a sitting councillor.

MATTHEW FORESTER, for the S.W. quarter
The brother of the prominent protestant, David Forester (see app. v) and the father of a radical in the 1580s, Alexander Forester (see app. x).

JOHN FREIR, for the N.W. quarter [skinner]
On the subscription list of 1562; assessed at 6s 8d in 1583; the brother of George Freir, writer to the signet (Pro. Bk. Guthrie, i, fos. 148, 172; see also Edin. Tests., 12 Aug. 1573 for George's testament).

*ROBERT GOURLAY, treasurer [merchant]
He died in 1590, leaving £1,330 (Edin. Tests., 4 July 1597); see app. vii for further details.

*JOHN HARWOOD [merchant]
See app. vii for further details; a sitting councillor.

*WILLIAM NAPIER [of WRIGHTHOUSES], for the N.E. quarter [merchant]
See app. vii for further details.

JAMES NICOLSON [advocate]
The brother-in-law of the protestant veteran, Edward Hope; see apps. v & vii for further details.

*PATRICK RIG, for the S.W. quarter [merchant]
B.&G. 15 Sept. 1563 by rt. of his wife, the dr. of John Hope, so also a brother-in-law of Edward Hope; assessed at £10 in 1565; he died in 1578, leaving £1,566 (Edin. Tests., 20 April 1579).

[blank] WOOD, for the N.W. quarter
Possibly the baxter, James Wood, mentioned later in the year as a collector for the poor and an elder 1584-5.

Deacons

GEORGE BARRIER [sword sharpener]
B. 5 Aug. 1573 for his good service in Leith.

THOMAS BROWN [cordiner]
He died in 1588, leaving £33 (Edin. Tests., 20 July 1592); a well-known activist in the 1560s; see apps. v & vii for further details.

WILLIAM ELLIS [merchant]
B. 29 Jan. 1561; assessed at £4 in 1581 and £2 in 1583; he died in 1585, leaving £324 (Edin. Tests., 21 April 1586).

JOHN HOGG [merchant]
There are a number of merchants of this name in the burgess roll, although only one of them appeared on the tax roll of 1565, assessed at £20.

m. JOHN KENE [writer]
See *Edin. Recs.*, iv, 193.

JAMES MASTERTOWN, for the S.W. quarter [merchant]
B. 19 Aug. 1570; G. 16 Jan. 1593; assessed at £3 in 1581 and 30s in 1583; his wife died in 1594, leaving £1,176 and he died in 1623, leaving £11,160 (Edin. Tests., 5 May 1595, 18 Feb. 1624).

*WILLIAM MENTEATH, for the N.E. quarter [bowmaker]
A craft councillor 1573-4; see app. vii for further details.

*JOHN MORRISON, for the N.E. quarter [merchant]
Probably J. M., younger, who died in 1615, leaving £11,056 (Edin. Tests., 17 July 1615); see app. vii for further details.

THOMAS PATERSON, for the S.E. quarter [merchant]
B.&G. 17 Jan. 1571; assessed at 10s in 1581 and 1583; he died in 1620, leaving £8,406 (Edin. Tests., 16 May 1620); also a deacon 1584-5.

RICHARD THOMSON, for the N.W. quarter [merchant]
B.&G. 6 March 1556; assessed at £5 in 1565 and 1581 and at £3 6s 8d in 1583.

ANDREW SIMPSON, for the N.W. quarter [tailor]
B. 6 May 1561; he died in 1581, leaving £1,163 (Edin. Tests., 18 Oct. 1583).

References: BGKE, fos. 1r, 2v, 5r, 6v, 8r, 10r, 11v, 12v.

The kirk session of 1574-5

Elders

JOHN JOHNSTON, writer, for the S.E. quarter
He had been associated with the burgh's protestants since at least 1559; see apps. v & vii for further details.

*ADAM FULLARTON, merchant, for the S.E. quarter
See apps. v, vii & x for further details.

ALEXANDER HAY, writer, for the N.E. quarter
He later became clerk register and died in 1594, leaving £1,424 (Edin. Tests., 26 March 1597); see app. vii for further details.

*m. JAMES McGILL, clerk register, for the N.E. quarter
He had had long-standing connections with the burgh's protestants; see apps. v & vii for him and apps. iv & x for his wife, Janet Adamson.

*JOHN ADAMSON, merchant, for the S.E. quarter and keeper of the poor box
See app. vii for further details.

*HENRY NISBET, merchant, for the S.W. quarter
B.&G. 23 Jan. 1562; assessed at £20 in 1565, £12 in 1581 and £20 in 1583; also a councillor of 1574-5.

*NICOL UDDART, merchant, for the S.W. quarter
A sitting bailie; see app. vii for further details.

*ANDREW SLATER, merchant, for the S.W. quarter
See apps. v, vii & x for details.

GEORGE GIBSON, scribe, for the N.W. quarter
On the subscription list of 1562; see app. vii for further details.

m. ALEXANDER MAUCHAN [of Overbarnton], advocate, for the N.W. quarter
Admitted as an advocate in 1564, although he had already appeared on the subscription list of 1562; assessed at £60 in 1565; he was married to the daughter of the wealthy goldsmith, Michael Gilbert (see app. viii and *Faculty of Advocates, 1532-1943*, 145).

*JOHN ARNOT, merchant, for the N.W. quarter
A sitting bailie; he became provost of the burgh in 1589 and died over £17,000 in debt (Edin. Tests., 24 May 1616); see app. vii for further details.

DAVID KINLOCH, baxter, for the N.E. quarter
Deacon of his craft 1574-5; see app. vii for further details.

Deacons

*GILBERT PRIMROSE, surgeon, for the N.W. quarter
B. 19 Feb. 1566; deacon of his craft from 1575; assessed at £3 in 1583; he became principal surgeon to James I in England and died in 1616, leaving £18,075 (Edin. Tests., 18 April, 10 May 1616).

*ALEXANDER BARCLAY, apothecary, for the N.E. quarter
B.&G. 20 Oct. 1570; assessed at £5 in 1581 and £2 in 1583; his wife, Janet Auchmowtie, died in 1571, leaving £242 (Edin. Tests., 17 March 1571); he was a councillor 1576-7.

*JOHN FAIRLIE, merchant, for the S.W. quarter
B. 1 June 1563; the brother of the laird of Braid; assessed at 10s in 1581 and 6s 8d in 1583; a councillor 1581-2; he died in 1585, leaving £2,928 (Edin. Tests., 31 Dec. 1586).

NICOL SIM, goldsmith, for the S.W. quarter
B. 4 Aug. 1562; deacon of his craft 1574-5; his wife, Isobel Coling, died in 1587, leaving £161 (8 March 1594).

*ROBERT GALBRAITH, merchant, for the N.W. quarter
B. 1 Dec. 1563; assessed at £20 in 1565 and £3 in 1581; he died in 1581, leaving £2,339 (Edin. Tests., 22 Oct. 1586); a sitting councillor.

*MARK KERR, merchant, for the N.E. quarter
B.&G. 22 April 1573; assessed at £4 in 1581 and £7 in 1583 but left only £106 when he died in 1597 (Edin. Tests., 13 March 1599); he came on to the council in 1576.

JAMES MARSHALL, merchant, for the N.E. quarter
B.&G. 15 Oct. 1560; assessed at £10 in 1565 and £1 in 1581 and 1583.

JOHN ROBESON, cutler, for the S.E. quarter
B. 6 Oct. 1552; deacon of the hammermen 1561-3; assessed at 30s in 1583.

JAMES MATHESON, baxter, for the S.E. quarter
He died in 1576, leaving £592 (Edin. Tests., 29 Dec. 1576); see app. vii for further details.

MATTHEW JAMIESON, merchant, for the N.W. quarter
See app. vii for details.

*JOHN MAIN, merchant, for the N.W. quarter
B.&G. 27 March 1570 at the request of Alex. Mauchan (see above); assessed at £6 in 1581 and £5 in 1583; he became a councillor in 1579; he died in 1596, leaving £5,229 (Edin. Tests., 22 Oct. 1596).

*EDWARD MAUCHAN, merchant, for the S.W. quarter
B.&G. 31 Jan. 1562; assessed at £20 in 1565, £3 in 1581 and £2 in 1583; he became a councillor in 1582; his wife, Isobel Fisher, died in 1585, leaving £479 (Edin. Tests., 20 April 1586).

*ALEXANDER OUSTEAN, tailor, for the S.W. quarter
B. 26 May 1560; G. 24 July 1584; deacon of his craft 1580-82, a member of the council 1580-81 and 1583-4; assessed at 50s in 1583; his wife, Janet Anderson, died in 1602, leaving £12,047 and he left £9,152 when he died in 1604 (Edin. Tests., 8 July 1603, 7 July 1604 & 4 Feb. 1607).

JAMES HATHAWAY, merchant, for the N.E. quarter
B.&G. 27 May 1573.

JAMES CRAIG, barber, for the S.E. quarter
B. 15 June 1558; assessed at 6s 8d in 1583.

JOHN HARVEY, merchant, for the S.E. quarter
B.&G. by rt. of his wife, the dr. of John Charteris, 22 April 1573; the brother-in-law of Henry Charteris, the elder of 1573-4; he died in Plymouth in 1576, leaving £930 (Edin. Tests., 10 March 1580).

References: BGKE, fos. 21r, 23v, 25r, 50r, 54v; see also J. M. Kirk, 'The development of the Melvillian movement in late sixteenth century Scotland' (Edin. Ph.D., 1972), 734-43, for details of the sessions of 1574-6.

The kirk session of 1575-6

Elders

CLEMENT LITTLE, advocate, for the N.W. quarter
Admitted an advocate in 1560; on the subscription list of 1562; he died in 1580, leaving £3,997 (*Faculty of Advocates, 1532-1943*, 124-5); the brother of William Little, who had first served on the council in 1568 and would later become a provost of the burgh; see app. vii for further details of both.

*JOHN JOHNSTON, brother of the laird of Elphinstone, for the S.E. quarter
He came on to the council in 1578; see app. x for further details.

JOHN WILSON, skinner, for the N.W. quarter
B. 16 Jan. 1561; deacon of his craft 1568-9; he died in 1576, leaving £1,378 (Edin. Tests., 19 Sept. 1577).

m. ROBERT PONT, lord of Session, for the S.E. quarter
An elder of St. Andrews 1559-61, minister of Dunblane in 1562; since then he had, as well as being a senator of the College of Justice, served for a number of years as a commissioner without parochial charge until he became minister of Corstorphine in 1574 and of St. Cuthbert's in 1578 (*St. Andrews Kirk Session Register* (SHS, 1889), i, 2-4; Haws, *Scottish Parish Clergy*, 47, 69, 303; Kirk, 'Thesis', 648-9).

*m. MICHAEL CHISHOLM, merchant, for the S.W. quarter
A sitting bailie; see app. vii for further details.

*ARCHIBALD STEWART, merchant, for the S.E. quarter
An old friend of Knox; see app. vii for further details.

*m. JOHN PRESTON, merchant, for the N.E. quarter
He had a long and distinguished civic career behind him; see app. x for details.

*ROBERT HENDERSON, surgeon, for the N.E. quarter, keeper of the poor box
On the council 1573-5 and deacon of his craft twice in the previous four years; a prominent activist in the 1560s; see app. v for further details.

*m. RICHARD STRANG, advocate, for the S.W. quarter
B.&G. 11 Oct. 1549; a member of the Kilspindie council of 1559-60; on the subscription list of 1562; assessed, as a lawyer, at £40 in 1565.

*JAMES FORMAN, merchant, for the N.E. quarter
He died of the plague in 1585; see app. vii for further details; he was also an elder 1584-5.

*JOHN ROBERTSON, merchant, for the N.W. quarter
A sitting councillor; assessed at £15 in 1565, £14 in 1581 and £20 in 1583.

WILLIAM PATERSON, writer, for the S.W. quarter
B.&G. 22 April 1573; he died in 1576, leaving £1,400 (Edin. Tests., 15 Feb. 1578).

Deacons

JOHN FORSYTH, writer, for the N.W. quarter
B. *gratis* 23 Sept. 1573 for service to the town; he died in 1581, leaving £121 (Edin. Tests., 13 July 1583).

JAMES COLDEN, skinner, for the N.W. quarter
A radical in the 1580s; see app. x for further details.

THOMAS MILLAR, tailor, for the N.E. quarter
The only burgess of this name in either the burgess or tax rolls was a cutler, the son-in-law of the prominent protestant cutler, James Young (see app. vii).

*JOHN WILKIE, skinner, for the S.E. quarter
B. 10 April 1568; he became both deacon of his craft and a councillor in 1576; assessed at £5 in 1583.

HENRY BLYTH, surgeon, for the S.E. quarter
B. 1 Aug. 1567; G. 27 June 1583; assessed at £2 in 1583; he died in 1587, leaving £1,090 (Edin. Tests., 12 Dec. 1589).

JOHN BLACKBURN, merchant, for the S.W. quarter
He was one of the most militant members of the session of 1583-4; see apps. vii & x for details.

LAWRENCE MAXTON, apothecary, for the N.E. quarter
B.&G. 14 Aug. 1577 by rt. of his wife, the dr. of John Charteris; the brother-in-law of Henry Charteris, the elder of 1573-4; assessed at 30s in 1581 and 10s in 1583.

JOHN BAUTIE, merchant, for the S.E. quarter
See app. vii for details.

ADAM WALLACE, merchant, for the S.W. quarter
B. 3 June 1564; G. 9 Sept. 1570; assessed at £10 in 1581 and £4 in 1583.

*WILLIAM HARVEY, tailor
A craft councillor 1583-4; assessed at £3 in 1583; it is possible that he was the Canongate burgess who died in 1589, leaving £25 (Edin. Tests., 24 Dec. 1589).

ALEXANDER ELLIS, merchant, for the N.W. quarter
B. 12 July 1555; G. 14 April 1568; assessed at £7 in 1565.

ALAN McAULAY (McCALL), merchant, for the S.W. quarter
See app. viii for details.

*ROBERT ABERCROMBIE, saddler, for the N.E. quarter
On the council 1566-7; deacon of the hammermen 1576-9; see app. vii for further details.

GEORGE LITTLEJOHN, merchant, for the N.W. quarter
B. 10 Dec. 1560; assessed at £5 in 1565, £2 in 1581 and £1 in 1583; he died in 1585, leaving £307
(Edin. Tests., 29 Jan. 1607).

JOHN HENRYSON, writer [to the signet and indweller], for the N.E. quarter
He died in 1591, leaving £2,171 (Edin. Tests., 26 Nov. 1591).

GILBERT MASTERTOWN, merchant, for the S.W. quarter
The only burgess of this name in either the burgess or tax rolls was a tailor, made B. in 1573 and
assessed at £2 in 1583.

   References: BGKE, fos. 75v, 76r.

The kirk session of 1584-5

Elders

WILLIAM INGLIS, merchant
B.&G. 20 March 1573; assessed at £8 in 1581 and £6 13s 4d in 1583; he died in 1587, leaving £5,597
(Edin. Tests., 20 Aug. 1594).

*JOHN ROBERTSON, merchant
An elder 1575-6; see above for details.

DAVID LAWTIE, writer
B.&G. 29 July 1580.

*WILLIAM NAPIER [of WRIGHTHOUSES], merchant
An elder 1573-4; see above and app. vii for details.

*HENRY CHARTERIS, merchant
An elder 1573-4; see above for details.

JOHN HENRYSON, writer
A deacon 1575-6; see above for details.

JAMES WOOD, baxter
The sitting deacon of his craft; he had held the same office four times since 1567; assessed at 20s in
1583; he died in 1587, leaving £598 (Edin. Tests., 3 June 1587).

*JAMES FORMAN, merchant
An elder 1575-6; see above and app. vii for details.

*m. JOHN PROVAND, merchant
B.&G. *gratis* at Morton's request 27 April 1576; a councillor 1577-8; his wife, Katherine Henryson,
died in Oct. 1583, leaving £22,656 (Edin. Tests., 21 Aug. 1587).

U

*EDWARD HERIOT, goldsmith
B. 30 Dec. 1575; a councillor 1579-80 and in 1583; deacon of his craft 1579-81 and 1582-3; assessed at £1 in 1583.

m. HENRY BALFOUR, advocate
Admitted an advocate in 1570 (*Faculty of Advocates, 1532-1943*, 10).

m. OLIVER COLT, advocate
Admitted an advocate in 1573; sheriff-depute of Edinburgh; B.&G. 22 July 1580 (*Faculty of Advocates, 1532-1943*, 39).

Deacons

JOHN THOMSON, skinner
See app. x for details.

PATRICK ELLIS, merchant
B.&G. 19 Sept. 1579; assessed at £8 in 1581 and £6 13s 4d in 1583; he died in 1620, leaving £17,202 (Edin. Tests., 12 Dec. 1620).

JAMES SANDILANDS, tailor
B. 17 July 1583; G. 5 July 1588; assessed at £6 13s 4d in 1583; he died in 1604, leaving £6,171 (Edin. Tests., 18 May 1605).

THOMAS PATERSON, younger, merchant
This is either the deacon of 1573-4 or his son; see above for details.

ARCHIBALD MOODIE, apothecary
B. 17 July 1583; assessed at £1 in 1581 and 13s 4d in 1583; he died in 1609, leaving £4,787 (Edin. Tests., 8 June 1610).

JAMES SKAITHWAY, merchant
B. 27 Dec. 1560; assessed at £10 in 1565, £3 in 1581 and £1 in 1583; he died in 1598, leaving £605 (Edin. Tests., 27 March 1599).

JAMES BARCLAY, skinner
Assessed at £2 in 1583; on the council 1586-7, 1588-9.

ALEXANDER THOMSON, taverner
Assessed at £5 in 1565, £18 in 1581, when he was amongst the dozen highest assessments, and £10 in 1583.

THOMAS TAIT, merchant
B.&G. 16 Dec. 1574; assessed at £5 in 1581 and 26s 8d in 1583; he died of the plague in Aug. 1585, leaving £1,591 (Edin. Tests., 2 Feb. 1587).

WILLIAM PRINGLE, litster
B. 8 Jan. 1580; assessed at 30s in 1581 and 1583; he died in 1611, leaving £1,708 (Edin. Tests., 10 March 1612).

JOHN BORTHWICK, elder, baxter
B. 15 March 1565; assessed at 13s 4d in 1583.

JOHN DOUGAL, younger, merchant
Although he had never reached the council, Dougal was a wealthy merchant; see apps. vii and x for further details.

JOHN HERIOT, baxter
B. 2 Nov. 1577; deacon of his craft 1580-81; assessed at 6s 8d in 1583.

JOHN MacMORRAN, merchant
Although he was described by Calderwood as the richest merchant of his day, he did not reach the council until 1586; his tax assessments for the 1580s indicate that his fortune only reached spectacular proportions shortly before his death in 1596; see app. x for further details.

WILLIAM COURTAS, skinner
He died, probably of the plague, in July 1585, leaving £635 (Edin. Tests., 30 Aug. 1586); see app. vii for further details.

JOHN MUIR, merchant
B. 22 Jan. 1584; assessed at 30s in 1583; he died of the plague in Aug. 1585, leaving £684 (Edin. Tests., 23 March 1586).

Reference: *Edin. Recs.*, iv, 359.

Appendix iv
Edinburgh and Leith heretics, c.1534-c.1557

ADAMSON, ELIZABETH
'delighted much in the company' of Knox in the autumn of 1555; the wife of James Baron (see below; Knox, *History*, i, 119-20; Calderwood, *History*, i, 304).
She must have died by Nov. 1558, by which time Baron had remarried (Prot. Bk. John Guthrie, fo. 60).

ADAMSON, JANET
Knox wrote to her from Lyons in 1557 (*Works*, iv, 245); the wife of James McGill, clerk register and president of the burgh 1556-8. See also app. x for her and apps. v and vii for McGill.

ADAMSON, WILLIAM [merchant?]
one of the few in Edinburgh in the early 1540s (Knox, *History*, i, 43).
B. 30 Sept. 1542; his father, William, was on the council as a bailie 1527-8, 1530-31 and 1535-6, as dean of guild 1541-2 and 1543-4, and as a councillor 1536-7, 1538-9 and 1544-5 (*Edin. Recs.*, ii, 93; iii, 289-97). Although he himself was never on the council, both of his sons, John and Wm. were, both later supporters of the king's party (see apps. i and vii); he died sometime between Feb. 1561 and July 1564, when his sons gained their burgess-ships (*Edin. Burgs.*, 20-21); he was the cousin by marriage of Andrew Slater, one of the leaders of the protestant party of the 1560s, and the brother-in-law of Patrick Bellenden of Stenness (see *Edin. Recs.*, ii, 82; *Edin. Burgs.*, 438; Paul, *Scots Peerage*, ii, 64).

AIKMAN, FRANCIS apothecary
one of the few in the burgh in the late 1530s and early 1540s (Knox, *History*, i, 43; Calderwood, *History*, i, 134).
He was dead by 1549; two of his daughters, Elizabeth and Janet, married David Somer and Alan Dickson, two of the most prominent members of the protestant party in the 1560s (Prot. Bk. King, 24 Dec. 1549, i, fo. 113; also iii, fo. 125; see app. v).

ALDJOY, GEORGE merchant
one of the secret 'professors' in the late 1530s (Calderwood, *History*, i, 134).

BALCASKIE, MARTIN [burgess]
charged with possessing English heretical books (JC 1/5, 16 Dec. 1538 and 28 Feb. 1539; Pitcairn, *Trials*, i, 217-8); escheated 12 March 1539 (*RSS*, ii, 2936: see also *TA*, vii, 78); Thomas Redpath,

one of the leading craftsmen in the protestant party in the 1560s, was married to Elizabeth Balcaskie, who was probably Martin's daughter (Prot. Bk. King, ii, fo. 156; *Edin. Burgs.*, 419; *RMS*, ii, 2231).

BARON, JAMES [merchant]
his was one of the houses used in the mid-1550s for meetings of the privy kirk; delivered a letter to Knox in Geneva in May 1557 (Calderwood, *History*, i, 304, 320; Knox, *History*, i, 132).
B. & G. 5 Jan. 1547; dean of guild 1555-6 and a regular member of the council 1555-69; assessed at £50 in 1565 and so by then one of the dozen wealthiest merchants in the burgh; after the death of his first wife, Elizabeth Adamson (see above), he married Helen Leslie of Kinnaird; he died in 1569, leaving £5,410 (Edin. Tests., 21 April 1570 and 8 Feb. 1571); a prominent member of the protestant party in the 1560s (see app. v).

BORTHWICK, DAVID [advocate]
one of the Arran circle in the early 1540s (Knox, *History*, i, 48).
He was an assessor in 1560-61; appeared on the subscription list of 1562; was made one of the procurators for the town in its action against Leith in 1562 (*Edin. Recs.*, iii, 153); and was assessed at £100 in the stent of 1565; he married into the Guthrie family (Edin. Tests., 23 March 1582); see Janet Henryson, below.

BROWN, JOHN burgess
escheated for heresy 13 March 1539; he fled to England and was apparently still there in Feb. 1556 (*RSS*, ii, 2946; Ab. Prot. Bk. King, v, no. 77).

BROWN, RINGAW in the Canongate
one of the few in Edinburgh in the early 1540s (Knox, *History*, i, 43).

CAIRNS, HENRY skipper in Leith
summoned for heresy in 1534; he was probably one of those who recanted as he was escheated for heresy only four years later, when he fled into exile (Knox, *History*, i, 24; Calderwood, *History*, i, 108; *RSS*, ii, 2988; *TA*, vii, 79; see *Edin. Recs.*, ii, 66).

CAIRNS, JOHN
an elder or deacon of the privy kirk in Edinburgh in the mid-1550s; appointed a reader in May 1560 (Calderwood, *History*, i, 304; *Edin. Recs.*, iii, 63).

CANT, ROBERT burgess
granted escheat of his own goods after abjuring, 6 March 1539 (*RSS*, ii, 2915; *TA*, vii, 77).
B. & G. 12 Feb. 1536.

CHRISTISON, MICHAEL [merchant]
an elder or deacon of the privy kirk in Edinburgh in the mid-1550s (Calderwood, *History*, i, 304).
B. 2 Oct. 1554; G. 14 May 1560; he and his servant appeared in the muster roll of 1558 (MS Co. Recs., ii., fo. 128r); assessed at £5 in 1565; he was one of the extentors for the tax granted to the Congregation in April 1560 (ibid., iii, fo. 33v). The brother of William Christison, who became minister of Dundee in 1563 (see Edin. Tests., 20 Nov. 1582; Haws, *Scottish Parish Clergy*, 69).

CRAIG, ADAM [goldsmith servant]
an elder or deacon of the privy kirk in Edinburgh in the mid-1550s (Calderwood, *History*, i, 304).
Given as a servant of the goldsmith craft in the muster roll of 1558 (MS Co. Recs., ii, fo. 136r); B. 15 Sept. 1562; a deacon of his craft 1572-4 and on the council 1578-9; assessed at 10s in 1583.

DAYES, ADAM shipwright in Leith
summoned for heresy in 1534 but fled the country (Knox, *History*, i, 24; Calderwood, *History*, i, 108; *Diurnal*, 18).

DURHAM, MICHAEL [doctor of medicine]
a member of the Arran circle in the early 1540s (Knox, *History*, i, 48).
B. & G. *gratis* 15 Jan. 1556.

FORREST, DAVID general of the Mint
one of the Arran circle in the early 1540s; Wishart stayed at his house in 1546; visited by Knox when he came to Edinburgh in 1555; one of the teachers in the expanding privy kirk of 1558, but castigated by Knox as one of the 'temporizers' who tried to quell the St. Giles' day riot in Edinburgh in Sept. 1558 (Knox, *History*, i, 67, 128; Calderwood, *History*, i, 161, 193, 304, 333).

GRAY, JAMES [mason]
an elder or deacon of the privy kirk in Edinburgh in the mid-1550s (Calderwood, *History*, i, 304). See *Edin. Accts.*, i, 401.

HARLAW, WILLIAM tailor in the Canongate
a teacher in the privy kirk in Edinburgh in the mid-1550s; appointed minister of St. Cuthbert's in 1560 (Calderwood, *History*, i, 303; Keith, *History*, i, 150-51; Haws, *Scottish Parish Clergy*, 214).
It is possible that this was the tailor made B. 12 Nov. 1554, although he does not appear on the muster roll; if so, his son, William, was a prominent activist in the 1560s and later a member of the king's party; his son, John, in turn, was a radical in the 1580s (see apps. v, vii and x).

HENDERSON, HENRY schoolmaster
summoned for heresy in 1534, but fled to England where he died (Knox, *History*, i, 24; Calderwood, *History*, i, 108; *TA*, vii, 233-4; Pitcairn, *Trials*, i, 255).
A graduate of St. Salvator's College in 1524 (Knox, *Works*, i, 57n).

HENRYSON, JANET
Knox wrote to her from Geneva, probably in March 1557 (*Works*, iv, 247; cf. *ibid.*, v, 475-94; Ridley, *John Knox*, 170n, 543).
The wife of Alexander Guthrie, common clerk of the burgh and a leading figure in the protestant party in the 1560s (Edin. Tests., 23 May 1600); see also app. x. For further details of Guthrie, see apps. v and viii.

HOPE, ALEXANDER [merchant]
an elder or deacon of the privy kirk in Edinburgh in the mid-1550s (Calderwood, *History*, i, 304).
B. & G. as second son of John Hope, 20 Feb. 1552; appeared in the muster roll of 1558 as a merchant, but without servants; assessed at 10s in the stent roll of 1583; the brother of Edward.

HOPE, EDWARD [merchant]
one of the few in Edinburgh in the early 1540s (Knox, *History*, i, 43).
B. & G. as son and heir of John Hope, 27 Nov. 1540; the brother of Alex. (see above) and the brother-in-law of James Nicolson (see apps. iii, v and vii); three times on the council in the 1550s before becoming a bailie of the Kilspindie council of 1559-60; on the subscription list of 1562 and assessed at £5 in 1565, 20s in 1581 and 40s in 1583; a commissioner to the General Assembly in 1560, 1562 and 1569; a prominent member of the protestant party in the burgh, particularly in the early 1560s (see apps. v, vii and x).

JOHNSTON, WILLIAM [advocate]
summoned for heresy in 1534 but fled the country; he returned after 1542, but subsequently
apostatized (Knox, *History*, i, 24; Calderwood, *History*, i, 108; see Knox, *Works*, i, 57n; *RSS*, ii,
1583; iv, 909; *Epistolae Regum Scotorum*, ii, 200; *RMS*, ii, 1211).
A member of the Faculty of Advocates when it was founded in 1532; he was dead by Jan. 1558. His
son, Robert, married into the Baron family, appeared on the subscription list of 1562, and was
later a member of the king's party; Robert was also the nephew of Marjorie Roger, the wife of
Adam Fullarton, the spokesman for the Congregation in the burgh in 1559 (*Faculty of Advocates,
1532-1943*, 114; Pitcairn, *Trials*, i, 401; *Edin. Burgs.*, 279; see Edin. Tests., 30 Jan. 1584, for
Marjorie Roger's testament, and app. v for Fullarton).

KIRK, WILLIAM chaplain in Leith
summoned for heresy in 1534 (Knox, *History*, i, 124; *Diurnal*, 18; Calderwood, *History*, i, 108; see
Knox, *Works*, i, 57n).

LINDSAY, ALEXANDER friar
he and his brother, Patrick, were among the secret 'professors' in the late 1530s (Calderwood,
History, i, 134).

LINDSAY, PATRICK goldsmith
one of the few in the burgh in the late 1530s and early 1540s (*ibid.*, i, 134; Knox, *History*, i, 43).
A master of the goldsmith craft (MS Goldsmith Recs., fo. 3r); on the council 1544-5 (*Edin. Recs.*,
iii, 297); he was dead by Aug. 1551 (Prot. Bk. King, ii, fo. 157).

LINDSAY, SIBILLA
one of the few in the burgh in the early 1540s (Knox, *History*, i, 43).
She was the wife of John Fowler, common clerk of the burgh since 1520; their son, William, was
on the council 1564-7 and 1569-70 but never seems to have been a militant protestant (see app. viii;
Edin. Burgs., 191; Prot. Bk. King, ii, fo. 103).

MACKAW, JOHN in the Canongate
one of the few in the burgh in the early 1540s (Knox, *History*, i, 43).
Possibly a servant in Arran's household (see *TA*, viii, 100, 248).

MAIN, JOHN merchant
one of the secret 'professors' in the late 1530s (Calderwood, *History*, i, 134).
B. cramer 12 May 1535; G. 1 Sept. 1561; assessed at £5 in 1565; both he and his son were queen's
men in the civil wars (see app. viii).

SIM, JAMES [apothecary]
Knox lodged with him in 1555 and he delivered a letter to Knox in Geneva in 1557 (Knox, *History*,
i, 119, 132).
He and his four servants appeared in the muster roll of 1558 (MS Co. Recs., ii, fo. 129r); he had
been one of the largest contributors to the loan to d'Oysel in 1554 (*Edin. Recs*, ii, 206-7); he acted
as curator for the son of John Fowler and Sibilla Lindsay (see above; Prot. Bk. King, v, fo. 30); he
died sometime between 1558 and 1561 (Prot. Bk. Guthrie, i, fo. 212).

SMALL, GEORGE [saddler]
an elder or deacon of the privy kirk in Edinburgh in the mid-1550s (Calderwood, *History*, i, 304).
B. saddler 12 June 1557, when he also was made a master of his craft (MS Hammermen Recs., i, fo.
203v); G. *gratis*, 11 April 1561 for service 'in Goddis caus'; a protestant activist in the 1560s; see
app. v.

STEWART, JOHN in Leith
summoned for heresy in 1534; died in exile (Knox, *History*, i, 24; *Diurnal*, 18; Calderwood, *History*, i, 108).

WATSON, ROBERT [merchant]
the privy kirk sometimes met in his house in the mid-1550s (Calderwood, *History*, i, 304).
B. 2 Nov. 1555; on the Kilspindie council of 1559-60 and the subscription list of 1562; assessed at £20 in 1565. His father, Robert, made B. & G. in 1524, had married into the Baron family and been on the council 1536-7 and 1539-41; after his death, which took place before 1550, Edward Hope (see above) was made his son's curator (Prot. Bk. Foular, iv, fos. 47-8; Prot. Bk. King, iii, fo. 103). The son was a prominent member of the protestant faction in the 1560s and a king's man in the civil wars (see apps. v and vii).

Appendix v
The protestant party, 1560-1571

BARON, JAMES merchant
Bothwell arranged to meet Knox at his house in 1563 (Knox, *History*, ii, 37). Convicted in 1564 for his part in the Nicol Young affair. For further details of him and his first wife, Elizabeth Adamson, see app. iv; for details of his second wife, Helen Leslie, see app. viii.

CLARK, ALEXANDER merchant
one of the four captains of the protestants who mustered on the Crags in July 1565; pledged before the justiciary court by David Somer (see below), Lord Lindsay of the Byres and Robert Campbell of Kinzeancleuch (MSS Justiciary, JC 19/2, 13 July and 15 Aug. 1565; JC 1/12, 26 July 1565; Knox, *History*, ii, 153); implicated in the Riccio murder (*Diurnal*, 96; *RSS*, v, 3149).
B. & G. *gratis* at Moray's request, 13 Jan. 1565; on the council of 1564-5 and returned to it after being nominated by Mary in Oct. 1566; assessed at £30 in 1565; he had connections with Moray since at least the autumn of 1560 and with Cecil since early 1561, and was on very close terms with Randolph (*CSP Scot.*, i, nos. 913, 943; ii, nos. 161, 171); see also app. x.

CUNNINGHAM, ROBERT merchant
implicated in the Riccio murder and charged with holding the queen at Holyrood along with Hope, Fullarton and Robert Watson (see below; JC 1/13, 8 and 20 April 1566; *Diurnal*, 96).
B. & G. 17 June 1553; on the council 1561-3; assessed at £10 (1565), 20s (1581) and 30s (1583); a collector for the ministry from 1569 (*Edin. Recs.*, iii, 262; see also *ibid.*, iii, 240); see also app. vii.

DICKSON, ALAN merchant
one of the bailies dismissed by Mary in Oct. 1561 for the council's proclamation against priests and friars.
B. & G. 9 April 1538; been on the council 1556-8 and returned to it in 1562 until 1567; assessed at £10 in 1565; on the subscription list of 1562. He became, however, an active member of the queen's party in the civil wars. He died in 1577, leaving £9,123 net (Edin. Tests., 26 March 1578).

FORESTER, DAVID merchant
pledged in the sum of £1,000 to enter the tolbooth on six hours' notice 1 April 1566 (*RPC*, i, 444).
B. & G. at the request of the provost and bailies, 10 Jan. 1549; on the council for most of the period 1557-71; assessed at £10 in 1565; on the subscription list of 1562; he died in 1572, leaving £1,254 net (Edin. Tests., 21 July 1574).

FULLARTON, ADAM merchant
emerged as the spokeman for 'the haill brether of the congregatioun' in the town in July 1559; although he appeared on the Kilspindie council of 1559-60 and the two which followed it, he did not serve on the council again until 1567; charged with being involved in the riot which preceded Riccio's death (JC 1/13, 8 and 20 April 1566).
B. & G. 24 Dec. 1549; assessed at £15 in 1565, £8 in 1581 and £5 in 1583; the net total of his wife's testament was £10,717, although all but £441 of that was made up of unpaid debts. He acted as a burgh commissioner to parliament, the Convention of Royal Burghs and the General Assembly at various times from 1566 onwards. After the death of James Baron in 1569, Fullarton emerged as the undisputed secular leader of the protestant party and was the natural choice to head the king's men exiled from the burgh in 1571; see apps. vii and x for further details of him and his wife, Marjorie Roger.

GRAHAM, ARCHIBALD merchant
pledged on a surety of £1,000 for detaining the queen in Holyrood (JC 1/13, 8 and 26 April 1566; both entries were subsequently deleted).
B. & G. 21 June 1553; on the council 1554-7, 1560-61 and 1563-5; assessed at £5 in 1565 and 1581 and £4 in 1583; he was a client of Maitland and closely connected with Randolph, the English ambassador (*CSP Scot.*, ii, no. 419); he died in 1594 (Edin. Tests., 13 Jan. 1595).

GUTHRIE, ALEXANDER town clerk
one of the four captains of the protestants who mustered on the Crags in July 1565; he was imprisoned in the Castle but released after a succession of appearances before the Court of Justiciary; one of those who stood surety for him was Patrick Bellenden of Stenness; after becoming implicated in the Riccio murder, Guthrie fled along with Patrick's brother, John Bellenden of Auchnoull, and James McGill, the clerk register; he was declared a rebel and deprived of his office, despite protests from the council; he was restored after being granted a remission in Dec. 1566 (Knox, *History*, ii, 153, 183; JC 1/12, 26 July 1565; JC 19/2, 13 July and 15 Aug. 1565; *Diurnal*, 97; *RPC*, i, 463; *RSS*, v, 3149; *Edin. Recs.*, iii, 212).
B. & G. 10 Jan. 1549; made common clerk of the burgh in 1558; on the council 1560-65 and dean of guild 1561-4; assessed at £40 in 1565; on the subscription list of 1562; he had been closely connected with Randolph since 1560 (*CSP Scot.*, i, no. 916); he remained as town clerk until his death in 1582 (see Edin. Tests., 6 Dec. 1583).
See also Q.P. list and apps. iv and x for his wife, Janet Henryson, who had had connections with Knox since the mid-1550s and remained a militant protestant in her old age.

HENDERSON, ROBERT surgeon
granted a remission 24 Dec. 1566 for detaining the queen and his part in the Riccio murder (*RSS*, v, 3149).
B. & G. *gratis* 24 July 1563, but he had been on the council 1557-8; on the subscription list of 1562; deacon of his craft 1560-62; assessed at 20s in 1583.

HOPE, EDWARD merchant
a bailie on the Kilspindie council of 1559-60 and a councillor 1560-64 and 1568-9; he was implicated in the Riccio murder but eventually only charged with detaining the queen and was pledged on sureties of £1,000, put up by Adam Fullarton and others; he had also been imprisoned in the Castle in 1564, probably in connection with his conviction in the Nicol Young affair (*Diurnal*, 97; JC 1/13, 8 and 26 April 1566; JC 19/2, 2 July 1564).
A prominent protestant since the 1540s; see apps. iv, vii and x.

JOHNSTON, JOHN writer, clerk to the privy council
he was listed by Knox, along with Baron, Fullarton and Hope, as his most trusted contacts in

Edinburgh in June 1559. He and Nicolson (see below) were deeply involved in the Moray conspiracy of 1565 and fled to England after it failed (Knox, *Works,* vi, 27; *Diurnal,* 81, 87; *CSP Scot.,* ii, nos. 240, 343; *RSS,* v, 2541).

He was a burgess, although not on the burgess roll; exempted from a burgh tax in 1557 (*Edin. Accts.,* i, 35); on the subscription list of 1562 and an elder 1574-5; made a writer to the signet in 1558, a clerk to the privy council by 1562 and appointed commissary clerk of Edinburgh in 1565, although he forfeited the office to Sebastian Danelour (see app. viii) after the conspiracy (*RSS,* v, 937, 1936, 2323, 2712; *RMS,* iv, 1275).

He did not die until 1597, when he left £3,299 net (Edin. Tests., 15 May 1598).

KERR, ROBERT elder merchant
one of the bailies dismissed by Mary in Oct. 1561.
B. & G. 20 Feb. 1539; he had been on the Kilspindie council of 1559-60 and returned to the council 1563-5; on the subscription list of 1562; assessed at £15 in 1565; see K.P. list.

LAUDER, GILBERT
one of the four captains of the protestants who mustered on the Crags in July 1565; he was pledged by George Douglas of Borg and others (Knox, *History,* ii, 153; JC 1/12, 26 July 1565; JC 19/2, 13 July and 15 Aug. 1565).
B. & G. as son of Henry Lauder, advocate to the queen, 29 Jan. 1562; he was exempted from burgh taxation in Jan. 1565 because he no longer 'usis trafique' (MS Co. Recs., iv, fo. 124r).

McGILL, m. JAMES of Rankeillor Nether clerk register
he established contact with Thomas Randolph in Sept. 1560 and had fallen 'in familiarity' with Knox by early 1561; he fled the town after the Riccio murder, was denounced as a rebel and discharged from office (*CSP Scot.,* i, no. 966; ii, no. 371; Knox, *History,* i, 356-7; ii, 183; *Diurnal,* 89, 97; *RPC,* i, 436).
The eldest son of Sir James McGill, a provost of Edinburgh in the reign of James V; appointed clerk register in 1554, made a president of the burgh 1556-7 and a member of the privy council in 1561; he was restored as clerk register in 1567 (Paul, *Scots Peerage,* vi, 587-92; *Faculty of Advocates,* 132; *RSS,* v, 2705, 2725). On the subscription list of 1562, an elder 1574-5 and provost of the burgh 1570-72 (see app. vii). His wife, Janet Adamson, was one of Knox's 'dear sisters of Edinburgh' in the 1550s and still a radical protestant after McGill's death in 1579 (see Edin. Tests., 9 Aug. 1582; apps. iv and x).

MILLAR, JAMES writer, justice-clerk depute
implicated in the Riccio murder (*RSS,* v, 3149).
B. & G. 17 Sept. 1576; on the subscription list of 1562; assessed at £10 for the burgh loan of 1565; he represented John Ashlowaine, one of the town councillors involved in the Nicol Young affair in 1564 (*RSS,* v, 2604; *RPC,* i, 468; JC 19/2, 2 July 1564); see also app. vii.

NICOLSON, JAMES writer, clerk to the signet
he and John Johnston (see above) were deeply involved in the Moray conspiracy of 1565 and fled to England after it failed (*Diurnal,* 81; *CSP Scot.,* ii, no. 240; *RSS,* v, 2508).
On the subscription list of 1562; he was married to the sister of Edward Hope (see above), and was made B. & G. by her 22 Nov. 1564; an elder 1573-4; see also app. vii.

PATERSON, WILLIAM merchant
convicted of assisting Moray and the rebels (JC 1/12, 4 Dec. 1565); he had been involved in the murder of Nicol Young in 1564.
B. & G. 26 Feb. 1550; he married into the influential Uddart family; on the subscription list of 1562; on the council 1558-9 and 1564-7; assessed at £30 in 1565 and £10 in 1580; he died in 1582, leaving £4,901 net (Edin. Tests., 17 Feb. 1585).

REDPATH, THOMAS furrier
pledged by his brother, George, on a surety of £1,000 to enter the tolbooth on six hours' notice 30 March 1566 (*RPC*, i, 442).

G. 17 Aug. 1554; his wife, Elizabeth, was probably the daughter of Martin Balcaskie, one of the earliest of the burgh's protestant heretics; deacon of his craft 1557-8; three times on the council between 1558 and 1567; on the subscription list of 1562; he died in 1567, leaving £1,076 (Edin. Tests., 2 July 1568).

His brother's son, also named Thomas, was a king's man in the civil wars; see app. vii.

SHARP, m. JOHN advocate
pledged, along with a number of protestant burgesses, in the sum of £1,000 to enter the tolbooth on six hours' notice after the Riccio murder (*RPC*, i, 445, 452). A burgess, appointed an assessor in 1562 and assessed at £30 for the burgh loan of 1565 (*RMS*, iv, 1883; *Edin. Recs.*, iii, 150).

SLATER, ANDREW merchant
one of the four captains of the protestants who mustered on the Crags in July 1565; pledged by Andrew Kerr of Cesford and others (Knox, *History*, ii, 153; JC 1/12, 26 July 1565; JC 19/2, 13 July and 15 Aug. 1565).

G. 19 March 1561; he had been one of the members of the council of 1558-9 sent to negotiate with the Congregation in June 1559 (*Edin. Recs.*, iii, 44); again on the council in 1562-4 and 1567-70; on the subscription list of 1562; assessed at £15 in 1565 and 30s in 1581; a very prominent member of the king's party in the civil wars, he remained an influential figure in burgh politics until the 1580s, when he became involved in the dispute over the burgh's exiled radical ministers; see apps. vii and x.

SOMER, DAVID merchant
acted as a surety for Clark after the Crags affair (JC 19/2, 13 July 1565); pledged by Alan Dickson in the sum of £1,000 to enter the tolbooth on six hours' notice 30 March 1566 (*RPC*, i, 442); he was convicted for his part in the Nicol Young affair in 1564.

G. *gratis* at the request of the provost, Douglas of Kilspindie, 26 Oct. 1555; a bailie on the Kilspindie council of 1559-60 and on the council 1560-62 and 1563-5; assessed at £5 (1565), 30s (1581) and 13s 4d (1583).

THOMSON, THOMAS [apothecary]
Randolph complained in Nov. 1561 that he was 'much cumbered' by this 'mischievous man . . . a playne anabaptiste' (*CSP Scot.*, i, no. 1041).

B. & G. 15 Feb. 1538; he was a partner with David Forester (see above) in the 'Lion of Leith' (*ibid.*, i, no. 986); assessed at £15 in 1565; he died in 1572 leaving £1,784 net (Edin. Tests., 5 Feb. 1575).

WATSON, m. JAMES merchant
pledged in the sum of £1,000 to enter the tolbooth on six hours' notice 30 March 1566 (*RPC*, i, 442).

B. & G. 2 June 1553; a bailie on the Kilspindie council of 1559-60 and he remained on the council until 1563; on the subscription list of 1562; his wife, Katherine Bryce, however, was a practising catholic (see app. vi); assessed at £30 in 1565; he died in 1582, leaving £138 net (Edin. Tests, 12 Nov. 1584); see app. ix.

WATSON, ROBERT merchant
implicated in the Riccio murder but charged only with detaining the queen at Holyrood; pledged on a surety of £1,000 (*Diurnal*, 96; JC 1/13, 8 and 26 April 1566).

B. 2 Nov. 1555; on the Kilspindie council of 1559-60 and the subscription list of 1562; assessed at £20 in 1565; a prominent king's man in the civil wars; see apps. vii and ix.

YOUNG, JAMES cutler
implicated in both the Friar Black affair and the Riccio murder (*Diurnal*, 96; *RPC*, i, 463; Pitcairn, *Trials*, i, 475, 484; JC 19/2, 2 July 1566).
The most prominent craftsman in the protestant party; deacon of the hammermen six times and on the council three times in the 1550s, including the Kilspindie council of 1559-60 (see app. i and Smith, *Hammermen of Edinburgh*, xciii, 143); one of the members of the council sent to negotiate with the Congregation in June 1559 (*Edin. Recs.*, iii, 44); made G. *gratis* by the council, 24 Sept. 1560; deacon twice and a councillor three times in the 1560s; on the subscription list of 1562; a commissioner to the General Assembly, despite merchant protests, in 1562 and an overseer of the Blackfriars hospital (*Edin. Recs.*, iii, 138, 161); his close identity of interests with the protestant party was, however, compromised by his personal interests in the Nicol Young affair (see Pitcairn, *Trials*, i, 449-50); assessed at 10s in 1583; see app. vii.

Lesser figures

ARMSTRONG, ANDREW merchant
involved in the anti-catholic riot at Holyrood in 1563, charged with the wounding of Friar Black in 1566 and implicated in the Riccio murder (Knox, *History*, ii, 87-8, 101; Pitcairn, *Trials*, i, 434-5, 475, 485; JC 19/2, 23 Oct. 1563 and 10 July 1566; *CSP Scot.*, ii, no. 36; *Diurnal*, 96; *RPC*, i, 463; *RSS*, v, 3149).
G. 8 Jan. 1558; assessed at £5 in 1565; he was killed in action in 1571; see app. vii.

BROWN, THOMAS cordiner
implicated in both the Friar Black affair and the Riccio murder (Pitcairn, *Trials*, i, 475, 484; JC 19/2, 2 July 1566; *Diurnal*, 96; *RPC*, i, 463).
A deacon of the kirk session 1573-4; assessed at 6s 8d in 1583; he died in 1588 (Edin. Tests., 20 July 1592); see app. vii.

CRANSTON, PATRICK merchant
involved in the anti-catholic riot at Holyrood in 1563; he acted as a surety for the four protestant activists, Andrew Armstrong, Thomas Brown, William Johnston and James Young, who were charged with the first assault on Friar Black; implicated in the Riccio murder (Knox, *History*, ii, 87-8, 101; *CSP Scot.*, ii, no. 36; Pitcairn, *Trials*, i, 434-5; JC 19/2, 23 Oct. 1563; JC 1/12, 12 Feb. 1566; *Diurnal*, 96).
B. 22 Feb. 1555; G. 8 July 1561; assessed at £5 in 1565.

HARLAW, WILLIAM saddler
convicted of detaining the queen at Holyrood 1 April 1566; threatened with execution but banished after the intercession of Bothwell (Knox, *History*, ii, 184; *Diurnal*, 98; Pitcairn, *Trials*, i, 480; Spottiswoode, *History*, ii, 39; *RPC*, i, 447).
He had been a master hammerman since at least 1550 but was only made B. & G. 26 Dec. 1560; he was deacon of the craft 1560-61 when he was arrested as one of the leaders of the craftsmen's riot of 1561 and was saved by the intercession of Knox; on the council of 1569-70; an active supporter of the king's party in the civil wars (see app. vii); he died in 1578 (Smith, *Hammermen of Edinburgh*, xciii, 148, 170, 175; Knox, *History*, i, 355-6).
His father, William, was prominent in the privy kirk of the 1550s and his son, John, was a radical in the 1580s (see apps. iv and x).

JOHNSTON, WILLIAM bower
charged with the first assault on Friar Black (Pitcairn, *Trials*, i, 475; JC 1/12, 12 and 18 Feb. 1566); implicated in the Riccio murder and at first denounced for non-appearance 8 June 1566, but pledged by Robert Campbell of Kinzeancleuch 4 July (*Diurnal*, 96; *RPC*, i, 463; Pitcairn, *Trials*, i, 485).

MOWBRAY, JOHN merchant
convicted of detaining the queen in Holyrood 1 April 1566; threatened along with Harlaw with execution but subsequently banished (Pitcairn, *Trials*, i, 480; *Diurnal*, 97-8; Knox, *History*, ii, 184; *RPC*, i, 447).
Assessed at £5, 50s and £2 in the stents of 1565, 1580 and 1583; on the subscription list of 1562; made G. by rt. of his second wife, the dr. of Mungo Fairlie (see app. vii), 17 Nov. 1581; he died in 1593, leaving £1,963 net (Edin. Tests., 8 Aug. 1593).

NORVAL, ROBERT merchant
indulged in horseplay before the trial of the archbishop of St. Andrews in 1563 (Knox, *History*, ii, 76).
B. & G. for good service to the town 25 July 1561 after he had guarded the tolbooth during the craft riot of 1561 (*ibid.*, i, 358); discharged from tax contributions 24 Jan. 1565 as he no longer 'usis trafique' (MS Co. Recs., iv, 124r).

RHIND, GEORGE goldsmith
involved in the anti-catholic riot at Holyrood in 1563 (Pitcairn, *Trials*, i, 434-5).
B. 4 Aug. 1562; G. 7 Jan. 1564; acting deacon of his craft for part of 1562-3; Rhind, however, like the rest of his family, became involved with the queen's party in the civil wars; see app. viii.

SMALL, GEORGE saddler
implicated in the Riccio murder (*Diurnal*, 96).
A prominent figure in the privy kirk of the 1550s (see app. iv); he had been on the assize dealing with the craft riot of 1560 (JC 1/11, 19 Dec. 1560).

WHITE, WILLIAM cordiner in the Canongate
implicated in the Riccio murder (*Diurnal*, 96; Pitcairn, *Trials*, i, 483; *RSS*, v, 3151).
Deacon of the Canongate cordiners in 1574 (*Canongate Extracts*, Maitland Misc., ii, pt. ii, 329).

Appendix vi
Catholic recusants and sympathisers from Edinburgh and the Canongate, 1560-1575

TO avoid repetition, full references to the catholic worshippers at Holyrood in August 1563 have only been given in the first entry.

AIKMAN, JOHN
his child baptised by catholic rite in 1566 (*Canongate Bk.*, 91).
Probably a small Edinburgh merchant, made B. 7 Dec. 1562, assessed at £2 in south-east quarter in 1565, but discharged from a burgh tax in 1566 (*Edin. Accts.*, i, 61; ii, 147).

ALDINSTOUN, JOHN [baxter]
attended mass at Holyrood in Aug. 1563 (Pitcairn, *Trials*, i, 435; JC 1/12, 1 Oct. 1563).

ALLAN, ADAM merchant
present at the baptism of John Charteris's child at Holyrood in Dec. 1561; attended mass at Holyrood Aug. 1563; pledged by Andrew Stevenson, his wife's brother (see Q.P. list); excommunicated July 1569, but allowed to return to the burgh for eight days in Oct. 1570 (MS. Co. Recs., iv, fos, 48v, 243r, 264v).
Stented at £30 (1565); £5 (1581); 30s (1583); made G. 13 July 1583 by rt. of his wife; he died in Paris in 1584, leaving £1,062 net; his wife, Mause, died in 1583 (Edin. Tests., 27 and 28 April 1586); see app. viii.

AYTON, AGNES
attended mass at Holyrood in Aug. 1563; pledged by James Paterson.
The wife of John Paterson, Snowdon Herald, who lived in the Canongate; she must have died before he did, in Jan. 1571 (*Broughton Court Book*, 59; Edin. Tests., 11 Jan. and 13 May 1575).

BALFOUR, WILLIAM indweller in Leith
convicted in Dec. 1561 of trying to incite a riot in the Edinburgh tolbooth by abusing protestant doctrine (Pitcairn, *Trials*, i, 416-8; see also *Canongate Bk.*, 15).

BARRIE, THOMAS [keeper of the Netherbow port]
threatened with excommunication in Feb. 1566 for attending the mass and actually excommunicated for marrying by catholic rite (*Canongate Bk.*, 38-9, 74). See app. viii.

BROCAS, WILLIAM smith
attended mass at Holyrood in Aug. 1563.
A master of the hammermen craft since at least 1546; elected deacon of the craft in May 1562 but dismissed by the council (Smith, *Hammermen of Edinburgh*, 130; *Edin. Recs.*, iii, 134-5; *RPC*, i, 210). See Q.P. list.

BROWN, JOHN merchant
attended mass at Holyrood in Aug. 1563; denounced rebel 1 Oct. 1563.
There are three of this name made burgesses between 1531 and 1540, but only one merchant in the 1565 roll, assessed at £3, who died in 1574, leaving £2,596 (Edin. Tests., 5 April 1574).

BRYCE [or FISHER], KATHERINE
attended mass at Holyrood in Aug. 1563; pledged by her protestant husband, James Watson (Pt. Bk. Guthrie, iii, fo. 85; see also *RSS*, v, 565); for details of Watson, see app. v.

CASS (KAUERIS), DAVID [smith]
agreed to renounce the mass and papistry 30 Dec. 1574 (BGKE, fo. 36v).
B. locksmith 25 Jan. 1570; 'dagmaker', assessed at 10s in 1583 roll.

CHALMER, JANET
she and her husband, Archibald Trench, attended mass at Holyrood in Aug. 1563.

CHARTERIS, JOHN younger [merchant]
had his child baptised at Holyrood in Dec. 1561 (*Edin. Recs.*, iii, 153).
B. & G. 17 May 1554; the son of John Charteris, who was on the councils of 1558-60, and the brother of Henry, who was on the council after 1574.

CLARKSON, JOHN baxter
attended mass at Holyrood in Aug. 1563.
Given as a freeman baxter in the muster roll of 1558 (MS Co. Recs., ii, fo. 136v); see his son-in-law, John Paterson, below; see Q.P. list.

CLARKSON, THOMAS [skinner]
attended mass at Holyrood in Aug. 1563; pledged by John Clarkson (see above). A visitor of his craft 1555-6; a master skinner in 1531 (*Edin. Recs.*, ii, 61).

CURROR, ISOBEL
attended mass at Holyrood in Aug. 1563; pledged by her husband, James Aikman (Pt. Bk. King, iv, fo. 40; Edin. Tests., 20 Oct. 1573).
Aikman was made B. & G. 17 March 1530, was on the councils of 1560-61 and 1563-4, and died in June 1569.

DOUGLAS, JOHN
accused of attending the mass while in France and refused under questioning to condemn it as idolatry, 23 April 1574 (*Edin. Recs.*, iv, 13).
Probably the servant of the laird of Whittingham (see *ibid.*, iii, 179).

EASTON, HENRY [candlemaker]
admitted absenting himself from communion for the previous fourteen years on 14 July 1575 (BGKE, fo. 67r).
B. candlemaker 4 July 1567; assessed as such at 6s 8d in 1583; see Edin. Tests., 30 April 1603, for his wife, Katherine Yetts.

FOWLER, ROBERT swordslipper [hammerman]
admitted in Aug. 1566 never having attended communion, but promised to do so in the future and asked for his child to be baptised (*Canongate Bk.*, 92; see also *Broughton Court Bk.*, 241).

GALLOWAY, MARGARET
attended mass at Holyrood in Aug. 1563; pledged by James Clarkson.

GILCHRISTON, WILLIAM
attended mass at Holyrood in Aug. 1563; pledged by James Arnot, a baxter, but there is no trace of Gilchriston as such in the muster or tax rolls.

GRAHAM, JOHN [cramer and draper]
his child baptised by a catholic priest in Nov. 1562; called before the council for upholding the mass in June 1563; pledged both Andrew Kennedy and Walter Scott in Oct. 1563 (see below); excommunicated July 1569 and banished from the town but, as the session complained in March 1575, he continued to frequent the burgh (*Edin. Recs.*, iii, 152, 162; MS Co. Recs., iv, fo. 243r; BGKE, fos. 12v, 49v).
B. 8 Jan. 1555; G. 24 April 1568; see his entry in the Q.P. list.

HAY, m. EDMUND [advocate and assessor]
a witness to the baptism of John Graham's child in Nov. 1562 (*Edin. Recs.*, iii, 153).
Assessed at £30 in 1565; an assessor 1576-8; the brother of Fr. John Hay, who referred to him in 1579 as a faithful catholic (*Catholic Narratives*, 146); he died in 1589 (Edin. Tests., 26 Jan. 1591).

HILL, BESSIE
attended mass at Holyrood in Aug. 1563; pledged by James Paterson.
The wife of Peter Thomson, Islay herald, who made B. 14 March 1559 (see her will made in Aug. 1572, Edin. Tests., 17 May 1574, and Thomson's entry in the Q.P. list).

HOPPRINGLE, DAVID apothecary
released from ward following a letter from the queen 21 June 1566 for marrying the daughter of Thomas Crichton, royal macer, by catholic rite (*Edin. Recs.*, iii, 215; MS Co. Recs., iv, fo. 151r; see also *RSS*, vi, 1929, 2486); the son of James Hoppringle, a member of the Seton council of 1559-60; given B. *gratis* by rt. of the provost, Preston of Craigmillar, 9 April 1568; assessed at 13s 4d in 1583; he died in 1593, leaving £554 net (Edin. Tests., 17 Feb. 1602).

INNES (ANIS), WILLIAM
excommunicated after being summoned before the session for breaking previous promises to renounce idolatry and attend communion in Feb. 1566 (*Canongate Bk.*, 38, 74).

JOHNSTON, AGNES
her illegitimate child was baptised in the chapel royal in 1566 (*Canongate Bk.*, 39); see Nicol Spens.

JOHNSTON, HELEN
a witness to the baptism of John Graham's child in Nov. 1562; attended mass at Holyrood in Aug. 1563, and pledged by her husband, Andrew Stevenson; the sister of Friar James Johnston of the Friars Preachers (Pt. Bk. King, i, fos. 118, 120; v, fo. 206); he was probably the friar who appeared before the justiciary court 10 Sept. 1563 for contravening the proclamation of Aug. 1561 (JC 19/2). For further details of Stevenson, who gained his burgess-ship through her, see his entry in the Q.P. list. She died in 1588; among her bequests was one of £20 to Edinburgh's poor, to be distributed by the kirk session (Edin. Tests., 21 July 1589).

KENNEDY, ANDREW merchant
attended mass at Holyrood in Aug. 1563; pledged by John Graham (see above). He was released from paying a burgh tax in 1564 as a pauper (*Edin. Accts.*, i, 48).

KENNEDY, JOHN [wright]
captured along with the ex-chaplain, James Tarbot, in April 1565 attending a private mass (Knox, *History*, ii, 143; *CSP Scot.*, ii, no. 171(1)).
B. 24 May 1555; see Q.P. list.

KERR, HENRY [merchant]
attended mass at Holyrood in Aug. 1563; pledged by James Watson.
The son of William Kerr, the bailie of the Seton council of 1559-60; he died in 1570 (Edin. Tests., 1 March 1571); he is probably the merchant assessed at £2 in 1565.

LAMB, JOHN [tailor]
excommunicated July 1569; the session complained 17 March 1575 that he, although still an excommunicate, was publicly frequenting the burgh (MS Co. Recs., iv, fo. 243r; BGKE, fo. 49v).
Made G. 27 June 1561, but he had been a tailor since at least 1552 (see Pt. Bk. King, iii, fo. 68).

LOCH, JOHN [furrier or skinner]
captured along with the ex-chaplain, James Tarbot, in April 1565 attending a private mass (*CSP Scot.*, ii, no. 171(1); given as 'Low' in Knox, *History*, ii, 143).
G. furrier 4 Sept. 1549; deacon of the skinners 1561-2; he died in Danzig in 1579, leaving £214 net (Edin. Tests., 9 March 1580).

LOCKHART, SIMON [wright in the Canongate]
his child baptised by catholic rite in 1565 (*Canongate Bk.*, 25; see *Broughton Court Bk.*, 96).

LOGAN, DAVID baxter
attended mass at Holyrood in Aug. 1563.
See his son's entry in the Q.P. list.

LYELL, JAMES
the session complained 17 March 1575 that he, although an excommunicate, was publicly frequenting the burgh (BGKE, fo. 49v).

McKIE, WILLIAM [ex-priest and schoolmaster]
convicted of saying the mass 13 June 1572, but he was executed for treason rather than for this (see his entry in the Q.P. list and cf. Sanderson, 'Catholic recusancy', 88).

MARJORIBANKS, BESSIE
present at the baptism of John Charteris's child in Dec. 1561; the wife of John Spottiswood (MS Co. Recs., iv, fo. 48v; Prot. Bk. King, iv, fo. 211); see below.

MARJORIBANKS, JAMES [ex-chaplain and notary]
excommunicated in 1568 or 1569 for refusing to deny the mass as a sacrifice for the dead; reconciled to the kirk 17 June 1574 (BGKE, fo. 10r).
Assessed as a man of law at £10 in 1565; see also *Edin. Recs.*, iii, 31; *Edin. Accts.*, i, 71; Pt. Bk. King, ii, fo. 2.

MOSSMAN, JOHN [notary, sheriff clerk]
convicted of attending the mass (*Canongate Bk.*, 74; see *Broughton Court Bk.*, 13; *Edin. Accts.*, i, 35).

MURRAY, CUTHBERT [merchant]
attended the mass at Holyrood in Aug. 1563; pledged by John Moscrop; excommunicated July 1569 but allowed to return to the burgh for eight days 6 Oct. 1570 (MS Co. Recs., iv, 243r, 264v). B. 31 Dec. 1555; G. 21 Jan. 1561; stented at £20 (1565), £3 (1581) and 20s (1583); he died in 1584, leaving £544 net (Edin. Tests., 20 Nov. 1592). See Q.P. list for both him and Moscrop.

OGLE, WILLIAM [notary and deputy director of Chancellory]
excommunicated July 1569; his servant, Robert Borthwick, was granted licence by the session to confer with him 2 Sept. 1574 to try to secure his conversion (MS Co. Recs., iv, fo. 243r; BGKE, fo. 17v). He died in May 1576 (see Edin. Tests., 25 May 1576; see also Prot. Bk. Guthrie, ii, fo. 136).

PATERSON, JOHN [causay maker, mason]
attended mass at Holyrood in Aug. 1563.
B. 25 April 1578 by rt. of w. Margaret, dr. of John Clarkson (see above); assessed at 5s in 1583.

PEACOCK, HENRY [tailor]
excommunicated July 1569; finally submitted to the kirk 12 May 1575 (MS Co. Recs., iv, fo. 243r; BGKE, fo. 55v).
A master tailor in the muster roll of 1558 (MS Co. Recs., ii, fo. 133v).

PINKERTON, CHRISTIAN
attended mass at Holyrood in Aug. 1563; the wife of James Roger.
See him and their sons in the Q.P. list.

PURVES, ALEXANDER [saddler]
excommunicated July 1569 for refusing to approve 'the word now trewlie prechit' and deny the efficacy of the mass as a sacrifice; reconciled 17 June 1574 (MS Co. Recs., iv, fo. 243r; BGKE, fo. 10r).
Made a master of his craft in 1555 (Smith, *Hammermen of Edinburgh*, 158); see Q.P. list.

RAMSAY, JANET
attended mass at Holyrood in Aug. 1563; the widow of Hector Blackadder, who was made B. & G. 7 Jan. 1550; she died in 1589 (Edin. Tests., 2 July 1590).

RAMSAY, MARGARET
a witness to the baptism of John Graham's child in Nov. 1562; the wife of James Lindsay (*Edin. Recs.*, iii, 153; Pt. Bk. King, ii, fo. 165).
Lindsay was a prominent member of the catholic faction in burgh politics in the 1560s; for further details of him see app. viii.

RUSSELL, ARCHIBALD [merchant]
one of the excommunicates who were allowed to return to the town briefly in Oct. 1570 (MS Co. Recs., iv, fo. 264v).
He appears, from the evidence of a customs roll of 1563, to have traded in a small way in skins, but was discharged from a burgh tax in 1566 (see MS Edinburgh Customs Accounts, E 71/30/12, fos. 32r, 47v, 51v; *Edin. Accts.*, i, 67).

SCOTT, sir JOHN schoolmaster [ex-chaplain and notary]
protected by the queen in 1564 and sheltered by Sir John Bellenden of Auchnoull and the laird of Fordel in 1566 (*Canongate Bk.*, 8, 11, 41, 74; see *Broughton Court Bk.*, 181-2, 298).

SCOTT, WALTER [slater]
attended the mass at Holyrood in Aug. 1563; pledged by John Graham (see above).
B. slater 5 March 1560; assessed at 5s in 1583.

SKENE, m. ALEXANDER [advocate]
called before the council 30 May 1561 for taking communion the previous Easter; put in the
tolbooth but released 16 June on the promise of good behaviour; excommunicated July 1569 (*Edin.
Recs.*, iii, 115, 117; MS Co. Recs., iv, fo. 243r).
Admitted to the Faculty of Advocates in 1554 (*Faculty of Advocates, 1532-1943*, 193); assessed at
£30 in 1565.

SMIBERT, WILLIAM [burgess of the Canongate]
his child baptised in the chapel royal in 1564 (*Canongate Bk.*, 9, 11; see *Broughton Court Bk.*,
186).

SMITH, GEORGE saddler
attended mass at Holyrood in Aug. 1563; excommunicated July 1569 (MS Co. Recs., iv, fo. 243r;
see also *RPC*, i, 216).
Made a master of the hammermen craft in 1555; the records of his craft report that he was executed
in the Castle in 1573, but he is not included in either of the lists of Castillians made when the Castle
fell (Smith, *Hammermen of Edinburgh*, 157, 174; see *Edin. Burgs.*, 456, for his son, George, who
was made B. 10 June 1586).

SPENS, NICOL [tailor]
his illegitimate child was baptised in the chapel royal in 1566 (*Canongate Bk.*, 39); assessed, as a
tailor, at £2 in 1583.

SPOTTISWOOD, JOHN [merchant]
excommunicated July 1569 (MS Co. Recs., iv, fo. 243r); he had been one of the members of the
assize in the Nicol Young case who had voted to convict all four of the defendants (Pitcairn, *Trials*,
i, 448); like Herbert Maxwell and James Lindsay, also members of the same assize, he was
subjected to some harassment by the council (*Edin. Recs.*, iii, 197); all three were members of the
catholic faction in the burgh, although Spottiswood seems to have been a relatively minor figure.
B. & G. 4 Oct. 1555; on the council 1555-6; assessed at £12 in 1565; he died in 1574, £226 in debt
(Edin. Tests., 27 Jan. 1576); one of his creditors was James Marjoribanks, who was probably
related to his wife, Bessie (see both above).
See Q.P. list for Spottiswood and for further details of Maxwell and Lindsay.

STEDMAN, ALEXANDER [merchant, burgess of the Canongate]
called a 'papist' by the session when he presented his child for baptism in 1566 (*Canongate Bk.*,
88). He was dead by 1569; see app. ix for his son, Charles, who was one of the Edinburgh
burgesses whose houses were demolished in 1572 (*Broughton Court Bk.*, 58, 67, 86).

STEINSON, sir JOHN schoolmaster and ex-chaplain
summoned before the session in May 1566 for refusing to take communion although he approved
the doctrine of the new church, and agreed to make his children attend its services (*Canongate Bk.*,
74).

TOD, BESSIE
attended mass at Holyrood in Aug. 1563; pledged by James Watson.
She was the wife of John Watson, skinner, who was probably the brother of James (Edin. Tests.,
27 April 1583); she was, therefore, related to Katherine Bryce (see above) by marriage.

TRENCH, ARCHIBALD [merchant]
denounced as a rebel, along with his wife, Janet Chalmer, for attending mass at Holyrood in Aug. 1563; pledged by Peter Douglas, who had renounced his burgess-ship after disputing the authority of one of the bailies of the Kilspindie council.
B. 25 Sept. 1550; given as a merchant in the muster roll of 1558 (MS Co. Recs., ii, fo. 131r); assessed at 5s in 1583.

WALLACE (VALLIS)
repented for marrying by catholic rite (*Canongate Bk.*, 74).

YOUNG, BESSIE
the wife of David Tod; present at the baptism of John Charteris's child in Dec. 1561 (MS Co. Recs., iv, fo. 48v).
Tod was made B. & G. 12 Sept. 1531 but had died before 1557 (Ab. Prot. Bk. King, v, no. 214).

YOUNG, HARRY baxter
attended mass at Holyrood in Aug. 1563.
B. 7 Dec. 1538; see the Q.P. list.

Appendix vii
King's men

ABERCROMBIE, ROBERT saddler
replaced John Richardson as deacon of his craft in June 1579 on the basis that he had served the king during the town's occupation, although he had left his apprentice, David Hamilton, behind to protect his goods and property (*Edin. Recs.*, iv, 110; BGKE, fo. 56r; see Richardson and Hamilton in Q.P. list).
A master of the hammermen craft in 1560 (Smith, *Hammermen of Edinburgh*, 173); G. 9 June 1570; on the council 1566-7; deacon of his craft 1576-80; assessed at £11 in 1583.

ACHESON, JOHN [merchant]
one of the Edinburgh merchants whose goods were held in France early in 1571; a bailie on the council of 1570-71 which was expelled by the queen's lords in June 1571; he continued as a bailie on the council in exile at Leith (*CSP Scot.*, iii, no. 703; see council lists). Not on the burgess roll although his son John was made B. & G. 22 April 1573; first appeared on the council in 1569; his wife was the sister of Patrick Bellenden of Stenness, made clerk of the coquet in Edinburgh in 1572 (Paul, *Scots Peerage*, ii, 64).

ACHESON, THOMAS in Morton, master assayer of the Mint
appointed master assayer of the Mint in place of James Mossman (see Q.P. list) 24 April 1572 (*RSS*, vi, 1576); on an assize in Leith 17 July 1572, which convicted George Wilkie and others of treason (JC 1/13; see Pitcairn, *Trials*, I, ii, 33f; see also *TA*, xii, 249).
B. by rt. of Archibald Stewart, bailie, 20 Jan. 1574; he was married to the daughter of Helen Acheson, the widow of William Birnie, whose second husband was Archibald Stewart (Edin. Tests., 31 May 1586; see Acheson and Stewart in Q.P. list).

ADAMSON, DAVID
he and John Adamson (see below) were apprehended by Grange, 29 April 1571; on an assize at Leith, 30 Nov. 1571, convicting John McHarg of slaughter (*Diurnal*, 209; JC 1/13, where he is described as a burgess).

ADAMSON, JOHN merchant
a bailie on the council of 1570-71 and one of the deputation sent to confer with Grange, 28 April 1571 (*Edin. Recs.*, iii, 285); he continued as a bailie on the council in exile at Leith and in the following year, 1572-3 (see council lists); he was one of the thirty Edinburgh burgesses denounced as rebels of the queen 18 Aug. 1571 and was forfeited for treason by the parliament of queen's lords held at Edinburgh later that month, while he attended the rival parliament of king's lords

held at the same time as a commissioner for the burgh (*Diurnal*, 239, 244; *CSP Scot.*, iii, no. 898); he also served on an assize in Leith 23 Feb. 1572 (JC 1/13).

There are a number of burgesses of this name on the roll; the most likely was made B. & G. as son of William A., 12 Feb. 1561, and was also probably the brother of William Adamson (see below); John was on the town council from 1570 almost without a break until 1584; his assessment in 1581 was £4.

ADAMSON, CAPTAIN JOHN

apprehended by Grange in full armour 29 April 1571 (*Diurnal*, 209).

Captain John A., B. by rt. of his wife, 17 Feb. 1575; he died in 1584, leaving £401 net (Edin. Tests., 9 Nov. 1584).

ADAMSON, WILLIAM [merchant]

lent the king's lords £1,000 which was repaid Oct. 1572 (*TA*, xii, 253).

B. & G. as son of William A., 6 July 1564; probably the brother of John Adamson (see above); on the council 1573-5 and 1578-80 (see council lists); assessed at £25 in 1581 and £6 13s 4d in 1583; his wife, Margaret Park, the sister of Alexander Park, one of the wealthiest of the burgh's merchants in the period, had died in 1570, leaving £3,500, most of it the Park legacy (Edin. Tests., 13 April 1570).

AIKENHEAD, JAMES

on the assize which convicted nine burgesses of being involved in the action at the Crags in June 1572 (JC 1/13, 9 Feb. 1573; see Pitcarin, *Trials*, I, ii, 40).

Not on the burgess roll although described as a burgess; probably the son of Thomas Aikenhead, skinner and craft councillor 1568-9 and after (see *Edin. Recs.*, iv, 469 and council lists).

AIKENHEAD, JOHN [merchant]

on the assize which convicted Grange and James Cockie of treason 3 Aug. 1573 (JC 1/13; Pitcairn, *Trials*, I, ii, 46).

The brother of Thomas Aikenhead; he died 22 Feb. 1575, leaving £577 net (Edin. Tests., 30 May 1584).

AIKMAN, JAMES

on the assize which convicted Grange and Cockie, 3 Aug. 1573 (JC 1/13; Pitcairn, *Trials*, I, ii, 46). There were two burgesses of this name, both with a £10 contribution in the 1565 roll; *either* the son and heir of Captain Walter Aikman (see below; *RSS*, vi, 1896; *RPC*, ii, 209) which is the more likely, *or* the son of James Aikman and Isobel Curror, who was charged with attending mass at Holyrood in 1563 (JC 1/12, 1 Oct. 1563; Pitcairn, *Trials*, i, 435; Edin. Tests., 20 Oct. 1573), and died in 1579 (Edin. Tests., 27 Jan. 1580).

AIKMAN, THOMAS [maltman]

on the assize which convicted Richard Smith and others of vithholding of Paisley Abbey, 23 July 1573 (JC 1/13; see Pitcairn, *Trials*, I, ii, 45).

B. 24 March 1561; £2 contribution in 1565 roll; 10s assessment in 1581; see also *Edin. Accts.*, i, 62.

AIKMAN, WALTER

captain of the regent's men of war; killed Aug. 1571 (*Diurnal*, 238; *Hist. King James VI*, 86); included in the indictments drawn up against John Newlands, Patrick Anderson and others (JC 26/1, 31 July and 3 Nov. 1573; see also *RSS*, vi, 1660, 1895, 1896; *TA*, xii, 331, 334; *RPC*, ii, 209). See also James Aikman (above), who was probably his son.

ARMSTRONG, ANDREW [merchant]

a captain of the regent's men of war who was killed in 1571 (*RPC*, ii, 100; Edin. Tests., 24 Dec.

1571). His testament was registered at Leith; it showed a net estate of £431. A prominent protestant activist in the 1560s; for further details, see app. v.

ARNOT, JOHN [merchant]
forfeited for treason by the parliament of queen's lords in Aug. 1571 (*Diurnal*, 244).
There are two merchants of this name in the 1565 roll, at £5, elder, and £20; the latter is the more likely, assessed at £10 in 1581 and £3 in 1583, on the council 1573-8 (see app. i).

BARBER, JOHN soldier [and tanner]
he and Cuthbert Ferguson (see below) killed 10 June 1572 (JC 1/13, 13 June 1572; Pitcairn, *Trials*, I, ii, 32; also the indictments against John Newlands and Patrick Anderson, JC 26/1, 31 July 1573 and 3 Nov. 1573).
B. tanner 23 April 1556.

BAWTIE, JOHN [merchant]
on assize in Leith, 23 Feb. 1572, which acquitted James Fiddes of remaining away from a raid (JC 1/13).
G. 2 May 1561; £15 contribution in 1565; he died in 1574, leaving £219 net (Edin. Tests., 18 Feb. 1575).

BLACKBURN, JOHN younger [merchant]
denounced as a rebel of the queen 18 Aug. 1571 (*Diurnal*, 239).
B. & G. *gratis* 11 Sept. 1573 ' for sa mekill det awand be baillies and counsall to him'; £5 contribution in 1565, assessed at 10s in 1581 and 30s in 1583; he died in 1587, leaving £292 (Edin. Tests., 18 July 1589); a prominent radical in the 1580s (see app. x).

BLYTH, ALEXANDER [merchant]
denounced as a rebel of the queen 18 Aug. 1571; on the assize which convicted the twenty-six who had been captured in the Crags action, 13 June 1572, and the assize dealing with Andrew Gray in Corstorphine, 22 July 1572 (*Diurnal*, 239; JC 1/13; see Pitcairn, *Trials*, I, ii, 32, 34f).
B. & G. 3 Jan. 1570; assessed at £2 in 1581 and 13s 4d in 1583.

BRADY, MUNGO [goldsmith]
on the assize which convicted Grange and Cockie, 3 Aug. 1573 (JC 1/13; Pitcairn, *Trials*, I, ii, 46; see also *TA*, xii, 279).
A craft councillor on the council of 1570-71 which was expelled by the queen's lords; assessed at 10s in 1583 stent; see also *Edin. Recs.*, iii, 282, 284-5.

BROWN, THOMAS [cordiner]
accused by the queen's lords 18 July 1571 of bringing the English into Scotland, along with Robert Cunningham, John Harwood (see below), and Mungo Fairlie (see Q.P. list) (*Memorials*, 176; Calderwood, *History*, iii, 113; but cf. *Diurnal*, 233, where he is given as Hew Brown). There was a merchant of this name, with a £20 contribution in 1565 and assessments of £9 in 1581 and £4 in 1583, but it is more likely that this is the protestant activist of the 1560s (see app. v).

BROWN, WILLIAM [merchant]
granted the escheat of the goods of Thomas Alexander (see Q.P. list), 2 June 1572; on the assize which convicted the twenty-six captured in the Crags action, 13 June 1572, and on the one which convicted a further nine burgesses of the same, 9 Feb. 1573 (*RSS*, vi, 1630; JC 1/13; see Pitcairn, *Trials*, I, ii, 32, 40).
B. & G. 31 Dec. 1555; £5 contribution in 1565 and assessed at 20s in the stents of 1581 and 1583; he died in Nov. 1583, leaving £286 net (Edin. Tests., 10 March 1585).

BRYSON, WILLIAM macer
granted the escheat of the goods of Matthew Aikman, John Clavie and Matthew Easton (see Q.P. list), 5 Jan. 1572 (*RSS*, vi, 1416); paid fee for July 1571 (*TA*, xii, 275; see also *CSP Scot.*, iv, no. 615).
B. & G. 30 Oct. 1561.

CARMICHAEL, JAMES
he and Thomas Redpath (see below) under sentence of forfeiture by the queen's lords, 13 Aug. 1571.
It is unlikely that this is the same Carmichael who was warned to appear at Leith 31 Jan. 1572 (see Q.P. list) as he had been a prominent conservative figure in the 1560s (see *Edin. Recs.*, iii, 142; Pitcairn, *Trials*, i, 448) and had not been on the council since his testimony to the de la Brosse inquiry early in 1560, despite appearing on Mary's leet of 1565 (see council lists and *De La Brosse Report*, 110). Although Redpath was a burgess, it is possible that Carmichael was not.

CARMICHAEL, JOHN younger of that ilk
captain of one hundred light horse (*TA*, xii, 360, 363f, 369; *RSS*, vii, 1629).
B. & G., light-horseman to the regent, *gratis*, at the request of his kinsman, George Douglas of Parkhead, provost, 4 Jan. 1577.

CHISHOLM, MICHAEL
denounced and forfeited for treason by the parliament of queen's lords, Aug. 1571, while he attended the rival parliament of king's lords as a commissioner for the burgh (*Diurnal*, 239, 244; *CSP Scot.*, iii, no. 898); a bailie of the council in exile at Leith, Oct. 1571-Sept. 1572 and also on the council of 1572-3 (see lists); granted the escheat of the goods of William Craik (see Q.P. list), 11 Dec. 1572 (*RSS*, vi, 1786); lent a total of £1,239 16s 11d, the largest of the loans by Edinburgh burgesses recorded in the treasurer's accounts, and was repaid in Oct. 1572 and Oct. 1573 (*TA*, xii, 254, 363).
B. & G. 13 March 1566; on the council continuously from 1567-78; £20 contribution in 1565 and £4 assessment in 1581; his first wife, Christian Adamson, had died in 1569, leaving £2,249 (Edin. Tests., 23 Feb. 1570).

CLARK, JOHN [apprentice] tailor
on Leith assize 22 July 1572 (JC 1/13).
B. tailor 12 Sept. 1572.

CLARK, WILLIAM tailor
on assize of 23 July 1573 (JC 1/13; see Pitcairn, *Trials*, I, ii, 45).
B. 8 Aug. 1564; he died in 1578, leaving £218 (Edin. Tests., 4 Dec. 1578).

COCK, JOHN tailor
on Leith assize 22 July 1572 (JC 1/13; see Pitcairn, *Trials*, I, ii, 34f).
B. *gratis* by rt. of office of Archibald Douglas of Kilspindie, provost, 16 Nov. 1562; assessed at 6s 8d in 1583.

COOPER, JOHN tailor
lent over £450 to the king's lords which was repaid Oct. 1572 and Oct. 1573 (*TA*, xii, 254, 363).
B. 3 Jan. 1559; G. before the decreet arbitral, 30 Aug. 1588; assessed at 13s 4d in 1583 stent; on the subscription list of 1562; his brother, James, actively supported the queen's party.

COURTAS, WILLIAM [skinner]
although he had appeared on the list of those warned to appear at Leith 31 Jan. 1572, he did

present himself the next day before the Court of Justiciary (see Q.P. list) and served on an assize in Leith 23 Feb. 1572 (JC 1/13).

B. 2 June 1553; G. by rt. of wife, 23 Sept. *1573* (see under Courtie in the burgess roll); assessed at 6s 8d in 1583 stent.

CRAIG, ANDREW [merchant]
denounced as a rebel of the queen and forfeited for treason by the parliament of queen's lords in Aug. 1571 (*Diurnal*, 239, 244).
G. 22 Feb. 1555; he died in Calais late in 1572, leaving £873 (Edin. Tests., 2 Dec. 1572); see also *Edin. Accts.*, i, 449; a wine importer.

CRAIK, LUCAS servant of m. John Sharp, advocate
granted escheat of goods of William Anderson (see Q.P. list), 3 Feb. 1573 (*RSS*, vi, 1844A).
B. 24 Sept. 1568; G. 16 Dec. *1573* for Sharp's good service to the town.

CRAWFORD, THOMAS of Jordanhill
a captain of the regent's men of war (*Diurnal*, 238; *Hist. King James VI*, 86); as he had charge of the area above the butter tron on the south side of the High Street during the siege of the Castle which 'will be uterlie wrackit incaiss he tak nocht gret heid and cure', the council agreed 19 Dec. 1572 to grant m. Robert Purves (see below) a free B. & G. (MS Guild Register, fo. 102v; *Edin. Burgs.*, 5n); also granted the escheat of goods of Gilbert Balfour of Westray (see Q.P. list), 16 Sept. 1571 (*RSS*, vi, 1288).

CREECH, JOHN [merchant]
denounced as a rebel of the queen 18 Aug. 1571; on the assize which convicted nine burgesses of being involved in the skirmish at the Crags, 9 Feb. 1573 (*Diurnal*, 239; JC 1/13).
Not in the burgess roll but he was made B. & G. in 1557 (*Edin. Accts.*, ii, 64); £20 contribution in 1565 roll; he died in 1578, leaving £2,293 (Edin. Tests., 23 March 1579).

CUNNINGHAM, ROBERT [merchant]
one of the four burgesses tried by the queen's lords 18 July 1571 for bringing the English into Scotland and maintaining the king's authority (*Diurnal*, 233; *Memorials*, 176; Calderwood, *History*, iii, 113); forced to hand over the evidents and accounts which he had in his possession as collector of the kirk's annual rents before he left the town in Sept. 1571 (*Memorials*, 190-91).
The protestant activist of the 1560s; see app. v for further details.

DAVIDSON, PATRICK herald
burgess; forfeited for treason by the parliament of queen's lords at Edinburgh in Aug. 1571 (*Diurnal*, 244).
£5 assessment in 1583 stent.

DAVIDSON, THOMAS [apothecary]
forfeited for treason by the parliament of queen's lords in Aug. 1571 (*Diurnal*, 244).
B. & G. 2 Oct. 1563; £30 contribution in 1565; on the council 1568-9; he died in Oct. 1574, leaving £3,777 (Edin. Tests., 18 June 1575).

DICK, GILBERT [merchant]
denounced as a rebel of the queen and forfeited for treason by parliament of queen's lords in Aug. 1571 (*Diurnal*, 239, 244).
£20 contribution in 1565 and assessments of £14 and £18 in the stents of 1581 and 1583; on the council 1569-70, 1578-80 and 1581-3; the net amount left in his testament, of over £10,593, confirms his position as one of the wealthiest of the burgh's merchants (Edin. Tests., 5 Jan. 1590); see app. x.

DOUGAL, JOHN merchant
on the assize which convicted nine burgesses of being involved in the skirmish at the Crags in June 1572 (JC 1/13, 9 Feb. 1573; see Pitcairn, *Trials*, I, ii, 40).
There were two merchants, elder and younger, of this name, but this is probably not the father, who was married to Isobel Kerr (see Edin. Tests., 2 June 1586 for his testament and ibid., 1 March 1570, for that of Henry Kerr, Isobel's father, who died in 1570); the son was married to Isobel Slater (see below), who lent over £770 worth of cloth and merchandise to the king's party; he was assessed at £8 and £14 in the stents of 1581 and 1583 after being made B. & G. 3 April 1573 as apprentice to John Robertson. He died in 1601, leaving £26,013 (Edin. Tests., 14 Dec. 1601); see app. x.

DOUGLAS, THOMAS [merchant]
granted the escheat of the goods of John Cranston, 1 Sept. 1571 (*RSS*, vi, 1256).
B. mt. 14 Nov. 1556.

DUNBAR, JOHN
on the assize which convicted Grange and Cockie, 3 Aug. 1573 (JC 1/13; Pitcairn, *Trials*, I, ii, 46).
B. & G. *gratis*, at the desire of the regent Moray, 15 Nov. 1567.

ELLIS, ANDREW merchant
on a Leith assize 23 Feb. 1572 and also the assize which convicted nine burgesses of being involved in the skirmish at the Crags, 9 Feb. 1573 (JC 1/13; see Pitcairn, *Trials*, I, ii 40).
B. as son and heir of James E., 16 March 1552; G. 11 May 1585; £2 contribution in 1565 and assessments of 30s and 20s in 1581 and 1583; cf. his brother, Alexander (see Q.P. list).

FERGUSON, CUTHBERT of the Canongate [merchant]
gave some financial assistance to the king's party early on in the wars (*TA*, xii, 274); among those forfeited for treason by the parliament of queen's lords in Aug. 1571 (*Diurnal*, 244), but killed in action less than two months later (*Memorials*, 195); his name was included in the indictments drawn up against John Newlands and Patrick Anderson and others (see Q.P. list and Edin. Tests., 22 Oct. 1572); he traded in French wine (*Broughton Court Book*, 96, 239).

FERGUSON, JOHN [elder?; merchant]
denounced as a rebel of the queen 18 Aug. 1571 (*Diurnal*, 239); used as a surety for the appearance of Alexander Guthrie (see Q.P. list), 28 Dec. 1571 (JC 1/13); described by Killigrew as 'a man well thought of by them of the best sort' when sent by Morton to plead the case of the Scottish merchants who had suffered from English pirates in June 1574 (*CSP Scot.*, iv, no. 787). Both the father and son have contributions, of £10 and £5, in the 1565 roll; it is more likely that this is the father who only died in 1582 (Edin. Tests., 13 Dec. 1582), although his wife died in Edinburgh in May 1572 (Edin. Tests., 22 July 1573); for the son, see app. x.

FINLAY (FEINEWEIN), LYELL (or LYOUNE) [merchant]
denounced as a rebel of the queen 18 Aug. 1571 (*Diurnal*, 239); on the assize which convicted nine burgesses involved in the Crags action, 9 Feb. 1573 (JC 1/13).
See *Edin. Accts.*, i, 64.

FORMAN, JAMES [merchant]
on the assizes which convicted nine burgesses of being involved in the Crags skirmish of June 1572 and Grange and Cockie for treason (JC 1/13, 9 Feb. 1573 and 3 Aug. 1573; Pitcairn, *Trials*, I, ii, 40, 46).
B. 7 Nov. 1554; G. by rt. of wife, Elspeth, dr. of David Tait, 23 Dec. 1573 (see also Thomas Tait, his brother-in-law, below); £5 contribution in 1565 and assessments of £5 and £4 in the stents of

1581 and 1583; on the council 1568-9, 1579-80 and 1582-3; he died, leaving a net £5,540, in 1585 (Edin. Tests., 22 Feb. 1586).

FULLARTON, ADAM [merchant]
elected captain of the Edinburgh band by the two hundred burgesses who fled to Leith late in June 1571 (*Hist. King James VI*, 86; *Diurnal*, 227); denounced as a rebel of the queen and forfeited by the parliament of queen's lords at Edinburgh in Aug. (*Diurnal*, 239, 244); an artillery platform erected on his house by the queen's lords became a target for the guns of the king's party at the start of the siege of the burgh in Sept. (*Hist. King James VI*, 94); granted the escheat of the goods of Thomas MacCalzean (see Q.P. list), 4 Feb. 1572 (*RSS*, vi, 1470); he had been dean of guild in the council of 1570-71 expelled by the queen's lords and continued as such on the council in exile in Leith and was re-elected for a third term in Sept. 1572; he also acted as president of the council Aug.-Sept. 1572 in the absence of the provost, James McGill (MS Guild Register, fos. 101v, 102r; see council lists). He was one of the commissioners appointed by the convention at Leith in Jan. 1572 to negotiate the details of the Leith agreement with the regent (*BUK*, i, 208; Calderwood, *History*, iii, 171). As well as provisioning his band, he also lent considerable sums to the king's lords, although only the repayment of £324 16s 4d in October 1573 has been recorded (*TA*, xii, 363; see also 247, 286); the testament of his wife, Marjorie Roger, who died in 1583, reveals almost £1,800 of outstanding debts, owed by the regents Moray, Lennox and Mar; it also shows an action still pending against unspecified persons for the spoiling of their goods and property and the demolition of their houses in the burgh during the time of the troubles to the value of 5,500 merks (Edin. Tests., 30 Jan. 1584). A leading protestant activist since 1559; see apps. v and x.

GALBRAITH, EDWARD [skinner]
on the assize which convicted the twenty-six captured in the action at the Crags (JC 1/13, 13 June 1572; see Pitcairn, *Trials*, I, ii, 32).
B. 26 Aug. 1564 (*Edin. Accts.*, ii, 185); G. by rt. of fr., 11 Sept. *1573*; assessed at £3 in 1583 stent; a deacon 1569-70 and a further three times between 1573 and 1583; on the council 1580-81; he died in 1597, leaving £1,820 (Edin. Test., 23 March 1598).

GALLOWAY, JOHN tailor
on Leith assize 22 July 1572 (JC 1/13; see Pitcairn, *Trials*, I, ii, 34f); his wife died of the plague in 1585, leaving £760 net (Edin. Tests., 17 July 1593).

GEDDES, ARCHIBALD [tailor]
on the assize which convicted nine burgesses of being involved in the Crags action (JC 1/13, 9 Feb. 1573; see Pitcairn, *Trials*, I, ii, 40).
B. 8 Nov. 1553; G. 16 Dec. *1573*; assessed at £5 in 1583 stent.

GEDDES, CHARLES [merchant]
denounced as a rebel of the queen 18 Aug. 1571 (*Diurnal*, 239); on a Leith assize 22 July 1572 (JC 1/13; Pitcairn, *Trials*, I, ii, 34f).
B. cramer 17 Aug. 1554; G. 14 April 1568; £10 contribution in 1565; assessments of £9 and £6 13s 4d in the stents of 1581 and 1583; he died in 1583, leaving £2,219 (Edin. Tests., 29 Nov. 1586); he had supported the Congregation during its second occupation of the burgh in 1559 until his capture early in November (*De La Brosse Report*, 107).

GIBSON, GEORGE clerk of the Court of Session
ordered to remain in the town along with Robert Scott and John Wallace (see below) in May 1571 (Calderwood, *History*, iii, 77).
B. & G. 17 April 1581 for good service to the town; on the subscription list of 1562.

GILBERT, JOHN [goldsmith]
on Leith assize 23 Feb. 1572 (JC 1/13).
G. 11 Oct. 1549; assessed at 13s 4d in 1583 stent; visitor of his craft 1555-6.

GOURLAY, ROBERT [merchant]
denounced as a rebel of the queen 18 Aug. 1571 (*Diurnal*, 239); lent £1,000 to the king's lords which was repaid in two instalments, in Oct. 1572 and Oct. 1573 (*TA*, xii, 253, 363); house threatened Feb. 1572 (*CSP Scot.*, iv, no. 149). £30 contribution in 1565; £10 assessment in 1583; on the council 1568-9 and appointed custumar of Edinburgh 22 Dec. 1573 (*RSS*, vi, 2247). He should be distinguished from the dependant of Châtelherault who was forfeited for treason by the king's lords (*CSP Scot.*, iii, no. 898; *Diurnal*, 245; *Memorials*, 186).

GRAY, ROBERT [merchant]
denounced as a rebel of the queen 18 Aug. 1571 (*Diurnal*, 239).
G. 1 March 1555; £40 contribution in 1565 and assessments of £18 in 1581 and £10 for his widow in 1583; his testament showed a net total of £4,714 10s (Edin. Tests., 6 Dec. 1583).

HAISTIE, NICOL cordiner
granted the escheat of the goods of two other cordiners, John Pillan and William Weir (see Q.P. list), 10 June 1572 (*RSS*, vi, 1641).
G. 24 Jan. 1561; assessed at 10s in 1583 stent.

HARLAW, JOHN [saddler]
both he and his father, William, hurt in the king's service; appointed master saddler to the king, 8 Sept. 1576 (*RSS*, vii, 694).
B. & G. 31 May 1583; assessed at 20s in 1583 stent; a radical in the 1580s (see app. x).

HARLAW, WILLIAM saddler
denounced as a rebel of the queen (*Diurnal*, 239); on the assize which convicted the twenty-six captured in the Crags action, 13 June 1572, and that which convicted nine more for the same offence, 9 Feb. 1573 (JC 1/13; see Pitcairn, *Trials*, I, ii, 32, 40); hurt in the king's service (*RSS*, vii, 694).
A protestant activist in the 1560s; see app. v.

HARWOOD, ALEXANDER [merchant]
denounced as a rebel of the queen 18 Aug. 1571 (*Diurnal*, 239).
£3 contribution in the 1565 roll.

HARWOOD (or HARRAT), JOHN [merchant]
one of the four burgesses put to an assize by the queen's lords 18 July 1571 for bringing the English into Scotland and maintaining the king's authority (*Diurnal*, 233; *Memorials*, 176; Calderwood, *History*, iii, 113).
G. 27 Dec. 1560; £40 contribution in 1565; assessments of £12 and £10 in the stents of 1581 and 1583; he was a member of the deposed council of 1570-71 and had been on the council since 1566; he returned to it in 1575 (see lists); his testament showed net assets of £2,009 (Edin. Tests., 6 Dec. 1587).

HAY, ALEXANDER clerk to the privy council
continued as such until replaced in June 1572 (*TA*, xii, 275, 324).
B. & G. *gratis* for service to the town, 25 Sept. 1573; £10 contribution in 1565.

HENDERSON, EDWARD commissary of Edinburgh
continued as such in Leith throughout (see MS Commissary Court, Register of deeds and protests,

4 May 1572; *Diurnal*, 295); see also the other commissaries, Clement Little and Alexander Sim, below.

An ex-prebendar of St. Giles' and master of the song school; on the subscription list of 1562; assessed at £30 in 1565; he died in 1579 (Edin. Tests., 6 Nov. 1579).

HENRYSON, ANDREW [merchant]
apprehended in full armour along with David Adamson, Captain John Adamson and five others by Grange 29 April 1571 (*Diurnal*, 209).
G. mt. 16 Oct. 1549; £30 contribution in 1565.

HOPE, EDWARD [merchant]
on the assize which convicted Grange and Cockie of treason 3 Aug. 1573 (JC 1/13; Pitcairn, *Trials*, I, ii, 46).
A prominent protestant figure over a long period; see apps. iv, v and x; see James Nicolson, his brother-in-law, below.

HOWIESON, JOHN [merchant]
only Edinburgh burgess on the Leith assize which dealt with the case of Henry Balmanno, 15 Feb. 1572 (JC 1/13; see Pitcairn, *Trials*, I, ii, 29).
B. mt. 13 Dec. 1560; G. 16 Sept. 1561; £15 contribution in 1565 and assessments of £16 and £10 in the stents of 1581 and 1583; his testament showed net assets of £8,852 (Edin. Tests., 15 Aug. 1586).

INGLIS, JAMES merchant
denounced as a rebel of the queen 18 Aug 1571 (*Diurnal*, 239); lent £500 to the king's lords and was partly repaid in Oct. 1572 and Oct. 1573 (*TA*, xii, 253, 363).
Not in the burgess roll but see his sons Thomas, B. & G. 11 Jan. 1592, and Cornelius, B. & G. 18 Jan. 1587; assessed at £33, the maximum in the 1583 tax; his wife, Margaret Leach, left a net £5,059 after her death in 1575 (Edin. Tests., 4 June 1576).

INGLIS, JAMES tailor
the council and deacons of crafts appealed to Grange that he, a 'workman of the king' who had been returning from Stirling, had been taken by Arthur Hamilton of Myreton 23 April 1571 (*Memorials*, 111); he set up a booth in Leith, despite objections from an inhabitant, Dec. 1571 (MS PC 1/6, fo. 45; see *RPC*, ii, 101) and his appointment as tailor to the king, first made in 1567, was confirmed in Aug. 1573 (*RSS*, v, 3180; vi, 2049; see also *TA*, xii, 278, 295, 308).

JAMIESON, MATTHEW [merchant]
denounced as a rebel of the queen 18 Aug. 1571 (*Diurnal*, 238).
B. & G. 12 Dec. 1566; assessed at £11 and £13 6s 8d in the stents of 1581 and 1583; his testament showed net assets of £4,007 when he died in 1585 (Edin. Tests., 1 Feb. 1587).

JOHNSTON, EDWARD [merchant]
denounced as a rebel of the queen 18 Aug. 1571 (*Diurnal*, 238).
B. & G. mt. 26 Dec. 1560; £10 contribution in 1565 and assessments of £10 and 50s in the stents of 1581 and 1583.

JOHNSTON, JOHN writer [and clerk to the privy council]
denounced as a rebel of the queen 18 Aug. 1571 (*Diurnal*, 239); he and Nicol Uddart delivered a letter from the Edinburgh kirk session to Knox 4 Aug. 1572 (*Memorials*, 254; see also *TA*, xii, 256, and *Diurnal*, 295).
Elected an elder in 1574; he had long links with the burgh's protestants; see app. v for further details.

JOHNSTON, ROBERT [merchant]
brother of the laird of Elphinstone; denounced as a rebel of the queen 18 Aug. 1571 (*Diurnal*, 239).
G. by rt. of wife Janet, elder dr. of John Stevenson, 22 Sept. 1570; he died in 1574 with net assets of
£896 (Edin. Tests., 9 Jan. 1576).

JOHNSTON, ROBERT [merchant]
denounced as a rebel of the queen 18 Aug. 1571 (*Diurnal*, 238).
B. & G. 10 Sept. 1560; £10 contribution in 1565.

KERR, JAMES [merchant]
on Leith assize 23 Feb. 1572 (JC 1/13).
Assessed, as a merchant, at 20s in 1581 and 10s in 1583.

KERR, ROBERT [merchant]
on Leith Assize 23 Feb. 1572 (JC 1/13).
This could be either the father or son of the same name, who had contributions of £15 and £20
respectively in 1565; the son was made B. & G. 30 April 1567 but did not serve on the council until
1575, whereas the father had been on the Kilspindie council of 1559-60 and continued his
municipal career up until 1580 (see app. v).

KINLOCH, DAVID [baxter]
forfeited for treason along with his son, Francis, by the parliament of queen's lords in Aug. 1571
(*Diurnal*, 244); the only Edinburgh burgess on a Leith assize dealing with Robert Thomson in
Dalmahoy (JC 1/13, 28 April 1572; see Pitcairn, *Trials*, I, ii, 30, where the date is wrongly given as
24th).
A leading baxter, who had often been in dispute with the council in the 1560s over the common
mills and taxation, the voting of assessors in council elections and over his own ineligibility as a
craft councillor (*Edin. Recs.*, iii, 120, 126, 263f; see also iv, 34); on the subscription list of 1562; he
died in 1591, leaving £54 net (Edin. Tests., 16 May 1595); see also app. x.

KINLOCH, FRANCIS [merchant]
forfeited along with his father for treason by the parliament of queen's lords in Aug. 1571
(*Diurnal*, 244).
B. & G. 18 Sept. 1579; assessed at £4 and 50s in the stents of 1581 and 1583.

KNOX, WILLIAM [merchant]
the spouse of Janet Richardson (see below); he lent the king's lords a sum in the region of £1,115
10s for cloth and other merchandise which was repaid by instalments in Oct. 1572 and Oct. 1573,
although £200 remained outstanding then (*TA*, xii, 254, 363); he died in Sept. 1572 and his
testament showed, at that date, debts owed to him of £1,211, most of them by the captains of the
regent's men of war; the net total was much lower, at £469, which agrees more readily with his
contribution of £5 in 1565 (Edin. Tests., 18 Nov 1572).
B. 7 July 1564.

LAING, NEIL keeper of the signet
paid his Michaelmas term pension in Nov. 1571 (*TA*, xii, 293).
£50 contribution in 1565 and on the subscription list of 1562; he died in 1586 (Edin. Tests., 10 Aug.
1586).

LAMBIE, ANDREW
captain of the regent's men of war and served on an assize in Leith 22 July 1572 (*Diurnal*, 238; *Hist.
King James VI*, 86; JC 1/13).
B. *gratis* by act of council 22 July 1567.

LAUDER, JAMES
tutor of Lauder and a burgess; forfeited for treason by the parliament of queen's lords in Aug. 1571 (*Diurnal*, 244).

LEACH, WILLIAM [tailor]
set up a booth in Leith in Dec. 1571, despite objections from an inhabitant (PC 1/6, fo. 45; see *Reg. Privy Council*, ii, 101).
B. & G. tailor, servant to the regent by his request, *gratis* 5 June 1568; 30s assessment in 1583 stent.

LEKPREVIK, ROBERT printer
moved his press from Edinburgh to St. Andrews in April 1571 (*Memorials*, 110; Melville, *Diary*, 26); but the provost of St. Andrews was instructed in April 1572 to stop him printing ballads and books although his licence was renewed three months later (*TA*, xii, 312, where he is given as Alexander (*sic.*); *RSS*, vi, 111, 2044).

LINDSAY, ANDREW keeper of the Edinburgh tolbooth
his own house as well as the council house was invaded by the Castilians 3 May 1571; he continued his duties in Leith (*TA*, xii, 390; *RPC*, ii, 131); he died of the plague in 1585 (Edin. Tests., 12 Dec. 1586).

LITTLE, CLEMENT commissary of Edinburgh
continued as such in Leith (see *Diurnal*, 295 and MS Commissary Court, Register of deeds and protests, which continues, after a break, from 5 Dec. 1571); he accompanied Tullibardine for a conference in the Castle with Grange in 1572 (Melville, *Memoirs*, 248).
The son of Clement Little and the brother of William (see below); on the subscription list of 1562, an assessor on the council in 1561, a commissioner to the General Assembly in 1563 and paid a £60 contribution in 1565 (*Edin. Recs.*, iii, 127, 175); he died in 1580, leaving £3,997 (Edin. Tests., 20 Feb. 1583).

LITTLE, WILLIAM [merchant]
elected as a bailie on the town council in exile at Leith in Oct. 1572 (see council lists); he had been a member of the council 1567-70. The brother of Clement Little; made B. & G. as one of the sons of umq. Clement L., 25 Sept. 1567; he and his mother paid a joint contribution of £30 in 1565 and he was assessed at £14 and £26 in 1581 and 1583.

LIVINGSTONE, DUNCAN [merchant]
dismissed by the queen's lords from his office of collector of the quots of testaments as a rebel of the queen 28 April 1572 (*Diurnal*, 295; see *RSS*, v, 1659; vi, 45).
B. & G. 13 Nov. 1550; assessed at £10 in 1565 and 20s in 1583; on the council 1553-4 and 1565-6 after being nominated by Mary; sub-collector of thirds for Lothian 1565-6 (*Thirds of Benefices*, xl).

McCARTNAY, JAMES writer
paid his pension for the Whitsuntide and Martinmas terms in 1572 and the Whitsuntide term in 1571 (*TA*, xii, 256).
£20 contribution in 1565.

McGILL, DAVID writer
he and his father, James McGill, were forfeited by the queen's lords 25 June 1571 (*Diurnal*, 227).
B. & G. *gratis*, son of James M., 25 Sept. 1555; £50 contribution in 1565.

McGILL, m. JAMES clerk register
the provost of the town council of 1570-71 deposed and expelled by the queen's lords, but he con-

tinued as provost of the council in exile at Leith and was re-elected in Oct. 1571 (see council lists); before the council was dismissed McGill had been harassed by the Castilians (*Memorials*, 113, 119, 136) and forfeited by the queen's lords along with his son, 25 June 1571 (*Diurnal*, 227); his house in Edinburgh was demolished, probably in Feb. 1572 (*ibid.*, 257; but cf. *Memorials*, 234; *CSP Scot.*, iv, no. 149); he continued throughout as clerk register (*TA*, xii, 256).
An important ally of the protestant party in the burgh throughout the 1560s; see app. v for further details.

MASON, JOHN
on Leith assize which convicted those captured in the Crags action (JC 1/13; 13 June 1572; see Pitcairn, *Trials*, I, ii, 32); described as a soldier.
Either a mason assessed at £3 in 1583 stent or a merchant assessed at £5 in both stents (see also his wife's testament, Janet Spottiswood, Edin. Tests., 21 June 1577).

MATHESON, JAMES [baxter]
on Leith assize 17 July 1572 (JC 1/13; see Pitcairn, *Trials*, I, ii, 33f).
B. baxter 6 June 1560; he died in 1576, leaving £592 (Edin. Tests., 29 Dec. 1576).

MENTEATH, WILLIAM bower
on the assize which convicted nine burgesses of being involved in the action at the Crags in June 1572 (JC 1/13, 9 Feb. 1573; see Pitcairn, *Trials*, I, ii, 40).
B. 10 March 1564; a craft councillor 1573-4).

MILLAR, JAMES writer and depute to the justice clerk
continued as such throughout; denounced as a rebel of the queen 18 Aug. 1571 (*TA*, xii, 282; *Diurnal*, 239).
See app. v for further details.

MORRIS, DAVID [merchant]
denounced as a rebel of the queen 18 Aug. 1571 (*Diurnal*, 239).
B. 30 March 1562; £10 contribution in 1565 and assessments of £24 and £33 in the stents of 1581 and 1583.

MORRISON, JOHN elder [merchant]
denounced as a rebel of the queen 18 Aug. 1571 (*Diurnal*, 239).
B. & G. Aug. 1537; £40 contribution in 1565; he died at Dysart in May 1573, leaving net assets of £2,290; among the debts he owed was £8 to the town of Edinburgh as two months' wages for a man of war in the time of troubles (Edin. Tests., 16 Dec. 1573).

MORRISON, JOHN younger [merchant]
denounced as a rebel of the queen 18 Aug. 1571 (*Diurnal*, 239).
B. & G. mt. 27 Sept. 1570; on the council 1574-5 and 1581-3; assessed at £25 in 1583 and £34 in 1581, although this was reduced to £20 on appeal.

MOSSMAN, JOHN [goldsmith]
on Leith assize 22 July 1572 (JC 1/13; see Pitcairn, *Trials*, I, ii, 34f).
B. goldsmith 22 Sept. 1564; a visitor 1555-6 and deacon 1557-8; assessed at £2 in 1583 stent; probably the younger brother of James Mossman (see Q.P. list).

MUIR, JOHN [tailor]
granted the escheat of the goods of Alexander Ramsay, tailor (see Q.P. list), 3 June 1572 (*RSS*, vi, 1641).
B. & G. tailor 12 Nov. 1569.

W

MURRAY, WILLIAM valet to the king
granted escheat of the goods of John Wilson, maltman (see Q.P. list), 9 Jan. 1572 (*RSS*, vi, 1423).
B. & G. *gratis* 28 June 1587.

NAPIER, ANDREW [merchant]
brother of Archibald Napier of Merchiston; on the assize which convicted Grange and Cockie 3
Aug. 1573 (JC 1/13; Pitcairn, *Trials*, I, ii, 46).
Assessed at 40s and 20s in the stents of 1581 and 1583; see also *Edin. Recs.*, iv, 469).

NAPIER, WILLIAM of Wrighthouses [merchant]
lent £1,000 to the king's lords which was repaid in two instalments in Oct. 1572 and Oct. 1573; on
the assize which convicted Grange and Cockie (*TA*, xii, 253, 363; JC 1/13, 3 Aug. 1573; Pitcairn,
Trials, I, ii, 46).
B. & G. by rt. of his fr., Alexr. Napier, 8 Sept. 1570; assessed at £33 in the 1583 stent; his father
had been made B. & G. by rt. of his wife, the dr. of Clement Little, in 1553, so William was the
first cousin of Clement and William Little (see above); he was on the council intermittently after
1574 and an elder in 1573.

NEILL, JOHN skinner
granted his burgess-ship 13 Feb. 1573 because of his service to the king in Leith, although he had
been refused it by right of his father, Richard Neill, who had remained in Edinburgh (see Q.P. list;
MS Guild Reg., fo. 103v; *Edin. Burgs.*, 5n). The son died in debt in 1575 (see Edin. Tests., 22 June
1580).

NICOLSON, JAMES [writer]
on the assize which convicted the twenty-six captured in the Crags action (JC 1/13, 13 June 1572;
see Pitcairn, *Trials*, I, ii, 32). He had close links with the burgh's protestant party (see app. v); an
elder in 1573.

NICOLSON, JOHN [cordiner]
on two assizes in Leith as well as the assize dealing with the withholding of Paisley Abbey (JC
1/13, 13 June 1572, 17 July 1572, 23 July 1573; see Pitcairn, *Trials*, I, ii, 32, 33f, 45).
Both father and son were cordiners, made B. 29 Jan. 1561 and 8 Nov. 1564; the father died in 1574,
leaving net assets of £104 (Edin. Tests., 19 Jan. 1575) and the son was assessed at 50s in the stent of
1583; the son was deacon of his craft three times between 1575 and 1582 and probably also 1570-
71.

NYMMILL, JOHN [merchant]
on the assize of 9 Feb. 1573 which convicted nine burgesses of being involved in the Crags action
(JC 1/13; see Pitcairn, *Trials*, I, ii, 40); he had been held in the Castle in April 1571 (*Memorials*,
111).
B. & G. 16 Oct. 1549; a £60 contribution in 1565 and an assessment of £3 on his widow in 1581,
although his testament only reveals a net £456 (Edin. Tests., 19 April 1581).

PRESTON, JOHN [merchant]
a commissioner for the town at the parliament of the king's lords in Edinburgh in Jan. 1573 (*CSP
Scot.*, iv, no. 515); acted as witness to the testament of James Nicol in June 1572 at Leith (Edin.
Tests., 4 May 1573). Preston had had a long and distinguished municipal career stretching back to
1549; he had been a member of the council of 1570-71 expelled from the burgh; he reappeared on
the council 1573-5; he had been on both Marian leets in the 1560s.
B. & G. 17 Jan. 1549; £40 contribution in 1565 and assessed at £10 and £5 in the stents of 1581 and
1583; see app. x.

PURVES, m. ROBERT furrier
acted as the agent for Captain Thomas Crawford (see above) in collecting the wages for his men of
war in April 1572; made B. & G. *gratis*, 19 Dec. 1572, at Crawford's request (*TA*, xii, 252; MS
Guild Reg., fo. 102v; *Edin. Burgs.*, 5n).
Assessed, as a merchant, at £5 in both stents of 1581 and 1583; he died in 1594, leaving a net £307
(*Edin. Recs.*, 18 May 1594).

RAMSAY, WILLIAM [merchant]
denounced as a rebel of the queen 18 Aug. 1571; on the assize which convicted Grange and Cockie
(*Diurnal*, 239; JC 1/13, 3 Aug. 1573; Pitcairn, *Trials*, I, ii, 46).
B. & G. 30 May 1559; £3 contribution in 1565 and assessments of 10s and 13s 4d in the stents of
1581 and 1583.

RANNALD, JAMES draper
denounced as a rebel of the queen 18 Aug. 1571 (*Diurnal*, 239).
Assessed, as a tailor, at 30s in the 1583 stent; see app. x.

REDPATH, THOMAS [merchant]
forfeited for treason by parliament of queen's lords in Aug. 1571 (*Diurnal*, 237, 244).
B. mt. 26 May 1564; he should be distinguished from the prominent craftsman of the same name
who died in 1567 (see app. v; *Edin. Recs.*, iii, 31, 208, and the council lists).

RICHARDSON, JANET
the widow of William Knox (see above); was repaid her husband's loans to the king's lords by
instalment in Oct. 1572 and Oct. 1573 (*TA*, xii, 254, 363).

RICHARDSON, m. ROBERT [treasurer]
repaid £660 in Oct. 1573 (*TA*, xii, 363).
B. *gratis* 28 Feb. 1554; on the subscription list of 1562.

ROSS, JAMES [merchant]
repaid £133 6s 8d in Oct. 1573 (*TA*, xii, 363).
G. 11 April 1567; £40 contribution in 1565 and assessments of £20 and £20 5s in the stents of 1581
and 1583 are confirmed by the net £7,526 which he left on his death in 1588 (Edin. Recs., 2 Sept.
1588); on the council without a break 1573-9.

RUSSELL, MUNGO (or KENTIGERN) [merchant]
denounced as a rebel of the queen Aug. 1571 (*Diurnal*, 239); lent £590 to the king's lords which
was repaid in Oct. 1572 (*TA*, xii, 254); a bailie of the town council in exile at Leith, Oct. 1571-
Sept. 1572 and re-elected for the following year; he had been on the deposed council of 1570-71
(see council lists for his career after 1573).
His burgess-ship is not recorded in the roll, but he was made B. & G. 13 March 1573 during his
second term as bailie (MS Guild Reg., fo. 104r); £20 contribution in 1565 and assessments of £25
and £33 in the stents of 1581 and 1583; his wife, who died of the plague in 1585, left £4,139 (Edin.
Tests., 28 Feb. 1587). See Q.P. list for his servant, William Yule, who was probably instructed by
his master to remain in the town.

SANDILANDS, PATRICK [tailor]
on the assize which convicted those captured in the Crags action in June 1572 (JC 1/13, 13 June
1572; see Pitcairn, *Trials*, I, ii, 32).
B. 22 April 1562, tailor (*Edin. Accts.*, ii, 149); G. before the decreet arbitral, 22 March 1588;
assessed at 20s in the 1583 stent.

SCARLETT, JOHN mason
deceased; made trenches for the siege of the Castle in 1573 (*RSS*, vi, 1975).
B. 13 Feb. 1568.

SCOTT, ROBERT clerk of the Court of Session
he was ordered to remain in Edinburgh by James McGill, the clerk register, to preserve the register books of the Court of Session for the duration of the troubles along with George Gibson and John Wallace; all three were warned not to act in an official capacity or attempt to leave the burgh by Grange in May 1571 (*RPC*, ii, 138; *Memorials*, 123; Calderwood, *History*, iii, 77; *TA*, xii, 256). His name appeared on the contribution list of 1562 and he made a contribution of £66 13s 4d in 1565; he died in 1592 (see Edin. Tests., 23 Aug. 1592).

SEGGAT, ALEXANDER
lent £350 to the king's lords, which was repaid in Oct. 1572 (*TA*, xii, 254). Although he was a burgess of the Canongate, he was assessed at £5 in the Edinburgh tax roll of 1583.

SEINYEOR, ARCHIBALD [merchant]
on the assize which convicted those captured in the action at the Crags (JC 1/13, 13 June 1572; see Pitcairn, *Trials*, I, ii, 32).
But see his entry in the Q.P. list.

SIM, ALEXANDER commissary of Edinburgh
continued as such, apparently throughout (see MS Commissary Court, Register of deeds and protests, 4 May 1572; *Diurnal*, 295).
An assessor on the council of 1562-3; on the subscription list of 1562; £40 contribution in 1565; he died in 1584 (see Edin. Tests., 5 July 1587); see also Clement Little and Edward Henderson, above.

SIM, JOHN [merchant]
a bailie on the council of 1570-71, but refused permission by the queen's lords 12 May 1571 to go to the regent (*Memorials*, 120).
£5 contribution in 1565; assessed at 20s in 1583; although there are more than one of this name on the roll, he was probably made B. & G. 12 Nov. 1561, was on the council 1564-7, after recommendation by Mary in one instance, and again 1580-82 (see council lists); he was the cousin of Alexander Sim (Pro. Bk. Guthrie, iii, fo. 124).

SINCLAIR, ANDREW
burgess; forfeited for treason by the parliament of queen's lords in Aug. 1571 (*Diurnal*, 244).

SLATER, ANDREW [merchant]
denounced as a rebel of the queen 18 Aug. 1571 (*Diurnal*, 239); a bailie of the council in exile, Oct. 1571-Sept. 1572; he petitioned the council in Aug. 1574 for repayment of £750 raised by John Adamson and him to finance men of war at Leith (*Edin. Recs.*, iv, 22).
A prominent protestant activist over a long period; see apps. v and x.

SLATER, ISOBEL
lent £770 in cloth and merchandise to the king's lords and was repaid in two instalments, in Oct. 1572 and Oct. 1573 (*TA*, xii, 254, 363); she was by then the wife of John Dougal (see above), but her first husband was James McCartnay, a bailie of the 1570-71 council until his death in Feb. 1571; he left a net £2,255 to his wife, son and two daughters; the two executors of his estate were his wife and Robert Gourlay, another of those who gave financial support to the king's party (see above and Edin. Tests., 18 Dec. 1572).

SMITH, JOHN cramer
on the Leith assize of 17 July 1572 (JC 1/13; see Pitcairn, *Trials*, I, ii, 33f).
B. 21 Oct. 1569; given as a draper in the muster roll of 1558 (MS Co. Recs., ii, 129r).

SOMERVILLE, THOMAS [merchant]
on the assize which convicted those captured in the Crags action, 13 June 1572 (JC 1/13; see Pitcairn, *Trials*, I, ii, 32).
B. 17 April 1562, mt. (*Edin. Accts.*, ii, 149); a commissioner to the General Assembly in March 1571 (*Memorials*, 96).

STRANG, RICHARD advocate
forfeited for treason by the parliament of queen's lords in Aug. 1571 (*Diurnal*, 244).
B. & G. mt. (?), 11 Oct. 1549; on the subscription list of 1562; a £40 contribution as one of the 'men of law' in 1565; frequently been an assessor on the council as well as a commissioner for the burgh to the Reformation parliament of 1560 and to the General Assembly in 1566 (*Edin. Recs.*, iii, 71, 266).

TAIT, THOMAS [merchant]
wounded in action against the forces of the queen's party led by John Newlands, probably in June 1572 (see the indictment against Newlands, JC 26/1, 3 Nov. 1573, and the collective one against Patrick Anderson and others, ibid., 31 July 1573).
B. & G. 16 Dec. *1573*; assessed at £5 and 26s 8d in the stents of 1581 and 1583; he died in 1583, leaving a net £159 (Edin. Tests., 2 Feb. 1587).

THORNTON, GILBERT writer to the signet
denounced as a rebel of the queen 18 Aug. 1571; granted the escheat of the goods of Alexander Job (see Q.P. list), 16 Jan. 1572 (*Diurnal*, 239; *RSS*, vi, 1437).
B. & G. by rt. of William Stewart, his father-in-law (see Q.P. list), 20 Feb. 1571; married to Katherine Stewart and died in 1579 (see Edin. Tests., 13 March 1581).

TOWERS, WILLIAM
burgess; on Leith assize 23 Feb. 1572 (JC 1/13).

TRENCH (TRINSS), THOMAS flesher
killed by forces of the queen's party in the action at the Crags in June 1572 (JC 1/13; Pitcairn, *Trials*, I, ii, 32).
B. 1 March 1566.

TURNET, PETER [skinner]
forfeited for treason by the parliament of queen's lords in Aug. 1571; he set up a booth in Leith in Dec. 1571 (*Diurnal*, 244; PC 1/6, fo. 45; see *RPC*, ii, 101).
A deacon 1559-60 and a craft councillor 1561-2, but he had been in dispute with the council over the voting rights of the crafts in elections (*Edin. Recs.*, iii, 54, 123); on the contribution list of 1562; assessed at 10s in 1583 stent.

UDDART, ALEXANDER [merchant]
on the assize which convicted Grange and Cockie 3 Aug. 1573 (JC 1/13; Pitcairn, *Trials*, I, ii, 46).
B. & G. 3 July 1566; £20 contribution in 1565 and assessed at £15 in 1583; he had been on the council 1564-70, once on the recommendation of Mary, and reappeared on it intermittently between 1573 and 1582. He died in 1597, leaving £11,991 net (Edin. Tests., 22 June 1597); see app. x.

UDDART, NICOL [merchant]
one of the Edinburgh merchants whose goods were held in France early in 1571; his house was one
of those burned down by the queen's lords in Feb. 1572; he conveyed a letter from the Edinburgh
kirk session to Knox in St. Andrews 4 Aug. 1572 (*CSP Scot.*, iii, no. 703; iv, 149; *Diurnal*, 258,
288; *Memorials*, 234, 254); he had acted as the major money broker for the council in exile; the
total amount lent by him was in some dispute, but eventually a figure of £3,600 was agreed upon
in December 1573 which the town met by setting the common mills in tack to him for seven years
(MS Co. Recs., v, fos. 7v-10r); the sum involved was almost three times as great as the largest loan
made to any of the regents (cf. Michael Chisholm).
B. & G. 14 Sept. 1563; he was assessed at £30 in 1565 and at the top rate of £33 in 1581 and 1583;
he had been the treasurer of the deposed council of 1570-71 and reappeared on it 1574-6; his father
was Thomas Uddart, the dean of guild in the unpopular Seton council of 1559-60, who had died at
Veere in 1569 (Edin. Tests., 13 May 1569, 4 Sept. 1570).

VAUS, DAVID [in Leith]
lent £500 to the king's lords and repaid in Oct. 1572 (*TA*, xii, 253; see *CSP Scot.*, iii, no. 192; *Edin.
Recs.*, iv, 169).

VAUS, THOMAS [merchant]
on the assize of 9 Feb. 1573, which convicted nine burgesses of being involved in the Crags action
(JC 1/13; see Pitcairn, *Trials*, I, ii, 40).
B. mt. 29 April 1558; G. 8 July 1561; £15 contribution in 1565 and assessments of £12 and £10 in
1581 and 1583.

WALKER, MURDO [mason]
set up a booth in Leith in Dec. 1571 despite objection from an inhabitant (PC 1/6, fo. 45; see *RPC*,
ii, 101).
B. mason 14 Nov. 1556; deacon 1561-2 and 1570-71.

WALLACE, ADAM [merchant]
on a Leith assize 30 Nov. 1571 (JC 1/13; see David Adamson, above).
B. mt. 3 June 1564; G. 9 Sept. 1570; assessed at £10 and £4 in 1581 and 1583.

WALLACE, JOHN clerk of the Court of Session
ordered to remain in the town with Robert Scott and George Gibson (see above), but not to act in
his official capacity (*Memorials*, 123; Calderwood, *History*, iii, 77).
B. & G. *gratis* for good service to the town, 3 Nov. 1556; on the subscription list of 1562 and made
a contribution of £30 in 1565; he died in Edinburgh late in 1572; his testament complained of the
'greit chargis' made on him during the troubles which forced his wife to sell or pledge her jewels
and valuables (see Edin. Tests., 11 Feb. 1575).

WATSON, JOHN merchant
on three assizes in Leith (JC 1/13, 23 Feb. 1572, 13 June 1572, 22 July 1572) as well as the assize
which convicted nine burgesses of being involved in the Crags action 9 Feb. 1573 (see Pitcairn,
Trials, I, ii, 32, 34-5, 40).
£5 contribution in 1565 and an £8 assessment in 1581; he died in 1582, leaving a net £656 (Edin.
Tests., 24 Oct. 1582).

WATSON, ROBERT [merchant]
replaced as custumar of Edinburgh by Cuthbert Ramsay (see Q.P. list), 20 July 1571 (*Diurnal*, 234;
but see *Exch. Rolls*, xx, 98, which show that he handed in his accounts for the period 1567-Aug.
1572 on 13 Oct. 1572); forfeited for treason by the parliament of the queen's lords in Aug. 1571
(*Diurnal*, 244).

A prominent protestant activist in the 1560s; see app. v for further details.

WEIR, DAVID [skinner]
on the assize which convicted those captured in the Crags action (JC 1/13, 13 June 1572; see Pitcairn, *Trials*, I, ii, 32).
B. 14 May 1557.

WIGHT, JOHN cramer
on a Leith assize 22 July 1572 (JC 1/13; see Pitcairn, *Trials*, I, ii, 34-5).
B. 23 Nov. 1566; G. 21 May 1577; assessed at £4 and £3 6s 8d in 1581 and 1583.

WILSON, JOHN merchant
on the assize of 9 Feb. 1573 which convicted nine burgesses of being involved in the Crags action (JC 1/13; see Pitcairn, *Trials*, I, ii, 40). There are a number of this name on the burgess roll, two on the 1565 roll and three on the 1583 roll.

WILSON, JOHN
on the same assize of 9 Feb. 1573.

WILSON, MICHAEL
on Leith assize 23 Feb. 1572 (JC 1/13).

YORSTON, WILLIAM [merchant]
on Leith assize 23 Feb. 1572 (JC 1/13).
B. & G. 30 Oct. 1561; assessed at 30s in the 1583 stent.

YOUNG, JAMES [cutler]
set up a booth in Leith in Dec. 1571 (PC 1/6, fo. 45; see *RPC*, ii, 101); on the assize which convicted Grange and Cockie (JC 1/13, 3 Aug. 1573; Pitcairn, *Trials*, I, ii, 46).
A prominent protestant activist in the 1560s; see app. v for further details.

Appendix viii
Queen's men

ABERCROMBIE, m. ANDREW
recruited John Moon, Marian agent (*CSP Scot.*, iii, no. 519).
B. & G. 16 July 1550.

ABERCROMBIE, DAVID [baxter]
one of the forty-five who entered pledges 17 Aug. 1573 (JC 1/13).
B. baxter 27 July 1570.

ACHESON, HELEN
widow of William Birnie; she and her second husband, Archibald Stewart, were involved in the
transfer and loan of money and jewels to Grange early in 1571 (*CSP Scot.*, iii, nos. 495, 638; iv,
no. 728); when she died in 1586, leaving a net £10,496, she was still owed £758 by Grange (Edin.
Tests., 31 May 1586); see Stewart and William Aikman (below).

ACHESON, JOHN saddler
summoned to appear at Leith 31 Jan. 1572 (*Memorials*, 219; wrongly transcribed in Dalyell ed.,
314, as 'Hutchesone'; see Advocates MS, fo. 238r).

ADAMSON, HEW
summoned to appear at Leith 31 Jan. 1572 (*Memorials*, 220).

ADAMSON, JAMES writer
summoned to appear at Leith 31 Jan. 1572 (*ibid.*, 220).

ADAMSON, JOHN smith outside the West Port
composition for taking part (*TA*, xiii, 345).

ADAMSON, JOHN younger [merchant]
charged with treasonably assisting the rebels 13 Aug. 1573 (JC 1/13; Pitcairn, *Trials*, I, ii, 47);
remission of £33 6s 8d granted for taking part and supplying victuals 18 Aug. 1573 (*RSS*, vi, 2109;
TA, xii, 266); called before the session 23 Dec. 1574 for remaining although he did not bear
armour, watch or ward, or approve their acts (BGKE, fos. 35r, 36v). B. & G. 12 Jan. 1571.

ADAMSON, WILLIAM writer
summoned along with John Adamson, younger, 23 Dec. 1574 for the same offence (ibid., fos. 35r,
36v).

AIKMAN, JAMES in the Over Bow [merchant]
summoned to appear at Leith 31 Jan. 1572 (*Memorials*, 219; wrongly transcribed in Dalyell ed., 315, as 'N. Bowe'; see Advocates MS, fo. 238). There are two merchants of this name in the 1565 roll, both assessed at £10, but it is likely that he was the son of James Aikman and Isobel Curror, who was charged with attending mass at Holyrood in 1563 (see Edin. Tests., 20 Oct. 1573 and app. vi); he died in 1579 (Edin. Tests., 27 Jan. 1580); but see his namesake in the K.P. list.

AIKMAN, MATHEW apothecary
summoned to appear at Leith 31 Jan. 1572 (*Memorials*, 219); at the horn and goods escheated 5 Jan. for assisting, fortifying, subscribing bands and entering into battle; remission granted 2 Aug. 1577 for taking part and other offences (*RSS*, vi, 1416; vii, 1122).
B. & G. 17 Sept. 1567; he died in 1582, leaving a net £20 (Edin. Tests., 13 Feb. 1584).

AIKMAN, WILLIAM [merchant]
'well-known to Mr. Secretary'; the factor of William Birnie, whose widow, Helen Acheson, petitioned for the return of 'great sums of money' which Aikman still owed (*CSP Scot.*, iii, nos. 390, 495). Mt. 6 March 1556. See also Sebastian Danelour (below).

ALDINSTOUN, HENRY baxter
Grange complains to Killigrew that those who remained in the town, including him, were being forced to submit to the session, Sept. 1572 (Calderwood, *History*, iii, 225; *Memorials*, 275, where given as 'Andersone'); one of the ninety-two penitents who gave in their supplications to the session Nov. 1572 (SP 52/23, fo. 254r); enters pledge 17 Aug. 1573 (JC 1/13).
B. baxter, servant to David Logan, 21 April 1569; see Logan also (below).

ALEXANDER, JOHN [tailor]
gives in supplication to the session April 1574 for remaining in the town (BGKE, fo. 1v).
B. & F. tailor, 20 Nov. 1565; he died in 1575, leaving £132 net (Edin. Tests., 19 Nov. 1589).

ALEXANDER, THOMAS merchant [bookseller]
goods escheated after his conviction for withholding the burgh and subscribing bands 2 June 1572; remission granted 8 June 1573 for taking part and other offences (*RSS*, vi, 1630, 1980).
B. bookseller 19 March 1561; G. 30 April 1567.

ALEXANDER, THOMAS tailor
summoned to appear at Leith 31 Jan. 1572 (*Memorials*, 219).
13s 4d in 1583 roll.

ALEYZART, FIRMIAN cordiner
Frenchman and burgess, granted remission 1 Jan. 1574 for remaining, taking part and other offences (*RSS*, vi, 2252).
30s in 1583 roll; he died in 1584, leaving £1,246 net (Edin. Tests., 16 Jan. 1585); he was almost certainly the 'French sutar' summoned to appear at Leith 31 Jan. 1572 (*Memorials*, 220).

ALLAN, ADAM merchant
summoned to appear at Leith 31 Jan. 1572 (*Memorials*, 219); failed to appear before the Court of Justiciary 13 Aug. 1573; granted remission for remaining, taking part and other offences (£33 6s 8d) on 18 Aug. (JC 1/13; *RSS*, vi, 2091; *TA*, xii, 266).
A catholic recusant in the 1560s; see app. vi for further details.

ALLAN, DAVID baxter
submitted to session 9 Dec. 1574 for remaining during a 'greit part' of the burgh's occupation although he did not watch or ward or approve their acts (BGKE, fo. 33v).

ALLAN, ROBERT
convicted 13 June 1572 of treasonably taking up arms; one of those captured after the skirmish on
10 June (JC 1/13; see *CSP Scot.*, iv, no. 363(1); *Diurnal*, 265).
Two of this name in 1583 roll; a fishman, 5s; a brewster, 5s (also in 1581 roll at 10s).

ANDERSON, JOHN flesher
summoned to appear at Leith 31 Jan. 1572 (*Memorials*, 220).
10s in 1583 roll.

ANDERSON, PATRICK maltman
granted remission of £10 for taking part (*TA*, xii, 267).

ANDERSON, PATRICK smith dwelling at the Castlehill
one of the forty-seven inhabitants accused 31 July 1573 of conspiring between April and June 1571
to the number of a thousand men to expel a 'greit part' of the burgesses and inhabitants from the
burgh, of depriving the provost and bailies of their offices, assembling weekly to the number of
two thousand men and entering into battle, killing Adam Wauchope (June 1571), William Shaw
and Captain Michael Wemyss at the head of the Canongate (June 1571), soldiers under the
command of Captain Walter Aikman (Aug. 1571), Cuthbert Ferguson (Oct. 1571), Methven
(March 1572) and John Barber, soldier (June 1572); all to appear under pain of rebellion and
horning on 26 Aug. (JC 26/1); continued 10/11 Aug. (ibid.), and finds pledge on 17 and 26 Aug.
(JC 1/13).
A master of the hammermen craft in 1560 (Smith, *Hammermen of Edinburgh*, 174); he died in
1579, leaving £24 net (Edin. Tests., 16 March 1579).

ANDERSON, WILLIAM candlemaker
summoned to appear at Leith 31 Jan. 1572 (*Memorials*, 219); goods escheated and at the horn for
failing to find surety for involvement in the killing of Shaw and Wemyss (see previous entry) 3
Feb. 1573 (*RSS*, vi, 1844A); granted remission for remaining, taking part and other offences 25
April 1573 (*ibid.*, vi, 1941).
10s in 1583 roll.

ANDERSON, WILLIAM baxter
in the Potterrow; granted remission of 40s on 28 Feb. 1576 for inter-communing (*TA*, xiii, 345).

ANDREW, THOMAS walker
summoned to appear at Leith 31 Jan. 1572 (*Memorials*, 219); goods escheated for failing to find
surety for taking part *or* supplying victuals *or* remaining 14 Sept. 1571; granted remission 20 July
1573 for taking part and other offences (*RSS*, vi, 1286, 2040); one of the penitents who gave in
their supplications to the session Nov. 1572 (SP 52/23, fo. 254; *CSP Scot.*, iv, no. 487); replaced
June 1579 as deacon of the walkers for remaining and serving the rebels (*Edin. Recs.*, iv, 110).
B. 17 April 1561; assessed at 20s in 1583 roll; deacon 1567-8, 1579-81 and 1582-3.

ARBUTHNOT, ALEXANDER [merchant and bookseller]
involved with Archibald Seinyeor (see below) in the conveying of money from France to Grange in
June 1571 (*Misc. Papers*, Maitland Club, xxvi (1834), 67-8; SRO, RH 1/2/415).
B. & G. 4 Aug. 1565; assessed at 20s in 1581 roll; he died in 1585, leaving £115 net (Edin. Tests., 22
April 1586); see Thomas Bassenden, below.

ARNEIL, NINIAN flesher
enters pledge 4 Feb. 1573 for assisting the rebels (JC 1/13; Pitcairn, *Trials*, I, ii, 39); finds surety
again 17 Aug. 1573 (JC 1/13).
B. 11 April 1565; assessed at 5s in 1583 roll.

ARNOT, HERCULES baxter
summoned to appear at Leith 31 Jan. 1572; enters pledge 17 Aug. 1573 (*Memorials*, 221; JC 1/13).
B. 28 Sept. 1570; assessed at 10s in 1583 roll.

ARTH, JOHN flesher
finds surety 17 Aug. 1573 (JC 1/13).

AUCHTERLONIE, ALEXANDER [baxter]
finds surety 17 Aug. 1573 (ibid.).
B. baxter 28 June 1564.

BAIRD, ROBERT
one of the penitents who gave in their supplications to the session Nov. 1572 (SP 52/23, fo. 254; *CSP Scot.*, iv, no. 487).

BALFOUR, GILBERT of Westray [merchant]
forfeited by the king's lords at Stirling 30 Aug. 1571 for assisting Grange, fortifying St. Giles' and other parts of the town (JC 26/1; see also Herbert Maxwell, John and Patrick Moscrop, Patrick Thomson, Cuthbert Ramsay, William Henderson and Alexander Home); goods escheated 9 Sept. and his lands in Haddington forfeited 16 Sept. (*RSS*, vi, 1274, 1288).
B. & G. 20 Nov. 1551; £20 in 1565 roll; a councillor 1557-8 and on the subscription list of 1562; he died in 1576, leaving £5,211 net (Edin. Tests., 12 Feb. 1577).

BALFOUR, m. JAMES of Pittendreich
made provost of Edinburgh 2 Oct. 1571 (see council lists).

BALLANTINE, STEPHEN litster
summoned to appear at Leith 31 Jan. 1572 (*Memorials*, 219; wrongly transcribed as 'Hewin' B. in Dalyell ed., 315; see Advocates MS, fo. 238).
There is a Stephen B. in the 1558 muster roll (MS Co. Recs., ii, fo. 130r; see also *Edin. Accts.*, i, 61).

BARBER, JOHN [cordiner]
gave in supplication to the session April 1574 for remaining in the town (BGKE, fo. lv).
B. tanner 23 April 1556; J.B., cordiner assessed at 3s in 1583 roll; he died in 1585, leaving £24 net (Edin. Tests., 11 Oct. 1586).

BARON, CHRISTINE *alias* GOODSON
finds surety along with her spouse, William Hutchison (see below), for assisting the rebels 2 April 1573; disagreement as to whether the remission he was granted also applied to her (JC 1/13; Pitcairn, *Trials*, I, ii, 42); her name appeared on the subscription list of 1562.

BARON, JOHN [officer]
goods escheated after his death 14 March 1573 for taking part, victualling and appearing in the field with the rebels (*RSS*, vi, 1896). J.B., officer (*Edin. Accts.*, i, 47).

BARRIE, THOMAS keeper of the Netherbow port
reconciled 3 March 1575 for remaining, accepting armour, acting as keeper of one of the ports of the burgh and accepting the office of messenger (BGKE, fo. 46r); he foiled the attempt of the king's lords to breach the Netherbow port in Aug. 1571; his hand struck off for forgery (*Hist. King James the Sext*, 87; *CSP Scot.*, iii, no. 892).
A catholic, who had been excommunicated by the Canongate session; see app. vi.

BARTILMO, ALEXANDER baxter
'burneman', summoned to appear at Leith 31 Jan. 1572 (*Memorials*, 221); baxter, finds surety 17 Aug. 1573 (JC 1/13).

BARTON, ANDREW merchant
summoned to appear at Leith 31 Jan. 1571 (*Memorials*, 220); finds surety 4 Feb. 1573 (Michael Gilbert, see below), but failed to appear on 9 Feb. (JC 1/13; Pitcairn, *Trials*, I, ii, 39); granted a remission 14 March 1574 for remaining, taking part and supplying the rebels with victuals, money and powder between Jan. 1571 and Aug. 1572 and for handling counterfeit coin between Aug. 1572 and Jan. 1573 (*RSS*, vi, 2376); submitted to the session April 1574 for remaining in the town (BGKE, fos. 1v, 20v); see also Prot. Bk. William Stewart, elder (B 22/1/57), 28 Jan. 1572.
B. & G. 6 April 1549; £20 in 1565 roll; he died in 1579, leaving £424 (Edin. Tests., 5 Aug. 1579); he should be distinguished from Andrew Barton of Leith, the son of Robert Barton; the Edinburgh merchant appeared on the subscription list of 1562.

BARTON, ANDREW [ex-chaplain]
the second of this name to be summoned to appear at Leith 31 Jan. 1572 (*Memorials*, 221); this is probably the 'Sir Andro' who submitted to the session in April 1574 for remaining in the town (BGKE, fos. 1v, 20v; see *Edin. Recs.*, ii, 251).

BASSENDEN, THOMAS printer
summoned to appear at Leith 31 Jan. 1572 (*Memorials*, 219); goods escheated and at the horn for withholding the Castle and town, keeping watch and ward and paying stents to the rebels 7 Jan.; granted remission of £66 13s 4d for remaining and taking part 7 Feb. 1573 (*RSS*, vi, 1420, 1847; *TA*, xii, 265, 337); submitted to the session for remaining, coming into battle, accepting the office of deacon of the kirk under a false minister, who taught perverse doctrine, and printing fifteen Marian books and tracts.
Only five hundred copies remained unsold (BGKE, fos. 2v, 29r). Bassenden, however, did print the 'Brief declaration . . .' of the king's party 1 Jan. 1573 (*CSP Scot.*, iv, no. 507). He died in 1577, leaving £2,009 net, including £500 owed to him by Alexander Arbuthnot (see above and Edin. Tests., 6 Feb. 1580).

BAUTIE, ALEXANDER [unfree] maltman
finds surety 17 Aug. 1573 (JC 1/13).
B. as *son* to Ninian B. 3 April 1579 (see next entry).

BAUTIE, NINIAN merchant
summoned to appear at Leith 31 Jan. 1572; granted remission 20 Oct. 1573 for remaining, taking part and other offences (*Memorials*, 219; *RSS*, vi, 2159).
£5 in 1565 roll.

BAXTER, WILLIAM outside the West Port
granted remission (40s) for intercommuning and another offence in 1568, 1 March 1576 (*TA*, xiii, 347).

BELL, ALEXANDER
submitted to the session 16 June 1575 for remaining and accepting armour (BGKE, fo. 62v).

BELL, FRANCIS skinner
summoned to appear at Leith 31 Jan. 1572 (*Memorials*, 221); one of the forty-seven charged with conspiracy 31 July 1573 (JC 26/1; see Patrick Anderson); finds surety 26 Aug. (JC 1/13).
G. 16 Oct. 1549; assessed at 10s in 1583 stent.

BELL, JOHN seedman
summoned to appear at Leith 31 Jan. 1572 (*Memorials*, 220).
B. 1 May 1563; at £3 in 1565 roll and 13s 4d in 1583.

BENNET, JOHN [in Edinburgh]
submitted to session April 1574 for remaining in the town (BGKE, fo. 1v). See *Broughton Court Book*, 7.

BICKERTON, JAMES apprentice smith
one of the penitents who submitted to the session Nov. 1572, but also (?) in the Castle, 'smith's boy', at its surrender (SP 52/23, fo. 254; *CSP Scot.*, iv, no. 487; SP 52/25, fos. 73r, 118r).

BINNIE, DAVID glasswright
summoned to appear at Leith 31 Jan. 1572 (*Memorials*, 221); one of the penitents who submitted to the session Nov. 1572 (SP 52/23, fo. 254); charged with conspiracy 31 July 1573 (JC 26/1; see Patrick Anderson); appears again in the processes of 10/11 Aug. and 13/14 Aug. (ibid.) and finds surety 26 Aug. (JC 1/13).
B. & G. 13 April 1569; he died in 1576, leaving only £7 net (Edin. Tests., 13 Nov. 1577).

BINNIE, WALTER painter
summoned to appear at Leith 31 Jan. 1572 (*Memorials*, 220); charged with conspiracy 31 July 1573 (JC 26/1; see Patrick Anderson); finds surety 26 Aug. (JC 1/13); see also Prot. Bk. John Aitkin, fo. 69r.
5s in 1583 roll.

BISSET, PATRICK [wineseller, merchant]
convicted 13 June 1572 of treason after his capture three days earlier (JC 1/13; Pitcairn, *Trials*, I, ii, 32; see Robert Allan); submitted to the session 23 Dec. 1574 for remaining, accepting armour and coming into battle (BGKE, fos. 35r, 36r).
B. & G. 16 Jan. 1549; *Edin. Accts.*, i, 479; £5 in 1565 roll.

BLACK, JOHN outside the West Port
granted a remission (£3) for intercommuning 28 Feb. 1576 (*TA*, xiii, 346).

BLYTH, GEORGE skinner
summoned to appear at Leith 31 Jan. 1572 (*Memorials*, 219); granted remission (£26 13s 4d) for taking part and other offences (*RSS*, vi, 1987; *TA*, xii, 266).
He died in 1582, leaving £1,207 (Edin. Tests., 16 Feb. 1583).

BLYTH, THOMAS webster
replaced as deacon of the websters June 1579 for serving in the town during its occupation by the queen's party (*Edin. Recs.*, iv, 110).

BLYTHMAN, JOHN flesher
summoned to appear at Leith 31 Jan 1572 (*Memorials*, 221); found surety 17 Aug. 1573 (JC 1/13); £10 composition for taking part (*TA*, xii, 267).
13s 4d in 1583 roll; three times a deacon in the 1560s.

BLYTHMAN, NICHOLAS flesher
summoned to appear at Leith 31 Jan. 1572 (*Memorials*, 221) and also exactly follows John Blythman in all respects except the amount of his composition, which was £6 13s 4d (JC 1/13, 17 Aug. 1573; *TA*, xii, 267).
5s in 1583 roll.

BORTHWICK, JOHN baxter
summoned to appear at Leith 31 Jan. 1572; one of the penitents who submitted to the session Nov. 1572 (*Memorials*, 221; SP 52/23, fo. 254).
B. baxter as servant and apprentice to Wm. Fiddes (see below) 15 March 1565; 13s 4d in 1583 roll.

BORTHWICK, ROBERT writer
summoned to appear at Leith 31 Jn. 1572 submitted to session April 1574 for remaining in the town (*Memorials*, 221; BGKE, fo. 1v).
He died in 1592, leaving £424 net (Edin. Tests., 6 June 1593).

BOW[IE], ALEXANDER [stabler]
convicted of treason 13 June 1572 after his capture three days earlier (JC 1/13; Pitcairn, *Trials*, I, ii, 32; see Robert Allan). Alexr. Bowie, stabler, assessed at 5s in 1583 roll.

BROCAS, WILLIAM smith
summoned to appear at Leith 31 Jan. 1572 (*Memorials*, 220); charged with conspiracy 31 July 1573 (JC 26/1; see Patrick Anderson); entered pledge 26 Aug. (JC 1/13).
A militant catholic; see app. vi for further details.

BROWN, GEORGE saddler
charged with conspiracy 31 July 1573 (JC 26/1; see Patrick Anderson); found surety 13/14 Aug. (ibid; marked 'gl') and again 26 Aug. (JC 1/13).
B. 6 June 1561; 6s 8d in 1583 roll.

BROWN, JOHN tailor
in the Castle at its surrender; given as a tailor in one version and as a shoemaker in the other (SP 52/25, fos. 72r, 117r).
B. tailor 31 Jan. 1555.

BROWN, JOHN writer
submitted to the session 4 Nov. 1574 for remaining in the town (BGKE, fos. 22r, 25v).
A John Brown (unspecified) among the penitents who submitted to the session Nov. 1572 (SP 52/23, fo. 254; *CSP Scot.*, iv, no. 487).

BRUCE, THOMAS [cordiner]
submitted to the session Nov. 1572 (SP 52/23, fo. 254).
B. 15 Jan. 1556; G., cordiner 13 Jan. 1562; 13s 4d in 1583 roll; he appeared on the council 1583-5 under the new arrangements of the decreet arbitral.

BURNE, JOHN flesher
found surety 17 Aug. 1573 (JC 1/13).

BURNETT, ALEXANDER [merchant]
summoned to appear at Leith 31 Jan. 1572 (*Memorials*, 221).
B. 8 Nov. 1560; G., mt., 19 July 1577; £10 in 1565 toll; he died in 1578, leaving £407 net (Edin. Tests., 14 Feb. 1587).

BURRELL, CUTHBERT [lorimer]
in the Castle at its surrender (SP 52/25, fos. 72r, 117v).
See Mungo B. lorimer B. as son to umq. Cuther B., *lorimer* B. 24 Dec. 1594.

BURRELL, MARION
she and her spouse, Robert Howie, paid composition of £3 for intercommuning (*TA*, xiii, 345).

See Edin. Tests., Marion B., daughter of Harry B., flesher, B. of Ed., 20 Jan. 1598; he had been an elder of the Canongate Kirk 1566-7 (*Canongate Bk.*, 51), one of those on the subscription list of 1562 and left £2,022 net when he died in 1587 (Edin. Tests., 26 Jan. 1591).

CALDER, VIRGIL wright
charged with conspiracy 31 July 1573 (JC 26/1; see Patrick Anderson); entered pledge 26 Aug. (JC 1/13); visitor of his craft 1555-6.

CALDERWOOD, JOHN saddler
summoned to appear at Leith 31 Jan. 1572 (*Memorials*, 219); charged with conspiracy 31 July 1573 (JC 26/1; see Patrick Anderson).

CALLANDER, MATHEW [cordiner dwelling beyond the Kirk of Field]
also charged with conspiracy 31 July 1573 (ibid.); pledge entered 26 Aug. (JC 1/13).
B. cordiner, as apprentice to Wm. Smith cordiner 11 March 1575 (but cf. the entry on 31 July, where he is given as a burgess); given as a 'birker' in the 1583 roll at 50s.

CANT, THOMAS of Sanct-Gely-Grange [merchant]
granted a free remission for taking part between Dec. 1570 and Aug. 1572 on 13 March 1576 (*TA*, xiii, 346).
B. & G. 27 Nov 1550; at £10 in 1565 roll, £6 in 1581 and 40s in 1583; see the testament of his wife, Margaret Tweedie, who died in 1573 (Edin. Tests., 1 Dec. 1573).

CARMICHAEL, JAMES merchant
summoned to appear at Leith 31 Jan. 1572 (*Memorials*, 219).
There are two of this name in the 1558 muster roll, one described as 'yr'; there is only one J.C. in the 1565 roll, at £10; but cf. the J.C. who was forfeited by the queen's lords Aug. 1571 (see K.P. list).

CARNBEE, ADAM [baxter]
one of the penitents who submitted to the session Nov. 1572 (SP 52/23, fo. 254).
B. baxter 27 July 1554.

CARNEY, ANDREW [tailor]
pledge entered 17 Aug. 1573 (JC 1/13).
B. *scissor* 13 May 1559; he died in 1587, leaving £481 net (Edin. Tests., 3 Oct. 1587).

CARNEY, JAMES baxter
one of the penitents who submitted to the session Nov. 1572; found surety 17 Aug. 1573; composition of £6 13s 4d for taking part (SP 52/23, fo. 254; JC 1/13; *TA*, xiii, 9).
B. 22 April 1561; 30s in 1583 roll.

CARRICK, JOHN [cordiner]
gave in supplication to the session that he only remained in the town during the troubles, 3 June 1574 (BGKE, fos. 8v, 9r).
B. cordiner 29 May 1567.

CASTLELAW, JOHN brewer
in the Castle at its surrender (SP 52/25, fos. 72r, 117r); a deacon of the Canongate Kirk 1567-8 (*Canongate Bk.*, 72-3).

CATHKIN, ALEXANDER smith outside the West Port
40s composition for intercommuning 28 Feb. 1576 (*TA*, xiii, 346).

CHALMER, JAMES merchant
convicted of conspiracy 13 June 1572 after his capture during a skirmish three days before (JC
1/13; Pitcairn, *Trials*, I, ii, 32; see Robert Allan); gave in supplication to the session April 1574 for
remaining in the town (BGKE, fo. 1v).
B. by rt. of wife, Helen, dr. of John Ferguson (see K.P. list) 31 Jan. 1562; 40s in 1565 roll, 20s in
1581, 6s 8d in 1583.

CLARKSON, ANDREW [tailor?]
submitted to the session Nov. 1572 (SP 52/23, fo. 254).
An Andro Clark, tailor, 13s 4d in 1583 roll (?).

CLARKSON, JOHN baxter
in the list of penitents who submitted Nov. 1572 (SP 52/23, fo. 254); he had been one of those
charged with attending mass at Holyrood in 1563, when he had been pledged by James Rhind (see
below and app. vi).

CLAVYE, JOHN candlemaker
at the horn for withholding the burgh, taking part in the killing of Shaw and Wemyss, subscribing
bands and taking oaths, 5 Jan. 1572 (*RSS*, vi, 1416; see Mathew Aikman and Mathew Easton);
summoned to appear at Leith 31 Jan. (*Memorials*, 219); he and Easton granted a remission (£80)
for remaining, taking part and other offences 7 Feb. 1573 (*RSS*, vi, 1846; *TA*, xii, 265, 337); submitted to the session Nov. 1572 (SP 52/23, fo. 254).
20s in 1583 roll; he died in 1586 in debt (Edin. Tests., 15 Feb. 1587).

COCHRANE, JOHN maltman
summoned to appear at Leith 31 Jan. 1572 (*Memorials*, 219).

COCKIE, JAMES goldsmith
in the Castle at its surrender (SP 52/25, fos. 72r, 117v); convicted of treason along with m. James
Kirkcaldy 3 Aug. 1573 (JC 1/13; Pitcairn, *Trials*, I, ii, 45); executed the same day along with
Grange and James Mossman (see below; *CSP Scot.*, iv, no. 712).
B. eldest son of umq. Jas. C., 4 Aug. 1562; deacon 1563-5.

COCKIE, WILLIAM *alias* SALTCRAIG [goldsmith, brother of James]
convicted of treason 13 June 1572 after his capture (JC 1/13; Pitcairn, *Trials*, I, ii, 32; see Robert
Allan).
B. goldsmith, second son of umq. Jas. C., 4 Aug. 1562; goldsmith, 30s in 1583 roll.

COOPER, JAMES tailor
summoned to appear at Leith 31 Jan. 1572 (*Memorials*, 219); one of the forty-seven charged with
conspiracy 31 July 1573 (JC 26/1; see Patrick Anderson).
B. *gratis* 12 Nov. 1561, his brother *John* C. surety for his stob and staik (see John C., who was
actively involved with the king's party, in K.P. list).

COOPER, PATRICK tailor
charged 9 Feb. 1573 with assisting the rebels by being involved in the skirmish at the Crags 10 June
1572 (JC 1/13; Pitcairn, *Trials*, I, ii, 40).

COOPER, THOMAS [apprentice] litster
one of the penitents who submitted to the session Nov. 1572 (SP 52/23, fo. 254; *CSP Scot.*, iv, no.
487); granted a remission (of £20) for remaining and taking part 18 Aug. 1573 (*RSS*, vi, 2107; *TA*,
xii, 266).
B. litster by rt. of fr. 19 July 1574.

COOPER, WILLIAM [carrier?]
one of the penitents who submitted to the session Nov. 1572 (SP 52/23, fo. 254); see *Edin. Accts.*, i, 316ff.

COR, LAWRENCE cordiner
charged with conspiracy 31 July 1573 and continued 13/14 Aug. (JC 26/1); entered pledge 26 Aug. (JC 1/13); had submitted to the session Nov. 1572 (SP 52/23, fo. 254; *CSP Scot.*, iv, no. 487); see Patrick Anderson.
3s in 1583 roll.

CORSAR, JOHN merchant
summoned to appear at Leith 31 Jan. 1572 (*Memorials*, 221).
£3 in 1565 roll.

CORSAR, JOHN writer [and macer]
summoned to appear at Leith 31 Jan. 1572 (*Memorials*, 221).
5s, macer, in 1583 roll.
There is a John Corsar, but unspecified, in the list of penitents of Nov. 1572 (SP 52/23, fo. 254) and is also mentioned in Prot. Bk. Wm. Stewart, elder, 28 Jan. 1572.

CORSBIE, ALEXANDER
summoned to appear at Leith 31 Jan. 1572 (*Memorials*, 219).

CORSBIE, DAVID merchant
a bailie of Edinburgh from Oct. 1571 (Prot. Bk. Aitkin, i, fo. 63r; see the council lists); summoned to appear at Leith 31 Jan. 1572 (*Memorials*, 218); charged with treasonably assisting the rebels 13 Aug. 1573 (JC 1/13; see also Pitcairn, *Trials*, I, ii, 47, and John Adamson, younger); granted a remission (of £20) for remaining and taking part on 18 Aug. (*RSS*, vi, 2097; *TA*, xii, 266).
G. 25 Sept. 1548; £5 in 1565 roll, 10s in 1581 and 5s in 1583. He died in 1612, leaving £3,607 net, most of it in the form of uncollected loans (Edin. Tests., 6 Jan. 1613).

COURTAS, WILLIAM skinner
summoned to appear at Leith 31 Jan. 1572 (*Memorials*, 221); he appeared before the Court of Justiciary the next day (JC 1/13).
B. 2 June 1553; assessed at 6s 8d in 1583 roll.

COUTTS, JOHN writer
summoned to appear at Leith 31 Jan. 1572 (*Memorials*, 221).
£10 in 1565 roll, and his widow at 10s in 1581 and 6s 8d in 1583.

COWIE, JAMES [in Edinburgh]
one of the thirty-nine who entered pledges 26 Aug. 1573 (JC 1/13).
See *Broughton Court Book*, 78.

COWIE, THOMAS
charged with treasonably assisting the rebels 13 Aug. 1573 (JC 1/13; see also Pitcairn, *Trials*, I, ii, 47, and John Adamson, younger).
B. by rt. of fr. 5 May 1575.

CRAGG, JOHN
one of the penitents who submitted to the session Nov. 1572 (SP 52/23, fo. 254).
Either a goldsmith (assessed at 5s in 1583) *or* a carter (assessed at 10s in 1581 and 5s in 1583; see also *Edin. Accts.*, ii, 101ff).

CRAIG, WILLIAM maltman
summoned to appear at Leith 31 Jan. 1572; one of the penitents who submitted to the session Nov.
1572 (*Memorials*, 221; SP 52/23, fo. 254).
B. maltman 29 April 1568.

CRAIK, WILLIAM merchant
summoned to appear at Leith 31 Jan. 1572 (*Memorials*, 219); goods escheated and at the horn for
failing to find surety to underly the law at Leith for treason 11 Dec. 1572 (*RSS*, vi, 1786).
The son of William Craik, provost of the burgh 1551-3 (*Edin. Recs.*, iii, 299); he was the brother-
in-law of both Archibald Seinyeor and Patrick Thomson and his mother had remarried Cuthbert
Ramsay, all three of them leading supporters of the queen's party (see below and the testament of
Janet Fleming (Edin. Tests., 3 Oct. 1570), who left £8,941 net when she died in 1570).

CRAMOND, JOHN servant of Alexander King, advocate
summoned to appear at Leith 31 Jan. 1572 (*Memorials*, 220); one of those still in the Castle at its
surrender 28 May 1573 and hurt (SP 52/25, fos. 72r, 117v); granted a remission for remaining and
taking part 31 May (*RSS*, vi, 1971); reconciled by the kirk session for entering into battle, entering
the Castle and taking part in the demolition and firing of parts of the town, Oct. 1574 (BGKE, fos.
22v, 25v).
B. & G. advocate by rt. of w. 12 Sept. 1589; see King below *and* in K.P. list.

CRANSTON, GEORGE [town officer]
granted a remission along with John Cramond for remaining and taking part 31 May 1573 (*RSS*,
vi, 1971); see *Edin. Accts.*, ii, 90.

CRAWFORD, JOHN shoemaker
in the Castle at its surrender 28 May 1573 (SP 52/25, fo. 72r, gives him as a shoemaker; ibid., fo.
117r as a tailor — cf. John Brown, above).

CRAWFORD, MUNGO
among the penitents who submitted to the session Nov. 1572 (SP 52/23, fo. 254).

CRAWFORD, THOMAS [stabler in the Cowgate]
convicted of treason 13 June 1572 after being captured at the skirmish on the 10th (JC 1/13;
Pitcairn, *Trials*, I, ii, 32, but this omits the fact that he was delivered to Captain Home by
command of the regent). In 1581 roll at 10s and 1583 roll at 6s 8d, but a burgess of the Canongate
(*Broughton Court Book*, 89); he died in 1585, leaving £194 net (Edin. Tests., 8 June 1586).

CRICHTON, JOHN baxter
summoned to appear at Leith 31 Jan. 1572 (*Memorials*, 221); granted a remission (of £20) for
taking part, victualling and circulating false coin 18 Aug. 1573 (*RSS*, vi, 2095; *TA*, xii, 266).
Alexr. C., B. as eldest son of *John C.* baxter B. 27 July 1580.

CRICHTON, THOMAS messenger and macer
summoned to appear at Leith 31 Jan. 1572; deceased by 13 April 1573 when his goods were
escheated for remaining, taking part and non-appearance (*Memorials*, 219; *RSS*, vi, 1929).
B. 22 Feb. 1555.

CUNNINGHAM, JOHN wright
summoned to appear at Leith 31 Jan. 1572 (*Memorials*, 221).
Deacon of his craft 1554-5, for part of 1559-60 and six times between 1560 and 1571.

CUNNINGHAM, MARGARET
in the Castle at its surrender 28 May 1573; after 'long reasoning with voting' she and the other women who remained in the Castle ordered to submit by the session 3 Feb. 1575 (BGKE, fo. 41r; SP 52/25, fos. 73r, 118r).

CURLE, JAMES [merchant]
according to the confession of Alexander Hamilton in June 1574, Curle was with Seton in France in 1571 (*CSP Scot.*, iv, 781; see also *ibid.*, iv, 772); 'allegit chanteor' of Dunkeld (*RSS*, vi, 1346).
B. & G. 16 Jan. 1549; £10 in 1565 roll; he had been on the council 1557-60, but did not serve after his appearance on the Seton council, despite being nominated by Mary in 1565; his name did appear on the subscription list of 1562; see also his son, William.

CURLE, WILLIAM
denounced for failing to appear before the privy council 27 Oct. 1571; forfeited 6 Nov. (*RPC*, ii, 90; *RSS*, vi, 1346).

DALYELL, JAMES [merchant]
convicted and executed for treason 13 June 1572 after his capture at the skirmish at the Crags on the 10th (JC 1/13; Pitcairn, *Trials*, I, ii, 32; *RSS*, vi, 2150; *Diurnal*, 265); he is probably the same man as the J.D. *elder*, who was summoned to appear at Leith 31 Jan. 1572 (*Memorials*, 219); cf. his son who was a prominent burgess throughout the 1570s (e.g. see *Edin. Recs.*, iv, 32).
B. & G. 4 Jan. 1550.

DANELOUR (or DEVILLOR), SEBASTIAN [merchant]
a 'dependant' of Mary; involved with William Aikman in the seizure of Archibald Stewart's goods (*CSP Scot.*, iii, no. 491); the bishop of Ross requested a passport for him to come from France with part of Mary's dowry in Dec. 1569 (*ibid.*, iii, no. 68); goods escheated and at the horn for taking part at Langside (*RSS*, vi, 2764).
£10 in 1565 roll.

DARLING, ANDREW baxter
summoned to appear at Leith 31 Jan. 1572 (*Memorials*, 220); one of the penitents who submitted to the session Nov. 1572 (SP 52/23, fo. 254); one of the forty-five who were pledged 17 Aug. 1573 (JC 1/13); granted a remission (of £6 13s 4d) on 18 Aug. for taking part, victualling and circulating false coin (*RSS*, vi, 2111; *TA*, xii, 267).
B. baxter 11 May 1554; 5s in 1583 roll.

DAVIDSON, WILLIAM son and heir of John
summoned to appear at Leith 31 Jan. 1572 (*Memorials*, 221).
B. as son and heir of umq. John D. flesher 27 Feb. 1556.

DENNAN, ROBERT flesher
one of the forty-five who entered pledges 17 Aug. 1573 (JC 1/13).

DEWAR, WILLIAM tailor
summoned to appear at Leith 31 Jan. 1572 (*Memorials*, 219); 'one Dewar, a tailor' and Patrick Thomson (see below) carried the ensigns of the queen's lords after the election of the new bailies, 7 July 1571 (*ibid.*, 175; Calderwood, *History*, iii, 111).

DICKSON, ADAM apothecary
summoned to appear at Leith 31 Jan. 1572 (*Memorials*, 219); granted a remission 16 Jan. 1573 for remaining and taking part of £333 6s 8d, which had been discharged 31 Dec. 1572 (*RSS*, vi, 1818; *TA*, xii, 265, 330).

Formerly the servant of Thomas Thomson, apothecary, a prominent member of the protestant faction (see *Edin. Recs.*, iii, 33-4, and app. v); G. by rt. of w. Janet, dr. of Thomas Thomson, 27 Sept. 1570; £10 in 1565 roll, £4 in 1581, 30s in 1583; see also Patrick Thomson (below), son of Thomas Thomson.

DICKSON, ALAN [merchant]
He and his son William summoned to appear at Leith 31 Jan. 1572 (*Memorials*, 219); pledged 13 Aug. 1573 after being charged along with John Adamson and others of treasonably assisting the rebels; pledged again on 17 Aug. and 24 Oct. (JC 1/13; see Pitcairn, *Trials*, I, ii, 47; *TA*, xii, 336, 364); ordered to appear in the place of repentance April 1574 as a relapsed fornicator (BGKE, fo. 1v); session agreed that he, John Moscrop and John Frood be 'advertised gently' to receive the injunctions of the kirk 30 June 1575; given a second private admonition 7 July, after which he twice promised to submit himself without result; warned three further times on 18 Aug., 8 and 29 Sept., along with Moscrop, Frood, Thomas MacCalzean, Peter Martin and Mungo Fairlie; finally promised to satisfy the kirk 20 Oct. 1575 for remaining, assisting and 'being officer in counsell' (ibid., fos. 65r, 65v, 67v, 68v, 70r, 71v, 73v, 75r).
A member of the protestant party for most of the 1560s (see app. v); another prominent queen's man, Herbert Maxwell (see below), was one of the witnesses to his testament.

DICKSON, THOMAS furrier
convicted of treason and conspiracy 13 June 1572 after capture in the Crags skirmish (JC 1/13; Pitcairn, *Trials*, I, ii 32; see Robert Allan); one of the forty-seven accused of active conspiracy 31 July 1573 (JC 26/1; see Patrick Anderson); given as a cordiner here and as a mason when pledged 13/14 Aug. (ibid.), but as a furrier when again pledged 26 Aug. (JC 1/13); one of the penitents who submitted to the session Nov. 1572 (SP 52/23, fo. 254); replaced as deacon of the furriers June 1579 for serving in the town during its occupation (*Edin. Recs.*, iv, 110).
B. furrier 10 July 1563; assessed at 6s 8d in 1583 roll; deacon 1567-70 and a further eight times between 1574 and 1584.

DICKSON, WILLIAM
summoned, along with his father Alan (see above), to appear at Leith 31 Jan. 1572; one of the penitents who submitted to the session Nov. 1572 (*Memorials*, 219; SP 52/23, fo. 254; *CSP Scot.*, iv, no. 487).

DICKSON, WILLIAM flesher
summoned to appear at Leith 31 Jan. 1572 (*Memorials*, 220; Calderwood, *History*, iii, 204).
B. flesher 2 March 1563; assessed at 20s in 1583 roll; he died in 1584, leaving £1,285 net (Edin. Tests., 1 April 1585).

DOBIE, JAMES flesher
summoned to appear at Leith 31 Jan. 1572 (*Memorials*, 220); possibly one of those still in the Castle at its surrender 28 May 1573 (SP 52/25, fo. 72v, but given as John Dobie in the second list, fo. 117v).
B. flesher as p. to Thomas Dobie, 21 March 1565; he died in 1593, leaving £25 net (Edin. Tests., 2 Aug. 1594).

DOBIE, WILLIAM flesher
summoned to appear at Leith 31 Jan. 1572 (*Memorials*, 220).
B. flesher by rt. of fr. Thomas Dobie, 2 April 1568.

DONALDSON, PETER soldier and 'man of Edinburgh'
hanged at Leith 8 Sept. 1571 for conspiring to betray the town (*Memorials*, 187).

DONALDSON, ROBERT baxter
one of the forty-five who entered pledges 17 Aug. 1573 (JC 1/13).
B. baxter 14 Jan. 1570.

DOUGLAS, JOHN [apprentice] tailor
one of the two penitents of that name who submitted to the session Nov. 1572 (SP 52/23, fo. 254; *CSP Scot.*, iv, no. 487); one of the forty-seven charged with active conspiracy 31 July 1573 (JC 26/1; see Patrick Anderson), and pledged 26 Aug. (JC 1/13).
B. tailor as p. to Thomas Ross, 1 Oct. 1574; there are two tailors of this name in the 1583 roll, assessed at 50s and 40s.

DOUGLAS, JOHN
one of the two penitents of that name who submitted to the session Nov. 1572 (SP 52/23, fo. 254).

DUNCAN, DAVID smith
one of the forty-seven charged with active conspiracy 31 July 1573 (JC 26/1; see Patrick Anderson); given as a locksmith when pledged 26 Aug. (JC 1/13).
B. blacksmith by rt. of w. 12 May 1559; assessed at 2s in 1583 roll.

DUNCAN, JOHN [slater]
one of the penitents who submitted to the session Nov. 1572 (SP 52/23, fo. 254); see *Broughton Court Book*, 204.

DUNCAN, MARK maltman
one of the forty-five pledged 17 Aug. 1573 (JC 1/13).

DUNDAS (DUNESS), THOMAS [apprentice tailor]
he and Alexander Ramsay (see below) reconciled 12 May 1575; both remained and were compelled to accept armour (BGKE, fo. 56r).

DUNLOP, ROBERT merchant
summoned to appear at Leith 31 Jan. 1572 (*Memorials*, 220).
40s in 1565 roll.

EASTON, MATTHEW candlemaker
at the horn for withholding the burgh, taking part in the killing of Shaw and Wemyss, subscribing bands and taking oaths, 5 Jan. 1572 (*RSS*, vi, 1416; see Matthew Aikman and John Clavye); granted a remission (of £80) for remaining, taking part and other offences (*ibid.*, vi, 1846; *TA*, xii, 265, 337; see also *RSS*, vi, 1884).
B. 15 March 1561; assessed at 5s in 1583 roll; he died in 1585, leaving £106 net (Edin. Tests., 23 Feb. 1587).

EASTON, THOMAS [brewster]
a hagbutter in the Castle at its surrender May 1573 (SP 52/25, fos. 72v, 117v).
B. 30 Dec. 1562; brewster, assessed at 2s in 1583 roll.

EDGAR, PATRICK merchant
summoned to appear at Leith 31 Jan. 1572 (*Memorials*, 220); his house on the Castlehill used as a guard house by Grange Feb. 1571 and as a site for the English cannon in the siege of the Castle in May 1573 (*Diurnal*, 199; Pitscottie, *History*, ii, 302; Birrell, *Diary*, 20). B. & G. 10 Oct. 1549; his name appeared on the subscription list of 1562; although his contribution of 1565 would indicate that he was one of the wealthiest merchants in 1565, he was over £340 in debt when he died in 1579 (Edin. Tests., 13 June 1579).

ELDER, JOHN mealman
summoned to appear at Leith 31 Jan. 1572 (*Memorials*, 220).
B. 9 April 1568.

ELLEN (or EWING), ROBERT
summoned to appear at Leith 31 Jan. 1572 (*Memorials*, 220; mistranscribed as 'Ewane' in Dalyell ed., 317 — see Advocates MS, fo. 238); submitted to the session April 1574 for remaining in the town (BGKE, fo. 1v). He was probably the brother of Thomas Ewing, goldsmith (see Edin. Tests., 17 Jan. 1570), but he was never admitted to the craft (see MS Goldsmiths' Recs., fo. 3r).

ELLIS, ALEXANDER merchant
summoned to appear at Leith 31 Jan. 1572 (*Memorials*, 220; mistranscribed as 'Cleish' in Dalyell ed., 316 — see Advocates MS. fo. 238); goods escheated and at the horn for withholding the Castle and town, keeping watch and ward and paying stents to the rebels 7 Jan. (*RSS*, vi, 1420; see also Thomas Bassenden); granted a remission of £66 13s 4d for remaining and taking part 7 Feb. 1573 (*ibid.*, vi, 1848; *TA*, xii, 265, 337); also among those who submitted to the session Nov. 1572 (SP 52/23, fo. 254).
B. as second son of Jas. E. 12 July 1555; G. mt. 14 April 1568; he died in 1576, leaving £549 net (Edin. Tests., 16 April 1578); see his brother, Andrew Ellis, in K.P. list.

ELPHINSTONE, THOMAS
reconciled to the kirk April 1574 for 'cumin in oppin and plane battell' (BGKE, fo. 1r).

ERSKINE, WILLIAM [merchant]
on the list of penitents who submitted to the session Nov. 1572 (SP 52/23, fo. 254; *CSP Scot.*, iv, no. 487).
See *Edin. Accts.*, i, 66, where he is assessed among the merchants in a stent of 1566.

FAIRFOUL, DAVID cooper
one of the smiths still in the Castle at its surrender in May 1573 (SP 52/25, fos. 73r, 118r); he and two other soldiers within the Castle pressed the session for satisfaction but were referred to the whole congregation because of the 'hienusnes of thair offences', 17 Feb. 1575 (BGKE, fos. 43r, 45v; see John Main and James White).

FAIRLIE, DAVID tailor
summoned to appear at Leith 31 Jan. 1572 (*Memorials*, 219); granted a remission (£13 6s 8d) for remaining, taking part and other offences 26 March 1573 (*RSS*, vi, 1917; *TA*, xii, 267); although summoned to appear on the same day as his brother, Mungo (see below), 13 Aug. 1573 before the justiciary court no further action was taken (JC 1/13); reconciled on the basis that he only remained in the town, Sept. 1574 (BGKE, fo. 19r).
B. & G. mt. tailor as third son of Jas. F. 7 Aug. 1583; assessed at £4 in 1583 roll.

FAIRLIE, MUNGO merchant
although he was one of the bailies of the council of 1570-71 dismissed by the queen's lords in June 1571 and put to an assize by them in July for maintaining the king's authority, he seems to have remained in the town, even though freed on surety (*Diurnal*, 226, 233; *Memorials*, 176; cf. the three others tried with him, Thomas Brown, Robert Cunningham and John Harwood); summoned to appear at Leith 31 Jan. 1572 (*ibid.*, 219), and was discharged on his appearance before the justiciary court the next day (JC 1/13); but he was among those charged with treasonably assisting the rebels 13 Aug. 1573 (ibid., see Pitcairn, *Trials*, I, ii, 47, and John Adamson, above) and was granted a remission (£33 6s 8d) on 18 Aug. for remaining and taking part (*RSS*, vi, 2098; *TA*, xii, 266); the session decided 18 Nov. 1574 after putting it to the vote that he should publicly satisfy

the kirk for remaining in the town, but he still had not done so over ten months later when he, Alan Dickson and Peter Martin were warned to do so (BGKE, fos. 28r, 73v).

B. & G. as eldest son of Jas. F., 31 Aug. 1570; brother of David (see above); £30 in 1565 roll, £12 in 1581 and £4 in 1583; he had also been on the council 1567-8, but did not return to it after 1573, although the youngest brother, William, did come on to the council in 1579.

FERGUSON, THOMAS outside the West Port
a £10 composition for supplying victuals to the rebels, 28 Feb. 1576 (*TA*, xiii, 344).

FIDDES, WILLIAM baxter
summoned to appear at Leith 31 Jan. 1572 (*Memorials*, 220); one of the penitents who submitted to the session Nov. 1572 (SP 52/23, fo. 254); one of the forty-five pledged 17 Aug. 1573 (JC 1/13); replaced as deacon of the baxters June 1579 for serving in the town during its occupation (*Edin. Recs.*, iv, 110).

Not in the burgess roll, but his son, William, is, gaining B. by rt. of fr., 18 April 1582; assessed at 13s 4d in 1583 Roll; deacon of his craft 1569-70.

FISHER, ANDREW [merchant]
summoned to appear at Leith 31 Jan. 1572 (*Memorials*, 219); fined £40 for failing to appear to answer a charge of assisting and supplying the rebels, 4 Feb. 1573 (JC 1/13; Pitcairn, *Trials*, I, ii, 40; see James Fleming, who was charged with the same offence).

B. & G., second son of John F., 16 Jan. 1549; younger brother of William Fisher (see below).

FISHER, m. JOHN [merchant]
pledged 13 Aug. 1573 (JC 1/13).

Possibly the father of Andrew and William Fisher, G. 20 Feb. 1539, but more probably the merchant assessed at £3 in 1581 and £2 in 1583, a councillor in 1578-9.

FISHER, WILLIAM
he and his father, Andrew, were summoned to appear at Leith 31 Jan. 1572 (*Memorials*, 219); judicial proceedings were taken against him or his uncle, William.

FISHER, WILLIAM [merchant]
summoned to appear at Leith 31 Jan. 1572 (*Memorials*, 219); charged with treasonably assisting the rebels 13 Aug. 1573 (JC 1/13; see Pitcairn, *Trials*, I, ii, 47, and John Adamson, above); pledged again 17th (JC 1/13) and granted a remission (£50) on 18th for remaining and taking part (*RSS*, vi, 2099; *TA*, xii, 266); it was probably his nephew, William, who was still in the Castle on its surrender in May 1573 (SP 52/25, fos. 72v, 117v).

B. & G. son and heir of John F., 9 April 1538; assessed at £3 in 1580 Roll.

FLEMING, ALAN [merchant]
one of the forty-five pledged 17 Aug. 1573 (JC 1/13); individually assessed at 10s in 1581 roll.

FLEMING, JAMES [apprentice] flesher
summoned to appear at Leith 31 Jan. 1572 (*Memorials*, 220); charged 4 Feb. 1573 with supplying the Castilians with a great quantity of wine, flesh, fish and malt and spreading false coin Aug.-Dec. 1572 (JC 1/13); must have re-entered the Castle as is given as a 'bowcher' in the lists of those in the Castle in May 1573 (SP 52/25, fos. 73r, 118r); admitted to the session 23 June 1575 that he had remained and accepted armour and after the end of the abstinence had re-entered the Castle (BGKE, fos. 59r, 63v).

B. as p. to umq. John Garman 8 Aug. 1583; in the 1581 roll at 15s (as an unfree flesher?) and the 1583 roll at 6s 8d.

FLEMING, WILLIAM [merchant]
summoned to appear at Leith 31 Jan. 1572 (*Memorials*, 219); *either* G. by rt. of w. 10 Oct. 1549 *or*, more probably, B. 15 April 1579 and assessed at 10s in 1581 roll and 30s in 1583 roll.

FORESTER, JOHN maltman
summoned to appear at Leith 31 Jan. 1572; one of the penitents who submitted to the session Nov. 1572 (*Memorials*, 219; SP 52/23, fo. 254).
B. 16 Dec. 1558.

FORESTER (FOSTER), NICOL [apprentice flesher]
submitted to the session April 1574 for remaining in the town (BGKE, fo. 1v).
B. flesher as only son to umq. *Thomas F.*, flesher, 7 June 1583 (see below).

FORESTER (FOSTLAWE), THOMAS [flesher]
one of the penitents who submitted to the session Nov. 1572 (SP 52/23, fo. 254; *CSP Scot.*, iv, no. 487).
See previous entry.

FORMAN, JOHN
a burgess, granted a remission 2 Oct. 1573 (£3 6s 8d) for remaining and taking part (*RSS*, vi, 2144; *TA*, xiii, 115).

FORRET, ANDREW skinner
submitted to the session 10 Oct. 1575 for remaining in the town (BGKE, fo. 77v).

FORRET, JAMES skinner
summoned to appear at Leith 31 Jan. 1572 (*Memorials*, 219; mistranscribed as 'Forrest' in Dalyell, ed., 314; see Advocates MS., fo. 238r); charged with treasonably assisting the rebels 13 Aug. 1573 (JC 1/13; see Pitcairn, *Trials*, I, ii, 47, and John Adamson, above); £20 composition (*TA*, xii, 266). Not himself on the burgess roll, but his son is: James F., B. & G. skinner as son to umq. Jas. skinner, 17 Feb. 1585. Forret had been one of the members of the assize in the Nicol Young case in 1564 who had voted to convict all four defendants; he had also been on the assize that convicted Henry Yair of the murder of Riccio in 1566 (Pitcairn, *Trials*, i, 448, 481); twice a deacon in the 1550s and died in 1583, leaving £325 net (Edin. Tests., 21 Jan. 1584).

FORSYTH, WALTER
one of the penitents who submitted to the session for remaining in the town, April 1574 (BGKE, fo. 1v).

FORSYTH, WILLIAM cordiner
charged 9 Feb. 1573 with assisting the rebels by being involved in the action at the Crags in June 1572 (JC 1/13; Pitcairn, *Trials*, I, ii, 40).

FOULIS, m. JAMES [of Colinton, advocate]
initially refused to submit to the kirk for remaining in the town, 17 June 1574, claiming that he was only a servant to those who did remain, but he had submitted by Oct. 1574 (BGKE, fos. 10r, 20v). James F., B. as son of umq. m. *James F. of Colinton* clerk of register B., 19 Jan. 1591; he died in 1593 (Edin. Tests., 28 Dec. 1599); see app. x for his father, Henry, laird of Colinton.

FOWLER, WILLIAM [merchant]
one of the merchants who brought letters from Mary to the bishop of Ross, for whom he interceded with Cecil and Leicester, May 1571; his goods had been held in France since early in 1571

(*CSP Scot.*, iii, nos. 695, 703); but he also acted as a messenger and source of information for Lennox (*ibid.*, iii, nos. 865, 889). He died in Jan. 1572 and his testament (Edin. Tests., 13 Aug. 1575) reveals almost £3,000 of debts owed to him, including Lennox, Ruthven and James McGill among the king's men, and Atholl, m. James Kirkcaldy and Gilbert Balfour among the queen's men; there are also a large number of burgesses of both parties among his debtors reflecting his substantial property holdings within the burgh.

£20 in the 1565 roll, and his widow was assessed at £12 in 1583 and £6 in 1581, which would support the impression that the bulk of his income came from property rather than trade. B. & G. 7 Jan. 1564; he came from an early protestant family (see app. iv, Sibilla Lindsay); his son, William, was an agent for Walsingham (see *CSP Scot.*, vi, no. 196).

FRASER (FRESELL), HENRY
submitted to the kirk June 1574 for remaining in the town (BGKE, fos. 8v, 9r).

FRENCH, ALEXANDER
submitted to the session April 1574 for remaining in the town (BGKE, fo. 1v).

FROOD, m. JOHN advocate
summoned to appear at Leith 31 Jan. 1572 (*Memorials*, 220); mistranscribed as 'Sende' in Dalyell ed., 317 — see Advocates MS., fo. 238); he, Moscrop and Alan Dickson were 'gentillie' and privately urged to submit themselves to the kirk as promised, 30 June 1575; despite three further private admonitions and a further promise to submit, he had not complied by Oct. 1575, when the session charged him with slander (BGKE, fos. 65, 67v, 68v, 69v, 71v, 75r).

FULLARTON, PATRICK cordiner
summoned to appear at Leith 31 Jan. 1572 (*Memorials*, 220; mistranscribed as a 'gardener' in Dalyell ed., 317; see Advocates MS., fo. 238).

GAIT, HEW [wright]
'quheillmaker'; he and a number of other wrights, smiths and gunners defected to the queen's lords in March 1572 (*RSS*, vi, 1530).

GALLOWAY, THOMAS town officer
charged 9 Feb. 1573 with assisting the rebels by being involved in the action at the Crags in June 1572 (JC 1/13; Pitcairn, *Trials*, I, ii, 40); submitted to the session in May and June 1575 for having remained in the burgh, borne armour and accepted office under 'intrusit magistrattis' (BGKE, fos. 58r, 64r).

GARDENER, JOHN litster
summoned to appear at Leith 31 Jan. 1572 (*Memorials*, 219; wrongly transcribed as 'Gordon' instead of 'Guarden' in Dalyell ed., 315; see Advocates MS., fo. 238); a pledge entered for him the next day (JC 1/13, but out of sequence, coming after an entry dated 23 Feb. 1572).

B. as apprentice and servant of umq. David G., 13 April 1565; assessed at 40s in 1581 roll and 50s in 1583.

GARDENER, PATRICK flesher
pledged 4 Feb. 1573 for assisting the rebels (JC 1/13; Pitcairn, *Trials*, I, ii, 39); listed among the forty-five inhabitants of the burgh who found surety 17 Aug. 1573, but marked 'remissione' in margin (JC 1/13); a composition of £13 6s 8d (*TA*, xii, 266).

B. 11 Feb. 1559; assessed at 5s in 1583 roll.

GARLAND, JOHN slater
charged 9 Feb. 1573 with assisting the rebels by being involved in the action at the Crags in June 1572 (JC 1/13; Pitcairn, *Trials*, I, ii, 40).

GARMAN, PATRICK stabler
one of the forty-seven accused 31 July 1573 of active conspiracy (JC 26/1; see Patrick Anderson); pledged 26 Aug. (JC 1/13).
B. & G. 4 May 1580; assessed at 10s in 1581 roll and 5s in 1583.

GEMMELL (GEMICE), THOMAS merchant
one of the penitents who submitted to the kirk in Nov. 1572; pledged 13 Aug. 1573 (SP 52/23, fo. 254; *CSP Scot.*, iv, no. 487; JC 1/13). £10 in 1565 roll; he died in 1573 or early 1574, leaving only £15 net (Edin. Tests., 20 Feb. 1574).

GIBSON, JAMES bower
submitted to the session April 1574 for remaining in the town (BGKE, fo. 1v).

GIBSON, JOHN bower
one of the twenty-three charged with treasonably assisting the rebels 13 Aug. 1573 (JC 1/13; see Pitcairn, *Trials*, I, ii, 47, and John Adamson, above); a composition of £13 6s 8d (*TA*, xii, 266); also in the list of those who submitted to the kirk in Nov. 1572 (SP 52/23, fo. 254); variously given as lancemaker or spearmaker.
B. bower 26 May 1564; he died in 1578, leaving £454 net (Edin. Tests., 20 Feb. 1579).

GIBSON, ROBERT cordiner in the Cowgate
executed by Lennox and Morton after the siege of Brechin, 12 Aug. 1570 (*Diurnal*, 183; see *Edin. Accts.*, ii, 218, 233, where he is listed among the cordiners paying chop mail in 1556-7 and 1565-6).

GIBSON, THOMAS bower
one of the penitents who submitted to the kirk in Nov. 1572 (SP 52/23, fo. 254).
A T.G., bower, assessed at 13s 4d in 1583 roll; see Agnes Hall, his wife (Edin. Tests., 22 Oct. 1588).

GILBERT, MICHAEL [goldsmith]
one of the Edinburgh burgesses whose goods were held in France early in 1571; also one of the Edinburgh merchants who brought letters from Mary to the bishop of Ross in May 1571; as well as acting as a go-between for letters and information, Gilbert offered to arrange the transfer of money for the bishop between London and Edinburgh at a profitable rate of exchange in July 1571; however, his house was one of those demolished by the queen's lords in Feb. 1572 (*CSP Scot.*, iii, nos. 695, 703; iv, 149).
B. & G. 10 Oct. 1549; the wealthiest craftsman in Edinburgh in this period, assessed at £33 in the 1583 stent and he left over £22,000 at his death in 1590 (Edin. Tests., 31 Jan. 1592); one of the two most prominent craftsmen on the council in the 1560s and a burgh commissioner at the coronation of James in 1567 (*Edin. Recs.*, iii, 238). But cf. John Gilbert, goldsmith (see K.P. list).

GILCHRIST, JOHN smith
summoned to appear at Leith 31 Jan. 1572 (*Memorials*, 220); one of the forty-seven accused of active conspiracy 31 July 1573 (JC 26/1; see Patrick Anderson); pledged 26 Aug. (JC 1/13); granted a remission for remaining and taking part between Jan. 1571 and Aug. 1572, 13 Feb. 1576 (*RSS*, vii, 456A); assessed at 10s in 1583 stent.

GIRDWOOD, DAVID [baxter]
one of the forty-five for whom pledges entered 17 Aug. 1573 (JC 1/13).
B. baxter 17 Dec. 1561; assessed at 20s in 1583 stent; he died in 1585, leaving £672 net (Edin. Tests., 20 Jan. 1587).

GLASFORD, THOMAS soldier and ordinary gunner within the Castle
one of those still in the Castle at its surrender in May 1573 (SP 52/25, fo. 118r); reconciled to the
kirk 20 May 1574 for taking 'plain parte' with the rebels in demolishing houses and raising fire
within the burgh (BGKE, fo. 7v); been listed as one of those who were 'attached' to Mary early in
1569 (*CSP Scot.*, ii, no. 1013).

GORDON, JOHN wright
one of the penitents who submitted to the kirk in Nov. 1572 (SP 52/23, fo. 254); one of the forty-
seven inhabitants charged with active conspiracy 31 July 1573 (JC 26/1; given here as 'Gowane';
see Patrick Anderson, above); pledged 26 Aug. (JC 1/13).
B. *carpentarius* 17 Aug. 1554; assessed, as a wright, at 30s in 1583 stent.

GOTTERSON, ANDREW smith
charged 9 Feb. 1573 with assisting the rebels by being involved in the action at the Crags in June
1572 (JC 1/13; Pitcairn, *Trials*, I, ii, 40); a locksmith and master in his craft in 1560 (Smith,
Hammermen of Edinburgh, 174-5).

GOWANLOCK, JOHN [brewster]
summoned to appear at Leith 31 Jan. 1572 (*Memorials*, 220).
B. brewster *gratis*, by rt. of office of the provost, Sir Simon Preston of Craigmillar, 22 Aug. 1567;
assessed at 10s in both stents of 1581 and 1583.

GRAHAM, JOHN draper and cramer
summoned to appear at Leith 31 Jan. 1572 (*Memorials*, 219); although called before the Court of
Justiciary 13 Aug. 1573, no further action was taken (JC 1/13).
A catholic, who had been excommunicated in 1569; see app. vi for further details.

GRAINGER, ARTHUR merchant
summoned to appear at Leith 31 Jan. 1572 (*Memorials*, 219).
B. 25 Jan. 1554; G. by rt. of wife 26 Dec. 1560; on the council 1561-3 and 1566-7 and on the subscription list of 1562; £15 contribution in 1565, but he only left £140 when he died in 1589; it
appears he gave up his burgess-ship at some point (Edin. Tests., 9 Aug. 1589).

GRAY, JOHN fishmonger
summoned to appear at Leith 31 Jan. 1572; charged 4 Feb. 1573 with assisting the rebels
(*Memorials*, 220; JC 1/13; Pitcairn, *Trials*, I, ii, 39).
B. herring seller 30 Dec. 1562.

GREGOR, DAVID [tailor]
submitted to the session July 1575 that he remained and bore armour (BGKE, fos. 67v, 69r); he
died in 1578, leaving £164 net (Edin. Tests., 20 Feb. 1580).

GUILLIAM, [JACQUES] smith
summoned to appear at Leith 31 Jan. 1572 (*Memorials*, 220), but appointed as a gunner in the
Castle 12 June 1573 'for good and thankful service' (*RSS*, vi, 1991).
B. Frenchman *gratis* for service to the town, 30 June 1568.

GUTHRIE, ALEXANDER [town clerk]
pledged 28 Dec. 1571 after being charged with treason by assisting the rebels in Edinburgh (JC
1/13; Pitcairn, *Trials*, I, ii, 29); when asked by the session if he had remained in the town after the
proclamation made at Michaelmas, 7 Sept. 1571, before the second siege of the town (see *CSP
Scot.*, iii, no. 941(4)), Guthrie replied that he had only stayed a day or two after that, but denied

that he had fenced courts in the queen's name; no further action seems to have been taken (BGKE, fo. 65v); Guthrie's protocol book (B 22/1/25) continued steadily until 9 June 1571 but there is then a gap until 10 Nov. 1573.

Guthrie had been a leading member of the protestant faction in the burgh throughout the 1560s; see app. v for further details.

HAIR, JOHN [tailor]
one of the penitents who submitted to the session in Nov. 1572 (SP 52/23, fo. 254).
B. tailor 12 June 1556; assessed, as a tailor, at 5s in 1583 stent.

HAISTIE, ALEXANDER millwright
summoned to appear at Leith 31 Jan. 1572 (*Memorials*, 221).

HAISTIE, ALEXANDER [merchant]
the second of this name in the list of those summoned to appear at Leith 31 Jan. 1572 (*ibid.*, 221; see Dalyell ed., 320; there *are* two in both manuscripts; see Advocates MS., fo. 238 and Univ. MS., fo. 81v); one of the two (but unspecified) was charged with being involved in the action at the Crags in June 1572 on 9 Feb. 1573 (JC 1/13; Pitcairn, *Trials*, I, ii, 40).
B. mt. 12 Dec. 1561; at £5 in 1565 roll.

HALL, ANDREW
submitted to the session April 1574 that he had taken up arms (BGKE, fo. 1r).

HALLIDAY, ALEXANDER smith outside the West Port
40s composition for intercommuning, 28 Feb. 1576 (*TA*, xiii, 346).

HAMILTON, ADAM smith
he and other smiths, wrights and gunners defected to the queen's lords in March 1572 (*RSS*, vi, 1530); he and his wife were in the Castle at its surrender in May 1573 (SP 52/25, fos. 72v, 118r).
B. blacksmith 20 Oct. 1560; assessed at 5s in 1583 roll.

HAMILTON, ANDREW of Cottis merchant
he and his son John forfeited by parliament 19 Aug. 1568 (JC 26/1); summoned to appear at Leith 31 Jan. 1572 (*Memorials*, 219); submitted to the session 23 Sept. 1574 that only remained in the town (BGKE, fo. 19r).

HAMILTON, DAVID [apprentice saddler]
one of the forty-five pledged 17 Aug. 1573 (JC 1/13); reconciled 12 May 1574 for remaining in the town at the desire of his master, Robert Abercrombie (a master saddler and one of the leading craftsmen in the king's party), and being compelled to bear arms (BGKE, fo. 56r).

HAMILTON, JAMES skinner
summoned to appear at Leith 31 Jan. 1572 (*Memorials*, 221), charged 9 Feb. 1573 with being involved in the action at the Crags in June 1572 (JC 1/13; Pitcairn, *Trials*, I, ii, 40).

HAMILTON, ROBERT cutler [hammerman]
captured along with the wives of John Moscrop and Fernihurst by the king's lords, 29 Sept. 1571; submitted to the session April 1574 for remaining in the town (*Memorials*, 192; BGKE, fo. 1v).
(See Moscrop below.)

HAMILTON, THOMAS of Priestfield [merchant]
one of the bailies chosen by Grange 20 June 1571; in Lennox's summons of forfeiture, 30 Aug.

1571, along with Herbert Maxwell and John Moscrop (*Diurnal*, 226, 245; *Memorials*, 186; *CSP Scot.*, iii, nos. 897, 898; Calderwood, *History*, iii, 137); recommended Francis Linton (see below) as a faithful supporter of the queen (*CSP Scot.*, iii, no. 697).
B. & G. as s. and h. of Thomas H., 8 Nov. 1561; although he appears among the merchants in the stents of 1565 (£20), 1581 (£3) and 1583 (£2), a council minute of 15 Jan. 1585 indicates that by then he did not practise 'tred nor trafficque' (*Edin. Recs.*, iv, 385); on the subscription list of 1562 and he had been on the council 1568-9; he did not reappear after 1573.

HANNAY, ROBERT
reconciled to the session Oct. 1574 for remaining, coming into battle, entering the Castle and firing shot into the town, helping in the demolition and firing of parts of the town (BGKE, fos. 22v, 25v).

HARDIE, PATRICK [cordiner in the Cowgate]
one of the penitents who submitted to the session Nov. 1572 (SP 52/23, fo. 254).
B. cordiner 14 Jan. 1567; assessed at 10s in 1583 stent; one of the 'faithful brethren' of the subscription list of 1562; he died in 1585, leaving £439 net (Edin. Tests., 8 May 1588).

HARLAW, JAMES writer
granted a remission for taking part, 8 June 1573 (*RSS*, vi, 1982).
£20 in 1565 roll; a witness for William Roberton, master of the grammar school and a catholic, in 1562 (*Edin. Recs.*, iii, 142).

HAY, JOHN [merchant]
convicted of treason along with twenty-five others after their capture in the Crags action, 13 June 1572 (JC 1/13; Pitcairn, *Trials*, I, ii, 32). J.H. of Tallo, yr., B. 29 Jan 1555; see also *Edin. Accts.*, i, 63.

HENDERSON, JAMES maltman outside the West Port
summoned to appear at Leith 31 Jan. 1572 (*Memorials*, 219); pledged 13 Aug. 1573 (JC 1/13); £10 composition for supplying the rebels and contravening the malt acts (*TA*, xiii, 347). He died in 1576, leaving £121 (Edin. Tests., 31 Aug. 1584).

HENDERSON, JOHN baxter
summoned to appear at Leith 31 Jan. 1572 (*Memorials*, 219); Grange complained to Killigrew that those who had remained in the town, including Henderson, were being forced to submit to the session, although they denied this when called before the superintendent; he does appear in the list of penitents of Nov. 1572; perhaps the reason for their willingness to submit was that the session could be asked to intercede on their behalf with the civil magistrate (*ibid.*, 264-6; Calderwood, *History*, iii, 225; SP 52/23, fo. 254); however, Henderson's case was still continuing before the Court of Justiciary 17 Aug. 1573 (JC 1/13); he seems to have submitted again to the session 30 Dec. 1574 for remaining in the burgh (BGKE, fo. 36v).
B. 23 Oct. 1560; assessed at 30s in 1583 stent.

HENDERSON, RICHARD [flesher]
one of the forty-five pledged 17 Aug. 1573 (JC 1/13).
See *Edin. Recs.*, iii, 43, 54; four times a deacon between 1556 and 1563.

HENDERSON, WILLIAM blacksmith
variously referred to as 'bloudrodd' or 'bloudwet'; summoned to appear at Leith 31 Jan. 1572 (*Memorials*, 219; wrongly transcribed from the Advocates MS., fo. 238 as 'Hackerson' in the Dalyell ed., 314); warded along with Cuthbert Ramsay and Patrick Thomson (see below) April [*sic*] 1573 for the fortifying of St. Giles' and other parts of the town (JC 26/1); all three had been

forfeited by parliament and were in the Castle at its fall (*CSP Scot.*, iv, no. 638; SP 52/25, fos. 72v, 117v).
A burgess of the Canongate (*Broughton Court Book*, 54).

HEPBURN, JOHN baker in the Potterrow
a £3 composition for intercommuning, 28 Feb. 1576 (*TA*, xiii, 345); his widow died in 1597, without assets, owing £13 (Edin. Tests., 9 June 1597); a burgess of the Canongate (*Broughton Court Book*, 137).

HERIOT (HERRET), ALEXANDER flesher
summoned to appear at Leith 31 Jan. 1572 (*Memorials*, 220).

HERIOT, GEORGE goldsmith
summoned to appear at Leith 31 Jan. 1572 (*Memorials*, 219; Calderwood, *History*, iii, 204); granted a remission for remaining and taking part (*RSS*, vi, 1969); replaced as deacon of his craft June 1579 for serving in the town during its occupation (*Edin. Recs.*, iv, 110).
B. 4 Aug. 1562; assessed at 40s in 1583 stent; deacon of his craft 1565-8.

HERIOT (HERROT), GEORGE baxter
one of the forty-five pledged 17 Aug. 1573 (JC 1/13).
B. baxter 5 Feb. 1561.

HERIOT, JOHN [apprentice] baxter
reconciled to the kirk 6 Jan. 1575 for remaining in the town (BGKE, fo. 38r).
B. baxter as apprentice to umq. Thomas Craig, 2 Nov. 1577; assessed at 6s 8d in 1583 stent.

HERIOT, JOHN litster
summoned to appear at Leith 31 Jan. 1572; one of those who submitted to the kirk in Nov. 1572 (*Memorials*, 221; SP 52/23, fo. 254; *CSP Scot.*, iv, no. 487).

HILL, JOHN [unfree] walker outside the West Port
fined an unspecified amount, probably for taking part, 28 Feb. 1576 (*TA*, xiii, 345).
B. walker 23 March 1585.

HOGG, THOMAS cordiner
one of the forty-seven charged with active conspiracy 31 July 1573 (JC 26/1; see Patrick Anderson); pledged 13/14 Aug. (ibid.) and again 26 Aug. (JC 1/13).
Assessed at 10s in 1583 stent; deacon 1560-61 and 1563-4.

HOGG, THOMAS flesher
appears as witness to a notarial process 28 Jan. 1572 (Prot. Bk. Wm. Stewart, elder; Prot. Bk. Aitkin, i, fo. 84r), and one of those summoned to appear at Leith three days later (*Memorials*, 220). A Thomas Hogg, probably the cordiner, is on the list of penitents who submitted to the kirk in Nov. 1572 (SP 52/23, fo. 254).

HORN, JOHN skinner
summoned to appear at Leith 31 Jan. 1572 (*Memorials*, 220); one of the forty-seven, including Patrick Anderson (see above), charged with active conspiracy 31 July 1573 (JC 26/1); pledged 10/11 Aug. (ibid.) and again 26 Aug. (JC 1/13); assessed at 30s in 1583 roll.

HOWDEN, JOHN [merchant]
one of the penitents who submitted to the kirk in Nov. 1572; one of the thirty-nine who pledged 26

Aug. 1573 (SP 52/23, fo. 254; *CSP Scot.*, iv, no. 487; JC 1/13).
B. mt. 28 March 1556; assessed at 40s in 1565 roll.

HOWIE, ROBERT [unfree baxter] in Potterrow
he and his wife, Marion Burrell (see above), paid compensation of £3 for intercommuning, 28 Feb. 1576 (*TA*, xiii, 345).
He died in 1583, leaving £169 (Edin. Tests., 11 June 1583).

HOWIE, THOMAS [unfree baxter] in Potterrow
a £3 composition for intercommuning, 28 Feb. 1576 (*TA*, xiii, 345).
His widow, Agnes Anderson, died in 1593, leaving £37 net (Edin. Tests., 31 Jan. 1593).

HOWIESON, JOHN smith
one of the forty-seven, including Patrick Anderson (see above), charged with active conspiracy 31 July 1573 (JC 26/1); reappeared 10/11 Aug. (ibid.) and pledged 26 Aug. (JC 1/13).

HUNTER, JAMES swordslipper [lorimer]
summoned to appear at Leith 31 Jan. 1572 (*Memorials*, 219), and produced a discharge the following day (JC 1/13); one of the forty-seven, including Patrick Anderson (see above), charged with active conspiracy 31 July 1573 (JC 26/1) and pledged 26 Aug. (JC 1/13).
He died in 1580, leaving £182 (Edin. Tests., 7 Nov. 1580).

HUNTER, JOHN
one of the penitents who submitted to the kirk Nov. 1572 (SP 52/23, fo. 254; *CSP Scot.*, iv, no, 487).
Either a merchant, B. 12 Dec. 1561, G. 20 Feb. 1571, assessed at £5 in 1565, and his widow at £3 in 1581 and £3 10s in 1583 *or* a tailor, B. 5 Feb. 1567.

HUNTER, MUNGO smith
one of the forty-seven, including Patrick Anderson (see above), charged with active conspiracy 31 July 1573 (JC 26/1) and pledged 26 Aug. (JC 1/13). Deacon of the hammermen 1545-51 (Smith, *Hammermen of Edinburgh*, xciii) and on the council twice in the 1550s and once in the 1560s.

HUTCHISON, WILLIAM skinner
one of the penitents who submitted to the kirk Nov. 1572; given as 'Hewcherim' (SP 52/23, fo. 254; *CSP Scot.*, iv, no. 487); he and his wife, Christine Baron (see above), pledged for assisting the rebels, 2 April 1573 (JC 1/13; Pitcairn, *Trials*, I, ii, 42); one of the forty-seven charged under the blanket indictment of active conspiracy, 31 July (JC 26/1; see Patrick Anderson, above), and listed with those pledged 26 Aug. but marked *'remissione'* (JC 1/13); his grant of remission, for a composition of £26 13s 4d, given as 18 March, predated all of these justiciary proceedings (*RSS*, vi, 1905; *TA*, xii, 265), but only referred to remaining and taking part.
B. tanner 27 July 1560.

JACKSON, THOMAS mason
one of the forty-seven, including Patrick Anderson (see above), charged with active conspiracy 31 July 1573 (JC 26/1) and pledged 26 Aug. (JC 1/13). Deacon of the masons 1556-7, 1559-60 and 1567-8; see also (Robert?) Sinclair (below), his apprentice; Jackson died, in debt, in 1576 (Edin. Tests., 5 June 1576).

JOB, ALEXANDER baxter
at the horn 16 Jan. 1572 for taking part or supplying victuals; granted a remission for remaining and taking part, 4 May 1573 (*RSS*, vi, 1437, 1956); assessed at £3 in 1583 stent; his wife's testament reveals a net £326 (Edin. Tests., 28 Jan. 1577).

JOHNSTON, GEORGE waxmaker
summoned to appear at Leith 31 Jan. 1572 (*Memorials*, 219); assessed at 10s in 1581 stent and 5s in 1583; he died in 1590, leaving £190 (Edin. Tests., 15 Dec. 1591).

JOHNSTON, JOHN flesher
summoned to appear at Leith 31 Jan. 1572 (*Memorials*, 220); assessed at 5s in 1583 stent; his wife's testament involved only very small amounts and was £1 in debt (Edin. Tests., 21 June 1577).

JOHNSTON, JOHN saddler
one of the twenty-three charged with treasonably assisting the rebels, 13 Aug. 1573 (JC 1/13; see John Adamson, above, and Pitcairn, *Trials*, I, ii, 47); paid a composition of £13 6s 8d for taking part (*TA*, xii, 267).
B. 24 July 1563; assessed at 30s in 1583 stent.
One J.J. was among the penitents who submitted to the kirk in Nov. 1572, and the other submitted in April 1574 for remaining in the town, but no further details are given (SP 52/23, fo. 254; *CSP Scot.*, iv, no. 487; BGKE, fos. 1v, 9r).

JOHNSTON, SIMON baxter
one of those who, as Grange complained to Killigrew, was forced to submit to the session for remaining in the town; he is included in the list of penitents of Nov. 1572, but also was one of the twenty-nine or thirty inhabitants, including Henry Anderson and John Henderson (see above), who appealed to the session to intercede with the civil magistrate on their behalfs since, although they had fought for the queen's lords, they had not interfered with their neighbours' property (Calderwood, *History*, iii, 225; SP 52/23, fo. 254; *CSP Scot.*, iv, no. 487; *Memorials*, 274-6).
B. 12 April 1563.

JOLLIE, WILLIAM
summoned to appear at Leith 31 Jan. 1572 (*Memorials*, 221).

KELLO, BERNARD [unfree] stabler
summoned to appear at Leith 31 Jan. 1572 (*Memorials*, 221).
B. 6 May 1580; assessed at 13s 4d in 1583 stent.

KELLO, JOHN [unfree stabler?]
a hagbutter in the Castle at its fall in May 1573 (SP 52/25, fos. 72v, 117v).
B. stabler 6 May 1580; assessed at 10s in the stents of 1581 and 1583.

KENNEDY, JOHN wright
summoned to appear at Leith 31 Jan. 1572 (*Memorials*, 221).
A catholic recusant; see app. vi.

KENNEDY, THOMAS wright
one of the forty-seven, including Patrick Anderson (see above), charged with active conspiracy, 31 July 1573; reappeared 13/14 Aug. (JC 26/1) and pledged 26 Aug. (JC 1/13); had appeared among the penitents who submitted to the kirk in Nov. 1572 (SP 52/23, fo. 254).
Assessed at 5s in 1583 roll.

KERR, THOMAS of FERNIHURST
appointed provost of the burgh by the queen's lords, 20 June 1571 (*Diurnal*, 226).

KIDD, JOHN [webster]
'worset maker', summoned to appear at Leith 31 Jan. 1572 (*Memorials*, 221).

KIDD, JOHN
the second of this name to be summoned to appear at Leith 31 Jan. 1572 (*Memorials*, 221).

KINCAID, EDWARD maltman
summoned to appear at Leith 31 Jan. 1572 (*Memorials*, 219); charged with assisting the rebels, 4 Feb. 1573 and reappeared 9 Feb. (JC 1/13; Pitcairn, *Trials*, I, ii, 39); granted a remission 5 March for taking part, provisioning and circulating false coin (*RSS*, vi, 1876); the composition of £400 was the second largest exacted from an Edinburgh burgess (*TA*, xii, 265).
Assessed at £5 in 1565, £3 in 1581 and 35s in 1583; he died in 1577, leaving £1,085 net (Edin. Tests., 12 Nov. 1577); he had figured in the Nicol Young case of 1564 as one of the eight members of the assize who voted to convict all four defendants (see also James Forret, Herbert Maxwell, John Spottiswood and John Wilson, also prominent members of the catholic faction in the burgh in the 1560s and supporters of the queen's party; Pitcairn, *Trials*, i, 448).

KING, ALEXANDER advocate
summoned to appear at Leith 31 Jan. 1572 (*Memorials*, 220) and a pledge entered for him the following day (JC 1/13); cf. his servant, John Cramond (above).
On the subscription list of 1562; £10 as one of the 'men of law' in 1565 roll; had been an assessor, procurator-fiscal and commissioner for the burgh (*Edin. Recs.*, ii, 298; iii, 150, 227).

KNELAND, WILLIAM [unfree maltman under the Castle wall]
one of the forty-five for whom pledges entered 17 Aug. 1573 (JC 1/13).
B. & F. maltman by rt. of wife 27 July 1580; assessed at 15s in 1581 and 5s in 1583; he died in 1589, leaving £30 net (Edin. Tests., 24 Feb. 1590).

LAING, WILLIAM merchant
summoned to appear at Leith 31 Jan. 1572 (*Memorials*, 220).
B. 30 May 1560; assessed at 40s in 1565 roll.

LAMB, JAMES
submitted to the session April 1574 for remaining in the town (BGKE, fo. 1v). A burgess of the Canongate (*Broughton Court Book*, 137).

LAUDER, GEORGE maltman
summoned to appear at Leith 31 Jan. 1572; at the horn for non-appearance to answer charges of remaining in the town and assisting the rebels, 1 April 1572 (*Memorials*, 221; *RSS*, vi, 1543). He died in 1585, leaving £171 (Edin. Tests., 22 April 1586).

LAUDER, HEW [merchant]
one of the bailies intruded by Grange 20 June 1571, although he had only been made a burgess less than a month before; on 3 Oct. 1571, the day after fresh elections, he was made sergeant-major of all the men of war in the burgh (*Diurnal*, 226, 250; *History of King James VI*, 86); summoned to appear at Leith 31 Jan. 1572 (*Memorials*, 218, where he is third listed); granted a remission 8 Oct. 1572 for assisting the rebels and taking part in the burning of Dalkeith in Dec. 1571 (*RSS*, vi, 1766); although he was first admonished, privately and 'gentillie', in June 1575, it was not until 15 Sept. that Lauder presented his supplication to the session that he had appeared in battle and accepted the 'office of ane crounderschipe'; the session had also arranged that his child's upbringing be guaranteed to be in the 'trew feir and knawledge of God' by making James Nicolson (see K.P. list) responsible for it (BGKE, fos. 62v, 63r, 65v, 67v, 69v, 70r, 72r).
Capt. Hew L., B. & G. by rt. of wife 30 May 1571; assessed at 50s in 1581 and £3 in 1583.

LAURIE, GEORGE (LAWRIESTON) [unfree] maltman
one of those who submitted to the kirk in Nov. 1572; one of the forty-five who entered pledges 17

Aug. 1573 (SP 52/23, fo. 254; *CSP Scot.*, iv, no. 487; JC 1/13).
George Lawrieston B. & F. 11 May 1580; assessed at 10s in 1581 and 5s in 1583.

LAURIE, JOHN maltman at the West Port
at the horn 8 Aug. 1572 for furnishing the Castle with 'ane gret quantitie of victuall'; granted a remission for assisting and supplying with victuals, 8 Oct. 1572, with a composition of £200 (*RSS*, vi, 1702, 1763; *TA*, xii, 265); also charged 4 Feb. 1573 with assisting the rebels in the Castle (JC 1/13; Pitcairn, *Trials*, I, ii, 39).
B. 17 Oct. 1569; assessed at 40s in 1581 and 20s in 1583. His composition is the fourth largest recorded.

LAWSON, DAVID tailor
gift of an annual rent owing to him because of his failure to appear in Leith to answer a charge of helping to fortify the burgh, 22 April 1572 (*RSS*, vi, 1574).
Assessed at 15s in 1583 stent.

LAWSON, JAMES bonnetmaker
submitted to the session 16 June 1575 for remaining and accepting armour (BGKE, fo. 62v).
See *Edin. Recs.*, iii, 54, 91; six times a deacon of the craft between 1556 and 1566.

LAWTIE, DAVID writer [to the signet]
summoned to appear at Leith 31 Jan. 1572 (*Memorials*, 220).
£10 as one of the 'men of law' in 1565 roll; see also *Diurnal*, 202.

LEKPREVIK (LAPUIK), ALEXANDER [notary]
one of those who submitted to the kirk in Nov. 1572 (SP 52/23, fo. 254). See *Broughton Court Book*, 113.

LENNOX (LEVENAX), JOHN 'cadgear' outside the West Port
an unspecified composition, probably for taking part, 28 Feb. 1576 (*TA*, xiii, 345).

LESLIE, HELEN of Kinnaird
the widow of James Baron, one of the most prominent protestants in Edinburgh in the 1560s; after his death in 1569, she married James Kirkcaldy, the cousin of Grange, who was put to the horn by the king's lords in Sept. 1571 (see Edin. Tests., 21 April, 1570; *RSS*, vi, 1295). Her second marriage was as unhappy as the first; she betrayed her husband to Morton but was found strangled shortly after he escaped (see Grant, *Memoirs of Sir William Kirkcaldy*, 321-3).

LIBERTON, WILLIAM baxter
one of the forty-five pledged 17 Aug. 1573 (JC 1/13).
Assessed at 5s in 1583 stent.

LIDDEL, WILLIAM merchant
summoned to appear at Leith 31 Jan. 1572 (*Memorials*, 220).
B. mt. 20 May 1561; he died in 1587, leaving £158 (Edin. Tests., 28 March 1588).

LIDDEL, WILLIAM smith
also on the list of 31 Jan. 1572 (*ibid.*, 221).
A master of his craft in 1550; he died in 1582 (Smith, *Hammermen of Edinburgh*, 149, 176).
A William Liddel appears on the list of those who submitted to the kirk in Nov. 1572, but no further details are given (SP 52/23, fo. 254).

LINDSAY, m. JAMES merchant
his testament was made in his house in Edinburgh 22 April 1572; one of the witnesses was the ex-chaplain, William McKie (see below and app. vi).
G. Sept. 1548; the brother of the early protestant craftsman, Patrick Lindsay (see app. iv); James, however, was a member of the deposed Seton council of 1559-60 and became a prominent member of the catholic faction in the 1560s; he voted to convict all four defendants in the Nicol Young case (Pitcairn, *Trials*, i, 448); his wife, Margaret Ramsay, had connections with catholic recusants (see app. vi), although he appeared on the protestant subscription list of 1562; assessed at £10 in 1565; he left £315 net (Edin. Tests., 26 March 1574).

LINTON, FRANCIS [merchant]
recommended by Thomas Hamilton of Priestfield as a 'true subject' of Mary, April 1571 (*CSP Scot.*, iii, no. 697).
G. 11 July 1561; a £30 contribution in 1565 roll; on the subscription list of 1562.

LITTLE, EDWARD merchant
the go-between of Verac and Mothe Fénélon, April 1571; Maitland and Grange passed on a request from him and other Edinburgh merchants engaged in the wine trade for a passport to France to Drury, Sept. 1571 (*CSP Scot.*, iii, nos. 680, 907). Little was a prominent member of the catholic faction in the burgh, had been a bailie on the Seton council of 1559-60, testified to the inquiry of February 1560 (*De La Brosse Report*, 122), and twice figured in Mary's leets in the 1560s; he was assessed at £20 in 1565.

LOCH, STEPHEN glasswright
summoned to appear at Leith 31 Jan. 1572 (*Memorials*, 221); one of the forty-seven, including Patrick Anderson (see above), charged with active conspiracy 31 July 1573 (JC 26/1) and pledged 26 Aug. (JC 1/13); yet his supplication to the session in April 1574 only mentioned his remaining in the town (BGKE, fo. 1v). He died in 1578, leaving £198 net (Edin. Tests., 24 Nov. 1580).

LOCKHART, ALEXANDER
among those who submitted to the kirk in Nov. 1572 (SP 52/23, fo. 254); charged 31 July 1573 along with Patrick Anderson (see above) and others with active conspiracy (JC 26/1); pledged 26 Aug. (JC 1/13).

LOGAN, DAVID [baxter apprentice]
his supplication to the session pleaded that he only remained for part of the time and bore armour only because he assumed his father's responsibility to watch and ward (BGKE, fos. 59r, 62v).
B. baxter by rt. of fr. David L., 26 Feb. 1574; assessed at 20s in 1583 stent; he died in 1589, leaving £257 (Edin. Tests., 18 May 1597). His father was a catholic; see app. vi.

LOVE, DAVID [baxter?]
40s composition for intercommuning, 28 Feb. 1576 (*TA*, xiii, 345).
Probably a baxter like the other bracketed with him.

LUMSDEN, HENRY [apprentice barber]
one of those who submitted to the kirk in Nov. 1572 (SP 52/23, fo. 254; *CSP Scot.*, iv, no. 487).
B. barber 29 Nov. 1576; G. 6 Sept. 1587; assessed at 20s in 1583 stent.

McAULAY (McCALLER), ALAN [merchant]
summoned to appear at Leith 31 Jan. 1572 (*Memorials*, 221); presented a discharge the next day before the Court of Justiciary (JC 1/13, but out of sequence).
G. 13 Nov. 1561; assessed at £13 in 1581 and £4 in 1583.

McCALL, JOHN merchant
charged along with John Adamson and others 13 Aug. 1573 with treasonably assisting the rebels
(JC 1/13; see Pitcairn, *Trials*, I, ii, 47, and Adamson, above); granted a remission, with a composition of £20, for remaining and taking part on 18 Aug. (*RSS*, vi, 2100; *TA*, xii, 266); submitted
to the session April 1574 for remaining in the town (BGKE, fo. 1v).
B. 5 Feb. 1562; G. 31 Aug. 1570; a £10 contribution in 1565 and assessed at £6 in 1581 and £3 in
1583.

MacCALZEAN, m. THOMAS [later Lord Cliftonhall] advocate and lord of session
summoned to appear at Leith 31 Jan. 1572 (*Memorials*, 218, where he is first on the list); put to the
horn and his goods escheated four days later for his failure to appear; granted a remission for
treasonably taking part, 2 May 1572 (*RSS*, vi, 1470, 1586). He was involved in a protracted
dispute with the session over his slandering of the minister, John Durie, which culminated in Nov.
1574 with him being ordered 'to departe out of thair session', but more seriously, over his refusal to
accept the injunctions of the kirk for remaining in the town, which resulted in his being barred
from the communion table. MacCalzean appealed to the General Assembly, which decided 11
Aug. 1574 that he be asked to produce evidence in writing; he did this 3 March 1575, arguing, with
justification, that he had been one of the first protestant adherents in the town; his case was that he
had been unable to leave the town because of his fear of falling into the hands of Archibald
Ruthven, who had pursued a *vendetta* against him ever since his daughter's marriage to Patrick
Moscrop in Dec. 1570 (given as 1571, but cf. *Diurnal*, 196); he maintained that he had been
'extremelie handillit' during his stay because of his loyalty to the king; he denied the charge of
accepting the office of eldership, though his defence that he had served in that current year and the
preceding one would seem to indicate that he continued as such after the town's occupation. The
session agreed, after a vote, to adhere to the recommendation of the General Assembly of 10
March that he be readmitted to the communion, but apparently only after he made a public
repentance in sackcloth, the same treatment, he protested on 9 June, as meted out to 'murtheraris
and raiseris of fyre'; he still had not submitted 8 Sept. 1575 when the session resolved on a further
private admonition to him, John Moscrop, Frood and Dickson before resorting to a public
admonition (BGKE, fos. 6r, 20v, 26r, 27v, 28r, 46v-48r, 52v, 53r, 60v, 61r, 71v; *Memorials*, 229;
Calderwood, *History*, iii, 343).
B. & G. 15 Nov. 1538; a £100 contribution in 1565 roll; frequently an assessor, appointed provost
in Oct. 1561, a commissioner to the General Assembly for the burgh in 1565 (*Edin. Recs.*, iii, 43,
127, 153, 211; see also Pitcairn, *Trials*, I, iii, 247f and the council lists); also a burgess of the
Canongate (*Broughton Court Book*, 82); he died in 1581, leaving £4,481 net (Edin. Tests., 3 July
1582).

MacCARTNAY, WILLIAM [writer]
submitted to the session April 1574 for remaining in the town (BGKE, fo. 1v).
B. & G. writer 'in respect of his office of customarye', 14 Feb. 1578.

McCASKIE, WALTER cooper
summoned to appear at Leith 31 Jan. 1572 (*Memorials*, 219).

McGILL, JOHN merchant
summoned to appear at Leith 31 Jan. 1572 (*Memorials*, (Dalyell ed.,), 315; cf. Bann. ed., 219,
which gives him as 'McGow').
B. & G. 31 May 1538.

McKIE, WILLIAM schoolmaster
convicted of treason and saying the mass 13 June 1572 after his capture in the Crags skirmish;
executed, although sixty years of age and coerced into the field by the provost under threat of

hanging (JC 1/13; Pitcairn, *Trials*, I, ii, 32; *Diurnal*, 265, 301; *CSP Scot.*, iv, no, 363(1); see app. vi).

MAIN, JOHN elder merchant
charged with being involved in the action at the Crags in June 1572 (JC 1/13, 9 Feb. 1573; Pitcairn, *Trials*, I, ii, 40).
This seems to be one of the burgh's earliest protestants; see app. iv.

MAIN, JOHN merchant
summoned to appear at Leith 31 Jan. 1572 (*Memorials*, 220); he and two others, who were soldiers in the Castle pressed their suit to the session, but were referred to the whole congregation because of the seriousness of their offences, 17 Feb. 1575 (BGKE, fos. 43r, 45v). Two merchants of this name in 1583 stent, one assessed at £5 (and £6 in 1581), the other at 20s.

MARJORIBANKS, m. JOHN merchant
warned, along with Fairlie, Peter Martin and Alan Dickson to appear before the session 29 Sept. 1575 (BGKE, fo. 73v).
B. & G. 10 Aug. 1561; on the council 1561-4 and the subscription list of 1562; paid a £30 contribution in 1565; he, while a bailie, opposed the council's attempts to dismiss the catholic master of the grammar school (*Edin. Recs.*, iii, 142); he returned to the council in 1576.

MARJORIBANKS, LEONARD
one of ninety-two who submitted to the kirk Nov. 1572 (SP 52/23, fo. 254; *CSP Scot.*, iv, no. 487).

MARJORIBANKS, MICHAEL clerk to the kirk session
made clerk to the rival commissaries set up in Edinburgh in April 1572 (*Diurnal*, 295); made public repentance 14 Oct. 1574 for remaining in the town (BGKE, fo. 22r). Appointed clerk 1565, and reappointed 23 Sept. 1575, replacing Adam Moscrop (*Edin. Recs.*, iii, 206; iv, 42).
B. & G. 22 June 1564.

MARTIN, PETER [merchant]
elected as one of the bailies of the queen's party in Oct. 1571, which was one of the charges, along with helping to take the steeple of St. Giles' and expelling the lawful magistrates (presumably in June 1571) when put to the horn 13 Jan. 1572 (Prot. Bk. Aitkin, i, fo. 69r; *RSS*, vi, 1431); figures prominently in the list of those summoned to appear at Leith 31 Jan., along with his son Thomas (*Memorials*, 218); granted a remission, 4 May 1573, for remaining, taking part and other offences, with a hefty composition of £200 (*RSS*, vi, 1954; *TA*, xii, 265); he had not submitted to the session as late as Sept. 1575 when he, Mungo Fairlie and Alan Dickson were warned to do so (BGKE, fo. 73v). On the subscription list of 1562; £20 contribution in 1565 roll, but only assessed at 10s in 1583; he had not been on the council before 1571 and did not reappear after 1573; a burgess of the Canongate (*Broughton Court Book*, 82); he died in 1584, leaving £460 net (Edin. Tests., 11 March 1584).

MARTIN, THOMAS [merchant]
the son of Peter M., summoned to appear at Leith 31 Jan. 1572 (*Memorials*, 218).
£5 contribution in 1565.

MATHESON, CUTHBERT webster
summoned to appear at Leith 31 Jan. 1572 (*Memorials*, 220); one of the ninety-two who submitted to the kirk Nov. 1572 (SP 52/23, fo. 254); one of the forty-seven, including Patrick Anderson (see

above), charged with active conspiracy 31 July 1573 (JC 26/1) and among those pledged 26 Aug. (JC 1/13).
B. & G. 29 Jan. 1561; assessed at 5s in 1583; deacon of his craft 1570-71.

MATHESON, JAMES baxter
summoned to appear at Leith 31 Jan. 1572 (*Memorials*, 220); Mungo Brady (see K.P. list) entered a pledge on his behalf before the Court of Justiciary the next day (JC 1/13; the entry is out of sequence, following one of 23 Feb.).
B. 6 June 1560.

MATHESON, WILLIAM [merchant]
one of those submitted to the kirk Nov. 1572 (SP 52/23, fo. 254).
B. & G. mt. by rt. of wife, 5 March 1558.

MATHIE, ROBERT [bonnetmaker]
also on the list of penitents of Nov. 1572 (SP 52/23, fo. 254).
B. bonnetmaker 6 April 1566.

MAXWELL, HERBERT [merchant]
one of the bailies intruded by the queen's lords 20 June 1571; forfeited for treason 30/31 July 1571 along with a number of other prominent burgh supporters of the queen's party (see Gilbert Balfour, above) for fortifying the steeple of St. Giles' and assisting Grange (*Diurnal*, 226, 235; JC 26/1; *CSP Scot.*, iii, no. 898; *Memorials*, 186; Calderwood, *History*, iii, 117); he submitted to the kirk 18 Nov. 1574 for remaining, coming into battle and accepting the 'pretendit office of ane bailye' (BGKE, fos. 29r, 30r).
B. & G. 29 March 1538; his contribution of £25 in 1565 was reduced, on appeal, to £15. He was one of the leading figures in the catholic faction in the burgh in the 1560s, had been one of the unpopular bailies on the Seton council of 1559-60, had fought a running battle with the council over fairly trivial matters since then, including his tax assessment, and appeared on the assize in the significant Nicol Young case in 1564 (see council lists; *Edin. Recs.*, iii, 189, 197; M. Wood, 'The domestic affairs of the burgh, 1554-1589: unpublished extracts from the records', *B.O.E.C.*, xv (1928), 49; MS Co. Recs., iv, fos. 28r, 115v, 184v, 210r, 257v; Pitcairn, *Trials*, i, 448). His son, John, had been taken prisoner by the king's lords in Sept. 1570 (*CSP Scot.*, iii, no. 449); a burgess of the Canongate (*Broughton Court Book*, 82); he should be distinguished from Herbert Maxwell of Cavannes, who died in 1573 (Edin. Tests., 12 Aug. 1579); he was still alive in 1577 (see Alan Dickson, above).

MAXWELL, RICHARD baxter in the Potterrow
a composition of £6 13s 4d for taking part with the rebels from Dec. 1570 until 1 Aug. 1572, made 28 Feb. 1576 (*TA*, xiii, 346).

MEID, ROBERT webster
one of the forty-seven, including Patrick Anderson (see above), charged with active conspiracy 31 July 1573 (JC 26/1) and pledged 26 Aug. (JC 1/13); he had been one of those who submitted to the kirk in Nov. 1572, before the main judicial processes began (SP 52/23, fo. 254). Not in the burgess roll, although he had been deacon of his craft 1559-60 and 1564-5; assessed at 5s in 1583.

MEIN, BARTIE cooper
summoned to appear at Leith 31 Jan. 1572 (*Memorials*, 221; mistranscribed as 'Barlie' in Dalyell ed., 319; see Advocates MS., fo. 238v).
Bartilmo Mein B. by rt. of wife, 2 May 1567.

MELROSE (MEWROS), JOHN wright
summoned to appear at Leith 31 Jan. 1572 (*Memorials*, 221); pledged 13 Aug. 1573 (JC 1/13).

MELVILLE, WILLIAM [merchant]
granted remission 22 Sept. 1573, with a composition of £6 13s 4d, for remaining and other offences (*RSS*, vi, 2135; *TA*, xii, 266).
Assessed at 30s in 1581 and 10s in 1583.

MERCER, LAURENCE [unfree] pewterer
among the forty-seven, including Patrick Anderson (see above), charged with active conspiracy 31 July; he reappeared 10/11 Aug. and was pledged 13/14, although the entry is marked 'acqt' (JC 26/1); however, he was again among those pledged 26 Aug. (JC 1/13).
B. by rt. of wife 20 April 1582; assessed at 5s in 1583 stent.

MILLAR, HANS (i.e. Dutch Hans) ordinary gunner in the Castle [skinner]
summoned to appear at Leith 31 Jan. 1572 (*Memorials*, 221); granted a remission for remaining, taking part and victualling, 10 Nov. 1573 (*RSS*, vi, 2199); reconciled by the session 20 May 1574 for taking part in the most wicked deeds of the rebels, including the firing and demolition of houses in the town (BGKE, fo: 7v).
B. & F. by rt. of wife 23 June 1569; he died in 1578, leaving £337 (Edin. Tests., 8 Feb. 1581).

MILLAR, JAMES [merchant]
one of the ninety-two who submitted to the kirk Nov. 1572 (SP 52/23, fo. 254); later charged, along with Patrick Anderson (see above) and others, with active conspiracy; reappeared 10/11 Aug. (JC 26/1), but no further mention of him.
There are a number of burgesses of this name — a smith assessed at 6s 8d in the roll of 1583, a lorimer made B. in 1578, a writer made B. & G. in 1567, but the likeliest is a merchant made B. 15 July 1563 (*Edin. Accts.*, ii, 168, but not on the burgess roll) with a £5 contribution in 1565.

MILLAR, JOHN skinner
summoned to appear at Leith 31 Jan. 1572 (*Memorials*, 221).
B. 27 June 1561; assessed at 5s in 1583.

MILLAR, RICHARD butterman
summoned to appear at Leith 31 Jan. 1572 (*Memorials*, 221).
B. 13 Aug. 1568; assessed at 30s in 1581 and 10s in 1583.

MILNE, JOHN wright
one of the smiths, wrights and gunners who defected to the queen's party in March 1572; still in the Castle at its fall in May 1573 (*RSS*, vi, 1530; SP 52/25, fos. 72v, 118r).

MITCHELLHILL, GEORGE [clothier and tailor]
one of the forty-seven charged, including Patrick Anderson (see above), with active conspiracy 31 July 1573 (JC 26/1); pledged 26 Aug. (JC 1/13).
B. & G. clothier 7 April 1558; assessed, as a tailor, at 5s in 1583.

MITCHELSON, THOMAS tailor and merchant
variously given as Michell and Mitchelson; summoned to appear at Leith 31 Jan. 1572; convicted of treason and executed after being captured in the Crags action, 13 June 1572 (*Memorials*, 219; JC 1/13; Pitcairn, *Trials*, I, ii, 32; *Diurnal*, 265; *RSS*, vi, 1888).
B. mt. 11 Feb. 1559.

MOFFAT, JOHN maltman
charged 4 Feb. 1573 with assisting the rebels in the Castle; pledged 9 Feb. (JC 1/13; Pitcairn, *Trials*, I, ii, 39).
B. 13 Oct. 1561 (*Edin. Accts.*, ii, 146, but not on the burgess roll); £20 contribution in 1565 and assessed at £6 in 1581 and £2 in 1583.

MOFFAT, ROBERT wright and ordinary gunner in the Castle
defected to the queen's lords in March 1572 and still in the Castle at its fall in May 1573 (*RSS*, vi, 1530; SP 52/25, fos. 72v, 118r); their appeal to the session was referred to the whole congregation because of the offences (see Thomas Glasford and Hans Millar), April/May 1574 (BGKE, fos. 3r, 7v).
See *Edin. Accts.*, ii, 105ff.

MOODIE, JOHN maltman
summoned to appear at Leith 31 Jan. 1572 (*Memorials*, 220).
B. 19 Dec. 1550; £5 contribution in 1565; he died in 1581, leaving £632 (Edin. Tests., 29 May 1580).

MOODIE, WILLIAM [tailor]
although he appeared as a witness to a notarial process in Leith 1 Nov. 1571 (Prot. Bk. Robesoun, xvii, fo. 130), his name was included in the list of those warned to appear at Leith 31 Jan. 1572 (*Memorials*, 219). The son of John Moodie (see above), and the son-in-law of William Anderson (see above), who acted as surety when he made B. 29 April 1568; appears in both rolls of 1581 and 1583, at 50s and £4, so probably a draper by then.

MORTON, ALAN
one of those who submitted to the kirk Nov. 1572 (SP 52/23, fo. 254).

MOSCROP, ANDREW
he and William Stevenson (see below), both burgesses of Edinburgh, denounced as rebels 4 Oct. 1571 for failing to appear before the privy council (*RPC*, ii, 83).

MOSCROP, JOHN [advocate]
forfeited by the king's lords 30/31 Aug. 1571 along with other leading Edinburgh supporters of the queen's party for fortifying the steeple of St. Giles' etc. (see Gilbert Balfour etc.); his goods and those of his son, Patrick, escheated to Archibald Ruthven, a personal enemy since the marriage of his son to the daughter of Thomas MacCalzean (see above; JC 26/1; *CSP Scot.*, iii, no. 898; *Diurnal*, 245; Calderwood, *History*, iii, 117; *RSS*, vi, 1260; *Memorials*, 186). His wife was captured by the king's lords 29 Sept. (*ibid.*, 191-2); he, his wife and son were all granted a remission 2 Dec. 1573 for being at Langside in 1568 (*RSS*, vi, 2214). Moscrop was the first recorded as asking to be readmitted to the communion table 13 May 1574; his appeal was rejected because he refused to accept the injunctions of the kirk as others had done on the grounds that he had left the burgh long before the first siege. The session, however, maintained that he had committed 'greater slander nor uyeris inferiores' who had remained by being the 'author' of the troubles between Fernihurst and the town of Jedburgh; when Moscrop finally agreed to submit, 22 Sept. 1575, this charge was ordered to be deleted; in the meantime, Moscrop appealed to the General Assembly, arguing that he had satisfied the civil authorities and received a pardon and the restitution of his lands and goods, but without success; after three private admonitions and one public, Moscrop submitted (BGKE, fos. 5v, 20v, 65, 67v, 68v, 69v, 71v, 72, 73r).
Procurator-fiscal of the burgh since 1559 (*Edin. Recs.*, iii, 28f); B. & G. 3 Sept. 1560; on the sub-scription list of 1562, and assessor on the council 1562-3 and a £100 contribution, the largest, in 1565; a burgess of the Canongate (*Broughton Court Book*, 106); see also Pitcairn, *Trials*, I, ii, 248.

MOSCROP, PATRICK [merchant]
the son of John Moscrop, married to the daughter of Thomas MacCalzean in Dec. 1570, resulting in a bitter dispute with Archibald Ruthven (*Diurnal*, 196); forfeited along with his father 30/31 Aug. 1571 and his goods escheated to Ruthven; included in his father's remission 2 Dec. 1573 (JC 26/1; *CSP Scot.*, iii, no. 898; *Diurnal*, 245; *Memorials*, 186; *RSS*, vi, 1260, 2214); although he, along with his father, initially refused to receive the injunctions of the kirk, he capitulated earlier, probably because he also wanted his child to be baptised (BGKE, fos. 20v, 43r).
Assessed at £5 in 1583 stent.

MOSSMAN, JAMES goldsmith
master assayer of the Mint, but replaced by Thomas Acheson 24 April 1572 and put to the horn 29 June on a blanket indictment of assisting or supplying victuals or remaining (*RSS*, vi, 1576, 1660, 1896); forfeited by the parliament of king's lords in April 1573 for assisting the rebels, furnishing of the steeple and other places within the burgh and making of false coin (JC 26/1; *CSP Scot.*, iv, no. 636); executed 3 Aug. 1573 (*Hist. King James VI*, 145).
B. & G. by rt. of fr. John Mossman (see K.P. list), 3 Oct. 1558; on the subscription list of 1562; a craft councillor and deacon 1568-9.

MUIR, MATTHEW burgh officer
admitted to the session that he accepted the post of officer during the occupation, although he merely continued in that capacity (BGKE, fo. 9r); recorded as witness to a notarial process 2 Jan. 1572 (Prot. Bk. Aitkin, i, fo. 73r).
B. officer 1 Feb. 1566.

MUIR, ROBERT stabler
summoned to appear at Leith 31 Jan. 1572; on the list of penitents who submitted to the kirk Nov. 1572 (*Memorials*, 220; SP 52/23, fo. 254).

MURDO, PATRICK swordslipper [lorimer]
on the list of those warned to appear at Leith 31 Jan. 1572 and one of the penitents who submitted to the kirk Nov. 1572 (*Memorials*, 221; SP 52/23, fo. 254).
B. 24 Oct. 1561.

MURRAY, CUTHBERT merchant
goods escheated for failing to find surety to answer the charge of involvement in the slaughter of Shaw, Wemyss and Hume (May-June 1571; see details in entry relating to Patrick Anderson); summoned again to appear at Leith 31 Jan. 1572; granted a remission, with a composition of £10, for remaining and taking part, 18 Aug. 1573 (*RSS*, vi, 1271, 2102; *Memorials*, 220; *TA*, xii, 266).
A catholic, who had been excommunicated in 1569; see app. vi.

MURRAY, THOMAS
in the list of penitents who submitted to the kirk Nov. 1572 (SP 52/23, fo. 254).

MUTTOK, [blank] soldier and cordiner
one of the six who were executed after their conviction for treason 13 June 1572 after the action at the Crags (*Diurnal*, 265, but not given as such in the official list of those convicted; see JC 1/13 and Pitcairn, *Trials*, I, ii, 32).

NEIL, RICHARD skinner
his son John refused his burgess-ship by right of his father 13 Feb. 1573 because Richard remained within the town during its occupation, even though John was in Leith (MS. Guild Reg., fo. 103v; *Edin. Burgs.*, 5n).
B. 28 June 1535.

NEILSON, JOHN [cordiner]
one of the forty-five pledged 17 Aug. 1573 (JC 1/13).
B. 23 March 1569; see *Edin. Accts.*, ii, 233.

NEWLANDS, JOHN [variously described as a butterman, woolseller and traveller]
one of the ninety-two inhabitants who submitted to the kirk Nov. 1572 (SP 52/23, fo. 254); singled out in a long and exhaustive indictment of 3 Nov. 1573 as the ringleader behind the riots and disturbances in the town from April 1571 onwards, raising 'the maist part of the comontie of . . . the burgh seditiouslie in armor' to the number of a thousand men, expelling 'a greit part' of the burgesses from the town and depriving the provost and magistrates of their offices; between then and Aug. 1572 he and his fellow conspirators convened regularly in numbers of two thousand men, and were guilty of the slaughter of many supporters of the king's party, including William Shaw, Michael Wemyss, Captain Walter Aikman, Cuthbert Ferguson, Thomas Tait and Methven; ordered to reappear before the court in a month's time (JC 26/1); granted a remission 21 Dec. 1573 for remaining and taking part since Jan. 1571 (*RSS*, vi, 2245).
£3 contribution in 1565; assessed at 10s in 1581 and 6s 8d in 1583; he died of the plague in 1585, leaving £101 (Edin. Tests., 17 Aug. 1587).

NEWTON, ANDREW barber
summoned to appear at Leith 31 Jan. 1572 (*Memorials*, 221).

NICOL, WILLIAM [burgh officer]
in the list of penitents who submitted to the kirk Nov. 1572 (SP 52/23, fo. 254). See *Edin. Accts.*, ii, 59.

NISBET, WILLIAM merchant
one of the queen's party bailies elected Oct. 1571 (Prot. Bk. Aitkin, i, fo. 66v); warned to appear at Leith 31 Jan. 1572 (*Memorials*, 218, where he figures seventh on the list); it is probably he, the 'one Nesbitt' and Alexander Ramsay (see below) who lent Grange two hundred crowns in April 1572, and this may have been what Killigrew warned Morton about in Jan. 1573 (*CSP Scot.*, iv, nos. 293, 533). Nisbet was granted a remission 16 March 1573, with a fairly hefty composition of £100, for remaining, taking part and other offences (*RSS*, vi, 1899; *TA*, xii, 265).
B. & F. 9 July 1567; G. 22 Sept. 1570; he had not been on the council before 1571, but reappeared on it after 1582 (see council lists); by that time, his assessments, of £8 in 1581 and £15 in 1583, indicate that he was one of the twenty wealthiest merchants in Edinburgh; he died of the plague in 1585, leaving £3,656 (Edin. Tests., 31 May 1588); his brother, Henry Nisbet, had been on the expelled council of 1570-71 and returned to it in 1573.

NIVEN, GILBERT
one of the forty-five pledged 17 Aug. 1573 (JC 1/13).

NORVAL, JAMES tailor
warned to appear at Leith 31 Jan. 1572 (*Memorials*, 220); one of the forty-seven, including Patrick Anderson (see above), charged with active conspiracy 31 July 1573 (JC 26/1); pledged 26 Aug. (JC 1/13); he had previously submitted himself to the kirk in Nov. 1572 (SP 52/23, fo. 254). Twice deacon of the tailors and a craft councillor 1569-70.

NWTALE, JOHN
convicted of treason 13 June 1572 after his capture in the action at the Crags (JC 1/13; Pitcairn, *Trials*, I, ii, 32).

OGILVIE, JAMES maltman
warned to appear at Leith 31 Jan. 1572 (*Memorials*, 220).

OSBORNE, WILLIAM drummer
convicted of treason·13 June 1572 after his capture in the Crags action (JC 1/13; Pitcairn, *Trials*, I, ii, 32).

PADYN, JOHN hekkil maker
granted a remission 19 March 1577 for remaining and taking part between Jan. 1571 and Aug. 1572 (*RSS*, vii, 966).
B. by rt. of wife 8 Nov. 1560; she died, in debt, in 1574 (Edin. Tests., 16 May 1575); assessed at 13s 4d in 1583 stent.

PALMER, JOHN [merchant]
granted a remission 22 June 1573 for remaining, taking part and other offences (*RSS*, vi, 2002).
B. 11 May 1552; G. 15 Nov. 1570; £10 contribution in 1565, and assessed at £5 in 1581 and 50s in 1583; he died in 1584, leaving £2,263 (Edin. Tests., 17 May 1585).

PATERSON, ANDREW maltman
warned to appear at Leith 31 Jan. 1572 (*Memorials*, 219).

PATERSON, EDWARD maltman
charged with assisting the rebels in the Castle 4 Feb. 1573 (JC 1/13; Pitcairn, *Trials*, I, ii, 39); granted a remission 18 March for taking part, supplying with provisions, receiving and circulating false coin (cf. John Wilson and Edward Kincaid, both maltmen and charged in the same terms but given much heavier fines); a composition of £26 13s 4d (*RSS*, vi, 1903; *TA*, xii, 265).
£10 contribution in 1565; he died in 1577, leaving £32 net (Edin. Tests., 15 Nov. 1577).

PATERSON, RICHARD merchant
warned to appear at Leith 31 Jan. 1572 (*Memorials*, 219).
£2 contribution in 1565.

PATERSON, ROBERT merchant
warned to appear at Leith 31 Jan. 1572 (*Memorials*, 220); summoned to appear before the Court of Justiciary 13 Aug. 1573 and refused a further extension of time (JC 1/13); granted a remission 18 Aug. for remaining, taking part and other offences (*RSS*, vi, 2103).
There are three merchants of this name in the 1565 roll.

PATERSON, THOMAS merchant
warned to appear at Leith 31 Jan. 1572 and a pledge entered on his behalf the next day (*Memorials*, 220; JC 1/13, but out of sequence and follows an entry of 23 Feb.).
B. & G. 17 Jan. 1571; assessed at 10s in the stents of 1581 and 1583.

PATERSON, WILLIAM baxter
warned to appear at Leith 31 Jan. 1572 (*Memorials*, 221); charged with treasonably assisting the rebels 13 Aug. 1573 (JC 1/13; see John Adamson, above, and Pitcairn, *Trials*, I, ii, 47); granted a remission 18 Aug., with a composition of £20, for remaining, taking part, supplying with victuals, receiving and circulating false coin (*RSS*, vi, 2106; *TA*, xii, 266).
His son was granted his burgess-ship by rt. of his father 11 March 1574; see James P. baxter; . assessed at 30s in 1583 stent.

PATON, GEORGE
one of those who submitted to the kirk Nov. 1572 (SP 52/23, fo. 254).

PETTIGREW (PETAROWSE), DAVID smith and ordinary gunner in the Castle
one of the smiths who defected to the queen's party in March 1572 and still in the Castle at its fall

in May 1573 (*RSS*, vi, 1530; SP 52/25, fos. 73r, 118r).
See Edin. Tests., 5 Jan. 1592.

PILLAN, JOHN cordiner
he and William Weir (see below) escheated for non-appearance or assisting, 10 June 1572 (*RSS*, vi, 1641).
B. 7 Nov. 1566.

PIRIE, ALEXANDER maltman [outside the West Port]
warned to appear at Leith 31 Jan. 1572 and presented a discharge the next day (*Memorials*, 220; JC 1/13, but out of sequence; one of two entries of this date which follow an entry of 23 Feb.).
£5 contribution in 1565 roll; he died in 1580, leaving £937 net (Edin. Tests., 10 Nov. 1580).

PORTEOUS, JOHN weaver in Backraw
fined an unspecified amount, almost certainly for taking part, 28 Feb. 1576 (*TA*, xiii, 345).
A burgess of the Canongate (*Broughton Court Book*, 185).

PORTEOUS, NINIAN [merchant]
son of Patrick (see below); warned to appear at Leith 31 Jan. 1572 (*Memorials*, 219); charged, along with John Adamson (see above) and others 13 Aug. 1573, with treasonably assisting the rebels (JC 1/13; see Pitcairn, *Trials*, I, ii, 47) and granted a remission, with a composition of £33 6s 8d, five days later (*RSS*, vi, 2092; *TA*, xii, 266). Assessed, as a merchant, at 20s in 1581; he died in 1582, leaving £472 net (Edin. Tests., 9 Oct. 1584).

PORTEOUS, PATRICK [merchant]
like his son, warned to appear at Leith 31 Jan. 1572; charged with the same offence 13 Aug. 1573 and also granted a remission, with a composition of £33 6s 8d, on 18 Aug. (*Memorials*, 219; JC 1/13; *RSS*, vi, 2093; *TA*, xii, 266); he also submitted to the session April 1574 for remaining in the town (BGKE, fo. 1v).
B. mt. 12 July 1555; G. 26 March 1571; assessed at 30s in 1581 stent; he died in 1582, leaving £309 (Edin. Tests., 1 April 1584).

PRIOR, MURDO
one of those convicted of treason 13 June 1572 after their capture in the Crags action (JC 1/13; Pitcairn, *Trials*, I, ii, 32).

PURVES, ALAN skinner
also one of the forty-seven charged with conspiracy 31 July 1573 (JC 26/1) and pledged 26 Aug. (JC 1/13); but his submission to the session in April 1574 only mentioned his remaining in the town (BGKE, fo. 1v).
B. 10 May 1554; deacon 1564-6.

PURVES, ALEXANDER saddler
one of the forty-seven, including Patrick Anderson (see above), charged with active conspiracy 31 July 1573; although he failed to appear 10/11 Aug. (JC 26/1), he was pledged 13 Aug. and again on 26th (JC 1/13).
A catholic, who had been excommunicated in 1569; see app. vi.

PURVES, WILLIAM macer
Replaced as macer 3 Oct. 1571; granted remission 31 May 1573 for treasonably remaining, taking part and other offences since Jan. 1571 (*RSS*, vi, 1301, 2432, 2449).
B. 13 Dec. 1560.

PURVES, WILLIAM apothecary
warned to appear at Leith 31 Jan. 1572 (*Memorials*, 221).
B. 24 Aug. 1564; G. 24 March 1568; assessed at 20s in 1581 and 1583; he died in 1588, leaving £476 (Edin. Tests., 10 July 1590).

PYOTT, JAMES [unfree litster]
one of those who submitted to the kirk Nov. 1572 (SP 52/23, fo. 254; *CSP Scot.*, iv, no. 487).
B. litster 25 Sept. 1583; he died in 1588, leaving a net £40 (Edin. Tests., 5 April 1592).

RAE, ROBERT, younger notary
pledged on a charge of murdering Darnley and the two regents, 24 July 1572 (JC 1/13; wrongly dated as 28 July in Pitcairn, *Trials*, I, ii, 36).

RAE, WILLIAM cutler
warned to appear at Leith 31 Jan 1572 (*Memorials*, 219); although there is a note that arrangements were being made 25 Jan. 1573 for his trial and that of Alan Dickson (see above; *TA*, xii, 336), there is no mention of him in the justiciary records until 13 Aug. 1573, when he was charged with treasonably assisting the rebels, along with John Adamson (see above) and others, and 17 Aug. when he reappeared, this time along with Dickson (JC 1/13); although no record of a grant of remission is recorded, he paid a composition of £20 for treasonably assisting the rebels (*TA*, xii, 266).
B. & G. 14 Dec. 1551; assessed at 13s 4d in 1583 stent; see *Edin. Recs.*, iii, 90.

RAMSAY, ALEXANDER tailor
warned to appear at Leith 31 Jan. 1572 (*Memorials*, 220); probably the Sandy Ramsay who, along with Nisbet (see above), lent Grange 200 crowns in April 1572 and was pointed out by Killigrew to Morton in Jan. 1573 (*CSP Scot.*, iv, nos. 293, 533); put to the horn 3 June 1572 for taking part and subscribing bands, but granted a remission, 16 Aug. 1573, with a hefty composition of £100, for remaining, taking part and other offences (*RSS*, vi, 1633, 2085; *TA*: xii, 266); submitted to the session 12 May 1574 that he remained and was compelled to bear arms (BGKE, fo. 53r).
B. 23 Nov. 1552; G. 19 May 1570; assessed at £2 in 1583 stent; he died in 1584, leaving £516 (Edin. Tests., 2 April 1585).

RAMSAY, ALEXANDER stabler
warned to appear at Leith 31 Jan. 1572 (*Memorials*, 220).

RAMSAY, CUTHBERT merchant
one of the bailies intruded by Grange 20 June 1571; he replaced Robert Watson, a long-standing prominent figure in the protestant faction in the burgh and king's party supporter (see K.P. list), as custumar of Edinburgh 20 July and so was a key figure in the pressure put by the Marian party on the Edinburgh merchants trading in France (*Diurnal*, 226, 234); his goods were escheated in favour of George Douglas of Parkhead Dec. 1571 and this was confirmed in Oct. 1574 after his forfeiture by the king's party parliament in Edinburgh in April 1573; he was charged, along with the other most prominent burgh supporters of the queen's lords, with fortifying St. Giles' and its steeple and other parts of the burgh, and assisting Grange (see Herbert Maxwell, Gilbert Balfour, the two Moscrops, William Henderson and Patrick Thomson); the charge on which he was still pursued eighteen months later was for his part in the slaughter of William Shaw in the action at the head of the Canongate in June 1571 (*RSS*, vi, 2696; *CSP Scot.*, iv, nos. 94, 636; JC 26/1). He had figured prominently in the list of those warned to appear at Leith 31 Jan. 1572 (*Memorials*, 218) and was one of the very few prominent Edinburgh Marian supporters still in the Castle when it fell in May 1573 (SP 52/25, fos. 73r, 118r).
B. & G. 16 Nov. 1560; his first wife had been Agnes Stewart, sometime Countess of Bothwell

(Paul, *Scots Peerage*, ii, 156-7; iii, 94); but he had remarried Janet Fleming, the widow of William Craik, thus linking himself indirectly with Patrick Thomson, Archibald Seinyeor and William Craik (see above); on the subscription list of 1562 and his £60 contribution in the 1565 roll indicates that he was one of the wealthiest merchants in Edinburgh. Although he had been on the council of 1563-4, he was acquitted in the Nicol Young case (see council lists and Pitcairn, *Trials*, i, 447f).

RANKIN, JOHN [apprentice tailor]
in the list of penitents who submitted to the kirk Nov. 1572, but seems to have submitted again April 1574 for remaining in the town (SP 52/23, fo. 254; BGKE, fo. 1v).
B. tailor as apprentice to Alexander Gothray, 30 Jan. 1579.

REACH (RECHE), ROBERT [baxter]
one of the penitents who submitted to the kirk Nov. 1572 (SP 52/23, fo. 254; *CSP Scot.*, iv, no. 487).
Assessed, as a baxter, at 6s 8d in 1583 stent.

REID, JOHN cordiner in the Cowgate
executed by Lennox and Morton after the siege of Brechin, 12 Aug. 1570 (*Diurnal*, 183).
See *Edin. Accts.*, ii, 200, 218, 233.

REID, JOHN maltman
warned to appear at Leith 31 Jan. 1572 (*Memorials*, 219); a remission granted, with a composition of £50, for taking part, victualling and circulating false coin, 18 Aug. 1573 (*RSS*, vi, 2094; *TA*, xii, 266). There is also a record of a composition of £6 13s 4d, paid by a John Reid who may or may not be the same man, 28 Feb. 1576, for intercommuning, supplying victuals and breaking the malt acts (*TA*, xiii, 344); he is probably 'fat John', maltman under the wall, made B. 17 April 1562. There is another maltman, who was also a wright, of the same name in the burgess roll, 19 Aug. 1562; however, there is only one maltman of this name in the 1581 and 1583 rolls, assessed at £3 and 20s; he died in 1585, leaving £384 net (Edin. Tests., 7 May 1586).

REID, JOHN wright
warned to appear at Leith 31 Jan. 1572 (*Memorials*, 220; he is given as 'Rind' in the Advocates MS., fo. 238v and Dalyell ed., 318); the only one of the twenty-three charged with treasonably assisting the rebels 13 Aug. 1573 to be discharged (JC 1/13; see Pitcairn, *Trials*, I, ii, 47, and John Adamson, above).
There is a wright of this name in the burgh in the mid-1550s (see *Edin. Accts.*, i, 143, 179; ii, 51), but he might be the wright and maltman made B. in 1562 noted in the previous entry.
Two of the penitents who submitted to the kirk Nov. 1572 had this name (SP 52/23, fo. 254).

REID, JOHN writer
summoned to appear at Leith 31 Jan. 1572 (*Memorials*, 220).

REID, ROBERT maltman
one of the forty-five who were pledged 17 Aug. 1573 (JC 1/13).
Assessed at 30s in the stents of 1581 and 1583.

RENTON, JOHN [unfree maltman]
one of the penitents who submitted to the kirk Nov. 1572 (SP 52/23, fo. 254).
B. 13 April 1580; assessed at 10s in 1581 and 5s in 1583.

RHIND, GEORGE goldsmith
warned to appear at Leith 31 Jan. 1572; one of the twenty-six convicted of treason after their

capture in the Crags action 13 June 1572; submitted to the session 17 March 1575 for remaining in the town and coming into battle, but innocent of any interference with his neighbours' goods (*Memorials*, 220; JC 1/13; Pitcairn, *Trials*, I, ii, 32; BGKE, fo. 49).
B. as eldest son of Thomas R., goldsmith, 4 Aug. 1562.

RHIND, JAMES merchant
warned to appear at Leith 31 Jan. 1572 (*Memorials*, 220).
B. & G. 12 Sept. 1531; £10 contribution in 1565 roll.

RHIND, MICHAEL goldsmith
warned to appear at Leith 31 Jan. 1572; also one of those convicted of treason after capture in the Crags action, 13 June 1572 (*Memorials*, 220; JC 1/13; Pitcairn, *Trials*, I, ii, 32; see George Rhind, above).
B. & G. by rt. of fr. 4 March 1564.

RICHARDSON, JOHN saddler
one of the twenty-three including John Adamson (see above), who were charged 13 Aug. 1573 with treasonably assisting the rebels (JC 1/13; see Pitcairn, *Trials*, I, ii, 47); a composition of £33 6s 8d for taking part (*TA*, xii, 266); dismissed as deacon of his craft June 1579 for serving in the town during its occupation (*Edin. Recs.*, iv, 110).
B. 14 Feb. 1565; assessed at £4 in 1583 stent; he died in 1589, leaving £3,574 net (Edin. Tests., 27 May 1590).

ROBESON, ANDREW skinner
warned to appear at Leith 31 Jan. 1572; granted a remission in March 1573 with a composition of £6 13s 4d (*Memorials*, 220; *RSS*, vi, 1912; *TA*, xii, 265). He died in 1581, leaving £1,225 net (Edin. Tests., 21 Oct. 1581).

ROBESON, GEORGE tailor
one of the twenty-six convicted of treason 13 June 1572 after their capture in the Crags action (JC 1/13; Pitcairn, *Trials*, I, ii, 32).

ROBESON, JAMES locksmith [outside the West Port]
warned to appear at Leith 31 Jan. 1572 (*Memorials*, 221).
B. 16 June 1564; he died in 1585, leaving £28 net (Edin. Tests., 19 Dec. 1586).

ROBESON, WILLIAM [flesher]
one of the penitents who submitted to the kirk Nov. 1572 (SP 52/23, fo. 254).
Deacon of his craft 1557-8 and 1570-71.

RODGER, ALAN mason
warned to appear at Leith 31 Jan. 1572 (given as 'Alan' in Advocates MS., fo. 238 and as 'Alexander' in Univ. MS., fo. 81v; *Memorials*, 221; Dalyell ed., 318).

RODGER, JAMES [merchant]
he and his sons warned to appear at Leith 31 Jan. 1572 (*Memorials*, 221).
B. & G. 12 Nov. 1538; see William R., made B. 6 May 1566, as son and heir to him, a tailor. Only one son, *James*, is mentioned in his testament, in which he left £203 net (Edin. Tests., 8 Jan. 1580); a third, *Alexander*, is referred to in *Edin. Recs.*, iv, 132.

ROSS, MUNGO [cook]
remitted by the session to the magistrate, but reconciled 14 Oct. 1574 for remaining, coming into

battle, entering the Castle, helping in the firing and demolition of houses as well as indiscriminately firing shot into the town (BGKE, fos. 22v, 25v); he was in the Castle when it fell (SP 52/25, fos. 72v, 117v).
B. pastry cook, *gratis* by rt. of the provost (Sir Simon Preston of Craigmillar) 12 Nov. 1565; assessed as a baxter at 6s 8d in 1583 stent.

ROWAN, THOMAS merchant
warned to appear at Leith 31 Jan. 1572 (*Memorials*, 220).
B. 22 Nov. 1550.

SANDERSON, JOHN flesher
submitted to the session 3 June 1574 that he only remained in the town (BGKE, fos. 8v, 9r, 13v); deacon 1560-61, but dismissed by the council for adultery (*Edin. Recs.*, iii, 89).

SANDILANDS, JAMES merchant
warned to appear at Leith 31 Jan. 1572 (*Memorials*, 221); warned to appear before the Court of Justiciary 13 Aug. 1573 and refused a further extension (JC 1/13); granted a remission 22 Jan. 1574 for remaining, taking part and other offences (*RSS*, vi, 2278).
B. merchant 20 Sept. 1567 (*Edin. Accts.*, ii, 232).

SAUCHIE (SONTEE/SONSIE), ALEXANDER [tailor]
one of the twenty-six convicted of treason after their capture in the Crags action, 13 June 1572 (JC 1/13; Pitcairn, *Trials*, I, ii, 32); although he is reported to have been one of the six subsequently executed, there is a man of the same name among the penitents who submitted to the kirk in Nov. 1572 (*Diurnal*, 265; SP 52/23, fo. 254; *CSP Scot.*, iv, no. 487).
B. tailor 28 Feb. 1551; G. 12 June 1557; a craft councillor 1560-61 and 1564-5 and five times deacon of his craft after 1558 (see council lists); on the subscription list of 1562.

SCOTT, JOHN
warned to appear at Leith 31 Jan. 1572 (*Memorials*, 221).
There are a number of this name in the burgess roll and the stent roll of 1583.

SEINYEOR, ARCHIBALD merchant
secured a discharge for 268 *escus de soleil* which he carried from France to Grange, 21 Nov. 1571 (*Misc. Papers illustrative of events in the reigns of Queen Mary and King James VI*, Maitland Club, xxvi (1834), 67f; SRO, RH 1/2/415); but Seinyeor also appeared on the assize at Leith which convicted the twenty-six men captured in the action at the Crags 13 June 1572 (JC 1/13; see Pitcairn, *Trials*, I, ii, 32).
B. & G. by rt. of wife, the dr. of Wm. Craik, provost of the burgh 1551-3, 12 Aug. 1562; he was the brother-in-law of William Craik (see above and also Patrick Thomson and Cuthbert Ramsay); £15 contribution in 1565 roll and he left £1,345 net when he died in 1575 (Edin. Tests., 12 May 1576).

SHANG, DAVID wright
in the Castle at its fall (SP 52/25, fos. 73r, 118r).
B. 18 Nov. 1552; deacon of the wrights 1558-9.

SHANKS, ARCHIBALD
submitted to the session April 1574 for remaining in the town (BGKE, fo. 1v).

SHARP, JAMES baxter
submitted to the session April 1574 for remaining in the town (BGKE, fo. 1v).
B. baxter 6 Sept. 1536.

SIMPSON, ANDREW maltman outside the West Port
£10 composition for supplying and contravening the malt acts, 1 March 1576 (*TA*, xiii, 347).
His widow assessed at 30s and £3 in 1581 and 1583 stents.

SIMPSON, JOHN
one of the twenty-six convicted of treason after their capture in the Crags action, 13 June 1572 (JC 1/13; Pitcairn, *Trials*, I, ii, 32); in the list of penitents who submitted to the kirk Nov. 1572 (SP 52/23, fo. 254; *CSP Scot.*, iv, no. 487).
There are a number of burgesses of this name in the roll, but he was probably one of the keepers of the kirk; (see *Edin. Recs.*, iii, 128, 221).

SIMPSON, LAURENCE tailor
warned to appear at Leith 31 Jan. 1572 (*Memorials*, 220).
G. 19 March 1561; he died in 1579, leaving £2,631 net (Edin. Tests., 28 Jan. 1580); his brother-in-law was Thomas Paterson (see above); on the subscription list of 1562.

SIMPSON, WILLIAM litster
warned to appear at Leith 31 Jan. 1572 (*Memorials*, 220).
B. 18 April 1551; his widow assessed at 20s in 1583 stent.

SINCLAIR, [ROBERT?] mason
a mason called Sinclair among those warned to appear at Leith 31 Jan. 1572 (*Memorials*, 221).
Robert Sinclair B. mason as apprentice to Thomas Jackson (see above), 23 Aug. 1566.

SLATER, JOHN mealman
warned to appear at Leith 31 Jan. 1572; one of the penitents who submitted to the kirk Nov. 1572 (*Memorials*, 220; SP 52/23, fo. 254; *CSP Scot.*, iv, no. 487).

SMITH, GEORGE tailor
one of the deputation sent by the council to confer with Grange 28 April 1571 (*Edin. Recs.*, iii, 285); in the list of those warned to appear at Leith 31 Jan. 1572 and he obtained a discharge the following day (*Memorials*, 219; JC 1/13, but out of sequence coming after an entry of 23 Feb.; see also Prot. Bk. Stewart, elder, 28 Jan. 1572); he was granted a remission 4 Oct. 1572 for remaining and taking part and submitted to the session in April 1574 for remaining in the town (*RSS*, vi, 1758; BGKE, fo. 1v).
B. 9 May 1559; G. 10 July 1564; assessed at 20s in 1583 stent; deacon 1570-71.

SMITH, JOHN
in the list of penitents who submitted to the kirk Nov. 1572 (SP 52/23, fo. 254).
Probably either a cordiner, B. 25 Feb. 1566, or a cramer, B. 21 Oct. 1569.

SMITH, MATTHEW blacksmith
warned to appear at Leith 31 Jan. 1572 (*Memorials*, 220).
B. as apprentice to William Smith (see below), 10 Jan. 1565; assessed at 10s in 1583 stent.

SMITH, ROBERT baxter
one of the twenty-six convicted of treason after their capture in the Crags action, 13 June 1572 (JC 1/13; Pitcairn, *Trials*, I, ii, 32); one of the forty-five pledged 17 Aug. 1573 (JC 1/13).
He died in 1575, leaving £14 net (Edin. Tests., 12 March 1577).

SMITH, WILLIAM blacksmith
warned to appear at Leith 31 Jan. 1572 (*Memorials*, 220); one of the forty-seven inhabitants of the

burgh, including Patrick Anderson (see above), charged with active conspiracy 31 July 1573 (JC 26/1); pledged 26 Aug. (JC 1/13).
G. 20 Dec. 1560; a master of his craft since at least 1550; deprived in 1574 (Smith, *Hammermen of Edinburgh*, 149, 175).

SOMERVILLE, PETER skinner
one of the forty-seven, including Patrick Anderson (see above), charged with active conspiracy 31 July 1573 (JC 26/1); pledged 13/14 Aug. (ibid.) and again 26 Aug. (JC 1/13).
Assessed at 13s 4d in 1583 roll.

SORLEY, JAMES
submitted to the session April 1574 for remaining in the town (BGKE, fo. 1v).

SPENS, JOHN litster
warned to appear at Leith 31 Jan. 1572 and a pledge entered on his behalf the next day (*Memorials*, 219; JC 1/13, but out of sequence following an entry of 23 Feb.).
B. 15 June 1563.

SPENS, PATRICK [baxter]
one of the forty-five pledged 17 Aug. 1573 (JC 1/13).
Assessed, as a baxter, at 13s 4d in 1583 stent; he left £736 net (Edin. Tests., 28 June 1586).

SPOTTISWOOD, JAMES draper
warned to appear at Leith 31 Jan. 1572 (*Memorials*, 219).
B. cramer 30 Aug. 1553; £5 contribution in 1565 and assessed at 10s in 1581.

SPOTTISWOOD, JOHN merchant
warned to appear at Leith 31 Jan. 1572 (*Memorials*, 219); one of the twenty-three, including John Adamson (see above), charged 13 Aug. 1573 with treasonably assisting the rebels (JC 1/13; see Pitcairn, *Trials*, I, ii, 47); granted a remission, with a composition of £33 6s 8d, for remaining, taking part and other offences, 18 Aug. (*RSS*, vi, 2096; *TA*, xii, 266).
A catholic, who had been excommunicated in 1569; see app. vi for further details.

STALKER, WILLIAM [apprentice] goldsmith
warned to appear at Leith 31 Jan. 1572 (*Memorials*, 220); one of the forty-seven, including Patrick Anderson (see above), charged with active conspiracy 31 July 1573; he was warned 10/11 Aug. to find surety within six days and was pledged 13/14 Aug. (JC 26/1).
B. by rt. of wife, dr. of Michael Rhind, goldsmith (see above), 10 June 1586; G. 13 Dec. 1588.

STANHOPE, HENRY maltman outside the West Port
£10 composition for supplying and contravening the malt acts, 28 Feb. 1576 (*TA*, xiii, 346).

STEEL, JOHN [day labourer]
warned to appear at Leith 31 Jan. 1572 (*Memorials*, 221).
See *Edin Accts.*, i, 210, 249.

STEVENSON, ALEXANDER merchant
warned to appear at Leith 31 Jan. 1572 (*Memorials*, 220); a pledge entered on his behalf the next day (JC 1/13, but out of sequence following an entry of 23 Feb.); been warned to appear before the Court of Justiciary 13 Aug. 1573 along with the others who had pledges entered that day and no further extension to be given to him (ibid.).

STEVENSON, ANDREW [merchant]

forfeited by the parliament of king's lords in Aug. 1571; charged, along with John Adamson (see above) and twenty-one others, with treasonably assisting the rebels; pledged until 17 Aug. when a further surety, this time for £200, was given; the surety was increased to £400 on his next appearance on 24 Oct. (JC 1/13); there is no further trace of him in the justiciary records which peter out soon after this date, although there is a record of arrangements being made for his trial along with Alan Dickson, who appeared with him throughout (*TA*, xii, 364); there is no record either of any remission or composition, although there is one for his son, John (see below). He had been put in charge of the evidents of the kirk which he handed over 6 Jan. 1574 (*Edin. Recs.*, iv, 9); his submission to the session in April 1574 only mentioned that he had remained in the town (BGKE, fo. 1v).

B. & G. mt. by rt. of wife, Helen Johnston, 10 Oct. 1549; his £60 contribution in the 1565 roll and his assessments of £20 in 1581 and £13 6s 4d in 1583 indicate that he was one of the wealthiest merchants in the burgh. Although he was on the subscription list of 1562, his wife had catholic sympathies (see app. vi); even so, he appeared on the council in the second half of the 1560s, though not again until 1578 (see council lists); he had been appointed also as one of the three merchant inventors of the chaplainries in the town in 1565 (*Edin. Recs.*, iii, 208); his widow left £2,026 net when she died in 1588.

STEVENSON, GEORGE

submitted to the session in April 1574 for remaining in the town (BGKE, fo. 1v).

STEVENSON, JOHN

the son of Andrew Stevenson; also charged with his father 13 Aug. 1573 with treasonably assisting the rebels (JC 1/13); a composition of £66 13s 4d for taking part with the rebels (*TA*, xii, 266), although his submission to the session of June 1574 stipulated that he had only remained in the town (BGKE, fos. 9r, 20v).

STEVENSON, PATRICK baxter

one of the forty-five pledged 17 Aug. 1573 (JC 1/13).
Not in the burgess roll but see James S. baxter, apprentice to Patrick S., B. 13 April 1586.

STEVENSON, ROBERT [tailor]

submitted to the session April 1574 for remaining in the town (BGKE, fo. 1v).
B. tailor 12 Nov. 1565.

STEVENSON, WILLIAM

he and Andrew Moscrop (see above), both burgesses of Edinburgh, denounced as rebels 4 Oct. 1571 for failing to appear before the privy council (*RPC*, ii, 83); one of those who submitted to the kirk Nov. 1572 (SP 52/23, fo. 254).
Either a cramer, B. 30 Sept. 1564, and assessed at 6s 8d in 1583 stent or a wright (*Edin. Accts.*, i, 208).

STEWART, ARCHIBALD [merchant]

an 'old acquaintance' of Thomas Randolph, who pressed his suit with both Cecil and Leicester; Lennox also assured Cecil that he was a faithful supporter of the regent who was in difficulty because his goods had been seized by Danelour (see above), a dependant of Mary; she agreed to allow Stewart's goods to be released in Nov. 1570 with the hint that more might be done for him if and when his 'sincerity' became 'more manifest'; probably in this connection Stewart three months later agreed to deliver 1,000 crowns to Grange. The Marian agent, John Chisholm, however, was sceptical of the value of the manoeuvre, believing that the Edinburgh merchants whose ships and goods had been held in France were more likely to have been alienated, not least because the partial release of the ships was done without Mary's knowledge. In the covering letter with the

1,000 crowns Chisholm again warned Grange to 'be war of them of the town' (*CSP Scot.*, iii, nos. 489, 490, 491, 495, 566, 627, 638).
B. & G. *gratis* at the request of the regent, 17 Sept. 1569; assessed at £10 in 1581 and £8 in 1583; he left £4,128 net when he died in 1584 (Edin. Tests., 25 Jan. 1585); he appeared on the council 1573-5 and was provost 1577-9.

STEWART, JOHN wright
one of the craftsmen who defected to the queen's lords in March 1572 (*RSS*, vi, 1530); still in the castle when it fell in May 1573 (SP 52/25, fos. 72v, 118r); submitted to the session 22 April 1574 but referred to the whole congregation because of the seriousness of his offences (BGKE, fo. 3r).

STEWART, WILLIAM, elder notary
warned to appear at Leith 31 Jan. 1572 (*Memorials*, 220); made public repentance for remaining in the town 14 Oct. 1574 (BGKE, fo. 22r). Volume three of his protocol book (B/22/1/57) shows that he remained in the town throughout the period of its occupation.
B. 29 Oct. 1553; G. *gratis* for his good service in writing the common business of the town, 20 Sept. 1560.

STODDARD, ALEXANDER, elder [merchant]
one of the forty-seven, including Patrick Anderson (see above), charged with active conspiracy 31 July 1573; reappeared 10/11 Aug. (JC 26/1). See his son, Alexander; among the merchants in 1558 muster roll (MS. Co. Recs., ii, fo. 129v).

STODDARD, ALEXANDER, younger
charged with the same offence as his father 31 July 1573; also reappeared 10/11 Aug. (JC 26/1).
B. as son and heir of Alexr. S., 8 Nov. 1560.

STODDARD, JOHN merchant
warned to appear at Leith 31 Jan. 1572 (*Memorials*, 221); charged 13 Aug. 1573 along with John Adamson (see above) with treasonably assisting the rebels (JC 1/13; see Pitcairn, *Trials*, I, ii, 47); granted a remission for remaining, taking part and other offences 18 Aug., with a composition of £13 6s 8d (*RSS*, vi, 2110; *TA*, xii, 267).
B. & G. by rt. of wife, 16 Feb. 1558; £10 contribution in 1565 and assessed at £3 in 1580 and 20s in 1583.

STODDARD, JOHN webster
one of the forty-seven charged, including Patrick Anderson (see above), with active conspiracy; given six days to find surety, 10/11 Aug. (JC 26/1).

STURGEON, THOMAS [cobbler]
warned to appear 31 Jan. 1572 at Leith (given as 'barker' in Advocates MS., fo. 238 and as a baxter in Univ. MS., fo. 81; *Memorials*, 221; Dalyell ed., 319). Assessed, as a cobbler, at 10s in 1583 stent.

TELFER, JAMES [merchant]
warned to appear at Leith 31 Jan. 1572 (*Memorials*, 221).
B. mt. 29 Dec. 1569; assessed at 10s in stents of 1581 and 1583.

TENNANT, ALEXANDER merchant
warned to appear at Leith 31 Jan. 1572 (*Memorials*, 220); one of the penitents who submitted to the kirk Nov. 1572 (SP 52/23, fo. 254).
B. cramer 17 Aug. 1553.

TENNANT, FRANCIS [merchant]

forfeited by Moray's parliament of Aug. 1568 (JC 26/1; *CSP Scot.*, ii, no. 766; *Diurnal*, 136); captured by the king's lords along with nineteen other Edinburgh burgesses 30 Aug. 1571 (*ibid.*, 246; Pitscottie, *History*, ii, 262; *History of King James VI*, 88); goods escheated because of his forfeiture for treason, 24 March 1576 (*RSS*, vii, 531).

Although he is described as 'ane gret rular in Edinburgh' in 1571, Tennant had not held office since the time he had been provost in 1550-51; his contribution to burgh politics since then had been confined to criticisms of the bailies and stubborn opposition to the new doctrines and ministry (*Edin. Recs.*, ii, 198, 221f, 239; iii, 162; M. Wood, *Lord Provosts of Edinburgh*, 18); he had also been made B. & G. as long ago as 2 Oct. 1543, which would put him in his mid- to late fifties, rather old for active politics, although Maxwell would have been fifty-eight by 1571 (see 'Report by De La Brosse and D'Oysel', *Scottish History Soc., Misc.*, ix (1958), 120); also a burgess of the Canongate (*Broughton Court Book*, 185).

THOMSON, DAVID [merchant]

warned to appear at Leith 31 Jan. 1572 (*Memorials*, 220).
Assessed at £3 in 1565; G. 29 April 1580.

THOMSON, JOHN litster

warned to appear at Leith 31 Jan. 1572 (*Memorials*, 219).
Assessed at £2 in 1581 stent.

THOMSON, JOHN merchant

granted a remission 18 Aug. 1573, with a composition of £6 13s 4d, for remaining and other offences (*RSS*, vi, 2105; *TA*, xii, 268).
B. 19 Sept. 1560; the brother-in-law of Mungo Fairlie (see above); he died in 1576, leaving £118 (*Edin. Tests.*, 19 Nov. 1576).

THOMSON, PATRICK apothecary

he and William Dewar (see above) carried the ensigns of the queen's lords which were paraded after the intrusion of the new bailies, 7 July 1571 (*Memorials*, 175; Calderwood, *History*, iii, 111); warned to appear at Leith 31 Jan. 1572 (*Memorials*, 218, where he figures high on the list); the process of forfeiture against him had already begun by the time he emerged from the Castle in May 1573 after his conviction for treason in the parliament held in Edinburgh the month before; he had been charged, along with Gilbert Balfour, Herbert Maxwell, William Henderson, Cuthbert Ramsay and the two Moscrops (see above), with assisting Grange and fortifying St. Giles', its steeple and other parts of the town (JC 26/1; *CSP Scot.*, iv, no. 636; *RSS*, vi, 1967; iv, 451; SP 52/25, fos. 73r, 118r).
B. 12 Dec. 1561. He was the son of Thomas Thomson, also an apothecary, who was a prominent and active protestant figure in the burgh until his death in 1572 (see app. v; *CSP Scot.*, i, no. 1043) and on the council in 1558-9 and 1560-61 (see lists); he was married to the sister of William Craik (see above).

THOMSON, PETER Islay herald

convicted along with eight others 9 Feb. 1573 of being involved in the Crags action in June 1572; he was also convicted of 'ryving of the nobill menis armes' (JC 1/13; Pitcairn, *Trials*, I, ii, 40).
B. & G. Islay herald *gratis*, 14 March 1559.
His wife, Bessie Hill, was a catholic recusant; see app. vi.

THOMSON, ROBERT skinner

one of the forty-seven, including Patrick Anderson (see above), charged with active conspiracy 31

July 1573; he reappeared 10/11 Aug., was pledged 13/14 Aug. (JC 26/1) and again 26 Aug. (JC 1/13).
B. 2 Nov. 1563.

THOMSON, THOMAS *alias* SMITH [unfree maltman] outside the West Port
40s composition for intercommuning with the rebels (*TA*, xiii, 345) 28 Feb. 1576.
B. maltman 4 April 1582; assessed at 10s in 1583 stent.

THOMSON, WILLIAM
convicted of treason along with the others captured in the action at the Crags, 13 June 1572; submitted to the session 4 Nov. 1574, though only for remaining in the town (JC 1/13; Pitcairn, *Trials*, I, ii, 32; BGKE, fo. 25v).
Either a taverner, B. 12 June 1557, or a merchant, B. & G. 16 Feb. 1563; their contributions in the 1565 roll were £15 and £5.

TOWERS, MAURICE macer
reconciled by the session 12 May 1575 as an aged man who, lacking 'all support of freindis nather haveand stoir of money in redines for his sustantation nor place to pas' to for safety, was compelled to act as macer in the tolbooth and to officiate at the parliament of queen's lords in the burgh (BGKE, fo. 56v). He was granted a respite 3 May 1576 for three years for treasonably remaining and taking part during the whole period of the town's occupation (*RSS*, vii, 578).
B. & G. 4 March 1531; £10 contribution in 1565; see *TA*, xii, 235.

TULLOCH, THOMAS [unfree] litster
warned to appear at Leith 31 Jan. 1572 (*Memorials*, 219).
B. 'worset seller' 5 July 1587; assessed at 5s in 1583 roll.

TURNBULL, WILLIAM [merchant]
submitted to the session 19 May 1575 that he had remained but also entered the Castle after the abstinence had expired on 1 Jan. 1573 (BGKE, fo. 58v); his name is not included in either of the lists of Castilians.
Assessed, as a merchant, at £5 in the stents of 1581 and 1583.

TWEEDIE, WILLIAM [cramer]
at the horn for assisting the rebels, 21 May 1572 (*RSS*, vi, 1618).
B. cramer 7 May 1555.

UCHILTRE, JOHN maltman
one of the forty-five pledged 17 Aug. 1573 (JC 1/13).

UR(OR), JAMES flesher
warned to appear at Leith 31 Jan. 1572 (*Memorials*, 220); one of the penitents who submitted to the kirk Nov. 1572 (SP 52/23, fo. 254); charged 4 Feb. 1573 with assistance given to Grange in withholding the burgh and Castle (JC 1/13; Pitcairn, *Trials*, I, ii, 39); a composition of £13 6s 8d for taking part (*TA*, xii, 265).
B. 2 April 1568; assessed at 13s 4d in 1583 roll; deacon of the fleshers 1582-4; his widow left £47 net (Edin. Tests., 28 Jan. 1587).

VALLANCE, ANDREW
one of the penitents who submitted to the kirk Nov. 1572 (SP 52/23, fo. 254; *CSP Scot.*, iv, no. 487).
Either a merchant, B. 8 Nov. 1553, or a skinner, B. 3 May 1573.

VAUS, JAMES [unfree or apprentice tailor]
submitted to the session April 1574 for remaining in the town (BGKE, fo. 1v).
B. draper 18 Nov. 1586; assessed, as a draper, at 10s in 1581 and 6s 8d in 1583.

WADDEL, JOHN barber
warned to appear at Leith 31 Jan. 1572 (*Memorials*, 221).
B. June 1555.

WALKER, JOHN [apprentice webster?]
one of the penitents who submitted to the kirk Nov. 1572 (SP 52/23, fo. 254); charged, along with forty-six others including Patrick Anderson (see above), with active conspiracy 31 July 1573; reappeared 10/11 Aug. and pledged 13/14 Aug. (JC 26/1) and again 26 Aug. (JC 1/13).
B. webster as apprentice to Andrew W., 22 July 1574, and assessed at 30s in 1583 stent, although there is also a walker, assessed at 10s in the same roll, who died in 1583 (Edin. Tests., 22 March 1585).

WALLACE, JOHN draper
one of the penitents who submitted to the session Nov. 1572 (SP 52/23, fo. 254); charged 13 Aug. 1573 with treasonably assisting the rebels (JC 1/13; Pitcairn, *Trials*, I, ii, 47); granted a remission 16 Aug., with a composition of £13 6s 8d, for remaining, taking part and other offences (*RSS*, vi, 2088; *TA*, xii, 266).

WALSH, GEORGE [barber]
submitted to the session 26 May 1575 for fornication and remaining in the town during its occupation (BGKE, fo. 57v).
B. barber 15 Nov. 1563.

WALSH, ROBERT merchant
warned to appear at Leith 31 Jan. 1572 (*Memorials*, 220).
£2 contribution in 1565 roll and assessed at 10s in 1581 and 5s in 1583; apparently only gained his burgess-ship 9 Jan. 1579.

WARDLAW, ANDREW servant
one of those convicted of treason 13 June 1572 after their capture in the Crags action (JC 1/13; Pitcairn, *Trials*, I, ii, 32); there is a halberdier of the same name in the list of Castilians of May 1573 (SP 52/25, fos. 72v, 118r).

WATSON, JOHN smith
warned to appear at Leith 31 Jan. 1572 (*Memorials*, 220); charged, individually, with assisting the rebels, 1 April 1573 (JC 1/13; Pitcairn, *Trials*, I, ii, 42). However, he seems already to have obtained a remission, 31 Jan. 1573, for remaining and taking part, paying a composition of £20 (*RSS*, vi, 1839; *TA*, xii, 265).
There is no further trace of him after 1 April in the justiciary records. He submitted to the session 3 June 1574 for having remained within the town, although someone with the same name had already presented his supplication to the session in Nov. 1572 (BGKE, fo. 8v; SP 52/23, fo. 254; *CSP Scot.*, iv, no. 487).

WATSON, WILLIAM draper
warned to appear at Leith 31 Jan. 1572 (*Memorials*, 221).
B. 4 Aug. 1562; £2 contribution in 1565.

WATT, JOHN smith
warned to appear at Leith 31 Jan. 1572 (*Memorials*, 219); one of the forty-seven, including Patrick

Anderson (see above) charged with active conspiracy 31 July 1573; he reappeared 10/11 Aug., was pledged 13/14 Aug. (JC 26/1), and again 26 Aug. (JC 1/13).

Although the only possible entry in the burgess roll is B. smith as s. and h. of umq. John, 10 Jan. 1575, who was assessed at 13s 4d in the 1583 stent and was a deacon-councillor in 1583-4 (*Edin. Recs.*, iv, 578), it is more likely that the man involved was his father; two protocol book entries of 28 Jan. 1572 specifically refer to him as a burgess (Prot. Bk. Stewart, elder, under that date; Prot. Bk. Aitkin, i, fo. 84r).

WAUCHOPE, GEORGE merchant

warned to appear at Leith 31 Jan. 1572 (*Memorials*, 219, where he figures fairly high on the list; Calderwood, *History*, iii, 204); granted a remission, 18 Aug. 1573, for remaining, taking part and other offences, with a composition of £20 (*RSS*, vi, 2108; *TA*, xii, 266); submitted to the session 19 Aug. 1574 that he had remained in the town and borne armour (BGKE, fo. 16r).

B. 3 Nov. 1564; G. 2 Oct. 1576; £5 contribution in 1565, but his assessments of £18 in 1581 and £20 in 1583 indicate that by then he was among the dozen wealthiest merchants in the burgh.

WAUCHOPE, JOHN furrier

one of the penitents who submitted to the kirk Nov. 1572 (SP 52/23, fo. 254); charged, along with Patrick Anderson (see above) and others, with active conspiracy 31 July 1573; pledged 13/14 Aug. (JC 26/1) and again 26 Aug. (JC 1/13); he made his public confession before the congregation 10 June 1574 (BGKE, fo. 9r); deacon of his craft 1565-6; he died in 1578, leaving £162 net (Edin. Tests., 29 Jan. 1580).

WAWANE, WALTER tailor

an ex-deacon of the tailors; he carried Grange's new ensign which was paraded through the town 27 Feb. 1571; warned to appear at Leith 31 Jan. 1572 (*Memorials*, 85, 221); a halberdier in the Castle when it fell in May 1573 (SP 52/25, fos. 72v, 118r); see council lists for 1568-9 and 1569-70.

WEIR, WILLIAM cordiner

he and John Pillan (see above) escheated for non-appearance or assisting, 10 June 1572 (*RSS*, vi, 1641); submitted to the kirk Nov. 1572 (SP 52/23, fo. 254, where given as 'Vere'); one of the forty-five pledged 17 Aug. 1573 (JC 1/13); replaced as deacon of the cordiners June 1579 for serving in the town during its occupation (*Edin. Recs.*, iv, 110).

B. 8 Nov. 1564; assessed at 30s in 1583 stent.

WEMYSS, JOHN merchant

warned to appear at Leith 31 Jan. 1572 (*Memorials*, 221).

Either a wine seller, who was deprived of his guildry for breaking the wine acts 15 Feb. 1564, or a merchant made B. & G. 16 Dec. 1569.

WHIPPO, GAVIN [baxter]

one of the forty-five pledged 17 Aug. 1573 (JC 1/13).

Not in the burgess roll, although his son John is, made B. 17 April 1599; but his burgess-ship is recorded in the dean of guild accounts for 29 June 1562 (*Edin. Accts.*, ii, 149).

WHITE, m. JAMES [master of the grammar school]

one of the rival commissaries appointed in Edinburgh in April 1572 (*Diurnal*, 295); granted a remission 16 Jan. 1573 for remaining and taking part (*RSS*, vi, 1817); when asked by the session why he had absented himself from the communion table, he replied that he had not yet been reconciled for remaining in the town; his public confession was finally made 14 Oct. 1574 (BGKE, fos. 14v, 22r). Appointed by the council in 1563 as master of the grammar school (*Edin. Recs.*, iii, 157).

WHITEHILL, JOHN
one of those convicted of treason after their capture in the Crags action, 13 June 1572 (JC 1/13; Pitcairn, *Trials*, I, ii, 32).
Probably a burgess of the Canongate (see *Broughton Court Book*, 283).

WILKIE, JOHN maltman
warned to appear at Leith 31 Jan. 1572 (*Memorials*, 219); one of the penitents who submitted to the session Nov. 1572 (SP 52/23, fo. 254).
B. by rt. of wife, dr. of Adam Carnbee (see above), 17 Sept. 1569.

WILLIAMSON, ANDREW wright
replaced as deacon of the wrights for serving in the town during its occupation, June 1579 (*Edin. Recs.*, iv, 110).
Assessed at 10s in 1583 stent.

WILSON, JAMES baxter [of the Canongate]
one of the forty-five pledged 17 Aug. 1573 (JC 1/13).
See *Broughton Court Book*, 406.

WILSON, JOHN [unfree] shoemaker in the Potterrow
fined an unspecified amount 28 Feb. 1576, probably for taking part (*TA*, xiii, 345).

WILSON, JOHN pewterer
warned to appear at Leith 31 Jan. 1572 (*Memorials*, 219); charged 13 Aug. 1573 with treasonably assisting the rebels (JC 1/13; see John Adamson, above, and Pitcairn, *Trials*, I, ii, 47); a £10 composition for taking part (*TA*, xii, 267).
B. 13 April 1568; dismissed by the council 8 May 1568 after the hammermen had submitted a petition that their deacon was 'ane man of na religioun', but he had regained the office within eight months, presumably after being reconciled by the session; he was a member of the deputation sent by the council to confer with Grange 28 April 1571 (*Edin. Recs.*, iii, 248, 268, 285); assessed at 13s 4d in 1583 stent; also deacon 1569-71; he died in 1585 of the plague, leaving £29 net (Edin. Tests., 3 Dec. 1586).

WILSON, JOHN maltman beside the West Port
goods escheated 9 Jan. 1572 for withholding the burgh, keeping watch and ward and paying stents to the rebels (*RSS*, vi, 1423); warned to appear at Leith 31 Jan. (*Memorials*, 219, where he figures quite high on the list); charged 4 Feb. 1573 with assisting the rebels (JC 1/13; Pitcairn, *Trials*, I, ii, 39); granted a remission 19 Feb. for taking part, supplying with provisions, receiving and circulating false coin, but the composition stood at £666 13s 4d, the largest recorded (*RSS*, vi, 1857; *TA*, xii, 265).
With a contribution of £40 in 1565 and assessments on £16 and £8 in 1581 and 1583, Wilson was the wealthiest maltman in Edinburgh (cf. John Howieson in the two rolls). It seems likely that the size of the fine was related more to his wealth and the scale of his trading operations than to any particularly strong commitment to the queen's party.

WILSON, PATRICK [merchant]
one of the penitents who submitted to the kirk Nov. 1572 (SP 52/23, fo. 254).
Listed among the merchants in the muster roll of 1558 (MS. Co. Recs., ii, fo. 129r); see also Harry Smith, made B. & G. by rt. of wife, the dr. of Patrick Wilson, *B. & G.*, 18 Aug. 1564.

WINRAM, THOMAS maltman outside the West Port
charged 4 Feb. 1573 with assisting the rebels (JC 1/13; Pitcairn, *Trials*, I, ii, 39); granted a

remission, dated the previous day, for remaining, taking part, supplying with victuals, receiving and circulating false coin (*RSS*, vi, 1844B); a composition of £50 (*TA*, xii, 265; see also xiii, 345). He died in 1583, leaving £208 net (Edin. Tests., 9 Jan. 1585).

WINTON, ANDREW barber
in the Castle when it fell in May 1573 (SP 52/25, fos. 72r, 117r); one of the forty-five, including Patrick Anderson (see above), charged with active conspiracy 31 July 1573; warned 10/11 Aug. to find surety within six days (JC 26/1).

WRIGHT (WRICH), THOMAS [unfree; later a merchant]
one of the penitents who submitted to the kirk Nov. 1572 (SP 52/23, fo. 254; *CSP Scot.*, iv, no. 487).
B. mt. 7 Sept. 1582.

YOUNG, ANDREW brewster
one of those convicted of treason 13 June 1572 after their capture in the skirmish at the Crags (JC 1/13; Pitcairn, *Trials*, I, ii, 32); submitted to the session 30 June 1575, admitting that he remained in the town and took 'plane parte' with the rebels (BGKE, fos. 64v, 66r).

YOUNG, HENRY baxter
one of the forty-five whose cases were continued 17 Aug. 1573 (JC 1/13); paid a composition of £6 13s 4d for taking part (*TA*, xii, 267).
A catholic recusant (see app. vi); the father of Michael Young (see below).

YOUNG, JOHN tailor
warned to appear at Leith 31 Jan. 1572 (*Memorials*, 219, where he figured in the first twenty on the list); been warned to appear before the Court of Justiciary 13 Aug. 1573 along with the others who had pledges entered for them that day and refused a further extension (JC 1/13); granted a remission 16 Aug., with a composition of £33 6s 8d, for remaining, taking part and other offences (*RSS*, vi, 2087; *TA*, xii, 266).
B. 30 April 1552; G. 8 June 1586; assessed at 50s in 1583 stent.

YOUNG, MICHAEL baxter
one of the forty-five whose cases were continued 17 Aug. 1573 (JC 1/13).
Assessed at 10s in 1583 stent; he died in 1584, leaving £542 net (Edin. Tests., 30 Aug. 1584); the son of the catholic baxter, Harry Young (Protocol Bk. King, iv, fo. 164; see app. vi and above).

YULE, WILLIAM [servant or apprentice to a merchant]
gave in his supplication to the session 3 June 1574 that he had only remained in the town (BGKE, fo. 8v).
B. mt. as apprentice to Mungo Russell, 6 Feb. 1583; G. 14 April 1590; he died in 1592, leaving £3,361 net (Edin. Tests., 6 April 1593). His master was one of the most prominent supporters of the king's party in the burgh and one of the bailies in exile at Leith 1571-2.

Appendix ix
Edinburgh inhabitants whose houses were demolished, February-June 1572

**ACHESON, HELEN
in May 1572 (*Diurnal*, 299).

*ACHESON, JOHN
in July 1572 (*Diurnal*, 307).

BURRELL, HARRY flesher
in June 1572 (*Diurnal*, 303).
B. 18 Jan. 1559; on the subscription list of 1562; an elder of the Canongate parish 1566-7 (*Canongate Bk.*, 51); deacon of his craft 1569-70; see his daughter, Marion, and her husband, Robert Howie, in the Q.P. list.

COLINTON, [FOULIS, m. HENRY], laird of
in July 1572 (*Diurnal*, 307).
His son, James, remained in the town (see Q.P. list); he died in Dec. 1571 (Edin. Tests., 14 Jan. 1576 and 31 Aug. 1577).

ERSKINE, JOHN, earl of MAR
in May 1572 (*Diurnal*, 299).

FREIR, JOHN merchant [skinner]
in June 1572 (*Diurnal*, 303).
on the subscription list of 1562, as was his brother, George, an advocate (Pt. Bk. Guthrie, i, fos. 148, 172); an elder 1573-4; assessed, as a skinner, at 6s 8d in 1583.

**GILBERT, MICHAEL
in Feb. 1572 (*CSP Scot.*, iv, no. 149).

*GOURLAY, ROBERT
in Feb. 1572 (*CSP Scot.*, iv, no. 149).

GRAHAM, ARCHIBALD [merchant]
in May 1572 (*Diurnal*, 296).
B. & G. 21 June 1553; assessed at £5 in 1565 and 1580 and £4 in 1583; a prominent member of the protestant party in the 1560s; on the council six times between 1554 and 1565.

HATTON, [LAUDER, WILLIAM] laird of
in July 1572 (*Diurnal*, 307).
See Edin. Tests., 21 Feb. 1598.

*HENRYSON, ANDREW
in July 1572 (*Diurnal*, 307).

JOSSY, JAMES merchant
in June 1572 (*Diurnal*, 303).
G. mt. 12 Feb. 1561; assessed at £15 in 1565 and his widow at £5 and £10 in 1580 and 1583.

KENNOCH (CARNOCHANE), JOHN [flesher]
in July 1572 (*Diurnal*, 307).
His son, William, was made B. 22 Feb. 1559 by rt. of his fr. (*Edin. Burgs.*, 286).

KENNOCH (KENOTH), MATTHEW flesher
he was dead when his house was demolished in June 1572 (*Diurnal*, 303).

*KINLOCH, DAVID
in May or June 1572 (*Diurnal*, 299, 301).

*McGILL, DAVID
in May 1572 (*Diurnal*, 299).

*McGILL, m. JAMES
the first to be demolished in Feb. 1572; a second lodging of his was also demolished in July
(*Diurnal*, 257, 288, 307; *Memorials*, 234; *CSP Scot.*, iv, no. 149).

*PRESTON, JOHN
probably had two houses demolished in April and May 1572 (*Diurnal*, 295, 299).

RAMSAY, [CAPTAIN] JOHN
in April 1572 (*Diurnal*, 295).
Rebated £20 of the duty he paid as farmer of the petty customs to compensate for his losses during
the siege of the Castle (*Edin. Recs.*, iv, 11); assessed at 10s in 1583.

*RICHARDSON, m. ROBERT
in July 1572 (*Diurnal*, 307).

SHANG, PATRICK [wright]
in July 1572 (*Diurnal*, 307).
On the subscription list of 1562; deacon of his craft three times in the 1560s and twice in the 1570s.

SIMPSON, JOHN merchant
in July 1572 (*Diurnal*, 307).
B. & G. 12 Sept. 1531; on the council 1553-6; a guard house had been erected close to his house in
1570 (*Edin. Recs.*, iii, 270).

*SLATER, ANDREW
in June 1572 (*Diurnal*, 303).

STEDMAN, CHARLES cook
in June 1572 (*Diurnal*, 303).
B. 1 Sept. 1562; assessed at £3 in 1565; his father, Alexander, had remained a catholic until the middle of the 1560s (see app. vi).

**STODDARD, JOHN
in July 1572 (*Diurnal*, 307).

STRANG, GEORGE [advocate]
in July 1572 (*Diurnal*, 307).
B. & G. by rt. of his wife 13 March 1564; on the subscription list of 1562.

*UDDART, NICOL
in Feb. 1572 (*Diurnal*, 258, 288; *Memorials*, 234; *CSP Scot.*, iv, no. 149).

WATSON, JAMES
in May 1572 (*Diurnal*, 299; *Memorials*, 234).
A prominent protestant; see app. v for further details.

*WATSON, ROBERT
in April 1572 (*Diurnal*, 295).

*YOUNG, JAMES
in July 1572 (*Diurnal*, 307).

 * see K.P. list
** see Q.P. list

Appendix x
Edinburgh Radicals, 1582-1584

THIS is nothing like a comprehensive list, nor could it be, given the paucity of sources; it is included as an impressionistic one to illustrate the striking social dichotomy amongst Edinburgh's radicals in the early 1580s. At times a rather fine line has had to be drawn; generally, it does not include pro-Morton or pro-Ruthven supporters if they took part in the factional struggles inside the council chamber.

ADAMSON, JANET
banished from the town along with the wives of the exiled ministers in the autumn of 1584 (Calderwood, *History*, iv, 200).
The widow of James McGill (see Edin. Tests., 9 Aug. 1582; *CSP Scot.*, vi, no. 423); a protestant since the 1550s (see app. iv).

ADAMSON, JOHN merchant
one of the eighteen burgesses exiled from the town 6 June 1584; he had been a member of the session of 1583-4 and petitioned the king to allow Durie to return in 1582 (Calderwood, *History*, iii, 633, 646; iv, 2; viii, 225, 260).
See K.P. list and the council index.

ARCHIBALD, WILLIAM [in the Dean village]
a witness to the formal taking of instruments by Pont and Balcanquhal 25 May 1584 (Calderwood, *History*, iv, 65).
He died in 1633 (Edin. Tests., 24 Oct. 1633).

BAIRNSFATHER, JOHN [tailor]
one of the members of the session of 1583-4 who refused to subscribe to the king's reply to the exiled ministers (Calderwood, *History*, viii, 269). B. 15 Feb. 1567; a craft councillor 1582-3; assessed at 13s 4d in 1583.

BICKERTON, HARRY [clerk to the session]
warned to leave the town during the king's residence 4 Oct. 1584 (*RPC*, iii, 692). Appointed as session clerk 20 May 1584 (*Edin. Recs.*, iv, 339); B. & G. 10 Nov. 1587; he died in 1602 (Edin. Tests., 15 March 1602).

BLACKBURN, JOHN merchant
one of the most militant members of the session of 1583-4; put into irons after his confrontation with the king at Falkland on 28 June 1584 over the Adamson letter; warned to appear before the

privy council on 4 Oct. and denounced as a rebel 11 Nov. (Calderwood, *History*, iv, 123, 425; *RPC*, iii, 692, 699; *CSP Scot.*, vi, no. 193).
See K.P. list.

BOYD, JAMES of the Kippis [merchant]
a caution of £500 entered for him in June 1582 (*RPC*, iii, 488).
Assessed at 10s in 1583; B. & G. by rt. of his wife 3 Nov. 1587; he died in 1595, leaving £1,419 net (Edin. Tests., 28 July 1595).

BOYD, ROBERT merchant
exiled from the town 6 June 1584 (Calderwood, *History*, viii, 260).

BROWN, JOHN stabler [burgess]
a caution of 100 merks entered for him in June 1582 (*RPC*, iii, 488).
Assessed at 5s in 1583; see the testament of his wife, Marion Simpson (Edin. Tests., 10 June 1597).

CARMUIR, JAMES merchant
warned to leave the town 4 Oct. 1584 (*RPC*, iii, 692).
Sommelier for wine sellers in the burgh in 1599 (*Edin. Recs.* (1589-1603), 260).

CATHKIN, EDWARD [skinner]
refused to subscribe to the Adamson letter; he was probably on the session of 1583-4, although Calderwood is not clear on this point; summoned before the privy council for causing a disturbance during Adamson's sermon but fled to England (Calderwood, *History*, iv, 79, 351).
Assessed, as a skinner, at 6s 8d in 1583; B. 9 June 1592; he later became a bookseller; he was involved in the riot of 1596 (see Calderwood, *History*, v, 511; Edin. Tests., 4 June 1601; *Edin. Recs.* (1589-1603), 65, 192).

CATHKIN, JAMES [skinner]
like Edward, he refused to subscribe to the Adamson letter and fled after being summoned before the privy council for his part in the same disturbance (Calderwood, *History*, iv, 79, 351).
Like his brother, he was also a skinner who later became a bookseller; B. 9 June 1592; also involved in the riot of 1596; he died in 1631 (Calderwood, *History*, v, 520, 535; *Edin. Recs.* (1589-1603), 65, 192; Edin. Tests., 19 April 1632).

CLARK, ALEXANDER merchant [of Balbirnie]
the 'chief of the best sort' on the council of 1583-4 who refused to subscribe to the Adamson letter; his career 1581-4, however, amply bore out Davison's opinion that he had been 'too pliable' to the court (*CSP Scot.*, vii, nos. 171, 180).
Provost 1579-84; see app. v. for further details; he died in 1591, leaving £3,111 net (Edin. Tests., 19 Jan. 1592).

CLARK, JOHN skinner
warned to leave the town 4 Oct. 1584; a caution of 500 merks entered for him 31 Oct. (*RPC*, iii, 692, 695-6).
Assessed at 30s in 1583; he died in 1604 (see Edin. Tests., 14 June 1605 and ibid., 10 Feb. 1598 for his wife, Elizabeth Kene).

COLDEN, JAMES skinner
exiled from the town 6 June 1584; put in Blackness Castle 4 Oct. and a caution of £1,000 entered for him 31 Oct. (Calderwood, *History*, viii, 260; *RPC*, iii, 692, 696).
Assessed at £3 in 1583.

DANIELSTONE, DAVID goldsmith
warned to leave the town 4 Oct. 1584; a caution of 500 merks entered for him by Alex. Thomson of Duddingston 31 Oct. (*RPC,* iii, 692, 695).
B. 6 Feb. 1562; G. by rt. of his wife, the dr. of Thomas Thomson, the protestant party man of the 1560s (see app. v) 27 Sept. 1570; on the council 1577-8; craft deacon 1581-2; assessed at 40s in 1583.

DARLING, PHILIP merchant
exiled from the town 6 June 1584; warned to leave on 4 Oct. and a caution of 500 merks entered for him on 31 Oct. (Calderwood, *History,* viii, 260; *RPC,* iii, 692, 696).
B. 27 Aug. 1574; G. by rt. of his wife 22 Feb. 1587; assessed at 40s in 1581 and £4 in 1583; he died in 1596, leaving £3,578 net (Edin. Tests., 29 March 1597).

DICK, GILBERT [merchant]
dismissed from office and imprisoned in Doune Castle by Lennox in 1582 but enjoyed the 'favour of all the godly'. Arran attempted to escheat him, according to Bowes, on a trumped-up charge in Sept. 1583 (*CSP Scot.,* vi, nos. 218, 644).
Assessed at £20 (1565), £14 (1581), £18 (1583); he died in 1587, leaving £10,593 net (Edin. Tests., 5 Jan. 1590); on the council 1569-70, 1578-80 and 1581-2.

DOUGAL, JOHN younger [merchant]
exiled from the town 6 June 1584 (Calderwood, *History,* viii, 260).
B. & G. 3 April 1573; assessed at £8 in 1581 and £14 in 1583 and died in 1601 as a very wealthy man; for further details, see app. vii.

DOUGLAS, JOHN skinner
a caution of 100 merks entered for him 21 June 1582 not to intercommune with rebels outside the realm (*RPC,* iii, 488).
B. 3 April 1573 at the regent's special request; a second skinner, apprenticed to the same master, was made B. 27 June 1583.

DUNNING, DAVID saddler
a caution of 200 merks entered for him in June 1582 on the same basis as Douglas (*RPC,* iii, 488).
B. 19 Dec. 1572; G. 19 Sept. 1592; assessed at 40s in 1583; he died in debt in 1596 (Edin. Tests., 5 May 1598).

FERGUSON, JOHN [merchant]
one of the 'best affected to religion', who were persecuted for the joyful welcome given to Durie on his return in Sept. 1582 (Calderwood, *History,* iv, 425).
This was probably J.F. younger; the father died in May 1582 (see K.P. list).

FIDDES (TIDDESS), WILLIAM baxter
exiled from the town 6 June 1584 (Calderwood, *History,* viii, 260).
Assessed at 13s 4d in 1583; this may be either the father or the son, who was made B. 18 April 1582. It is more likely to be the son as the father remained in the town during the civil wars (see Q.P. list); he died in 1605, leaving £1,118 net (Edin. Tests., 7 Jan. 1607 and 28 Jan. 1608).

FISHER, THOMAS [merchant]
one of the members of the session of 1583-4 who refused to subscribe to the Adamson letter (Calderwood, *History,* viii, 269).
Either the merchant assessed at £6 in 1581 and £3 10s in 1583 or the son of Wm. Fisher (see Q.P. list), made B. & G. 24 May 1583; the former is more likely; on the council 1589-90 and a bailie

1591-2; his wife, Margaret, was the sister of James Carmuir (see above and Edin. Tests., 4 June 1580).

FORESTER, ALEXANDER
a caution of 500 merks entered for him 4 Aug. 1582 to avoid dealings with traitors outside the realm (*RPC*, iii, 505).
The son of Matthew F., the brother of the protestant party man of the 1560s, David Forester (see David's testament, Edin. Tests., 21 July 1574).

FULLARTON, ADAM [merchant]
one of the 'best affected' persecuted for the reception given to Durie in 1582; exiled from the town 6 June 1584; put into Dumbarton Castle in Oct. 1584 (Calderwood, *History*, iv, 425; viii, 260; *RPC*, iii, 692).
See apps.v and vii; he had last been on the council in 1577.

GALBRAITH, EDWARD skinner
exiled from the town 6 June 1584; imprisoned in Blackness Castle in Oct. 1584 (Calderwood, *History*, viii, 260; *RPC*, iii, 692).
See K.P. and council lists.

GILBERT, JANET
banished from the town along with the wives of the exiled ministers in the autumn of 1584 (Calderwood, *History*, iv, 200).

GORDON, GEORGE tailor
exiled from the town 6 June 1584 (Calderwood, *History*, viii, 260).
Assessed at 6s 8d in 1583; he died in 1593, leaving £135 net (Edin. Tests., 5 April 1593).

HARLAW, JOHN saddler
exiled from the town 6 June 1584; a caution of 500 merks entered for him 17 July 1584 to obey the authority of the king, provost and bailies, not to dispute acts of parliament or to communicate with rebels (Calderwood, *History*, viii, 260; *RPC*, iii, 678).
Appointed master saddler to the king in 1576 (*RSS*, vii, 694), but not made B. & G. until 31 May 1583; the son of the protestant activist and king's man, Wm. Harlaw (for details of both, see apps. v and vii).

HENRYSON, JANET
banished from the town along with the wives of the exiled ministers in the autumn of 1584 (Calderwood, *History*, iv, 200).
The widow of Alexander Guthrie, common clerk of the burgh, who died in 1582; she had been one of Knox's 'dear sisters' of Edinburgh in the later 1550s (see app. iv).

HOPE, EDWARD [merchant]
engaged in a dialogue with Henry Nisbet over the subscribing of the Adamson letter in 1584 (Calderwood, *History*, iv, 144ff).
A long-serving protestant activist (see apps. iv, v and vii).

JOHNSTON, JOHN of Elphinstone
a caution of £1,000 entered for him by his brother James Johnston of Elphinstone in June 1582; an elder of the session of 1583-4; warned to appear before the privy council 4 Oct. 1584 and denounced for non-appearance 11 Nov.; he was a witness to James Lawson's testament made in London in Oct. 1584 (*RPC*, iii, 488, 692, 699; *Edin. Recs.*, iv, 319; Calderwood, *History*, iv, 205).

B. & G. 25 Oct. 1577 by rt. of his wife, the dr. of the important early protestant, James Baron (see apps. iv and v); assessed at 20s in 1583; on the council 1578-84.

JOHNSTON, JOHN, younger [merchant]
warned to leave the town 4 Oct. 1584 (*RPC*, iii, 692).
Assessed at 20s in 1581 and £4 in 1583.

KINLOCH (KILLOUGH), DAVID [baxter]
Fénélon was informed that he and Durie conspired to attack him during his visit in 1583 (*CSP Scot.*, vi, no. 336).
See K.P. for further details.

LAWSON, ALEXANDER [merchant]
a caution of 100 merks entered for him 21 June 1582 (*RPC*, iii, 488).
Assessed at £3 in 1581 and 10s in 1583; he died in London in about 1626 (Edin. Tests., 15 Feb. 1627).

LINDSAY, ROBERT stabler
exiled from the town 6 June 1584; warned to leave the town again in Oct. 1584 (Calderwood, *History*, viii, 260; *RPC*, iii, 692).

LITTLE, WILLIAM [merchant]
one of the minority on the 1583-4 council who refused to subscribe the Adamson letter (Calderwood, *History*, viii, 269).
See the K.P. list and council list; he was, however, nominated by the leet of Sept. 1583.

LIVINGSTONE, ROBERT baxter
exiled from the town 6 June 1584 (Calderwood, *History*, viii, 260).
Assessed at 20s in 1583.

MacMORRAN, JOHN merchant
a caution of 1,000 merks entered for him 2 Aug. 1582 to avoid dealings with traitors outside the realm (*RPC*, iii, 504; see also Melville, *Memoirs*, 267).
Assessed at £8 in 1581 and £5 in 1583 but described by Calderwood as the richest merchant of his day (*History*, v, 382); he left £37,861 when he died in 1596 (Edin. Tests., 23 July 1596); he had been a client of Morton (*Broughton Court Book*, 293).

McQUHIRRIE, JOHN merchant
exiled from the town 6 June 1584; a caution of £500 entered for him 17 July 1584 (Calderwood, *History*, viii, 260; *RPC*, iii, 678).
Assessed at 20s in 1581 and 50s in 1583; his testament described him as a 'worsetman'; he left £366 net (Edin. Tests., 22 May 1607).

MALCOLM, ANDREW merchant
warned to leave the town 4 Oct. 1584; a caution of 500 merks entered for him 31 Oct. (*RPC*, iii, 692, 695).
Assessed at £3 in 1581 and £3 6s 8d in 1583; he died in 1589, leaving £1,209 net (Edin. Tests., 28 June 1591).

MARK, ROBERT [cramer]
a witness to the formal taking of instruments by Pont and Balcanquhal 25 May 1584; banished for

refusing to subscribe the Adamson letter; probably a member of the session of 1583-4 (Calderwood, *History*, iv, 65, 79).
Assessed, as a cramer, at 5s in 1583; B. 12 Jan. 1586.

MITCHELLHILL, JOHN merchant
imprisoned in Tantallon Castle 4 Oct. 1584, but released on a caution of 500 merks 31 Oct. (*RPC*, iii, 692, 696).
B. & G. 9 Jan. 1579; assessed at £3 in 1581 and 50s in 1583; he died in 1625 (Edin. Tests., 15 Nov. 1625).

MOFFAT, JOHN [merchant]
a caution of £500 entered for him in June 1582 (*RPC*, iii, 488).
Probably the merchant assessed at £20 (1565), £6 (1581), 40s (1583).

NAPIER, ANDREW merchant
exiled from the town 6 June 1584 (Calderwood, *History*, viii, 260).
See K.P. list.

NYMILL, JOHN merchant
warned to leave the town 4 Oct. 1584 (*RPC*, iii, 692).
Possibly the son of the K.P. merchant who died in 1582 (see app. vii).

OUSTEAN, ALEXANDER [tailor]
one of the minority on the 1583-4 council who refused to subscribe the Adamson letter (Calderwood, *History*, viii, 269).
B. 26 May 1560; deacon 1580-82, craft councillor 1581-2; assessed at 50s in 1583; he died in 1604, leaving £9,152 net (Edin. Tests., 7 July 1604 and 4 Feb. 1607); his son, John, was involved in the riot of 1596 (MS Register of the Privy Seal (PS 1/69), 24 Feb. 1597).

PRESTON, JOHN [merchant]
a spokesman for the rump of the session summoned to Falkland in June 1584 for refusing to subscribe the Adamson letter (Calderwood, *History*, iv, 124).
B. & G. 17 Jan. 1549; on the council near-continuously from 1549-1575; a commissioner to the General Assembly in 1565, 1567, 1571 and 1580, and to the Convention of Royal Burghs in 1555, 1556, 1574 and 1578-81; a collector for the ministry in 1564, 1570 and 1573; by 1584 he was 71 years of age (*Edin. Recs.*, ii, 233; iii, 176, 208, 211, 279; iv, 3, 379-80; *BUK*, i, 471; Calderwood, *History*, ii, 383; iii, 38; *Burghs Conv. Recs.*, i, 9, 24-5, 36, 66, 71, 80, 121). See also app. vii.

PRIMROSE, GILBERT surgeon
exiled from the town 6 June 1584; imprisoned in Dumbarton Castle 4 Oct. and released on a caution of £1,000 on 31 Oct. (Calderwood, *History*, viii, 260; *RPC*, iii, 692, 695).
B. 19 Feb. 1566; appointed surgeon to the king in 1577 (*RSS*, vii, 1160); assessed at £3 in 1583; deacon of the barbers 1575-8 and 1580-83; on the council 1575-6 and in 1583; he moved to London after 1603 and died there in 1616, leaving £18,075 net (Edin. Tests., 10 May 1616).

RANNALD, JAMES merchant
imprisoned in Tantallon Castle 4 Oct. 1584; released on a caution of £1,000 on 31 Oct. (*RPC*, iii, 692, 696).
A draper; see K.P. list.

RICHARDSON, THOMAS [tailor?]
one of the 'best affected' persecuted for the reception given to Durie in 1582 (Calderwood, *History*, iv, 425).
B. tailor 5 July 1555 but not in the 1583 roll.

ROSS, THOMAS
Fénélon was informed that Durie, Kinloch and Ross conspired to attack him during his visit in 1583 (*CSP Scot.*, iv, no. 336).
B. 6 Dec. 1578; G. 17 May 1588 as the son of James Ross (see K.P. list and *RPC*, ii, 344).

SLATER, ANDREW merchant
one of the minority on the 1583-4 council who refused to subscribe the Adamson letter (Calderwood, *History*, viii, 269).
A prominent protestant radical since the 1560s (see apps. v and vii).

SOMERVILLE, THOMAS maltman
exiled from the town 6 June 1584; a caution of 1,000 merks entered for him 17 July (Calderwood, *History*, viii, 260; *RPC*, iii, 678).
See K.P. list; he died of the plague in 1584, leaving £640 net (Edin. Tests., 3 July 1605).

THOMSON, ALEXANDER skinner
exiled from the town 6 June 1584; a caution of 500 merks entered for him 17 July (Calderwood, *History*, viii, 260; *RPC*, iii, 678).
B. 5 June 1577; G. 16 Oct. 1588; assessed at 20s in 1583; his wife died of the plague in 1585 leaving a net estate of £537; he died in debt in 1620 (Edin. Tests., 2 Sept. 1586, 27 Dec. 1623).

THOMSON, JOHN skinner
warned to leave the town 4 Oct. 1584; a caution of 500 merks entered for him 31 Oct. (*RPC*, iii, 692, 696).
B. 17 Sept. 1578; his master, Robert Thomson, had been a queen's man (see app. viii); assessed at 20s in 1583; he died in 1586, leaving a mere £8 net (Edin. Tests., 26 Jan. 1592).

UDDART, ALEXANDER merchant
one of the session of 1583-4 who refused to subscribe the Adamson letter (Calderwood, *History*, viii, 269).
See K.P. and council lists; he returned, however, to the Arran council of 1584-5.

WHITE, HENRY cordiner
exiled from the town 6 June 1584 (Calderwood, *History*, 260).
B. 27 July 1560; assessed at 10s in 1583; deacon of his craft in 1583.

Appendix xi
Tax Roll of September 1565

(MS Co. Recs., iii, fos. 136r-138v)

THIS was not a normal stent on the burgh but part of an effort to raise a loan of 10,000 merks for the purchase of the superiority of Leith. This explains the unusually large sums involved and is why it includes lawyers, who were normally exempt from burgh taxation. There are, in all, 357 merchants or neighbours on the roll, who were assessed individually. In addition, there are 31 'men of law and scribes', although 5 of them were subsequently deleted. Craftsmen were assessed corporately. The total merchant contribution was £4,197 and the average contribution approximately £11 16s. The totals for the four quarters were: £1,255 (N.W.) from 105 merchants; £815 (N.E.) from 58; £1,165 (S.W.) from 89; £962 (S.E.) from 105. The total for the lawyers was £1,156 13s 4d and for the crafts £1,347 8s. Original spelling has been retained.

£60	Burnye, William	(8)
	Edyear, Patrik	
	Nymbill, John	
	Park, Alexander	
	Ramsay, Cuthbert	
	Stevinsoun, Andro	
	Uddert, Thomas	
	Wilsoun, Luke	
£50	Achesoun, Alexr.	(3)
	Barroun, James	
	Hammyltoun, John	
£40	Adamsoun, James	(13)
	Adamsoun, John	
	Gray, Robert	
	Harwod, John	
	Hendersoun, Thomas	
	Jhonnisoun, James of Kello	
	Moreiss, Alexander	
	Moresoun, John	
	Oliphant, James	
	Prestoun, m. John	
	Roiss, James	
	Westoun, John	
	Wilsone, John	

£30	Allane, Adam	(16)
	Andersoun, William	
	Chaipe, Alexr.	
	Clerk, Alexander	
	Dauidsoun, John	
	Dauidsoun, Thomas	
	Fairlie, Mungo	
	Glen, m. Robert	
	Gourlay, Robert	
	Hendiresoun, Andro	
	Litill, Clement, his relict and son	
	William	
	Lyntoun, Francis	
	Merioribankis, m. John	
	Patersoun, William	
	Robesone, William	
	Uddert, Nicholas	
£25	Aslovane, John	(3)
	Henry, Thomas	
	Lowry, James	
£20	Arnot, John	(37)
	Balfour, Gilbert	
	Bartane, Andro	
	Baverage, David	

Broun, Hew
Broun, Thomas
Chisholme, m. Michell
Craig, Robert
Creiche, John
Dik, Gilbert
Dowgall, John
Dundas, Ewfame
Foular, William
Guthre, James
Galbraythe, Robert
Halliday, John
Hamyltoun, Thomas of Preist-
field
Hendersoun, William, somelier
Hog, John
Kar, Robert, younger
Litill, Edward
Marioribankis, Symon
Mertyne, Peter
Mauchame, Edward
Moffet, John
Murray, Cuthbert
Nycholis, James
Nysbet, George
Nysbet, Henry
Norvell, John
Patersoun, Robert
Russell, Mongow
Smallyer, Lyonn
Tagnal, Sir Temothie
Uddert, Alexr.
Uddert, John
Watsoun, Robert

£15   Adamsoun, John   (31)
Arthbuthnat, Alexr.
Banxs, John
Bawty, John
Bortuik, James
Broun, James
Bruntoun, James
Chalmer, Andro
Charterhouss, Henry
Clerk, Michael
Dougalsoun, Roger
Fullartoun, Adam
Grahame, John, elder
Graunger, Arthur
Hume, Alexr.
Home, David
Hopper, George

Howesoun, John
Johnnestoun, James of the Coittis
Jowsye, James
Ker, Robert
Lyall, David
Maxwell, Harbert
Nysbet, Hew
Robertsoun, John
Senyeor, Archibald
Sklatter, Andro
Symsoun, Deme
Thomsoun, Thomas
Thomsoun, William
Waus, Thomas

£12   Gray, Adam   (2)
Spottiswod, John

£10   Aicheso[n], John, relict of   (62)
Aikman, James
Aikman, James
Auchtmouty, John
Baird, James
Broun, Mark
Burnet, Alexander
Cant, Thomas
Carmichaell, James
Carmichaell, John
Cokburn, Thomas
Couttis, John
Cunynghame, Robert
Curle, James
Devillor, Sebastian
Diksoun, Adam
Dikesoun, Allane
Fairly, Charles
Fergussoun, John, elder
Forester, David,
Fortoun, Mungo
Geddes, Charles
Gemmyl, Thomas
Grahame, John, Younger
Gryntoun, William
Hendersoun, John
Hendersoun, William
Home, Edward
Jhonnistoun, Edward
Johnistoun, John of the Coittis
Jhonnistoun, Robert
Kennedy, Archibald
Kincaid, Edward
Lindesay, m. James

Levingstoun, Duncane
Lyntoun, Robert
Makcall, John
Makcarny, James
Merschell, James
Moryss, David
Murdesoun, Andro
Norvell, James
Ostiane, George
Ostiane, John
Palmer, John
Patersoun, Edward
Purdy, John
Purvess, Wa., pottinger
Quyntun, Robert
Rig, Patrik
Robertsoun, John
Row, John, maltman
Rynde, James
Scott, William
Skaythwyre, James
Spens, m. John
Stoddart, John
Strang, William
Towris, David
Watsoun, m. James
Wigholme, Thomas
Yorstoun, John

£8   Lyall, Alexr.   (1)

£7   Helleis, Alexr.   (1)

£6   McQuhyrie, Gilbert   (2)
      Todyner, Thomas

£5   Acchesoun, Henry   (87)
      Adamsoun, John
      Arnot, John, elder
      Armstrang, Andro
      Bannatyne, Henry
      Bassendyn, Michael
      Bawtye, Ninian
      Bennet, Thomas
      Bisset, m. Patrick
      Blackburne, John
      Blackburne, John, younger
      Broun, William
      Byrnye, John
      Corsby, David
      Cranstoun, Patrick
      Crystesoun, Michael

Cunnynghame, John
Dalgleiss, James
Dalyell, James
Dalyell, James, younger
Denholme, Robert
Farime, Andro
Fergesoun, John
Ferquhair, John
Fischear, Patrik
Flemyng, John
Forman, James
Forrat, Robert
Galbrayth, William
Grahame, Archibald
Grahame, Mark
Haistie, Alexr.
Hammyltoun, m. Jon.
Hamyltoun, Robert
Harper, Robert, in trowoppis
    close
Hereis, John
Houpie, Edward
Huntar, John
Hunter, John
Kar, William
Kincaid, Edward
Knox, William
Lawrie, James
Lawrye, Thomas
Lillie, Matthew
Littiljohne, George
Lowrie, Gilbert
Lowrye, William
Mathew, Thomas
Merioribankis, James
Mertene, Thomas
Myller, James
Mowbray, John
Mudie, John, elder
Napier, Alexr.
Nysbet, Robert
Patersoun, Robert
Perye, Alexander
Portuouss, Patrik
Raburne, Nicoll
Robertsoun, William
Rowene, John
Russell, Alexr.

Russell, Alexr.

Scott, David
Scot, Nicol
Schaw, James

Small, John
Somer, David
Speir, Williame
Spottiswod, James
Stark, Robert
Stutie, John
Sym, John
Tadder, Alexr.
Thomsoun, Alexander
Thomsoun, Edward
Thomsoun, Richert
Thomsoun, William
Wallace, James
Wardlaw, James
Watsoun, John
Wauchop, George
Williamsoun, Andro
Williamsoun, William
Winkstoun, laird of
Wod, George

£4   Scott, Adam   (1)

£3   Andersoun, Robert   (45)
Arth, John
Bassendene, James, relict of
Bell, John, seidman
Bog, William
Broun, John
Cochrane, Patrik
Cosser, John
Crystesoun, Adam
Dalgleiss, Robert
Donaldsoun, James
Dundas, Andro
Forman, Arch., cuke
Gardyn, John, lister
Geichamie, Gilbert
Grahame, William
Harrowar, Patrik
Harwod, Alexr.
Hill, John
Huchesoun, William
Johnestoun, William
Kincaid, James
Kincaid, William
Lowrie, Martin
Mane, John
Meile, Andro
Michell, Alexr.
Newlandis, Andro
Newlandis, John

Park, John
Patersoun, Robert
Quhyte, Gilbert
Quhytman, Alexander
Ramsay, William
Richie, Andro
Rynd, Alexander
Sandersoun, George
Shankis, Thomas
Studman, Charles
Thomsoun, David
Udwart, John
Weir, Jon.
Wilsoun, Deme
Wilsoun, Williame
Young, John

40s   Aikman, John   (43)
Aikman, Thomas
Blakstok, Agnes
Burne, John
Chalmer, James
Craig, James
Dennan, James
Douglas, Andro
Dunlop, Robert
Eistoun, John
Eleis, Andro
Fyldour, Nycholl
Fuyrd, Alex.
Galbrayth, Gilbert
Gilcrist, William
Grachame, John
Craig, Gilbert
Gray, Alex.
Haliburton, Adam
Haldane, John
Hammyltoun, John, merchand
Hay, Gilbert
Kar, Henry
Laing, William
Loch, James, relict
Lufe, George
Merschell, John
Mwyre, John
Napier, Mongow
Nicholsoun, John
Patersoun, Peter
Patersoun, Richart
Purvok, George
Ra, William
Russall [blank] in ye boll

Skloter, Thomas
Sydsarth, Thomas
Thomsoun, Jon, r[elict]
Todrik, George
Watsoun, Williame
Welshe, Robert
Wilsoun, John, cramer
Young, John, taverner

Amount not given
    Govenne, Patrik

Men of Law and Scribes

£100   Borthuik, Mr. David
           Creyctoun, Mr. George
           McCalyeane, Mr. Thomas
           Moscrop, Mr. Johnne

£66 13s 4d   Scott, Robert

£60   Litill, Mr. Clement
           Mauchane, Mr. Alexr.

£50   Laing, Sir Neil
           McGill, Mr. David

£40   Bannatyne, James [del.]
           Guthre, Alexr.
           Strange, Mr. Richert
           Sym, Mr. Alexr.
           Young, John

£30   Hay, Mr. Edmond
           Hendersoun, Mr. Edward
           Scharp, Mr. Jon
           Skene, Mr. Alexr.
           Wallace, John

£20   Abercrummby, Mr. Alexr.
           Harlaw, James
           Makkartnay, James
           Patersoun, William

£10   Freir, Mr. George
           King, Alexr.
           Kynroiss, Mr. Henry
           Lawty, David [del.]
           Merioribankis, James [del.]
           Myller, James [del.]
           Spens, Mr. Peter
           Smiber, Thomas [del.]

Crafts

Skinners & furriers	£307 8s
Tailors	£107
Baxters	£210
Hammermen	£150
Fleshers	£190
Cordiners	£80
Wrights & masons	£95
Goldsmiths	£60
Websters, walkers & bonnetmakers	£40
Barbers	£45

Appendix xii
Tax Roll of June 1583

(MS Stent Rolls, i, fos. 15-30)

AFTER 1583, as a result of the decreet arbitral, all inhabitants, including craftsmen, were subject to individual tax assessment. This is the first tax roll to follow the new arrangements. There are a total of 1,245 inhabitants on the roll. The sum actually raised was £2,105 3s 4d. The returns from the individual quarters were £592 11s 4d from 259 inhabitants (N.W.); £457 10s from 222 (N.E.); £404 11s 8d from 351 (S.E.); £650 10s 4d from 413 (S.W.). The average assessment overall was just over 33s 4d. An attempt has been made to discriminate between merchants or neighbours, who are given in upper case, and craftsmen, given in lower. Anyone who does not easily fit into either category is given separately at the end of each section. However, at times the distinction is not a very significant one, particularly towards the lower end of the roll; anyone who was assessed individually in previous rolls is given in upper case. It is, therefore, not possible to give a firm figure for the number of merchants proper in the burgh, although 527 were assessed individually in a roll of 1581, the last before the decreet. Two of the crafts present the same problem: there are 116 tailors on the roll but also 26 drapers or merchant tailors, who were assessed individually up until 1583; the same distinction applied between the 8 bonnetmakers and 6 hatmakers. Otherwise, there are 60 skinners; 55 baxters; 43 hammermen (including cutlers, saddlers and pewterers, although, according to the craft's own records, it had 91 masters in 1576); 40 fleshers; 29 cordiners; 20 websters; 19 goldsmiths and wrights; 18 candlemakers; 15 barbers or surgeons; 13 masons; 9 coopers and lorimers; 6 walkers; 5 bowmakers; 3 furriers and dyers; and 2 slaters. Original spelling has been retained.

The tax roll of 1581, the last to be drawn up before the decreet, is reproduced in full in my thesis, 'Edinburgh and the Reformation', 425-36; the average assessment on merchants in it was £3 4s.

£33	INGLIS, JAMES	(6)	£20	NISBET, HENRY	(3)
	MOREIS, DAVID			ROBERTSOUN, JHOUN	
	NAPER, WILLIAM			WAUCHOP, GEORGE	
	RUSSELL, MUNGO				
	UDDART, NICHOLAS		£18	DIK, GILBERT	(1)
	Gilbert, Michaell, goldsmyth				
			£15	NESBET, WILLIAM	(2)
£26	LITTILL, WM.	(1)		UDDERT, ALEXR.	
£25	MORESOUN, JON.	(2)	£14	DOWGALL, JHOUN, elder	(2)
	PROVAND, m. JHOUN			DOWGALL, JON., younger	
£20 5s	ROSS, JAMES	(1)	£13 6s 8d	ABIRCRUMBIE, RYT.	(4)

378

	JAMIESOUN, MATHO			INGLIS, WILLIAM	
	SOMERVELL, BARTILMO			KARKETLE, GEORGE	
	STEVINSOUN, ANDROW			LOWRY, JAMES	
				MAKNACHT, ROGER	
£12	FOWLER, r[elict] of WILLIAM	(5)		SMYTH, ROBERT	
	JAKSOUN, JHOUN			Alexr., George, saddler	
	WARDLAW, JON.			[hammerman]	
	WILLIAMSOUN, DAVID				
	WILSOUN, LUCAS		£6	HAMMILTOUN, JON.	(3)
				KER, ROBERT	
£11	COCHRANE, PATRIK	(2)		SMART, ROBERT	
	Abircrumbie, Rot., saidler				
	[hammerman]		£5	AICHESOUN, ALEXR. of	(27)
				Gosfurd	
£10	AMULIGEN, THOMAS	(16)		AIKYNIHEID, THOMAS	
	DALGLEISHE, JAMES			CARKETTLE, JON.	
	GLEN, mr. ROT, eldar			COKBURNE, WILLIAM	
	GOURLAY, ROBERT, customer			COR, CLEMENCE	
	GRAY, r[elict] of ROT.			DAVIDSOUN, PATRIK, herald	
	HARWOD, JHOUN			FULLERTOUNE, ADAM	
	HOWESOUN, JOHNE, maltman			GILLASPIE, ROBERT	
	JOWSY, r[elict] of JAMES			GOTHRAY, JONAT	
	LEYIS, JHOUN			JOWSIE, ANDROW	
	LOWRIE, THOMAS			LILLIE, JAMES, cook	
	MAKMATH, HECTOR			McMORAM, JON.	
	PURDIE, JAMES, herald			MAYNE, JHOUN	
	SPEIR, r[elict] of WILLIAM			MASOUN, JHOUN	
	THOMESOUN, ALEXR., tavirnir			MOSCROP, PATRIK	
	VAUSS, THOMAS			NAP[ER], ALEXR.	
	Fowlis, Thomas, goldsmyth			OLIPHANT, JAMES	
				PRESTOUN, m. JON.	
£8	DOBIE, RYT	(8)		PURVIS, m. ROBERT	
	HERREIS, ROT.			STRANG, WILLIAM	
	LOWES, NINIANE			THOMSOUN, JAS.	
	RAA, HECTOR			TRUMBLE, WILLIAM	
	STEWART, ARD.			TUEDY, JOHNE, tutor	
	WILSOUN, JON., elder, maltman			Wilky, Jhoun, skinner	
	Burell, Harie, flesher			Cowy, Robert, tailor	
	Eillot, David, baxter			Geddis, Ard., tailor	
				Seggat, Alexr. [of the Canon-	
£7	COLPLAND, THOMAS	(4)		gate; see K.P. list]	
	KER, MARK				
	NICOLL, JAMES		£4 10s	McMORANE, NINIANE	(2)
	Porterfield, Jhoun, tailor			Hunter, James, glaysinwricht	
£6 13s 4d	ADAMSOUN, JAMES	(13)	£4	ACHESOUN, GEORGE	(36)
	ADAMSOUN, WILLIAM			ADAMESOUN, r[elict] of JON.	
	BERNARD, WILLIAM			BROUN, JAS.	
	ELEIS, PATRIK			BROUN, THOMAS	
	FAIRLIE, JHOUN			COR, r[elict] of ANDRO and	
	GEDDES, CHARLES			hir sone	
	HAMMILTOUN, WILLIAME			DARLING, PHILP	

FAIRLIE, DAVID [B. & G. mt.
   tailor 7 Aug. 1583]
FAIRLIE, MUNGO
FORMAN, JAS.
FORTOUN, JON.
GALBRAYTH, WALLANTYNE
GECHAME, WILLIAM
GOURLAW, JHOUN
GRAHAME, mr. ARD
GRAHAME, JON. spouse
HORN, WILLIAM
INGLIS, ARCHIBALD
JHONESTOUN, JHOUN
LAWSONE, JOHNE
LOWRIE, JAS.
LOWRY, JHOUN
McCALAW, ALLANE
MAKMATH, ALEXR.
MAILYILL, JAMES
MUDIE, WILLIAM
MURRAY, JHOUN
OLIPHANT, ROBERT
SCOTT, MUNGO
STARK, ROBERT
THOMESOUN, EDWARD
TODDMER, r[elict] of
   LAWRENCE
WALACE, ADAME
Patersoun, Jon., flesher
Richartsoun, Jon., saddler
Weir, Jhoun, pewdrer
   [hammerman]
Dik, Jhoun, tailor

£3 10s   DREW, JOHNE   (5)
FISCHEAR, THOS.
HUNTER, r[elict] of JOHN
LOWDIANE, THOMAS
RIG, WM.

£3 6s 8d   EGLISHAME, JHOUN   (10)
HENDERSOUN, JAMES
LOKKIE, QUYNYENE
MALCUM, ANDRO
MAWLE, WILLIAM
SCOTT, ROBERT
THOMESOUN, RYT.
WICHT, JHOUN
YOUNG, THOMAS
Sandelandis, James, tailor

£3   ARNOTT, JHOUN   (30)
BOG, ROBERT

BONNYMAN, GEORGE
BOYNTOUN, ALLANE
CANT, JAMES
CUNNGHAME, JON.
McCALL, JON.
MARIORIBANKIS, r[elict] of
   SYMON
MILLER, JHOUN
MILLER, WM.
MONTEYTH, JHOUN
MUREHEID, WILLIAM
MYNTO, WALTER
PATERSOUN, r[elict] of
   WILLIAM
RAMSAY, ROT.
SYMSOUN, r[elict] of ANDROW
TENNENT, PATRIK
TRIMYEANE, JON., hatmaker
WILLIAMSOUN, WILLIAM
Galloway, Jon., barber
Primirose, Gilbert, barber
Job, Alexr., baxter
Masoun, Jhoun, masoun
Coldane, Jas., skinner
Galbrayth, Edward, skinner
Wilsoun, Richert, skinner
Harvie, Jon., tailor
Smaill, Wm., tailor
Walker, Alexander, walker

50s   BROUN, HEW   (34)
DAUIDSOUN, JHOUN
DONELDSOUN, JOHNE
FENTOUN, JON., litster
FLEMING, THOMAS, maltman
GAIRDIN, JOHNE, litster
HARPER, WILLIAM
HENRYSOUN, THOS.
HUCHESOUN, JOHNE
HUNTER, ALEXR.
JOHNISOUN, EDUARD
JONSTOUN, EDWARD, younger
KYNLOCH, FRANCES
LYCHTOUN, JAMES
McMICHAELL, THOMAS, elder
McMATH, JOHNE
McQUHIRIE, JON.
MASTERTOUN, JAMES
MAXTOUN, LOWRENCE, ypot.
MICHELHILL, JHOUN
PALMER, JHOUN
RICHESOUN, ANDRO

SOMERVELL, JAMES
TENNENT, FRANCES
TINDALE, ANDRO
WALLACE, WILLIAM
WILSOUN, GILBERT
Stewart, Henrie, baxter
Callender, Matho, birker
  [cordiner]
Nicolsoun, Jhoun, cordiner
Dowglas, Jhoun, tailor
Hoppringle, William, tailor
Owsten, Alexr., tailor
Young, Jon., tailor

| 45s | HOME, ANTHONE | (4) |

Huchesoun, William, cordiner
Dannelstoun, Robert, tailor
Lindsay, Alexr., tailor

| 43s 4d | SCOTT, WALTER | (1) |

| 40s | AYTYKN, JHOUN | (62) |

ANDERSOUN, JHOUN, chaynger
ANDERSOUN, WILLIAM
ASLOWAME, JON.
BARCLAY, ALEXR., apothecar
BLYTH, JON.
CALDER, ALEXR.
CANT, THOMAS
CHARTERIS, HENRY
CREICH, r[elict] of JON.
CUNNINGHAME, WM.
ELEIS, WILLIAM
FAIRLIE, MUNGO, younger
FERIE, JAS.
FISCHEAR, JON.
FOULLAR, WILLIAME
GEDDIS, THOMAS, son of
  Charles G., m[erchant]
HAMILTOUN, THOMAS of
  Preistiffield
HARVIE, ALEXANDER
HENRYSOUN, JHOUN
HOWP, EDWARD
HUCHESOUN, JAMES
HUCHESOUN, WILLIAM, cook
JOHNESOUN, JAMES
JUSTICE, WILLIAM
KYNNAIRD, JHOUN
LAYNG, ARCHIBALD

McCUBIN, JOHN[1]
McMICHELL, THOMAS
MAWCHAME, EDWARD
MAWCHAME, JAMES
MOFFET, JOHNE, maltman
MOWBRAY, JOHNE
OWSTEAND, r[elict] of JON.
RICHESOUN, JAMES
SCOTT, ALEXR.
SLOWMAN, ALEXR.
SMYTH, ROT.
STEWART, ALEXR.
WALLACE, JON., draper
WILSOUN, RYT.
WRYT, JAS.
WRYT, THOMAS, tailor,
  m[erchant]
YOUNG, JAS., cramer
Bisset, Wm., chirurgeane
Blyth, Henrie, barber
Newtoun, Adame, baxter
Wilkie, Jon., candlemaker
Annand, Thomas, goldsmith
Dennelstoun, David, goldsmith
Herutt, George, goldsmith
Mosman, Jon., elder, goldsmith
Duning, David, saddler
Barclay, James, skinner
Dowglas, Jon., tailor
Duncane, George, tailor
McCurny, Andro, tailor
Maisterstoun, Gilbert, tailor
Ramsay, Alexr., tailor
Spens, Nicholl, tailor
Cant, Walter[2]
Howme, David

| 35s | KYNKAID, EDWARD | (1) |

| 30s | ACHIESOUN, JON. | (80) |

ALLANE, ADAM
AUCHMOWTIE, DAVID
BAWTIE, JON.
BLAIKBURNE, JAMES
BLAIKBURNE, JHOUN, younger
BOYDE, JHOUN
CALDIR, JAMES
CHALMERIS, JOHNE
CRYSTIE, JAMES
CUNNINGHAME, JHOUN, elder

[1] [B., mt. 15 July 1580].
[2] [of Sanct-Gely-Grange, B. & G. 21 Oct. 1586].

CUNNINGHAME, ROBERT
DAVIDSOUN, JAS., apot.
DIKSOUN, ADAM, apot.
DUNGALSOUN, ROGER
EDASLIE, JAS.
FLEMMING, WILLIAM
GILMURE, THOMAS
GILRY, JOHNE
HAMMILTOUN, ROT. of Lairkin
HERREIS, WM.
HEREOTE, GAWIN, maltman
HEREOTT, JAMES, maltman
HOPPER, WM.
HOPPRINGLE, WM., litster
LOCHE, JOHNE
LOCHE, ROBERT, maltman
LOWRIE, GILBERT
MAR, ALEXR.
MERCHELL, JOHN
MICHELL, JAMES
MILLER, CUDBERT
MORESOUN, JON.
MURE, JOHNE
MUREHEID, JAMES
PATERSONE, r[elict] of ROBERT
PEIRSOUN, ALEXR., litster
POOR, ROBERT
RAMSAY, ARD.
REID, ROT.
RIDDELL, ANDRO
SCOTT, ROBERT
SOMERVELL, THOMAS,
    maltman
SOMERVELL, WILLIAM
TEMPILTOUN, HEW
THOMSOUN, ALEXR.
TURNBILL, ANDRO
TUEDY, JOHN
WALKER, THOMAS, maltman
WILSOUN, JON.
WILSOUN, JOHNE
WILSOUN, ROT.
YORSTOUN, WILLIAM
Cairnie, Jas., baxter
Hendersoun, Jon., baxter
Patersoun, William, baxter
Elizer, Fermer, cordiner
Weir, Wm., cordiner
Hailywell, Robert, beltmaker
Cokkie, William, goldsmith
Robiesoun, Jon., cutlar
Jonstoun, Jon., saddler

Symontoun, Edward, saddler
    [hammermen]
Allane, Rot., skinner
Clerk, Jon., skinner
Cortas, Thomas, skinner
Horne, Jhoun, skinner
Ross, Thomas, skinner
Androw, Jon., tailor
Creche, Andro, tailor
Fyshare, Nicol, tailor
Leche, William, tailor
Nicolsoun, James, tailor
Rannald, James, tailor
Robiesoun, Alexr. tailor
Walkir, Johne, webster
Gordoun, Jon., wright
Wod, Thomas, wright
Lowchame, Gilbert
Marioribankis, James, younger

26s 8d   COK, THOMAS   (6)
JHONESTOUN, ARCHIBALD
TAIT, THOMAS
Weir, Quyntene, pewdrer
    [hammerman]
Ballantyne, Jhoun, skinner
Corsbie, Thomas, skinner

25s   Penndrink, Alexr., skinner   (1)

20s   ANDRO, DAVID   (131)
AUCHTMOWTY, r[elict] of
    THOMAS
BARTANE, JAS.
BAVERAGE, DAVID
BLYT, r[elict] of GEORGE
BROUN, WILLIAM
CALDWELL, JON.
CAMPBELL, OOSTIAME
CHALMERIS, RICHART,
    buthman
COCHRANE, GEORGE,
    maltman
COLDANE, PETER
CONHAITH, JAMES
CRAIG, ANDROW,
    m[erchant], tailor
CRYSTESOUN, MICHAEL
CUDBERT, ANDROW
DAVIDSOUN, JON.
DOBIE, THOMAS, messenger,
    m[erchant]

DROW, ROBERT, draper
(H)ELEIS, ANDRO
FAIRUM, GEORGE, maltman
FLEMING, THOMAS, maltman
FOSTLAW, WILLIAM
FRUME, WM.
GALBRAYTH, JHOUN, draper
GALBRAYTH, r[elict] of
    ROBERT
GIBSOUN, ADAME, draper
GRAHAME, JAS.
GRAY, mr. JAS., advocate
HOME, ARCH.
HOPPRINGLE, DAVID, taverner
JOHNESTOUN, GILBERT
JONSTOUN, JON. of Elphing-
    stoun
KER, THOMAS, m.
LEIRMONT, HENRIE,
    taverner
LATILLJHOUNE, GEORGE
LEVINGSTOUN, DUNCANE
LOWRY, JOHNE, maltman
MAKFARYEANE, WILLIAM
McQUHIRRIE, GILBERT
MAIN, JON.
MARIORIBANKIS, JAS.
MARTENE, JON.
MASOUN, r[elict] of ALEXR
MERCHELL, JAMES
MOFFET, PATRIK
MOYSES, JAMES, fischeman
MUIR, JOHN, cramer
MURRAY, CUDBERT
NAPER, ANDROW
NICOLSOUN, ROBERT,
    butterman
OGRIE, WM.
PRESTON, m. QUINTENE,
    apot[hecary]
PURVES, WM., apot[hecary]
QUARE, JAMES
REID, ALEXR., writer
REID, JOHNE, maltman
ROBERTSOUN, GEORGE
ROBERTSOUN, r[elict] of
    JHOUN
SCOTT, JAMES
SCOTT, NYCHOLL

SHAW, ROT.
SKATHWY, JAMES
SMAILL, JOHNE
SPENS, JHOUN
STEVINSOUN, JON.
STIRLING, DAVID, travelor
STIRLING, r[elict] of ROBERT
STODDERT, JON.
SYM, JOHNE
SYMSOUN, r[elict] of
    WILLIAM[3]
THOMSOUN, JON.
THOMESOUN, JOHNE
TODRIK, r[elict] of GEORGE[4]
UDWART, JON.
VETCHE, MUNGO
WILLIAMSOUN, ANDRO
WILSOUN, JAMES
WILSOUN, JON.
YOUNGER, HARIE
Culame, Walter, baxter
Donaldsoun, Jon., baxter
Forest, Jon., baxter
Girdwod, David, baxter
Levingstoun, Rot., baxter
Logane, David, baxter
Patersoun, James, baxter
Purdee, Jon., baxter
Robertsoun, Patrik, baxter
Wod, James, baxter
Bruce, r[elict] of Alexr., barber
Henrysoun, Rot., chirurgeane
Lumisdane, Henrie, barber
Fairgussoun, Jas., bower
Clavy, Jhoun, candlemaker
Mirrne, Bartilmo, cordiner
Pullous, Jon., cordiner
Maine, Patrik, couper
Boncle, Thos., cutler
    [hammerman]
Wryt, Jon., swordslipper
    [cutler]
Diksoun, William, flesher
Hendersoun, Jon., flesher
Neische, Mathew, flesher
Robesoun, Jon., flesher
Robiesoun, Thomas, flesher
Bartane, Jon., goldsmith
Hart, Edward, goldsmith

[3] [Deme Symsoun in 1565 stent].
[4] [in 1565 stent].

Thomson, George, lorimer
Harlaw, Jon., saddler
[hammerman]
Bischope, Frances, skinner
Eillot, Jon., skinner
Hepburn, Andro, skinner
Quhyte, Thomas, skinner
Reidpeth, George, skinner
Reid, Jas., skinner
Rig, Jon., fisheman, skinner
Thomsoun, Alexr., skinner
Thomesoun, Johne, skinner
Betoun, Wm., browdinster[5]
Inglis, James, tailor
Lumisdane, Andro, tailor
Miller, Robert, tailor
Murdo, Jhoun, tailor
Portuous, James, tailor
Sandelandis, Patrik, tailor
Smyth, George, tailor
Vauss, Hew, damasker[6]
Andro, Thomas, walker
Dowglas, Ard.
Jhonestoun, r[elict] of Roger
Scrymegor, Captene Wm.
Westoun, mr. Thomas

15s LEVINGSTOUN, WILLIAM, (7)
hatmaker
LINDSAY, GEORGE,
hatmaker
LYELL, WILLIAM, elder,
fishman
STARK, JOHNE
Watsoun, James, cordiner
Aitkyne, r[elict] of William
[goldsmith][7]
Lawsoun, David, tailor

13s 4d ANDERSOUN, JOHNE (89)
ARMESTRANG, r[elict] of
ANDRO
BELL, JHOUN, seidman
[merchant][8]
BANKYS, JON.
BLYTH, ALEXR.

COLVILLE, RICHERT
COWPER, THOMAS, maltman
CRAIG, ROT.
FERRY, DAVID, cook
HART, JON., cook
HENRISOUN, JOHNE, customer
HOPPRINGLE, DAVID,
apothercary
KELLO, BARNARD, stabler
KER, JAMES, draper
McCARTNAY, WM.[9]
MOSMAN, JON., younger
MUDY, ARCHIBALD,
apot[hecary]
NEILSOUN, JHOUN, cramer
RAMSAY, WILLIAM
RIED, JON.
RICHESOUN, JAS.
ROBISOUN, ROBERT
RUSSALL, ALEXR.
SMYTH, HARY
SOMER, DAVID
SYMSOUN, LOWRY
TODDMER, THOMAS
TRAYNARE, JAMES, pultreman
UCHILTRIE, JON., writer
VANNAND, HENRIE
WATSOUN, ANDRO
WATSOUN, WILLIAM,
seidman
WILLIAMESOUN, NINIANE
Adamsoun, Henrie, baxter
Andersoun, Thomas, baxter
Borthuik, Jhoun, baxter
Broun, Alexr., baxter
Fargusson, Andro, baxter
Fiddes, William, baxter
Hog, David, baxter
Hunter, Thomas, baxter
Jonstoun, Symon, baxter
Knowes, Jon., baxter
Lawsoun, Treyulas, baxter
Logane, Alexr., baxter
Michelsoun, Moyses, baxter
Spens, Patrik, baxter
Cudbertsoun, Deme, wedow[10]

[5] [tailor?].
[6] [tailor?].
[7] [G., goldsmith, 10 Oct. 1549].
[8] [in the 1565 stent].
[9] [B. & G., writer, 14 Feb. 1578].
[10] [John C., bonnetmaker, B. 6 April 1566].

Gibsoun, George, bow[er]
Gibsoun, Thomas, bower
Bruce, Thomas, cordiner
Cloggie, Jon., cordiner
Millar, Thomas, cutler
Raa, Wm., cutler
Smyt, Henrie, cutler
Wat, Jon., smith
Wilsoun, Jon., pewdrer
    [hammerman]
Blytman, Jon., flesher
Clavie, Andro, flesher
Davidsoun, Jas., flesher
Dobie, Jon., flesher, taverner
Fairbairne, William, flesher
Hammiltoun, David, flesher
Richesoun, Andro, flesher
Ur, James, flesher
Gilbert, Jon., goldsmith
Palmer, David, goldsmith
Purvis, Nicholl [lorimer]
Bikkertoun, William, mason
Taillirfer, Mungo, mason
Courte, Wm., skinner
Lowrestoun, Rot., skinner
Someruell, Petir, skinner
Tuedie, Walter, skinner
Wallace, Moyses, skinner
Abirnethy, Thomas, tailor,
    meilman
Alexr., Thomas, tailor
Bairnisfayer, Jhoun, tailor
Broun, Andro, tailor
Clerk, Andro, tailor
Cowper, Jhoun, tailor
Kennedy, Jhoun, tailor
Makcuir, Jhoun, tailor
Rattray, Patrik, tailor
Wauchop, Rot., wright
Dowgal, Rot., fidlar
Padene, Jon.[11]
Ryssie, Deme

10s   AICHESOUN, JHOUN   (163)
ADAMSON, JHOUN
ANDERSOUN, ROT., maltman
ANGUS, CRISTIANE, brewster
BAWCHOP, ANDRO, tailor,
    cramer
BAWTY, ALEXR.
BLAIR, JOHN

BROUN, JHOUN, collictor
BROUN, THOMAS
BROUNRIG, THOMAS, cook
CAIRNS, JHOUN, chapman
CAMPBELL, ROBERT
CAVERIS, DAVID, hatmaker
CHAP, WM.
COCHRANE, r[elict] of HEW
COKBURNE, WILLIAM
CRAIG, ROBERT, apot[hecary]
CRAWFURD, JON., maltman
CRAWFURD, JHOUN
DALGLEISHE, ROBERT
DIKSOUN, JON.
DRYSDAILL, WILLIAM
DUNDAS, ANDRO
DURIE, PATRIK
FARUN, JAS., maltman
FARQUHAR, JON.
FELL, THOMAS, cramer
FIDDES, mr. JAS., taverner
FINDLIE, JOHNE, draper
FISHEAR, m. JHOUN
FISHEAR, WILLIAM
FLEMYNG, JON.
FUIRD, NYCHOLL, maltman
FYNELASUN, JOHNE, meilman
GAVELOK, JOHNE, brewster
GIB, STEVEN, tailor, draper
GLEN, JOHNE, litster
GORDOUN, JAS.
GRENESOUN, JON.
HAMMILTOUN, DAVID,
    maltman
HAMMILTOUN, THOMAS,
    butterman
HAIRT, GAWIN, fishman
HARVIE, mr. WM., advocate
HEPBURNE, JON., hatmaker
HEREWTE, JAS., maltman
HOG, JON., stabler
HOME, WM., draper, tailor
HOWPE, EDWARD
JONSTOUN, JON., stabler
JHONNESOUN, PATRIK
JHONESTOUN, SYMON
JOHNESTOUN, WM.
KELLO, JON., stabler
KER, JAS.
LAWSOUN, ANDROW
LILLE, ANDRO, draper

[11] [B. by r. of w. Katherine, 8 Nov. 1560].

B1

LOWRIE, MARTENE
LOWTHIAN, r[elict] of
  WILLIAM, draper
LYELL, WILLIAM
LYNTOUN, r[elict] of
  FRANCES
MANNE, ALEXR., fishman
MARTENE, PETER
MELVILL, WM.
MILLERE, RYCHART, butter-
  man
MOREYS, ALEXR., tapster[12]
MOWBRAY, r[elict] of JAS.
MURRAY, THOMAS, suddert,
  tapster
PATERSOUN, THOMAS
PENNIND, ANDRO, stabler
QUHYTE, GILBERT, cr[amer],
  tailor
QUNTENE, ROT.
SAMUELL, MICHAELL
SCOTT, JON., stabler
SCOTT, WM.
SOMERVELL, ARD., butterman
STALKER, JON., maltman
STEONDLINE, WM., draper
TAILIEFER, JAMES
TAILYER, JOHNE, draper
TAIT, WILLIAM, cramer
THOMSOUN, ALEXR.
THOMESOUN, ROT.
THOMSOUN, THOMAS,
  maltman
TWEDY, WALTER, woolseller
UDDERT, ALESOUN, taverner
WALLACE, WILLIAM
WERE, JOHNE
WILLIAMSOUN, THOMAS
WILSOUN, JAMES, draper
YOUNG, WILLIE, butterman
YULE, WILLIAM
Lourisoun, Jon.[13]
Mekiliohne, Edward, barber
Arnott, Hercules, baxter
Hunter, Andro, baxter
Louristoun, James, baxter
Wod, Patrik, baxter
Young, Michaell, baxter
Young, Thomas, baxter

Andersoun, William, candle-
  maker
Haistie, Nycholl, cordiner
Hardie, Patrik, cordiner
Hog, Thomas, cordiner
Quhyte, Henry, cordiner
Strudgeann, Thomas, cobbler
Hammiltoun, Robert, couper
Adamesoun, Wm., flesher
Andersoun, Jon., flesher
Dobie, Thomas, flesher
Fische, Wm., flesher
Pursell, Rot., flesher
Bradie, Mungo, goldsmith
Craig, Adam, goldsmith
Gilbert, Alexr., goldsmith
Stalker, Jas., goldsmith
Kerss, David, dagmaker
Gilcryst, Jon., smith
Smyth, Mathew, smith
Thomsoun, Alexr., cutler
Young, Jas., cutler
  [hammermen]
Grib, Alexr., lorimer
Windyettis, Thomas, sheith-
  maker [lorimer]
Tailliefer, Robert, mason
Bell, Frances, skinner
Bowie, Jas., skinner
Broun, Patrik, skinner
Forrett, Jhoun, skinner
McDowgall, Alexr., skinner
Mairtene, Archibald, skinner
Ramsay, Jas., skinner
Robesoun, James, skinner
Turnet, Peter, skinner
Watsoun, Jon., skinner
Watsoun, Jon., skinner
Barclay, George, tailor
Baxter, Jon., tailor
Birges, William, tailor
Carmichaell, Jhoun, tailor
Carnbie, Rot., tailor
Duncane, Jon., tailor
Farquher, Lawrence, tailor
Grenlaw, Jon., tailor
Hay, William, tailor
Holme, James, tailor
Howp, Alexr., [tailor][14]

[12] [B. mt. 18 May 1580].
[13] [B. barber, 7 May 1567].
[14] [B. tailor, as p. to David Fairlie, tailor, 30 Jan. 1579].

Kennedie, Jon., [tailor][15]
Moresoun, Wm., tailor
Reid, Murdow, tailor
Rowame, Jhoun, tailor
Sanddlandis, George, tailor
Wod, Johne, tailor
Bankis, Jhoun, walker
Walker, Jhoun, walker
Stevensoun, Jon., wright
Williamsoun, Andro, wright
Bassendene, David
Boyd, James, of ye Kips[16]
Cunninghame, Cudbert
Gibsoun, Jonet, ladieboxmont
Mayne, John, cachpillar
Ramsay, Capitane Jon.
Weir, Bessie

6s 8d BALLANTINE, THOMAS, (135)
stabler
BAWCHOP, ROBERT
BELL, JON., fishman
BOWIE, THOMAS, stabler
BROUN, ALEXR.
BROUN, ANDRO
BROUN, JAMES, draper
CALDUN, ROBERT, maltman
CAMPBELL, r[elict] of
ROBERT, writer
CHALMER, JAS.
COUTIS, r[elict] of JOHN
CRAWFURD, THOMAS, stabler
DIKSOUN, THOMAS,
brewster, maltman
DUN, WILLIAM, maltman
DUNCANE, JON., chaynger
FAIRLIE, JON.
FOIRBRAND, GEORGE
GEORGE, DIONRIS, doy-
ledderman
GILLASPIE, MICHAELL,
stabler
GRAY, UMPHRA
HAMILTON, ARD.,
m[erchant]
HAMMILTOUN, GEORGE,
maltman

INGLIS, ROT., litster
KYNKAID, THOMAS, maltman
KNELAND, ALEXR., maltman
McMILLANE, ALEXR.[17]
MAKMATH, WM., litster
MAXWELL, r[elict] of
HARBERT[18]
MENYIES, THOMAS, cook
MILLARE, WILLIAM, fishman
MOFFET, WILLIAM, woolseller
NEMOK, GEORGE
NEWLANDIS, JHOUN, woolseller
NYCHOLL, r[elict] of DAVID[19]
NORWELL, r[elict] of
THOMAS
NORWELL, WILLIAM, stabler
OGILWY, ALEXR., litster
PATERSOUN, GEORGE
PATERSOUN, JON., stabler
PATERSOUN, JOHNE
QUAIRD, JAS., chapman
REID, ROBERT, draper, tailor
ROBESOUN, WALTER,
maltman
RUSSELL, JOHNE
SCOTT, r[elict] of THOMAS,
brewster
STEVINSOUN, WILLIAM,
cramer
SYMSOUN, r[elict] of WM.,
litster
THOME, ARTHOR, stabler
TWEDIE, THOMAS
WAUS, JAMES, draper
WATT, JON., customer
WILSOUN, JOHNE, younger
maltman
Bassenden, Michaell, barber
Craig, James, barber
Lowsoun, Jhoun, barber
Lynsay, Jas., barber
Adamsoun, Jas., baxter
Arnott, Rot., baxter
Fiddes, Alexr., younger, baxter
Hammiltoun, Jon., baxter
Hendersoun, George, baxter
Henrysoun, James, baxter

[15] [B. tailor as p. to Andrew Cowie, tailor, 18 April 1582].
[16] [B. & G. by r. of w. Marian, dr. to Ninian Barclay mt., 3 Nov. 1587].
[17] [B. stabler, ordinary officer, 18 Aug. 1585].
[18] [in the 1565 stent].
[19] [heritor; see *Edin. Recs.*, iv, 89].

Hereote, Jon., baxter
Purdiee, Andro, baxter
Riche, Rot., baxter
Ros, Mungo, baxter
Torrence, Ard., baxter
Mathe, Jon., bonnetmaker
Patersoun, Rot., bonnetmaker
Rannald, Patrik, bonnetmaker
Somer William[20]
Mayne, Wm., bower
Clavie, William, candlemaker
Eistoun, Henrie, candlemaker
Broun, Thomas, cordiner
Callender, Patrik, birker
   [cordiner]
Davidsoun, Alexr., cordiner
Douglas, William, cordiner
Ellot, Jon., cordiner
Ellot, William, cordiner
McIldunden, Peter, cordiner
Murray, Jon., cordiner
Nicolsoun, William, cordiner
Barnard, James, couper
Reid, Jhoun, couper
Bartilmo, Alexander, tinctor
   [dyer]
Adamesoun, Stewin, flesher
Fleming, Jas., flesher
Fyndlaw, Jon., flesher
Russell, Jon., flesher
Weir, Wm., flesher
Diksoun, Thomas, furrier
Fostlaw, Jas., swordslipper
   [cutler]
Lynsay, David, smith
Millar, Jas., smith
   [hammerman]
Windyettis, Jon., sheithmaker
   [lorimer]
Masoun, Paul, mason
Nesbett, James, mason
Broun, George, saddler
Dunsmore, Jon., saddler
Hammiltoun, David, saddler
   [hammermen]
Cathkene, Edward, skinner
Cortes, William, skinner
Freir, Jon., skinner
Loch, Mungo, skinner

Neill, Jhoun, skinner
Rynde, Peter, skinner
Vallange, Andro, skinner
Weir, Frances, skinner
Robesoun, Wm., slater
Anstruyer, Jon., tailor
Cok, Jon., tailor
Galbrayth, Umfray, tailor
Gordoun, George, tailor
Hoppringill, Patrik, tailor
Huchesoun, Lawrence, tailor
Ker, Jon., tailor
Makkie, Jon., tailor
Muir, Alexr., tailor
Mure, Robert, tailor
Patersoun, David, tailor
Penstoun, Suilliam, tailor
Rynd, Nicholl, elder[21]
Sanndelandis, Nycholl, tailor
Wallace, James, tailor
Wicht, Adam, tailor
Wilsoun, William, tailor
Lyle, Jon., webster
Stevinsoun, Jon., webster
Cowtis, Wm., walker
McKilveill, Alexr., nolt driver
Castellaw, r[elict] of Alexr.
Watsoun, Stevin

6s   CHAIP, r[elict] of ALEXR.[22]   (1)

5s   ADAMESOUN, JOHNE,   (247)
      stabler
    ADINSTOUN, JAS., hatmaker
    AIKMAN, WILLIAM, draper
    ALLANE, ROT., fishman
    ALLANE, JHOUN, maltman
    ALLANE, ROBERT, brewster
    ANGUSS, WILLIAM
    ATKYNE, ROBERT
    BAIRD, WM., stabler
    BAIRINSFAYER, GEORGE,
      cramer
    BALAM, JON., stabler
    BAWTY, ALEXR., brewster
    BLYTH, JAS., brewster
    BOW, JAMES, draper
    BUWIE, ALEXR., stabler

---

[20] [B. bonnetmaker, 25 Nov. 1577].
[21] [tailor; *Edin. Recs.*, iv, 365].
[22] [merchant; in 1565 stent].

BROUN, ANDRO
BROUN, JON., stabler
BURNE, JON., stabler
CAMPBELL, JON., driver
CANT, ALEXR.
COLEYNE, ABRAHAM, draper
CORSBIE, DAVID
CORSER, JHOUN, maser[23]
COWPER, JAMES
CRAIG, JOHNE, carter
DAVIDSOUN, r[elict] of
    JHOUN[24]
DOUGLAS, r[elict] of ANDRO
FORSYTH, WM., maltman
FRELANDS, MAURIOUN, tapster
FYNLAW, MICHAELL, draper
GARMONT, PATRIK, stabler
GIBSOUN, JON., bookbinder
GLEN, ROT., fishman
GORLAY, ROT., bookbinder
GRAHAME, r[elict] of JHOUN
GREG, GILBERT, fishman
HAGY, CRISTIANE, cramer
HAMMILTOUN, ROT., stabler
HAMMILTOUN, WILLIE, stabler
HARDIE, ALEXR., brewster
HAY, r[elict] of GILBERT[25]
HAY, ROBERT, cook
HENDERSOUN, EDUARD
HENRESOUN, ALEXR.,
    cramer
HENRESOUN, r[elict] of JAS.,
    maltman
HENRYSOUN, r[elict] of
    ADAM
HENRYSOUN, GEORGE
HUCHESOUN, WALTER
JAK, PETIR, butterman
JONSTOUN, r[elict] of
    GEORGE
JOHNISTOUN, GEORGE,
    waxmaker
JOHNESTOUN, ROBERT,
    meilman
JOWYS, JONAT, tapster
KER, HENRIE
KNELAND, WM., maltman
LESLIE, WM., brewster

LOGANE, JON., stabler
LOURISTOUN, GEORGE,
    meilman
McQHUAIRE, JOHNE, brewster
MARIORIBANKIS, r[elict] of
    JAMES
MARK, ROT., cramer
MINTEITH, WILLIAM, stabler
MICHELL, MICHELL, brewster
MOWBRAY, JAS., brewster
MYLNE, PATRIK, stabler
NEILSOUN, ROT., maltmaker
NEWLANDS, ROT., stabler
PATERSOUN, RYT., brewster
PENTLAND, GEORGE
PRESTOUN, JAMES
QUHYTE, JAMES, cramer
RAA, JON., fishman, tapster
RAA, WILLIAM
REID, JAS., stabler
REID, r[elict] of JON.,
    brewster
REYNTOUN, JOHNE, meilman
ROBESOUN, r[elict] of WM.
ROGER, HEW, meilmaker
ROSS, JON., cook
SCOTT, JOHNE, meilmaker
SHAW, r[elict] of JAS.[26]
SMYTH, JON., brewster
SMYTH, THOMAS, maltmaker
SNEILL, WM., brewster
STRABROK, ALEXR., stabler
STRUDGEVIN, THOMAS,
    chapman
SLOWAME, WILLIAM
SONSIE, ALEXR., cramer
STARK, JON., butterman
STEVINSOUN, ROGER
SYMSOUN, NYCHOL, cook
SYMSOUN, THOMAS,
    butterman
TARBAT, THOMAS
THOMESOUN, WILLIAM
TRINSHE, ARD.
VAUS, THOMAS, stabler
VERNUR, GEORGE, pultreman
WALKER, HARIE, hatmaker
WATSOUN, ROT., cramer

[23] [merchant; in 1565 stent].
[24] [merchant; in 1565 stent].
[25] [merchant; in 1565 stent].
[26] [merchant; in 1565 stent].

WELSCHE, ROT.
WILKYN, ALEXR., maltman
WILSOUN, JHOUN, tapster
YOUNG, JON., stabler
YOUNGER, WALIE, brewster
Brussatt, Nowie, barber
Crytoun, Abraham, baxter
Darling, Andro, baxter
Libbertoun, William, baxter
Purves, Patrik, baxter
Rennald, William, baxter
Thomsoun, Thos., baxter
Wilsoun, Jon., baxter
Walker, William, bonnetmaker
Broun, Jon., bower
Dudgeon, Jon., candlemaker
Eistoun, Mathew, candlemaker
Wilkey, Henrie, candle[maker]
Logane, Jon., cordiner
Moresoun, Wm., cordiner
Pvmfra, Jon., cordiner
Walker, Thomas, cordiner
Balkaskie, Walter, couper
Dalyell, Jas., couper
Dy[on]eis, George, couper
Thomsoun, Andro, couper
Turnble, Jon., couper
Cunnynghame, Hewe, tinctor
    [dyer]
Yule, Adam, tinctor
Arneill, Niniane, flesher
Blythman, Nycholl, flesher
Gardner, Patrik, flesher
Hagie, Jas., flesher
Hagie, r[elict] of Walter[27]
Hall, Jon., flesher
Henderoun, Rot., flesher
Jonstoun, Jon., flesher
Kennoche, William, flesher
Neilsoun, Jon., flesher
Patersoun, Peter, flesher
Patersoun, William, flesher
Patersoun, William, flesher
Pursell, William, flesher
Cranstoun, Cudbert, furrier
Craig, John, goldsmith
Henrysoun, George, goldsmith
Broun, Hes, smith
Bruce, Thomas, saddler
Fostlaw, Androw, swordslipper
    [cutler]

Hammiltoun, Adam, smith
Henrisoun, Cudbert, cutler
Heslope, George, swordslipper
Mersir, Lawrence, pewdrer
Ross, Jon., smith
Spens, Peter, smith
Sprottie, William, smith
Trotter, Thomas, smith
Wilsoun, Jhoun, younger,
    pewdrer [hammermen]
Michel, David, lorimer
Rannild, George, lorimer
Wedirspone, Thomas, lorimer
Patersoun, Jhoun, causemaker
    [mason]
Pierie, Gavin, mason
Robesoun, Allane, mason
Thomsoun, Jhoun, mason
Watt, Thomas, mason
Weir, Thomas, mason
Bell, Thomas, skinner
Eldar, Frances, skinner
Gottersoun, Frances, skinner
Miller, Jon., skinner
Mowbray, Robert, skinner
Symontoun, Johne, skinner
Tennent, Alexr., skinner
Thomesoun, Thomas, skinner
Vallange, Peter, skinner
Watsoun, William, skinner
Scott, Walter, slater
Aitkyn, David, tailor
Arratt, David, tailor
Bonkle, Wm., tailor
Brysun, Steven, tailor
Cathcart, Michaell, tailor
Diksoun, Jas., tailor
Dowglas, Robert, tailor
Dury, Jhoun, tailor
Dyoneis, Jas., tailor, brewster
Fleming, Andro, tailor
Gilbert, r[elict] of Jon., tailor,
    brewster
Grene, Jhoun, tailor
Haire, Jon., tailor
Henrysoun, Thomas, tailor
Houp, Alexr., tailor
Hunter, Adam, tailor
Inglis, Wm., tailor
Leggat, Hew, tailor
Leggat, Hew, tailor

[27] [unfree flesher; in 1581 stent].

Makcuir, Rot., tailor
Makcuir, Robert, tailor
Martene, Alexr., tailor,
  brewster
Michelhill, George, tailor   3s
Patersoun, Cudbert, tailor
Purdie, Ryt., tailor
Pursell, George, tailor
Purvess, Jhoun, tailor
Raynie, William, tailor
Schaw, Patrik, tailor
Blak, Andro, webster
Blak, Andro, webster
Blak, Jon., webster
Blak, Jon., webster
Donaldsoun, James, webster
Gemmell, George, webster
Mathesoun, Cudbert, webster
Meid, Rot., webster
Mewriss, Jas., webster
Filp [Philop], Jon., webster
Pook [Pollock], Wm., webster
Pook, Wm., webster
Thomesoun, Leonard, webster
Tulloc[h], Thomas, worsetmaker
Wardlaw, Ard, webster
Wryt, Thomas, webster   2s
Brewhous, Jhone, worsetmaker
Baxter, Jas., wright
Bog, Thomas, wright in
  norowaye
Bynning, Walter, painter[28]
Fender, Jon., younger, wright
Kennedy, Thomas, wright
Killimure, William[29]
Mansoun, Frances, wright
Quhytlaw, John, wright
Schang, Jon., wright
Symsoun, William, wright
Touris, James, glasswright
Weymis, David, glasswright
Wilkie, Jon., glasswright
Currie, Symon
Diksun, Elizabeth
Fairburne, Jonat
Fischear, Katherene
Kersell, Jhoun
McGevein, Rot., gaird,
Porteous, Wm., messenger

Rook, Jhoun, boulyure
Wilsoun, Katheren, widow
Wod, Katherene

GRAY, ISOBELL, cramer   (21)
WOD, WM., brewster
Welshe, George, barber
Davidsoun, Mathew, bonnetmaker
Tullo, Jon., bonnetmaker
Barbor, Jon., cordiner
Bikkartoun, Jon., cordiner
Chepman, Jas., cordiner
Cor, John, cordiner
Cor, Lowrence, cordiner
Cunde, David, cordiner
Gibsoun, Jon., cobbler
Lympetlaw, Thomas, cordiner
Smyth, Jon., cordiner
Richeman, William, mason
Aikyne, Jhoun, tailor
Carruyeris, Johne, tailor
Corlaw, Andro, tailor
Cowpir, r[elict] of Androw,
  tailor
Cudbertsoun, Andro, tailor
Lowdeane, Jon., tailor

AIRTH, ISOBELL, tapster   (71)
ALEXR., ROBERT, tapster
BELL, AGNES, brewster
BLAK, DAVID, brewster
BROUN, KATHERENE, cramer
BRUCE, AGNES, tapster
CARMICHAEL, JOHNE, stabler
CRANSTOUN, ADAM, tapster
DIK, WALTER, tapster
DONALDSOUN, JON., cook
DONELDSOUN, MATHO,
  brewster
EISTOUN, THOMAS, brewster
FLEMING, JON., brewster
FREIR, r[elict] of m. GEORGE[30]
GODDISKIRK, r[elict] of
  JHOUN, butterman
GRAY, DAVID, tapster
HAIRE, ISOBELL, brewster
HALL, HECTOR, chapman
IRWING, JONAT, cramer
JONSTOUN, WILLIAM,
  brewst[er]

[28] [see Ryt. B., made B. 7 Aug. 1583 as p. to Walter B., glasswright].
[29] [B. wright, 3 Feb. 1571].
[30] [advocate; in 1565 stent].

KERSELL, JON., suddert,
  tapster
KNELAND, ALESOUN,
  brewster
KNOWES, BESSE, brewster
LAWSOUN, LOWRENCE,
  brewster
LOGANE, DAVID, cramer
LOWRIE, HENRIE, brewster
McDULL, PATRIK, brewster
McGLINTO, ROT., brewster
MALAN, HECTOR, litster
MALAN, HECTOR, litster
MICHELSOUN, JON., meilmaker
OCULTRIE, BARTILMO,
  brewster
PATERSOUN, DAVID, tailor,
  cramer
REID, JHOUN, brewster
RUSSELL, ADAM, brewster
STRANG, JONET, tapster
STRONG, KATHERENE, tapster
THOMSOUN, DAVID, brewster
THOMESOUN, MARIOUN,
  brewster
THOMSOUN, NICOLL, tapster
VERNOR, r[elict] of PATRIK,
  brewster
WIGHOLME, MAIRJORIE,
  tapster
WILSOUN, ISABLL, brewster
YOUNG, ALLANE, tapster
YOUNG, r[elict] of ROT.,
  fishman
Minteith, Andro, baxter
Clavy, r[elict] of Patrik,
  candlemaker
Quhyte, William, cordiner,
  tapster

Dowglas, Alexr., couper
Patirsoun, Thomas, flesher,
  brewster
Mure, Cudbert, furrier
Duncane, David, smith
Mair, Roger, smith
Robesoun, Jon., smith,
  brewster [hammermen]
Patersoun, Laurence, mason
Templetoun, Rot., mason
Jonstoun, Jas., saddler
Corsby, David, skinner
Turnor, George, skinner
Cherilaw, Rot., tailor, brewster
Law, Andro, tailor, brewster
Layng, Jhoun, tailor
Libertoun, Patrik, tailor
Littill, Thomas, tailor
Lynsay, Jon., tailor, tapster
Cunnghame, Bessie
Cochrane, Jas.
Fergussoun, Robert
Scott, Jas.
Thomesoun, r[elict] of Gilbert

No amounts given
  ADAMSOUN, JON., baillie
  CHISHOLME, m.
    MICHAELL, baillie
  FAIRLIE, WILLIAM, bailie
  SCLATER, ANDRO, baillie
  MYLNN, r[elict] of DAVID,
    brewster
  Mylare, David, goldsmith
  Grahame, James, skinner
  Wilsoun, Jonat, widow

Deleted   Jonstoun, Edward, younger

List of Events in Scotland and beyond, and in Edinburgh, 1542-1585

Scotland and beyond

Dec. 1542: Death of James V and minority of Queen Mary.

Jan. 1543: Arran proclaimed governor.

July 1543: Two Treaties of Greenwich. Riots against religious houses in Perth and Dundee.

Dec. 1543: Parliament rejects treaties.

1544-5: First stage of the 'Rough Wooing'.

Sept. 1547: English victory at Pinkie.

1548-50: English garrisons set up in Borders and Lothian, including Haddington, eighteen miles from the town.

1549, 1552: Provincial councils of the Church suggest reforms.

April 1554: Regency of Mary of Guise.

1555: Act of parliament abolishes office of craft deacon, but restored to the burgh's crafts by charter from the regent in 1556.

1556: Perpetual tax suggested by the regent.

Dec. 1557: First Band of the Congregation.

April 1558: Marriage of Mary and Francis; execution of Walter Miln.

Nov. 1558: Succession of Elizabeth I.

Jan. 1559: Beggars' Summons.

March-April 1559: Treaty of Cateau-Cambrésis.

May 1559: Riot at Perth nine days after Knox's return; Ayr town council dismisses its chaplains.

Edinburgh

1543: Protestant preacher, John Rough, given hostile reception in the town; an attack on the Blackfriars repulsed by the inhabitants.

Aug. 1543: Riot in the council chamber.

May 1544: Part of the town sacked by Hertford.

1545: Outbreak of the plague.

1548: Economic blockade of the town; riot against French troops quartered in the town.

1550-51: Severe food shortages in the town.

1555: Protestant privy kirks begin to meet in the town.

1556: Threat to the town's jurisdiction over its port; dispute over the office of water bailie of Leith involves the regent.

May 1556: Knox preaches for ten days.

1556-7: Series of heavy taxes imposed on the burgh by the regent.

July 1558: Theft of image of St. Giles puts council under threat of excommunication.

Sept. 1558: St. Giles' Day riot.

1558-9: Series of clashes between the council and its provost, Seton.

March-April 1559: Reforming council of the Church sits in the town.

Scotland and beyond

June 1559: St. Andrews and Dundee purged by the Congregation; Perth recaptured on 25th, Scone Abbey sacked, Linlithgow purged.

July 1559: Death of Henry II of France. Truce between the regent and the Congregation.

Aug.-Sept. 1559: Arrival of c.2,000 French troops.
Oct. 1559: Congregation depose the regent.

Feb. 1560: Treaty of Berwick.

March-April 1560: English troops march into Scotland, making camp at Restalrig outside Edinburgh; regent retires into the Castle, the French troops to Leith, which is put under siege.

June 1560: Death of Mary of Guise.

July 1560: Treaty of Edinburgh.

Aug. 1560: Reformation parliament abolishes papal authority and the mass; adopts the Confession of Faith.
Aug.-Dec. 1560: First Book of Discipline in process of revision.

Dec. 1560: Death of Francis II.
Jan. 1561: Convention of nobility gives qualified approval to First Book of Discipline.

Edinburgh

June 1559: The council concerned that the imprisonment of one of its bailies by the provost will provoke a riot; an attack on the friaries on 14th prompts the council to take the town's religious treasures into safe-keeping. Congregation enter the town and Knox preaches in St. Giles' on 29th.
July 1559: Knox appointed burgh minister on 7th but leaves with the Congregation on 24/25 July. Willock continues in St. Giles' and the mass is celebrated at Holyrood.
Sept.-Oct. 1559: Regent intervenes in council elections; Seton continues as provost.
Oct. 1559: Congregation's second occupation; council dismissed; new council under Kilspindie appointed; tax of 2,000 merks on the burgh.
Nov. 1559: Congregation abandon the town 6/7 Nov. French troops retake it; St. Giles' reconsecrated; Seton council resumes control.
Feb. 1560: Inquiry held in town by de la Brosse and d'Oysel.
April 1560: Congregation enter the town for the third time; altars in St. Giles' thrown down; Kilspindie council resumes control; tax of £1,600 on the burgh.

May 1560: Council ceases to pay chaplains and prebendaries and bans payment of annuals due to chaplainries.
June 1560: Council passes ordinance against 'idolatreris and harlottis'.
July 1560: Council assumes control of property and income of friaries; collectors appointed to bring in their revenues for the new ministry.
Aug. 1560: Church vestments and treasures sold off by public auction, including those from craft altars.
Oct.-Nov. 1560: Sunday flesh market abolished as part of policy of strict Sabbatarianism; deacon of fleshers dismissed for adultery.
Nov. 1560: Craft riot.

March 1561: Council ordinance expelling all ex-priests and ex-religious who refuse to conform; compulsory attendance at the sermon enforced; agreement with the crafts for voluntary collection for the poor.
July 1561: Craft riot.

Scotland and beyond

Edinburgh

Aug. 1561: Mary arrives at Leith on 19th; proclamation enforcing a standstill in religion on 25th.

Aug. 1561: Celebration of mass in queen's household on 24th provokes a minor riot; Knox preaches against the mass on 31st.
Oct. 1561: Mary dismisses provost and bailies after they reissue the ordinance of March 1561.

Feb. 1562: Compromise financial settlement with the new church; all monastic lands within burghs revert to the crown.

April-July 1562: Council begins its attempts to dismiss catholic master of grammar school; dismisses catholic deacon of hammermen; appoints second minister; institutes voluntary tax for the ministry; imposes religious test on office-holders.

Oct. 1562: Huntly defeated and killed at Corrichie.

Aug.-Dec. 1562: Knox away on visitation in the west.
Nov. 1562: Appeal for funds for new poor hospital; town granted Blackfriars' lands and income four months later by the queen.
1563: Council's appeal for funds to support the ministry in June, followed in Nov. by a flat-rate compulsory tax; protestant riot in the chapel royal in Aug. and demonstration when Knox called before privy council in Dec.

Jan. 1564: Mary revokes the burgh ordinance of 1562 enforcing a religious test.

1564: Council reverts to a voluntary tax for the ministry in May; Nicol Young affair; Knox on visitation to the north for six weeks.
1565: Compulsory quarterly tax for poor and ministry instituted in Jan. Full-scale catholic riot as result of Tarbot affair in April.

July 1565: Marriage of Mary and Darnley on 29th triggers off the Moray rebellion. After failing to rouse Edinburgh, it peters out in the Chaseabout Raid.

Leaders of protestants found drilling arrested early in July. Mary dismisses the provost when she re-enters the town in Aug. but the council resists attempts to silence Knox temporarily. She intervenes in the Oct. council elections. Knox accepts a commission in the south in Dec. of indefinite length.
Feb. 1566: First assault on Fr. Black.

March 1566: Riccio murder.

March 1566: Fr. Black killed on night of Riccio murder; Knox and the town clerk flee eight days later; more than twenty burgesses pursued for their part in Riccio affair.

June 1566: Birth of James.
Oct., Dec. 1566: Further financial concessions to the reformed church granted by Mary.

Oct. 1566: Mary intervenes again in the council elections.
Dec. 1566: Knox granted six-month leave of absence in England.

Feb. 1567: Murder of Darnley at the Kirk o' Field.
May 1567: Marriage of Mary and Bothwell at Holyrood.

March 1567: Edinburgh and other burghs granted remaining land and income of old church within burghs.

Scotland and beyond

June 1567: Mary defeated at Carberry.
July 1567: Mary abdicates; James VI crowned at Stirling.
Aug. 1567: Moray proclaimed regent.

Dec. 1567: Parliament re-enacts leglislation of 1560.
May 1568: Mary defeated at Langside and flees to England.

Jan. 1570: Murder of Moray.

July 1570: Lennox appointed regent.

May 1571: 'Creeping parliament' of king's lords in the Canongate.

Sept. 1571: Lennox killed at Stirling and Mar succeeds as regent.

Jan. 1572: Convention of Leith.

July 1572: Five-month truce negotiated.
Aug. 1572: Massacre of St. Bartholomew.
Nov. 1572: Morton succeeds Mar as regent.

Feb. 1573: Pacification of Perth.
May 1573: End of civil war.

March 1578: Morton temporarily deposed as regent by confederate lords.

1580: Esmé Stewart created earl of Lennox; Morton arrested.
1581: Negative Confession; Morton executed.

1582: Ascendancy of Lennox and Arran.

Edinburgh

June 1567: Knox returns ten days after Carberry.

Nov. 1567: Gift of Trinity College to the town.

April 1568-Aug. 1569: Severe food shortages, followed by an outbreak of the plague.
Oct. 1569: Kirkcaldy of Grange elected provost.

April 1570: Queen's lords temporarily occupy the town.

Dec. 1570: Grange's 'outrage'.
April-May 1571: Fighting between the rival forces at the Netherbow; council expelled from the town and a Marian one substituted; Knox leaves for St. Andrews.
Oct. 1571: Abortive siege of the town by king's party; rival elections in Leith and Edinburgh.
Feb.-July 1572: Demolition of houses in the town by queen's party; economic blockade of the town by the king's party.
July 1572: Return of the exiles to the town; deposition of Marian council shortly after.
Nov. 1572: Death of Knox three months after his return to the burgh.

April-May 1573: English pioneers land at Leith; Castle rendered after eleven-day bombardment.
1574: 'Common collection' for the ministry instituted; outbreak of plague; imprisonment of leading merchants by Morton for exporting bullion.
1575: Compulsory weekly collection for poor instituted but abandoned in 1576.
April 1578: Confederate lords purge council of Morton supporters.
Sept. 1578: Morton faction regains control after a leet imposed at council elections.

1581: Pro-Morton burgesses exiled during his trial.
May 1582: Council agree to expel Durie temporarily for criticism of the court.

Scotland and beyond	Edinburgh
	Aug. 1582: Craft riot induces commission into the government and constitution of the burgh.
Aug. 1582: Ruthven Raid.	Sept. 1582: Return of Durie; Ruthven lords purge the council at its elections.
Dec. 1582: Lennox leaves for France.	
	April 1583: Decreet-arbitral.
June 1583: Fall of Ruthven lords.	
	Sept.-Oct. 1583: Comprehensive purge of Ruthven supporters from the council at its elections.
May 1584: Arran made chancellor; parliament passes 'Black Acts'.	May 1584: Two ministers, Lawson and Balcanquhal, flee to England.
	June-July 1584: Number of radicals exiled from the town; council and kirk session asked to subscribe Archbishop Adamson's letter to the burgh's exiled ministers.
	Oct. 1584: Further leet imposed on the council; Arran made provost; kirk session nominated by the purged council.
Oct.-Nov. 1585: Return of Ruthven lords from England, followed by radical ministers; fall of Arran.	1585: Severe outbreak of the plague.

Bibliography

THIS is not a complete bibliography of all the works used in writing this book. It is intended, firstly, along with the list of abbreviated titles given earlier, to provide a full reference for works cited frequently in the notes or appendices. A number of works which have been cited only once or twice in the notes have been omitted; in these cases a full reference has been given when they were first cited. The bibliography is also intended to act as a guide for reading in Edinburgh and Scottish burgh history as well as in more general Scottish history of the sixteenth century. It has not attempted, however, to be comprehensive in any of these and would have to be many times even its present length to be so.

1. MANUSCRIPT SOURCES

EDINBURGH CITY ARCHIVES

Council register, vols. ii-vii.
Guild register, vols. i-ii.
Bailies' and treasurers' accounts, vol. i.
Bailies' accounts, vol. i.
Accounts of the common good and proper revenue of the burgh, vol. i.
Accounts of the collector of kirk rents, vol. i.
Dean of guild accounts, vols. i-ii.
Dean of guild court book, vols. i-ii.
Act book of the deacons of crafts, vol. i.
Minutes of the hammermen of Edinburgh, vols. i-ii.
Stent rolls, vol. i.
Moses bundles, inventory no. 195.
Abstracts of the protocol books of Alexander King, vols. i-v; John Guthrie, vol. i; Alexander Guthrie, vols. i-iii, ix.

SCOTTISH RECORD OFFICE, EDINBURGH

Commissary court records:
  Register of Edinburgh testaments (CC 8/8/1-).
  Register of acts and decreets (CC 8/2/5).
  Register of deeds and protests (CC 8/17/1).
  Minute book of deeds and protests (8/18/1).
Exchequer records:
  Edinburgh customs accounts, 1551-73 (E71/30/8-17).
  Wool customs book, 1573 (E71/31/20).

Justiciary court records:
  Court books, old series (JC 1/6-13).
  Register of bonds of caution (JC 19/1-2).
  Small papers, main series (JC 26/1).
  Books of adjournal, old series (JC 2/1).
  High court minute books, old series (JC 6/1-2).
Privy council records:
  Register of *acta* (PC 1/6-8).
  Register of acts of caution (PC 6/1).
  Register of the privy seal, old series (PS 1/41-3).
State papers:
  State papers, correspondence (SP 1/1/287-8).
Burgh records:
  Edinburgh burgh register of deeds (B 22/8/1-2).
  Edinburgh burgh court book (B 22/23/1).
  Protocol books of Alexander King (B 22/1/14-18).
  Protocol book of John Guthrie (B 22/1/19).
  Protocol books of Alexander Guthrie (B 22/1/20-30).
  Protocol books of William Stewart, elder (B 22/1/55-7).
  Protocol books of John Aitkin (B 22/1/59, 61).
  Protocol books of William Stewart, younger (B 22/1/61-2).
Notarial records:
  Protocol book of John Robeson (NP 1/17; also in transcript, RH 2/1/22).
Church of Scotland records:
  Edinburgh, general session minutes, 1574-5 (Buik of the General Kirk of Edinburgh, CH
    2/450/1; also partly in transcript, RH 2/1/35).
Edinburgh and Leith papers:
  Notebook of provosts and magistrates of Edinburgh (RH 9/14/1).
  Resolution of the Edinburgh kirk session and subscription list, 26 November 1562 (RH 9/14/8).
Gifts and deposits:
  Records of the goldsmith craft of Edinburgh (GD 1/482/1).
Transcripts:
  Discharge by Archibald Seigneur, 21 November 1571 (RH 1/2/415).

NATIONAL LIBRARY OF SCOTLAND, EDINBURGH

Advocates MS 29.2.9a   Balcarres papers, *inter alia*, papers relating to Morton's dealings with
                        Edinburgh merchants.

Advocates MS 29.2.8   Two papers concerning the teaching of the catechism in Edinburgh,
                        1581.

Advocates MS 33.6.1   Wodrow collection, the small MS of David Calderwood's History of
                        the Church of Scotland.

NLS MS 189   Extract from the Edinburgh council minute book, with list of members
                        of the council, 12 December 1572.

PUBLIC RECORD OFFICE, LONDON

State papers, Scotland, Edward VI (SP 50/4-5).
State papers, Scotland, Mary (SP 51).
State papers, Scotland, Elizabeth (SP 52/1-36).

BRITISH LIBRARY, LONDON

Cotton collection:

Caligula B. viii-x	Papers relating to Anglo-Scottish relations, 1525-70.
Caligula C. i-viii	Papers relating to Anglo-Scottish relations, 1567-86.

Harleian collection:

289	Collection of papers, mostly sixteenth century, relating to the affairs of Scotland.
291	Collection of papers relating to the affairs of Scotland, 1572-86, including the dialogue between Edward Hope and Henry Nisbet of 1584.

Additional MSS:

4,736	The larger MS of David Calderwood's History of the Church of Scotland.
33,531	State papers and correspondence relating to the affairs of Scotland, 1449-1594.
48,117	Beale papers, mostly relating to Scottish religious affairs.

2. PRINTED PRIMARY SOURCES

All books were printed in London unless otherwise stated.

A. Public Records

Acts of the Lords of Council in Public Affairs, 1501-1554: Selections from the Acta Dominorum Concilii introductory to the register of the Privy Council of Scotland, ed. R. K. Hannay (Edinburgh, 1932).

The Acts of the Parliaments of Scotland 1124-1707, ed. T. Thomson and C. Innes, 12 vols. (Edinburgh, 1814-75).

Calendar of State Papers, Foreign of the reign of Edward VI, 1547-1553, ed. W. B. Turnbull (1861).

Calendar of State Papers, Foreign of the reign of Mary, 1553-1558, ed. W. B. Turnbull (1861).

Calendar of State Papers, Foreign of the reign of Elizabeth, 1558-1589, ed. J. Stevenson and others (1863-1950).

Calendar of the State Papers relating to Scotland and Mary Queen of Scots, 1547-1603, ed. J. Bain and others, 14 vols. (Edinburgh, 1898-1969).

Calendar of State Papers, Rome, ed. J. M. Rigg, 2 vols. (1916-26).

Calendar of State Papers, Spanish, ed. G. A. Bergenroth and others, 13 vols. and 2 supplements (1862-1954).

Compota Thesaurariorum Regum Scotorum: Accounts of the Lord High Treasurer of Scotland, ed. T. Dickson and others, 13 vols. (Edinburgh, 1877-).

Hamilton Papers: Letters and papers illustrating the political relations of England and Scotland in the XVIth century, ed. J. Bain, 2 vols. (Edinburgh, 1890-92).

The Register of the Privy Council of Scotland, 1545-1625, ed. J. Hill Burton and D. Masson, 14 vols. (Edinburgh, 1877-98).

Registrum Magni Sigilli Regum Scotorum: The Register of the Great Seal of Scotland, ed. T. Thomson and others, 12 vols. (Edinburgh, 1814-1914).

Registrum Secreti Sigilli Regum Scotorum: The Register of the Privy Seal of Scotland, ed. M. Livingstone and others, 8 vols. (Edinburgh, 1908-).

Rotuli Scaccarii Regum Scotorum: The Exchequer Rolls of Scotland, ed. J. Stewart and others, 23 vols. (Edinburgh, 1878-1908).

B. Source Collections

Aberdeen Council Letters (1552-1633), ed. L. B. Taylor (1943-50).

Aberdeen. *Ecclesiastical Records of Aberdeen* (Spalding Club, 1846).

Aberdeen. *Extracts from the Council Register of the Burgh of Aberdeen, 1398-1570,* ed. J. Stuart, 2 vols. (Aberdeen, 1844-48).

Acts and Proceedings of the General Assemblies of the Kirk of Scotland (1560-1618), ed. T. Thomson (Bannatyne & Maitland Clubs, 1839-45).

Anderson, W. J., 'Narratives of the Scottish Reformation, ii: Thomas Innes on Catholicism in Scotland', *Innes Review,* xiii (1962), 112-21.

Ayr Burgh Records, 1534-1624, ed. G. Pryde (SHS, 1937).

Bannatyne Miscellany, ed. W. Scott and D. Laing, 3 vols. (Edinburgh, 1827-55).

Brown, P. H., *Early Travellers in Scotland* (Edinburgh, 1891).

Brown, P. H., *Scotland before 1700 from contemporary documents* (Edinburgh, 1893).

Canongate. *The Buik of the Kirk of the Canagait, 1564-1567,* ed. A. B. Calderwood (SRS, 1961).

Canongate. *Court Book of Regality of Broughton and Burgh of the Canongate, 1569-1573,* ed. M. Wood (Edinburgh, 1937).

Catholic Tractates of the Sixteenth Century, 1573-1600, ed. T. G. Law (Scot. Text. Soc., 1901).

The Compt Buik of David Wedderburne, 1587-1630, ed. A. H. Millar (SHS, 1898).

Dickinson, G., ed., *Two missions of Jacques de la Brosse: An Account of the Affairs of Scotland in the year 1543 and the Journal of the Siege of Leith, 1560* (SHS, 1942).

Dickinson, G., ed., 'Report by De La Brosse and D'Oysel on conditions in Scotland, 1559-1560' (SHS, *Misc.,* 1958).

Donaldson, G., *Accounts of the Collectors of Thirds of Benefices, 1561-1572* (SHS, 1949).

Dunfermline. *The Burgh Records of Dunfermline, 1488-1584,* ed. E. Beveridge (Edinburgh, 1917).

Dunfermline. *Extracts from the Burgh Records of Dunfermline in the 16th and 17th Centuries,* ed. A. Shearer (Dunfermline, 1951).

Edinburgh. *Commissariat Record of Edinburgh: Register of Testaments,* i (SRS, 1897).

Edinburgh. *Edinburgh Records,* ed. R. Adam, 2 vols. (Edinburgh, 1899).

Edinburgh. *Extracts from the Records of the Burgh of Edinburgh, 1403-1603,* ed. J. D. Marwick and M. Wood, 6 vols. (Scot. Burgh Rec. Soc., 1869-92, 1927).

Edinburgh. *Roll of Edinburgh Burgesses and Guild Brethren, 1406-1700,* ed. C. B. B. Watson (SRS, 1929).

Forbes-Leith, W., *Narratives of Scottish Catholics under Mary Stuart and James VI* (Edinburgh, 1885).

Glasgow. *Extracts from the Records of the Burgh of Glasgow,* i, ed. J. D. Marwick (Scot. Burgh Rec. Soc., 1876).

Hannay, R. K., ed., 'Letters of the Papal Legate in Scotland, 1543', *SHR,* xi (1911), 1-26.

Reports of the Royal Commissioners of the Historical Manuscripts Commission:

       1st Report (1870).

       3rd Report (1872).

       4th Report (1874).

       5th Report (1876).

       6th Report (1877).

       7th Report (1879).

       9th Report: Calendar of the Manuscripts of the Marquess of Salisbury, vols. i-iv (1883-5).

       12th Report, Part iv: The Manuscripts of the Duke of Rutland, vol. i (1888).

Hunt, C. A., *Book of the Perth Hammermen, 1518 to 1568* (Perth, 1889).

Liber Conventus S. Katherine Senensis prope Edinburgum (Abbotsford Club, 1841).

Maitland Miscellany, eds. A. Macdonald and others, 4 vols. (Maitland Club, 1833-47).

Mary of Lorraine. *The Foreign Correspondence with Marie de Lorraine, Queen of Scotland from the originals in the Balcarres Papers,* ed. M. Wood, 2 vols. (SHS, 1923, 1925).

Mary of Lorraine. *The Scottish Correspondence of Mary of Lorraine, 1542-1560,* ed. A. I. Cameron (SHS, 1927).

Miscellaneous Papers principally illustrative of events in the Reigns of Queen Mary and King James VI, ed. W. J. Duncan (Maitland Club, 1834).

Papal Negotiations with Mary Queen of Scots during her reign in Scotland, 1561-1567, ed. J. H. Pollen (SHS, 1901).

Pitcairn, R., *Criminal Trials in Scotland from 1488 to 1624,* 3 vols. (Edinburgh, 1833).

Records of the Convention of Royal Burghs of Scotland, ed. J. D. Marwick (Edinburgh, 1866-90).

Register of Ministers, Exhorters and Readers and of their Stipends after the Period of the Reformation (Maitland Club, 1830).

Registrum cartarum ecclesie Sancti Egidii de Edinburgh (Bann. Club, 1859).

Registrum Honoris de Morton (Bann. Club, 1853).

Satirical Poems of the time of the Reformation, ed. J. Cranstoun (Scot. Text Soc., 1891).

Smith, J., *The Hammermen of Edinburgh and their Altar in St. Giles Church with Extracts from the Original Records, 1494-1558* (Edinburgh, 1905).

A Source Book of Scottish History, ed. W. C. Dickinson and others, 3 vols. (Edinburgh, 1953-4).

Spalding Miscellany, ed. J. Stuart, 4 vols. (Spalding Club, 1844-5).

Spottiswoode Miscellany, vol. ii (Spottiswoode Club, 1845).

St. Andrews. *Register of the Ministers, Elders and Deacons of St. Andrews, 1559-1600,* ed. D. H. Fleming (SHS, 1889-90).

Stirling. *Extracts from the Records of the Royal Burgh of Stirling,* ed. R. Renwick, 2 vols. (Glasgow, 1887-9).

Teulet, J. A. B., ed., *Papiers d'état, pièces et documents inédits ou peu connus relatifs à l'histoire de l'Ecosse au XVIe siècle,* 3 vols. (Bannatyne Club, 1852-60).

Teulet, J. A. B., ed., *Relations politiques de la France et de l'Espagne avec l'Ecosse au XVIe siècle,* 5 vols. (Paris, 1862).

The Warrender Papers, ed. A. I. Cameron (SHS, 1931).

Wodrow Miscellany, ed. D. Laing (Edinburgh, 1844).

C. Narrative Sources, Tracts etc.

Bannatyne, Richard, *Journal of the Transactions in Scotland,* ed. J. G. Dalyell (Edinburgh, 1806).

Bannatyne, Richard, *Memorials of Transactions in Scotland, 1569-1573,* ed. R. Pitcairn (Bann. Club, 1836).

Birrel. Diary of Robert Birrel, 1532-1605, in *Fragments of Scottish History,* ed. J. G. Dalyell (Edinburgh, 1798).

Bowes. *The Correspondence of Robert Bowes,* ed. J. Stevenson (Surtees Soc., 1842).

Buchanan. *The History of Scotland, by George Buchanan,* ed. J. Aikman, 4 vols. (Glasgow, 1827).

Calderwood. *History of the Kirk of Scotland by Mr. David Calderwood,* ed. T. Thomson and D. Laing, 8 vols. (Wodrow Society, 1842-49).

Castelnau, Michel de, *Mémoires,* ed. J. Le Laboureur, 3 vols. (Paris, 1731).

Chronicle of Perth: A register of remarkable occurrences, chiefly connected with that city, from the year 1210 to 1668, ed. J. Maidment (Maitland Club, 1831).

Colville. *Original Letters of Mr. John Colville, 1582-1603,* ed. D. Laing (Bann. Club, 1858).

A diurnal of remarkable occurrents, that have passed within the country of Scotland, since the death of King James the Fourth, till the year 1575, ed. T. Thomson (Edinburgh, 1833).

Fergusson, David, *Tracts, 1563-1572,* ed. J. Lee (Bann. Club, 1860).

The First Book of Discipline, ed. J. K. Cameron (Edinburgh, 1972).

Herries. *Historical memoirs of the reign of Mary, Queen of Scots, and a portion of the reign of King James the Sixth,* ed. R. Pitcairn (Edinburgh, 1836).

The Historie and Life of King James the Sext, ed. T. Thomson (Bann. Club, 1825).

Holinshed, R., *The Chronicle of England, Scotland and Ireland,* ed. H. Ellis, 6 vols. (1807-08).

Knox. *The Works of John Knox,* ed. D. Laing, 6 vols. (Edinburgh, 1846-64).

Knox. *John Knox's History of the Reformation in Scotland*, ed. W. C. Dickinson, 2 vols. (Edinburgh, 1949).

La Mothe-Fénélon, B. de S. de, *Correspondence diplomatique*, ed. J. A. B. Teulet, 7 vols. (Bann. Club, 1840).

Lesley. *Diary of John Leslie, Bishop of Ross*, ed. D. Laing (Bann. *Misc.*, iii, 1855).

Lesley. *The Historie of Scotland, wrytten first in Latin by the most reverend and worthy Jhone Leslie, Bishop of Rosse, and translated in Scottish by Father James Dalrymple 1596*, eds. E. G. Cody and W. Murison, 2 vols. (Scot. Text Soc., 1888-95).

Maitland, J., *Maitland's Narrative of the principal Acts of the Regency, during the Minority, and other Papers relating to the History of Mary, Queen of Scots*, ed. W. S. Fitch (Ipswich, 1833).

Majoreybanks, George, *Annals of Scotland, 1514-1591*, ed. J. G. Dalyell (Edinburgh, 1814).

Melville, James, *The Autobiography and Diary of Mr. James Melville*, ed. R. Pitcairn (Wodrow Soc., 1842).

Melville, Sir James of Halhill, *Memoirs of his Own Life, 1549-93*, ed. T. Thomson (Bann. & Maitland Clubs, 1827).

Pitscottie, *The Historie and Cronicles of Scotland by Robert Lindesay of Pitscottie*, ed. J. G. Mackay, 3 vols. (Scot. Text Soc., 1899-1911).

Spottiswoode, *History of the Church of Scotland, by John Spottiswoode*, ed. M. Russell and M. Napier, 3 vols. (Spottiswoode Soc., 1847-51).

The State Papers and Letters of Sir Ralph Sadler, ed. A. Clifford (Edinburgh, 1809).

Winzet, Ninian, *Certain Tractates together with the Book of Four Score Three Questions*, ed. J. K. Hewison, 2 vols. (Scot. Text Soc., 1888-90).

3. SECONDARY SOURCES: PUBLISHED BOOKS AND ARTICLES

Adams, I. H., *The Making of Urban Scotland* (1978).

Anderson, W. J., 'The excommunication of Edinburgh town council, 1558', *Innes Review*, x (1959), 289-94.

Angus, W., 'The incorporated trade of the skinners of Edinburgh, with extracts from their minutes, 1549-1603', *BOEC*, vi (1913), 11-106.

Arnot, H., *The History of Edinburgh* (Edinburgh, 1779).

Bain, E., *Merchant and Craft Guilds, a History of the Aberdeen Incorporated Trades* (Aberdeen, 1887).

Ballard, A., 'The theory of the Scottish burgh', *SHR*, xii (1916), 16-27.

Barbé, L. A., *Sidelights on the History, Industries and Social Life of Scotland* (1919).

Baxter, J. H., 'Dundee and the Reformation', *Abertay Historical Society Publications*, vii (1960), 26.

Brown, P. H., *John Knox: a Biography*, 2 vols. (Edinburgh, 1895).

Brown, P. H., *Scotland in the Time of Queen Mary* (1904).

Brunton, G. and Haig, D., *Historical Account of the Senators of the College of Justice* (Edinburgh, 1832).

Bryce, W. M., 'The Black Friars of Edinburgh', *BOEC*, iii (1910), 13-104.

Bryce, W. M., *The Black Friars of Edinburgh* (Edinburgh, 1911).

Bryce, W. M., *The Scottish Grey Friars*, 2 vols. (Edinburgh, 1909).

Bulloch, J. B. P., 'The Johnstones of Elphinston', *Trans. of the East Lothian Antiquarian and Field Naturalists Soc.*, iv (1948), 34-50.

Burleigh, J. H. S., *A Church History of Scotland* (Oxford, 1960).

Burns, J. H., 'Catholicism in defeat: Ninian Winzet', *History Today*, xvi (1966), 788-95.

Burrell, S. A., 'Calvinism, capitalism and the middle classes: some afterthoughts on an old problem', *Journal of Modern History*, xxxii (1960), 129-41.

Bush, M. L., *The Government Policy of Protector Somerset* (1975).

Campbell, A. J., 'The burgh churches of Scotland', *RSCHS*, iv (1932), 185-94.

Campbell, W., *History of the Incorporation of Cordiners in Glasgow* (Glasgow, 1883).

Chalmers, G., *Caledonia*, 8 vols. (Paisley, 1887-1902).

Chambers, R., *Edinburgh Merchants and Merchandise in Old Times* (Edinburgh, 1859).

Clair, C., 'Christopher Plantin's trade connections with England and Scotland', *Library*, xiv (1959), 28-45.

Colston, J., *The Guildry of Edinburgh: is it an Incorporation?* (Edinburgh, 1887).

Colston, J., *The Incorporated Trades of Edinburgh* (Edinburgh, 1891).

Colville, J., *By-ways of History: Studies in the Social Life and Rural Economy of the Olden Time* (Edinburgh, 1897).

Cormack, A., *Poor Relief in Scotland* (Aberdeen, 1923).

Cowan, I. B., 'Church and society in post-Reformation Scotland', *RSCHS*, xvii (1969-71), 185-201.

Cowan, I. B., *Regional Aspects of the Scottish Reformation* (Historical Assoc., 1978).

Davidson, J. and Gray, A., *The Scottish Staple at Veere: a Study in the Economic History of Scotland* (1909).

Devine, T. M. and Lythe, S. G. E., 'The economy of Scotland under James VI', *SHR*, 1 (1971), 91-106.

Dickinson, W. C., 'Burgh life from burgh records', *Aberdeen University Review*, xxi (1946), 214-26.

Dickinson, W. C. and Duncan, A. A. M., *Scotland from the Earliest Times to 1603* (rev. ed., Oxford, 1977).

Donaldson, G., *Mary, Queen of Scots* (1974).

Donaldson, G., *Scotland: James V to James VII* (Edinburgh, 1965).

Donaldson, G., *The Scottish Reformation* (Cambridge, 1960).

Donaldson, G., *The Sources of Scottish History* (Edinburgh, 1978).

Donaldson, G., 'Map of the siege of Leith, 1560', *BOEC*, xxxii (1966), 1-7.

Donaldson, G., 'The legal profession in Scottish society in the sixteenth and seventeenth centuries', *Juridical Review*, new series, xxi (1976), 1-19.

Donaldson, G., 'Scottish presbyterian exiles in England, 1584-8', *RSCHS*, xiv (1962), 67-80.

Dunlop, A. I., *Royal Burgh of Ayr* (Edinburgh, 1953).

Durkan, J., 'Care of the poor: pre-Reformation hospitals', *Innes Review*, x (1959), 268-80.

Edinburgh, 1329-1929 (Edinburgh, 1929).

Fleming, D. H., *Mary Queen of Scots* (2nd ed., 1898).

Fleming, D. H., *The Reformation in Scotland: Causes, Characteristics, Consequences* (Edinburgh, 1910).

Flinn, M., ed., *Scottish Population History from the 17th Century to the 1930s* (Cambridge, 1977).

Foster, W. R., *The Church before the Covenants, 1596-1638* (Edinburgh, 1975).

Fraser, A., *Mary Queen of Scots* (1969).

Fraser, D., *Edinburgh in Olden Times* (Montrose, 1976).

Grant, F. J., ed., *The Faculty of Advocates in Scotland, 1532-1943* (SRS, 1944).

Grant, I. F., *The Social and Economic Development of Scotland before 1603* (Edinburgh, 1930).

Gray, W. F., 'The incorporation of candlemakers of Edinburgh, 1517-1884', *BOEC*, xvii (1930), 91-146.

Gross, C., *The Gild Merchant* (Oxford, 1890).

Haws, C. H., *Scottish Parish Clergy at the Reformation, 1540-1574* (SRS, 1972).

Horn, D. B., 'The origins of the University of Edinburgh', *Edinburgh University Journal*, xxii (1966), 213-25, 297-312.

Houston, J. M., 'The Scottish burgh', *The Town Planning Review*, xxv (1954), 114-27.

Innes, C., *Ancient Laws and Customs of the Burghs of Scotland*, 2 vols. (Scottish Burgh Recs. Soc., 1868-9).

Innes, C., *Sketches of Early Scotch History and Social Progress* (Edinburgh, 1861).

An Inventory of the Ancient and Historical Monuments of the City of Edinburgh (Royal Comm. on the Ancient Monuments of Scotland, Edinburgh, 1951).

Irons, J. C., *Leith and its Antiquities*, 2 vols. (Edinburgh, 1898).

Janton, P., *John Knox, ca. 1513-1572. L'homme et l'oeuvre* (Paris, 1967).

Johnston, T., *The History of the Working Classes in Scotland* (Glasgow, 1923).

Keith, R., *The History of the Affairs of the Church and State in Scotland from the beginning of the Reformation . . . to 1568*, 3 vols. (Spottiswoode Soc., 1844-50).

Keith, R., 'Trading privileges of the royal burghs of Scotland', *English Historical Review*, xxviii (1913), 545-71, 678-90.

Kennedy, W., *Annals of Aberdeen from the Reign of King William the Lion to the End of the Year 1818* (Aberdeen, 1818).

Kerr, T. A., 'The early ministry of John Craig at St. Giles', 1562-1566', *RSCHS*, xiv (1962), 1-17.

Kerr, T. A., 'The later ministry of John Craig in St. Giles', 1567-1572', *RCHS*, xiv (1962), 81-99.

Kirk, J. M., 'The influence of Calvinism on the Scottish Reformation', *RSCHS*, xix (1976), 157-79.

Lamond, R., 'The Scottish craft gild as a religious fraternity', *SHR*, xvi (1916), 191-212.

Lang, A., *John Knox and the Reformation* (1905).

Lee, J., *Lectures on the History of the Church of Scotland*, 2 vols. (Edinburgh, 1860).

Lee, M., 'The fall of the regent Morton: a problem in satellite diplomacy', *Journal of Modern History*, xxviii (1956), 111-29.

Lee, M., *James Stewart, Earl of Moray* (New York, 1953).

Lee, M., 'John Knox and his History', *SHR*, xlv (1966), 79-88.

Lees, J. C., *St. Giles', Edinburgh* (1889).

Little, W. C., 'An historical account of the hammermen of Edinburgh', *Trans. Soc. of Antiquaries of Scotland*, i (1702), 170-83.

Lockie, D. M., 'The political career of the bishop of Ross, 1568-80', *Univ. of Birmingham Hist. Journal*, iv (1953), 98-145.

Lynch, M., 'The "faithful brethren of Edinburgh": the acceptable face of protestantism', *Bulletin of the Institute of Historical Research*, li (1978), 194-9.

Lynch, M., 'The two Edinburgh town councils of 1559-60', *SHR*, liv (1975), 117-39.

Lythe, S. G. E., *The Economy of Scotland in its European Setting, 1550-1625* (Edinburgh, 1960).

Lythe, S. G. E., *Life and Labour in Dundee from the Reformation to the Civil War* (Abertay Historical Society, 1958).

Lythe, S. G. E. and Butt, J., *An Economic History of Scotland, 1100-1939* (Glasgow and London, 1975).

MacAdam, J. H., *The Baxter Books of St. Andrews* (Leith, 1903).

McCrie, T., *Life of Andrew Melville*, 2 vols. (Edinburgh, 1819).

McCrie, T., *Life of John Knox*, 2 vols. (Edinburgh, 1839).

MacKenzie, W. M., *The Scottish Burghs* (Edinburgh, 1949).

Mackie, J. D. and Pryde, G. S., *The Estate of Burgesses in the Scots Parliament and its Relation to the Convention of Royal Burghs* (St. Andrews, 1923).

Mackinnon, J., *Social and Industrial History of Scotland from the Earliest Times to the Union* (Edinburgh, 1920).

Mackintosh, J., *History of Civilization in Scotland*, 4 vols. (Aberdeen, 1887-8; Paisley, 1896).

Maclennan, B., 'The Reformation in the burgh of Aberdeen', *Northern Scotland*, ii (1974-7), 119-44.

McNeill, P. and Nicholson, R., *An Historical Atlas of Scotland, c. 400-c. 1600* (St. Andrews, 1975).

McRoberts, D., ed., *Essays on the Scottish Reformation, 1513-1625* (Glasgow, 1962).

Makey, W. H., *The Church of the Covenant, 1637-1651: Revolution and Social Change in Scotland* (Edinburgh, 1979).

Makey, W. H., 'The elders of Stow, Liberton, Canongate and St. Cuthbert's in the mid-seventeenth century', *RSCHS*, xvii (1970), 155-67.

Maitland, W., *The History of Edinburgh* (Edinburgh, 1753).

Malcolm, C. A., 'The incorporation of cordiners of the Canongate, 1538-1773', *BOEC*, xviii (1932), 100-150.

March, M. C., 'The trade regulations of Edinburgh during the fifteenth and sixteenth centuries', *Scottish Geographical Magazine*, xxx (1914), 483-8.

Marwick, J. D., *Edinburgh Guilds and Crafts. A Sketch of the History of Burgess-ship, Guild Brotherhood and Membership of Crafts in the City* (Scottish Burgh Recs. Soc., 1909).

Marwick, W. H., 'The incorporation of tailors of the Canongate', *BOEC*, xxii (1938), 91-131.

Mathieson, W. L., *Politics and Religion, 1550-1695*, 2 vols. (Glasgow, 1902).

Maxwell, A., *The History of Old Dundee* (Edinburgh and Dundee, 1884).

Maxwell, A., *Old Dundee, Ecclesiastical, Burghal and Social, prior to the Reformation* (Edinburgh and Dundee, 1891).

Meek, D. E. and Kirk, J. M., 'John Carswell, superintendent of Argyll: a reassessment', *RSCHS*, xix (1975), 1-22.

Merriman, M. H., 'The assured Scots: Scottish collaborators with England during the Rough Wooing', *SHR*, xlvii (1968), 10-34.

Miller, A. C., *Sir Henry Killigrew, Elizabethan Soldier and Diplomat* (Leicester, 1963).

Miller, R., *John Knox and the Town Council of Edinburgh* (Edinburgh, 1898).

Mitchison, R., *A History of Scotland* (1970).

Morris, D. B., *The Development of Burghal Administration in Scotland* (Edinburgh, 1917).

Morris, D. B., *The Stirling Merchant Gild and Life of John Cowane* (Stirling, 1919).

Murray, D., *Early Burgh Organization in Scotland, as illustrated in the History of Glasgow and some neighbouring Burghs*, 2 vols. (Glasgow, 1924-32).

Murray, P. J., 'The excommunication of Edinburgh town council in 1558', *Innes Review*, xxvii (1976), 24-34.

Napier, M., *Memoirs of John Napier of Merchiston, his Lineage, Life and Times* (Edinburgh, 1834).

Nicholson, R., *Scotland: the Later Middle Ages* (Edinburgh, 1974).

Pagan, T., *The Convention of Royal Burghs of Scotland* (Glasgow, 1926).

Paton, H. M. and Smith, J., 'St Leonard's lands and hospital', *BOEC*, xxiii (1940), 111-46.

Paul, J. B., 'Edinburgh in 1544 and Hertford's invasion', *SHR*, viii (1910), 113-31.

Paul, J. B., 'Social life in Scotland in the sixteenth century', *SHR*, xvii (1919), 296-310.

Percy, E. S. C., *John Knox* (1937).

Pryde, G. S., 'The burgh courts and allied jurisdictions', in 'An Introduction to Scottish Legal History', *Stair Society*, xxv (1958), 384-94.

Read, C., *Mr. Secretary Walsingham and the Policy of Queen Elizabeth*, 3 vols. (Oxford, 1925).

Reid, W. S., 'The coming of the Reformation to Edinburgh', *Church History*, xlii (1973), 27-44.

Reid, W. S., 'The middle class factor in the Scottish Reformation', *Church History*, xvi (1947), 137-53.

Reid, W. S., *Skipper from Leith: the History of Robert Barton of Over-Barnton* (Philadelphia, 1962).

Reid, W. S., *Trumpeter of God: a Biography of John Knox* (New York, 1974).

Renwick, R., *Peebles during the Reign of Queen Mary* (Peebles, 1903).

Ridley, J., *John Knox* (Oxford, 1968).

Ritchie, J., 'James Henrysoun, "chirurgian to the poor"', *Medical History*, iv, 70-79.

Robertson, D., *The Bailies of Leith* (Leith, 1915).

Robertson, D. and Wood, M., *Castle and Town: Chapters in the History of the Royal Burgh of Edinburgh* (Edinburgh, 1928).

Robertson, J., *History of the Reformation in Aberdeen* (Aberdeen, 1887).

Rogers, C., *Social Life in Scotland from Early to Recent Times*, 3 vols. (Edinburgh, 1884-6).

Rooseboom, M. P., *The Scottish Staple in the Netherlands: an Account of the Trade Relations between Scotland and the Low Countries from 1292 till 1676* (The Hague, 1910).

Ross, A., 'Reformation and repression', *Innes Review*, x (1959), 338-81.

Ross, T., 'The Magdalene Chapel and the Greyfriars Churches, Edinburgh', *Trans. Scottish Ecclesiological Soc.*, iv (1912-13), 95-102.

Ross, T. and Brown, G. B., 'The Magdalen Chapel, Cowgate, Edinburgh', *BOEC*, viii (1916), 1-78.

Russell, E., *Maitland of Lethington . . . a Study of his Life and Times* (1912).

Sanderson, M. H. B., 'Catholic recusancy in Scotland in the sixteenth century', *Innes Review*, xxi (1970), 87-107.

Scott, H., ed., *Facti Ecclesiae Scoticanae*, 8 vols. (Edinburgh, 1915-50).

Shaw, D., *The General Assemblies of the Church of Scotland, 1560-1600: their Origins and Development* (Edinburgh, 1964).

Shaw, D., ed., *John Knox: a Quartercentenary Reappraisal* (Edinburgh, 1975).

Smout, T. C., 'The development and enterprise of Glasgow, 1556-1707', *Scottish Journal of Political Economy*, vii (1960), 194-212.

Smout, T. C., 'The Glasgow merchant community in the seventeenth century', *SHR*, xlvii (1968), 53-71.

Smout, T. C., *A History of the Scottish People* (1969).

Steuart, A. F., 'Gilbert Balfour of Westray', in A. W. Johnston, *Old-Lore Miscellany of Orkney, Shetland, Caithness and Sutherland*, iv (1911), 146-50.

Tytler, P. F., *The History of Scotland*, 9 vols. (Edinburgh, 1828-43).

Warden, A. J., *The Burgh Laws of Dundee with the History and Extracts from the Records of the Guild of Merchants and Fraternities of Craftsmen* (1872).

Watson, C. B. B., 'List of owners of property in Edinburgh, 1635', *BOEC*, xiii (1924), 93-145.

Watt, H., *John Knox in Controversy* (Edinburgh, 1950).

Webster, B., *Sources of History: Scotland from the Eleventh Century to 1603* (1975).

Wilson, D., *Memorials of Edinburgh in the Olden Time*, 2 vols. (Edinburgh, 1848, 1891).

Wood, M., 'Domestic affairs of the burgh: unpublished extracts from the records', *BOEC*, xv (1928), 1-53.

Wood, M., 'Edinburgh poll tax returns', *BOEC*, xxv (1945), 90-126.

Wood, M., 'The hammermen of the Canongate', *BOEC*, xix (1933), 1-30; xx (1935), 78-110.

Wood, M., *The Lord Provosts of Edinburgh, 1296-1932* (Edinburgh, 1931).

Wood, M., 'The neighbourhood book', *BOEC*, xxiii (1940), 82-100.

Wood, M., 'Survey of the development of Edinburgh', *BOEC*, xxiv (1974), 23-56.

Wright, R. S., *The Kirk in the Canongate* (Edinburgh, 1956).

Yair, J., *An Account of the Scotch Trade in the Netherlands and of the Staple Port in Campvere* (1776).

4. UNPUBLISHED THESES

Anderson, A. H., 'The burgh of the Canongate and its court' (Edinburgh University Ph.D., 1949).

Kerr, T. A., 'John Craig, 1512-1600' (Edinburgh University Ph.D., 1954).

Kirk, J. M., 'The development of the Melvillian movement in late sixteenth century Scotland' (Edinburgh University Ph.D., 1972).

Lynch, M., 'Edinburgh and the Reformation' (London University Ph.D., 1977).

Macniven, D., 'Merchant and trader in Aberdeen in the early seventeenth century' (Aberdeen University M.Litt., 1977).

Merriman, M. H., 'The struggle for the marriage of Mary, Queen of Scots: English and French intervention in Scotland, 1543-1550' (London University Ph.D., 1975).

Pound, J. F., 'Government and society in Tudor and Stuart Norwich, 1525-1675' (Leicester University Ph.D., 1975).

Index

Aberdeen, population of, 11; burgh government in, 6, 24n, 28, 60, 62-3; social tensions in, 50; Reformation in, 75, 214.

Acheson, Helen, widow of William Birnie, 129, 139. *See also* Stewart, Archibald.

Acheson, John, mt., 127, 129, 137, 139, 156.

Adamson, Alexander, mt., 194. *See also* Dundas, Euphemia.

Adamson, James, mt., 106.

Adamson, John, mt., 132, 137, 162, 163, 173.

Adamson, Patrick, archbishop of St. Andrews, 41, 45, 158, 162.

Adamson, William, mt., 83.

Aikenhead, Thomas, skinner, 17.

Aikman, Francis, apothecary, 83-4.

Aikman, James, mt., 173, 189. *See also* Curror, Isobel.

Aikman, William, mt. and Marian agent, 129, 175-6.

Aitkin, John, notary, protocol book of, 201.

Aldinstoun, John, baxter, 175, 189.

Allan, Adam, mt., 174, 189.

Alva, Fernando de Toledo, duke of, 128, 144.

Anderson, Patrick, smith, 59.

Arbroath, 60.

Argyll, earl of, *see* Campbell.

Armstrong, Andrew, mt., and attacks on catholics, 104, 114, 175, 182; and Riccio murder, 115.

Arnot, John, mt., 156.

Arran, earls of, *see* Hamilton, James *and* Stewart, James.

Ashlowaine, John, mt., 84.

Atholl, earl of, *see* Stewart.

Balcanquhal, Walter, minister of Edinburgh (1574-1616), 157, 159, 161, 164, 167; payment of, 35.

Balcaskie, Martin, burgess, 84.

Balfour, Gilbert, of Westray, mt., 176, 210.

Balfour, Sir James, of Pittendreich, provost (1571-2), 110, 210.

Balfour, William, indweller in Leith, 99, 176.

Bannatyne, Richard, secretary to Knox, author of *Memorials*, 129, 135, 137-8, 141, 143, 200.

Barber, William, 'minister' of hammermen craft in 1560, 57-8.

Baron, Alexander, mt., 74, 194-5. *See also* Baron, James, his cousin.

Baron, James, mt., 17, 29, 74, 80, 102, 119, 173; early protestant, 82-4; status of, 80, 184; family connections, 84; and protestant party, 106, 167, 175, 184; and Knox, 84, 221.

Bassenden, Thomas, printer, 48n.

Beaton, David, archbishop of St. Andrews and cardinal, 69.

Beaton, James, archbishop of Glasgow, 133.

Bedford, Francis Russell, 2nd earl of, 165.

Bell, John, seed seller, mt., 80.

Bellenden, Sir John, of Auchnoull, justice-clerk, 106, 183.

Bellenden, Patrick, of Stenness, 183.

Birnie, William, mt., 72, 203; wealth of, 52-3, 179. *See also* Acheson, Helen.

Black, John, Dominican friar, 37, 76, 99; attack on in 1565, 114-5, 175-6.

Black Friars, Dominican friary of, 26, 75, 82; income and property of, 21, 30-31, 34, 103-4, 179.

Blackburn, John, mt., 162-3.

Borthwick, m. David, advocate, 83.

Bothwell, earl of, *see* Hepburn.

Bowes, Sir Robert, 159-61, 164.

Brady, Mungo, goldsmith, 128.

Brand, John, minister of Canongate, 142.

Brechin, 51.

Bristo, barony of, 3.

Bristol, 52; population of, 11.

Brocas, William, smith, 93, 174; elected deacon of hammermen in 1562, 57-8, 100-1, 175, 180, 189-90, 207.

Brown, John, mt., 189.

Brown, Thomas, cordiner, 114, 116, 127, 175.

Bruce, Alexander, barber, 101.